Madagascar

THE BRADT TRAVEL GUIDE

'France, Spain, Italy and the Indie... must be ransackt to make sauce for our meat; while we impoverish the land, air and water to enrich our private table... Besides, these happy people have no need of any foreign commodity, nature having sufficiently supplied their necessities wherewith they remain contented. But it is we that are in want, and are compelled like famished wolves to range the world about for our living, to the hazards of both our souls and bodies, the one by the corruption of the air, the other by the corruption of religion.'

Walter Hamond, *A Paradox Prooving that the Inhabitants of ... Madagascar ... are the Happiest People in the World*, 1640

Madagascar

THE BRADT TRAVEL GUIDE

Eighth Edition

Hilary Bradt

Bradt Travel Guides Ltd, UK
The Globe Pequot Press Inc, USA

Eighth edition 2005

First published in 1988 by Bradt Publications

Bradt Travel Guides Ltd
19 High Street, Chalfont St Peter, Bucks SL9 9QE, England
Published in the USA by The Globe Pequot Press Inc, 246 Goose Lane,
PO Box 480, Guilford, Connecticut 06475-0480

British Library Cataloguing in Publication Data
A catalogue record for this book is available from the British Library

ISBN-10: 1 84162 104 8
ISBN-13: 978 1 84162 104 3

Photographs
Cover Crowned lemur and baby (Duncan Murrell)
Text Kate Booth (KB), Hilary Bradt (HB), Nick Garbutt (NG), Peter Havelock (PH)

Illustrations Cherry-Anne Lavrih (orchids), Carole Vincer (baobabs),
Nick Garbutt (others)
Maps Alan Whitaker

Typeset from the author's disc by Wakewing
Printed and bound in Italy by Legoprint SpA, Trento

Author/Contributors

Hilary Bradt (author) has visited Madagascar around 25 times since her first trip in 1976, mostly as a tour leader. She lectures, broadcasts and writes on the joys and perils of travelling in Madagascar and other countries. She is also the founder of Bradt Travel Guides.

Ony Rakotoarivelo (updater) is an English teacher at Akany Avoko in Antananarivo. She maintains links between school children in Madagascar and the UK.

SPECIALIST CONTRIBUTORS

Ian Anderson (*The Music of Madagascar*) is the editor of the magazine *Folk Roots* and a regular broadcaster on the subject of folk music.

Oliver and Camilla Backhouse (*Blindness in Madagascar, Malagasy Hats*) spent a year in Madagascar and set up the charity MOSS (see pages 151–2).

Samantha Cameron (*Traditional Healing...*, and Fianar update) works for Feedback Madagascar, co-ordinating their health programme.

Rob Conway (*Marine Beasties*) is a medical student and projects co-ordinator for Blue Ventures.

Joanna Durbin (*DWCT's Madagascar Programme* and updates) manages the Madagascar programme for Durrell Wildlife Conservation Trust. She has been working in conservation in Madagascar since 1988.

Nick Garbutt (photos, *A Layman's Guide to Lemurs, Madagascar's Mammals* ... plus other contributions) is a zoologist, photographer, tour leader and author.

Matthew Hatchwell (*Count Benyowski* and Masoala update) is the European Co-ordinator for the Wildlife Conservation Society.

Jonathan Hughes (*Natural History*) is an author and lecturer in ecology in London.

Tim Ireland (*Geology* and *Gemstones*) is an Australian geologist.

Angus McCrae (*Ant-lions* and *Wild Silk*) worked as a medical entomologist in Africa for 25 years.

John and Valerie Middleton (various) have made several extended trips to Madagascar to indulge their passion for worldwide cave and karst exploration.

Colin Palmer (*Pangalanes* and *Cargo Boats*) is a consultant who specialises in the role of water transport in developing countries.

Derek Schuurman (*Birding in Madagascar* plus other contributions) works for Rainbow Tours in London. He is the author of two books and countless articles on Madagascar.

Seraphine Tierney (*Famadihana Diary*) is the attaché at the Madagascar Consulate in London.

Jane Wilson-Howarth is a medical doctor and zoologist. She has worked in clinics in the developing world for 11 years and writes about travel health for *Wanderlust* magazine. She has written three travel health books and a travel narrative about Madagascar.

Contents

LIST OF MAPS

Acknowledgements

MISAOTRA! (THANK YOU)

Even a cursory flip through this book will show how much I owe to the readers and specialists who help to update each edition. As I re-read them, there are always some that stand out because of the enthusiasm of the traveller. This time the honour belonged to 'FRB'. Despite discomforts that would make a tough man weep, she managed to love every minute of her solo trip through the east of Madagascar. Here's a typical remark: 'The taxi-brousse ride from Mananara back to Tamatave was a delight – even though it was a 26-hour delight of which only three hours were spent asleep!' Then there are the veteran Madadventurers, John and Valerie Middleton. At an age when many people are happy simply to draw their pensions, they are an inspiring example to the younger people who write to me asking 'Is it safe?'

But 24 hours after I'd delivered the first proofs to the typesetter and it was absolutely too late to make changes I received a rather fat package containing two school exercise books obviously bought in Madagascar. Inside were 56 pages of notes and update information, including carefully drawn maps. It was from Stuart Riddle and of course I stopped everything to make sure that all the important information was included in this 8th edition. Deadlines are important, but accurate, inspiring information is something I can't do without. So thank you Stuart, and thank you everyone else who wrote letters or sent emails, whether in the form of a postcard or numerous pages. They are all read, all appreciated, and if possible all used.

I particularly love the ones that make me laugh. Like this: 'Hotel XXX is not open to the public any more. The owner uses it as a slaughterhouse.' It's a relief to know that Madagascar is not becoming too normal!

My heartfelt thanks to the following:

Kelyn Akuna, Wendy Applequist, Leo Barasi, Kathryn Baskerville, Johan Bjørkås, Laura Brandstetter, Irene Boswell, Sebastian Bulmer, Samantha Cameron, Christopher deCharms, Christina Dodwell, Joanna Durbin, Stuart Edgill, Ilya Eigenbrot, Alexander Elphinstone, Nick Garbutt, Jamie Gibbs, Sheena Gibson, Melanie Gomes, Tom Gray, Richard Green, John Grehan, Alex Hall, Al Harris, Keri Harvey, Onno Heuvel, Alison Jolly, Ben Kelly, Gary Lemmer, Richard Lewis, Kiersten Lortz, John & Valerie Middleton, Duncan Murrell, Erik Patel, John & Leigh Pitterle, Nivo Ravelojaona, Fiona Riddall Bell, Sally Rieder, Alex Sandell, Tom Savage, Øyvind Sæthre, Erik & Jacqueline Verhagen, Tom Voth & Helen Bomsta, Charlie Welch & Andrea Katz.

Forgive me if I have omitted anyone.

Introduction

Nearly 30 years ago I attended a slide show in Cape Town given by a zoo collector who had just returned from a country called Madagascar. By the end of the evening I knew I had to go there. It wasn't just the lemurs, it was the utter otherness of this little-known island that entranced me. So I went, and I fell in love, and I've been returning ever since.

Last September I was back with a small group of family and friends. They had mixed interests and not all wanted to see wildlife; some were more interested in the people. So we asked the driver if we could stop at a school – any school – along the road between Antsirabe and Fianarantsoa. The head teacher was delighted by our request and took us to the single classroom where the assorted boys and girls were crammed together on benches chanting their lessons. To say that our appearance created a diversion would be an understatement – the photos we took show facial expressions ranging from suspicion to radiant delight. However, three little children in the front row hid their faces on their arms. Their teacher explained: they were siblings who lived many kilometres away in the mountains and they had never seen white people at close quarters before. They were afraid. Yet this was on one of the most popular tourist routes in Madagascar.

Our next request, since it was Sunday, was to look in on a church service. We chose one of the many imposing Protestant churches near Fianar and again our driver and guide asked permission for us to sit at the back. But the priest was late (this was, after all, Madagascar) so after half-an-hour the congregation offered to sing a hymn especially for us. They sang beautifully, in seemingly effortless harmony. It was one of the most moving musical performances I have ever experienced and most of us were dabbing our eyes by the end.

This is what's so magical about Madagascar. In even the most visited areas you can experience something special, or guarantee it by venturing well off the beaten track. Or you can join other tourists in a fail-safe wildlife experience or luxuriate in one of the new fly-in beach resorts.

The choice is yours – lucky you!

* * * * * *

Some day, when I am old and worn and there is nothing new to see, I shall go back to the palm-fringed lagoons, the sun-drenched, rolling moors, the pink villages, and the purple peaks of Madagascar.

E A Powell, *Beyond the Utmost Purple Rim*, 1925

KEY TO STANDARD SYMBOLS

—·—·—	International boundary	𝐢	Tourist information
------	District boundary	🏺	Museum
[National park]	National park or reserve	⁙	Archaeological or historic site
[Forest park]	Forest park or reserve	⊞	Historic building
✈	Airport (international)	🏰	Castle/fortress
✈	Airport (other)	✝	Church or cathedral
✚	Airstrip	ℂ	Mosque
✈	Helicopter service	⚑	Golf course
══════	Railway	🏃	Stadium
----------	Featured footpath/trek	•	Other place of interest
----------	Other footpath	▲	Summit/peak name height (in metres)
--🚢--	Car ferry	△	Water depth
--⛴--	Passenger ferry	⊶	Border post
--⛴--	Pirogue ferry	◉	Cave/rock shelter
🛢	Petrol station or garage	◻—●—◻	Cable car, funicular
P	Car park	⦚	Waterfall
🚐	Taxi-brousse/bus station etc	☀	Scenic viewpoint
🚲	Cycle hire	❀	Botanical site
⌂	Hotel, inn etc	♧	Specific woodland feature
▲	Campsite	🗼	Lighthouse
♠	Hut	≍	Marsh
⚑	Wine bar	⚲	Mangrove
✗	Restaurant, café etc	✈	Bird watching/nesting site
☆	Night club		Coral reef
⊠	Post office		Sandy beach (extensive)
ℓ	Telephone	➤	Sandy beach
e	Internet access	↯	Scuba diving
✚	Hospital, clinic etc	⌐	Fishing sites
✚	Pharmacy/health centre		
$	Bank		
⚱	Statue or monument		

*Other map symbols are sometimes shown in
separate key boxes with individual
explanations for their meanings.*

Perspectives on Madagascar

'[Madagascar is] the chiefest paradise this day upon earth.'

Richard Boothby, 1630

'I could not but endeavour to dissuade others from undergoing the
miseries that will follow the persons of such as adventure themselves for
Madagascar ... from which place, God divert the residence and adventures
of all good men.'

Powle Waldegrave, 1649

As it was in the 17th century, so it is today – although very few people these days
are disappointed. My love affair with Madagascar has lasted 28 years and, like any
lover, I tend to be blind to its imperfections and too ready to leap to its defence. I
am therefore fortunate to receive so much feedback from travellers both new and
experienced, wide-eyed or blasé, to help me see Madagascar with fresh eyes. It is,
I suppose, not a holiday island in the conventional sense, and as an exotic
destination it lacks tangible tourist sights and events. As one disappointed traveller
put it: 'I need to be hit in the face with garish temples, outrageous costumes,
bizarre practices. I agree toying with Grandad's bones is pretty bizarre but what
chance has a tourist like me of seeing a *famadihana*?'

Madagascar faces the dilemma of many developing countries: its government is
anxious to encourage tourism and there are a large number of potential visitors
who have seen television programmes about the island's natural history or are
looking for a new holiday destination. And yet this is one of the poorest countries
in the world and it is, perhaps, one of the most corrupt. Change will continue to
be slow, not helped by the fact that Malagasy culture is based on respect for the past
rather than anticipation of the future.

Nevertheless, I still rejoice that so much is special: the wildlife (of course), the
people – their beauty and gentle friendliness – the scenery, the food, and above all
the serendipity. Wander away from the main tourist places in any town and you are
likely to stumble across a market, a street fair, a group of musicians, or a gathering
that brings home what we seem to have lost in our culture: the ability to be joyful
despite poverty.

Here are some comments from letters I've received over the years (the last four
are 2003/4).

'The beauty of the land I had expected, but the gentle openheartedness
and hospitality of the people took me by storm. I have lived and travelled
extensively in South America, Europe and Eastern Africa but I have never
encountered such lovely people as the Malagasy!'

'My advice is to see Madagascar before the Malagasy finish with it.'

'The experience was wonderful, all that I had hoped for and more...the Malagasy people are simply amazing, the scenery wonderful, every day an adventure I shall never forget.'

'I loved the place and the people. I made so many friends in so few days that I will never be able to keep up the correspondence. I am already devising reasons to go back there again.'

'I found it an extraordinary island with an immense wealth of interest and some very real and unshakeable problems. Madagascar offers various trials of patience alongside infinite potential for the independent traveller.'

Some of our favourite things:

- Sailing a pirogue in Mangily/Ifaty
- The drive from Tana to Fianar
- Amber Mountain off-season when we had the whole park to ourselves.
- The natural swimming pool/showers in Amber Mountain, Andringitra and Isalo
- Just wandering around.

✳ ✳ ✳ ✳ ✳ ✳

YOUR PERSPECTIVES WANTED!

One of the joys of publishing new editions of this guide is the chance to add readers' views on Madagascar as well as the all-important hard information on favourite hotels, restaurants, and travel off the beaten track. With the inevitable changes following the presidential struggle for power in 2002, this feedback is even more needed.

Whatever your experiences in Madagascar, irrespective of whether you travelled there independently or as part of an organised group, do write to tell me about it. Particularly welcome is hard information with accurately noted addresses and prices, and readers who include a map to show the location of their new find have me almost weeping with joy.

Whether you have loved Madagascar or hated it, I'd like to hear from you in time for the next edition which is scheduled for 2007.

Happy travelling

Hilary Bradt

Hilary Bradt

19 High Street, Chalfont St Peter, Bucks SL9 9QE, England
Tel: 01753 893444 Fax: 01753 892333
Email: info@bradtguides.com
www.bradtguides.com

Part One

General Information

MADAGASCAR AT A GLANCE

Geography

Name Madagascar or The Malagasy Republic; *Repoblikan'i Madagasikara*
Location 400km off the east coast of Africa, south of the Equator.
Size 587,040km². 2½ times the size of Great Britain; slightly smaller than Texas. The world's fourth largest island.
Capital Antananarivo (Tana; Tananarive)
Main towns Fianarantsoa, Antsirabe, Toliara (Tuléar), Taolagnaro (Fort Dauphin), Toamasina (Tamatave), Mahajanga (Majunga), Antsiranana (Diego Suarez). The French colonial names in parentheses are still commonly used.
Highest point Mt Maromokotro (Tsaratanana massif) 2,876m (9,450ft)
Climate Tropical, with most rain falling between December and March

Human statistics

Population 16 million approx (15,660,000 at the last census in 2001)
Population growth per year 2.9%
GNI per capita US$240 (2002). Half the population earns less than US$1 per year.
Life expectancy 53
Language Malagasy, French; some English spoken
Religion Mainly Christian, roughly divided between Protestants and Catholics. Some Muslims and Hindus largely in the Asian communities.

Politics/administration/economy

President Marc Ravalomanana
Prime minister Jacques Sylla
Main exports Prawns, vanilla
GDP growth 5.9% (2001); −11.9% 2002 (the year of 'The Crisis')
Flag White, green and red (white vertical band, green and red horizontal bands)
Public holidays Jan 1, Mar 29, May 1, Jun 26, Aug 15, Nov 1, Dec 25, Dec 30
Motto Fatherland, Liberty, Justice

Natural history

Fauna and flora Cut off from mainland Africa for millions of years, the island's flora and fauna has evolved into unique species: about 10,000 endemic plants, 316 reptiles, and 109 birds. The 71 species and sub-species of lemur make Madagascar the world's top priority for primate conservation.
Protected areas Until 2003 only 3% of the island's vulnerable habitats were protected. In September of that year the new government pledged to increase this to 10% within the next five years.

Practical details

International airport Ivato, Antananarivo
Time GMT+3
Electricity Voltage 220, plugs two-pin (continental style)
International telephone code 261 20
Currency The franc Malgache (Fmg) is being replaced by the ariary
Rate of exchange (October 2004) £1 = 17,750Fmg, €1 = 11,300Fmg, US$1 = 10,000Fmg

The Country

1

GEOGRAPHY

A chain of mountains runs like a spine down the east-centre of the island descending sharply to the Indian Ocean, leaving only a narrow coastal plain. These eastern mountain slopes bear the remains of the dense rainforest which once covered all of the eastern section of the island. The western plain is wider and the climate drier, supporting forests of deciduous trees and acres of savannah grassland. Madagascar's highest mountain is Maromokotro (9,450ft/2,876m), part of the Massif of Tsaratanana, in the north of the island. In the south is the 'spiny forest' also known as the 'spiny desert'.

CLIMATE

Madagascar has a tropical climate: November to March – summer (wet season), hot with variable rainfall; April to October – winter (dry season), mainly dry and mild. That said, climate change is affecting every country in the world and Madagascar is no exception. The once reliable weather pattern has gone. Rain can come early or late. You can be lucky or unlucky.

The normal pattern of weather is that southwest trade winds drop their moisture on the eastern mountain slopes and blow hot and dry in the west. North and northwest 'monsoon' air currents bring heavy rain in summer, decreasing southward so that the rainfall in Taolagnaro is half that of Toamasina. There are also considerable variations of temperature dictated by altitude and latitude. On the summer solstice of December 22 the sun is directly over the Tropic of Capricorn, and the weather is very warm. Conversely, June is the coolest month.

Average midday temperatures in the dry season are 77°F (25°C) in the highlands and 86°F (30°C) on the coast. These statistics are misleading,

RAINFALL CHART

Region	Jan	Feb	Mar	Apr	May	Jun	Jul	Aug	Sep	Oct	Nov	Dec
West	●	●	●	●	✳	✳	✳	✳	✳	✳	✳	●
Highlands	●	●	●	●	✳	○	○	○	✳	✳	✳	●
East	●	●	●	●	●	●	●	✳	✳	✳	✳	✳
South	●	●	●	✳	○	○	○	○	✳	✳	✳	●
North	●	●	●	●	✳	✳	✳	✳	✳	✳	✳	●
Northwest (Sambirano)	●	●	●	●	✳	✳	✳	✳	✳	✳	✳	●

● = rain ✳ = driest months ○ = fine but cool

CYCLONES

Madagascar has always suffered from cyclones which generally receive scant attention from the media. Between 1968 and 1999 the country suffered 21 severe cyclones which affected 5.2 million people, making 445,000 homeless and killing 1,291. In 2000, cyclones Eline, Gloria and Hudah affected over a million people and killed 1,292.

The year 2004 was a devastating one. In February Cyclone Elita killed 29 people, injured 100, and rendered 44,000 homeless. But worse was to come: on March 7 Cyclone Gafilo made its first strike on the island in the region of Antalaha in the northeast, with winds of 120km/h (75mph) gusting up to 200km/h. These southwesterly winds scythed across the island to Mahajanga. Three days later Gafilo returned from the west, doing further damage to Morondava and neighbouring towns. The final death toll was 222 dead, 170 missing and 895 injured. More than 260,000 were made homeless, 621 items of infrastructure – roads and bridges – have been damaged and agriculture severely disrupted, with 37,057ha of land damaged and over 10,000 farm animals killed. The north of the country suffered the most, with the worst damage inflicted on Antalaha, in the northeast, though Antsiranana in the far north and neighbouring towns were also severely affected. Some meteorologists consider Gafilo to be Madagascar's most destructive cyclone ever.

The high death toll is partly accounted for by the sinking of the *Samson* ferry bound for Mahajanga from Moroni, in the Comoro Islands; 113 people were on board the vessel and only two survivors have been found. These, a young Comoran couple, managed to reach a life raft and landed near the village of Ampasimariny the following day.

however, since in June the night-time temperature can drop to near freezing in the highlands and it is cool in the south. The winter daytime temperatures are very pleasant, and the hot summer season is usually tempered by cool breezes on the coast.

The east of Madagascar frequently suffers from cyclones during February and March and these may brush other areas in the north or west.

The map and chart in this section give easy reference to the driest and wettest months and regions but remember: even in the rainiest months there will be sunny intervals, and in the driest there may be heavy showers. For more advice on the best months to visit Madagascar see *When to Go, Chapter 4*.

Climatic regions
West
Rainfall decreases from north to south. Variation in day/night winter temperatures increases from north to south. Average number of dry months: seven or eight. Highest average annual rainfall within zone (major town): Mahajanga, 152cm. Lowest: Toliara, 36cm.

Central
Both temperature and rainfall are influenced by altitude. Day/night temperatures in Antananarivo vary by 14°C. The major rainy season usually starts at the end of November. Highest average annual rainfall within zone (major town): Antsirabe, 140cm.

East

In the northeast and central areas there are no months (or weeks) entirely without rain; but drier, more settled weather prevails in the southeast. Reasonably dry months: May, September, October, November. Possible months for travel: April, December, January (but cyclone danger in January). Difficult months for travel (torrential rain and cyclones) are February, March. Highest annual rainfall in zone: Maroantsetra, 410cm. Lowest: Taolagnaro (Fort Dauphin), 152cm.

Southwest

The driest part of Madagascar. The extreme west may receive only 5cm of rain a year, increasing to around 34cm in the east.

North

This is similar to the east zone except for the dry climate of the Antsiranana (Diego Suarez) region, which gets only 92cm of rain per year, with a long and fairly reliable dry season.

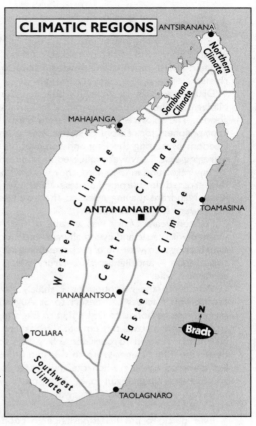

Northwest (Sambirano)

Dominated by the Massif of Tsaratanana, this region includes the island of Nosy Be and has a micro-climate with frequent heavy rain alternating with sunshine.

A BRIEF HISTORY

This is just a glance at Madagascar's fascinating history. For a full account read A History of Madagascar *by Mervyn Brown. See page 453.*

The first Europeans

The first Europeans to sight Madagascar were the Portuguese in 1500, although there is evidence of earlier Arab settlements on the coast. There were unsuccessful attempts to establish French and British settlements during the next couple of centuries; these failed due to disease and hostile local people. Hence a remarkably homogeneous and united country was able to develop under its own rulers.

By the early 1700s, the island had become a haven for pirates and slave-traders, who both traded with and fought the local kings who ruled the clans of the east and west coast.

ROBERT DRURY

The most intriguing insight into 18th-century Madagascar was provided by Robert Drury, who was shipwrecked off the island in 1701 and spent over 16 years there, much of the time as a slave to the Antandroy or Sakalava chiefs.

Drury was only 15 when his boat foundered off the southern tip of Madagascar (he had been permitted by his father to go to India with trade goods). The shipwreck survivors were treated well by the local king but kept prisoners for reasons of status. After a few days they made a bid for freedom by seizing the king and some of his courtiers as a hostage and marching east. They were followed by hundreds of warriors who watched for any relaxation in the guard; they were without water for three days as they crossed the burning hot desert and just as they came in sight of the River Mandrare (having released the hostages) they were attacked and many were speared to death.

For ten years Drury was a slave of the Antandroy royal family. He worked with cattle and eventually was appointed royal butcher, the task of slaughtering a cow for ritual purposes being supposedly that of someone of royal blood – and lighter skin. Drury was a useful substitute. He also acquired a wife.

Wars with the neighbouring Mahafaly gave him the opportunity to escape north across the desert to St Augustine's Bay, some 250 miles away. Here he hoped to find a ship to England, but his luck turned and he again became a slave, this time to the Sakalava. When a ship did come in, his master refused to consider selling him to the captain, and Drury's desperate effort to get word to the ship through a message written on a leaf came to nothing when the messenger lost the leaf and substituted another less meaningful one. Two more years of relative freedom followed, and he finally got away in 1717, nearly 17 years after his shipwreck.

Ever quick to put his experience to good use, he later returned to Madagascar as a slave trader!

See *Further Reading* (page 453) for a new book on Robert Drury.

The rise of the Merina Kingdom

The powerful Merina Kingdom was forged by Andrianampoinimerina (be thankful that this was a shortened version of his full name: Andrianampoinimerin-andriantsimitoviaminandriampanjaka!).

Succeeding to the tiny kingdom of Ambohimanga in 1787, by 1808 he had united the various Merina kingdoms and conquered the other highland tribes. In many ways the Merina Kingdom at this time paralleled that of the Inca Empire in Peru: Andrianampoinimerina was considered to have almost divine powers and his obedient subjects were well provided for: each was given enough land for his family's rice needs, with some left over to pay a rice tribute to the king, and community projects such as the building of irrigation canals were imposed through forced labour (though with bonuses for the most productive worker). The burning of forests was forbidden.

Conquest was always foremost in the monarch's mind, however, and it was his son, King Radama I, who fulfilled his father's command to 'Take the sea as frontier to your kingdom'. This king had a friendly relationship with Britain, which in 1817

TANGENA

When James Hastie, royal tutor, arrived in Madagascar in 1817 he witnessed and described one of the more barbaric tortures that King Radama I was using on his subjects: the Ordeal of *Tangena*. *Tangena* is a Malagasy shrub with a poisonous kernel in its fruit. This poison was used to determine the guilt or innocence of a suspected criminal. A 'meal' consisting of three pieces of chicken skin, rice and the crushed *tangena* kernel was prepared. The suspect was then forced to drink large quantities of water to make him – or her – vomit. If all three pieces of chicken skin reappeared the person was innocent (but often died anyway as a result of the poison). If the skin remained in the stomach the unfortunate suspect was killed, usually after limbs, or bits of limbs and other extremities, had been lopped off first.

One of the successes of Hastie's influence on the king was that the monarch agreed that, although the Ordeal by *Tangena* should continue, dogs could stand in for the accused. This decision was ignored by Queen Ranavalona who used it freely on the Christian martyrs she persecuted with such enthusiasm. Sir Mervyn Brown (from whose book, *A History of Madagascar*, this information is extracted) estimates that several thousand Malagasy met their deaths through the *tangena* shrub during Queen Ranavalona's long reign. Even during this period of xenophobia the queen was reluctant to subject the Europeans under arrest to the ordeal because of the inevitable political repercussions. Prudently, the poison was administered to chickens; all but one promptly died (the 'innocent' chicken/European was a bit too useful to condemn).

The Ordeal by *Tangena* was finally abolished by Queen Ranavalona's son, King Radama II, in 1861.

and 1820 signed treaties under which Madagascar was recognised as an independent state. Britain supplied arms and advisers to help Radama conquer most of the rest of the island.

The London Missionary Society

To further strengthen ties between the two countries, the British Governor of Mauritius, which had recently been seized from the French, encouraged King Radama I to invite the London Missionary Society to send teachers. In 1818 a small group of Welsh missionaries arrived in Tamatave (now Toamasina). David Jones and Thomas Bevan brought their wives and children, but within a few weeks only Jones remained alive; the others had all died of fever. Jones retreated to Mauritius, but returned to Madagascar, along with equally dedicated missionary teachers and artisans, in 1820 to devote the rest of his life to its people. The British influence was established and a written language introduced for the first time (apart from some ancient Arabic texts) using the Roman alphabet.

'The wicked queen' and her successors

Radama's widow and successor, Queen Ranavalona I, was determined to rid the land of Christianity and European influence, and reigned long enough (33 years) largely to achieve her aim. These were repressive times for Malagasy as well as foreigners. One way of dealing with people suspected of witchcraft or other evil practices was the 'Ordeal by Tangena' (see box above).

It was during Queen Ranavalona's reign that an extraordinary Frenchman arrived in Madagascar: Jean Laborde, who, building on the work of the British missionaries, introduced the island to many aspects of Western technology. He remained in the queen's favour until 1857 – much longer than the other Europeans (see box on page 401).

The queen drove the missionaries out of Madagascar and many Malagasy Christians were martyred. However, the missionaries and European influence returned in greater strength after the Queen's death and in 1869 Christianity became the official religion of the Merina Kingdom.

After Queen Ranavalona I came King Radama II, a peace-loving and pro-European monarch who was assassinated after a two-year reign in 1863. There is a widely held belief, however, that he survived strangulation with a silk cord (it was taboo to shed royal blood) and lived in hiding in the northwest for many years (see box on page 401). There is also a belief (less widely held) that he was assassinated because he was the illegitimate son of Queen Ranavalona I and Jean Laborde.

After the death of Radama II, Queen Rasoherina came to the throne, but the monarchy was now in decline and power shifted to the prime minister who shrewdly married the queen. He was overthrown by a brother, Rainilaiarivony, who continued the tradition by marrying three successive queens and exercising all the power. During this period, 1863-96, the monarchs (in title only) were Queen Rasoherina, Queen Ranavalona II and lastly Queen Ranavalona III.

The French conquest

Even during the period of British influence the French maintained a long-standing claim to Madagascar and in 1883 they attacked and occupied the main ports. The Franco-Malagasy War lasted thirty months, and was concluded by a harsh treaty making Madagascar a form of French protectorate. Prime Minister Rainilaiarivony, hoping for British support, managed to evade full acceptance of this status but the British government signed away its interest in the Convention of Zanzibar in 1890. The French finally imposed their rule by invasion in 1895. For a year the country was a full protectorate and in 1896 Madagascar became a French colony. A year later Queen Ranavalona III was exiled to Algeria and the monarchy abolished.

The first French Governor-General of Madagascar, Joseph Simon Gallieni, was an able and relatively benign administrator. He set out to break the power of the Merina aristocracy and remove the British influence by banning the teaching of English. French became the official language.

British military training and the two World Wars

Britain has played an important part in the military history of Madagascar. During the wars which preceded colonisation British mercenaries trained the Malagasy army to fight the French. During World War I 46,000 Malagasy were recruited for the allies and over 2,000 killed. In 1942, when Madagascar was under the control of the Vichy French, the British invaded Madagascar to forestall the possibility of the Japanese Navy making use of the great harbour of Diego Suarez (see box on pages 362–3).

In 1943 Madagascar was handed back to France under a Free French Government. An uprising by the Malagasy against the French in 1947 was bloodily repressed (some 80,000 are said to have died) but the spirit of nationalism lived on and in 1960 the country achieved full independence.

The first 30 years of independence

The first president, Philibert Tsiranana, was 'pro-France' but in 1972 he stepped down in the face of increasing unrest and student demonstrations against French

MADAGASCAR AND THE JEWS OF EUROPE
John Grehan

During the latter years of the 1930s, German Nazis, as well as many anti-Semites across Europe, wanted to rid the continent of all Jews. Their solution to the 'Jewish Question' was the wholesale deportation of European Jews to Madagascar. What became known as 'The Madagascar Plan' was first discussed as early as November 1938, a year before the outbreak of World War II. (As Madagascar was a French colony one can only wonder at what degree of collusion there was between the French and German governments over this proposal at that time.)

The annexation of Poland in 1939 brought yet more Jews under German administration. This led to a revival of The Madagascar Plan and prompted the President of the Academy of German Law – Hans Franc – to suggest that as many as three million Jews should be shipped to Madagascar. This would have meant the German occupation of the island and this was certainly discussed in 1940 within days of the fall of France. Indeed, Franz Rademacher of the German Foreign Office drew up firm arrangements for installing the Jews in Madagascar in September 1940, and he planned to visit the island to 'map out' the details.

It was intended that the island would be under the authority of Heinrich Himmler though largely administered by the Jews themselves. Franc, in a speech in July 1940, even claimed that Jewish leaders had accepted the Madagascar Plan. But the Jews had been deceived if they thought that Madagascar had been chosen as the place for a sustainable Jewish homeland. Madagascar was to be a vast 'reservation' in which, because of the poor climatic and agricultural conditions, the Jews would slowly die out. Some have gone even further and suggested that Madagascar was to be the place where the mass extermination of the Jews – with the gas chambers, ovens and all the associated paraphernalia of the death camps – would take place. Certainly the remoteness of Madagascar would have provided the Germans with the privacy they wanted for conducting such atrocities.

Until well into 1941 The Madagascar Plan was Germany's stated 'Final Solution'. It was only when such a policy became impractical, and it was the Royal Navy's mastery of the seas which made the plan impractical, that exportation gave way to extermination and another, and more terrible, Final Solution to the Jewish Problem took its place.

John Grehan is the author of The Forgotten Invasion, *see Further Reading in the Appendix.*

neo-colonialism. An interim government headed by General Ramanantsoa ended France's special position and introduced a more nationalistic foreign and economic policy.

In 1975, after a period of turmoil, a military directorate handed power to a naval officer, Didier Ratsiraka, who had served as Foreign Minister under Ramanantsoa. Ratsiraka established the Second Republic, changing the country's name from The Malagasy Republic to The Democratic Republic of Madagascar. He introduced his own brand of 'Christian-Marxism' and his manifesto, set out in a 'little red book', was approved by referendum. Socialist policies such as the nationalisation of banks

RACIAL DISHARMONY

Astute travellers will notice that there is a degree of racial unease between the Merina people in the highlands, historically the rulers of Madagascar, and the other clans. Probably no society is free of racism since no multiethnic society has evolved without wars or at least internal dissent. Traditionally the Malagasy have reserved most of their racial hatred for what they perceive to be a common enemy: the Indians and Pakistanis who own many of the businesses and are accused of exploiting the Malagasy and failing to integrate. However, one of the repercussions of La Crise was that it heightened the ethnic divisions between the Merina, followers of Marc Ravalomanana, and the Betsimisaraka who rallied behind their kinsman, Ratsiraka.

followed. Within a few years the economy had collapsed and has remained in severe difficulties ever since. Ratsiraka was nevertheless twice re-elected, though there were claims of ballot rigging and intimidation.

Into the 21st century

In 1991 a pro-democracy coalition called the Forces Vives, in which the churches played an important part, organised a series of strikes and daily demonstrations calling for Ratsiraka's resignation. Around 500,000 demonstrators marched on the president's palace. Though unarmed and orderly, they were fired on by the presidential guards and an estimated 100 died. This episode further weakened Ratsiraka and at the end of the year he relinquished executive power and agreed to a referendum which approved a new constitution and fresh elections in 1992/93. Albert Zafy won the election.

The Third Republic, born in 1993, soon ran into trouble. Albert Zafy refused to accept the limitations on his presidential role required by the new constitution and in 1995 won a referendum which gave him, rather than the Assembly, the right to appoint the prime minister. Zafy's continuing breaches of the constitution led to his impeachment by the National Assembly, and in the ensuing presidential election former president Ratsiraka emerged the winner. Ratsiraka then piloted through major amendments to the constitution which restored most of the dictatorial powers that he had formerly enjoyed.

The first round of presidential elections was held in December 2001. The official results showed the mayor of Antananarivo, Marc Ravalomanana, leading with 46% so that a second round would be necessary. However, results collected by various observer groups indicated that Ravalomanana was the outright winner with 52%.

'La crise politique' January – July 2002

Even in the sometimes bizarre politics of the developing world the spectacle of two 'presidents' in two 'capitals' with two set of 'ministers' was unusual. Friends of Madagascar watched appalled as the country unravelled itself to the indifference of the leaders of the industrialised world.

Every day the people marched peacefully, backed by the Protestant Church of which Ravalomanana is a prominent member. Ratsiraka declared Martial Law which was countered by Ravalomanana declaring himself president and installing his own ministers in government offices. Ratsiraka retreated with his government to his home town of Toamasina and was supported by the Governors of the other coastal provinces. All this was accomplished with the minimum of violence. But then Ratsiraka's supporters isolated the capital by blocking all roads leading to the city and by dynamiting the bridges. The people of Antananarivo faced a tenfold increase in the price of fuel, and basic staples such as rice, sugar and salt disappeared from the shops. Air Madagascar was grounded. The army was split behind the two leaders. As the months passed, the blockade caused malnutrition and death to the vulnerable in Tana and hardship to all. Many businesses faced bankruptcy.

In May, the balance of power started to shift. A court-monitored recount confirmed that Ravalomanana had won the election, and he was sworn in as president. Ratsiraka steadfastly refused to accept this and the blockades continued and the death toll, hitherto kept remarkably low, started to rise. As the army's support for Ratsiraka dwindled and switched to Ravalomanana, it became possible to use force to dismantle the barricades and to take Ratsiraka strongholds such as Mahajanga and Antsiranana. The USA, Norway and Switzerland were the first nations to recognise Ravalomanana as the rightful president. France, which had prolonged the crisis by delaying recognition because of its close links with Ratsiraka, was finally compelled to go along, followed by most European countries, which had been awaiting a lead from France. However most African presidents, who had supported Ratsiraka as a fellow member of their dictators' club, continued to reject Ravalomanana's legitimacy, and it was nearly a year before Madagascar was re-admitted into the African Union.

GOVERNMENT AND POLITICS

Madagascar is governed by a presidential system, but the powers of the president have varied under the various constitutions adopted over the last 40 years. At independence the constitution was based closely on the French, with the president head of the government as well as head of state. Under the 'socialist revolution' (1975–91) President Ratsiraka had virtually dictatorial powers, supported by large majorities for his party AREMA in the National Assembly. The strength of older left-wing parties prevented him from establishing a formal one-party state, but the constitution provided that only socialist parties could compete in elections. After his overthrow in 1991 the pendulum swung to a parliamentary constitution similar to the German or the British, with a largely ceremonial president and power vested in a prime minister elected by the National Assembly. But this was effectively destroyed by President Zafy's refusal to accept the constitutional limits on his power and when Ratsiraka subsequently returned to power he rewrote the constitution to restore nearly all his old powers; it is this rewritten constitution that is still in force.

Since colonial times the country has been divided for purposes of local government into six provinces, each consisting of hundreds of communes or municipalities with Governors and Prefects appointed by the central government but, in an effort to move towards decentralisation, other systems of local government are being considered.

An important factor in politics has been the coastal people's mistrust of the Merina who conquered them in the nineteenth century. The numerical superiority of the coastal people has ensured their dominance of parliament and government, helped by deep divisions among the Merina (radicals, communists, conservatives, Catholics and Protestants). When Ratsiraka was in trouble in 1991 and again in 2002 he stirred up coastal hostility to the Merina. However the emergence of Marc Ravalomanana as the first Merina elected president indicates that the coastal/plateau divide is now much less significant, though some coastal politicians such as ex-President Zafy still try to exploit it.

Party politics have in general been based on support for individual leaders rather than ideology. Since the involvement of the IMF in the late eighties most parties play lip service to the liberalisation of the economy, but there is nostalgia for a large central government with its greater opportunities for political patronage. Recent parliamentary elections have established President Ravalomanana's party TIKO as the largest in the Assembly but it is essentially a coalition of supporters of the President with no particular ideology or programme other than the President's commitment to democracy and the liberal economy. Ratsiraka's old party AREMA still has a lot of support and it is the most important opposition party. But there are many others, motivated mainly by the leader's ambition for office.

Corruption was virtually unknown during the post-independence government of Tsiranana. It became firmly established during Ratsiraka's Second Republic and is now widespread. President Ravalomanana has launched a major campaign against corruption but it is likely to have only limited success, if only because the salaries of even senior civil servants are so low that they cannot support their families without exacting bribes for their services.

ECONOMY

Over the past 30 years Madagascar has declined from being modestly prosperous to becoming one of the poorest countries in the world. Under Tsiranana's post-independence government, a combination of careful management and political stability produced a steady growth in GNP and an improvement in living standards. However, from the late 70s Ratsiraka's unwise policies of nationalisation and centralisation, coupled with a worsening of the terms of trade following successive oil-price shocks, led to the collapse of the economy. For 25 years the average GNP growth was zero so that, with the population doubling, living standards were halved. Reluctant recourse to the IMF and its policies of austerity and liberalisation led to some improvement in the late 80s but the disruptions of successive political crises, notably those of 1991 and 2002, checked and sometimes reversed this recovery. In particular the blockading of the capital by Ratsiraka's forces in 2002 virtually halted external trade and seriously damaged the growing industrial sector which was largely dependent on exports. The outlook seems brighter under Ravalomanana, a successful businessman who genuinely believes in the liberal economy. But it will take a long time to repair the damage and restore confidence.

Madagascar has always had an adverse balance of trade, but in the post-independence days the deficit was modest and covered by various payments from France. The economic collapse under the Second Republic greatly increased the deficit, and the country has since been dependent on massive support from the IMF, the World Bank, the European Union and various bilateral donors led by France, with USA also playing an important role. The local currency, the *franc malgache* (Fmg), was maintained in parity with the French franc long after its real value had declined. From the eighties onward pressure from the IMF to liberalise the exchange rate led to successive substantial devaluations, but at the beginning of this century the exchange rate appeared to have stabilised, fluctuating around 10,000Fmg = £1. But in 2003 President Ravalomanana's abolition of a wide range of import taxes, designed to stimulate the economy, led in the short term to a rapid increase of imports without a corresponding rise in exports. The consequent increase in the trade gap caused a spectacular collapse of the currency in the first half of 2004, with the Fmg losing over half its value.

The economy has always been based on agriculture, with rice by far the largest crop, providing enough to feed the population and leave some over for export.

However, under the Second Republic the severe decline in the road infrastructure isolated many rice-growers from the markets, while the low official price paid to the growers discouraged them from growing a surplus for sale and led them to revert to a subsistence economy. Rice production accordingly failed to keep pace with the growing population so that the country now has to import some 30% of its needs, at considerable expense in foreign exchange. The main cash crops for export have been vanilla, of which Madagascar is the world's largest producer, and coffee; but while vanilla has remained a leading export earner, coffee production has declined along with the world price and the sector seems unlikely to recover. In the last decade prawns, either fished or farmed in the inlets on the west coast, have become a major export item. Much hope has been invested in tourism, for which the potential is enormous, but expansion has been held back by poor infrastructure and the successive political crises have discouraged tourists.

In the last few years the US Africa Bill, offering privileged access to the American textile market to Madagascar and certain African countries, caused a rapid growth in the industrial sector with many textile factories springing up in industrial tax-free zones (ZFIs). But the blockade of the capital in 2002 and the cutting off of exports was disastrous for this sector. Most factories closed with investors losing their money and scores of thousands of workers losing their jobs. The American market remains available for textiles and some other items but it is likely to be some time before investor confidence returns. The small mining sector (semi-precious stones, mica and chromite) has recently expanded with the discovery of large deposits of sapphire but, partly because of government corruption, nearly all the gems have been exported illegally so that the economy has not benefited. A Canadian subsidiary of the British mining firm RTZ will shortly begin exploiting substantial deposits of ilmenite on the southeast coast (see page 277). This is on such a scale that it could in due course add as much as 10% to the country's export earnings.

Tourism statistics

The target for tourism in 2000 was 200,000 visitors but numbers dropped from 155,000 in 1999 to 138,000 because of bad publicity about cyclones and cholera. The figures for 2002 were little better, and in 2003 tourism was brought to a virtual standstill by 'La crise politique'. It still has not returned to its former levels. By comparison Mauritius receives 500,000 visitors a year. The majority of visitors to Madagascar are French (55%), then Italians (12.1%), Americans (4.2%) and Swiss, with German and British at 2% each.

PRICE WARNING!

At the time of going to press, Madagascar is suffering from serious inflation. The formerly stable exchange rate has doubled in less than a year, so Fmg prices in this book will no longer be accurate. Prices quoted in euros or US$ should be more or less correct, however.

The People

ORIGINS

Archaeologists believe that the first people arrived in Madagascar from Indonesia/Malaya about 2,000 years ago. A journey in a reconstructed boat of those times has proved that the direct crossing of the Indian Ocean – 6,400km – was possible, though most experts agree that it is much more likely that the immigrants came in their outrigger canoes via Southern India and East Africa, where they established small Indonesian colonies. The strong African element in the coastal populations probably derived from later migrations from these colonies since their language is also essentially Malayo-Polynesian with only slightly more Bantu-Swahili words than elsewhere in the island. The Merina people of the highlands retain remarkably Indonesian characteristics and may have arrived as recently as 500–600 years ago.

Later arrivals, mainly on the east coast, from Arabia and elsewhere in the Indian Ocean, were also absorbed into the Malagasy-speaking population, while leaving their mark in certain local customs clearly derived from Islam. The two-continent origin of the Malagasy is easily observed, from the highland tribes who most resemble Indonesians, to the African type characterised by the Bara or Makoa in the south. In between are the elements of both races which make the Malagasy so varied and attractive in appearance. Thus there is racial diversity but cultural uniformity.

BELIEFS AND CUSTOMS

The Afro-Asian origin of the Malagasy has produced a people with complicated and fascinating beliefs and customs. Despite the various tribes or clans, the country shares not only a common language but a belief in the power of dead ancestors (*razana*). This cult of the dead, far from being a morbid preoccupation, is a celebration of life since the dead ancestors are considered to be potent forces that continue to share in family life. If the *razana* are remembered by the living, the Malagasy believe, they thrive in the spirit world and can be relied on to look after their descendants in a host of different ways. These ancestors wield considerable power, their 'wishes' dictating the behaviour of the family or community. Their

---

DID YOU KNOW?

- Earthquakes mean that whales are bathing their children.
- If a woman maintains a bending posture when arranging eggs in a nest, the chickens will have crooked necks.
- If the walls of a house incline towards the south, the wife will be the stronger one; if they incline towards the north it will be the husband.
- Burning a knot on a piece of string causes the knees to grow big.

property is respected, so a great-grandfather's field may not be sold or changed to a different crop. Calamities are usually blamed on the anger of *razana*, and a zebu bull may be sacrificed in appeasement. Large herds of zebu cattle are kept as a 'bank' of potential sacrificial offerings.

Belief in tradition, in the accumulated wisdom of the ancestors, has shaped the Malagasy culture. Respect for their elders and courtesy to all fellow humans is part of the tradition. But so is resistance to change.

Spiritual beliefs

At the beginning of time the Creator was Zanahary or Andriananahary. Now the Malagasy worship one god, Andriamanitra, who is neither male nor female. (Andriamanitra is also a word for silk, the fabric of burial shrouds).

Many rural people believe in 'secondary gods' or nature spirits, which may be male or female, and which inhabit certain trees, rocks (which are known as *ody*) or rivers. People seeking help from the spirit world may visit one of these sites for prayer. Spirits are also thought to possess humans who fall into a trance-like state, called *tromba* by the Sakalava and *bilo* by the Antandroy. Some clans or communities believe that spirits can also possess animals, particularly crocodiles.

The Malagasy equivalent of the soul is *ambiroa*. When a person is in a dream state it can temporarily separate from the body, and at death it becomes an immortal *razana*. Death, therefore, is merely a change and not an end. A special ceremony usually marks this rite of passage, with feasting and the sacrifice of zebu. The mood of the participants alternates between sorrow and joy.

Fady

The dictates of the *razana* are obeyed in a complicated network of *fady*. Although *fady* (the plural is also *fady*) is usually translated as 'taboo' this does not truly convey the meaning: these are beliefs related to actions, food, or days of the week when it is 'dangerous to...'. *Fady* vary from family to family and community to community, and even from person to person.

The following are some examples related to actions and food among the Merina: it may be *fady* to sing while you are eating (violators will develop elongated teeth); it is also *fady* to hand an egg directly to another person – it must first be put on the ground; for the people of Andranoro it is *fady* to ask for salt directly, so one has to request 'that which flavours the food'. A *fady* connected with objects is that the spade used to dig a grave should have a loose handle since it is dangerous to have too firm a connection between the living and the dead.

Social *fady*, like *vintana* (see below), often involve the days of the week. For example, among the Merina it is *fady* to hold a funeral on a Tuesday, or there will be another death. Among the Tsimihety, and some other groups, it is *fady* to work the land on Tuesdays; Thursday is also a *fady* day for some people, both for funerals and for farming.

A *fady* is not intended to restrict the freedom of the Malagasy but to ensure happiness and an improved quality of life. That said, however, there are some cruel *fady* which Christian missionaries have been trying, over the centuries, to eliminate. One is the taboo against twins among the Antaisaka people of Mananjary. Historically twins were killed or abandoned in the forest after birth. Today this is against the law but still persists and twins may not be buried in a tomb. Catholic missionaries have established an orphanage in the area for the twins born to mothers torn between social tradition and maternal love. Many mothers who would otherwise have to suffer the murder or abandonment of their babies can give them to the care of the Church.

FADY AND THEIR ORIGINS
The intruders and the geese
During the rule of King Andrianampoinimerina, thieves once attempted a raid on the village of Ambohimanga. The residents, however, kept geese which caused a commotion when the intruders entered the compound, thus alerting the people who could take action. Geese are therefore not eaten in this part of Madagascar.

The baby and the drongo
Centuries ago the communities of the east coast were persecuted by pirates who made incursions to the hills to pillage and take captives. At the warning that a pirate band was on its way the villagers would flee into the jungle. When pirates approached the village of Ambinanetelo the women with young children could not keep up with the others so hid in a thicket. Just as the pirates were passing them a baby wailed. The men turned to seek the source of the cry. It came again, but this time from the top of a tree: it was a drongo. Believing themselves duped by a bird the pirates gave up and returned to their boats. Ever since then it has been fady to kill a drongo in Ambinanetelo.

The tortoise and the pot
A Tandroy man put a tortoise in a clay pot of boiling water to cook it, but the tortoise kicked so hard that the pot shattered to smithereens. The man declared that his descendants would never again eat tortoise because it broke his pot.

Many *fady* benefit conservation. For instance the killing of certain animals is often prohibited, and the area around a tomb must be left undisturbed. Within these pockets of sacred forest, *ala masina*, it is strictly forbidden to cut trees or even to burn deadwood or leaf litter. In southeast Madagascar there are *alam-bevehivavy* (sacred women's forests) along a stretch of river where only women may bathe. Again, no vegetation may be cleared or damaged in such localities.

For an in-depth study of the subject try to get hold of a copy of *Taboo* (see *Books* in the *Appendix*).

Vintana
Along with *fady* goes a complex sense of destiny called *vintana*. Broadly speaking, *vintana* is to do with time – hours of the day, days of the week, etc – and *fady* usually involves actions or behaviour. Each day has its own *vintana* which tends to make it good or bad for certain festivals or activities. Sunday is God's day; work undertaken will succeed. Monday is a hard day, not a good day for work although projects undertaken (such as building a house) will last; Tuesday is an easy day – too easy for death so no burials take place – but all right for *famadihana* (exhumation) and light work; Wednesday is usually the day for funerals or *famadihana*; Thursday is suitable for weddings and is generally a 'good' day; Friday, *Zoma*, is a 'fat' day, set aside for enjoyment, but is also the best day for funerals; Saturday, a 'noble' day, is suitable for weddings but also for purification.

As an added complication, each day has its own colour. For example Monday is a black day. A black chicken may have to be sacrificed to avoid calamity, dark-coloured food should not be eaten and people may avoid black objects. Other day-colours are: Tuesday multicoloured, Wednesday brown, Thursday black, Friday red, Saturday blue.

Tody and Tsiny

A third force shapes Malagasy morality. In addition to *fady* and *vintana*, there is *tody* and its partner *tsiny*. *Tody* is somewhat similar to the Hindu/Buddhist kharma. The word means 'return' or 'retribution' and indicates that for any action there is a reaction. *Tsiny* means 'fault', usually a breach of the rules laid down by the ancestors.

After death

Burial, exhumation and second burial are the focus of Malagasy beliefs and culture. To the Malagasy, death is the most important part of life, when a person abandons his mortal form to become a much more powerful and significant ancestor. Since a tomb is for ever whilst a house is only a temporary dwelling, it follows that tombs should be more solidly constructed than houses.

Burial practices differ among the various tribes but all over Madagascar a ritual known as *sasa* is practised immediately after a death. The family of the deceased go to a fast-flowing river and wash all their clothes to remove the contamination of death.

Funeral practices vary from clan to clan. The Antankarana (in the north) and Antandroy (south) have 'happy' funerals during which they may run, with the coffin, into the sea. An unusual ritual, *tranondonaky*, is practised by the Antaisaka of the southeast. Here the corpse is first taken to a special house where, after a signal, the women all start crying. Abruptly, after a second signal, they dance. While this is happening the men are gathered in the hut of the local chief from where, one by one, they go to the house where the corpse is lying and attach money to it with a special oil. The children dance through the night, to the beat of drums, and in the morning the adults wrap the corpse in a shroud and take it to the *kibory*. These tombs are concealed in a patch of forest known as *ala fady* which only men may enter, and where they deliver their last messages to the deceased. These messages can be surprisingly fierce: 'You are now at your place so don't disturb us any more' or 'You are now with the children of the dead, but we are the children of the living.'

More disturbing, however, is the procedure following the death of a noble of the Menabe Sakalava people. The body may be placed on a wooden bench in the hot sun until it begins to decompose. The bodily fluids which drip out are collected in receptacles and drunk by the relatives in the belief that they will then take on the qualities of the deceased.

It is after the first burial, however, that the Malagasy generally honour and communicate with their dead, not only to show respect but to avoid the anger of the *razana* who dwell in the tombs. The best-known ceremony in Madagascar is the 'turning of the bones' by the Merina and Betsileo people: *famadihana* (pronounced 'famadeean'). This is a joyful occasion which occurs from four to seven years after the first burial, and provides the opportunity to communicate with and remember a loved one. The remains of the selected relative are taken from the tomb, rewrapped in a new burial shroud (*lamba mena*) and carried around the tomb a few times before being replaced. Meanwhile the corpse is spoken to and informed of all the latest events in the family and village. The celebrants are not supposed to show any grief. Generous quantities of alcohol are consumed amid a festive atmosphere with much dancing and music. Women who are trying to

TOMB ARCHITECTURE AND FUNERARY ART

In Madagascar the style and structure of tombs define the different clans or tribes better than any other visible feature, and also indicate the wealth and status of the family concerned. Below is a description of the tombs.

Merina In early times burial sites were near valleys or in marshes. The body would be placed in a hollowed-out tree trunk and sunk into the mud at the bottom of a marsh. These *fasam-bazimba* marshes were sacred. Later the Merina began constructing rectangular wooden tombs, mostly under the ground but with a visible structure above. In the 19th century the arrival of the Frenchman Jean Laborde had a profound effect on tomb architecture. Tombs were built with bricks and stone, no longer just from wood. It was Laborde's influence which led to the elaborate structure of modern tombs, which are often painted with geometric designs. Sometimes the interior is lavishly decorated.

Sakalava During the *Vazimba* period, the Sakalava tombs were simple piles of stones. As with the Merina the change occurred with the introduction of cement and a step design was added. At a later stage, wooden stelae, *aloalo*, were placed on the tombs, positioned to face east. These were topped with carvings of a most erotic nature. Since Sakalava tombs are for individuals and not families, there is no attempt at maintaining the stelae as it is believed that only when the wood decays will the soul of the buried person be released. Not all the carvings, however, are erotic – they may just depict scenes from everyday life or geometric paintings.

Tomb construction commences only after the person's death and can take up to six weeks, the body meanwhile being kept in a house. While a tomb is under construction, many zebu are sacrificed to the ancestors. The Sakalava call their tombs *izarana*, 'the place where we are separated'.

Antandroy and Mahafaly The local name of these tombs is *fanesy* which means 'your eternal place'. Zebu horns are scattered on the tomb as a symbol of wealth (on Sakalava tombs, zebu horns are only a decoration, not an indication of status). The Antandroy and Mahafaly tombs have much the same architecture as those of the Sakalava, but are more artistically decorated. The Mahafaly *aloalo* bear figures depicting scenes from the person's life, and the entire length is often carved with intricate designs. These tombs are carefully maintained, and it is probably the Mahafaly tombs in the southern interior which are the most colourful and striking symbols of Malagasy culture. Antandroy tomb paintings tend to be merely decorative and do not represent scenes from the deceased person's life.

conceive take small pieces of the old burial shroud and keep these under their mattresses to induce fertility.

By law a *famadihana* may take place only in the dry season, between June and September. It can last up to a week and involves the family in considerable expense, as befits the most important celebration for any family. In the Hauts Plateaux the practice of *famadihana* is embraced by rich and poor, urban and rural, and visitors

FAMADIHANA DIARY

Seraphine Tierney Ramanantsoa

I travelled across the seas to be here today. This day was long awaited, I would soon be in contact with my mother again. She had died seven years previously and I had not been able to be at her funeral. Tradition had always been so important to her so I knew she would be happy that I have come for her *famadihana*.

The meeting point is at 6am outside Cinema Soa in Antananarivo. My household woke up at about 4am to pack the food that had been prepared during the previous week. Drinks and cutlery are all piled into the car. A great number of people are expected as it is also the *famadihana* of the other members of my mother's family.

Fourteen cars and a big taxi-brousse carrying in all about 50 people, squashed one on top of the other, turn up. Everybody is excited. It is really great to see faces I haven't seen since my childhood. Everybody greets each other and exchanges news.

At 8am we all set off. We are heading towards Ifalimanjaka (meaning 'Joy Reigns Here'), in the *fivondronana* of Manjakandriana. Driving through villages with funny names like Ambohitrabiby (the 'Town of Animals') brings me back to the time when such names were familiar. We make one stop at Talatan'ny volon'ondry for a breakfast of rice cakes and sausages: another opportunity to re-acquaint myself with long lost cousins with whom I spent the long summer holidays as a child. We used to run around together playing games like catching grasshoppers and then finding carnivorous plants and dropping the insect in to see how long it took the plant to close its top to eat its prey.

10am. We arrive at the tombs. Faces are bright, full of expectancy. I ask what the day means to them. They all agree that it's a day for family togetherness, a day for joy, for remembrance.

We are in front of my mother's tomb. It is made out of stone and marble, very elegant. The family will have spent more money on keeping that tomb nice and well maintained than on their own house.

Everybody stands around in front of the tomb waiting for the main event to start: the opening of the tomb door. We have to wait for the president of the *fokon'tany* ('local authority') to give permission to open the tomb. Although it had been arranged beforehand he cannot be found anywhere. This wait, after such anticipation, is taken patiently by all – just one of those things.

Mats are laid on the ground on one side of the tomb. The atmosphere of joy is so tangible! Music is blaring out. Permission is finally granted to enter the tomb. The *ray aman-dreny* ('the elders') are the first to enter.

The inside of my mother's tomb looks very comfortable with bunk beds made out of stone. It is very clean. There are names on the side of the beds. The national flag is hoisted on top of the tomb as a sign of respect. The conversation goes on happily on the little veranda outside the tomb's door, people chatting about the event and what they have been doing in the last few days.

They start to take the bodies out. Voices could be heard above the happy

fortunate enough to be invited to one will find it a strange but very moving occasion; it's an opportunity to examine our own beliefs and rituals associated with death. For an account of what *famadihana* means to a sophisticated London-based Merina woman, see box above.

murmur: 'Who is this one? This is your ma! This one your aunt! Here is your uncle! Just carry them around!' The closest relations carry the body but others could touch and say hello. When carrying them, they make sure that the feet go first and the head behind. Everybody carries their loved ones out of the tomb in a line, crying but happy.

When all the bodies are out, they are put on the ground on the front side of the tomb, the head facing east, with their immediate family seated around their loved one. This is a very important moment of the *famadihana*: the beginning of the wrapping of the body. The old shroud in which the body was buried is left on and the new silk shroud put on top of it, following the mummified shape and using baby safety pins to keep it in place. There are three new silk shrouds for my mother which have been donated in remembrance and gratitude. The belief is that she won't be cold and the top shroud befits her, being of top quality silk with beautiful, delicate embroidery. This is the time to touch her, give her something, talk to her. Her best friend is there, making sure that my mother is properly wrapped, as the ritual has to follow certain rules. Lots of touching as silent conversation goes on, giving her the latest news or family gossip, and asking for her blessing. Perfume is sprinkled on her and wishes made at the same time.

The music plays on, everyone happily sitting around the mummified bodies. Flowers are placed on the bodies. The feeling of togetherness and love is so strong. This occasion is not just for the immediate family, but for cousins, and cousins of cousins, uncles and aunts and everybody meeting, bonded by the same ties, belonging to one unique extended family.

Photographs of the dead person are now put on top of each body. There is a photograph of a couple on top of one body: they were husband and wife and are now together for ever in the same silk shroud.

Food is served in the forest area just next to the tombs. The huge feast and celebration begins.

Back to the bodies. We lift them, carrying them on our shoulders. We sing old rhymes and songs and dance in a line, circling the tomb seven times, moving the body on our shoulder and making it dance with us.

The last dance ends. The bodies have to be back inside the tombs by a precise time and the tomb is immediately closed after a last ritual cleaning. This moment of goodbye is very emotional. The next time the tomb will be opened will not be for happiness but grief because it will be for a burial. *Famadihana* happens only once every seven or ten years.

Everybody returns to the cars and drives to the next meeting place – my uncle's, where a huge party finishes the day. Everyone is happy at having done their duty, *Vita ny adidy*!

It has been a very special day for me. My mother was extremely traditional, spending endless energy and money during her lifetime to keep the traditions. It all makes sense now because this *famadihana* brought so much joy, a strong sense of belonging and identity, and give a spiritual feeling that death is not an end but an extension into another life, linked somehow with this one.

Misaotra ry neny ('Thank you Mum').

Variations of *famadihana* are practised by other tribes. The Menabe Sakalava, for example, hold a *fitampoha* every ten years. This is a royal *famadihana* in which the remains of deceased monarchs are taken from their tomb and washed in a river. A similar ritual, the *fanampoambe*, is performed by the Boina Sakalava further north.

Healers, sorcerers and soothsayers

The 'Wise Men' in Malagasy society are the *ombiasy*; the name derives from *olona-be-hasina* meaning 'person of much virtue'. Traditionally they were from the Antaimoro clan and were the advisors of royalty: Antaimoro *ombiasy* came to Antananarivo to advise King Andrianampoinimerina and to teach him Arabic writing.

The astrologers, *mpanandro* ('those who make the day'), work on predictions of *vintana*. There is a Malagasy proverb, 'Man can do nothing to alter his destiny'; but the *mpanandro* will advise on the best day to build a house, or hold a wedding or *famadihana*. Though nowadays *mpanandro* do not have official recognition, they are present in all levels of society. A man (or woman) is considered to have the powers of a mpanandro when he has some grey hair – a sign that he is wise enough to interpret *vintana*. Antandroy soothsayers are known as *mpisoro*.

The Malagasy have a deep knowledge of herbal medicine and all markets display a variety of medicinal plants, amulets and talismans. The Malagasy names associated with these are *ody* and *fanafody*. Broadly speaking, *ody* refers to fetishes such as sacred objects in nature, and *fanafody* to herbal remedies – around 60% of the plants so far catalogued in Madagascar have healing properties. Travellers will sometimes come across conspicuous *ody* in the form of stones or trees which are sacred for a whole village, not just for an individual. Such trees are called *hazo manga*, 'good tree', and are presided over by the *mpisoro*, the senior man of the oldest family in the village. Another type of *ody* is the talisman, *aoly*, worn for protection if someone has transgressed a *fady* or broken a promise. *Aoly* are sometimes kept in the house or buried. *Ody fiti* are used to gain love (white magic) but sorcerers also sell other forms of *ody* for black magic and are paid by clients with either money, zebu or poultry (a red rooster being preferred).

Mpamonka are witch doctors with an intimate knowledge of poison and *mpisikidy* are sorcerers who use amulets, stones, and beads (known as *hasina*) for their cures. Sorcerers who use these in a destructive way are called *mpamosavy*.

On their death, sorcerers are not buried in tombs but are dumped to the west of their villages, barely covered with soil so that feral dogs and other creatures can eat their bodies. Their necks are twisted to face south.

Thanks to Nivo Ravelojaona, of Za Tours, who provided much of the above information.

The way it is...

Visitors from the West often find the beliefs and customs of the Malagasy merely bizarre. It takes time and effort to understand and respect the richness of tradition that underpins Malagasy society, but it is an effort well worth making.

Leonard Fox, author of *Hainteny*, sums it up perfectly:

> Whoever has witnessed the silent radiance of those who come to pray… at
> the house of Andrianampoinimerina in Ambohimanga and has
> experienced the nobility, modesty, unobsequious courtesy, and balanced
> wholeness of the poorest Merina who has remained faithful to his heritage
> can have no doubt as to the deep integrative value of the Malagasy
> spiritual tradition.

MALAGASY SOCIETY
Marriage and children

The Malagasy have a strong sense of community which influences their way of life. Just as the ancestors are laid in a communal tomb, so their descendants share a communal way of life, and even children are almost considered common property within their extended family. Children are seldom disciplined but learn by example.

Marriage is a fairly relaxed union and divorce is common. There is no formal dowry arrangement or bride price, but a present of zebu cattle will often be made. In rural communities the man should bring his new wife home to his village (not vice versa) or he will lose face. You often see young men walking to market wearing a comb in their hair. They are advertising their quest for a wife.

Most Malagasy (and all Christians) have only one wife, but there are exceptions. There is, for example, a well-known man living in Antalaha, in the northeast, who has 11 wives and 120 children. This arrangement seems to work surprisingly well, with each wife working to support her own children, and a head wife to whom the others defer. The man is wealthy enough to provide housing for all his family.

The village community

Malagasy society is a structured hierarchy with two fundamental rules: respect for the other person and knowing one's place. Within a village, the community is based on the traditional *fokonolona*. This concept was introduced by King Andrianampoinimerina when these councils of village elders were given responsibility for, among other things, law and order and the collection of taxes. Day-to-day decisions are still made by the *fokonolona*.

Rural Malagasy houses are always aligned north/south and generally have only one room. Furniture is composed of mats, *tsihy*, often beautifully woven. These are used for sitting and sleeping, and sometimes food is served on them. There are often *fady* attached to *tsihy*. For example you should not step over a mat, particularly one on which meals are eaten.

Part of the Malagasy culture is the art of oratory, *kabary*. Originally *kabary* were the huge meetings where King Andrianampoinimerina proclaimed his plans, but the word has now evolved to mean the elaborate form of speech used to inspire and control the crowds at such gatherings. Even rural leaders can speak for hours, using highly ornate language and many proverbs; a necessary skill in a society that reached a high degree of sophistication without a written language.

The market plays a central role in the life of rural people, who will often walk 15–20km to market with no intention of selling or buying, but simply to catch up on the gossip or continue the conversation broken off the previous week. You will see well-dressed groups of young people happily making their way to this social centre. Often there is a homemade tombola, and other outlets for gambling.

Festivals and ceremonies

Malagasy Christians celebrate the usual holy days, but most tribes or clans have their special festivals.

Ala volon-jaza

This is the occasion when a baby's hair is cut for the first time. With the Antambahoka people in the south the haircut is performed by the grandparents. The child is placed in a basin filled with water, and afterwards bathed. Among the Merina the ceremony is similar but only a man whose parents are still alive may cut a baby's hair. The family then have a meal of rice, zebu, milk and honey. Coins are placed in the bowl of rice and the older children compete to get as many as possible.

Circumcision

Boys are usually circumcised at the age of about two; a baby who dies before this operation has been performed may not be buried in the family tomb.

MALAGASY HATS
Camilla Backhouse

During my year working in Madagascar I was particularly struck by the wonderful array of different hats that were worn there. Market stalls were piled high with hats of all shapes, colours and sizes. I had done some millinery before and was extremely interested in all the different weaves and so spent time learning about them.

Little had been noted about Malagasy headwear until the missionaries came in the early 19th century. At that time, apparently, few hats were worn as a person's hairstyle was regarded as more important and a sign of beauty. People from each region of Madagascar had different ways of plaiting their hair and they would often incorporate shells, coins or jewels. Oils and perfumes were massaged into the hair – the richer people used *Tseroka*, a type of castor oil mixed with the powdered leaf of *Ravintsara*, which produced a nutmeg scent, while the poorest population were satisfied with the fat of an ox or cow.

The chiefs wore simple headdresses but it was not until the Europeans came that hats became more popular. Although plaiting and the art of weaving were already very well established, there was little or no evidence of woven hats. The cutting of hair was introduced in 1822 which may have changed the Malagasy attitudes to wearing hats – to cover an unplaited head certainly would not be any detriment to their beauty. Initially hats were worn by the more wealthy people. Chiefs could be seen wearing caps made of neatly woven rushes or coarse grass and the people of Tana began to wear hats of more costly and durable material (often imported from overseas). It was Jean Laborde in the 1850s who started the industry of hat-making and helped to increase the production of them.

The operation itself is often done surgically, but in some rural areas it may still be performed with a sharpened piece of bamboo. The foreskin is not always simply discarded. In the region of the Antambahoka it may be eaten by the grandparents, and in Antandroy country it could be shot from the barrel of a gun!

Different clans have their own circumcision ceremonies. Among the Antandroy, uncles dance with their nephews on their shoulders. But the most famous ceremony is *Sambatra*, which takes place every seven years in Mananjary.

Tsangatsaine
This is a ceremony performed by the Antankarana. Two tall trees growing side by side near the house of a noble family are tied together to symbolise the unification of the tribe, as well as the tying together of the past and present, the living and the dead.

Fandroana
This was the royal bath ceremony which marked the Malagasy New Year. These celebrations used to take place in March, with much feasting. While the monarch was ritually bathed, the best zebu was slaughtered and the choicest rump steak presented to the village nobles. The day was the equivalent of the Malagasy National Day, but the French moved this to July 14, the date of the establishment of the French Protectorate. This caused major resentment among the Malagasy as effectively their traditional New Year was taken from them. After independence

In each region the hats vary – they use different plant fibres (depending on what grows well near them), different weaves and occasionally dyes. The colours used are not the vegetable or plant dyes I had imagined but imported from China. The fibres are usually from palms (raffia, *badika*, *manarana*, *dara*), reeds (*penjy*, *harefo*) or straw. Some of the best regions that I came across for seeing weaving were near Lac Tritriva (straw), Maroantsetra (raffia), Mananjary (*penjy*, *dara*), Mahsoabe near Fianarantsoa (*badika*) and Vohipeno (*harefo*).

The ways of preparing the fibres differ, but in general they are dried, flattened and then, if necessary, using a sharp knife, are stripped into thin fibres. They are then ready for weaving. Some are woven into strips which are eventually machined together, while other regions use a continuous weave method to make the entire hat. The latter method can be extremely complicated and is an amazing art to watch. The weaver will place their foot on the central part of the woven circle and gradually intertwine hundreds of different fibres into position. One of my lasting memories was spending time in Maroantsetra where they make the most beautiful crochet-style raffia hat. Women sit on palm mats outside their houses weaving, while children play, plait hair or busily prepare food for the next meal. Occasionally the hats are blocked (a method of shaping a crown or brim over a wooden block). There are places in Tana where they heat steel blocks on a fire and then press the woven hat into a trilby style for example. This was a fascinating sight to see as normally these blocks are electrically heated.

The variety of hats is astounding. It can take a day for a woman to weave a hat, and this can be a main source of family income. If you are interested in getting a Malagasy hat, it is worthwhile getting to know a weaver so they may be able to make one large enough for the *vahaza* head!

the date was changed to June 26 to coincide with Independence Day. These days, because of the cost of zebu meat and the value attached to the animals, the traditional meat has been replaced by chicken, choice portions again being given to the respected members of the community. In the absence of royalty there is, of course, no royal bath ceremony.

Music

Music infuses the lives of the Malagasy people, and like Hainteny it is the outward expression of their feelings towards nature and human relationships. Traditional musical instruments are often unadapted natural objects – dried reeds or gourds rubbed together or shaken to the beat of the music – while the words reflect the spiritual essence of the culture. Pop music is encroaching on this tradition, of course, but the charity Valiha High (see page 000) is helping preserve the traditions.

ETHNIC GROUPS

This section was originally taken from A Glance at Madagascar *by Ken Paginton in 1973 (and at that time the only authoritative source on Madagascar) and has subsequently been added to from a variety of sources.*

The different clans of Madagascar are based more upon old kingdoms than upon ethnic grouping. Traditions are changing: the descriptions below reflect the tribes at the time of Independence, rather than in the more fluid society of today.

THE VAZIMBA

Vazimba is the name given to the earliest inhabitants of Madagascar, pastoralists of the central plateaux who were displaced or absorbed by later immigrants. Once thought to be pre-Indonesian aboriginals from Africa, it is now generally accepted that they were survivors of the earliest Austronesian immigrants who were pushed to the west by later arrivals.

Vazimba come into both the legends and history of the Malagasy. *Vazimba* tombs are now places of pilgrimage where sacrifices are made for favours and cures. It is *fady* to step over such a tomb. *Vazimba* are also thought to haunt certain springs and rocks, and offerings may be made here. They are the ancestral guardians of the soil.

Antaifasy (People-of-the-sands)

Living in the southeast around Farafangana, they cultivate rice, and fish in the lakes and rivers. Divided into three clans, each with its own 'king', they generally have stricter moral codes than other tribes. They have large collective burial houses known as *kibory*, built of wood or stone and generally hidden in the forest.

Antaimoro (People-of-the-coast)

These are among the most recent arrivals and live in the southeast around Vohipeno and Manakara. They guard Islamic tradition and Arab influence and still use a form of Arab writing known as *sorabe*. They use verses of the Koran as amulets.

Antaisaka

Centred south of Farafangana on the southeast coast but now fairly widely spread throughout the island, they are an off-shoot of the Sakalava tribe. They cultivate coffee, bananas and rice – but only the women harvest the rice. There are strong marriage taboos amongst them. Often the houses may have a second door on the east side which is used only for taking out a corpse. They use the *kibory*, communal burial house, the corpse usually being dried out for two or three years before finally being put there.

Antankarana (Those-of-the-rocks)

Living in the north around Antsiranana (Diego Suarez) they are fishermen or cattle raisers whose rulers came from the Sakalava dynasty. Their houses are usually raised on stilts. Numerous *fady* exist amongst them governing relations between the sexes in the family; for example a girl may not wash her brother's clothes. The legs of a fowl are the father's portion, whereas amongst the Merina, for instance, they are given to the children.

Antambahoaka (Those-of-the-people)

The smallest tribe, of the same origin as the Antaimoro and living around Mananjary on the southeast coast. They have some Arab traits and amulets are used. They bury in a *kibory*. Group circumcision ceremonies are carried out every seven years.

Antandroy (People-of-the-thorns)

Traditionally nomadic, they live in the arid south around Ambovombe. A dark-skinned people, they wear little clothing and are said to be frank and open, easily

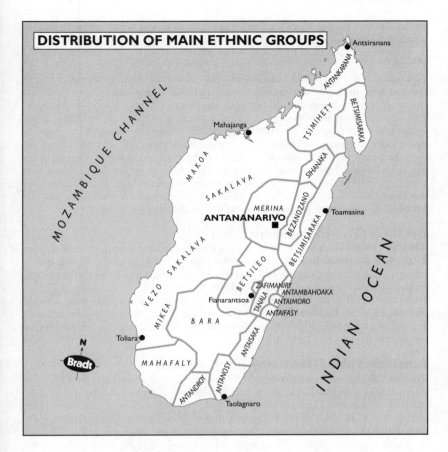

DISTRIBUTION OF MAIN ETHNIC GROUPS

roused to either joy or anger. Their women occupy an inferior position, and it is *fady* for a woman to milk a cow. The villages are often surrounded by a hedge of cactus plants. Until recently they ate little rice, their staples being maize, cassava and sweet potatoes. They believe in the *kokolampo*, a spirit of either good or bad influence. Their tombs are similar to those of the Mahafaly tribe. Sometimes it is *fady* among them for a child to say his father's name, or to refer by name to parts of his father's body. Thus he may say *ny fandiany* (the-what-he-moves-with) for his feet, and *ny amboniny* (the-top-of-him) for his head.

Antanosy (People-of-the-island)

The island is a small one in the Fanjahira River. They live in the southeast, principally around Taolagnaro (Fort Dauphin). Their social structure is based on clans with a 'king' holding great authority over each one. There are strict *fady* governing relationships in the family. For example, a brother may not sit on or step over his sister's mat. As with many other tribes there are numerous *fady* regarding pregnancy: a pregnant woman should not sit in the doorway of the house; she should not eat brains; she should not converse with men; people who have no children should not stay in her house overnight. Other *fady* are that relatives should not eat meat at a funeral and the diggers opening a tomb should not wear clothes. When digging holes for the corner posts of a new house it may be *fady* to stand up so the job must be performed sitting down.

Bara

Originally in the southwest near Toliara, these nomadic cattle raisers now live in the south-central area around Ihosy and Betroka. Their name has no special meaning but it is reputed to derive from an African (Bantu) word. They may be polygamous and women occupy an inferior position in their society. They attach importance to the *fatidra* or 'blood pact'. Cattle stealing is regarded as proof of manhood and courage, without which a man cannot expect to get a wife. They are dancers and sculptors, a unique feature of their carved wooden figures being eyelashes of real hair set into the wood. They believe in the *helo*, a spirit that manifests itself at the foot of trees. In the past a whole village would move after somebody died owing to the fear of ghosts. They use caves in the mountains for burial. It is the custom to shave the head on the death of a near relative.

Betsileo (The-many-invincibles)

They are centred in the south of the Hauts Plateaux around Fianarantsoa but about 150,000 of them also live in the Betsiboka region. They are energetic and expert rice-producers, their irrigated, terraced rice-fields being a feature of the landscape. *Famadihana* was introduced to their culture by the Merina at the time of Queen Ranavalona I. It is *fady* for the husband of a pregnant woman to wear a *lamba* thrown over his shoulder. It may be *fady* for the family to eat until the father is present or for anyone to pick up his fork until the most honourable person present has started to eat.

Betsimisaraka (The-many-inseparables)

They are the second largest tribe and live on the east coast in the region between Nosy Varika and Antalaha. Their culture has been influenced by Europeans, particularly pirates. They cultivate rice and work on vanilla plantations. Their clothes are sometimes made from locally woven raffia. Originally their society included numerous local chiefs. The *tangalamena* is the local official for religious rites and customs. The Betsimisaraka have many superstitious beliefs: *angatra* (ghosts), *zazavavy an-drano* (mermaids), and *kalamoro*, little wild men of the woods, about 25 inches high with long flowing hair, who like to slip into houses and steal rice from the cooking pot. In the north coffins are generally placed under a shelter, in the south in tombs. It may be *fady* for a brother to shake hands with his sister, or for a young man to wear shoes while his father is still living.

Bezanozano (Many-small-plaits)

The name refers to the way in which they do their hair. They were probably one of the first tribes to become established in Madagascar and now live in an area between the Betsimisaraka lowlands and the Merina highlands. Like the Merina, they practise *famadihana*. As with most of the coastal tribes their funeral celebrations involve the consumption of considerable quantities of *toaka* (rum).

Mahafaly (Those-who-make-taboos or Those-who-make-happy)

The etymology of the word is sometimes disputed but the former meaning is generally regarded as being correct. They probably arrived around the 12th century and live in the southwest desert area around Ampanihy and Ejeda. They are farmers, with maize, sorgho and sweet potatoes as their chief crops; cattle rearing occupies a secondary place. They kept their independence under their own local chiefs until the French occupation and still keep the bones of some of their old chiefs – this is the *jiny* cult. Their villages usually have a sacrificial post, the *hazo manga*, on the east side where sacrifices are made. Some of the blood is generally put on the foreheads of the people attending.

The tombs of the Mahafaly attract a great deal of interest. They are big rectangular constructions of uncut stone rising some three feet above the ground and decorated with *aloalo* and the horns of the cattle slain at the funeral feast. The tomb of the Mahafaly king Tsiampody has the horns of 700 zebu on it. The *aloalo* are sculpted wooden posts set upright on the tomb, often depicting scenes from the person's life. The burial customs include waiting for the decomposition of the body before it is placed in the tomb. It is the practice for a person to be given a new name after death – generally beginning with 'Andria'.

The divorce rate is very high and it is not at all uncommon for a man to divorce and remarry six or seven times. It is very often *fady* for children to sleep in the same house as their parents. Their *rombo* (very similar to the *tromba* of the Sakalava) is the practice of contacting various spirits for healing purposes. Amongst the spirits believed in are the *raza* who are not real ancestors and in some cases are even supposed to include *vazaha* (white foreigners), and the *vorom-be* which is the spirit of a big bird.

Makoa
The Makoa are descended from slaves taken from the Makua people of Mozambique, and although sometims classified as Vezo, they maintain a separate identity. Typically of larger stature than most Malagasy, Makoa men were often employed by the French as policemen and soldiers, thus reinforcing their distinction from other Malagasy.

Merina (People-of-the-Highlands)
They live on the Hauts Plateaux, the most developed area of the country, the capital being 95% Merina. They are of Malayo-Polynesian origin and vary in colour from ivory to very dark, with straight hair. They used to be divided into three castes: the Andriana (nobles), the Hova (freemen) and the Andevo (serfs); but legally these divisions no longer exist. Most Merina houses are built of brick or mud; some are two-storey buildings with slender pillars, where the people live mainly upstairs. Most villages of any size have a church – probably two, Catholic and Protestant. There is much irrigated rice cultivation, and the Merina were the first tribe to have any skill in architecture and metallurgy. *Famadihana* is essentially a Merina custom.

Mikea
The term 'Mikea' refers not so much to a tribe as to a lifestyle. They subsist by foraging in the dry forests of the west and southwest. Various groups of people up the west coast are called Mikea, although their main area is the Forêt des Mikea between Morombe and Toliara. The Mikea are Malagasy of various origins, having adopted their particular lifestyle (almost unique in Madagascar) for several reasons, including fleeing from oppression and taxation etc exerted on them by various powers: Sakalava, French, and the Government of the 2nd Republic. (Information from Dr J Bond.)

Sakalava (People-of-the-long-valleys)
They live in the west between Toliara and Mahajanga and are dark skinned with Polynesian features and short curly hair. They were at one time the largest and

HAINTENY

References in this book to the Merina have hitherto been focused on their military abilities, but this tribe has a rich and complex spiritual life. Perhaps the shortest route to the soul of any society is through its poetry, and we are fortunate that there is a book of the traditional Malagasy poetry, *Hainteny*. Broadly speaking, *hainteny* are poems about love: love between parent and child, between man and woman, the love of nature, the appreciation of good versus evil, the acceptance of death. Through the sensitive translations of Leonard Fox, the spiritual and emotional life of the Merina is made available to the reader who cannot fail to be impressed by these remarkable people. As Leonard Fox says: 'On the most basic level, *hainteny* give us an incomparable insight into a society characterised by exceptional refinement and subtlety, deep appreciation of beauty, delight in sensual enjoyment, and profound respect for the spiritual realities of life.'

There are two examples of *hainteny* below, and others are scattered throughout this book.

What is the matter, Raivonjaza,
That you remain silent?
Have you been paid or hired and your mouth tied,
That you do not speak with us, who are your parents?
– I have not been paid or hired
and my mouth has not been tied,
but I am going home to my husband
and am leaving my parents,
my child, and my friends,
so I am distressed,
speaking little.
Here is my child, dear Mother and Father.
If he is stubborn, be strict, but do not beat him;
and if you hit him, do not use a stick.
And do not act as though you do not see him
when he is under your eyes, saying:
'Has this child eaten?'
Do not give him too much,
Do not give him the remains of a meal,
and do not give him what is half-cooked,
for I will be far and will long for him.

Do not love me, Andriamatoa, as one loves
the banana tree exposed to the wind,
overcome and in danger from cold.
Do not love me as one loves a door:
It is loved, but constantly pushed.
Love me as one loves a little crab:
even its claws are eaten.

most powerful tribe, though disunited, and were ruled by their own kings and queens. Certain royal relics remain – sometimes being kept in the northeast corner of a house. The Sakalava are cattle raisers, and riches are reckoned by the number of cattle owned. There is a record of human sacrifice amongst them up to the year

1850 at special occasions such as the death of a king. The *tromba* (trance state) is quite common. It is *fady* for pregnant women to eat fish or to sit in a doorway. Women hold a more important place amongst them than in most other tribes.

Sihanaka (People-of-the-swamps)
Their home is the northeast of the old kingdom of Imerina around Lake Alaotra and they have much in common with the Merina. They are fishermen, rice growers and poultry raisers. Swamps have been drained to make vast rice-fields cultivated with modern machinery and methods. They have a special rotation of *fady* days.

St Marians
The population of Ile Sainte Marie (Nosy Boraha) is mixed. Although Indonesian in origin there has been influence from both Arabs and European pirates.

Tanala (People-of-the-forest)
These are traditionally forest-dwellers, living inland from Manakara, and are rice and coffee growers. Their houses are usually built on stilts. The Tanala are divided into two groups: the Ikongo in the south and the Menabe in the north. The Ikongo are an independent people and never submitted to Merina domination, in contrast to the Menabe. Burial customs include keeping the corpse for up to a month. Coffins are made from large trees to which sacrifices are sometimes made when they are cut down. The Ikongo usually bury their dead in the forest and may mark a tree to show the spot.

Some recent authorities dispute that the Tanala exist as a separate ethnic group.

Tsimihety (Those-who-do-not-cut-their-hair)
The refusal to cut their hair (to show mourning on the death of a Sakalava king) was to demonstrate their independence. They are an energetic and vigorous people in the north-central area and are spreading west. The oldest maternal uncle occupies an important position.

Vezo (Fishing people)
More usually referred to as Vezo-Sakalava, they are not generally recognised as a separate tribe but as a clan of the Sakalava. They live on the coast in the region of Morondava in the west to Faux Cap in the south. They use little canoes hollowed out from tree trunks and fitted with one outrigger pole and a small rectangular sail. In these frail but stable craft they go far out to sea. The Vezo are also noted for their tombs, which are graves dug into the ground surrounded by wooden palisades, the main posts of which are crowned by erotic wooden carved figures.

Zafimaniry
A clan of some 15,000 people distributed in about 100 villages in the forests between the Betsileo and Tanala areas southeast of Ambositra. They are known for their woodcarvings and sculpture, and are descended from people from the Hauts Plateaux who established themselves there early in the 19th century. The Zafimaniry are thus interesting to historians as they continue the forms of housing and decoration of past centuries. Their houses, which are made from vegetable fibres and wood with bamboo walls and roofs, have no nails and can be taken down and moved from one village to another.

In the last few years there have been several anthropological books published in English about the people of Madagascar. See *Books* in the *Appendix*.

The tribes may differ but a Malagasy proverb shows their feeling of unity: *Ny olombelona toy ny molo-bilany, ka iray mihodidina ihany*; 'Men are like the lip of the cooking pot which forms just one circle'.

LANGUAGE

The Indonesian origin of the Malagasy people shows strongly in their language which is spoken, with regional variations of dialect, throughout the island. (Words for domestic animals, however, are derived from Kiswahili, indicating that the early settlers, sensibly enough, did not bring animals with them in their outrigger canoes.) Malagasy is a remarkably rich language, full of images, metaphors and proverbs. Literal translations of Malagasy words and phrases are often very poetic. 'Dusk' is *Maizim-bava vilany*, 'Darken the mouth of the cooking pot'; 'two or three in the morning' is *Misafo helika ny kary*, 'When the wild cat washes itself'. The richness of the language means that there are few English words that can be translated into a single word in Malagasy, and vice versa. An example given by Leonard Fox in his book on the poetry of Madagascar, *Hainteny*, is *miala mandry*. *Miala* means 'go out/go away' and *mandry* means 'lie down/go to sleep'. Together, however, they mean 'to spend the night away from home, and yet be back in the early morning as if never having been away'!

Learning, or even using, the Malagasy language may seem a challenging prospect to the first-time visitor. Place names may be 15 characters long (because they usually have a literal meaning, such as Ranomafana: Hot water), with seemingly erratic syllable stress. However, as a courtesy to the Malagasy people you should learn a few Malagasy words. There is a Malagasy vocabulary on page 445. Dictionaries and phrase books can be bought in Antananarivo. A useful one

SOME MALAGASY PROVERBS

Tantely tapa-bata ka ny foko no entiko mameno azy.
This is only half a pot of honey but my heart fills it up.

Mahavoa roa toy ny dakam-boriky.
Hit two things at once like the kick of a donkey.

Tsy midera vady tsy herintaona.
Don't praise your wife before a year.

Ny omby singorana amin' ny tandrony, ary ny olona kosa amin' ny vavany.
Oxen are trapped by their horns and men by their words.

Tondro tokana tsy mahazo hao.
You can't catch a louse with one finger.

Ny alina mitondra fisainana.
The night brings wisdom.

Aza manao herim-boantay.
If you are just a dung beetle don't try to move mountains.

Aza midera harena, fa niter-day.
Do not boast about your wealth if you are a father.

Ny teny toy ny fonosana, ka izay mamono no mamaha.
Words are like a parcel: if you tie lots of knots you will have to undo them.

MALAGASY WITHOUT (TOO MANY) TEARS
Janice Booth

Once you've thrown out the idea that you must speak a foreign language correctly or not at all, and that you must use complete sentences, you can have fun with only a few words of Malagasy. Basic French is understood almost everywhere, but the people – particularly in villages – warm instantly to any attempts to speak 'their own' language.

If you learn only three words, choose *misaotra* ('thank you'), pronounced 'misowtr'; *veloma* ('goodbye'), pronounced 'veloom'; and *manao ahoana* (pronounced roughly 'manna owner'), which is an all-purpose word meaning 'hello', 'good morning' or 'good day'. If you can squeeze in another three, go for *tsara* ('good'); *aza fady* ('please'), pronounced 'azafad'; and *be* (pronounced 'beh'), which can be used – sometimes ungrammatically, but who cares! – to mean 'big', 'very' or 'much'. Thus *tsara be* means very good; and *misaotra be* means a big thank you. Finally, when talking to an older person, it's polite to add *tompoko* (pronounced 'toompk') after 'thank you' or 'goodbye'. This is equivalent to Madame or Monsieur in French. If your memory's poor, write the vocabulary on a postcard and carry it round with you.

In a forest one evening, at dusk, I was standing inside the trunk and intertwining roots of a huge banyan tree, looking up through the branches at the fading sky and a few early stars. It was very peaceful, very silent. Suddenly a small man appeared from the shadows, holding a rough wooden dish. Old and poorly dressed, probably a cattle herder, he stood uncertainly, not wanting to disturb me. I said '*Manao ahoana*,' and he replied. I touched the bark of the tree gently and said '*tsara*'. '*Tsara*,' he agreed, smiling. Then he said a sentence in which I recognised *tantely* ('honey'). I pointed questioningly to a wild bees' nest high in the tree. '*Tantely*,' he repeated quietly, pleased. I pointed to his dish – '*Tantely sakafo?*' Yes, he was collecting wild honey for food. '*Tsara. Veloma, tompoko.*' I moved off into the twilight. '*Veloma*,' he called softly after me. So few words, so much said.

Another day, in Tana, a teenaged girl was pestering me for money. She didn't seem very deserving but wouldn't give up. Then I asked her in Malagasy, 'What's your name?' She looked astonished, eyes suddenly meeting mine instead of sliding furtively. 'Noro.' So I asked, very politely, 'Please, Noro, go away. Goodbye.' Nonplussed, she stared at me briefly before moving off, the cringing attitude quite gone. By using her name, I'd given her dignity. You can find that vocabulary – all seven words of it! – in the language appendix on page 445.

'What's your name?' is probably the phrase I most enjoy using. Say it to a child and its eyes grow wider, as a timid little voice answers you. Then you can say '*Manao ahoana*', using the name, and you've forged a link. Now find out from *Appendix 2* how to say 'My name is...' – and you're into real conversation!

When I'm in Madagascar I still carry a copy of the language appendix in my bag. It's dog-eared now, and scribbled on. But it's my passport to a special kind of contact with friendly, gentle and fascinating people.

(published by Hippocrene Books, New York) combines dictionary and phrase book in one volume; website (UK): www.wermter.fsnet.co.uk.

Natural History

This section, with the exception of Geology and as far as Conservation, is written by Jonathan Hughes with additional information by Jim Bond, Nick Garbutt and others.

INTRODUCTION

Madagascar's natural history is its most striking single feature. There are over 200,000 species on the island, living in habitats ranging from rainforests to deserts and from mountain tops to mangrove swamps. The residents are as unique as they are diverse, so that a list of Malagasy species reads like a hurried appendix tagged on the end of a catalogue of the world's wildlife – 'The ones found nowhere else'. Six whole plant families exist only on Madagascar, as do 1,000 orchid species, many thousands of succulents, countless insects, over 300 species of frog, at least 270 kinds of reptile, five families of birds and more than 100 different mammals, including an entire group of primates, the order to which we belong. One thing is certain: whatever animal or plant you gaze upon during your visit, you are unlikely to see it anywhere else.

This magnificent menagerie is the product of a spectacular geological past. More than 165 million years ago, Madagascar was a land-locked plateau at the centre of the largest continent the Earth has ever seen, Gondwanaland or Gondwana. This was during the age of the reptiles at about the time when the flowering plants were beginning to blossom and primitive mammals and birds were finding a niche among their giant dinosaur cohabitants. With a combination of sea-level rises and plate movements Gondwanaland subsequently broke into the island continents of Australia, Antarctica, South America and Africa. As the Indian Ocean opened up between once neighbouring territories, Madagascar cast away from the African coast, setting itself adrift as one of the Earth's great experiments in evolution.

Some of the plants and animals present on the island today are the results of adaptation from the original, marooned Gondwanaland stock. Ancient groups such as the ferns, cycads, palms and pandans, and primitive reptiles such as the boas and iguanids, are descendants of this relic community. Yet the magic of Madagascar is that a select band of species have enriched the community by arriving *since* the break-up. Flying, swimming, journeying as seeds or riding the floodwaters of the east African rivers in hollow trunks, wave after wave of more recent plants and animals came from over the horizon during a period of 100 million years, bringing with them the latest adaptations from the big world beyond. Colonisers, such as the lemurs and carnivores, may have had a helping hand from a partial land-bridge which is thought to have appeared from beneath the waves of the Mozambique Channel about 40 million years ago.

Yet, whatever their mode of transport, upon landfall each species spread outwards in every direction, through the tremendous range of habitats on offer, changing subtly as they encountered new environments, sometimes to the extent that new species were formed. This evolutionary process is termed 'adaptive radiation' and it results in the creation of an array of new species found nowhere else.

The patterns in the island's diversity tell us something of the timing of these

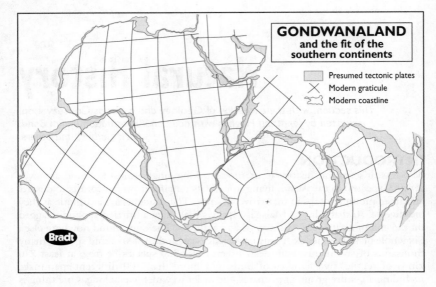

GONDWANALAND
and the fit of the
southern continents

> Presumed tectonic plates
> ✕ Modern graticule
> Modern coastline

colonisations. A large number of unique succulent plants indicates an early arrival from Africa in the dry west, followed by a radiation eastwards ending in the rainforests. On the contrary, the two Malagasy pitcher plants found on the east coast probably arrived at about the same time as the Malagasy, and from the same direction. The remoteness of Madagascar's rainforests, positioned as they are across a stretch of dry plateaux and over a spine of high mountains, may have made these humid lands tantalisingly out of reach for African rainforest species. Certainly many of the Malagasy species seem to have closer associations with Asian and South American groups with which they share Gondwanaland ancestors. As a result of these various evolutionary processes and chance events, the island is blessed with animals and plants of many descriptions, most unique to the island and many still unstudied.

GEOLOGY

Tim Ireland

Note: Ma = millions of years ago, Ga = billions of years ago

The geology of Madagascar raises plenty of interesting questions, many of them unanswered, and attracts geologists and mining companies from around the world. Madagascar comprises three main geological terranes: a **crystalline core** comprising the central highlands, a **sedimentary shelf** that flanks this core on the west, and dispersed **volcanic edifices**.

The **crystalline core** dates to the Late Proterozoic (900–550 Ma), a period long before the evolution of complex life, and before the assembly of the continents as we know them. Yet these rocks contain tiny crystals of the resistant mineral zircon which testify to a far greater antiquity (2.6 Ga). At that stage the atmosphere was rich in carbon dioxide, the now-geologically distinctive continents and oceans differed less than they do today … little is known confidently about those times. Probably the zircon crystals record the formation of a continent that would later become part of Gondwana. Other continental masses also existed, several that would later become the northern continents, and one that would split and become South America and Africa.

Two of these (South America-Africa and Australia-Antarctica-India-Madagascar) had been drifting slowly closer together, and then at 690 Ma, almost at the same time as the first large multicellular marine creatures evolved, they collided, as India and Asia collided to form the Himalaya. During such collisions the edges of the continents crumple and snap, and kilometre-thick sheets are thrust over each other. Mountain ranges (orogenic belts) are thus created that suture together the original continental blocks. This so-called 'Mozambique Belt' of mountains (Pan-African Orogen) was immense, extending 7,000km from modern Kenya to Antarctica, and Madagascar was at the centre of it. The rocks buried during mountain building are recrystallised and partially melted under the subsequent pressure and heat. The Central Highlands of Madagascar are just a small part of the exhumed roots of this vast and ancient mountain belt, and consist of intensely recrystallised rocks such as gneisses and granulites (formed in the solid-state), and subordinate migmatites and granites (crystallised from molten rock). The ramparts of the 'Mozambique Belt' then stood sentinel, slowly eroding but largely unchanged, for several hundred million years, while soft-bodied life in the oceans experimented with the idea of greater progression.

The **sedimentary shelf** began to form early in the Palaeozoic (500 Ma), as three-dimensional macroscopic organisms with external skeletons evolved and explosively diversified. The old mountain belt had been eroded down near sea-level, and the waning of an ice age caused marine flooding of the land. Across the world, life evolved dramatically toward a climax of vegetation productivity in the Carboniferous (when much of the world's coal was deposited: 320 Ma) and then shivered through its most severe ice age and most catastrophic extinction only 30 million years later (96% of marine species vanished). That ice age scraped all evidence of the preceding sedimentation from proto-Madagascar, and the geological record there is reset, beginning with gravel and boulder deposits laid down as the glaciers retreated. In the middle Permian (270 Ma), the southern continents were still assembled as one (Gondwana) in which Madagascar was a central part without identity, bound on the west by Africa, the east by India and the south by Antarctica.

Gondwana began to split apart soon after, toward the modern continental distribution. As a continent divides, rifts form (like modern East Africa), then become nascent seas (like the Red Sea), and eventually widen into oceans. The rocks of the sedimentary shelf record 100 million years of deposition spanning that cycle, for the rift separating Madagascar from Africa. The earliest (basal) sediments are mixed glacial and river and lake (terrestrial) deposits that contain a fossil flora common to all the modern southern continents. Later, the land was inundated and marine carbonates were deposited in this new shallow sea, which preserve the remains of some primitive fish. During the Triassic (240–210 Ma) the landscape was uplifted (rejuvenated) and terrestrial gravels and sands were deposited, including those exposed in Isalo National Park. Major marine transgression followed, and from this time, until after the demise of the dinosaurs (63 Ma), fossiliferous marine limestone (carbonate) sedimentation dominated in the growing Mozambique Channel. These sediments today make up the Bemahara Plateau and the *tsingy* landscapes of western Madagascar. The shallow marine ecosystems at that stage were characterised by the super-abundance of squid-like animals with planar, segmented, spiral shells (*ammonites*), and the west-Madagascan sedimentary carbonate sequences are an incredible repository of these fossils. Tectonic landscape rejuvenation occurred again between 50 and 30 Ma as a major eastern rift developed between India and Madagascar, and ended sedimentation on the shelf.

The **volcanic edifices** of Madagascar are less obvious than related volcanoes responsible for the Comoros, Réunion and Mauritius islands. They are widespread in the north and along the east coast, and inland, make up the Ankaratra Massif, Itasy Highlands, and Montagne d'Ambre. Underwater volcanic activity began during the Cretaceous (120 Ma), related to the eventual departure of India, and has persisted off the north Malagasy coast up to the present day, due to anomalously high heat flow similar to the case in Hawaii. The lavas and intrusive rocks produced have rare and bizarre chemistry, consisting of a bimodal super-alkalic (Na-rich) suite dominated by basaltic andesites and Na-amphibole-bearing syenitic rocks. The most recent major volcanism occurred less than two million years ago, of note giving birth to Nosy Be, where modern hot springs testify to the relative youth of volcanic activity. There are suggestions that the volcanic focus is moving southeast, from the Comoros toward Madagascar; the volcanic record in the island is potentially far from over.

Significant **landscape evolution** has occurred over the last 40 Ma. At and after the time India began to head northeast, the rift between Africa and Madagascar stabilised and topographic relief was regenerated by activity on major NNE- and NNW-oriented faults. These orientations can be recognised across the country bounding smaller sedimentary basins and mountain ranges, and most noticeably, control the geometry of the east coast. The centre and east were uplifted more than the west, providing the basis for the modern geomorphology of the island. Completely emergent for the first time for several hundred million years, during this time land plants and animals evolved and proliferated toward the present unique flora and fauna for which Madagascar is famous. Local lake and river deposits developed in the lowlands, and erosion cut back the highlands. In the centre and east, the entire marine record was stripped away, revealing the crystalline core and resulting in undulating dome-like mountains (eg: Pic d'Imarivolanitra, aka Pic Boby). In the west, the sedimentary sequences were eroded flat, to near sea-level. Tectonic activity in the last million years has again uplifted the Malagasy terrain, and this ancient erosional surface (peneplain) now defines the Bemaraha (and other) plateaux of the west, dissected by the modern west-flowing rivers.

The final chapter starts just two thousand years ago, when skilled Malay boatmen found their way to then uninhabited Madagascar (while their brethren discovered all but two of the Pacific Islands). Humans can affect geological processes; reduction in primary forest since the colonisation of Madagascar has indisputably influenced the shape of the land. Soils stabilised by deep root systems and high inputs of organic matter become susceptible to erosion, and the sediment load in the rivers has increased. In the 50 years to 1945, 40m of clay was deposited in the delta of the Betsiboka River at Mahajanga, immensely more than the underlying sedimentary record suggests was usual prior to deforestation. Ubiquitous hillside scars called *lavaka* are the inland testimony to this accelerated redistribution of material from highlands to coast, an inexorable environmental response to deforestation that is sending the Malagasy highlands toward eventual peneplanation at an incredible rate; if mean annual erosion of 1mm takes place continuously without volcanic or tectonic rejuvenation, Madagascar will be reduced to near sea level in a short three million years.

MADAGASCAR'S BIODIVERSITY

Madagascar is one of the 12 most important countries for biodiversity on the planet. It is home to so many species for two reasons: it is near to the Equator and it contains an astonishing array of habitats. The tropical climate is a perfect host to the processes of life – far more living things survive within the tropics than in

THE EXTINCT MEGAFAUNA

Today, Madagascar's wildlife is as rich as anywhere on Earth. The tragedy is that it was once richer still. When, just 2,000 years ago, humans arrived, they found a world covered with forests and populated by huge tortoises, dwarf hippos, lemurs the size of gorillas and the 'elephant bird' which, at three metres high, made an ostrich look like a goose. All are now extinct, possibly as a result of both direct hunting and indirect effects such as competition with humans for food, habitat or space. It is no accident that these animals represent what, at the time, would have been the 'biggest ones' on the island – the megafauna. Large animals are not only more worthwhile prey for humans, but they are also more impinged by human activities for they have higher demands on the environment.

The 16 or so species of lemur that became extinct were all larger than the present title-holders – the indri and diademed sifaka. Some species hung like a sloth from branches, while others browsed on the forest floor. The elephant bird, or *Aepyornis*, was not one species but several, one of which, *A. maximus*, weighing over 300kg, may have been the largest bird that has ever lived. Recent finds reveal that the birds became extinct only a few hundred years ago. Indeed tales of '*vorombe*', or big bird, are still fresh in Malagasy folklore. Such tales may have filtered through to Marco Polo who wrote of the giant roc able to lift an elephant, on the island south of Zanzibar.

The roc as visualised by an artist in 1598

cooler regions, while the habitat variety provides more opportunity for animal and plant variation. It is in this evolutionary playground that every now and then a member of a mainland plant or animal group has found itself marooned. Little wonder, then, that Madagascar has such biodiversity – a feature that has served to fascinate centuries of travellers, but one that has also placed a tremendous responsibility upon a poor nation.

FLORA

Madagascar has one of the richest floras in the world. The upper estimates of its diversity, at 12,000 species, make the island the world's number one floral hotspot for an area of its size. The key to this richness is its endemism – 80% of Madagascar's plant species are not found anywhere else. The fortuitous break from

Africa and Asia at a time when the flowering plants were just beginning to diversify, allowed many groups to develop their own lineage, supplemented occasionally by the later colonisations of more advanced forms.

Ferns and cycads

Ferns were in their heyday before even Gondwanaland was formed. Their best efforts were the impressive tree-ferns, which had large spreading fronds sprouting from a tall, scaly stem. These structures created vast forests in all warm, humid areas during the Carboniferous Period, 350 million years ago; forests that were later to persist only as coal seams in the rocks. Although they eventually lost ground to seed-bearing plants in the age of the dinosaurs, it is a credit to the fern design that they are still abundant and successful. Indeed the soft, symmetrical foliage of ferns very much symbolises the lushness of wet, hot places. It's true that they have been relegated to a life in the shade of more recently evolved plants, but at this they excel, out-competing all others.

Although some species are present in dry habitats, the vast majority of Madagascar's ferns decorate the branches and trunks of the eastern rainforest. One noticeable species is the huge **bird's nest fern** (*Asplenium nidus*), which adorns most of the large trunks with luxuriant balconies of leaves. The ancient **tree-ferns** (*Cyathea* spp) that once supplied the forest canopy are still present on its floor, contributing to the prehistoric atmosphere of the forest. Many other species inhabit the shady world among the tree roots or swell the foliage at riverbanks. In all, the diversity and delicacy of the ferns much enhance the rainforest experience.

Often mistaken for a tree-fern, the **cycad** (*Cycas* spp), is significantly different. It is one of the original seed-bearing plants, an innovation leading eventually to the evolution of the flowering plants which currently command all of the world's habitats, which marked the end of the ferns' dominance on Earth. Ironically, cycads are much more unusual today than their fern predecessors. Resembling a

MADAGASCAR'S DINOSAURS

Visitors to the museum in Tsimbazaza, in Tana, will see a display of dinosaur bones, confirming that these ancestors of today's remarkable lizards lived on Madagascar before the break up of Gondwanaland. The oldest dinosaur fossils yet discovered were found in 2000 in southern Madagascar and date back 230 million years! Another find was of a bizarre blunt-snouted herbivorous crocodile, *Simosuchus clarki*, discovered in northwest Madagascar, which dates from the late Cretaceous era, between 97 million and 65 million years ago. Hitherto, crocodiles were assumed to have changed little for millions of years.

The discovery of 2001 was of *Masiakasaurus knopfleri*, possibly the first animal to be named after a pop star – the palaeontologists called it after the lead guitarist of Dire Straits, because whenever they played his music they found dinosaur fossils. *M. knopfleri* was a ferocious little two-legged carnivore, whose larger cousin *Majungatholus atopus* was discovered by the same team from the State University of New York Stony Brook. *Majungatholus atopus*, which lived between 70 and 65 million years ago, has recently been discovered to have been a cannibal. An examination of distinctive tooth marks on the fossilised bones suggest that they could only have come from the teeth of the same species. Cannibalism has been documented in only one other species of dinosaur.

tree-fern with palm-like leaves, the single Malagasy representative of the genus *Cycas* is found only in the eastern rainforest. If seen, it is worth a close look. The cone that it bears holds seeds which, 300 million years ago, became the most significant single plant adaptation in Earth's history.

Palms

Madagascar is home to one of the world's richest palm floras. There are around 170 species, three times more than in the rest of Africa put together, and of these 165 are found nowhere else. The dominance of species with Asian relatives betrays the fact that Madagascar severed with India millions of years *after* it left Africa's shores.

The species present range from the famous to the recently discovered, from dwarf to giant, and almost all have intriguing characteristics. One palm has led to a Malagasy word entering our language – the **raffia palm** (*Raphia ruffia*). The fibres from its leaves are woven into the hats, baskets and mats. Of the 50 new palm species discovered in the last decade, one is worth particular attention: *Ravenea musicalis*, the world's only 'water palm'. It starts life actually underwater in only one of Madagascar's rivers. As it grows it surfaces, eventually bears fruit, and then seeds. Its discoverer named it *R. musicalis* after being charmed by the chimes of its seed pods as they hit the water below. There are other riverside palms in Madagascar adapted to tolerate the recurrent floods of the island's lowland rainforest, but none as perfectly as the musical water palm.

Another unusual group is named the '**litter-trapping palms**'. The crown of their leaves is arranged like an upturned shuttlecock, sprouting at first from the forest floor, and then gaining height as the stem grows from below. Its watertight crown catches leaves falling from the canopy, perhaps to obtain trace minerals, but no one really knows. A strange consequence of this growth is that the roots of other plants, which originally grew through the soil into the crown by mistake, later dangle down from its heights as alabaster-white zigzags.

Although the vast majority of palms live among the hardwoods of the lowland rainforest, there are species which brave the more arid environments, notably the **feather palms** (*Chrysalidocarpus* spp), which nestle in the canyons of Isalo National Park and stand alone amongst the secondary grasslands of the west. An extremely rare and unusual palm, *Ravenea xerophila*, is even to be found within the semidesert of the spiny forest.

A distinct lack of large herbivores in Madagascar has left its palms spineless and without poisons. Pollination is mostly by bees and flies, but some species have tiny flowers to entice unknown insect guests. For seed dispersal lemurs are often employed. The ring-tailed, black, red-ruffed and the browns all assist in scattering the seeds. The bright colours of some fruits serve to attract birds and forest pigs. While the few African palms, which normally use elephants as dispersers, presumably make do with zebu.

Looking like a messy cross between a palm and a pine tree, **pandan palms**, or screw pines (*Pandanus* spp), are different from those above, but equally fond of Madagascar. Their foliage consists of untidy grass-like mops which awkwardly adorn rough branches periodically emerging from their straight trunks. Common in both rain and dry forests, there are 75 species, only one of which is found elsewhere, placing the country alongside Borneo in the pandan diversity stakes.

Trees

Until the arrival of humans, Madagascar was probably largely cloaked in forest. There remain examples of each of the original forests, but vast areas of Madagascar have become treeless as a result of *tavy* (slash and burn) agriculture

SCIENTIFIC CLASSIFICATION

Since many animals and plants in Madagascar have yet to be given English names, I have made use of the Latin or scientific name. For those not familiar with these and the associated terminology, here is a brief guide:

Having been separated into broad classes like mammals (mammalia), angiosperms (angiospermae) – flowering plants – etc, animals and plants are narrowed down into an order, such as Primates or Monocotyledons. The next division is family: Lemur (Lemuridae) and Orchid (Orchidaceae) continue the examples above. These are the general names that everyone knows, and you are quite safe to say 'in the lemur family' or 'a type of orchid'. There are also subfamilies, such as the 'true lemurs' and 'the indri subfamily' which includes sifakas. Then come genera (genus in the singular) followed by species, and the Latin names here will be less familiar-sounding. It is these two names that are combined in the scientific name precisely to identify the animal or plant. So *Lemur catta* and *Angraecum sesquipedale* will be recognisable whatever the nationality of the person you are talking to. We call them ring-tailed lemur and comet orchid; the French say maki and orchidée comète. With a scientific name up your sleeve there is no confusion.

and soil erosion. Most of the **evergreen trees** remaining form the superstructure of the rainforest. They are normally 30m high, with buttressed roots, solid hardwood trunks and vast canopies. There can be up to 250 species of trees per hectare in the lowland rainforest, but from the ground they all look very similar. To identify a species, botanists must often wait for flowering, an event that is not only extremely difficult to predict, but also one that takes place 30m above the ground. One obvious tree is the **strangler fig** (*Ficus* spp), which germinates up in the canopy on a branch of its victim, grows down to the floor to root, and then encircles and constricts its host leaving a hollow knotted trunk. The Malagasy prize the forest hardwoods; one canopy tree is called the 'kingswood' because its wood is so hard that, at one time, any specimens were automatically the property of the local king.

The only evergreen species to be found outside the rainforest are the **tapia tree** (*Uapaca bojei*), the nine species of **mangrove tree** and some of the **succulent trees** to be found in the extreme southwest where sea mists provide water year-round. In tolerating the conditions of west Madagascar, these evergreens have borne their own unusual communities.

The rest of Madagascar's trees are **deciduous**, that is they lose their leaves during the dry season. The taller dry forests of the west are dappled with the shadows of **leguminous trees** such as *Dalbergia* and *Cassia*, characterised by their long seed pods and symbiotic relationships with bacteria which provide fertilisers within their roots. Sprawling **banyan figs** (*Ficus* spp), and huge **tamarind trees** (*Tamarindus indica*), create gallery forest along the rivers of the west and south, yielding pungent fruit popular with lemurs. In drier woodland areas Madagascar's most celebrated trees, the **baobabs** (*Adansonia* spp), dominate. See page 47 for an expert's description of Madagascar's baobabs.

One last species deserves a mention. The **traveller's tree** (*Ravenala madagascariensis*) is one of Madagascar's most spectacular plants. It earns its name from the relief it affords a thirsty traveller: water is stored in the base of its leaves and can be released with a swift blow with a machete. A relation of the banana, its elegant fronds are arranged in a dramatic vertical fan, which is decorative enough to have earned it a role as Air Madagascar's symbol. Its large, bulbous flowers sprout from the leaf axils and, during the 24 hours that they are receptive, are visited by unusual pollinators – ruffed lemurs. The lemurs locate flowers which have just opened, and literally pull them apart to get at the large nectary inside. Keeping a lemur fed is quite a demand on the tree, but it produces flowers day after day for several month's, and during this time, the lemurs eat little else. The traveller's tree is perhaps the only native species to have benefited from *tavy* agriculture, for it dominates areas of secondary vegetation on the central plateau and east coast.

Pitcher plants

There are only two species of pitcher plant (*Nepenthes* spp) on Madagascar, but they are spectacular enough to deserve a mention. In wetlands in the south, they poke out of the marsh beds like triffids planning an ambush. One of their leaves wraps upon itself to create a fly trap, which then serves up trace elements, from the flies' remains, unobtainable from the mud below. The rest of the family live thousands of miles away in Southeast Asia, and it is thought that the arrival of these two species stemmed from a fortuitous migration along the same path that originally brought the Malagasy – perhaps they inadvertently shared the boats!

Succulents

In Madagascar, wherever rainfall is below about 400mm a year, succulents reign. The entire southwest of the island is dominated by their swollen forms. Further north they decorate the natural rock gardens of Isalo, Itremo and the countless outcrops on the central plateau. They also appear within the sparse dry forests of the west, among the stone chaos of the *tsingy*, and even venture on to the grasslands and into the rainforests.

XEROPHYTES AND SUCCULENTS – PLANTS IN DRY HABITATS

Unlike animals, plants cannot escape harsh environments. The plants of Madagascar's dry southwest have therefore adapted to tolerate strong sunlight, high temperatures and, most restricting of all, desiccation. Here, as elsewhere in the world, these high demands have produced unusual-looking but fascinating plant species called xerophytes.

All xerophytes have deep root systems to acquire what little water there is available. Their leaves are usually small and covered in hairs, and much of the photosynthesis is done by the green stems. This design lowers the surface area of the plant and traps still air adjacent to the leaf, reducing water loss – the key aim. In addition to desiccation, overheating is as much a problem for plants as it is for animals. Many xerophytes are therefore orientated to minimise heating, usually having their narrowest edge facing the sun, and they often add grey pigments to their leaves to deflect the intense light of midday.

The most extreme adaptations for a dry life are to be seen in the succulents. This general term describes all xerophytes which store water in their waxy leaves, roots or stems. Such water is a valuable commodity in a dry habitat, and one that must be protected from thirsty grazers. Succulents usually employ toxins, or spines, and this need for defence has given rise to the most spectacular plants on the island – the didierea 'trees' of the spiny forest.

The **euphorbias** are the most widespread group. They have diversified into a thousand different forms, from bushes resembling strings of sausages, to trees sprouting smooth green branches but few leaves, to spiny stalks emerging from an underground swollen tuber. Many species shed their leaves at the start of the dry season, but when present they are swollen with water and shining with wax. To replace the leaves they often yield wonderful flowers and, in so doing, brighten up the landscape. Another succulent group, the **pachypodia**, are perhaps even more unusual. They are stem succulents with sometimes grotesquely swollen bodies, so that the tallest look like short, fat trees sprouting at their tips, whereas the smaller species resemble grey bottles sprouting either stubby leaves or flowers, depending on the season. **Aloes**, **kalanchoes** and **senecios** are leaf succulents, existing essentially as a collection of swollen leaves sprouting from the earth. The leaves are often ornamental, tinged with terracotta and bearing harsh spines, but also

ORCHIDS IN MADAGASCAR
Clare and Johan Hermans

Like so many other living things on the island, the orchids of Madagascar are extremely varied and well over three-quarters are endemic. More than 950 different species have been recorded so far and new ones are still being discovered. The orchids have adapted to every possible habitat, including the spiny forest and the cool highland mountain ranges, but their highest density is in the wet forests of the east. Whilst orchid habitats are becoming scarcer, something can be seen in flower at most times of the year; the best season for flowers is the rainy season from January to March.

Some of the most memorable orchids are to be found in the eastern coastal area, which is the habitat of large Angraecums, Eulophiellas and Cymbidiellas. Many orchids here are epiphytes – they live on tree branches or stems with their roots anchoring the plants and although they scramble over their host, collecting moisture and nutrients, they are not parasites.

Angraecum eburneum can be seen in flower from September to May, its thick leathery leaves form a half-metre wide fan shape; the flower stems reach above the leaves carrying a number of large greenish-white fragrant flowers. Like many Malagasy orchids the blooms are strongly night-scented and white in colour to attract pollinating moths.

The comet orchid, *Angraecum sesquipedale*, is one of the most striking. It flowers from June to November and the plants are similar to eburneum but slightly more compact. Individual flowers can be almost 26cm across and over 30cm long including the long nectary spur, characteristic for the Angraecoid orchids, at the back of the flower. The flower was described by Charles Darwin at the end of the 19th century when he predicted that there would be a moth with a very long tongue that could reach down to the nectar at the bottom of the spur. This idea was ridiculed by his contemporaries but in 1903 a moth with a proboscis of over 30cm was found in Madagascar!

Aeranthes plants look similar to Angraecums. Their spider-like greenish flowers are suspended from a long thin stem, gently nodding in the breeze.

Eulophiella roempleriana is now very rare. One of the few remaining, almost two-metre-high plants can be seen on Île aux Nattes, off Île Sainte Marie. The large, deep pink flowers are well worth the pirogue trip to the island. A few more of these plants survive in the reserves around Andasibe. The plant is normally in flower from October onwards.

display showy red flowers during the drought. Some species do have stems to raise their broad foliage above the ground. The largest aloes have stocky 3m stems covered in untidy dead scales which sport the huge succulent leaves and, in June and July, a large, red inflorescence. Other succulents in Madagascar include *Adenia neohumbertii*, which looks even more rock-like than the pachypodia, swollen, straggling milkweed and succulent relatives of the cucumber family with disc-shaped leaves.

Didierea

To botanists the **Didiereaceae** of the arid southwest are the most intriguing plants in Madagascar, for they are an entire family of bizarre plants found nowhere else on Earth. The common name of one species, the octopus tree, gives some indication of their eccentricities. They look similar to some forms of cacti and they are often quoted

Cymbidiella orchids are also very striking; they generally flower from October to January. *Cymbidiella pardalina*, with its huge crimson lip, cohabits with a stag-horn fern, while *Cymbidiella falcigera*, with large black-spotted yellow flowers, prefers the exclusive company of the raffia palm.

The highlands of Madagascar with their cooler and more seasonal climate are inhabited by numerous terrestrial orchids, growing in soil or leaf litter; underground tubers produce deciduous leaves and flower stems – not dissimilar to orchids seen in temperate regions.

Eulophia plantaginea is a relatively common roadside plant; large colonies can sometimes be found, especially in boggy areas.

Cynorkis can also be seen along the roads. Many are terrestrials, others grow on wet rock or in swamps. Epiphytes like Angraecum and Aeranthes can still be found in the few remaining pockets of forest in the highlands.

Aerangis plants are instantly recognisable by their shiny, dark green foliage. The flowers superficially resemble those of Angraecum but they are often much smaller, carried on elegant racemes, and their scent is exquisite. The plants are commonly seen in the wet shade of the rainforest reserves of Périnet and Ranomafana.

Jumellea are again similar but have a more narrow, folded back single flower on thin stems.

Bulbophyllum orchids are easily missed by the untrained eye; their rounded, plump pseudo-bulbs are often seen on moss-covered trees. They are always worthwhile investigating: small gem-like blooms may be nestled amongst the foliage.

Oeonia with its huge white lip and two red dots in its throat can be found rambling amongst the undergrowth.

The apparently bare higher peaks of the Hauts Plateaux, like Ibity near Antsirabe, also contain a very specialised community of orchids. The thick-leaved, sun-loving Angraecoids and Bulbophyllums share the rock faces with succulents; these rock dwellers are known as lithophytes.

One of the best and easiest places to see orchids, such as Angraecum, Cymbidiella and Gastrorchis, is in the ground of hotels and private gardens but one must be aware that these domesticated collections may contain the odd foreign interloper. Orchids from the Orient and South America are brought in as pot plants, the flowers being often bigger and brighter than the natives.

Import and export permits are required to take orchids out of Madagascar.

as examples of convergent evolution – where two separate groups of organisms have adapted similar features to cope with a similar environment. However, they do differ from typical cacti in that they do not have green swollen stems, but instead bear small, deciduous leaves, protected by immense thorns, on grey, wooded branches. A number of these spiny branches sprout from near the base of each plant and soar unsteadily into the sky, so that the entire structure has an unkempt and uninviting appearance from afar. In various guises, these magnificent didierea join the succulent trees to create the unworldly landscape of the spiny forest in the southwest.

At first sight the mass of thorns and branches confuses the eye, let alone identification, but if you want to name a species try to recognise individual silhouettes and look for the following features:

- **Didierea madagascariensis**, the octopus tree – most abundant between Morondava and Toliara (Tuléar), the erratic branches of this tree, which sprout from close to the base, are covered with very long thorns and, in the wet season, long thin leaves, giving it a fuzzy appearance.
- **Didierea trolli** – when adult they are similar to *D. madagascariensis*, but are distinguished when younger by having lateral branches at the base of the stem, which creep over the ground and keep browsing animals at a distance.
- **Decaryia madagascariensis**, the zigzag plant – found between Ampanihy and Ambovombe, it has a complex crown of thorny, zigzagging branches and produces small, white flowers.
- **Alluaudiopsis fiherenensis** – found north of Toliara (Tuléar), it is bushy but short (up to 2m) and sprouts yellow-white flowers.
- **Alluaudia procera** – this is the most abundant of the trees in much of the spiny forest. When young it is little more than a mesh of wild, extremely thorny bush. However, when closer to its maximum height of 15m, it takes on a more regal appearance with a single trunk crowned by a series of substantial branches. Its leaves sprout in curious lines which spiral up the branches during the wet season to be shed at the start of the dry. Thorns patrol the leaves on each side and hence themselves form further spirals. Tiny flowers sometimes adorn tufts on the tips of the branches.
- **Alluaudia ascendens** – Up to 20m tall, this tree shares the skies with *A. procera*. A solitary woody trunk divides into a series of long slim, skyward branches, hence the Latin name. Even when juvenile the single stem is present with its spiralling thorns.
- **Alluaudia montagnacii** – only found near Itampolo, it has few leaning branches, covered in spirals of thorns and finishing in bouquets of leaves and flowers. The fact that they look like a cross between *A. procera* and *A. ascendens* has led some to suggest that they are nothing more than hybrids.
- **Alluaudia comosa** – common along the road from Toliara (Tuléar) to Andranavory, these trees resemble very thorny, squat acacia, their dark crowns often formed into an anvil shape.
- **Alluaudia dumosa** – grows between Ampanihy and Taolagnaro (Fort Dauphin). It has a woody trunk with few leaves and even fewer spines. The diverging greyish-brown branches above the main trunk carry out most of the photosynthesis. The flowers are white with red stigmas.

Foreigners

In common with many islands around the globe, Madagascar has suffered from accidental or intended introductions of 'alien' species. Referred to as 'weedy' species, these are the botanical equivalents of cats and rats – species that should not really be there, but that cause havoc when they arrive. Out-competing native species, sharp tropical grasses from South America permanently deface the burnt woodlands of the west and, avoided by cattle, their populations explode. Where thick forest is cleared, fast-growing *Eucalyptus* and *Psidium* trees step in. They either suffocate competitors with their dense growth or poison the soil with their toxins. In drier areas, superbly adapted and profoundly damaging cacti spread from the nearby sisal plantations and flourish where there was once spiny forest. Needless to say, the native animal populations, unable to adapt to these invaders, also suffer, and this, perhaps more than the endangerment of plant species, has prompted action from conservation bodies.

The value of the flora

Many Malagasy plants crop up in garden centres throughout Europe. Familiar to horticulturalists are the dragon tree (*Dracaena marginata*), the crown of thorns (*Euphorbia millii*), the *Areca* palm, the flamboyant tree (*Delonix regia*) and the Madagascar jasmine (*Stephanotis floribunda*) of bridal bouquet fame. Other natives are valued for their uses rather than their aesthetic qualities. Recent interest has grown in Madagascar's various wild coffees, *Rubiaceae*. Many are naturally decaffeinated and hybrids with tastier coffees are currently being produced. More seriously, the rosy periwinkle (*Catharanthus roseus*) is a champion of those who campaign to conserve natural habitats. It contains two alkaloid chemicals proven to assist treatment of leukaemia and other cancers in children. There may well be other plants in a position to offer equally useful products, but the rate of forest destruction may be extinguishing these before we have a chance to appreciate them. Slowly we are learning that there is great value in diversity alone.

Baobabs
Jim Bond

The baobabs (*Adansonia* sp.) of Madagascar are one of its main attractions and a 'must see' on the list of many visitors on account of their extraordinary size and beauty. To the Malagasy who live alongside them, they are important economically, yielding highly nutritious fruits, oil from the seeds, strong fibre for rope and bark for roofing material, as well as often having a deeper spiritual significance by providing a home for the ancestors. The Malagasy name for the largest species, the magnificent *Adansonia grandidieri,* is *renala* or *reniala,* literally: 'mother-of-the-forest' – which is particularly apt, considering the 'keystone' role these trees play in the dry forest ecosystems.

Diversity

There are eight baobab species in the world, of which six are endemic to Madagascar, with only one found in the whole of Africa and one in NW Australia. The diversity in Madagascar would suggest that this is where baobabs first evolved, a theory that has now been supported by molecular studies of the baobab 'family tree'. It also appears that this happened long after the separation of the continents, which means that the African and Australian species must have arisen from colonising fruits floating across the Indian Ocean, rather than any Gondwanaland explanation.

Within Madagascar, the other six species each evolved to fit their own niche within the dry forest zones. What kept them isolated from each other here, unlike in Africa, was partly a north-south divide (the Sambirano barrier) and partly having three different flowering seasons within both northern and southern groups. However, even within the same species, baobabs can assume quite widely different forms, or 'ecotypes', depending on local conditions. For example, some of the *renala* near Morondava are almost 30 metres tall, smooth, columnar giants, but in the spiny scrub by Andavadoaka, mature trees of the same species reach only three metres, are quite knobbly, almost spherical in shape, and wonderfully grotesque-looking! (See illustrations on opposite page.) It is not always easy, even to the trained eye, to tell the species apart so below are some working guidelines that I use when in doubt.

Form and function

Baobabs are dryland plants, in the sense that they are 'drought survivors'. They are able to take up and store water from a sporadic downpour very efficiently within the soft, porous 'wood' of their big, fat trunks, which acts like a giant sponge. However, they do not like getting their roots too wet, which is why they are not found in the east, nor do they tolerate frost well, which limits their distribution inland. The thick bark is relatively (but not completely) fire-resistant and can be removed in moderation without causing the tree too much harm. All baobabs are deciduous in the dry season, although two Malagasy species also flower at this time, providing an important source of pollen for bees when few other plants are in flower.

Taxonomy

There are technically seven species in Madagascar, although one is a bit of a red herring, as it is the African species, *A. digitata,* which was introduced by Arab traders and planted as street trees in a few towns such as Diego and Mahajanga. These should be fairly obvious.

The six true Malagasy species fall into two sub-genera, based on flower characters: the Brevitubae ('short-tubed') and the Longitubae ('long-tubed'). This may all seem rather academic, but understanding the function behind these differences should help to explain the overall shape and position of the tree, and hence point to which one it might be…

Brevitubae

These comprise *A. grandidieri* in the south and *A. suarezensis* in the north. The distinctive feature of both is that they have flat-topped crowns of predominantly horizontal branches, which emerge just above the canopy height of the forest in which they grow. The *reason* these species invest so much extra energy is thought to be to make things easier for their favoured ancestral pollinator, a large and clumsy fruit bat, to fly in to at night. The idea is that the bats could land easily on the flat, bare branches and hop about between flowers. These in turn are short in length and sit presented nicely upwards like cups and saucers, their long stamens fanning out ready to brush the bats' chins when they feed on the nectar. The flowers only come out at dusk and are cream-coloured in order to catch the moonlight, although by the next morning they start to wilt, turning red before falling off about four days later. The flowers are also visited by sunbirds, bees and small lemurs.

Longitubae

The remaining Malagasy species, *A. za* and *A. rubrostipa* (or *A. fony*) in the south, and *A. perrieri* and *A. madagascariensis* in the north, have long floral parts, mostly yellow or red, which tend to dangle down. The nectaries are at the end of a long tube, so have almost certainly evolved to accommodate the tongues of large hawkmoths. The trees have no need to emerge from the canopy and they have round crowns, with branches forking upwards and outwards. Where they happen to live is more determined by soil type and manner of seed dispersal.

ESTIMATING THE AGE OF A BAOBAB

Baobabs are fairly long-lived, but do not grow as old as previously thought. Recent studies indicate that even the biggest, fattest *renala* that we know of, in the Mangoky Valley, are probably no more than 600 years old, and that's being generous! Most are far younger. From a conservation point of view, this is quite significant since older-living trees do not need such a high rate of regeneration in order to replicate their numbers and so maintain a sustainable population.

Identification

So, for the simplified guide to working out which baobab is which:

1 Is it really a baobab? – there are other big, fat grey trees in the dry zones, eg: *Pachypodium* sp. (which has spines towards the top) or *Moringa* (bean-shaped pods). If it has large, round or ovoid, hard fruits with a velvety coat then you can be pretty sure it's a baobab.
2 Does it have a flat-topped, emergent crown or a round-topped crown at the level of the other trees? Are its branches trying to be horizontal or generally reaching up?
3 Can you see any flowers and what are they like? (They all shrink in size and turn red on the ground.) Is there thick foliage at the same time?
4 Is it in the northern dry zone or in the south/west?
5 What is the soil or underlying geology like – sandy, alluvial, calcareous, volcanic?
6 Other special characters (see below) – fruit, stalk, trunk constriction, leaf margin, staminal tube proportions…
7 What do the *local* people call it? In areas with two or three baobab species coexisting, especially in the south and west, they are usually right.

Individual species
'Southern three'

Adansonia grandidieri. Malagasy name: *renala* or *reniala*
Perhaps the most famous of the Malagasy baobabs and certainly the grandest of them all, it was actually named in honour of the pioneering French botanist and explorer, Alfred Grandidier. This is generally the largest of the three 'southern species', although as mentioned earlier, this all depends on the natural height of the surrounding vegetation. Heights of over 30m have been recorded and a diameter of 7.5m.

A. grandidieri
Andavadoaka

Some have even been hollowed out to house people. Usually found on richer alluvial soils, ie: flood-plains, or near watercourses where it grows tallest, but also adjacent to mangroves and salt marshes, which may be the cause of characteristic ring patterns on the bark in some areas. It has quite a restricted distribution, between the Manambolo lakes system in the north and the fringes of the Mikea Forest in the south. Best examples, in relatively undisturbed forest, are to be seen in the Mangoky Valley. Flowering season: May–August.

A. grandidieri
Morondava

Adansonia za. Malagasy name: *za*
Intermediate in size of the southern species, this one has the widest distribution, from just west of Fort Dauphin up to Analalava. It tends to prefer calcareous soils and is the only species in the spiny forest on limestone of the Mahafaly Plateau in the deep south. Probably more frost tolerant than the others, it is found more inland, notably around Zombitsy. Typically it has a tall, straight trunk with grey bark and round crown, although there are stunted versions in the very dry south. Fruits are more ovoid than round and have a peculiarly swollen stalk. Flowering season: Nov–Jan.

Adansonia rubrostipa (syn. *A. fony*). Malagasy name: *fony*
(Originally described and named in 1890 as *A. fony*, after the local name, by the French botanist, Baillon, this species was officially renamed in 1995 on a technicality relating to the original publication. Not surprisingly, this has caused much offence in Madagascar and there are now moves afoot to try and get the old name conserved. Out of respect to all concerned, I shall therefore refer to it only by the Malagasy name.)
    Fony is generally the smallest of the southern group and it tends to grow on sandy soil. It may be found up the west coast from Itampolo to Soalala. The classic form is the bottle-shaped tree in the spiny forest, although further north at Kirindy, a taller and more slender model appears, which is in fact the dominant tree in some parts of that forest. *Fony* do not seem to mind growing almost on top of one another and they can often be quite concentrated, presumably due to their thin-walled fruits not being naturally carried very far. Definitive characters include: a characteristic constriction in the trunk just below the branches (not necessarily in every tree) and a serrated leaf margin. *Fony* also tend to have more of a reddish tinge to the bark, but there is some overlap either way on this with other species. Flowering season: February–March.

'Northern three'
In the north, the local names, *bojy* or *bozy,* are not specific, presumably because baobabs have less economic importance.

Adansonia suarezensis
This is the northern 'flat-top', and a much smaller version of its cousin the *renala*. It has an even more restricted distribution in various small patches of remaining woodland around Diego plus the forests of Mahory and Analamera to the south. The conservation status of *A. suarezensis* is listed as 'critical' due to ongoing clearance of the surrounding vegetation. However, some individual trees are regarded as sacred and are locally protected, together with one intact small wood on a basalt outcrop near the village of Ambilo, about 6km east of Mahavanona – do be generous in your encouragement of this if you visit! Flowering season: May–July.

Adansonia perrieri
This is the largest baobab in the north and the rarest. It has the most restricted distribution of all, limited to only four known populations in and around the Montagne d'Ambre massif. Sometimes known as 'the rainforest species', this baobab appears to have found a very specialised niche on the sheltered banks of small streams running off the old volcano. One of the best sites to see it in its full glory is on the

stream in the park that runs down from the Grande Cascade, although you need to walk down an entirely separate path. Rising tall and majestic up to 25m from the steep valley floor, its crown merges neatly with those of other trees on the slopes. Note how few there are though! Key features are: somewhat thickened distal branches and a distinctive large, pale yellow flower, with relatively wide petals and stamens fused for most of their length, a bit like a hibiscus. Flowering season: November–December.

Adansonia madagascariensis
This is another extremely plastic species that is often mistaken for others! Growing beside *A. suarenzensis* in at least two places, *A. madagascariensis* looks much smaller and scruffier with its irregular tangle of branches. However, given more favourable soil and water conditions it can grow much taller, such as at the east entrance to Ankarana, where it starts to resemble the stature of *A. perrieri*. Up on the nearby karst itself, it looks quite wee and delicate with a pear-shaped trunk. Essentially, it is found only from the Ankara (sic) plateau, just south of Mahajanga, north. It can be distinguished most readily from *A. za* by having round or grapefruit-shaped fruits and a lack of swollen stalk, as well as having other minor floral differences. Flowering season: March–April.

Conservation and respect
Although they are generally left standing by people when forests are cleared, this is not always the case. Where there is regular burning of the undergrowth to stimulate new grazing, like in the *renala* forest south of Lac Ihotry, a few mature trees fall each year. Few young trees survive the flames and those that do are promptly eaten by zebu, so there is little regeneration. Left unchecked it will not take long before such healthy-looking forests resemble the sad scene around the famous 'avenue de baobabs' north of Morondava – just imagine how tall the surrounding forest there must have been there before it was all degraded!

There are many complex interactions in the dry forests, which are only now becoming appreciated. Baobabs are known to provide food, support and homes to all sorts of creatures, both directly and indirectly, including: ants, moths, bees, sunbirds, eagles, geckos, fruit bats, lemurs, humans, fungi and even other plants. Reflect a moment on all these potential dependants before you take your photos. Pay your respects to these true mothers of the forest and be seen to do so. And, if possible, ask permission first – that tree might be sacred *(faly)* to someone!

FAUNA
Compared with the breathtaking ecosystems of mainland Africa, Madagascar's fauna has far more subtle qualities. A combination of ancient Gondwanaland stock and the descendants of the last 165 million years' wayfarers, it is more intriguing than dynamic. Here are a seemingly random collection of animal groups that had the opportunity to prove themselves in the absence of big predators and herbivores. The resulting 180,000 species existing in habitats from rainforests to coral reefs bring human opportunity too, for dozens of truly unique safaris.

Invertebrates
There are well over 150,000 species of invertebrate on Madagascar, the majority in the eastern rainforests. To spot them turn over leaves and logs on the forest floor, peer very closely at the foliage or switch on a bright light after dark. Although creepy, let alone crawly, they do contribute substantially to the experience of wild

ANTS BEWARE!

Angus McCrae

Should you come across perfectly conical little craters up to 5cm across with little or no evidence of spoil around them in dry, sandy places, you're looking at evidence of ant lions (Fam. Myrmeleontidae, of the minor order Neuroptera). Out of sight at the bottom of each pit may lurk the strange and ravenous ant lion larva, buried but for the tips of its needle-sharp mandibles. Should an unwary ant or other small prey stray over the brink and loosen some sand, a blur of action may suddenly erupt: showers of sand are hurled back by the ant lion's jerking head and the resultant landslide carries the intruder helplessly down into the waiting jaws. Only if you're British might they come as a big surprise – ant lions are found in most countries. In North America their common name is doodle-bug.

Seen close up, the larval ant lion looks like some kind of termite-like alien with a large, hard and somewhat flattened head attached apparently upside down to its softer, hunched body. It has eyes arranged in a group on each side of the head, and thin vibrissae sprout from around its sickle-like jaws. Its mouth is permanently sealed, and it feeds instead through a narrow groove between each mandible and its close-fitting maxilla, thus being incapable of chewing or taking in anything but liquid. With no solids to be excreted the stomach ends blindly, disconnected from the hind-gut. On pupation the larva digs deeper and makes a stout, round cocoon of silk secreted by its malpighian tubules (the insect equivalent of kidneys) and stored in its rectum. The silk simply oozes out from its otherwise unused anus which is unmodified with any kind of spinneret. Sand adheres to the outside as the cocoon is formed.

The adults are seldom noticed by non-specialists as most are of unexciting grey to pale fawn colours and they usually fly only at dusk or at night. They superficially resemble dragonflies but fly more clumsily and have smaller eyes and short, stout and clubbed antennae. At rest they fold their wings lengthwise, hiding the abdomen. Unlike their larvae they have a fully functional mouth, chewing mouthparts and a complete gut, but very little is known about their food or how they catch it.

The genus *Palpares* includes several endemic Malagasy species of striking size and colour which sometimes take to flight by day under dull conditions or when disturbed, as well as at night. Of these, *P. voeltzkowi* is one of the largest and perhaps the most handsome of any ant lion in the world with its violet-black and white-blotched wings more than 16cm in span and its reddish-brown body exceeding 16cm.

About 20 ant lion species have been described from Madagascar but more can be expected as they have not been revised for half a century. Their greatest diversity is in the dry west and south, but so far no endemic Malagasy genera are known and their affinities appear strongly African.

areas on the island and, providing you can suppress the spine shivers, your mini-safaris will be well worthwhile.

It is a difficult task to pick out the most impressive invertebrates, but notable are the huge **golden orb-web spiders** (*Nephila madagascariensis*), which gather on telephone lines in all the towns. Their silk is so strong that it was once used as a textile – Queen Victoria even had a pair of Nephila silk stockings! Equally oversized are the **pill millipedes** (*Sphaerotherium* spp) which roll up when startled to resemble a striped, brown golf ball. Among the forest foliage are superbly camouflaged **praying mantis**, **net-throwing spiders**, which cast their silk nets at fliers-by, and **nymphs** and bugs of all shapes, colours and adornments. Among the leaf litter there are spectacular, striped **flatworms** and vast numbers of wonderful **weevils**.

The 300 species of **butterfly** are all descendants of African voyagers. The most visible are the heavily-patterned swallowtails, and the nymphalids with their dominant blue and orange liveries. Madagascar's **moths** are significantly older in origin and are probably descendants of the Gondwanaland insects marooned on the island. This explains the diversity in place – there are 4,000 species, and many groups are active in the daylight, filling niches that elsewhere are currently the realm of butterflies. Most dramatic is the huge, yellow comet moth (*Argema mittrei*), which has a wingspan of up to 25cm, and the elaborate urania moths (*Chrysiridia*), which look just like swallowtails decorated with emeralds. A very close relative is found in the Amazon rainforest.

Fish
Additional information from Derek Schuurman

The inhabitants of Madagascar's abundant lakes, marshes, estuaries, rivers and mountain brooks have been as much isolated by history as those of the land. The most interesting species are the **cichlids** (known locally as *Damba*), with their huge variety, colourful coats and endearing habits of childcare – they protect their young by offering their mouths as a retreat in times of danger. Other Malagasy species demonstrate the parental instinct, a feature rare in fish. Some of the island's **catfish** also mouth-brood and male **mudskippers** in the mangroves defend their nest burrows with the vigour of a proud father.

Another major group is the **killifish**, which resemble the gouramis to be found in pet shops. Specialised **eels** live high up in mountain brooks, and in the underground rivers of west Madagascar blind **cave fish** live, sometimes entirely on the rich pickings of bat guano. The one problem with the island's fish is that they are not big and tasty. Consequently many exotic species have been introduced into the rivers and are regularly on display in the nation's markets. These new species naturally put pressure on the native stock and, as is often the story, the less-vigorous Malagasy species have been all but wiped out. The main culprit seems to be the Asian snakehead (*Channa* cf.*striata*). North Koreans farmed them in Madagascar in the 1980s but following the first floods they spread and are now present in all the major lakes of Madagascar. The snakehead is a voracious predator and has severely reduced populations of endemic fish wherever it occurs. The other predatory fish which has decimated indigenous fish is the black bass, *Micropterus salmoides*.

More robust are the marine species to be found swimming off the island's 4,000km of coastline. Madagascar is legendary for its **shark** populations and a quick dip off the east coast should be considered carefully, but on the west coast there are **coral reefs** bursting with life, outdoing even the Red Sea for fish diversity. The reefs are host to a typical Indo-Pacific community of clownfish, angelfish, butterflyfish, damselfish, tangs and surgeons, triggerfish, wrasse, groupers, batfish, blennies and gobies, boxfish, lionfish, moray eels, flutefish, porcupinefish, pufferfish, squirrelfish, sweetlips and the Moorish idol.

Frogs

The only amphibians on Madagascar are frogs. Newts, salamanders and toads are absent, but the frog abundance more than makes up for these omissions. On

LEECHES
Hilary Bradt

Few classes of invertebrates elicit more disgust than leeches. Perhaps some facts about these extraordinarily well-adapted animals will give them more appeal.

Terrestrial leeches such as those found in Madagascar are small (1–2cm long) and find their warm-blooded prey by vibrations and odour. Suckers at each end enable the leech to move around in a series of loops and to attach itself to a leaf by its posterior while seeking its meal with the front end. It has sharp jaws and can quickly – and painlessly – bite through the skin and start feeding. When it has filled its digestive tract with blood the leech drops off and digests its meal. This process can take several months since leeches have pouches all along their gut to hold as much blood as possible – up to ten times their own weight. The salivary glands manufacture an anticoagulant which prevents the blood clotting during the meal or period of digestion. This is why leech wounds bleed so spectacularly. Leeches also inject an anaesthetic which is why you don't feel them biting.

Leeches are hermaphrodite but still have pretty exciting sex lives. To consummate their union they need to exchange packets of sperm. This is done either the conventional way via a leechy penis or by injection, allowing the sperm to make its way through the body tissues to find and fertilise the eggs.

Readers who are disappointed with the small size of Malagasy leeches will be interested to hear that an expedition to French Guiana in the 1970s discovered the world's largest leech: at full stretch 45cm long!

average a new species of Malagasy frog is discovered every eight weeks. There are currently 170 catalogued species, but the actual number may be closer to 300 and all but two of these are endemic.

Most of the species, restricted by their permeable skins, spend their lives in the humid forests of the east. With their bulbous finger tips, which help them to grip on to the waxy forest leaves, large brightly coloured eyes and loud whistles, the **tree frogs** are appealing to most visitors. They either return to small streams to breed, hang their egg batches from overhanging branches (a habit which demands high-dive routines from the tadpoles), or abandon the waterways altogether to raise their young in the miniature pools among pandan leaves or between the epiphytes of the canopy. Closer to the forest floor there are other, more brightly coloured frogs, such as the large, blushing **tomato frog** (*Dyscophus antongili*) and the magnificent miniature *Mantella* species, which resemble the famed poison arrow frogs from the Amazon in that they display their toxic inners with lurid coats of black, gold and blue.

Away from the mature forest, frogs congregate around fast-flowing mountain streams littered with mossy rocks, alongside the sticky marshes that house pitcher plants and even in the drier Hauts Plateaux and Isalo regions where they rumble through the floor litter defying dehydration.

Reptiles

The unique evolutionary history of Madagascar is typified by the reptiles on the island. There are 316 endemic reptile species. Some are derived from ancient

Gondwanaland stock, many of which are more closely related to South American or Asian reptiles than to African. There are also large groups of closely related species marking the radiations that stemmed from African immigrations in more recent times. The most dramatic example of the latter concerns chameleons. Madagascar is home to about half the world's chameleon species including the smallest and the largest. With impressive adaptive dexterity, they have dispersed throughout the habitats of the island to occupy every conceivable niche (see box, pages 56–57).

Similar in their success have been the **geckoes**. The 70-odd gecko species seem to be split between those that make every effort imaginable to camouflage themselves and those that are quite happy to stick out like a sore thumb. The spectacular **day gecko** (*Phelsuma madagascariensis*) and its relatives can be seen by passing motorists from some distance. Their dazzling emerald coats emblazoned with day-glo orange splashes are intended for the attentions of the opposite sex and competitors. Once in their sights they bob their heads and wave their tails as if an extra guarantee of visibility is needed. In contrast a magnificently camouflaged **leaf-tailed gecko** (*Uroplatus* spp) could easily be next to your hand on a tree trunk without you noticing it. With its flattened body, splayed tail, speckled eyes, colour-change tactics and complete lack of shadow, you may remain ignorant until, nervous, it gapes a large, red tongue in your direction.

A quiet scuttle on the floor of a western forest may well be a **skink**, while louder ramblings could be due to one of the handsome **plated lizards**. However, the most significant disturbances, both in the forest and the academic world, are made by the **iguanids**. This group of large lizards is primarily found in the Americas, and never in Africa. Hence its presence on Madagascar is a sign that its ancestors were members of the original party that separated from Africa.

Madagascar's three **boas** are in the same boat. They exist only as fossils in Africa, supplanted by the more stealthy pythons, but they do have distant relatives in South America. Most often seen is the Madagascar tree boa (*Sanzinia madagascariensis*), which although decorated in the same marbled glaze, varies in colour from orange (when juvenile) to grey and black, brilliant green or brown and blue, depending on the location. Its larger relative the ground boa (*Acrantophis madagascariensis*) is also often spied at the edge of waterways in the humid east and north. Of the remaining species of snake, the one-metre long **hog-nosed snake** (*Leioheterodon madagascariensis*), in its dazzling checkerboard of black and yellow, is most frequently encountered, usually gliding across a carpet of leaves on the lookout for frogs.

Despite the fact that none of the island's snakes are a danger to humans, the Malagasy are particularly wary of some species. The blood-red tail of one harmless tree snake (*Ithycyphus perineti*), known to the Malagasy as the *fandrefiala*, is believed to have powers of possession. It apparently hypnotises cattle from up high, then drops down tail-first to impale its victim. Similar paranormal attributes are bestowed on other Malagasy reptiles. The chameleons, for example, are generally feared by the Malagasy, and when fascinated *vazaha* go to pick one up, there is often a bout of surprised gasps from the locals. Another reptile deeply embedded in the folklore is the **Nile crocodile** (*Crocodilus niloticus*) which, although threatened throughout the island, takes on spiritual roles in some areas (see Lac Antanavo).

A number of Madagascar's **tortoises** are severely threatened with extinction. Captive breeding programmes at Ampijoroa are currently successfully rearing the ploughshare (*Geochelone yniphora*) and flat-tailed tortoises (*Pyxis planicauda*) and further south, the Beza-Mahafaly reserve is protecting the handsome radiated tortoise (*Geochelone radiata*). Four species of fresh-water **turtle** inhabit the western waterways, the only endemic being the big-headed or side-necked turtle

CHAMELEONS
Hilary Bradt

Everybody thinks they know one thing about chameleons: that they change colour to match their background. Wrong! You have only to observe the striking *Calumma parsonii*, commonly seen at Périnet, staying stubbornly green while transferred from boy's hand to tree trunk to leafy branch, to see that in some species this is a myth. Most chameleons are cryptically coloured to match their preferred resting place (there are branch-coloured chameleons, for instance, and leaf-coloured ones) and some do respond to a change of background, but their abilities are mainly reserved for expressing emotion. An anxious chameleon will darken and grow stripes and an angry chameleon, faced with a territorial intruder, will change his colours dramatically. The most impressive displays, however, are reserved for sexual encounters. Chameleons say it with colours. Enthusiastic males explode into a riot of spots, stripes and contrasting colours, whilst the female usually responds by donning a black cloak of disapproval. Only on the rare occasions that she is feeling receptive will she present a brighter appearance.

Chameleons use body language more than colour to deter enemies. If you spot a chameleon on a branch you will note that his first reaction to being seen is to put the branch between you and him and flatten his body laterally so that he is barely visible. If you try to catch him, he will blow himself up, expand his throat, raise his helmet (if he has one) and hiss. His next action will be to either bite, jump, or try to run away. Fortunately they must be the slowest of all lizards, are easily caught, and pose for the camera with gloomy resignation (who can resist an animal that has a constantly down-turned mouth like a Victorian headmistress?). This slowness is another aspect of the chameleon's defence: when he walks, he moves like a leaf in the wind. This is fine when the danger is an animal predator, but less effective when it is a car. In a tree, his best protection is to keep completely still. He can do this by having feet shaped like pliers and a prehensile tail so he can effortlessly grasp a branch, and eyes shaped like gun-turrets which can swivel 180 degrees independently of each other, enabling him to view the world from front and back without moving his head. This is the chameleon's true camouflage.

The family Chamaeleonidae is represented by three genera, the 'true chameleons' *Calumma* and *Furcifer*, and the little stump-tailed chameleons,

---

(*Erymnochelys madagascariensis*), and beyond in the Mozambique Channel, there are **sea turtles** (Ridley, hawksbill and green) which periodically risk the pot as they visit their nesting beaches.

Birds

Madagascar's score sheet of resident birds is surprisingly short. There are only about 270 species of birds on the island. However, of these, 109 species are endemic, there are five endemic families, and 36 endemic genera – rendering Madagascar the hot-spot for bird endemism in Africa.

The key endemics include the three extremely rare **mesites** – the brown mesite (*Mesitornis unicolor*) in the rainforests, the white-breasted mesite (*Mesitornis variegata*) in the western dry forests and the subdesert mesite (*Monias benschi*) in the south's spiny forest. A similar allocation of habitats is more generously employed by the ten species of **couas** which brighten the forests throughout the island with their blue-masked faces. Six species are ground-dwellers, occupying the roles filled

Brookesia. Unlike the true chameleons, the Brookesia's short tail is not prehensile.

In chameleons there is often a striking colour difference between males and females. Many males have horns (occasionally used for fighting) or other nasal protuberances. Where the two sexes look the same you can recognise the male by the bulge of the scrotal sac beneath the tail, and a spur on the hind feet.

It is interesting to know how the chameleon achieves its colour change. It has a transparent epidermis, then three layers of cells – the top ones are yellow and red, the middle layer reflects blue light and white light, and the bottom layer consists of black pigment cells with tentacles or fingers that can protrude up through the other layers. The cells are under control of the autonomic nervous system, expanding and contracting according to a range of stimuli. Change of colour occurs when one layer is more stimulated than others, and patterning when one group of cells receives maximum stimulation.

In the early 17th century there was the firm conviction that chameleons subsisted without food. A German author, describing Madagascar in 1609, mentions the chameleon living 'entirely on air and dew' and Shakespeare refers several times to the chameleon's supposed diet: 'The chameleon ... can feed on air' (Two Gentlemen of Verona) and 'of the chameleon's dish: I eat the air promise-crammed' (Hamlet). Possibly at that time no-one had witnessed the tongue flash out through the bars of its cage to trap a passing insect. This tongue is as remarkable as any other feature of this remarkable reptile. It was formerly thought that the club-shaped tip was sticky, allowing the chameleon to catch flies, but researchers discovered that captive chameleons had been catching much larger prey – lizards, intended to coexist as cage-mates. These animals were far too heavy to be captured simply with a sticky tongue, so a high-speed video camera was brought into use. This showed that a chameleon is able to use a pair of muscles at the tip of its tongue to form a suction cup milliseconds before it hit its prey. The whole manoeuvre, from aim to mouthful, takes about half a second.

The name apparently comes from Greek: chamai leon, dwarf lion. I suppose a hissing, open-mouthed reptile could remind one of a lion, but to most visitors to Madagascar they are one of the most appealing and bizarre of the 'strange and marvellous forms' on show.

elsewhere by pheasants and roadrunners. Much harder to see are the **ground-rollers**, which patrol the rainforest floors in their pretty uniforms. One rebellious member of the family, the long-tailed ground-roller (Uratelornis chimaera), has left the forest for the challenge of living among the didierea in the southwest. More restricted in range are the **sunbird asities** (Neodrepanis spp) which appear as flashes of blue and green in the canopies of montane rainforests, their down-turned beaks designed for the nectaries of canopy flowers.

Yet beak variation is more the domain of Madagascar's most celebrated endemic family – the **vangas**. All 15 member species have perfected their own craft of insect capture, filling the niches of various absent African birds, so that, physically, they are very dissimilar. They often flock together, or with other Malagasy birds, presenting a formidable offensive for the local insects. The most prominent is the sickle-billed vanga (Falculea pallinata) which parallels the tree-probing habits of African woodhoopoes. The heavy carnivorous diet of the shrikes is adopted here by the hook-billed vanga (Vanga curvirostris), while the dramatic, blue-billed helmet vanga

BIRDING IN MADAGASCAR
Derek Schuurman

To see a fair spectrum of Madagascar's endemic birds, visit at least one site in each of the island's three chief climatic/floristic zones: eastern rainforest, southern 'spiny bush', and western dry deciduous forests. Each holds its own complement of regional endemics. In addition, a select band of birds is dependent on the dwindling wetlands so include these in your itinerary. The transition forest of Zombitse should also be visited. During a stay of two or three weeks and armed with two helpful field guides (see page 455) you should be able to tick off most of the island's sought-after 'lifers'.

Below is a review of the sites on the standard birding route.

Eastern rainforest
Rainforest birding is best in spring and early summer (mid September to January).

Ranomafana National Park
Above all, Ranomafana is known for its ground-rollers (pitta-like, short-legged and rufous-headed especially). Other 'megaticks' often seen include brown mesite, yellow-browed oxylabes, Crossley's babbler, grey-crowned greenbul, forest rock-thrush and Pollen's vanga. Velvet and common sunbird asitys are plentiful. On high ridges, look for yellow-bellied sunbird asity, brown emutail and cryptic warbler. In Vohiparara you might find Madagascar rail and grey emutail.

Andasibe-Mantadia National Park (Périnet)
At Andasibe (Périnet) you can see most of the broadly distributed rainforest endemics. 'Specials' include collared nightjar, red-fronted coua, Rand's warbler, coral-billed nuthatch vanga and Tylas vanga. In rank herbaceous growth, look for Madagascar wood-rail, White-throated rail and Madagascar flufftail.

In Mantadia, the pittalike, scaly (rare), rufous-headed and shortlegged ground-rollers occur, as do velvet asity, common sunbird asity, Ward's flycatcher and brown emutail. Two wetlands nearby, the Torotorofotsy Marsh (a four-hour walk), and the more accessible Ampasipotsy Marsh, hold Madagascar rail, Madagascar snipe, grey emutail and Madagascar swamp warbler.

Masoala National Park
Birding in this lowland rainforest is exceptional. Aside from nearly all the broadly distributed rainforest birds, 'specials' include brown mesite, red-breasted coua, scaly ground-roller and the helmet and Bernier's vangas. Two

(*Euryceros prevostii*) resembles a small hornbill. Other species mimic nuthatches, treecreepers and tits. In short, if *The Beagle* had been caught by the West Wind Drift and Darwin had arrived in Madagascar instead of the Galapagos, the vangas would certainly have ensured that his train of thought went uninterrupted.

Malagasy representatives of families found elsewhere make up the bulk of the remaining birdlife. Herons, coots, grebes and ducks take up their usual positions in the wetlands alongside endemics such as the Madagascar teal (*Anas bernieri*), an endangered species currently being studied in western Madagascar, and the Madagascar malachite kingfisher (*Alcedo vintsioides*). In the forests and open scrub small game birds, the impressive crested ibis (*Lophotibis cristata*), doves and the extremely rare species are protected here: the Madagascar serpent eagle and Madagascar red owl. But seeing them is extremely difficult as both are elusive.

Tropical dry deciduous forests (western region)
Ankarafantsika National Park (Ampijoroa)
An outstanding birding locality year round, this forest holds most of the 'specials' local to western Madagascar. They include white-breasted mesite, Coquerel's coua, Schlegel's asity and Van Dam's vanga. Several other vangas (sicklebill, rufous, Chabert's, white-headed, blue and rufous) abound. Raptors include the critically endangered Madagascar fish eagle as well as Madagascar harrier-hawk and Madagascar sparrow-hawk. Other sought-after species often seen include Madagascar crested ibis and Madagascar pygmy kingfisher. In the Betsiboka Delta (Mahajanga), look for Humblot's heron, Madagascar teal, Madagascar white ibis and Madagascar jacana.

Transition Forest
Zombitse-Vohibasia National Park
A serious 'OOE' all year (Orgasmic Ornithological Experience) and included in all birding itineraries for its 'megatick', the Appert's greenbul, Zombitse also holds an impressive variety of other endemics, like giant and crested couas.

Vangas include blue, sicklebill, hook-billed, rufous, white-headed and Chabert's. Look out for Madagascar partridge, Madagascar buttonquail, Madagascar sandgrouse, greater and lesser vasa parrots, grey-headed lovebird, Madagascar green pigeon, Madagascar hoopoe, Thamnornis warbler, common newtonia, common jery, longbilled green sunbird and Sakalava weaver.

Southern sub-arid thorn thicket ('spiny bush' or 'spiny forest')
Excellent birding year-round; start just before daybreak.

Ifaty/Mangily
Ifaty's bizarre euphorbia-didieraceae bush holds some extremely localised birds, notably sub-desert mesite, long-tailed ground-roller, La Fresnaye's vanga and Archbold's newtonia. Look for running coua and subdesert brush-warbler. Excellent for banded kestrel and Madagascar nightjar, too.

St Augustine's Bay
The spiny bush in St Augustine's Bay is lower and more scrubby than at Ifaty and holds Verreaux's coua, littoral rockthrush and the recently described red-shouldered vanga. At puddles along the road, look for Madagascar plover.

drab but tuneful vasa parrots (*Coracopsis* spp) occupy the various strata of the vegetation (see page 430). More colourful birds in the air include the grey-headed lovebird (*Agapornis cana*), the olive bee-eater (*Merops superciliosus*), the paradise flycatcher (*Terpsiphone mutata*) and the blushing pink hoopoe (*Upupa epops*) with bold black-and-white stripes and crest feathers. Unmistakable, and common, are the red fody (*Foudia madagascariensis*), which dance about the savannah landscape dressed in scarlet during the breeding season (November to April), and the crested drongo (*Dicrurus forticatus*), which has coal-black plumage and a strongly forked tail. The rock-thrushes (*Monticola* spp) of the drier south look just like European robins in morning suits. The real thing, the endemic Madagascar magpie robin (*Copsychus albospecularis*), sports black-and-white attire and has the habit of flirting fearlessly with humans.

The Madagascar kestrel (*Falco newtoni*) is joined by other **birds of prey** such as the banded kestrel (*Falco zoniventris*), the Madagascar harrier-hawk (*Polyboroides radiatus*), Frances's sparrow-hawk (*Accipiter francesii*), the Madagascar buzzard (*Buteo brachypterus*), the Madagascar cuckoo-falcon (*Aviceda madagascariensis*) and seven species of owl. The two eagles found on the island are both extremely rare. The Madagascar fish eagle (*Haliaeetus vociferoides*) is sparsely distributed on the west coast, fishing the freshwater lakes, mangroves and estuaries between Morondava and Antsiranana. The Madagascar serpent eagle (*Eutriorchis astur*) was recently rediscovered, after a period of 50 years, hunting on the Masoala Peninsula.

Mammals

Madagascar's mammals are the prize exhibit in the island's incredible menagerie. They exist as an obscure assortment of primates, insectivores, carnivores, bats and rodents, representing the descendants of parties of individuals who, curled up in hollow trunks or skipping across temporary islands, accidentally completed the perilous journey from eastern Africa to the island beyond the horizon at different times over the last 100 million years. Once established, they gradually spread through the diverse habitats of their paradise island, all the time evolving and creating new species.

Biologists often refer to Madagascar as a 'museum', housing 'living fossils'. This is because almost all the mammals on the island today closely resemble groups that once shone on the mainland but have since been replaced by more advanced species. Although evolution has certainly occurred on the island, it seems to have had less momentum than it had back in Africa. Hence, while their cousins on the mainland were subjected to extreme competition with the species that were to develop subsequently, the Malagasy mammals were able to stick more rigidly to their original physiques and behaviours.

The word 'cousins' is especially poignant when applied to the lemurs, for back in Africa primate evolution was eventually to lead to the ascent of humankind. How opportune then for an understanding of our own natural history that one of our direct ancestors managed to end up on this island sanctuary and remain, sheltered from the pressures of life elsewhere, relatively true to its original form for us to appreciate 35 million years later.

The lemurs

Lemurs are to a biologist what the old masters are to an art critic: they may not be contemporary, but historically they are very important and they are still beautiful to look at. Lemurs belong to a group of primates called the *prosimians*, a word which means 'before monkeys'. Their basic body design evolved about 40 to 50 million years ago. With stereoscopic-colour vision, hands that could grasp branches, a brain capable of processing complex, learned information, extended parental care and an integrated social system incorporating a wide range of sound and scent signals, the lemurs were the latest model in evolution's comprehensive range of arboreal (tree-living) mammals. Their reign lasted until about 35 million years ago, when a new model, the monkey, evolved. Monkeys were superior in a number of ways: they were faster, could think more quickly, used their vision more effectively and were highly dextrous. Thus monkeys quickly replaced the lemurs which, destined for the fossil records, vanished from the forests of the world. That is, all but one forest, for on the island of Madagascar, a few stowaway lemurs had managed to take refuge. Today we see the results of 35 million years of their evolution. The single ancestral species has adapted into 51 recognised varieties (see *Appendix 3*), and instead of gazing down at inanimate rocks, we have the luxury of being able to watch, hear and smell the genuine article.

Smell is an extremely important aspect of lemur lives. Through scents, lemurs communicate a wide range of information, such as who's in charge, who is fertile, who is related to whom and who lives where. They supplement this language with an audible one. Chirps, barks and cries reinforce hierarchies in lemur societies, help to defend territories against other groups and warn of danger. Socially the lemurs show a great variety of organisations and the strategy used by each species is largely dependent on the nature of their diet. The small, quick-moving, insectivorous lemurs such as the mouse lemurs and dwarf lemurs are nocturnal and largely solitary except during the mating season when they pair with a member of the opposite sex. Literally surrounded by their insect food, they require only small territories, hence they never cover large distances and spend their entire lives in the trees. A different way of life is led by the larger leaf-eating species such as the indri. In a rainforest there is no shortage of leaves; however, as a food source leaves are fairly poor in nutrients, hence each lemur needs to consume a large amount. Leaf-eaters therefore tend to collect in small groups, together defending their territory of foliage with scents and often loud calls which, in the dense forests, are the best forms of communication.

Their sex lives vary, but most of these species have 'family' groups in which a single male dominates. The most social lemurs on the island are those with a more varied diet concentrating on fruit, but also including seeds, buds and some leaves. This group includes the ring-tailed lemur, the ruffed lemur and the 'true' lemurs. The diet of these species requires active foraging over large areas during the day,

ARE LEMURS STUPID?

Most scientists have considered lemurs to be at the low end of the primate IQ scale. Now an experiment undertaken by Duke University has demonstrated that lemurs – or at least ring-tails – are not only cute but can solve quite complex problems. 'The little bit of research that's out there suggests their learning capacities are not as sophisticated as those of monkeys,' said psychologist Elizabeth Brannon, who led the research. 'So initially, I thought it very unlikely that I was going to get any cognitive experiments to really work with them.' But she found a combination of greed and the lure of a touch-screen computer worked to get the animals to co-operate. 'If a task involves a food reward, they can be amazing,' she said. 'They'll work for a couple of hundred trials because they want these sugar pellets, even though we do not deprive them of food in any way. Occasionally, one animal would come over and finish the sequence started by another to get the reward,' said Brannon.

Unexpectedly, the lemurs could remember sequences. For instance, they showed they could remember the order of appearance of random images by touching them in order when they reappeared as a group. 'It shows that the animal is actually learning some kind of strategy above and beyond what they're learning about the individual pictures in a given set,' Brannon said. But the lemurs were not especially dextrous. 'While monkeys will use their fingers, the ringtails use their nose or mouth to touch the screen'.

Information from Reuters, May 12 2004

so in order to defend their expansive territory, and to protect themselves in daylight, these lemurs form distinctive troops. The societies are run by matriarchs, which organise the troop's movement, courtship and defence, but there are also whole groups of males, which often separate for week-long excursions away from the home base. Usually operating in more open country these lemurs use a wide range of visual signals to accompany their scents and sounds. This makes them particularly entertaining to watch.

Perhaps the most entertaining of all the lemurs is the ring-tailed lemur (*Lemur catta*). Among lemurs it forms the largest and liveliest troops. Each troop typically stirs at dawn, warms up with a period of sunning and then, guided by the

A LAYMAN'S GUIDE TO LEMURS
Nick Garbutt

Unless you are a keen natural historian, sorting out Madagascar's 50 varieties (taxa) of lemur is challenging. The information below, together with the scientific classification (see box on page 42), should help you put names to faces: and if you know in which region/reserve the most common species are found you'll be better able to decide what that leaping animal high in the trees is likely to be.

Diurnal lemurs (active during the day)
The largest and the easiest to identify, these are usually found in groups of between three and twelve individuals.

Ring-tailed lemurs (*Lemur catta*) Recognisable by their banded tails, and more terrestrial than other lemurs, these are seen in troops of around 20 animals in the south and southwest, notably in Berenty reserve.

Ruffed lemurs These are large lemurs (genus *Varecia*) and commonly found in zoos but seldom seen in the wild. There are two species: black-and-white ruffed lemur and red ruffed lemur. Both live in the eastern rainforest, the black-and-white in Mantadia or Nosy Mangabe, and the red in Masoala.

True lemurs This family has only fairly recently been grouped under a new generic name, *Eulemur*. They are all roughly cat-sized, have long noses, and live in trees. A confusing characteristic is that males and females of each species are coloured differently. The best-known *Eulemur* is the black lemur, *E. macaco* (called maki by the Malagasy), of northwest Madagascar, notably Nosy Komba and Lokobe. Only the males are black; females are chestnut brown. Visitors to Ranomafana usually see the red-bellied lemur; the male has white 'tear-drop' face markings. In the northern reserves you'll find the crowned lemur, *Eulemur coronatus*.

Brown lemurs (*Eulemur fulvus*) present the ultimate challenge. There are six subspecies and, since the males mostly look quite different from the females, you have 12 animals to sort out. Fortunately for you their ranges do not overlap. Two neighbouring brown lemurs have beautiful cream or white eartufts and side whiskers: Sanford's brown lemur (*E. f. sanfordii*) is found in the northern reserves; the white-fronted brown lemur, *E. f. albifrons* (the males have bushy white heads and side whiskers of almost Santa Claus proportions), in the northeast. Moving south you'll find the common brown lemur (*E. f. fulvus*) matriarchs, heads off to forage, breaking at noon for a siesta. The troop moves along the ground, each individual using its distinctive tail to maintain visual contact with the others. If out of eyesight the troop members use the cat-like mews that prompted their scientific name. By dusk they return to the sleeping trees which they use for three or four days before the females move the group off to another part of the territory to harvest the food there. During the April breeding season, the males become less tolerant of each other and engage in 'stink-fights' where, after charging their tails with scent from glands on their wrists, they waft them antagonistically at opponents. Similar aggressive interactions occur when two ring-tailed troops meet, yet actual physical violence is rare.

in the east and also the west. The red-fronted brown lemur (*E. f. rufus*) lives in the southeast and southwest, as do the two collared lemurs, *E. f. collaris* and *E. f. albocollaris*. The two collared brown lemurs, *E. f. albocollaris* and *E. f. collaris* (white-collared and collared brown) are found in the southeast. Females all look pretty much the same – boring and brown.

Bamboo lemurs (genus *Hapalemur*) These are smaller than the 'true lemurs', with short muzzles and round faces. They occur in smaller groups (one to three animals), cling to vertical branches, and feed on bamboo. You may see these in the eastern reserves of Andasibe and Ranomafana; the commonest species is the grey bamboo lemur (*Hapalemur griseus*), although in Ranomafana you could see the golden bamboo lemur, *H. aureus*.

Indri The largest of the lemurs, and the only one without a tail, this black-and-white 'teddy bear' lemur is unmistakable. It is seen in Andasibe.

Sifakas (genus *Propithecus*) The sifakas (sometimes pronounced Shee-fahk) belong to the same family as the indri, sharing its characteristic long back legs; sifakas are the 'dancing lemurs' that bound upright over the ground and leap spectacularly from tree to tree. The commonest sifakas are white or mainly white and so are unlike any other lemur. The white sifaka (*P. verreauxi verreauxi*) shares its southern habitat with the ring-tailed lemur, while its cousin the Coquerel's sifaka (*P. V. coquerel*), which has chestnut arms and legs, is seen in Ampijoroa, in the northwest. You may also see the dark-coloured Milne-Edwards sifaka (*P. diadem edwardsi*) in Ranomafana.

Nocturnal lemurs

Two genera of nocturnal lemur helpfully sleep or doze in the open so are regularly seen by tourists: sportive lemurs (lepilemurs) and woolly lemurs or avahis (guides may use both popular and generic names). Most species of lepilemur spend the day in a tree-hole from which they peer drowsily, and the woolly lemur sleeps in the fork of a tree or shrub.

During guided night walks you may see the eyes of dwarf lemurs – most likely the greater dwarf lemur at Andasibe. The tiny mouse lemurs are quite common, and easiest to see at Ranomafana or Berenty.

You're very unlikely to see an unplanned aye-aye, but check the description on page 64 if you think you did…

See *Appendix 3* for a checklist of lemurs and where to find them.

THE AYE-AYE

Hilary Bradt

The strangest lemur is the aye-aye, *Daubentonia madagascariensis*. It took a while for scientists to decide that it was a lemur at all: for years it was thought to be a peculiar type of squirrel. Now it is classified in a family of its own, Daubentonidae. The aye-aye seems to have been assembled from the leftover parts of a variety of animals. It has the teeth of a rodent (they never stop growing), the ears of a bat, the tail of a fox and the hands of no living creature, since the middle finger is like that of a skeleton. It's this finger which so intrigues scientists, as it shows the aye-aye's adaptation to its way of life. In Madagascar it seems to fill the ecological niche left empty by the absence of woodpeckers. The aye-aye evolved to use its skeletal finger to winkle grubs from under the bark of trees. The aye-aye's fingers are unique among lemurs in another way – it has claws not fingernails (except on the big toe). When searching for grubs the aye-aye taps on the wood with its finger, its enormous ears pointing like radar dishes to detect a cavity. It can even tell whether this is occupied by a nice fat grub. Another anatomical feature of the aye-aye that sets it apart from other primates is that it has inguinal mammary glands. In other words, its teats are between its back legs.

This fascinating animal was long considered to be on the verge of extinction, but recently there have been encouraging signs that it is more widespread than previously supposed. Although destruction of habitat is the chief threat to its survival, it is also at risk because of its supposedly evil powers. Rural people believe the aye-aye to be the herald of death. If one is seen near a settlement it must be killed, and even then the only salvation may be to burn down the village.

Other mammals

Employing one of the most primitive mammalian body plans, the **tenrecs** have been able to fill the vacancies created by an absence of shrews, moles and hedgehogs, and in doing so have diversified into at least 24 different species. Five of the species are called the spiny tenrecs, most looking just like hedgehogs, some with yellow and black stripes. However, the largest of these, the tail-less common tenrec (*Tenrec ecaudatus*), has lost the majority of its spines. Not only is this species, at 1.5kg, the largest insectivore in the world, but it can also give birth to enormous litters, which the mother feeds with up to 24 nipples. The 19 species of furred tenrecs are mostly shrew-like in stature, although three species look and act more like moles, and one has become aquatic, capturing small fish and freshwater shrimps in the fast-flowing streams of the Hauts Plateaux.

Highly successful elsewhere, **rodents** have made little impression on Madagascar. There are 20 species, most of which are nocturnal. The easiest to see is the red forest rat (*Nesomys rufus*) which is active during the day. The most unusual are the rabbit-like giant jumping rat (*Hypogeomys antimena*) from the western forests and the two tree-dwelling *Brachytarsomys* species which have prehensile tails.

The island's eight **carnivores** belong to the civets and mongooses, *Viverridae*, which evolved 40 million years ago, at about the same time as the cats. The largest, known as the *fosa* (*Cryptoprocta ferox*), is very cat-like with an extremely long tail which assists balance during canopy-based lemur hunts. The size of a chubby cat, the striped civet (*Fossa fossana*) hunts in the eastern rainforests for rodents, and a third, very secretive animal, the *falanouc* (*Eupleres goudotii*) inhabits the northeastern

'I want to see an aye-aye'

A glimpse of Madagascar's weirdest lemur is a goal for many visitors. And many go away disappointed. When weighing up whether to try to see one in the wild or to settle for a captive animal, you should bear in mind that the aye-aye is a rare, nocturnal and largely solitary animal. Most of its waking hours are spent foraging for food in the upper canopy; only occasionally does it descend to the ground. So even in the reserve of Nosy Mangabe, which was created for aye-ayes, your chance of seeing more than two distant shining eyes in the beam of your torch is very small. I know of one visitor who spent a week on Nosy Mangabe and never saw this animal.

That leaves the choice between the semi-wild aye-aye on the eponymous island at Mananara or those caged in the two Malagasy zoos: Tsimbazaza in Tana and Ivoloina near Toamasina. Mananara seems to satisfy most people, providing they know what to expect. The animals are 'wild' in that they live free and find some of their food in their environment, but they are thoroughly accustomed to people so are easy to approach and photograph. Of the two zoos, Ivoloina is my choice. The animals are less stressed – because there are fewer visitors – and you can usually arrange to see the aye-aye at dusk when they are starting to be active. Tsimbazaza offers night-time visits to see the aye-ayes and this is an ideal farewell to Madagascar before flying home.

If you are not able to get to Ivoloina, there are an increasing number of zoos which have aye-ayes in specially designed 'night-into-day' cages which give you perfect viewing when the animals are active. The best are Zurich (in their wonderful Masoala exhibit), Jersey (the late Gerald Durrell's zoo) in the UK and Duke University Primate Center in the USA.

rainforests where it lives almost entirely on earthworms. Each of Madagascar's forest types play host to mongooses. There are five species in all, the most obvious being the ring-tailed mongoose (*Galidia elegans*) which varies in colour but is typically a handsome, rusty red.

Possessing, among mammals, the unique gift of flight, it is not surprising that most of Madagascar's **bats** are also found on mainland Africa or Asia. There are three species of fruit bat which are active during the day, very noisy, large (a wingspan of up to 1.5m) and unfortunately often on the Malagasy menu. If the fruit bats look like flying foxes (and they do), then the remaining 20 plus species are not unlike flying mice. These are nocturnal, prefer moths to figs and find them by echo-location, employing shell-like ears and distorted noses. It is known that some moths outdo the bats by chirping back at them in mid-flight, scrambling the echo and sending the aggressor off into the night.

The Bay of Antongil marks the northern extent of **humpback whale** migrations. The whales calve just beyond the coral reefs in July and August, and after this period migrate south as far as the Antarctic coast to feed. **Dugongs**, or sea cows, are extremely rare. The Vezo of the west coast share their fishing grounds with an abundance of **dolphins**, and regard them as kin. If a dolphin is discovered dead, they wrap it in shrouds and bury it with their ancestors.

MADAGASCAR'S ECOSYSTEMS

As mentioned earlier, Madagascar has an amazing array of habitats, the result of the effects of ocean currents, prevailing winds and geology. Rain is heaviest in the east and lightest in the west; but at the same time, heaviest in the north and lightest in the south. Since rainfall is the single most significant factor in creating habitat characteristics, a complex spectrum of the world's tropical and subtropical habitats is therefore accommodated in a relatively small area of land – the wettest of rainforests in the northeast to the driest of deserts in the southwest. In addition, Madagascar's geology brings further variety by creating undulating coastlines, broad riverbeds and estuaries, shallow ocean shelves for coral reefs, high mountainous slopes and plateaux, a wealth of soil types and even bizarre limestone 'forests' riddled with caves. These various habitats house a wealth of ecosystems, and in this section each of the dominant ecosystem types found on and around the island will be described.

Terrestrial ecosystems

Before the arrival of humans, Madagascar was almost entirely covered with forests, each suited to the rainfall and altitude of the local area. In the east, where rainfall was sufficient, there was evergreen rainforest, *'lowland'* near the coast and *'montane'* in the highlands. The peaks of the tallest mountains supported thicket communities isolated as if on an island in a 'low-altitude sea'. The Hauts Plateaux, or highlands, were covered with deciduous wet forests interrupted occasionally by rocky outcrops and succulents. The western slopes of the highlands bore tapia trees adapted to the rain shadow of the highlands, and on the western coast vast belts of dry deciduous forest composed of baobabs and leguminous trees were a paradise for troops of lemurs. The southern arid region did not give way to desert, but instead kept the forest theme with the remarkable succulent trees and didierea, and along the west coast there were smatterings of mangrove swamps maintaining the coast margin and bringing a violent green trim to the reddish-brown of the interior.

Much of this once-vast canopy which sheltered the soils of the entire island is now gone. In its place are poorer *secondary communities* of grasslands, forest mosaics and scrub, relying on impoverished soils which are constantly being washed into the sea. The communities are annually burnt in the practice of *tavy* (slash and burn) agriculture, and in the process foreign, virile species take the place of native plants. However, the original *primary communities* do exist in patches. There are still expanses of rainforest, spiny forest and mangroves. The great dry forest of the west is much reduced, but in evidence near to the coast. The remaining communities are particularly fragmented, harbouring amongst geological oddities such as the massif of Isalo and the *tsingy*, or depending on altitude or awkward slopes for their isolation. The one complete loss is the forest of the Hauts Plateaux which has been replaced by grasslands, ricefields and zebu.

Of these remnant communities, none is truly virgin. We know that there were many more lemurs, birds and plants on Madagascar before human settlement. These presumably became extinct as a result of the changes that occurred on the island after the advent of human colonisation. In removing such species communities are inevitably altered, but it is true to say that there are still good examples of natural communities on the island – and it is these primary communities that are of most interest to wildlife watchers.

Rainforests

The spine of mountains which border the central plateau force the wet air arriving from over the Indian Ocean to drop its moisture on the east coast of the island. Madagascar's rainforests therefore exist in a distinct band adjacent to the east coast where the continuous rainfall is high enough to sustain the evergreen canopy trees. Known as the *Madagascar Sylva*, this band of forest extends inland only as far as the mountain range, hence it is thickest in the northeast, even crossing to the west coast around Nosy Be, and becomes thinner as the mountain range approaches the coast towards Taolagnaro. The end of the mountain range, just northwest of Taolagnaro, forms a unique but fragile divide between the evergreen rainforest to the east and the arid spiny forest beyond. This region is particularly unusual in that it is actually *subtropical*, below the Tropic of Capricorn, and there are few areas in the world able to boast subtropical rainforests.

The *Sylva* is not one standard forest, but more a collection of local forest types. Variations occur due to latitude, underlying rock type, angle of slope, frequency of flooding and, towards Nosy Be, seasonality; but the most profound variation is due to altitude. In the tropics, temperature drops by up to 0.7°C for every 100m gained in altitude. As the climate changes so do the flora and fauna, hence rainforests are typically classified by their height above sea level.

Coastal rainforest (sea level)
Very little of Madagascar's unique coastal, or littoral, rainforest remains. Rooted in sand, washed with salty air, battered by cyclones and bordering lagoons and marshes the coastal forest harbours a very unusual community. The architecture of the forest is similar to the more widespread lowland forest, but the plants here are different: they are salt-tolerant and highly efficient at extracting water and nutrients from the shallow, porous sand beneath them. Good examples: Tampolo Forestry Station (*Chapter 12*).

Lowland rainforest (0–800m)
Most of the rainforest in Madagascar can be described as lowland rainforest, that is the forest rising from sea level to around 800m. This type of forest is hot and sticky, with a saturated humidity of 100% and annual rainfall of up to 5,000mm. The forest canopy is 30m above the ground, and there are few emerging trees beyond this height. As well as hardwoods, palms (including the litter-trappers) and pandans contribute to the canopy and under-storey. Most of Madagascar's orchid and fern species live epiphytically on the tree branches, providing rainwater pools for beautiful tree frogs and insects. Vast numbers of insect species hide amongst the foliage. The most obvious insects are the flitting butterflies, monstrous beetles and the myriad ants and termites which patrol the forest floor. Ant colonies infest every part of the forest within their territory on predictable days each month. Within the dark field layer of tree roots, tree-ferns and cycads, are leeches, spiders and occasionally chameleons.

The stars of the forest, the lemurs, skip among the forest branches and the liana climbers which serve as highways between the forest floor and the world above. Lemurs dominate the ecosystem and are quite capable of eating virtually every plant food that it yields. Preying on the lemurs, fosa are at home among the canopy branches, while above the leaves, birds of prey and fruit bats patrol. An unusual sight from ground-level are what look like strange fungi blossoming from the bark of the canopy trees. These are in fact the trees' flowers and fruit sprouting directly from their trunks and branches. A habit known as *cauliflory*, it is intended to make life easier for their pollinators and seed-bearers. Below this vivid display, tenrecs and forest birds rummage through the litter on the floor, and the Madagascar striped civet and mongooses wait to pick off any unsuspecting prey.

Good examples: Masoala Nosy Mangabe and the lower parts of Marojejy (all *Chapter 12*).

Montane rainforest (800–1,300m)
As altitude increases and air temperature drops, the tree species of the lowland rainforest give way to those more able to tolerate the cooler conditions. These

RAINFOREST COMMUNITIES

If a plant could pick a place to live, it would choose one with constant high temperatures and an abundance of water. The hottest, wettest places on Earth occur near to the Equator and they are covered in the world's greatest conglomerations of plants – the tropical rainforests. The rainforests have thrived here for millennia, bathing in the planet's most powerful sunlight and heaviest, most dependable rainfall. In this evergreen habitat there is no autumn, though leaves are individually shed as they age and become inefficient. This constant shower of leaf litter builds up on the forest floor to become the fodder of fungi and soil bacteria, which work unceasingly to decompose the material. A quick turn around of nutrients is vital in a habitat that bears high rainfall, for with each torrent much of the soil surface is washed into the river systems. For the same reason rainforest soils are remarkably shallow, yet rainforest trees are remarkably tall, so throughout the world the trees employ buttress or stilt roots to give them some stability. Another common feature is the broad-leaf which comes to a point, known as a drip-tip, designed to shed the heavy rain as it lands.

The dominant trees block out the sun from below with a solid canopy many metres above the ground. Their broad branches inadvertently support tonnes of epiphytic plants such as orchids and ferns which, embedded in tiny patches of soil, sip water directly from the super-saturated air with bizarre 'air roots'. Trapped amongst their foliage are numerous pools of rainwater used by insects to raise larvae, which in turn serve as food for the tadpoles of tree frogs. On emerging, the vast numbers of insect species harvest the leaves, buds and shoots around them, each specialised to tolerate its host's defensive poisons. The insects themselves are food for birds, bats, tree frogs,

species have lower canopies and are the foundation of a different type of rainforest known as *montane*. The change from lowland to montane forest is a gradual one, influenced by a number of factors. In southern Madagascar, due to the effects of higher latitudes, montane forest occurs further down the mountains, and in the north where it is warmer, lowland forest continues from sea level up to about 900m. To accommodate this variation an arbitrary altitude of 800m is often used to define the boundary between the two types of forest in Madagascar.

Once in true montane forest the landscape is very different from the lowland forest below. Not only is the canopy lower and the temperature very much cooler, but the under-storey is far more dense. Tree-ferns and bamboos litter the forest floor and the gallery above is festooned with epiphytes and mosses. There is a tight tangle of trunks, roots and woody lianas, all sporting furry lichens and lines of bright fungi. Some orchid species have abandoned the branches and have rooted on the forest floor, where they are joined by determined succulent species.

Montane reserves are excellent places to spot mammals and birds. At the three best sites there are many lemur species, some only recently discovered. Bright forest birds, chameleons and boas are also at large.

Good examples: Ranomafana (*Chapter 9*); Andasibe-Mantandia (*Chapter 11*); Montagne d'Ambre (*Chapter 15*); parts of Marojejy (*Chapter 12*).

Cloudforest (above 1,300m)

The forest beyond 1,300m has an even lower canopy and is characteristically thick with ferns and mosses. Its proper title is 'high-altitude montane' but because it is lizards, spiders and other insects, and to complete the food chain, there are predatory snakes within the canopy, birds of prey above, and mammalian carnivores below.

Rainforest animals have other roles. They are employed by plants to courier pollen about the forest. The plants advertise their nectar with magnificent, pungent flowers, each species timing the flowering event for a particular period in the month, year or even decade, so that its dispersed members can swap genes effectively. Once fertilised, the fruits and seeds of the plants are unwittingly dispersed by a different set of animal carriers, such as fruit bats, nut-cracking birds and the lemurs.

Many of the rainforest's residents never leave these hanging gardens, but below the canopy there is another world. An under-storey of smaller plants, such as palms and shrubs, lap up what light is allowed through from above. The huge trunks of the canopy trees are encumbered with lianas, creepers and ferns, and at their bases the forest floor, cloaked in darkness and largely devoid of plant growth, is the realm of fungi, ants and termites. Despite appearances, the floor is more dormant than dead, for its soil is riddled with baby trees, stunted by the darkness but waiting patiently for their one chance to join the others above – a tree fall. If this occurs, the light comes streaming down from above, and opportunistic saplings take their chance by throwing their growth into top gear. In the years it takes for the saplings to climb and close up the canopy once more, a flourish of 'chablis' plants and animals revel in this short-lived paradise, their entire lifecycles designed to support the precarious existence of jumping between tree fall events.

This, then, is the rainforest, the most complex, productive and dynamic community on Earth.

often cloaked in mists, the emotive label of 'cloudforest' is often applied. The low temperature of the cloudforest slows down decomposition, creating waterlogged peaty soils in valleys. Termites do not live this high up, so large earthworms and beetles take the role of detritivores. The canopy is as low as 10m above the ground and in places the under-storey gives way to a thicket of shrubs. Mosses, lichens and ferns inhabit every branch and stone, and cover the floor along with forest succulents and *Bulbophyllum* orchids. A variety of lemurs brave the low temperatures and thick vegetation.

Good examples: Marojejy (*Chapter 12*); Andringitra (*Chapter 9*).

Montane scrubland

On the peaks of Madagascar's tallest mountains there are extremely isolated and unusual communities. In a climate that often provides snow, the canopy here is so low that it eventually reaches a habitat which is less like a forest and more like dense scrub. It is characterised by a single stratum of strange, evergreen heath-trees belonging to the daisy family and an unusual genus called *Philippia*. Among these, and on exposed rocks, are specialist euphorbia and orchids. With the nearest equivalent habitat thousands of kilometres away, these species have evolved isolated on 'high-altitude islands' as remote as any in the ocean. Even at these heights lemurs are found, such as bamboo lemurs and troops of ring-tails with specialised diets.

Good example: Andringitra (*Chapter 9*).

Tapia woodland

Growing in fragmented clumps among the canyons of the rocky western slopes of the Hauts Plateaux are the wonderful tapia trees (*Uapaca bojeri*). Although deprived of rain by the highlands to their east and pounded by hot sunlight throughout the year, the tolerant tapias manage to maintain a canopy year round, supplied by the water that rolls down over the rocks into their canyon homes. Similar in appearance to the stunted cork oaks of the Mediterranean, they share the 10m high canopy with other evergreens, which, unable to withstand fires to the same degree, are becoming less of a feature. The canopy is not as closed as that of the rainforest, so an under-storey of shrubs is well developed, criss-crossed with lianas. Although pandans are common, in this drier habitat tree ferns and most palms and epiphytes are absent. One exception is the beautiful feather palm (*Chrysalidocarpus isaloensis*), endemic to Isalo National Park.

The tapia forests are the sole home of Madagascar's endemic silkworm. Mammals are uncommon, but troops of ring-tailed lemurs and Verreaux's sifaka are sometimes seen.

Good example: Isalo National Park (*Chapter 10*).

Dry deciduous forest

The magnificent dry forests of the west once covered the vast lowland plain west of the Hauts Plateaux. Now, this kind of forest is to be found only in patches, sharing the coast with the mangroves, bordering the largest rivers of the south and dotted about the plains near Isalo and inland from Mahajanga. The forest supports far fewer species than the eastern rainforests but has higher rates of endemism.The trees of these dry forests are less densely arranged and the canopy is lower, at 12–20m. It is too dry here for any epiphytes except some tolerant orchids in wetter areas.

There are several distinct types of dry deciduous forest varying with soil conditions. Growing on the richer, red soils near to the west coast are forests dominated by leguminous trees such as *Dalbergia* and *Cassia*. Where these forests meet the broad rivers of the west and south, enormous tamarind trees, *Tamarindus indica*, and sprawling banyan figs, *Ficus* spp, are common. The banyans, with typical fig audacity, can cover a significant area with their numerous stilt trunks, so that each individual creates its own miniature forest. On the drier limestone plateaux and sandy plains of the west coast, the baobabs (*Adansonia* spp) take over.

The title 'deciduous' refers to the shedding of the canopy during the seven or eight months of the dry season. A carpet of leaves begins to accumulate on the forest floor shortly after the rains stop in May and, through decomposition, they help to create a thick humus layer in the soil. During 'the dry' much of the animal life goes to ground, quite literally. Amphibians and insects bury themselves in the soil and await October when the rains return. Upon the advent of the first rainstorm the forest floor bubbles with emerging animal life and the canopy branches sprout leaves once again.

Foraging within this landscape are many bird and mammal species, each adapted to extract one element of the forest's bounty. Sifakas, sportive lemurs, brown lemurs and the ubiquitous mouse lemurs are particularly in evidence, but more obscure species also inhabit specialised niches within the forest ecosystem. The tamarind forests are the classic backdrop in pictures of ring-tail troops patrolling the floor with their tails in the air. Vangas and other birds form multi-species flocks within the canopy, and the tuneful vasa parrots make territories in the under-storey. The deep litter layer is home to tenrecs, tortoises, boas and hog-nosed snakes. Fosas and mongooses regularly run along their patrol trails, and are prepared to pursue prey into the canopy if the need arrives.

Good examples: Kirindy; Ampijoroa (both *Chapter 17*); Berenty (*Chapter 10*).

Inselberg and tsingy communities

Where the island's underlying rocks break through the landscape in the west, localised communities develop, composed of specialised plants and animals. Rain simply rolls off the rock surfaces or passes through its porous body, so all the residents must be tolerant to desiccation. These communities are particularly interesting in Madagascar because they are the sole retreat for many of the island's more ornamental succulents. Magnificent euphorbias, aloes, kalanchoes and pachypodia tuck themselves into the tiny pockets of soil available among the crevices, bringing foliage and flowers to the smooth rock face. Insects, birds and lemurs rely on these structures for sustenance, only retreating, in the heat of the day, to the copses of trees in nearby canyons.

Such plants are also to be found among the knife-edge pinnacles of three spectacular limestone karst massifs known locally as the *tsingy*. A result of erosion, the jigsaw landscape of the *tsingy* enables a complex mosaic of communities to live side-by-side. The towering pinnacles which sport the succulents are in fact the ornate roofs of extensive cave systems below. The caves are inhabited by bats, rodents and tonnes of arthropods feeding on the bat guano. Blind cave fish swim in the broad, dark rivers, as do, it is rumoured, cave crocodiles. Where the cave roofs have collapsed sunny gullies are crowded with dense, dry forests, rich in baobabs.

This diversity of habitat naturally supports a diversity of birds and mammals, and the *tsingy* massifs are good places to see a wealth of lemur species. It has even been said that Ankarana has the highest density of primates on Earth.

Good examples: Isalo National Park (*Chapter 10*); the *tsingy* massifs of Ankarana, Bemaraha and Namoroka (all *Chapter 17*).

Spiny forest

Whenever photographers wish to startle people with the uniqueness of Madagascar, they head for the 'spiny forest'. Its mass of tangled, spiny branches and swollen succulent trunks creates a habitat variously described by naturalists as 'a nightmare' and 'the eighth wonder of the world'. Stretching in a band around the southwest coast from Morombe to Taolagnaro, the spiny forest is the only primary community able to resist the extreme arid environment of this region. All the plants here are beautifully adapted to sporadic rainfall, even surviving without water for more than a year. The unworldly landscape of this community is largely a result of the striking forms of didierea trees (see descriptions in *Flora* section), which also provide most of the spines in the forest. Side-by-side with the didierea, forming impenetrable thickets, are emergent baobabs, bloated 'bottle-tree' pachypodia and, particular to Madagascar and Socotra, woody tree euphorbias. Of the latter group the most recognisable are the huge *E. enterophora*, with its umbrella-shaped crown of slender green branches atop a black trunk, the sausage tree, *E. oncoclada*, and the spiky grey-green *E. stenoclada* which is so designed to capture the condensing sea mist near the coast. Dramatic, tall aloes and broad-leaved grey kalanchoe 'trees' are found, and endemic orchids and palms, extremely specialised to withstand the aridity, are additional oddities. Where bordering the coast the community can benefit from condensing sea mists and is in places evergreen.

The most evident animal life, aside from reptiles and desert arthropods, are the groups of sifakas which somehow avoid the nasty spines of the didierea as they leap from one trunk to another.

Good examples: Berenty; Ifaty; along the Taolagnaro-Ambovombe road; Beza-Mahafaly (all *Chapter 10*).

Secondary communities

Plants are the foundation of any community. Wherever plants have been removed directly or indirectly by human activities the entire community collapses. It sometimes returns later but in a poorer form called a secondary community.

TAVY

Jamie Spencer

Slash and burn farming, or in Malagasy *tavy*, is blamed for the permanent destruction of the rainforest. Those practising *tavy* agree with this. They also respect this forest and they can see that *tavy* greatly jeopardises the future for the next generations. So why destroy what you love and need?

One answer to a very complex question is the practical need. In Madagascar the poverty is extreme and there are few options. Life's priority is to feed your family and children. Rice, the food staple, is grown both on the flat ground in sustainable paddy fields, and on the steep slopes of slashed and burned forest. Cyclones often wash away much of the paddy rice crop and wipe out the earth dams and irrigation waterways built at great cost and effort. Some farmers have invested a lifetime's savings employing labour for their construction. So if floods strike, people rely on the hill rice. Fertility in these fields is not replenished as in paddies where nutrients are carried in the water. The soil quickly becomes unproductive so new slopes must be cut after a few years.

The cultural explanation for *tavy* is less obvious. The people of 'my' village, Sandrakely, are Tanala, meaning 'people of the forest'. The forest is their world and to survive in this surprisingly harsh environment they clear the land with fire – the ancient agricultural technique brought by the original immigrants from Indonesia perhaps 2,000 years ago. In more recent history the Tanala were forced into the forest by warring neighbours and colonial occupants of more fertile areas.

As the traditional means of survival and provision, *tavy* can be seen as central to society's make-up and culture. The calendar revolves around it, land ownership and hierarchies are determined by its practice, and politics are centred on it. It is the pivot and subject of rituals and ceremonies. The forest is the domain of the ancestors and site of tombs and religious standing stones. *Tavy* is an activity carried out between the living and the dead: the ancestors are consulted and permit its execution to provide for the living. The word *tavy* also means 'fatness', with all the associations of health, wealth and beauty.

If they have the choice, many people are happy to pursue the sustainable kind of agriculture so Feedback is ready to help them. But the practical and cultural context must always be respected. The new alternatives must be rock solid when people's lives are at stake and to be truly enduring they must be accommodated within the culture by the people themselves. It is they who understand the problems and know the solutions that are acceptable. They must not be forced.

Jamie Spencer is the founder of the charity Feedback Madagascar; see page 150.

Madagascar is particularly prone to this degrading process as a result of its frightening rate of soil erosion. The resulting communities are typically infested with competitive foreign plants and are poor in animal life. There are several widespread secondary communities on the island but as with primary communities there are limitless gradations of these where two meet.

Savoka

This is the local name for the secondary rainforest that tends to grow back after *tavy*. It is sadly dominated by foreign tree species which will eventually infest all returning forest, changing Madagascar's rainforest communities for ever. Some native plants have managed to compete with these exotics. The traveller's tree (*Ravenala madagascariensis*) really comes into its own in *savoka*, dominating vast tracts. Malagasy bamboos and pandans also line the remaining primary forest, but there are few animals living in this vegetation. *Tavy* has reduced the rainforest to *savoka* along much of the east coast, particularly inland of the Pangalanes Canal where slash and burn has been ruthless.

Hauts Plateaux grassland (bosaka)

Over a thousand years of *tavy* has destroyed the wet forests that existed on the central highlands. At first the forest must have battled to return, but eventually it failed, smothered by vigorous grass species which provided grazing for the introduced zebu cattle. All that remains now is a barren, sterile grassland dominated by uninviting species such as the knife-sharp *Heteropogon*.

Once dependent upon zebu the Malagasy continued burning the high country in order to bring fresh 'green bite' grass shoots for their cattle. This has, over hundreds of years, left the landscape scarred with deep cuts in the topsoil, called *lavaka*. The soil from these unsightly scars is washed into Madagascar's rivers, turning them iron red in the process. Eventually the sediment flows out into the sea clogging up mangroves and coral reefs. The net loss of soil from the surface of Madagascar as a result of *tavy* is the country's most pressing problem.

Parts of the plateaux support plantations of imported *Eucalyptus* and pine trees. Quick-growing, they are used for firewood by the highlanders. The establishment of these trees is at least proof that in parts of the plateaux, the soils are still rich enough to support the forest that once covered the area.

Palm savannah

Further west where dry forests have suffered the same fate as those of the highland, a dramatic 'palm savannah' exists. Again, the majority of the ground is covered by tall grasses, but there are also scattered palm and baobab trees which can withstand the annual burning. Unfortunately this is likely to be a temporary landscape. The saplings of the trees are less resistant to the flames, so no new trees will be replacing the few remaining ones.

Southern cactus scrub

The harsh environment of the south prevented serious agriculture in this region until fairly recently, hence the spiny forest had remained relatively protected. New sisal plantations have, however, led to colonisation by Mexico's *Agave* cactus creating a secondary cactus scrub in some areas. Another import is the prickly pear cactus (*Raketa*) used for fencing and food for both humans and cattle. The cochineal beetle, introduced by the French in 1928/9, destroyed this important food source and, coupled with the drought of those years, contributed to wide-spread famine.

Aquatic ecosystems

Madagascar's aquatic ecosystems are underrated as sites of ecological interest. On the coast there are excellent stands of mangrove swamp, numerous lagoons and estuaries and, fringing the shore and forming barriers out at sea, magnificent coral reefs. Inland, the island's high lakes and marshes provide isolated havens for unusual bird species and even rare lemurs. Aquatic ecosystems are less restricted by the terrestrial climate and tend to offer more stable habitats for a rich diversity of species.

Wetlands

Wetlands everywhere are regarded as important habitats. Where water accumulates there is an abundance of plants and insects. The plants are terrestrial species adapted to tolerate waterlogging and periodic dry spells, and the insects depend on the water for reproduction, for many species have underwater larval stages. Lakes, swamps and marshes all over the island are therefore popular with birds, attracted by the shelter and materials of the reeds and rushes and the sustenance to be gained from the insect life. On open water and lagoons near the coast, flamingos group in large flocks, accompanied in their feeding by a variety of waders. The rare Madagascar fish eagle can be seen in some locations, and among the marshes that border the inland lakes are white-throated rails, cuckoo-rollers and the Madagascar pygmy kingfisher.

However, in Madagascar it is not only birds that make their homes among the reeds. In the reed beds of Lake Alaotra, a rare subspecies of the grey bamboo lemur, *Hapalemur griseus alaotrensis*, has given up bamboo for papyrus to become the world's only reed-dwelling primate. In southern Madagascar another marsh character hides among the foliage, although this time it's a fellow plant: the insectivorous pitcher plant, *Nepenthes madagascariensis*. Lakes and waterways also play host to healthy and even sacred populations of crocodiles.

CORAL REEF COMMUNITIES

Coral reefs earn their glamorous title, the 'rainforests of the sea', for they are easily as diverse as rainforests, and for similar reasons. The foundation species, the reef-building corals, are miniature relatives of the jellyfish, who have taken to living in vast colonies, surrounding themselves with a protective skeleton of calcium carbonate and grabbing plankton out of the water with their stinging tentacles. Together these colonies can, over many years, create massive solid structures, full of nooks and crevices, in and on which a myriad of fish and invertebrates live.

There are two basic types of corals – the slow-growing massive corals, which add 1cm each year to their bulk; and the more delicate branching corals, which grow ten times faster, but fracture easily during storms. The resulting architecture of a reef is similar to that of a rainforest for one very good reason – corals, like trees, grow towards the light. They do this in order to sustain the most intimate of symbiotic relationships, for, living within the tentacles of each coral individual, or polyp, are millions of single-celled algae. The algae, bathed in the tropical light, provide the polyp with food, while the polyp returns the favour by protecting the algae from predators. This in-house harvesting system works most efficiently in clear, tropical waters, where nutrient levels are poor enough to deter smothering seaweeds and temperatures high enough to permit active reef-building. It is therefore a very fruitful relationship for it creates a prosperity of life in waters that are essentially the subaqua equivalent of a desert.

Competition between corals for a place in the sun is remarkably heated. If two colonies of the same species grow close to each other they tend to fuse,

Good examples: Lake Tsimanampetsotsa (*Chapter 10*); Lake Alaotra; Lake Ravelobe (both *Chapter 11*); Lake Ampitabe (*Chapter 14*); Ampijoroa (*Chapter 17*).

Mangroves

Where trees dominate the wetlands instead of grasses, there are swamps. By far the most important swamps on the island are the mangroves. Madagascar possesses the largest area of mangroves in the western Indian Ocean. About 330,000ha of the land/water margin are dominated by their characteristic salt tolerant trees, which straddle the water at low tide with weight-bearing roots, their tips sticking upwards, unable to gain oxygen in the thick estuarine mud. Some of the trees get a headstart in life by germinating their seeds whilst still on the parent tree. Sporting a shoot and leaves, the seed then drops at low tide into the mud below to attempt a planting.

Mangroves are important and rich ecosystems. They support a wealth of bird species, which arrive to feast on the swarms of swamp insects above the water and shoals of fish below. Many marine fish and crustacean populations treat the underwater architecture of the mangroves as a nursery, coming in from the sea to mate, breed and rear their young in relative safety. Consequently, as mangroves are being uprooted to make way for hotels elsewhere around the Indian Ocean, the local fishermen are finding their livelihood disappearing. Mangroves are under threat in Madagascar.

Good examples: All the important mangrove sites are on the west coast: Anakao (*Chapter 10*); Katsepy and Marovoay (near Mahajunga); Morombe (*Chapter 17*);

Coral reefs

Madagascar has 1,000km of coral reef. As with other coral reefs, most of the species are from a community of globetrotting fish, corals and invertebrates, which crop

but if different species are neighbours warfare begins. The corals launch filaments which digest the skeleton of the enemy, and this explains the significant gaps between colonies on a reef. Their sex life is equally dramatic. It was only relatively recently that divers swimming at night, just after the full moon, stumbled upon corals engaging in mass spawning events, where the water is filled with sperm and eggs, all desperately trying to locate an ideal partner. Fish time their migrations to coincide with this phenomenon, which may take place only once a year, and feed in a frenzy on the abundant platter.

More permanent residents light up the habitat with their colours and behaviours. Unlike their ocean-going relatives, reef fish have an interest in defending their favourite location – a protective crevice or a bountiful patch of sponge. They do this with a combination of poisons, startling territorial displays and plain aggression. For human voyeurs the effect is one of constant theatre, each fish and invertebrate playing its role with finesse. Parrotfish have strong enough 'beaks' to chip away at the coral and extract polyps. Clownfish harbour among stinging anemones, free from harm due to an oily secretion on their scales. Cleaner wrasse run 'cleaning stations', which fish periodically visit to have their parasites removed, while a mimic of the wrasse exploits this chance for deception, and instead of removing unwanted hangers-on, removes chunks of flesh. The goby and the bulldozer shrimp team up to build burrows. The shrimp does the digging and the more vigilant goby watches for danger. All are kept on edge by small sharks patrolling the reef edges and trapped lagoons for stray prey.

up wherever the environment is just right.

There are 63 genera of reef-building corals working to manufacture the island's numerous fringing and barrier reefs. The 1,600km of latitude that Madagascar has to offer creates a gradual cooling of the waters towards the south of the island enabling different corals, and therefore different communities, to predominate. The continental shelf surrounding Madagascar also contributes to diversity. A speedy drop-off on the east coast into deep waters allows only limited fringing reef growth stretching in patches from Fenoarivo to the Masoala Peninsula. Off the west coast, the vast and shallow shelf spreading out under the Mozambique Channel, warmed by the Agulhas current coming down from the Equator, creates far more reef opportunities. Along this coast there are fringing and barrier reefs sporting remote cays and a wealth of fish and invertebrates. Loggerhead, green and hawksbill turtles cruise the underwater meadows between corals and nest on the beaches. International travellers such as boobies, terns and tropic birds feed on reef residents. From July to September, migrating humpback whales use the warm waters of eastern Madagascar for breeding, before heading to Antarctica for a plankton feast.

Good examples: Ile Sainte Marie (*Chapter 13*); islands off Nosy Be (*Chapter 16*); Ifaty, Anakao and Lokaro (all *Chapter 10*).

CONSERVATION
An age-old problem

When people first settled in Madagascar, the culture they brought with them depended on rice and zebu cattle. Rice was the staple diet and zebu the spiritual

THE DURRELL WILDLIFE CONSERVATION TRUST'S MADAGASCAR PROGRAMME
Joanna Durbin

The Durrell Wildlife Conservation Trust (formerly the Jersey Wildlife Preservation Trust), founded by Gerald Durrell in 1963 and with its headquarters at Jersey Zoo, is a non-profit organisation whose mission is 'To save species from extinction'. This is achieved by conserving biodiversity associated with isolated habitats of high animal species endemicity, by developing and promoting the tools used in management of endangered species, and by increasing capacity to carry out this conservation. Durrell Wildlife began operating in Madagascar in 1983 through a formal accord with the government. Our current efforts are concentrated in five sites in western forests or wetlands – fragile and poorly studied ecosystems with their own complement of Madagascar's endemic species, which have often been neglected by other conservation programmes.

The Menabe forests near Morondava on the west coast contain a remarkable cluster of locally endemic, endangered species including the giant jumping rat, the flat-tailed tortoise and the narrow-striped mongoose. They are threatened by slash and burn maize cultivation, which has created vast holes in the forest, and by unsustainable logging operations that damage the forest's structure and open up trails that lead to increased hunting and other extractive uses. Our work has been focused on raising awareness of the locally endemic species by defining their conservation status and threats; on working with local communities using traditional laws called 'dina' to agree on limits to cultivated areas in exchange for rights to cultivate on illegally deforested land; and working with Government and NGO partners to create a new style of protected area to ensure the survival of Menabe's forests and species.

staple, the link with the ancestors. Rice and zebu cannot be raised in dense forest, so the trees were felled and the undergrowth burned.

Two hundred or so years ago King Andrianampoinimerina punished those of his subjects who wilfully deforested areas. The practice continued, however. In 1883, 100 years later, the missionary James Sibree commented: 'Again we noticed the destruction of the forest and the wanton waste of trees.' The first efforts at legal protection came as long ago as 1927 when ten reserves were set aside by the French colonial government, which also tried to put a stop to the burning. Successive governments have tried – and failed – to halt this devastation.

Since independence in 1960, Madagascar's population has more than doubled (to nearly 16 million) and the remaining forest has been reduced by half. Only about 10% of the original cover remains and an estimated 2,000km^2 is destroyed annually – not by timber companies (although there have been some culprits) but by impoverished peasants clearing the land by the traditional method of *tavy*, slash and burn, and cutting trees for fuel or to make charcoal. However, Madagascar is not overpopulated: the population density averages only 21 people per square kilometre, while in Great Britain it is 228. The pressure on the forests is because so much of the country is sterile grassland. Unlike in neighbouring Africa, this savannah is lifeless because Malagasy animals evolved to live in forests; they are not adapted to this new environment.

Change in Madagascar's vegetation is by no means recent. Scientists have identified that the climate became much drier about 5,000 years ago. Humans have just speeded up the process.

The Durrell Wildlife Madagascar programme has focused on conservation of endemic wetland species through two projects. The Western Wetland Project concentrates on species such as Madagascar teal and side-necked turtle and the Eastern Wetland Project includes action for the Alaotran gentle lemur (bamboo lemur) and Meller's duck. These different habitats represent centres of endemism for many other species including fish and other waterbirds. In addition to their biodiversity importance, wetlands are highly productive and sustain large human populations through fisheries and agriculture. A wetland conservation campaign at Lac Alaotra, Madagascar's largest lake, linked to participative ecological monitoring has led to a significant reduction in marsh burning, stabilisation of the lemur population and an increase in fish catches, demonstrating how conservation can be good for biodiversity and for local livelihoods.

The ploughshare tortoise is a prime example of an extremely rare species occurring only at a single site that is vulnerable to a variety of pressures such as uncontrolled bush fires and collection for international trade. Our conservation action for this species, in Baly Bay National Park, which includes all remaining 5,500ha of tortoise habitat, demonstrates how concentrating on a single species can provide multiple benefits for the conservation of a range of endangered species typical of the highly threatened western dry forest and coastal habitats. In particular, we have helped to revive a traditional fire management technique based on burning firebreaks at the start of the dry season. We also run a captive breeding centre for the ploughshare tortoise, the flat-tailed tortoise and the side-necked turtle at Ampijoroa forestry station in Ankarafantsika National Park near Mahajanga with the aim of providing new juveniles to reinforce depleted wild populations.

The race against time

Madagascar has more endangered species of mammal than any other country in the world. The authorities are not unaware of this environmental crisis: as long ago as 1970 the Director of Scientific Research made this comment in a speech during an international symposium on conservation: 'The people in this room know that Malagasy nature is a world heritage. We are not sure that others realise that it is *our* heritage.' Resentment at having outsiders make decisions on the future of their heritage without proper consultation with the Malagasy was one of the reasons there was little effective conservation in the 1970s and early 1980s. This was a time when Madagascar was demonstrating its independence from Western influences. Things changed in 1985, when Madagascar hosted a major international conference on conservation for development. The Ministry of Animal Production, Waters and Forests, which administered the protected areas, went into partnership with the World Wide Fund for Nature (WWF). Their plan was to evaluate all protected areas in the country, then numbering 37 (2% of the country), and in their strategy for the future to provide people living near the reserves with economically viable alternatives. They have largely achieved their aims. All the protected areas have been evaluated and recommendations for their management made. They are now the responsibility of the National Association for Management of Protected Areas (Association Nationale pour la Gestion des Aires Protegées, ANGAP) which was established under the auspices of the Environmental Action Plan (EAP), sponsored by the World Bank. Among their successes has been the establishment of several new national parks and a three-year 'Debt for Nature' swap negotiated by the WWF with the Central Bank of Madagascar. France has agreed to cancel 50 million euros of debt by the end of 2004.

The WWF funds a number of projects in Madagascar. Other outside agencies involved in conservation include the Durrell Wildlife Conservation Trust (UK), DPZ (Germany), Conservation International, Missouri Botanical Gardens, Duke University Primate Center, and the Peregrine Fund; also USAID (US Agency for International Development), UNDP (United Nations Development Programme) and UNESCO. One of the most active Malagasy NGOs is FANAMBY.

The Durban Initiative, 2003

In a dramatic announcement at the 5th World Parks Congress in Durban, South Africa, in September 2003, President Marc Ravalomanana promised to triple the size of the areas of Madagascar under protection from 1.7 million to six million hectares over the next five years. That's an increase from the current 3% of the country's total area to 10%.

Under the plan, the government will expand its terrestrial coverage from 1.5 million to five million hectares and its coastal and marine-area coverage from 200,000 to one million hectares. Deforestation, the president said, has taken its toll on the island, reducing the country's forest by nearly half over the last 20 years. 'We can no longer afford to sit back and watch our forests go up in flames,' he said. 'This is not just Madagascar's biodiversity, it is the world's biodiversity. We have the firm political will to stop this degradation.'

The government will launch a science-based process to choose the best sites for protection, including the identification of threatened species that are currently outside the protected area network. These are called 'gap species'. The government also wants to create wildlife corridors that connect existing parks, preserve rare habitats and protect watersheds. Some of the new protected areas will be called Conservation Sites rather than National Parks.

The government aims to turn the country into a regional leader in ecotourism through sustainable conservation, helping to achieve its goal of reducing poverty by 50% over the next 12 years.

NATIONAL PARKS AND RESERVES
Categories
The six categories of protected area are becoming blurred, as more and more reserves become national parks and open to tourists.

1 Réserves Naturelles Intégrales (strict nature reserves)
2 Parcs Nationaux (national parks)
3 Réserves Spéciales (special reserves)
4 Conservation Sites (a new classification since 2003)
5 Forêts Classées (classified forests)
6 Périmètres de Reboisement et de Restauration (reafforestation zones).

The first three categories were established to protect natural ecosystems or threatened species, and are the ones of interest to tourists, as is the fourth, recently added category of Conservation Site (see www.sitedeconservation.com). Several of the former strict nature reserves that denied access to tourists have now been gazetted as national parks. These protect ecosystems and areas of natural beauty, and are open to the public (with permits). At the time of writing there are nine national parks: Montagne d'Ambre, Marojejy, Masoala, Andasibe, Andringitra, Ranomafana, Zombitse and Vohibasia, Andohahela, Isalo and Tsingy de Bemaraha.

A letter from an American adventurer prompts me to point out that national parks in Madagascar are very different to those in North America or even Europe. They are not huge areas of wilderness with a network of hiking trails where you can wander at will, but carefully controlled places which you may visit only with a guide who will require you to stick to prescribed circuits. If you want to get off the beaten track, don't try to do it within a national park.

There are 18 or so special reserves, of which Ankarana, Cap Sainte Marie, Beza-Mahafaly, Andranomena, Anjanaharibe-Sud and Nosy Mangabe are described in this book. These reserves are for the protection of ecosystems or threatened species. Not all are supervised. Access may be limited to authorised scientific research.

There are also an increasing number of private reserves, the most famous of which is Berenty.

Permits
Permits to visit the reserves and national parks cost foreigners 50,000Fmg per person per reserve. Half this entrance fee goes to ANGAP and half to local communities, so each visitor is playing his or her part. Permits are always available at the park/reserve entrance (be sure to get a receipt) but you may wish to visit the ANGAP office in Antananarivo for the latest information or a 'passport' which covers all the protected areas you want to visit (see page 184).

Hiring guides
After years of confusion and consequent resentment, fees for guides are more or less standardised and posted by the entrance to the popular parks and reserves. They do vary from park to park, however. Usually rates are for a maximum of three people – larger groups pay more. However, guides now expect a hefty tip on top of this fee. This is fair enough if the guide has been exceptional but if they have been sloppy or lazy be brave and omit the tip but explain why. Discourage guides

(again, with a polite explanation) from disturbing or frightening animals to make them move into range of your camera. When tipping, bear in mind the enormous earnings of these people compared with, say, the 160,000Fmg (£16/US$25) per month earned by a labourer in the sisal plantations. Always confirm the fee before setting out.

One 'problem' with guides is that they have been trained to give a standard tour with accompanying commentary and I have never met one with the flexibility to vary it according to the time available or the interests of the tourists they are accompanying. It can be frustrating to stand around in the heat listening to a long list of Latin names for plants or birds but there is nothing you can do about it without being rude. Marvel that these chaps have learned so much in two languages that are not their own!

Planning and Preparation

HOW MUCH WILL IT COST?

The airfare is the most expensive part of your trip. Once there, you will find Madagascar a cheap country. At the time of writing (May, 2004) it has suffered a massive devaluation so that the Malagasy franc/Ariary is now worth half its value of a year ago. No doubt prices will rise accordingly, so any information I give now may well have changed by the time you read this.

For those travelling mainly by bus or taxi-brousse and staying in *Category C* hotels, £15/US$25 per day for a couple is normally about average (considerably less today), and allows for an occasional splurge. Note that couples can travel almost as cheaply as singles, since most hotels charge by the room (with double bed). Sleep cheap and eat well is a good recipe for happy travels.

Costs mount up if you are visiting many national parks or reserves, which cost 50,000Fmg (about £4.00/US$6.80) along with another US$5 or so for the guide.

The easiest way to save money on a day-to-day basis is to cut down on bottled water: a bottle of *Eau Vive* costs over £1/US$1.70 in smart hotels (but half the price in a shop). Bring a water container and sterilising agent (and some herbal tea bags to make it taste nicer). If you are a beer drinker, be careful where you buy it: from a supermarket it costs about 30p/50c; in a cheap restaurant you could pay 50p/85c, and in the best hotels it could be £1/US$1.70 or more.

WHEN TO GO

Read the section on climate (page 3) before deciding when to travel. Broadly speaking, the dry months are in the winter between April and September, but rainfall varies enormously in different areas. The months you may want to avoid are August and during the Christmas holidays, when popular places are crowded, and February and March (the cyclone season) when it will probably rain – and worse. However, the off-peak season can be rewarding, with cheaper international airfares and accommodation and fewer other tourists. September is nice, but often windy in the south. April and May often have lovely weather, and the countryside is green after the rainy season.

Keen naturalists have their own requirements: botanists will want to go in February when many of the orchids are in flower, and herpetologists will also prefer the spring/summer because reptiles are more active – and brightly coloured – during those months. Bear in mind that giant jumping rats, dwarf lemurs, tenrecs and some reptiles are less active and so harder to see during the cold dry months of June, July and August.

My favourite months to visit Madagascar are October and November, when the weather is usually fine but not too hot, the jacarandas are in flower, the lemurs have babies, and lychees are sold from roadside stalls in the east.

RED TAPE
Visas

A visa is required by everyone and is normally issued for a stay of 30 days. A 30-day visa, costing €22 or the equivalent in US dollars, can be issued at the airport in Antananarivo on arrival. This is an easier and often cheaper option than applying through your local embassy or consulate, but only US dollars cash and Euros will be accepted. At the time of writing the 'without visa' queue at the airport in Antananarivo is much shorter so this is another advantage of waiting until you get to Madagascar. However, if you require more than 30 days or are travelling on business you should obtain your visa before leaving home. Long-term visas are usually available for stays of more than 90 days, but need authorisation from Antananarivo so can take about two months to process. Travellers who apply for a visa extension during their stay are usually successful.

Embassy and consulate addresses

Australia Consulate: 3rd level, 100 Clarence St, Sydney, NSW 2000; tel: 02 9299 2290; fax: 02 9299 2242; email: tonyknox@ozemail.com.au. Hours 09.00–13.00. Visas are issued within 24 hours and cost AUS$50.00. The Consul-General, Anthony Knox, is very enthusiastic and helpful. He is also the agent for Air Madagascar.

Austria Consulate: Pötzleindorferstr 94, A-1184 Wien; tel: 47 91 273; fax: 47 91 2734.

Belgium Embassy; 276 Av de Tervueren, 1150 Bruxelles; tel: 770 1726 & 770 1774; fax: 722 3731; email: ambassade.madagascar@skynet.be.

Canada Embassy: 649 Blair Rd, Gloucester, Ontario K1J 7M4; tel: 613 744 7995; fax: 613 744 2530; email: ambmgnet@inexpres.net. Honorary Consulate: 8530 Rue Saguenay, Brossard, Québec, J4X IM6; tel/fax: 450 672 0353. Honorary Consulate: 8944 Bayridge Drive SW, Calgary, Alberta T2V 3M8; tel: 403 262 5576; fax: 403 262 3556.

France Embassy: 4 Av Raphael, 75016 Paris; tel: 1 45 04 62 11; fax: 1 45 03 31 75. Visas take up to three days and cost €26 (single) or €31 (multiple). Consulate: 234 Bd Perrier, 13008 Marseille; tel: 4 91 15 16 91; fax: 4 91 53 79 58.

Germany Consulate: Seepromenade 92, D-14612 Falkensee; tel: 03322 23 140; fax: 03322 23 14 29. €30.

Italy Embassy: Via Riccardo Zandonai 84/A, Roma 400194; tel: 36 30 77 97; fax: 396 329 43 06.

Kenya Honorary Consulate: First floor, Hilton Hotel (PO Box 41723), Nairobi; tel: 225 286; fax: 252 347. Allow 24 hours for visas.

Mauritius Embassy: Av Queen Mary, Port Louis; tel: 686 3956; fax: 686 7040.

Réunion Consulate: 73 Rue Juliette Dodu, 97461 Saint-Denis; tel: 21 05 21/21 65 58. Visas cost the same as in France.

South Africa Consulate: No 13 6th St, Houghton Estate, Johannesburg; tel: 442 3322; fax: 442 6660; email: consul@infodoor.co.za; www.madagascarconsulate.org.za; 30-day visa, single entry R120, multiple entry R140; 90-day visa, single entry R180, multiple entry R200. Consulate; Hon Consul: David Fox; 201 Percy Osborne Rd, Morningside, Durban; tel/fax: 31 312 9704; email: mdconsul@icon.co.za. Visas issued for 90 days only, single entry R120, multiple entry R140.

Spain Honorary Consulate: Balmes 202–2a, 08006 Barcelona; tel: 415 1006; fax: 415 2953.

Switzerland Honorary Consulate: 2 Theaterplatz, 3011 Bern; tel: 311 3111; fax: 311 0871; email: Hocomad@Datacomm.ch.

UK Honorary Consulate: 16 Lanark Mansions, Pennard Rd, London W12 8DT; tel: 020 8746 0133; fax: 020 8746 0134. Hours 09.30–13.00. Visas supplied immediately or by post; very helpful. The visa form can be downloaded from the website: www.Madagascar.org.uk. £40 (single entry) or £50 (multiple entry). Business visas cost £55. Note: a visa can be easily

Previous page La Piscine Naturelle, Isalo National Park (NG)

Above Crossing the Manambolo river (NG)

Below right Confusing bank notes! (See page 125) (HB)

Below School children at the Centre Fihavanana, Antananarivo (KB)

10,000 Ariary
(50,000 Fmg; no equivalent Fmg banknote)

5,000 Ariary (25,000 Fmg)

Old 25,000 Fmg banknote

2,000 Ariary (10,000 Fmg)

Old 10,000 Fmg banknote

bought at the airport in Antananarivo for only £23, but for a short stay (max 30 days). Note that an embassy is scheduled to be opened in London – sometime.
United States Embassy: 2374 Massachusetts Av NW, Washington DC 20008; tel: 202 265 5525. Permanent Mission of Madagascar at the UN: 801 Second Street, New York NY 10017; tel: 212 744 3816; fax: 212 483 7603; www.embassy.org/madagascar.
Honorary Consulate: The Hon Consul in California is Monique Rodrigues, who runs the specialist tour operator, Cortez Travel, 124 Lomas Santa Fe Dr, No 208, Solana Beach, CA 92075; tel: 619 792 6999. Visas in the US usually cost US$33.45 for a single-entry visa.

Extending your visa
A visa extension is usually easy to obtain. As early in your trip as possible go to the Ministry of the Interior, five minutes from the Hilton Hotel in Antananarivo. For your *prolongation* you will need three photos, a photocopy of your currency declaration, a typewritten declaration (best done at home) of why you want to stay longer, a *Certificat d'Hébergement* from your hotel, your passport, your return ticket and the fee: about €25. Every provincial town has an immigration office, or at least a Commissariat de Police, so in theory you can extend your visa anywhere.

GETTING THERE
By air
If you are planning to take several domestic flights during your stay, Air Madagascar should be the international carrier since they offer a 'Visit Madagascar Pass' giving a 25% discount on flights between the most popular destinations in Madagascar, providing visitors also book their international flight (at the same time) on Air Madagascar. This pass is valid only for visitors staying one to four weeks; those on an extended visit pay the full rate. Also South Africa and Kenya count as 'regional' not international (so no discount).

Note that autumn flights are heavily booked (it's the most popular season and also the start of the off-peak cheaper tickets). Book as far in advance as possible.

From Europe
As with any longhaul flight it is often cheaper to book through an agency such as Trailfinders (tel: 020 7938 3366), WEXAS (tel: 020 7581 8768), STA (tel: 020 7361 6262), or the Flight Centre (tel: 01892 530030) rather than phoning the airline direct. At the time of writing only Air France flies to Madagascar from the UK (via Paris). Air Madagascar is the preferred alternative (from Paris) in order to take advantage of the discount on domestic fares. The prices here are the listed ones (ie the maximum you would pay).

Air Madagascar Headquarters: 31, Avenue de l'Indépendance, Antananarivo; tel: (261) 20 22 222 22; fax: (261) 20 22 337 60; email: airmad@wanadoo.mg. The country's national airline is now owned by Lufthansa. Their UK contact details remain the same, however: Air Madagascar, Oak House, County Oak Way, Crawley, West Sussex RH11 7ST; tel: 01293 596 665. The Air Mad website is: www.airmadagascar.mg; schedules are updated regularly but the website does not give prices. There are, as yet, no Air Madagascar flights from London – it is necessary to fly to Paris and connect with the Air Madagascar flight from CDG Airport (section 2a). Air Madagascar now has direct flights from Milan. Return flights in 2004 from Paris or Milan to Tana are quoted at €830 plus taxes, low-season is €649. Flight schedules are reviewed half-yearly so the best source of information is the Air Madagascar website. Currently there are three flights from Paris per week. These flights are overnight, taking approximately 14 hours. For information on domestic flights see page 129.

Air France www.airfrance.com. Flights depart from Heathrow via Paris on Mondays, Wednesdays, Fridays and Sundays. These are day flights (leaving CDG at 10.15), in contrast to Air Madagascar which flies overnight. The return flight is overnight (00.50). The high-season, undiscounted price from Paris is £1,016 and low season £886; these prices include taxes.

CORSAIR This is the cheapest option but tickets can be purchased only through Nouvelles Frontières, 3 Boulevard Saint-Martin, 75003 Paris; tel: 01 4027 0208; fax: 01 4027 0019; www.nouvelles-frontieres.fr. A word of warning from a recent user: 'We were 15 hours delayed going out and 30 hours delayed returning. Apparently this is not uncommon and has been the case for the last two years. As you can imagine it caused considerable stress and furthermore we found the staff on the plane somewhat curt. I would not feel confident flying with them again, despite their reasonable prices. Air Madagascar are a much better bet!' (R Pierce)

On most airlines serving Madagascar there are different rates according to the season (based on popularity). High season is usually July and August, and the Christmas holiday, and low season from January to the end of June.

From other Indian Ocean islands
Réunion
The following airlines fly from Paris to Réunion: Air France, AOM French Airlines, Air Liberté, and British Airways. From Réunion there are almost daily Air Madagascar flights to Antananarivo, and also to Toamasina, Mahajanga and Taolagnaro (Fort Dauphin). Air Austral flies three times a week to Nosy Be.

Mauritius
Air Mauritius and Air Madagascar fly between Mauritius and Antananarivo.

Comoro Islands
Air Madagascar flies from Mayotte and Air Mauritius from Moroni.

Seychelles
There is one flight a week (Tuesday) from the Seychelles.

From Africa
Kenya
There are several flights per week (Air Madagascar, Air Mauritius and Air France) from Nairobi. With so many cheap flights from London to Nairobi, this may be a good option. The current fare for a 30-day excursion is US$559 (excluding tax). Try to book a seat on the right-hand side of the plane for the wonderful view of Kilimanjaro shortly after take off.

South Africa
Air Madagascar (tel: 011 289 8222) flies from Johannesburg on Thursdays and Saturdays, and their partner InterAir (tel: 011 616 0636; www.interair.co.za) goes on Tuesdays. They return the following day. All flights leave Johannesburg at 08.30, getting you to Tana in the early afternoon. The flight takes four hours and, at a discounted rate through a tour operator, costs about R4,600 (about £385) high season.

InterAir can be contacted in London: tel: 0208 283 9742; fax: 0208 562 3600; email: gsa.1.gsa@britishairways.com.

From the USA
Madagascar is about as far from California as it is possible to be. Indeed, San Francisco and the southern Malagasy town of Toliara *are* as far apart as it is possible to be. Understandably, therefore, fares from the USA are expensive. Air France is probably the best carrier, or via United or Delta to Paris to connect with the Air Madagascar flight. From California you can travel west via Singapore or Bangkok (from where there are now Air Madagascar flights).

From Australia
Air Madagascar has an office in the same building as the Sydney consulate. Flights are usually routed via Singapore, from where there is an Air Madagascar flight to Antananarivo, via Réunion, on Wednesdays and Saturdays. Alternatively you can go from Melbourne or Perth to Mauritius (Air Mauritius) connecting with an Air Madagascar flight to Antananarivo, or fly from Perth via Johannesburg.

By sea
From South Africa
There is no longer a passenger-carrying cargo boat running from Durban, but many people sail their own yachts to Madagascar.

Yacht clubs
Royal Natal Yacht Club PO Box 2946, Durban 4000; tel: 031 301 5425; fax: 031 307 2590.
Point Yacht Club PO Box 2224, Durban 4000; tel: 031 301 4787; fax: 031 305 1234.
Zululand Yacht Club PO Box 10387, Meer'en'see 3901; tel: 035 788 0256; fax: 035 788 0254.
Royal Cape Yacht Club PO Box 777, Cape Town 8000; tel: 021 4211 354; fax: 021 4216 028.

Many yachts sail from Natal to Madagascar and the Durban consulate was set up to cope with their visas. It takes six to seven days to sail to Anakao, the most popular port (south of Toliara). Most stop en route at Europa Island, where a French garrison will advise on the next stage. Experienced sailors and divers will want to reach the atoll of Bassas da India which offers superb diving but has been responsible for the shipwreck of numerous vessels.

Because of the increasing number of yachts visiting the northwest of Madagascar, I give information for 'yachties' in the *Nosy Be* chapter.

WHAT TO TAKE
Luggage
A soft bag or backpack is more practical than a hard suitcase (and you may not be allowed to take a suitcase on a Twin Otter plane). Backpackers should consider buying a rucksack with a zipped compartment to enclose the straps when using them on airlines. Or – a cheaper option – roll up the straps and bind them out of the way with insulating tape. Bring a light folding nylon bag for taking purchases home, and the largest permissible bag to take as hand baggage on the plane. Pack this with everything you need for the first four days or so (security restrictions permitting). Lost or delayed luggage is then less of a catastrophe.

Clothes
Before deciding what clothes to pack, take a look at the *Climate* section on page 3. There is quite a difference between summer and winter temperatures,

particularly in the highlands and the south where it is distinctly cold at night between May and September. A fibre-pile jacket or a body-warmer (down vest) is useful in addition to a light sweater. In June and July a scarf (muffler) can give much-needed extra warmth. At any time of the year it will be hot during the day in low-lying areas, and very hot between October and March. Layers of clothing – T-shirt, sweatshirt, light sweater – are warm and versatile, and take less room than a heavy sweater. Don't bring jeans, they are too heavy and too hot. Lightweight cotton or cotton mix trousers such as Rohan Bags are much more suitable. The Bags have a useful inside zipped pocket for security. At any time of year you will need a light showerproof jacket, and during the wet season, or if spending time in the rainforest, appropriate raingear and perhaps a small umbrella. A light cotton jacket is always useful for breezy evenings by the coast. Don't forget a sunhat.

For footwear, trainers (running shoes) and sandals are usually all you need. 'Sports sandals' which strap securely to the feet are better than flip-flops. Hiking boots may be required in places like Ankarana, Andringitra and Isalo but are not necessary for the main tourist circuits.

Give some thought to beachwear if you enjoy snorkelling. You may need an old pair of sneakers (or similar) to protect your feet from coral and sea urchins, and a T-shirt and shorts to wear while in the water to prevent sunburn.

Toiletries

Although you can buy just about everything in Madagascar, it's still best to bring all you need. My indulgence is bringing a roll of my favourite brand of soft toilet paper; the local stuff is adequate, but that's all and you can't rely on the local WCs having any sort of paper. A correspondent notes with satisfaction that condoms are very cheap and reliable. Certainly Madagascar is addressing the problem of AIDS with enthusiasm: in the drawer of my posh Tana hotel was a Gideon's Bible and a condom!

Bring baby-wipes or – better – moist toilet tissues for freshening up during a long trip. There is also an excellent hand-gel which cleans and disinfects your hands. When used regularly, especially after shaking hands or handling money, I have found this a real help in preventing travellers' diarrhoea.

Some toilet articles have several uses: dental floss is excellent for repairs as well as for teeth, and a nail brush gets clothes clean too.

Don't take up valuable space with a bath towel – a hand towel is perfectly adequate.

Protection against mosquitoes
Repellents
With malaria on the increase, it is vital to be properly protected (see page 110). Buzz-Bands (made by Traveller International Products) which slip over the wrists and ankles are recommended as easy to use and effective. For hotel rooms, pyrethrum coils which burn slowly through the night and repel insects with their smoke are available all over Madagascar. They really do work. Plug-in repellents which work in a similar way are also effective.

Mosquito nets
Most *Category A* and *B* hotels either have effective screening or provide mosquito nets, but if you are staying in C hotels or travelling by overnight taxi-brousses (which may stop or break down) you should consider bringing a mosquito net. Because most hotels do not have anything to hang a net from, a

free-standing net is more practical (though a lot more expensive). They generally have a built-in groundsheet giving protection from bed bugs and fleas as well as mosquitoes. This means, however, that you must use your own sleeping bag inside it. You should also treat these nets with Permethrin, which kills bugs on contact. Most mosquito nets are white but Kelyn Akuna points out that insects are attracted to white and that it's harder to see through the white mesh. So look for a darker colour.

A range of mosquito nets and other anti-bug devices, plus advice, can be had from Nomad Travel Store in London: tel: 020 8889 7014; email: orders@nomadtravel.co.uk; www.nomadtravel.co.uk.

Backpacking equipment

Basic camping gear gives you the freedom to travel adventurously and can add a considerable degree of comfort to overland journeys. Nomad (see above) sells an excellent range of adventure travel gear.

The most important item is your backpack: this should have an internal frame and plenty of pockets. Protect it from oil, dirt and the effluent of young or furry/feathered passengers with a cover. You can buy a commercially-made one or make your own: the plastic woven rice sacks sold in Madagascar markets are ideal for this purpose (bring a large needle and dental floss to do the final custom-fitting in Tana). For security consider bringing a lockable mesh backpack cover, such as Pacsafe, available from Nomad.

In winter (June to August) a lightweight sleeping bag will keep you warm in cheap hotels with inadequate bedding, and on night stops on – or off – 'buses'. A sheet sleeping bag plus a light blanket (buy it in Tana) or space blanket are ideal for the summer months (October to May) and when the hotel linen may be missing or dirty.

An air-mattress or pillow pads your bum on hard seats as well as your hips when sleeping out. One of those horseshoe-shaped travel pillows lets you sleep sitting up (which you'll need to do on taxi-brousses).

A lightweight tent allows you to strike out on your own and stay in national parks, on deserted beaches and so forth. It will need to have a separate rain-fly and be well-ventilated.

Most people forgo a stove in order to cut down on weight, but if you will be camping extensively bring a stove that burns petrol (gasoline) or paraffin (kerosene). Meths (*alcohol à bruler*) is usually available as well. Fuel quality in Madagascar is poor so make sure your stove will burn local fuel while you are still in Tana. There are always fresh vegetables for sale in the smallest village so bring some stock cubes to make vegetable stew.

Take your own mug and spoon (and carry them with you always). That way you can enjoy roadside coffee without the risk of a cup rinsed in filthy water, and market yoghurt without someone else's germs on the spoon. Milk powder tastes (to most people) better in tea or coffee than condensed milk. You can buy it locally, or bring it from home. Don't forget a water-bottle.

Give some thought to ways of interacting with the locals. A Malagasy phrase-book (best bought in Tana) provides lots of amusement as you practise your skills on fellow-passengers, and playing cards are universally understood.

A good book allows you to retreat from interaction for a while (but you won't be able to read on a taxi-brousse). Bring enough reading matter with you – English-language books are not easy to find in Madagascar. If you want to read at night, buy a 100-watt bulb (bayonet type) to substitute for the 40-watt one supplied by *Category C* hotels.

Trekking equipment

If you are planning a lot of travel by foot, you'll need to choose your boots with care. Kelyn Akuna writes: 'Boots can make all the difference. I chose a pair of nice all-leather, Goretex lined, waterproof boots. I later learned that these were completely impractical. If you are planning on doing serious trekking [in the northeast] of Madagascar, abandon all hope of keeping your feet dry. At times the trail is a stream, or is flooded (sometimes up to your thighs) in run-off water from rice paddies. So you need to make sure that your boots dry out fast, but are still supportive enough. And while we are on the subject of feet, I brought a pair of socks for each day up to five days. I found that it was worth the extra weight as I could go for longer without having to worry about washing my socks.' Kelyn also adds ruefully that you should bring lots of Band-aids and moleskin for blisters.

Note that this advice is relevant for treks outside the national parks, such as The Smuggler's Path (see page 287) or the Trans-Masoala trail (page 324) but the well-engineered trails in national parks do not require anything special in the way of footwear.

Photographic equipment

These days most people use digital cameras. Apart from the obvious advantages it is great to be able to show local people their photo. Christopher deCharms reports: 'We brought a digital camera and it worked out very well. We found that in most major towns (we succeeded in Diego, Tana, Fianar, Toliara) it is possible to find a modern WinXP computer with a CD burner, buy CDR disks, copy your photos to the computer (bring your cable) and then to CD and then carry or mail home the CD.'

For those still using 35mm cameras, ordinary print film is widely available in Madagascar and can be competently developed in Tana, Fianarantsoa and Nosy Be. Slide film is harder to find. Bring twice as much film as you think you'll need. You will not need a telephoto lens for the lemurs of Berenty and Nosy Komba (wide-angle is more useful for these bold animals) but you'll want a long lens plus very fast film (400 ASA) and a flash for most forest creatures. For landscapes 100 or 200 ASA is ideal. A macro lens is wonderful for all the weird insects and reptiles. Don't overburden yourself with camera equipment – there's no substitute for the eye/brain combination!

Miscellaneous items for budget travellers

Bring a roll of insulating tape or gaffer tape which can be used for all manner of things. Blu-Tack is equally versatile; bring enough to make a plug for your sink, to stop doors banging or to hold them open. A Swiss Army knife (or similar) is essential (but remember not to pack it in your hand luggage). A rubber wedge will secure your hotel door at night, and a combination lock is useful in a variety of ways (see the section on safety, page 120). Other useful items are a light tarpaulin (multiple uses) and a length of strong, nylon cord (ditto). It's worth bringing two torches (flashlights) in case one breaks or is lost.

A small tape recorder/Walkman is a great asset during lone evenings in dingy hotel rooms or on an all-night taxi-brousse. Earplugs are just about essential, to block out not only the sounds of the towns but those of enthusiastic nocturnal animals when camping in reserves! (Personally I think it's worth being kept awake by these, but it can pall after several nights.) A large handkerchief or bandanna has many uses and protects your hair and lungs from dust, and the uses for a *lamba* (Malagasy sarong) are too numerous to list.

Checklist

Small torch (flashlight) with spare batteries and bulb, or headlamp (for nocturnal animal hunts), travel alarm clock (or alarm wristwatch), penknife, sewing kit, scissors, tweezers, safety pins, insulating tape or Sellotape (Scotchtape), string, felt-tipped pen, ballpoint pens, a small notebook, a large notebook for diary and letters home, envelopes, plastic bags (all sizes, sturdy; Zip-loc are particularly useful), universal plug for baths and sinks (though Blu-Tack does the job just as well), elastic clothes line or cord and pegs, concentrated detergent, ear plugs, insect repellent, sunscreen, lipsalve, spare glasses or contact lenses, sunglasses, medical and dental kit (see *Chapter 5*), dental floss, a water bottle, water purifying tablets or other sterilising agent, compact binoculars, camera and film, books, miniature playing cards, Scrabble/pocket chess set, French dictionary and Malagasy phrasebook.

Goods for presents, sale or trade

This is a difficult area. In the past tourists have handed out presents to children and created the tiresome little beggars you will encounter in the popular areas (if you don't now know the French for pen or sweets, you soon will). They have also handed T-shirts to adults with similar consequences. For more on this subject see *Chapter 7*. There are, however, plenty of occasions when a gift is appropriate, although as Will Pepper points out, 'On a number of occasions people said this souvenir of Ireland is all well and good but I would prefer cash.' Giving money in return for services is entirely acceptable so in rural areas it's best to pay cash and refrain from introducing a new consumer awareness.

In urban areas or with the more sophisticated Malagasy people, presents are a very good way of showing your appreciation for kindness or extra good service. Music cassettes often go down well with taxi-brousse drivers, but only pop music. It's worth bringing some duty-free cigarettes, however much you disapprove of smoking. It is probably the present most gratefully received.

If you want to contribute something a little more intellectually satisfying, here is a suggestion from Dr Philip Jones, who travels in Madagascar on behalf of the charity Money for Madagascar. 'I was asked several times for an English Grammar, so any such books would be valued gifts. If visitors take a French–English dictionary, why not leave it in Madagascar?' Frances Kerridge suggests English-language tapes as an alternative to books: 'Almost everyone seems to want to learn English.'

MONEY

Travellers' cheques In the old days everyone brought travellers' cheques, but now these are rarely seen and consequently are difficult to cash. If you do opt for travellers' cheques (and it is the safest option) they should be in euros or US dollars. Sterling travellers' cheques are almost impossible to change.

Cash It is far easier to change cash (euros or US dollars) so this is the best option if you are on a prepaid group tour. Be wary of bringing US$100 bills – these are not always accepted because of the large number of counterfeit ones doing the rounds. Bring $50 and $20 bills (or the equivalent in euros), and about 10 single dollar bills which are ideal for tips or handicrafts if you don't have local currency handy.

Credit cards Most of the large hotels now accept credit cards, but there are some notable exceptions. Visa is much more likely to be accepted than Mastercard (but bring both if you have them). Credit cards may be used to draw cash at many banks and *Bureaux de Change*. This will be an over-the-counter procedure so you don't normally need to know your pin number. For some reason that no-one can explain, credit cards don't work in Madagascar between 5 and 6pm!

ATM machines These exist but often don't work so you can't rely on them.

In summary, when I travel in Madagascar I bring my money in cash and credit cards (in a moneybelt). For independent travel (no pre-booked hotels) I would add some euro travellers' cheques.

WAYS AND MEANS

Over the years I've come to believe that everyone *can* enjoy Madagascar but not everyone does because they do not take sufficient care in matching the trip to their personality. When planning a holiday most people consider only their interests and how much they are prepared to spend. I feel that a vital component has been missed out.

What sort of person are you?

The Catch 22 of tourism in Madagascar is that the type of person who can afford the trip is often the type least suited to cope with the Malagasy way of life. In our culture assertiveness, a strong sense of right and wrong, and organisational skills are the personality traits which lead to success in business, and thus the income to finance exotic travel. But these 'A' type personalities often find Madagascar unbearably 'inefficient' and frustrating. By having control over their itinerary through a tailor-made tour, or by renting a vehicle and driver, such people are more likely to get the most out of their trip. A group tour, where they must 'go with the flow', may be the least successful option.

Conversely, the happiest travellers are often either those who choose to travel on a low budget (providing they're not obsessed with being ripped off) or those who can adopt the attitude of one elderly woman on a group tour who said 'I'm going to give up thinking; it doesn't work in Madagascar.' It doesn't, and she had a great time!

These days there is a trip to suit everyone in this extraordinary country. It won't be a cheap holiday, but it will be one you never forget so choose wisely.

Below are the main options, in descending order of price and comfort.

The luxury package

The owners of Tsarabanjina (Nosy Be) and Anjajavy (north of Mahajanga) have ensured that holidaymakers (such as honeymooners) looking for a trip-of-a-lifetime are shielded from the unexpected. International flights are met by a private plane which whisks passengers off first to a magnificent island surrounded by coral, and then to a beach resort and forest reserve where are lemurs as well as every activity imaginable. This is a well-rounded package (you visit small villages as well as wildlife) and well worth the expense. See pages 396 and 410 for details.

Expedition cruising

With ships you know that you will sleep in a comfortable bed each night and eat familiar food. It is thus ideal for the adventurous at heart who are no longer able to take the rigours of land travel. It is also sometimes the only way of getting to remote offshore islands and for snorkelling over some of the best reefs in the world. In the UK try Noble Caledonia (tel: 020 7752 0000; www.noble-caledonia.co.uk). And in the US, Zegrahm Expeditions (tel: 1 800 628 8747 or 206 285 4000; www.zeco.com) are recommended.

Tailor-made tours

This is the ideal option for a couple or small group who are not restricted financially. It is also the best choice for people with special interests or who like things to run as smoothly as possible. You will be the decision-maker and will choose where you want to go and your preferred level of comfort, but the logistics will be taken care of.

You can organise your tailor-made trip through a tour operator in your home country, in which case you will have the benefit of legal protection if things go wrong, or use email to contact some Malagasy tour operators. Let the tour operator know your interests, the level of comfort you expect, and whether you want to cram in as much as possible or concentrate on just a few centres.

Tour operators which specialise in tailor-made tours in Madagascar are listed later in this chapter.

Group travel

Group travel is usually a lot of fun, ideal for single people who do not wish to travel alone, and if you choose the tour company and itinerary carefully you will see a great deal of the country, gain an understanding of its complicated culture and unique wildlife, and generally have a great time without the need to make decisions (but you need to be able to relinquish the decision-making; not everyone can do this).

Many of the listed tour operators in the UK and the USA do set departures (ie: group tours rather than tailor-made trips) to Madagascar.

Working holidays

There is a growing interest in paying to be a volunteer in a scientific or community project in Madagascar. The pioneer here is **Earthwatch**. Among other things in Madagascar you can work with Dr Alison Jolly on lemur research. Addresses: 267 Banbury Road, Oxford OX2 6HU, England; tel: 01865 318838; www.earthwatch.org/europe/ and 3 Clock Tower Place, Suite 100, Box 75, Maynard, MA 01754, USA; tel: 1 800 776 0188 or 978 461 0081; email: info@earthwatch.org. A similar organisation for students is **World Challenge Expeditions**, Black Arrow House, 2 Chandos Rd, London NW10 6NF; tel: 020 8728 7200; email: welcome@world-challenge.co.uk. **Blue Ventures** co-ordinates teams of volunteers, working with local biologists, marine institutes, NGOs and communities whose livelihoods depend on marine ecosystems. For more information see www.blueventures.org, or email enquiries@blueventures.org. Another organisation for marine conservation is **Frontier**, 50–52 Rivington St, London EC2A 3QP; tel: 020 7613 2422, take paying volunteers for their marine research programmes. Their website is www.frontierprojects.ac.uk. **Pioneer Madagascar** is the volunteering scheme of Azafady (see page 150); tel: 020 8960 6629; www.madagascar.co.uk. The ten-week scheme is run four times a year, with volunteers working on conservation and community projects.

Semi-independent travel

If you have a fax machine or email and are willing to persevere with Madagascar's erratic telecommunications (which are rapidly improving), you can save money by dealing directly with a tour operator in Madagascar. The ones that I know or that have been recommended are listed later in this chapter, but there are many more. Now tourism is established in Madagascar, local operators have a clear understanding of tourists' needs and are impressively efficient. The downside to using a local operator is that they won't be bonded. If things go wrong there is no redress: you will not get a refund nor be able to sue the company.

Perhaps the ideal do-it-yourself trip is to hire a local driver/guide and vehicle when you arrive in Tana. This way you are wonderfully free to stop when you please and stay where you wish. There are some drivers listed in the Antananarivo chapter but some people have written to me happily about their experiences after being approached by a man with a car at Ivato Airport.

Independent travel

Truly independent travellers usually have a rough idea of where they want to go and how they will travel but are open to changes of plan dictated by local conditions, whim and serendipity. Independent travellers are not necessarily budget travellers: those who can afford to fly to major towns, then rent a vehicle and driver, can eliminate a large amount of hassle and see everything they set out to see – providing they set a realistic programme for themselves. What they may miss out on is contact with the local people, and some of the smells, sounds and otherness of Madagascar.

The majority of independent travellers use public transport and stay in B or C Category hotels. They are exposed to all Madagascar's joys and frustrations and most seem to love it. The key here is not to try to do too much, and to speak at least some French. *Chapter 6* tells you about the trials and tribulations of travelling by taxi-brousse: no problem providing you allow time for delays.

The seriously adventurous

Madagascar must be one of the very few countries left in the world where large areas are not yet detailed in a guidebook. A study of the standard 1:2,000,000 map of Madagascar reveals some mouth-watering possibilities, and a look at the more detailed 1:500,000 maps confirms the opportunities for people who are willing to walk or cycle. Or drive. Two of my most adventurous correspondents, Valerie and John Middleton, have travelled all over Madagascar by 4WD vehicle and their trusted Madagascar Airtours guide and driver. I asked them why they keep coming back. 'Why do we go where we do? Well, I have had a passion for worldwide cave and karst exploration for well over 40 years and in plants, and in particular their adaption to extreme conditions.' As John says, having a focus helps, especially when explaining your presence to bemused locals. The Middletons also support my theory that the seriously adventurous are often 'pensioners'.

Not that the youngsters don't do their bit for exploring Madagascar's uncharted areas. Throughout this book there are quotes from people who did just that, sometimes after a lot of preparation and sometimes on a whim. In the former category comes Meredith Sorenson and his friend, former Peace Corps volunteers who are currently walking the length of Madagascar (the hard way, along the eastern corridor) to raise money for local projects. Meredith has established an excellent website so you can follow his route on www.hikemadagascar.com.

Not everyone is courageous enough to step or pedal into the unknown like this, but in fact it's one of the safest ways to travel: the Malagasy that you meet will, once they have got over the shock of seeing you, invariably be welcoming and hospitable (see boxes on pages 420 and 246). The risk of crime is very low.

It's how I first saw Madagascar and why I fell in love with the place.

Serious adventurers will need to plan their trip beforehand with the FTM regional maps. The Middletons tell me: 'It is possible to obtain photocopies of the 1:100,000 maps that cover Madagascar plus a few of the 1:25,000 that cover only a small area. These can be obtained in person only from The Institute Geographique National, 2-4 Av Pasteur, 94165 Saint-Mande, Paris. This also applies to maps for other French ex-protectorates. ID is needed before entry is permitted. It may seem a long way to go but it does make an excellent excuse for a trip to Paris!' If you don't live within reach of Paris you will have to purchase the maps in Tana. See page 180.

Travelling alone

To travel alone may be a matter of choice or necessity. The trick is to make the necessity into choice by revelling in the opportunity to get close to the local people and to immerse yourself in their culture. The reports by 'FRB' in *Chapter 12* show just how rewarding this can be.

Lone travellers need to be prepared for the long evenings. Robert Bowker found nights at national parks particularly lonely: 'Dinner is early, and after that nothing to do but go to your bungalow. Take a powerful torch and lots to read. I got through a fair number of crossword puzzles. Also take music...'. For budding writers evenings alone are the perfect time to develop your diary skills. Another problem which needs to be borne in mind when planning a solo trip is that national parks and reserves will be expensive unless you team up with other travellers, because guides charge for a group of three. Trips like the Masoala Peninsula, where boat hire is involved, will be prohibitive. Conversely, one person can squeeze into any taxi-brousse.

Solo travellers should avoid the usual tourist routes where they may encounter hostility from the locals, as well as higher prices. The real rewards come when you travel off the beaten track.

Safety aspects of travelling alone are covered on page 123.

SPECIAL INTERESTS

Added to the points above are the tourists who are going to Madagascar to pursue a special interest.

Hiking, trekking and rock-climbing

Madagascar now has several options for enthusiastic hikers: organised trekking in the national parks or hiking in remote areas.

Trekking

It's a misnomer to call it trekking because Madagascar is not like the Himalayas or Andes where your gear is carried by porters or pack animals to a different campsite each night. There are two national parks that are set up for hiking, Andringitra and Isalo, but you usually do a circular hike and return to the same campsite at night. This does not diminish the experience, however. My most recent Madagascar trip (2003) was to explore the trekking possibilities, and I can count Andringitra as one of my best hiking experiences anywhere (see page 221). You need to be aware of how national parks work in Madagascar. American Christopher deCharms wrote to me: 'We went to Madagascar having heard tales, seen photos and hoping for wilderness adventure and trekking through the wilds on our own. While we had a fantastic trip, we found things to be quite different from our expectations, and a lot less wild. In our experience, the accessible wilderness is very limited and highly controlled. We went to five of the national parks (Ankarana, Mt Amber, Andringitra, Ronomafana, Isalo) hoping for wilderness trekking as we are accustomed to in US national parks – lots of land, and few rules other than not causing harm. We found that the national parks are more comparable to what we in the US call "state parks". They are small, only about 5–10 miles across or so, and surrounded by cultivated land. You have no choice but to take a fixed tourist route for a fixed tourist price led by a guide (and likely a cook and porters if overnighting), and to sleep in pre-built camp areas with cook huts. The motivation is clear: provide a safe, controlled tourist experience, prevent tourists from going anywhere other than the designated paths, and take money from the tourists to sustain the parks and community. Despite this, the walks are great, we enjoyed our visits, the animals are fascinating, the guides are friendly, and conservation is a good thing. However, if you are experienced in the wilderness and looking for adventure as several other travelers we spoke with were, you will need real advance planning and local information.'

Hiking
My advice to people like Christopher is to bear in mind that many of Madagascar's 'roads' are overgrown tracks, and ideal for hiking. There are a couple of well-known routes, the Smugglers' Path and the Trans-Masoala Trail, but these do not appeal to me nearly as much as the huge regions that have seen few, if any, foreigners. The country is well mapped and the local people are accustomed to travelling on foot. I find the FTM 1:500,000 maps mouth-watering in their possibilities – talking of which, be sensible about water supplies. Hiking in the south is fascinating from a cultural perspective but you will need to carry a lot of water. Conversely, if hiking in the east you will get very wet but never be short of a drink! Read the advice on page 148 on the cultural aspects of travelling off the beaten path safely and enjoyably.

Rock-climbing
The centre for rock-climbing is Andringitra and Camp Catta. See page 221.

Mountain biking
Madagascar is becoming increasingly popular for travelling using your own muscle-power. The advantages are obvious: bad roads and broken-down vehicles do not delay you, con-men will not overcharge you and – most important – by passing slowly through Madagascar's small villages and communities you will experience the Malagasy culture in an unforced way. These advantages far outweigh the inevitable security risks of being totally at the mercy of local people. You are far more likely to be overwhelmed by hospitality than robbed.

Lex Cumber sent me some invaluable advice stemming from his 3000km trip by mountain bike. See box on page 96. Also do check out the excellent website set up by Michael Ayers after his long solo ride through Madagascar in 2003. It gives the flavour (and hardship!) of travelling this way beautifully: www.terminalia.org/mad.

Caving
Madagascar has some fabulous caves, and several expeditions have been mounted to explore them. Caving is not a popular Malagasy pursuit, however, so cavers should take particular care to explain what they are doing and get the necessary permits for exploring protected areas. An experienced local tour operator will help with the red tape.

The best karst areas are in the north and west, as follows.

Ankarana Known for its *tsingy*, this is the best explored and mapped of all karst areas.
Narinda The longest cave, Anjohibe, is 5,330m.
Namoroka Access difficult and safety a problem in this area.
Bemaraha Excellent possibilities for exploration now this *tsingy* area is being opened up to tourism.
Toliara region Mickoboka Plateau to the north has pits to a depth of 165m, and the

Mahafaly Plateau to the south contains numerous small caves.

Diving

Liz Bomford, an experienced diver who has been visiting Madagascar for 25 years, provided the following information.

By far the best and most exciting diving is around Nosy Be and its galaxy of islands and reefs. The biodiversity in this area is outstanding. Coral bleaching caused by global warming has not affected the reefs to any degree and you can find almost every hard coral species known in the Western Indian Ocean. The fish life is stunning. You may see humpback whales as well as dolphins from the boat. Underwater you could get lucky and find whale shark. Nosy Be is extraordinarily good for nudibranchs so there's something for everyone. The diving operators in Nosy Be work with local fishermen to protect the environment with the aim of providing good diving conditions for tourists. You won't be disappointed.

DIVE SITES

At Ile Sainte Marie, off the east coast, there are several good dive sites, and the dive operators are a responsible bunch. However, visibility is often limited due to heavy rainfall in this area.

The west coast around Toliara used to offer very good diving (I first dived there in 1976) but these days over-fishing has taken its toll and the diving is a shadow of what it used to be. Medical facilities are poor and evacuation in the event of a diving injury is extremely difficult. The diving operators are variable. If you dive here, make sure you check your equipment carefully.

The water is colder in August and September (take a hood or a sweat) but the rest of the year a 5mm suit will do. Men will have no trouble hiring a suit but if you're a woman, consider taking your own wetsuit – otherwise you may have trouble finding one to fit.

If you are considering diving in Madagascar, read the box on *Diving Safety* on page 121.

River trips

Madagascar has some splendid rivers, particularly in the west. Some offer the perfect means to pass through otherwise inaccessible areas of the country. The

TRAVELLING BY MOUNTAIN BIKE IN MADAGASCAR
Lex Cumber

If you are thinking of taking a bike to Madagascar, do it, you'll love it. On most of the roads you will be more comfortable than anyone in motorised transport. The simplicity and strength of the humble bike will get you virtually anywhere, bring you closer to the wonderful people of the island and allow you to see things that you would miss if you travelled any other way. You're independent, flexible and a lot better off than in a taxi-brousse, trust me! Here are some tips.

The Bike A good quality hardtail mountain bike is the ideal vehicle for Madagascar. What you need to think is simplicity, strength and self sufficiency. If it can't be fixed with the tools you carry yourself, or by a Malagasy mechanic with a hammer, don't take it. Fit a new chain and block, carry spare spokes, brake blocks, cables, inner-tubes and take plenty of oil (the dust is unbelievable). Go with the strongest wheels you can afford, and the fattest tyres you can fit (1.95 minimum). You can pick up cheap bike parts in the larger towns but you have to be creative. My seat post clamp snapped and was held up by a bolt from an old Land Rover, for example!

On the bike Forget panniers unless you are staying on the good roads around Tana. If you are straying out of the highlands, the roads will simply shake your bike to pieces. A 20–35 litre backpack held away from your back with mesh for ventilation is ideal: it's more flexible, stays with you at all times, and you do get used to it. A rear rack with a rack bag is a good addition, and allows you to carry heavy tools/food/water away from your back.

Personal clothing You obviously need two sets, one for cycling and one for socialising/resting. If you are going to explore the deserts, I advise the 'Beau Geste' style of hat with peak on front, and flap on back. General purpose shorts, with cycling short inners underneath (two pairs minimum) are ideal. Also take leather cycling gloves (artificial materials disintegrate with the sweat and the heat); footwear of the trainer/walking boot variety is ideal, again go for natural materials; lightweight socks, with a clean set of underwear spare at all times. I find an Arabic scarf a fantastic all-purpose bit of kit: sleep under it, dry yourself with it, use it as a picnic blanket or head covering for dust-storms etc. Bandannas are a useful addition and keep the sweat out of your eyes. Just think tough kit for your contact points on the bike, and breathable kit everywhere else. The rule to apply for your clothing is 'one set wet, one set dry'. Take shorts, T-shirt, boots and hat for riding. At night consider a clean T-shirt/vest with a cotton or similar shirt, and lightweight trousers. Your appearance is always worth considering, as you never know who you are going to meet! Finally, take a lightweight fleece as it can get cold at night, and some sort of wind breaker/waterproof shell.

Personal hygiene Take a good first-aid kit, and Savlon for your backside. My colleague on our 3,000km Madagascar adventure had golf-ball sized boils on his behind for 3–4 weeks as a result of a) lots of saddle time b) sweat c) lack of 'arse discipline' (as we called it). Apply Savlon liberally, and if you get the chance to wash, take your time and be particular down below. Anti-fungal creams are a good idea as well. Take dehydration salts, imodium type pills and laxatives. Your body will not know what hit it, and you never know how it will react. Salt pills are useful as well. Remember to drink as much as you can at night. Filter/sterilise it. Always be cautious with open source water.

Remote towns When pulling into a town/village, always ride right the way through it first, select your likely bar/bunkhouse, and then cycle back to it. You don't want to miss the heavenly spot 500m up the road because you pulled over early. If in doubt look for a village elder [important, I would think. See page 148. HB]. If you are really remote, the locals will often run away, but just wait and the relevant person will find you. Don't presume to be able to buy food if you are away from the 'Route National'. Bear in mind villagers will often offer you food, and as result go without themselves. Finally, if you do buy food in remote villages make sure you give the women-folk the money, not the men.

Ride routine Be moving before sunrise if you're in the desert: 05.00 is about right. If you can finish your riding for the day by 11.00–12.00, that's perfect, but be realistic. Don't ride at midday unless you really have to. Just find/make some shade and rest. You'll probably be exhausted by then anyway, but after a few weeks you should be able to put in 6–8 hours riding per day. Rest days are vital, four days on and one day off is better than the standard five-day week routine.

Food Carry two days' rations if you can, because you just never know when you may have to spend a night out: peanuts, raisins/dates, processed cheese, salt, rice and boiled sweets. Pick up these supplies in Tana. This food stash will supplement your basic rice diet, which soon becomes boring, and lacks the calories required for hard riding. Otherwise, watch where the locals eat and don't be afraid of the road-side stands, they are fantastic. Carry a lightweight stove that does not rely on gas.

Camping Strangely in Madagascar there is a totally different attitude to camping. It is viewed as suspicious behaviour by many rural communities. Where possible avoid it. However you need to carry a sleeping bag and mat anyway, so a poncho or tent will allow you the flexibility to camp out should you need to. Best advice: try not to be too obvious or you will attract a lot of unwanted attention.

Security As a rule Madagascar is a very safe place, but on a bike you are exposed. Your best defence is learning the language, using humour and keeping some small denomination notes handy. Note that you will not find banks outside of the four or five main cities that know what a credit card is, so you will have to carry a lot of cash. Spread it around, hide some in your bike etc. Have photocopies of documentation on you, as well as originals. Leave details in Tana, and inform your national consulate of an approximate return date. If in trouble, don't raise your voice and negotiate calmly with the head man, be patient, and keep smiling.

Navigation Even the best maps available in Madagascar are inaccurate. Rely on local knowledge when navigating the minor roads. If you are travelling cross country, good compass work and the ability to read the terrain is essential. Again local knowledge, and the ability to stay calm when lost are essential.

Biking in Madagascar is breathtaking in every sense of the word. It's not easy, but you don't go to Madagascar to be pampered! I can promise you will see the country at its best, and the desert sunrises are worth the journey alone. Go for it!

range includes extended calm water floats to exciting white-water sections. See *River Trips* page 439.

Birdwatching

There are several tour operators that specialise in birding trips. 'Twitchers' travel with such a different focus to other wildlife viewers that it's well worth going with a like-minded group and use an expert tour-leader.

See pages 58–9 for full details on the best birding places. The following cover all the different habitats: Ampijoroa (and along the road from Mahajanga), Ranomafana, Marojejy, Masoala, Andohahela or Ifaty (spiny forest), and Zombitse.

Here's a special place for birders: a hotel/restaurant in Tana, the Tonga Soa (see page 172), is planning to become a birding centre. Nick Garbutt reports: 'Brian Finch, the owner's brother, is a well-known birding tour leader (what else could he do with a name like his?) in Madagascar and both he and Patrick are keen to establish Tonga Soa as a place for the exchange of up-to-date information about wildlife. Their intention is to establish a small reference library relating to Malagasy natural history and have a visitor's book that anyone can contribute to as they pass through Tana and say what's been seen where and when. Others looking in may then be able to take advantage of such recent news.'

Working or volunteering in Madagascar

Many tourists, having fallen in love with Madagascar, want to return to work. A few achieve it, but only after much perseverance. Madagascar does not have enough jobs for its own citizens, so welcomes only outsiders who have specialised skills. Although the American Peace Corps have an active and successful programme in Madagascar, the British equivalent, VSO, is not currently working there. However, the organisation set up by Christina Dodwell, the Dodwell Trust, welcomes volunteers. She tells me: 'The Ministry of Education has asked us to put

SOME DAYS IN THE LIFE OF A WILDLIFE RESEARCHER

Frances Kerridge (Frankie Be) worked for several years in the southeast of Madagascar, studying carnivores with the organisation MICET. Her letters from the field were a regular source of entertainment. Here are some extracts.

It took nearly two weeks to get from Tana to Vevembe. The vehicle broke down and we were stuck for two days in torrential rain. My fruit and veg started rotting, all the cardboard boxes full of food dissolved, rice and coffee went mouldy, and beans and peanuts started sprouting... Then the river we had to ford was too high for the (mended) car so I had to pay porters to carry everything – traps and other research equipment, tents, tarps, all the kitchen stuff, three months' supply of food etc – the rest of the way. Cost a bloody fortune but we're there. Rosette gets on with her mapping and the student and I get down to the radio-tracking. Then the student breaks his antenna, gets water in his receiver and tells me he really can't do the work, it's too hard and he will be ill. Back to Tana while I search for another student. Another highlight was my guide getting a leech on his eyeball. Mega shouting and screaming, and I thought the student was going to faint. Got it off by killing it (slowly) with a tobacco leaf.

[After setting my tent on fire] I stayed in the guide's tent overnight. This was indeed an experience and not one I wish to repeat ever. Iato lit the candle every 15 minutes to see what time it was (as he has to get up first to start cooking out a call for an increased number of volunteers (gap-year and career-break) to stimulate the young Malagasy to learn English. Volunteers are also needed in Madagascar for community development tasks. Our projects are carried out in collaboration with village community groups, school teachers, radio stations, and local environment groups. Volunteers spend two, three or six months living in a village or small town, taking part in the community and working to assist English teachers, create eco-tourist circuits, help build boats or carts, repair or repaint classrooms, hold a Sports Day, plant tree nurseries, make radio shows in English, hold English Club meetings in villages, and set up and decorate new local cultural centres. No skills are required, and weekends are free. See www.dodwell-trust.org, and page 150 for more details about the Dodwell Trust.

Many people fondly visualise a job working in conservation but this is very difficult to achieve unless you are already experienced in this area. It is probably best to start by being a paying volunteer through the organisations which sponsor such holidays (see page 91).

HIGHLIGHTS AND ITINERARIES

Having sorted out the 'whats' and 'hows' of travelling in Madagascar you must turn your attention to the all-important subject of 'where'. One of the hardest decisions facing the first-time visitor to a country as large and diverse as Madagascar is where to go. Even a month is not long enough to see everything, so itineraries must be planned according to interests and the degree of comfort wanted. First, the highlights, according to interests.

Highlights
Wildlife

The best reserves and national parks (starting from the north and going clockwise) are: Montagne d'Ambre, Ankarana, Masoala, Nosy Mangabe,

---

breakfast) but as he can't tell the time he had to wake Baby to read the watch. Zaman'dory got up every 15 minutes to go for a pee and Baby alternatively ground his teeth and talked in his sleep. I was very relieved when the night was over...

The next drama involved Baby, who was complaining of toothache. I got a shock when I looked inside his mouth – one tooth had a massive hole in it, another was just a splintered fragment and there were quite a few missing (remember he is only 22). I walked down to Vondrozo with him (25km) to see if the hospital would pull his tooth out, there being no dentist there. However, they were not very helpful so I arranged for him to go to Farafangana with me. This was to be his first trip beyond Vondrozo and his first sight of the sea, which he found suitably impressive; in fact he lost the power of speech for quite a while.

Zely's wife gave birth to their sixth offspring – a messenger arrived to say she was in labour and I sent down a knitted baby jacket and some sardines and chocolate to sustain her through the ordeal. When Zely returned from paternity leave he said we should choose his new son's name. I tried to make something suitable from our initials but the best I could manage was Frisbe, so we all chose a name and put them in a hat. Zely chose mine which was 'Faly' which means happy in Malagasy. It could have been much worse – we had run out of glue and a guide was going to Vondrozo to do some shopping. I had written down 'Araldite' on a piece of paper and somehow that got into the hat!

Andasibe-Mantadia (Périnet), Ranomafana, Berenty, Kirindy, Ankarafantsika (Ampijoroa). Others (wonderful, but only for the fit) are Marojejy, Andohahela and Tsingy de Bemaraha.

Scenery

The central highlands between Fianarantsoa and Ambalavao, Andringitra, Isalo and Andohahela National Parks, Avenue of the Baobabs (Morondava), Ankarana, Montagne d'Ambre.

Beaches and watersports

Madagascar's best beaches are on the west coast, but many people are disappointed because of the shallow water (it is often impossible to swim at low tide). The beautiful beaches of the east coast are for sunbathing only – sharks are a danger to swimmers. The very best beaches are in remote areas such as Anjajavy, islands around Nosy Be, Ile Sainte Marie and south of Toliara.

Diving is covered under *Special Interests*. Surfing is a growing sport in the southwest (see box on page 242). Sport fishing can be organised from Nosy Be.

Fun times

The people of southern Madagascar are the most outgoing on the island, with good discos in Taolagnaro and Toliara, but Nosy Be (and specifically Ambataloaka) is undoubtedly where the action is for tourists.

Museums

Madagascar has only a few good museums so it is worth listing them here. The best by far – really super! – is the Museum of the Antandroy in Berenty Reserve. Toliara has a good ethnological museum (and you can see a coelacanth at its marine museum). The Museum of Art and Archaeology in Antananarivo is nicely laid out and interesting, as is the Museum Akiba in Mahajanga. The only natural history museum that I am aware of is in Tsimbazaza in Tana.

People and tombs

Your tour operator may be able to organise a visit to a *famadihana* (only in the highlands and only between June and September). An unforgettable experience. Merina tombs can easily be seen between Antananarivo and Antsirabe, but the most intriguing and interesting tombs are those of the Mahafaly in the Toliara region. Many are well off the beaten track and make this a particularly interesting area to explore by mountain bike.

Itineraries
Luxurious Madagascar

The opening of several top-class hotels in recent years means that it is now possible to see the highlights of Madagascar in style. The following hotels are in the very good to luxury class: Anjajavy and Tsarabanjina (secluded beach resorts), Relais de la Reine (Isalo National Park), Vakôna Lodge (Andasibe-Mantadia/Périnet), Le Domaine de Fontenay (Joffreville, Montagen d'Ambre), Hotel Vanila (Nosy Be) and Princesse Bora Lodge (Ile Sainte Marie).

Reliability and comfort

An itinerary which includes the following will provide a good overview of the country and its wildlife, with hotels of international standard: Antananarivo, Antsiranana (Diego Suarez), Andasibe-Mantadia (Périnet), Antsirabe, Toliara,

DISTANCES FROM TANA IN KILOMETRES

Antananarivo–Ambositra	330km
Antananarivo–Antsirabe	170km
Antananarivo–Fianarantsoa	408km
Antananarivo–Mahajanga	572km
Antananarivo–Morondava	665km
Antananarivo–Perinet	142km
Antananarivo–Toamasina	365km
Antananarivo–Toliara	941km

Taolagnaro (Fort Dauphin) and Berenty, and Nosy Be or Ile Sainte Marie. The stretches between Antananarivo and Antsirabe should be done by taxi or private car, and the rest by plane.

Nature reserves in moderate comfort
These are accessible by good road or reliable private transport and have good-to-moderate accommodation: Ranomafana, Ankarafantsika (Ampijoroa), and Berenty. Also Bush House and its reserve (Pangalanes)

Camping only reserves
Camping at the edge of the best reserves is the best – some would say the only – way to appreciate the wildlife. The following are for tents only: Tsingy de Bemaraha, Ankarana, Marojejy, Masoala, Nosy Mangabe, and Andohahela.

Landscape, people and tombs, beaches
For those whose interest lies more in the people and the countryside, a journey overland is recommended. RN7 from Antananarivo to Toliara gives a wonderful overview from rice-paddies in the highlands to the magnificent granite mountains of Andringitra, and the small villages between Ihosy and Toliara. It also gives you a chance to see Isalo National Park. The journey is best done in a private vehicle so you can stop and look; there are good hotels in the main towns.

A more adventurous alternative (but still on a good road) is by plane or bus to Toamasina then north by public transport to Soanierana-Ivongo and by boat to Ile Sainte Marie.

Finally...
Remember that you are in Madagascar to enjoy yourself. Here's a comment from a traveller who did the unthinkable: spent eight days in Ranomafana without entering the national park.

'Now I will make my confession: I never actually went into the park itself! ... I'm not that keen on lemurs anyway – they look like half monkeys and half cat and I don't much like either animal. I absolutely love the thermal baths, though!'

Good for Sarah for knowing what she wants and doesn't want to do!

TOUR OPERATORS
UK
The internet is the ideal way of finding out the best tour operator for your purposes. ATTA (African Travel and Tourism Association) has a comprehensive listing for Madagascar, separated into different interests; www.ATTA.co.uk. Safaribookers (www.safaribookers.com) has a listing of Madagascar specialists;

check out their 'Last Minute' area for good deals at short notice. The organisation Responsibletravel.com promotes ethical tour operators.

If you're looking for an outstanding tour leader check www.nickgarbutt.com. Nick has contributed much information to this book and is one of the most knowledgeable people around.

Aardvark Safaris Tel: 01980 849160; fax: 01980 849161; email: mail@aardvarksafaris.com; www.aardvarksafaris.com. Exclusive tailor-made holidays.
Africa Travel Centre Tel: 0207 387 1211; fax: 0207 383 7512; email: info@africatravel.co.uk; www.africatravel.co.uk. Flights and tailor-made holidays.
Arc Journeys Tel: 020 7681 3175 (24hr phone and fax line); email: arcjourneys@travelarc.com. Tailor-made cultural and nature tours.
Cazenove + Loyd Tel: 020 7384 2332; fax: 020 7384 2399; www.cazloyd.com. Tailor-made trips.
Cox & Kings Travel Tel: 020 7873 5000; fax: 020 7630 6038; email: Cox.Kings@coxandkings.co.uk; www.coxandkings.co.uk. Dedicated group departures and tailor-made itineraries.
Discovery Initiatives Tel 01285 643333; www.discoveryinitiatives.com. Wildlife specialists. Group and tailor-made holidays.
Distinctive Destinations Tel: 020 8898 9320; email: info@sanjeeda.co.uk; www.sanjeeda.co.uk. Indian Ocean Sailing Dhow. Private & group charters.
Earthwatch Tel: 01865 318 838; fax: 01865 311 383; email: info@earthwatch.org.uk; www.earthwatch.org/Europe. Several trips focus on Madagascar (wildlife). See *Working holidays*, page 91.
Elite Vacations Tel: 01707 371 000; fax: 01707 371 800; email: hannah.janes@elitevacations.com; www.elitevacations.com. Flora, fauna, wildlife, forests, beaches.
Explore Worldwide Ltd Tel: 01252 760 000; fax: 01252 760 000; email: res@exploreworldwide.com; www.exploreworldwide.com. Regular Madagascar trips; no special focus.
Naturetrek Tel: 01962 733051; fax: 01962 736426; email: info@naturetrek.co.uk; www.naturetrek.co.uk. Special focus: birds and mammals.
Okavango Tours & Safaris Ltd; tel: 020 8343 3283; fax: 020 8343 3287; email: marguerite@okavango.com; www.okavango.com
Papyrus Tours Tel: 01405 785 232; email: rogermitchell44@aol.com. Wildlife tours led by Nick Garbutt.
Pulse Africa Tel: 0208 995 5909; pulseafricauk@easynet.co.uk; www.africansafari.org.uk. Beaches and lemurs galore!
Partnership Travel Tel: 020 8343 3446; fax: 020 8349 3439; email: info@partnershiptravel.co.uk
Rainbow Tours Tel: 020 7226 1004; fax: 020 7226 2621; email: info@rainbowtours.co.uk; www.rainbowtours.co.uk. Tailor-made trips for individuals and for small groups, with an emphasis on wildlife, birding, culture and community tourism. They also offer small group departures including wildlife and birding tours led by experts such as Nick Garbutt, Lyn Mair and Roger Garina.
Reef & Rainforest Tours Tel: 01803 866965; fax: 01803 865916; email: mail@reefandrainforest.co.uk, www.reefandrainforest.co.uk. Specialists in Madagascar with a wide variety of tours, including Family Adventures itineraries for children under 12 years old.
Safari Consultants Tel: 01787 228494; fax: 01787 228096; email: bill@safariconsultantuk.com; www.safari-consultants.co.uk. Private holidays through southern Madagascar.

Scott Dunn World Tel: 020 8682 5010; fax: 020 8767 2026; email: world@scottdunn.com; www.scottdunn.com

Steppes Africa Tel: 01285 650011; email: safari@steppesafrica.co.uk; www.steppesafrica.co.uk. Tailor-made holidays to Madagascar.

Sunbird Tel: 01767 682969; fax: 01767 692481; email: sunbird@sunbird.demon.co.uk. Regular Madagascar birding trips.

The Ultimate Travel Company Tel: 020 7386 4646; email: enquiry@theultimatetravelcompany.co.uk; www.theultimatetravelcompany.co.uk. Upmarket, tailor-made tours; leader Nick Garbutt.

Tim Best Travel Tel: 020 7591 0300; fax: 020 7591 0301; email: info@timbesttravel.com; www.timbesttravel.com. Wildlife, diving, whalewatching, Culture.

Vintage Africa; Tel: 01451 850 803; email: vintagelon@vintageafrica.com; www.vintageafrica.com. Nature, landscapes, special interest. Tel: +254 20 3742435; Kenya email: vintagenbo@vintageafrica.com

Wildlife Worldwide Tel: 020 8667 9158; fax: 020 8667 1960; email: chris@wildlifeworldwide.com; www.wildlifeworldwide.com. Tailor-made wildlife tours with expert naturalists.

Worldwide Adventures Abroad Tel: 0114 247 3400; fax: 0114 251 3210; email: abroad@globalnet.co.uk; www.adventures-abroad.com

Worldwide Journeys & Expeditions Tel: 020 7386 4646; fax: 020 7381 0836; email: enquiry@worldwidejourneys.co.uk. Tailor-made trips, and guided tours led by naturalist Nick Garbutt.

World Odyssey Tel: 01905 731373; fax: 01905 726872; email: info@world-odyssey.com; www.world-odyssey.com. Private, tailor-made, guided tours.

USA

The website for the Madagascar embassy has a selection of US tour operators: www.embassy.org/Madagascar/tours.html. Below are the specialists I know and trust.

Blue Chameleon Ventures PO Box 516, Alva, FL 33920, USA; tel: +239 728 2390; email: bill@bluechameleon.org; www.bluechameleon.org. 'Herp' trips with an expert.

Cortez Travel, Inc PO Box 1699, Solano Beach, CA 92075; tel: 619 755 5136 or 1 800 854 1029; fax: 1 858 481 7474; email: info@cortez.usa.com. Cortez is the specialist Madagascar operator in the US; Monique Rodriguez has been running trips there for over two decades and probably knows the practicalities better than anyone else in the travel business.

Field Guides, Inc PO Box 160723, Austin, Texas 78746; tel: 512 327 4953 or 800 728 4953; email: fieldguides@fieldguides.com; www.fieldguides.com. Birding tours.

Lemur Tours Inc 501 Mendell St, Unit B, San Francisco, CA 94124; tel: 1 800 73 lemur or 415 695 8880; fax: 415 695 8899; email Carol@lemurtours.com; www.lemurtours.com.

Remote River Expeditions PO Box 544, Boulder, CO 80206; email: info@remoterivers.com; www.remoterivers.com. Specialising in river journeys, birding and wildlife tours.

Australia

Adventure Associates Pty Ltd 197 Oxford St Mall, Bondi Junction, Sydney, NSW 2022 (PO Box 612, Bondi Junction, NSW 1355); tel: 02 9389 7466; fax: 02 9369 1853; email: mail@adventureassociates.com; www.adventureassociates.com

African Wildlife Safaris 259 Coventry St, South Melbourne VIC 3205; tel: 61 03 9696 2899; fax: 61 03 9696 4937; email: info@africanwildlifesafaris.com.au; www.africanwildlifesafaris.com. Contact: Anne-Marie Zambelli.

Wildlife Safari 213 Railway Rd; Subiaco WA 6008; tel: 61 08 9388 9900; fax: 61 08 9388 9232; e-mail: africa@wildlife-safari.com.au; www.wildlife-safari.com.au

South Africa
ecoAfrica Travel Tel: 021 809 2180; fax: 021 809 2189; email: katharinavg@ecoafrica.com; www.ecoAfrica.com. Wildlife and special interest trips.
Falcon African Safaris (Pty) Ltd PO Box 3490, Randburg, 2125; tel: 011 886 1981; fax: 011 886 1778; email: enquiries@falcon-africa.co.za; www.falcon-africa.co.za. 10 years experience of running trips into Madagascar.
Pulse Africa Tel: 011 325 2290; email: info@africansafari.co.za; www.africansafari.co.za. Beaches and lemurs.
Talking Travel P O Box 2079, Link Hills 3652, SA; tel/fax: 27 031 763 3904; email: safaris@talkingtravel.co.za; www.talkingtravel.co.za and www.africa-uncovered. Guided wildlife, birding, diving, kayaking.
Unusual Destinations PO Box 97508, Petervale 2151 Gauteng, SA; tel: 011 706 1991; fax 011 463 1469; email: info@unusualdestinations.com; www.unusualdestinations.com. The SA experts in Madagascar. Very helpful and knowledgeable. Regular group departures and specialist natural history trips.
Wildlife Adventures Tel: 021 422 2017; fax: 021 422 2712; email: sales@wildlifeadventures.co.za; www.wildlifeadventures.co.za. Cultural, diving and tailor-made tours.

Kenya
Origins Safaris Tel: 254 20 331191 or 222075; fax: 254 20 330698 or 216528; email: info@originsafaris.info; www.originsafaris. Specialist Safari Operator (including Madagascar)
Vintage Africa Tel: 254 20 3742435; email: vintagenbo@vintageafrica.com; www.vintageafrica.com. Nature, landscapes, special interest.

Madagascar
There are many tour operators in Madagascar. This is by no means a complete list, just a selection of those that I can recommend. For a complete list of accredited tour operators (members of TOP – Tours Opérateurs Professionnels) contact TOP: tel/fax: 22 665 82 or 22 788 59; email: topmad@dts.mg. Their website, with a complete list of tour operators, is www.madagascar-guide.com/top/.

The full telephone code for Tana is (261 20) 22 followed by the number.

Boogie Pilgrim Villa Michelet, Lot A11, Faravohitra, Antananarivo; tel: 22 258 78; fax: 22 625 56; email: bopi@dts.mg; www.boogie-pilgrim.net. Organise tours of every sort, including some by light aircraft. Owners of Bush House (Pangalanes). Recommended.
Cortez Expeditions 25 Rue Ny' Zafindraindiky, Antanimena, Antananarivo; tel: 22 219 74; fax: 22 247 87; email: cortezexpeditions@simicro.mg. One of the most experienced tour operators in Madagascar and owner of the Relais du Masoala in Maroantsetra.
Destinations Mada Lot 1 B K 45 bis, Amapasamadinika; tel: 22 310 72; fax: 22 310 67.
Kayak Masoala www.kayakmasoala.com
Mad Caméléon Lot II K6, Ankadivato, Antananarivo; BP4336; tel: 22 630 86; fax: 22 344 20; email: madcam@dts.mg. Specialise in river trips.
Madagascar Airtours 33 Av de l'Indépendance, Antananarivo; BP3874; tel: 22 241 92; fax: 22 641 90. Also at the Hilton Hotel. The most experienced agency, with offices in most major towns, they can organise a wide variety of specialist tours including natural history, ornithology, speleology, trekking, mineralogy, river trips, sailing, etc. Michel Rakotonirina is the very experienced guide used by the Middletons for all their serious adventures. 'His knowledge of all things Malagasy is exceptional and we found him invaluable.'

Madagascar Ecotours Lot VF72, Mahamasina Nord, Antananarivo; tel/fax: 22 262 15; email: ecotours@madagascar.hypermart.net or actionmd@wandadoo.mg; www.dts.mg/actionmd

Madagascar Discovery BP3597, Antananarivo; tel: 22 351 65; fax: 22 351 67; email: mda@dts.mg; www.madagascar-contacts.com/mda.

Madamax BP5133 Ampitatafika, 101 Antananarivo; tel: 22 351 01; fax : 22 354 50; email: madamax@madamax.com; www.madamax.com/madamax/go.htm. Specialise in 'high-adrenalin adventures' including white-water rafting and treks to Tsaratanana /Mt Maromokotro.

Malagasy Tours Lot VX29, Avaradrova, Antananarivo; tel: 22 627 24; fax: 22 622 13; www.malagasy.com. The owner, Olivier Toboul, runs specialised itineraries for ethnobotany (amongst other things) using local people who can explain the complexities of the Malagasy culture. Good for off-the-beaten-track exploration, too.

SETAM 56, Av du 26 Juin 1960, Analakely, Antananarivo; tel: 22 324 31 or 22 324 33; cellphone: 032 0732 433 or 032 0724 373; fax: 324 35 or 347 02; email: setam@dts.mg; www.takelaka.dts.mg. Very helpful and efficient.

Transcontinents 10 Av de l'Indépendance, Antananarivo; BP551; tel: 22 223 98; fax: 22 283 65; email: transco@dts.mg. Efficiently run. Recommended.

Tropic Tours Travel 30, Rue de Russie, Isoraka, Antananarivo; BP8019; tel: 22 580 75; fax: 22 445 62; email: tropic@tropic-tours.net; www.tropic-tours.net

Voyages Bourdon Tel: 22 296 96; email: voyagesbourdon@simicro.mg. 'Gatien is extremely efficient and everything worked like clockwork.' (RP)

Za Tour Lot ID 33 Bis, Ambohitsorohitra, Antananarivo 101; tel: 22 656 48; fax: 22 656 47; email: zatour@iris.mg; www.3dmadagascar.com/zatour. One of the most experienced and conscientious operators in Madagascar. Highly recommended.

RAINBOW TOURS

The leading specialist for Madagascar

Voted **Best Tour Operator 2004**
Guardian/Observer Travel Awards

**We offer the widest range of itineraries, based on our
extensive knowledge and experience and backed by our
expert Malagasy agents.**

For independent, individual travellers –
or your own group

Wildlife, birding, botanical and entomological trips
Beach and scuba diving holidays
Honeymoons
Music and cultural tours
Indian Ocean island combination holidays

Scheduled tours include:

Wildlife tours with *BBC Wildlife*
Botanical tours led by Jim Bond
Birding tours for *World Birdwatch* & BirdLife International

RAINBOW TOURS
Tel: +44 (0)20 7226 1004
Email: info @rainbowtours.co.uk
Or visit our website www.rainbowtours.co.uk

Health and Safety

5

HEALTH
Dr Jane Wilson-Howarth

Before you go
Malaria prevention

Take advice from a travel clinic, your GP or the website www.fitfortravel.scot.nhs.uk. Malaria (including cerebral malaria) is a risk in Madagascar and it is important to protect yourself by avoiding bites between dusk and dawn and also by taking tablets. There is some chloroquine resistance so Mefloquine (Lariam) taken weekly is probably the best prophylactic if it suits you. It is available only on prescription and would cost about £25 for a two-week trip. Perhaps around one quarter of people who try this tablet will experience unacceptable side effects, so take it for two and a half weeks (three doses) before departure and if it makes you feel weird or gives you nightmares stop it and take another regime. Malarone, a once a day preparation, is a new alternative although some doctors will only prescribe enough for up to 28 days because of current licensing restrictions. It is by far the most expensive prophylactic: it will cost you about £90 for a two-week trip. Another good alternative, although unsuitable in pregnancy, while breast-feeding or in children under 12, is Doxycycline capsules daily (also on prescription, at around £28). There is a possibility of photosensitivity (in up to 5% of users) and so this may not be the best prophylactic if you plan to do a lot of sunbathing. Ensure that you use factor 25+ SPF suncream and long clothes to protect you.

All prophylactics have the potential to cause side effects and are best taken after food (or milk or biscuits); nausea is more likely if they are taken on an empty stomach. If pregnant or planning a pregnancy take medical advice before travelling. Some travellers like to carry tablets for the emergency treatment of malaria; if you choose to do this make sure you understand when and how to take them. Pack a non-mercury thermometer.

Take plenty of insect repellent; DEET-based is best; try some before you go and if it irritates your skin look for a product based on Merck 3535. Having loose-fitting outfits with long-sleeved shirts and long trousers will allow you to cover up at dusk; for additional protection you can spray your evening clothes with Permethrin (eg: Bug Proof from Nomad). Consider carrying a mosquito net (see page 86). Bed-nets are most effective if treated with permethrin or a similar contact insecticide. Such treatment remains effective for six months and kits are sold at many travel clinics.

Immunisations

Seek advice about immunisations at least a couple of months before travel; in the UK you can see your GP or visit a travel clinic such as those operated by MASTA (tel: 01276 685040 for the nearest clinic); they offer constantly updated health briefs as well as immunisations. It's important that your immunisations for

CLOTS AND DVT
Dr Jane Wilson-Howarth

Long-haul air travel increases the risk of deep vein thrombosis. This has been understood since 1946 when a doctor reported his own thrombosis after a 14-hour non-stop flight. Fortunately he survived, as do the vast majority of people who develop clots in their leg veins. Indeed recent research has suggested that most of us develop clots when immobilised but nearly all of them resolve without us every having been aware of them. In certain susceptible individuals, though, large clots form and these can break away and lodge in the lungs. This is dangerous but happens in a tiny minority of passengers. Several conditions make the problem more likely. Immobility is the key and factors like reduced oxygen in cabin air and dehydration may also contribute. Moving about the cabin hourly should help avoid the problem and abstaining from excessive alcohol will prevent sedation and also dehydration which both exacerbate the situation. Taking sleeping pills on long flights is also unwise.

Studies have shown that flights of over five-and-a-half-hours are significant; also people who take lots of shorter flights over a short space of time form clots. People at highest risk are:

- Those who have had a clot before – unless they are now taking warfarin
- People over 80 years of age
- Anyone who has recently undergone a major operation or surgery for varicose veins
- Someone who has had a hip or knee replacement in the last three months
- Cancer sufferers
- Those who have ever had a stroke
- People with heart disease
- Those with close blood relatives who has had a clot – they may have an inherited tendency to clot because of LeidenV factor.

Those with a slightly increased risk:

- People over 40
- Women who are pregnant or have had a baby in the last couple of weeks

tetanus, polio and typhoid are up to date. Highly effective vaccines against hepatitis A are recommended for those travelling for several months. Two shots provide protection for ten years.

If you are flying to Tana from Nairobi you will need a yellow fever certificate.

'Ordinary' intramuscular shots against rabies are now available and may be worth arranging if you are travelling in remote areas. The disease is a problem in Madagascar because of the half-wild dogs found in many parts of the island. Remember that 'live' vaccines cannot be given within a fortnight of each other, so plan well ahead. There is a list of vaccination centres at the end of this section.

Teeth
Have a dental check-up before you go and if you have a lot of fillings and crowns carry a Dental Emergency Kit (from some pharmacies or ask your dentist).

Insurance
Make sure you have insurance covering the cost of an air ambulance and treatment in Réunion or Nairobi, which offer more sophisticated medical facilities than are

- People taking female hormones or on other oestrogen therapy
- Heavy smokers
- Those who have very severe varicose veins
- The very obese
- People who are very tall (over 6ft/1.8m) or short (under 5ft/1.5m)

A deep vein thrombosis (DVT) is a clot of blood that forms in the deep leg veins. This is very different from irritating but harmless superficial phlebitis. DVT causes swelling and redness of one leg and there is usually heat and pain in one calf and sometimes the thigh. A DVT is only dangerous if a clot breaks away and travels to the lungs (pulmonary embolus). Symptoms of a pulmonary embolus (PE) include chest pain which is worse on breathing in deeply, shortness of breath and sometimes coughing up small amounts of blood. The symptoms commonly start three to ten days after a long flight. Anyone who thinks that they might have a DVT needs to see a doctor who will arrange a scan. Treatment is usually for six months or more warfarin to thin the blood .

Prevention of DVT
- To reduce the risk of thrombosis on a long journey:
- Take a meal of oily fish in the 24 hours before departure
- Exercise before and after the flight
- Keep mobile before and during the flight; move around every couple of hours
- During the flight drink plenty of water or juices
- Avoid taking sleeping pills and excessive tea, coffee and alcohol
- Perform exercises that mimic walking and tense the calf muscles
- Consider wearing flight socks or support stockings (see www.legshealth.com)

The jury is still out on whether it is wise to take aspirin. If you think you are at increased risk of a clot ask your doctor if it is safe to travel.

available in Madagascar. Europ Assistance International, which has an office in Antananarivo, gives cover for scuba-diving. Divers Aware Network (DAN) is the best insurance available for scuba-diving. With all insurance make sure that you tell them about any pre-existing problems when applying.

Water sterilisation
Bringing water to the boil kills all the microbes that are likely to make you ill on your travels so tea, coffee or *ranovola* (the water rice is boiled in) bought in *hotelys* are probably the most convenient safe drinks. If travelling with small children you can take a thermos flask; almost-boiling water kept in this for 15 minutes will be thoroughly sterilised. Mineral water is not always available, causes a litter problem and can be quite expensive, and studies in other countries suggest it may be contaminated. Chemical sterilisation methods do not render water as safe as by boiling, but it is good enough for most purposes. The cheapest and most effective sterilising agent is iodine (preferable to chlorine and silver because it kills amoebic cysts). Iodine comes in liquid or tablet form. To make treated water more palatable, add vitamin C after the sterilisation time is complete or bring packets of

TRADITIONAL HEALING AND ETHNOBOTANY IN MADAGASCAR

Samantha Cameron

The author is a volunteer for the NGO Feedback Madagascar, and is co-ordinator of their health programme in the Fianarantsoa region. She recently led an RGS-supported expedition researching ethnobotanical knowledge in an area bordering the rainforest, and hopes that findings can be used to ease collaboration and understanding between traditional healers and the medical establishment, in the same way as is being done with traditional birth attendants. Anyone interested in borrowing an extensive photo exhibition, complete with captions, about village life in Madagascar, should write to: samcam77@hotmail.com.

Faced with environmental degradation and increasing exposure to Western medicine, there are many people who fear for the future of ethnobotanical knowledge. However, recent research in rural southeast Madagascar found that traditional healing practices continue to be widespread and that, although older people generally have more faith in them, the younger generation are also very knowledgeable about traditional remedies.

In this area of Madagascar, access to Western medicine is almost irrelevant to the use of traditional remedies. Villagers living far from the hospital do not necessarily use less Western medicine, or more traditional medicine, since most people go to the weekly market, near to the hospital, or are able to send someone in their place. Many people consult both healers and the hospital, the decision depending on the type of illness they are suffering from and, to a lesser extent, the cost of treatment. Often healers are seen when people have an illness that they believe Western medicine cannot cure. The two are also used in combination, or people resort to one having found the other ineffective. If symptoms of a disease are recognised, treatment is often self-administered. Some health problems of a sensitive nature, such as gynaecological problems and sexually transmitted diseases, are commonly treated by healers; women being afraid or too embarrassed to go to the hospital. Other conditions are often of a more psychological or supernatural nature, such as phobias and spirit possessions.

Healers commonly first receive their powers on the death of another healer, usually their parent or grandparent, and often through a dream. Many practise clairvoyance, using cards or mirrors in order to communicate with their ancestors so as to diagnose illness and treatment. Sometimes, even if the disease is known, there is no fixed recipe but treatment varies according to what is identified as the cause of that disease. So two people with the same

powdered drink. Silver-based sterilising tablets (sold in Britain under the trade name Micropur) are tasteless and have a long shelf life but are less effective than both iodine and chlorine products. An alternative is a water filter such as the Pur system or Aqua-pure Traveller, which provide safe water with no unpleasant flavour; they are expensive, however, and any filter is prone to blockage – or to being lost! Cheaper and more versatile is a plug-in immersion heater, so that you can have a nice hot cuppa (if you bring teabags).

Note that most travellers acquire diarrhoea from inadequately cooked, or reheated, contaminated food – salads, ice, ice-cream etc – rather than from disobeying the 'don't drink the water' rule.

illness would not necessarily be administered the same treatment. These diagnostic powers of healers are all-important, and are the reason why they could never be replaced. Some healers update treatments annually, on the advice of their ancestors, and many are blessed with healing hands; so the medicinal plants they use would not be as effective if self-administered. It is therefore difficult to know to what extent people are successfully cured by a plant's medicinal properties and how much is due to the healer's power or is just psychological.

Despite evident deforestation in the area, people living close to the forest do not suggest any consequent dramatic change in the abundance of medicinal plants, only stating that they have to go slightly further afield to find them. In fact, users of medicinal plants originating from secondary vegetation note that their abundance has actually increased as a direct result of environmental degradation. Other healers are unaware of availability since they are not responsible for plant collection. Some even claim to know nothing about medicinal plants or where they are found, being led to them whilst in a trance, their body possessed by ancestral spirits.

Although use of forest plants is generally higher in villages near the forest, some healers living near the forest use exclusively savannah-originating medicinal plants, and some living far from the forest use forest plants. Such patterns of medicinal-plant use can result from the method of plant collection; some healers have plants come to them overnight by a supernatural force, some send people to harvest them, and some buy in the market or elsewhere. Many healers also conserve plants by drying them, thus making frequent collection unnecessary. Migration is another cause, some healers originating from forested areas and later moving away but continuing to use the forest plants that tradition has passed on to them. Medicinal plant knowledge therefore changes more according to the speciality of the healer, and the healer's origin, as opposed to their proximity to the forest.

Although traditional healing does not appear to be dying out and Western medicine does not seem to pose a real threat, perhaps its greatest threat is from religion. Common belief has it that traditional healing is the devil's work as it comes from the power of the ancestors rather than the power of God. The risk is that young people may resist the healing power they inherit. Recording traditional medicine practices enhances understanding of the context in which it is used in Madagascar, by distributing the results to local communities, authorities and scientists. It is also necessary to increase appreciation and valuation of these secondary forest products, with the aim of conservation and sustainable natural resource management.

Some travellers' diseases
Malaria and insect-borne diseases
Tablets do not give complete protection from malaria, though they will make it less serious if it does break through; it's important to protect yourself from being bitten. The mosquitoes that give you malaria usually bite in the evening (from about 17.00) and throughout the night, so it's wise to dress in long trousers and long-sleeved shirts, and to cover exposed skin with insect repellent. *Anopheles* mosquitoes generally hunt at ankle level, and tend to bite the first piece of exposed flesh they encounter, so DEET-impregnated ankle bands are fairly effective in reducing bites. In most countries, malaria transmission is rare in urban

environments, but it does occur around Antananarivo because rice fields are so close to the city. Most hotels have screened windows or provide mosquito nets. Bring your own net if staying in cheap hotels. Burning mosquito coils reduces but does not eliminate the risk of bites.

Be sure to take your malaria tablets meticulously for the requisite time after you get home. Even if you have been taking your malaria prophylaxis carefully, there is still a slight chance of contracting malaria. The symptoms are fevers, chills, joint pain, headache and sometimes diarrhoea – in other words the symptoms of many illnesses including flu. Bear in mind that malaria can take as little as seven days to develop. Consult a doctor (mentioning that you have been abroad) if you develop a flu-like illness within a year of leaving a malarious region. The life-threatening cerebral malaria will become apparent within three months and can kill within 24 hours of the first symptoms.

Mosquitoes pass on not only malaria but also elephantiasis, dengue fever and a variety of other serious viral fevers. By avoiding mosquito bites you also avoid illness, as well as those itching lumps which so easily become infected. Once you've been bitten, tiger balm, calamine lotion or calamine-based creams help stop the itching.

Travellers' diarrhoea

Diarrhoea is very common in visitors to Madagascar, and you are more likely to suffer from this if you are new to tropical travel. Tourists tend to be obsessed with water sterilisation but, contrary to popular belief, travellers' diarrhoea usually comes from contaminated food not contaminated water. Ice-cream, sadly, is risky, especially if it is homemade and even factory-made ice-creams can be bad news if they are stored badly. So, especially if you have a sensitive stomach and/or haven't travelled much before, you should avoid ice-cream, and also ice, salads, fruit with lots of crevices such as strawberries, uncooked foods and cooked food that has been hanging around or has been inadequately reheated. Sizzling hot street food is likely to be far safer than the food offered in buffets in expensive hotels, however gourmet the latter may look. Yoghurt is usually safe, as are sorbets. Remember peel it, boil it, cook it or forget it!

The way to the quickest recovery from travellers' diarrhoea is to reduce your normal meals to a few light or high carbohydrate items, avoid milk and alcohol and drink lots of clear fluids. You need to replace the fluids lost down the toilet, and drinks containing salt and sugar are most easily absorbed. Add a little sugar to a salty drink, such as Marmite (available in Tana!) or Oxo, or salt to a sugary drink like Coca-Cola. Sachets of rehydration mixtures are available commercially but you can make your own by mixing a rounded dessertspoon (or four teaspoons) of sugar with a quarter-teaspoon of salt and adding it to a glass of boiled and cooled water. Drink two glasses of this every time you open your bowels – more often if you are thirsty. Substituting glucose for sugar will make you feel even better. If you are in a rural area drink young coconut water or *ranovola* (water boiled in the pot that rice is cooked in).

Hot drinks and iced drinks cause a reflex emptying of the bowel and cause belly-ache, so take drinks tepid or at room-temperature while the diarrhoea is at its worst. Once the bowel has ejected the toxic material causing the diarrhoea, the symptoms will settle quite quickly and you should begin to feel better again after 24–36 hours. Should the diarrhoea be associated with passing blood or slime, it would be sensible to have a stool check at some stage, but provided you continue to drink clear fluids, no harm will come from waiting for a few days.

Holiday schedules often make it impossible to follow the 'sit it out' advice. When a long bus journey or flight is anticipated you may wish to take a blocker such as Imodium. Just remember that such drugs slow up the action of the bowel so you tend to feel ill for a longer period of time and they are dangerous if you have dysentery. Safer and far more effective is the antibiotic Ciprofloxacin taken as a three-day course (500mg twice daily). Discuss this with your doctor or travel clinic. Drink lots whatever treatment you are taking and if you are worried or feel very ill, seek local medical advice. As long as you keep well hydrated the symptoms will usually settle without further treatment. Even bacillary dysentery and cholera will usually resolve within a week without treatment, as long as you drink plenty of clear fluids.

Cholera
In the last few years cholera has been a problem in Madagascar. By the end of 2000, 39,400 cases had been reported and 2,245 Malagasy had died. Although it has a fearsome reputation, cholera doesn't usually make healthy people ill. It takes the debilitated, poor and half-starved of famine or conflict zones, or it is present along with other gastro-intestinal infections. Cholera is avoided in the same way as other 'filth-to-mouth' diseases and – if there are symptoms – it can be treated with the usual oral rehydration fluids that all wise travellers know about.

Other hitchhikers
There is a high prevalence of tapeworm in Malagasy cattle, so eat your steaks well done. If you do pass a worm, this is alarming but treatment can wait.

Bilharzia
This is a nasty, debilitating disease which is a problem in much of lowland Madagascar. The parasite is also carried by pond snails and is caught by people who swim or paddle in clean, still or slow-moving water (not fast-flowing rivers) where an infected person has defecated or urinated. The parasite causes 'swimmer's itch' when it penetrates the skin. Since it takes at least ten minutes for the tiny worm to work its way through your skin, a quick wade across a river, preferably followed by vigorous towelling off, should not put you at risk. Bilharzia is cured with a single dose of Praziquantel. If you think you may have been exposed to the disease, ask your doctor to arrange a blood test when you get home. This should be done more than six weeks after but ideally within 12 weeks of the last exposure.

Sexually transmitted infections
These are common in Madagascar and AIDS is on the increase. If you enjoy nightlife, male or female condoms will make encounters less risky. The femidom doesn't rustle as much as it used to.

Rabies (Le rage)
Rabies is a disease that is feared wherever it occurs – for good reason. Once the symptoms of hydrophobia become apparent, the victim is doomed and the mode of death is awful. Cerebral fear centres are stimulated so that the victim experiences terror and there are fits, spasms and pain. That is the bad news. The good news is that although the disease occurs on Madagascar, the risk to visitors is small and there are highly effective vaccines that probably give absolute protection.

The rabies virus can be carried by any mammal, and the commonest route of infection is from a dog bite. Unfortunately, most rabid animals do not look mad or froth at the mouth so it is important to assume that any mammal bite sustained anywhere in Africa could potentially be dangerous. It is likely that lemurs could pass on rabies, and bats can certainly carry the disease.

LEMURS AND RABIES

When I was leading a trip in Madagascar in 2003 one of my group was bitten on the forearm by a female ring-tailed lemur. The animal was carrying a baby and was startled. It bit in self-defence. The skin was broken and there was a small amount of bleeding. In the days and weeks that followed, Susanne and I agonised about the possibility of rabies and what to do about it.

We asked advice from a local hotel manager (French) who reassured her that there was almost no possibility of the lemur being rabid. I felt the same way so Susanne decided to wait until she returned to Germany, but the uncertainty spoiled the rest of her trip. Even the tiniest chance of catching rabies is too terrible to contemplate – and she couldn't stop contemplating it.

She saw her doctor 18 days after the bite and was started on a course of anti-rabies injections. Rather than being reassuring, her doctors told her that she'd left it much too late, and that she would not know for three months whether or not she would get rabies – and die from it. Of course she is fine now, but what should we have done?

I've talked to several people about this dilemma including Madagascar residents. They all know that lemurs could carry rabies but what interests me is the likelihood of the animal becoming infected and then surviving long enough to bite a human. Lemurs tame enough to bite a tourist are found only in private reserves where dogs are excluded. Even if a rabid dog did get into the reserve would it be able to catch a lemur? And if it did catch one, would it inflict a bite which infected the animal but didn't kill it? The likelihood seems very small.

Alison Jolly, who has been studying lemurs for 40 years, says: 'I have never heard of anyone catching rabies from a lemur. I think that the chances are so small that I wouldn't dream of getting rabies shots after a lemur bite – as you say, the chance of a rabid dog catching a lemur which then got away seem not worth worrying about – except in one circumstance. If the lemur was hand-raised, either a current pet or a pet released into the wild, it may attack a human without provocation. In that case you get a deep bite with no warning. It probably is just misguided "normal" behaviour, treating you as one of its own species, but you can't be sure, so I would go and get shots. A bite in self-defence, though, isn't worth bothering about.'

After any animal bite it is wise to administer good first aid because infections are frequent. This means vigorously cleaning the wound with plenty of soap under running water (from a tap or poured from a water bottle) for five minutes – timed with a watch. Scrubbing under running water – if a brush can be found – will clean out even more virus. After the cleaning process, the wound should be flooded with rum, whiskey, vodka or any strong antiseptic solution. Next the victim should get the wound dressed – but not stitched – and post-bite jabs need to be arranged. Tetanus jabs may also be needed, and sometimes antibiotics are needed to treat wound infection.

If rabies virus enters the body, it slowly progresses along the nerves until it gets to the brain at which point it causes encephalitis and hydrophobia – fear of water including one's own saliva. The incubation period for rabies depends upon the severity of the bite and also the distance from the brain. If a toddler gets savaged on the face the child will become ill in as little as four days.

The dilemma is what to do if you have a small skin-break on a limb. Treatment clearly needs to be given, and as promptly as possible, but the options available in remote parts of Madagascar are less than ideal. Malagasy health assistants will still administer the less-than-safe and out-dated Semple vaccine; it gives some protection and is considerably better than nothing if there are no other options. But for those with the money and resources to get something better it is not a wise option. Semple vaccine is a 5% suspension of sheep or goat brain given – painfully – into the abdomen on 21 consecutive days followed by booster doses. Semple isn't used in many hospitals in Tana but it is outside the capital, eg: in Toliara. Serious reactions to it happen as frequently as 1 in 76 courses (with 41% of those affected dying), and its efficacy is poor. I have heard of people receiving Semple vaccine after a dog bite and dying of rabies anyway. There is also HIV/AIDS on Madagascar and so any treatment involving injections could give you HIV, as well as hepatitis B.

If I was bitten on an extremity, then I'd get to somewhere with rabies vaccine. Furthermore, if I hadn't been previously immunised I'd need to try to find a clinic that could give me rabies immune globulin too, but there have been difficulties obtaining this lately, even in Europe. Reputable travel health insurers should be able to advise where the nearest source of safe vaccine and immune globulin might be. Sometimes embassies can help with such information.

Infection and trivial breaks in the skin
The skin is very prone to infection in hot, moist climates, so anything that makes even the slightest break to its surface is likely to allow bacteria to enter and so cause problems. Mosquito bites – especially if you scratch them – are a common route of infection, so apply a cream to reduce the itching. Toothpaste helps if you are stuck for anything better. Cover any wounds, especially oozing ones, so that flies don't snack on them. Significant skin infections can arise through even a small nick or graze. Antiseptic creams are not advised, since they keep the wounds moist and this encourages further infection. A powerful antiseptic, which also dries out moist wounds, is potassium permanganate crystals dissolved in water. Another alternative is diluted tincture of iodine (which you may be carrying anyway as a water steriliser) or povadine-iodine. Large bottles of the latter are available at a reasonable price in the many pharmacies in Madagascar or can be bought in spray form as Betadine before arrival. Bathe the wound twice a day, more often if you can, by dabbing with cotton wool dipped in dilute potassium permanganate, or iodine solution. Bathing in sulphur springs cures too.

Sunburn
Light-skinned people burn remarkably quickly near the Equator, especially when snorkelling. Wearing a shirt, preferably one with a collar, protects the neck and back, and long shorts can also be worn. Use a sunscreen with a high protection factor (up to 25) on the back of the neck, calves and other exposed parts.

Prickly heat
A fine pimply rash on the trunk is likely to be heat rash; cool showers, dabbing (not rubbing) dry and talc will help relieve it. Treat the problem by slowing down to a relaxed schedule, wearing only loose, baggy 100% cotton clothes and sleeping naked under a fan; if it's bad you may need to check into an air-conditioned hotel room for a while.

Foot protection

Wearing shoes or sandals on the beach and when walking anywhere will protect the feet from injury and from parasites. Old trainers (running shoes) worn when you are in the sea will help you avoid getting coral or urchin spines in the soles of your feet and give some protection against venomous fish spines. Booties, which can be bought for about £25, will protect from coral but not venomous fish. If you tread on a venomous fish or stingray, or are charged by a lionfish, soak the foot (or affected part) in hot (up to 45°C) water until some time after the pain subsides; this may mean 20–30 minutes' immersion in all. If the pain returns re-immerse. Once the venom has been heat-inactivated, get a doctor or paramedic to check and remove any bits of fish spines in the wound (see box on pages 252–3).

The nasty side of nature
Animals

Malagasy land-snakes are back-fanged, and so are effectively non-venomous. Sea-snakes, although venomous, are easy to see and are rarely aggressive. However, if you are bitten then seek immediate medical treatment; try to keep the bitten part as still and as low as possible to slow the spread of venom.

Be wary of scorpions and centipedes, particularly when in the dry forest. Neither is fatal, but stings are very unpleasant. Scorpions often come out after rain. They are nocturnal but they like hiding in small crevices during the day. If you are camping in the desert or the dry forest, it's not unusual to find they have crept into the pocket of a rucksack – even if you have taken the sensible precaution of suspending it from a tree. Scorpion stings are very painful for about 24 hours. After a sting on the finger, I had an excruciatingly painful hand and arm for several days. The pain was only eased with morphine. My finger had no feeling for a month, and over 15 years later it still has an abnormal nerve supply.

Large spiders can be dangerous – the black widow is found in Madagascar, as well as an aggressive hairy spider with a nasty bite. Try to find out what you have been stung by. Navy digger wasps have an unpleasant sting, but it's only the scorpions that commonly cause problems because they favour hiding places where one might plunge a hand without looking. If you sleep on the ground, isolate yourself from these creatures with a mat, a hammock or a tent with a sewn-in ground sheet.

Leeches can be a nuisance in the rainforest, but are only revolting, not dangerous (AIDS cannot be spread via leeches). They are best avoided by covering up, tucking trousers into socks and applying insect repellent (even on shoes – but beware, DEET dissolves plastics). Once leeches have become attached they should not be forcibly removed or their mouthparts may remain causing the bite to itch for a long time. Either wait until they have finished feeding (when they will fall off) or encourage them to let go by applying a lit cigarette, a bit of tobacco, chilli, salt or insect repellent. A film canister is a convenient salt container. The wound left by a leech bleeds a great deal and easily becomes infected if not kept clean. For more on leeches see box on page 54.

Beware of strolling barefoot on damp, sandy riverbeds and areas of beach where locals defecate. This is the way to pick up jiggers (and geography worms). Jiggers are female sand fleas, which resemble maggots and burrow into your toes to feed on your blood while incubating their eggs. Remove them, using a sterilised needle, by picking the top off the boil they make and teasing them out (this requires some skill, so it's best to ask a local person to help). Disinfect the wound thoroughly to avoid infection.

Plants

Madagascar has quite a few plants which cause skin irritation. The worst one I have encountered is a climbing legume with pea-pod-like fruits that look furry. This 'fur' penetrates the skin as thousands of tiny needles, which must be painstakingly extracted with tweezers. Prickly pear fruits have the same defence. Relief from the secretions of other irritating plants is obtained by bathing. Sometimes it's best to wash your clothes as well, and immersion fully clothed may be the last resort!

Medical kit

Apart from personal medication taken on a regular basis, it's unnecessary to weigh yourself down with a comprehensive medical kit, as many of your requirements will be met by the Malagasy pharmacies.

Expeditions or very adventurous travellers should contact a travel clinic (see *Travel clinics and health information*, on page 118). The absolute maximum an ordinary traveller needs to carry (I always carry less) is: malaria tablets; lots of plasters (Band-Aid/Elastoplast) to cover broken skin, infected insect bites etc; antiseptic (potassium permanganate crystals to dissolve in water are best, or povidine-iodine); small pieces of sterile gauze or Melonin dressings and adhesive plaster; soluble aspirin or paracetamol (Tylenol) – good for fevers, aches and for gargling when you have a sore throat; Anusol or Sudocrem or some kind of soothing cream for a sore anus (after diarrhoea); also useful in cases of severe diarrhoea where a cough or sneeze can be disastrous are panti-liners or sanitary pads (these are also excellent for covering wounds); Canesten for thrush and athlete's foot; foot powder; Vaseline or Heel Balm for cracked heels; a course of Amoxycillin (or Erythromycin if you're penicillin-allergic) which is good for chest infections, skin infections and cystitis; Cicatrin (neomycin) antibiotic powder for infected bites etc; antibiotic eye drops; anti-histamine tablets; travel sickness pills (for those winding roads); tiger balm or calamine lotion for itchy bites; pointed tweezers for extracting splinters, sea-urchin spines, small thorns and coral.

HEALTH SUPPLIES IN MADAGASCAR

John Pitterle, a resident of Antananarivo has sent me this report. Dr Jane has added her comments in square brackets. 'Anti-mosquito stuff is easily available. Mosquito coils can be purchased very cheaply at grocery stores and small shops [these are useful because they continue to function during power cuts but they only reduce the bite rate by about half]. If you don't like the smoke, plug-in units that take a little rectangular pad every night can be purchased [if staying in large rooms you may need two – read the instructions that should tell you what room volume the vapour covers]. The most economical option is an electrical diffuser that comes with a little bottle of liquid that can last for about 45 nights.

'Anti-malarial medication is available at pharmacies here. We use Savarine. It is a combination of proguanil and chloroquine. I paid just under 200,000Fmg (about £14) for a box of 28 pills.' [Dr Jane adds: 'This is cheap but it is not the most effective prophylactic these days for Madagascar.']

If you do get ill in Madagascar try to get back to Tana which has a choice of quite good private clinics and a decent hospital. These are listed on page 182. There are also a handful of good clinics elsewhere. Check *Medical clinics* in the index.

Travel clinics and health information

A full list of current travel clinic websites worldwide is available on www.istm.org/. For other journey preparation information, consult ftp://ftp.shoreland.com/pub/shorecg.rtf or www.tripprep.com. Information about various medications may be found on www.emedicine.com/wild/topiclist.htm.

UK

Berkeley Travel Clinic 32 Berkeley St, London W1J 8EL (near Green Park tube station); tel: 020 7629 6233

British Airways Travel Clinic and Immunisation Service There are two BA clinics in London, both on tel: 0845 600 2236; www.britishairways.com/travelclinics. Appointments only at 111 Cheapside; or walk-in service Mon–Sat at 156 Regent St. Apart from providing inoculations and malaria prevention, they sell a variety of health-related goods.

The Travel Clinic, Cambridge 48a Mill Rd, Cambridge CB1 2AS; tel: 01223 367362; fax: 01223 368021; email: enquiries@travelcliniccambridge.co.uk; www.travelcliniccambridge.co.uk. Open 12.00–19.00 Tue–Fri, 10.00–16.00 Sat.

Edinburgh Travel Clinic Regional Infectious Diseases Unit, Ward 41 OPD, Western General Hospital, Crewe Rd South, Edinburgh EH4 2UX; tel: 0131 537 2822. Travel helpline open 09.00–12.00 weekdays. Provides inoculations and anti-malarial prophylaxis and advises on travel-related health risks.

Fleet Street Travel Clinic 29 Fleet St, London EC4Y 1AA; tel: 020 7353 5678; www.fleetstreet.com. Injections, travel products and the latest advice.

Hospital for Tropical Diseases Travel Clinic Mortimer Market Centre, 2nd Floor, Capper St (off Tottenham Ct Rd), London WC1E 6AU; tel: 020 7388 9600; www.thhtd.org. Offers consultations and advice, and is able to provide all necessary drugs and vaccines for travellers. Runs a healthline (tel: 09061 337733) for country-specific information and health hazards. Also stocks nets, water purification equipment and personal protection measures.

MASTA (Medical Advisory Service for Travellers Abroad), at the London School of Hygiene and Tropical Medicine, Keppel St, London WC1 7HT; tel: 09068 224100. This is a premium-line number, charged at 60p per minute. For a fee, they will provide an individually tailored health brief, with up-to-date information on how to stay healthy, inoculations and what to bring.

MASTA pre-travel clinics Tel: 01276 685040. Call for the nearest; there are currently 30 in Britain. Also sell malaria prophylaxis memory cards, treatment kits, bednets, net treatment kits.

NHS travel website www.fitfortravel.scot.nhs.uk. Provides country-by-country advice on immunisation and malaria, plus details of recent developments, and a list of relevant health organisations.

Nomad Travel Store 3–4 Wellington Terrace, Turnpike Lane, London N8 0PX; tel: 020 8889 7014; fax: 020 8889 9528; email: sales@nomadtravel.co.uk; www.nomadtravel.co.uk. Also at 40 Bernard St, London WC1N 1LJ; tel: 020 7833 4114; fax: 020 7833 4470; and 43 Queens Rd, Bristol BS8 1QH; tel: 0117 922 6567; fax: 0117 922 7789. As well as dispensing health advice, Nomad stocks mosquito nets and other anti-bug devices, and an excellent range of adventure travel gear.

Thames Medical 157 Waterloo Rd, London SE1 8US; tel: 020 7902 9000. Competitively priced, one-stop travel health service. All profits go to their affiliated company, InterHealth, which provides health care for overseas workers on Christian projects.

Trailfinders Immunisation Centre 194 Kensington High St, London W8 7RG; tel: 020 7938 3999.

Travelpharm The Travelpharm website, www.travelpharm.com, offers up-to-date guidance on travel-related health and has a range of medications available through their online mini-pharmacy.

Irish Republic

Tropical Medical Bureau Grafton Street Medical Centre, Grafton Buildings, 34 Grafton St, Dublin 2; tel: 1 671 9200. Has a useful website specific to tropical destinations: www.tmb.ie.

USA

Centers for Disease Control 1600 Clifton Rd, Atlanta, GA 30333; tel: 888 232 3228 (toll free and available 24 hours) or 800 311 3435; fax: 877 FYI TRIP; www.cdc.gov/travel. The central source of travel information in the USA. Each summer they publish the invaluable *Health Information for International Travel*, available from the Division of Quarantine at the above address.

Connaught Laboratories PO Box 187, Swiftwater, PA 18370; tel: 800 822 2463. They will send a free list of specialist tropical-medicine physicians in your state.

IAMAT (International Association for Medical Assistance to Travelers) 417 Center St, Lewiston, NY 14092; tel: 716 754 4883; email: info@iamat.org; www.iamat.org. A non-profit organisation that provides lists of English-speaking doctors abroad.

Canada

IAMAT (International Association for Medical Assistance to Travellers) Suite 1, 1287 St Clair Av W, Toronto, Ontario M6E 1B8; tel: 416 652 0137; www.iamat.org

TMVC (Travel Doctors Group) Sulphur Springs Rd, Ancaster, Ontario; tel: 905 648 1112; www.tmvc.com.au

Australia, New Zealand, Thailand

TMVC Tel: 1300 65 88 44; www.tmvc.com.au. 22 clinics in Australia, New Zealand and Thailand, including:

Auckland Canterbury Arcade, 170 Queen St, Auckland; tel: 9 373 3531

Brisbane Dr Deborah Mills, Qantas Domestic Building, 6th floor, 247 Adelaide St, Brisbane, QLD 4000; tel: 7 3221 9066; fax: 7 3321 7076

Melbourne Dr Sonny Lau, 393 Little Bourke St, 2nd floor, Melbourne, VIC 3000; tel: 3 9602 5788; fax: 3 9670 8394

Sydney Dr Mandy Hu, Dymocks Building, 7th Floor, 428 George St, Sydney, NSW 2000; tel: 2 221 7133; fax: 2 221 8401

IAMAT PO Box 5049, Christchurch 5, New Zealand; www.iamat.org

South Africa

SAA-Netcare Travel Clinics PO Box 786692, Sandton 2146; fax: 011 883 6152; www.travelclinic.co.za or www.malaria.co.za. Clinics throughout South Africa.

TMVC 113 DF Malan Drive, Roosevelt Park, Johannesburg; tel: 011 888 7488; www.tmvc.com.au. Consult the website for details of clinics in South Africa.

Switzerland

IAMAT 57 Voirets, 1212 Grand Lancy, Geneva; www.iamat.org

SAFETY

Before launching into a discussion of crime, it's worth reminding readers that by far the most common cause of death or injury while on holiday is the same as at home: road accidents. No-one seems to worry about this, however, preferring to focus their anxieties on crime. I have been taken to task by some readers for over-emphasising the danger of robbery, and certainly it is true that most visitors to Madagascar return home after a crime-free trip. However, this is one area where being forewarned is forearmed: there are positive steps that you can take to keep yourself and your possessions safe, so you might as well know about them, while knowing also that the vast majority of Malagasy are touchingly honest. Often you will have people call you back because you have overpaid them (while still unfamiliar with the money) and every traveller can think of a time when his innocence could have been exploited – and wasn't. In my experience, too, hotel employees are, by and large, trustworthy. So try to keep a sense of proportion. Like health, safety is often a question of commonsense. Keep your valuables hidden, keep alert in potentially dangerous situations, and you will be OK.

Bear in mind that thieves have to learn their profession so theft is common only where there are plenty of tourists to prey on. In little-visited areas you can relax and enjoy the genuine friendliness of the people.

Before you go

You can enjoy peace of mind by giving some time to making your luggage and person as hard to rob as possible before you leave home. Also make three photocopies of all your important documents: passport (information page and visa), airline ticket (including proof of purchase), travellers' cheques (sales advice slip), credit cards, emergency phone number for stolen credit cards, emergency phone number of travel insurance company and insurance documents. Leave one copy with a friend or relative at home, one in your main luggage and one in your handbag or hand luggage. A simpler alternative is to have a hotmail or yahoo account and email yourself scans of all these documents to access if necessary.

- Leave your valuable-looking jewellery at home. You do not need it in Madagascar. Likewise your fancy watch; buy a cheap one.
- Lock your bag when travelling by plane or taxi-brousse; combination locks are more secure than small padlocks. Make or buy a lockable cover for your backpack.
- Make extra deep pockets in your travel trousers by cutting the bottom off existing pockets and adding an extra bit. Fasten the 'secret' pocket with velcro.

Crime prevention

Violent crime is still relatively rare in Madagascar, and even in Antananarivo you are probably safer than in a large American city. The response to a potentially violent attack is the same in Madagascar as anywhere: if you are outnumbered or the thief is armed, it is sensible to hand over what they want.

You are far more likely to be robbed by subterfuge. Razor-slashing is very popular (with the thieves) and is particularly irritating since your clothes or bag are ruined, maybe just for the sake of the used tissue that caused the tempting-looking bulge in your pocket. When visiting crowded places avoid bringing a bag (even a daypack carried in front of your body is vulnerable, as is a bum-bag); bring your money and passport or ID in a moneybelt under your clothes, or in a neck pouch. Women have advantages here: the neck pouch can be hooked over their bra so no cord shows at the neck and a moneybelt beneath a skirt is safe since it needs an unusually brazen thief to reach for it! If you must have a bag, make sure it is difficult to cut, and that it can be carried across your body so it cannot be snatched (see box on page 167). Passengers in taxis may be the victims of robbery: the thief reaches through the open window and grabs your bag. Keep it on the floor by your feet.

Having escorted scores of first-timers through Madagascar, I've learned the mistakes the unprepared can make. The most common is wearing jewellery ('But I always wear this gold chain'), carelessness with money etc ('I just put my bag down while I tried on that blouse'), and expecting thieves to look shabby ('But he was such a well-dressed young man').

Passports and IDs

If you prefer to leave your passport in a safe place in your hotel room when you go out, carrying a photocopy of your passport is no longer sufficient for ID purposes, unless it is an authorised copy, with red stamps all over it, available either from the police (supposedly free) or from the office of the mayor (1,500Fmg per copy). You must provide your passport (photo page and visa page) and as many photocopies of it as you think you might need. This authorised copy is then valid for the police, for banks, for Western Union, or anyone else who might demand your ID.

This is all quite a hassle, but losing your passport is worse. I've never been stopped in all my trips to Madagascar, but have had plenty of reports of people (mostly young) who have.

Tips for avoiding robbery

- Remember that most theft occurs in the street not in hotels; leave your valuables hidden in a locked bag in your room or in the hotel safe.
- If you use a hotel safe at Reception, make sure your money is in a sealed envelope that cannot be opened without detection. There have been cases of the key being accessible to all hotel employees, with predictable results.

SCUBA DIVING SAFETY IN MADAGASCAR

Liz Bomford with additional information by Rob Conway

Madagascar has got some truly wonderful underwater opportunities but divers need to be cautious. There is no hyperbaric chamber in the country; diving casualties must be evacuated overseas by air. The nearest recompression facilities are in Kenya, South Africa, Réunion and Mauritius. As flying exacerbates decompression sickness, this is not an ideal situation so you need to keep risks to the minimum. Divers Aware Network (DAN) offers comprehensive diving insurance for evacuation from Madagascar and has experience in doing this.

If you are going to dive Madagascar you should be an experienced diver, taking responsibility for your own dives. Madagascar is not suitable for newly qualified PADI open-water divers. It is essential to dive within guidelines and take your own computer so you do not depend blindly on the local dive leaders. Do not dive with any outfit that does not carry oxygen on the boat. Make sure you ask about this; your life may depend on it.

There are no regulations in Madagascar and dive operators are not obliged to provide good quality octopus rigs, or to service equipment regularly, or indeed to carry out any of the 'housekeeping' that is required to provide safe diving. If you can manage it, bring your own equipment. Also make sure that you are conservative with your dive profiles and take an extra long safety stop on ascending.

Don't be afraid to ask about safety issues. You are not being a wimp. I had a 'bend' in Madagascar in 2003. If my instructor had not been equipped with oxygen, I would be dead. As it was, he didn't have enough and I now have mild but permanent neurological injuries. Don't let them tell you 'there are no accidents in Madagascar'. I was that statistic and I feel sure I'm not the only one.

- If staying in C Category hotels bring a rubber wedge (or Blu-Tack) to keep your door closed at night. If you can't secure the window put something on the sill which will fall with a clatter if someone tries to enter.
- Pay particular attention to the security of your passport.
- Carry your cash in a moneybelt, neck pouch or deep pocket. Wear loose trousers that have zipped pockets. Keep emergency cash (eg: a US$100 bill) in a Very Safe Place. Keep a small but reasonable amount of cash in a wallet that you can give away if threatened.
- Divide up travellers' cheques so they are not all in one place. Keep a note of the numbers of your travellers' cheques, passport, credit cards, plane ticket, insurance etc in your moneybelt. Keep photocopies of the above in your luggage.
- Remember, what the thief would most like to get hold of is money. Do not leave it around (in coat pockets hanging in your room, in your hand while you concentrate on something else, in an accessible pocket while strolling in the street). If travelling as a couple or small group have one person stand aside to keep watch while the other makes a purchase in the street.
- In a restaurant never hang your bag on the back of a chair or lay it by your feet (unless you put your chair leg over the strap). When travelling in a taxi, put your bag on the floor by your feet.
- For thieves, the next best thing after money is clothes. Avoid leaving them on the beach while you go swimming (in tourist areas) and never leave swimsuits or washing to dry outside your room near a public area.
- Bear in mind that it's impossible to run carrying a large piece of luggage. Items hidden at the bottom of your heaviest bag will be safe from a grab-and-run thief. Couples or small groups can pass a piece of cord through the handles of all their bags to make them one unstealable unit when waiting at an airport or taxi-brousse station.

A WOMAN TRAVELLING ALONE
FRB

I had a fantastic time travelling alone for a few weeks in rural Madagascar! Making a journey between S-Ivongo and Maroantsetra I'd expected to be left with overwhelming impressions of beautiful coastlines, an extraordinary ecosystem, improbable fauna and near-impossible transport conditions. I wasn't disappointed! Just as special though were the warmth and hospitality of the Malagasy people.

I'd landed in Tana with the doubtful benefit of four months' (poorly) self-taught French and only the vaguest idea of an itinerary, having booked the flight on a whim to satisfy a long-standing but uninformed curiosity about the island. In an almost *vazaha*-free area I must have been quite a novelty but I learnt a few words of Malagasy and tried to take an interest in everything – although after attempting to de-husk rice grains with a giant (6ft) pestle and mortar, I decided that this was best left to the experts!

Travelling alone is perhaps nobody's ideal but I really wouldn't have missed the experience for the world, at least in this part of the world; I was constantly touched by the friendship and companionship extended by local people. My limited linguistic skills were no bar to laughter and camaraderie in the back of a *camion*, as our lurching vehicle threw us among the sacks of rice, flour and sugar, the cooking pots and tomatoes, whilst the beer crates

- Avoid misunderstandings – genuine or contrived – by agreeing on the price of a service before you set out.
- Enjoy yourself. It's preferable to lose a few unimportant things and see the best of Madagascar than to mistrust everyone and ruin your trip!

...and what to do if you are robbed

Have a little cry and then go to the police. They will write down all the details then send you to the chief of police for a signature. It takes the best part of a day, but you will need the certificate for your insurance. If you are in a rural area, the local authorities will do a declaration of loss.

Women travellers

Things have changed a lot in Madagascar. During my travels in the 1980s my only experience of sexual harassment (if it could be called that) was when a small man sidled up to me in Nosy Be and asked: 'Have you ever tasted Malagasy man?'

Sadly, with the increase of tourism comes the increase of men who think they may be on to a good thing. A firm 'no' is usually sufficient; try not to be too offended: think of the image of Western women that the average Malagasy male is shown via the cinema or TV.

A woman Peace Corps volunteer gave me the following advice for women travelling alone on taxi-brousses: 'Try to sit in the cab, but not next to the driver; if possible sit with another woman; if in the main body of the vehicle, establish contact with an older person, man or woman, who will then tend to look after you.' All women readers agree that you should say you are married, whether or not you wear a ring to back it up.

Lone travellers, both male and female, seem to have a better time well off the beaten track. My correspondent 'FRB' (see box below) is not alone in saying that the true warmth of ordinary Malagasy is more likely to be found away from tourist areas.

crashed alarmingly on shelves just above our heads ... although it was sometimes difficult to see each other through the diesel fumes! My (all male) companions on this journey were unfailingly charming, lowering a plank which I used to enter and exit more easily as we made the numerous stops required to rebuild bridges and take on/offload people, poultry and produce.... and I found this pattern of courtesy and kindness repeated again and again in so many situations as I progressed via *kat-kats* and ferries, pirogues, on foot, by boat and even, briefly, on the back of a motorbike.

I should have at least one cautionary tale to tell of an intimidating experience – but I haven't! I enjoyed myself far more than I'd anticipated and am left humbled by the simple humanity of the people who made this possible. I never felt unsafe and while eating in *hotelys* or having bread and coffee from a roadside stall would generally find people willing to chat.

Having said that, it was a relief to speak English when happy chance found me a travelling companion! I think the solo experience might have been more uncomfortable among the groups of *vazaha* present in the more tourist-orientated areas. But if you're thinking of seeing Madagascar alone – do it! I found that the rural Malagasy respond with relief to someone who trusts them and will make you welcome. If you're in a touristy area, try to find a like-minded *vazaha* to enjoy it with – and don't forget to exchange email addresses, sharing the memories afterwards is as important as living them!

Men travellers

To the Malagasy, a man travelling alone is in need of one thing: a woman. Lone male travellers will be pursued relentlessly, particularly in beach resorts. Prostitutes are ubiquitous and very beautiful. Venereal disease is common. A recent added danger from prostitutes is lacing a tourist's drink with the 'date-rape' drug Rohypnol to render their victim unconscious in his room, then rob him of all his possessions.

The new government is clamping down hard on sex tourism. Considering the risks you would be foolish to succumb to temptation.

> *The mercies of God [be bestowed on] this people, whose simplicity hath herein made them more happy than our too dear-bought knowledge hath advantaged us.*
>
> Walter Hamond, 1640

In Madagascar

6

MONEY
The currency

Madagascar's currency has always been difficult to cope with. Here is an extract from an account written over a hundred years ago:

> The French five-franc piece is now the standard of coinage in Madagascar; for small change it is cut up into bits of all sizes. The traveller has to carry a pair of scales about with him, and whenever he makes a purchase the specified quantity of this most inconvenient money is weighed out with the greatest exactness, first on his own scales, and then on those of the suspicious native of whom he is buying.

So it is perhaps not surprising that the new government has kept up the tradition of confusing foreigners, and its own people, by changing the currency. The *franc malgache* (Fmg) is being replaced by the traditional Malagasy currency of *Ariary* (which was still in use in Madagascar when I first went there). This move, which was initiated in August 2003, is presumably intended to shake off another legacy of French colonialism. It has succeeded in shaking me while the Malagasy blithely ignore the change. The problem will become evident as you read this book. All the prices are still in Fmg because, to be honest, dividing them all by five to make Ariary is beyond me. You, dear reader, will just have to do this yourself! One Ariary is 5Fmg.

The Fmg will cease to be legal tender in August 2006. Until then both currencies will be used but considering that it took us British about ten years to adjust to our change of currency in the 1970s, I suspect that most Malagasy will be quoting Fmg when they tell you a price.

Ariary confusion

Now for the interesting bit. What's really clever about this changeover is that the new Ariary notes are printed in such a way that the unsuspecting tourist assumes they are francs and pays five times too much. The honest Malagasy will usually put you right but you can hardly blame the occasional opportunist to take advantage of your confusion. You therefore need to do your homework before you arrive, with the help of the colour photo of the new notes opposite page 83. You will see that there are three new Ariary notes: 10,000 Ariary (worth 50,000Fmg), 5,000 Ariary (25,000Fmg) and 2,000 Ariary (10,000Fmg). The two lower denominations have an equivalent note in Francs (shown in the photo) but the 10,000 Ariary is worth over £3/$5 at today's rate of exchange so is almost unusable: no-one ever has change! But perhaps inflation will soon take care of that.

Coins to the value of 10 and 20 Ariary are still in circulation – left-over from the last century when they were worth something. Now they are practically worthless.

Exchange rate and hard currencies

The franc malgache (and Ariary) floats against hard currencies but had, until 2004, remained pretty stable. Prices had also stayed largely unchanged since the last edition of this guide. In March 2004 the franc/Ariary was devalued by one third; it is now worth less than half its value of 2003. Most tourist hotels therefore quote their prices in euros, as have I when possible. It's likely to remain unchanged while the franc/Ariary prices rise.

Exchange rate in October 2004

£1 = 17,750Fmg/3,550 Ariary
US$1 = 10,000Fmg/2,000 Ariary
€1 = 11,300Fmg/2,260 Ariary

Changing money

There are no currency restrictions and you are permitted to make purchases using American dollars – indeed, the tourist-aware vendors in places visited by cruise ships are quite unhappy if offered Malagasy money.

See page 89 on the best way of bringing your money. Whether you opt for travellers' cheques, cash or credit cards, you will find privately owned *Bureaux de Change* more efficient than the banks where there are often long queues and where it's difficult to understand the procedure. The best bank for foreign exchange is the BFV, which has branches all over Madagascar and can change money through your Visa credit card. Tourist hotels will usually, but not always, change money but the rate may not be so good.

Towards the end of your trip change money cautiously. **You cannot change your local money back into hard currency, and once you're into the check-in hall at the airport there is nowhere to spend it.**

Transferring funds

Now that you can draw cash from many banks using your credit card you are less likely to need money transferred from home. If you are staying a long time in Madagascar, however, it's advisable to make the transfer arrangement beforehand. The best bank for this is Banque Malgache de l'Océan Indien, Place de l'Indépendance, Antananarivo. Its corresponding bank in the UK is Banque Nationale de Paris, 8–13 King William St, London EC4P 4HS; tel: 020 7895 7070.

If you need cash in a hurry there are Western Union offices in Madagascar to which money can be transferred from home in a few hours, or in minutes if your nearest and dearest are willing to go to a Western Union office with cash. The fee (in the UK) is £32 if done with a credit card but, for the obliging mum, partner or whatever in your home country, it is a simple procedure which can be done over the phone, saving the journey to a Western Union office. They need to phone Western Union on 0800 833 833 (in the USA: 800 325 6000) and know the town from where you wish to pick up the money. There are Western Union offices in Antananarivo, Mahajanga, Toamasina, Fianarantsoa and Nosy Be. Phone 261 20 22 313 07 for addresses or further information or check their website: www.westernunion.com.

PUBLIC TRANSPORT

You can get around Madagascar by road, air and water. And by rail. Whatever your transport, you'd better learn the meaning of *en panne*; it is engine trouble/breakdown. During these *en panne* sessions one can't help feeling a certain nostalgia for the pre-mechanised days when Europeans travelled by *filanzana* or palanquin. These litters were carried by four cheerful porters who, by all accounts, were so busy swapping gossip and telling stories that they sometimes dropped their unfortunate *vazaha* in a river. The average distance travelled per day was 30 miles – not much slower than a taxi-brousse today! The *filanzana* was used for high officials as recently as the 1940s. To get around town the locals depended on an earlier version of the current rickshaw, or *pousse-pousse*. The *mono-pousse* was a chair slung over a bicycle wheel. One man pulled and another pushed. The more affluent Malagasy possessed a *boeuf-cheval*: a zebu trained to be ridden. (I've seen a photo; the animal looks rather smug in its saddle and bridle.)

By road

> If I make roads, the white man will only come and take my country. I
> have two allies – hazo [forest] and tazo [fever]…
>
> King Radama I

Coping with the 'roads' is one of the great travel challenges in Madagascar. It's not that the royal decree has lasted 180 years but there's a third ally that the king didn't mention – the weather: torrential rain and cyclones destroy roads as fast as they are constructed. But they are being repaired and reconstructed, mostly with foreign aid. At the time of writing many of the most important roads (the *Routes Nationales*) are either paved or in the process of being paved. The others are dreadful, but then…that's Madagascar!

Taxi-brousse is the generic name for public transport in Madagascar. *Car-brousse*, *taxi-be* and *kat-kat* are also used, but they all refer to the 'bush-taxis' which run along every road in the country. These have improved a lot in recent years, especially along tourist routes. Even so, stories like those on page 128 are still not unusual.

Taxi-brousse
Vehicles
Taxi-brousses are generally minibuses or Renault vans with seats facing each other so there is no good view out of the window (a *baché* is a small van with a canvas top). More comfortable are the Peugeot 404s or 504s, sometimes known as *taxi-be* (although some people call the 25-seater buses *taxi-be*) designed to take nine people, but often packed with 14 or more. A *car-brousse* is usually a Tata sturdy enough to cope with bad roads. A *katkat* is a term used in the northeast for the 4WD vehicles which are needed to cope with the atrocious roads. The back is covered with a tarpaulin and there are no seats: you sit on your luggage. For even worse conditions, you may find a *tracteur-brousse*!

Practicalities
Vehicles leave from a *gare routière* (bus station) on the side of town closest to their destination. You should try to go there a day or two ahead of your planned departure to check times and prices, and for long journeys you should buy a ticket in advance (from the kiosk – don't give your money to a ticket tout). The following advice is from Frances Kerridge – a seasoned taxi-brousse traveller: 'Don't be embarrassed to ask to see the vehicle – the Malagasy do. Reserve your seat – they will write your name on a hand-drawn plan in an exercise book – and get them to write your place on the ticket. Once you have anything written on a piece of paper it is regarded as law and once it is typed it must be gospel!

'Never be late for a taxi-brousse. Some of them do leave on time, especially on popular journeys or if the departure time is horrendous, eg: 2am. Get there early

VIVE LE TAXI-BROUSSE!

Taxi-brousses are improving, especially on the main tourist routes, but I couldn't resist repeating these entertaining stories!

'At about 10 o'clock we (two people) went to the taxi-brousse station. "Yes, yes, there is a car. It is here, ready to go." We paid our money. "When will it go?" "When it has nine passengers." "How many has it got now?" "Wait a minute." A long look at notebooks, then a detailed calculation. "Two." "As well as us?" "No, no, including you." It finally left at about 7 o'clock.'

Chris Ballance

'After several hours we picked up four more people. We couldn't believe it – the driver had to sit on someone's lap!'

Stephen Cartledge

'At last we were under way. I had my knees jammed up against the iron bar at the back of the rows in front where sat a very sick soldier, who spent most of the journey with his head out of the window spewing lurid green bile at passers-by like something from a horror-movie... After about 20 minutes we had to stop at a roadside stall to buy mangoes. Since I was now on the sunny side of the vehicle the temperature of my shirt rose to what, had it been made of polyester, would have been melting point. Our next stop was Antsirabe where we were surrounded by about 50 apple vendors and all and sundry went absolutely beserk. I hadn't seen so many apples since...since we left Ambositra. At about 5pm the radio was turned on so we could listen to two men shouting at each other at a volume which would have caused bleeding of the eardrums in Wembley Stadium. When one passenger complained our driver managed to find a few extra decibels. At about 6pm it started to get decidedly brisk, and since the ailing squaddie in front of me showed no sign of having rid himself of toxic enzymes I now had to endure an icy blast in my face. Our next stop was for grapes. We now had enough fruit on board to start a wholesale business in Covent Garden, and I was a bit tetchy.'

Robert Stewart

'We eventually made it after an eventful four-hour taxi-brousse journey which entailed the obligatory trawl around town for more passengers, selling the spare tyre shortly after setting off, a 30-minute wait outside the doctor's as the driver wasn't feeling very well, and all of us having to bump-start the vehicle every time we stopped to pick anyone up.'

H & M Kendrick, 1998

'I woke up nice and early to get my taxi-brousse to Mahamasina from Diego. I clambered on to a nice new minibus, eager to hit the open road. There was one other passenger. We cruised around for three hours, frequently changing drivers, trying to get more customers. In this time our driver got into three fights, one lasting half an hour. There was even a tug-of-war with passengers, which looked quite painful, to persuade them to use their taxi-brousse.'

Ben Tapley, 2001

to claim your seat, then read your book, write your diary or whatever. Be ready with soap and towel for a bath stop. Follow the women and children to get some degree of privacy.'

Stuart Riddle has provided this recent advice on how to survive a long-distance taxi-brousse journey. 'The priority is to choose your seat carefully. You will not be able to reserve the window seat at the front – this is always taken by the co-driver. The best seats are on the row behind the driver because there is more leg room. The worst seats for leg room are the back row of Toyotas. This is also the noisiest area and you will be fighting for space with children and chickens.

'On overnight journeys prepare for the cold nights even though the sun may be beating down when you leave. Try to get a window seat so you can control the temperature. The warmest seat is next to the driver, because of the heat of the engine, but this can be uncomfortably hot and the driver will wake you each time he changes gear. The dazzle of oncoming headlights is also a problem.

'Your driver will play loud music throughout the night. The speakers are usually at the back so sitting near the front brings some relief. [Some travellers recommend bringing your own favourite cassettes and hoping to persuade the driver to play them.]

'Motion sickness is often a problem even if you've never experienced it before. Be prepared with pills as well as waterproof plastic bags and tissues.'

On short journeys and in remote areas, vehicles simply leave as soon as they fill up. Or if they have a schedule expect them to leave hours late, and always be prepared (with warm clothing, fruit, water etc) for a night trip, even if you thought it was leaving in the morning.

There is no set rate per kilometre; fares are calculated on the quality of the vehicle, the roughness of the road and the time the journey takes. They are set by the government and *vazaha* are only occasionally overcharged. Ask other passengers what they are paying, or trust the driver. Taxi-brousses are very cheap. It should not cost you more than US$10 for an all-day journey. Faster routes (tarred roads) may be a bit more expensive. Passengers are occasionally charged for luggage that is strapped on to the roof.

Drivers stop to eat, but usually drive all night. If they do stop during the night most passengers stay in the vehicle or sleep on the road outside.

There is much that a committed overland traveller can do to soften his/her experiences on taxi-brousses – see page 87. If you're prepared for the realities, an overland journey can be very enjoyable and gives you a chance to get to know the Malagasy. And before you get too depressed and cancel your trip, remember that on the popular routes there are normal buses with one seat per passenger. The above (and the box) mainly pertains to adventurous journeys away from the *Route Nationales*.

By air

Air Madagascar started its life in 1962 as Madair but understandably changed its name after a few years of jokes. Most people now call it Air Mad. It serves over 40 destinations, making it the most efficient way – and for some people the only way – of seeing the country. Here are some sample return fares (excluding tax) from Antananarivo: Mahajanga US$252, Nosy Be US$264, Antsiranana (Diego Suarez) US$252. Remember that you can get a 25% discount on domestic flights providing you chose Air Mad as your international carrier.

Air Madagascar has the following planes: Boeing 747 (jumbo) on the Paris to Antananarivo route, Boeing 737 to the larger cities and Nosy Be, the smaller ATR 49-seater turbo props, and the little Twin Otters to the smaller towns.

The recent rise in tourism in Madagascar has brought more passengers than Air Mad can cope with, particularly at peak holiday times. Try to book in advance through one of their agents (see page 83). If you are doing your bookings once you arrive, avoid the crush by getting to the Air Mad office when it opens in the morning, or use one of the many very competent travel agents in the capital. Often flights which are said to be fully booked in Antananarivo are found to have seats when you reapply at the town of departure. In any case, you should reconfirm your next flight as soon as you arrive at your destination (at the Air Mad office in town). Rupert Parker, a frequent traveller to Madagascar, reveals his secret: 'Because you are still allowed to make a reservation without payment, flights always appear full, but the trick is to go to the airport two hours in advance and put your ticket on the counter. The *liste d'attente* works on a first-come-first-served basis and half an hour before the flight is due to leave they start filling the empty seats, taking the tickets in order of arrival. We have never, in ten years, been disappointed – it just increases the stress level but we have always got on the plane.' Conversely, passengers with booked seats who check in late will find their seats sold to waiting-list passengers. Always arrive at least an hour before the scheduled departure.

There are no numbered seats on internal flights, which are non-smoking. It is useful to know that *Enregistrement Bagages* is the check-in counter and *Livraison Bagages* is luggage arrival.

And here's a warning: there are no toilets in a Twin Otter!

Air Madagascar schedules are reviewed twice-yearly, at the end of March and the end of October, but are subject to change at any time and without notice. Air Mad has a good website: www.airmadagascar.mg (though it doesn't give prices). Their phone number in Antananarivo is 26 120 22 22 222.

With a shortage of aircraft and pilots, planes are sometimes delayed or cancelled. Almost always there is a perfectly good reason: mechanical problems, bad weather. Air Mad is improving and on the whole they provide as reliable a service as one can expect in a poor country.

By boat

The Malagasy are traditionally a seafaring people (remember that 6,000km journey from Indonesia) and in the absence of roads, their stable outrigger canoes are used to cover quite long sea distances. Pirogues without outriggers are used extensively on the rivers and canals of the watery east. Quite a few adventurous travellers use pirogues for sections of their journeys. Romantic though it may be to sail in an outrigger canoe, it can be both uncomfortable and, at times, dangerous.

Ferries and cargo boats travel to the larger islands and down the west coast.

River rafting is becoming increasingly popular as a different way of seeing the country.

By rail

After years of deterioration, Madagascar's railways have been privatised (see box opposite). The line between Fianarantsoa and Manakara on the east coast is giving a reliable, enjoyable service, and there is talk about the line from Antananarivo to Andasibe being restored. The line from Antananarivo to Toamasina is unlikely to take passengers in the near future.

A posh rail option is the *Micheline*, a swanky white bus with rubber wheels that runs oh-so-smoothly on railway tracks. It's only used for groups of tourists and is usually booked through tour operators. At present it is based in Fianarantsoa and only runs on the first part of the Fianar to Manakara line, although Madarail is planning to use it on the Tana to Antsirabe route. To hire the train currently costs

Above Beach at Ile aux Nattes off Ile Sainte Marie (HB)

Left Sailing pirogue near Nosy Be (HB)

Below Grandidier's baobabs, *Adansonia grandidieri*, at sunset, near Morondava (NG)

Above Ground boa (*Acrantophis madagascariensis*) swallowing a lizard (NG)

Right Northern green tree frog (*Boophis luteus septentrionalis*) (NG)

Below Panther chameleon (*Furcifer pardalis*) (HB)

MADARAIL

At the end of the 19th century a British economist, Captain E W Dawson, wrote: 'Madagascar only requires the advent of railways… to make it one of the most prosperous commercial countries in the world.' Eventually three railway lines were built, from the capital to Tamatave, the main port, with a spur from Moramanga to Lake Alaotra; from Tana to Antsirabe, and from Fianarantsoa to Manakara. Thus it was not the rail network that Dawson probably envisaged but three prongs.

When I first started visiting Madagascar, RN2 to Toamasina (Tamatave) was in such poor condition that rail travel was the only option. It was a very crowded, but scenically marvellous journey. The engineering statistics were impressive: built between 1901 and 1913 by Chinese coolies, the track runs for 375km through numerous tunnels and over several viaducts. When RN2 was rebuilt in the 1980s it provided a much faster access to the main port and the track gradually fell into disuse and disrepair. Sabotage and cyclones finished the job.

Now there is new hope for the railways. Comazar, a private pan-Africa railway operator, has acquired a majority shareholding in Madagascar's railways. Under the name of Madarail, it has signed an agreement to revitalise the 'northern network' and bring it up to the standard of the 'southern network', Fianarantsoa to Manakara, which is now owned by an American company. However, the bad news for rail buffs is that the Tana to Toamasina line seems to be destined to carry freight only except for the last stretch between Moramanga and Brickaville where there is little local transport. 'If we didn't accommodate passengers, they would jump on the freight trains anyway,' says the Managing Director of Comazar philosophically.

Rail enthusiasts will be interested in the monogram Madagascar: Rail and Mail Services *published by The Indian Ocean Study Circle. See page 454.*

1,500,000Fmg (about £100 at today's exchange rate). More information from 261 20 513 54.

Transport within cities
Buses
Most cities have cheap buses but few travellers use these because of the difficulty of understanding the route system. No reason not to give it a try, however.

Taxis
Taxi rates have gone up in recent years because of a sharp rise in fuel prices, but they are still reasonable. Taxis have no meters, so you must agree on the price before you get in. Within most cities taxis operate at a set rate.

Rickshaws (Pousse-pousses)
Pousse-pousses were introduced into Madagascar by British missionaries who wanted to replace the traditional palanquin with its association with slavery. The name is said to originate from the time they operated in the capital and needed an additional man behind to push up the steep hills. They are now a Madagascar speciality (unlike the pedal rickshaws in other parts of the world, these are pulled

by a running man). Most towns have *pousse-pousses* – the exceptions are the hilly towns of the highlands.

Many Western visitors are reluctant to sit in comfort behind a running, ragged, sweating man and no-one with a heart can fail to feel compassion for the *pousse-pousse* pullers. However, this is a case of needing to abandon our own cultural hang-ups. These men want work. Bargain hard (before you get in) and make sure you have the exact money. It would be optimistic to expect change. A medium-length journey will generally cost around 5,000Fmg. If you don't feel like bargaining a dollar will do nicely. *Pousse-pousse* pullers love carrying soft-hearted tourists and have become quite cunning – and tiresome – in their dealings with *vazaha*. However, remember how desperately these men need a little luck – and an innocent tourist could make their day!

HIRING (OR BRINGING) YOUR OWN TRANSPORT

Tim Ireland puts it succinctly: 'The great pity is watching so many magnificent landscapes tear past your eyes as you strain your neck trying to get a better view past 15 other occupants of a taxi-brousse.' He goes on to recommend a mountain bike as the perfect means of transport, but a hired vehicle will achieve the same flexibility.

Car hire

More and more visitors have been renting cars or 4WD vehicles in recent years. You would need to be a competent mechanic to hire a self-drive car in Madagascar, and generally cars come with chauffeurs (providing a local person with a job and you with a guide/interpreter). A few days on Madagascar's roads will cure you of any regret that you are not driving yourself. Night-time driving is particularly challenging: headlights often don't work or are not switched on. Your driver will know that the single light bearing down on you is more likely to be a wide truck than a narrow motorbike and react accordingly. The Merina Highway Code (informal version) decrees that drivers must honk their horns after crossing a bridge to ensure that the spirits are out of the way.

There are car-hire firms in most large towns. A list of the international companies in Antananarivo is below. In addition the Maison du Tourisme has a more comprehensive list, and I have included them in town information outside the capital.

Prices currently work out at about £50/US$75 per day, including fuel and driver, for a small saloon car driving around Antananarivo. For a week's hire of a 4WD you should expect to pay about £750/US$1,125.

If you are planning to hire a vehicle, I suggest you consider doing so in Toliara (Tuléar) which has some of the most interesting people and scenery – and the worst roads – in Madagascar. A 4WD vehicle will allow you to get well off the beaten track.

Sheena Gibson comments that 'fuel pumps often have no fuel, but if you keep driving around you will probably find one in the area that does have fuel – often these are hand-pumped which is great at first but can get tiring!'

Major car rental firms (in Antananarivo) and prices

Aventour Tel: 22 317 61 or 22 613 42 or 22 609 66. Saloon: 189,500Fmg/day + 2350/km + VAT 20% with a driver, without petrol.

Europcar Tel: 22 336 47. 4WD: 722,005Fmg to 801,638Fmg/day with a driver, without petrol.

SIXT Tel: 22 297 66/ 22 621 50; email: intermad@dts.mg. 4WD: 150,000Fmg + 1,500/km + insurance 110,000Fmg + VAT 20%/day; saloon car: 90,000Fmg + 900/km + insurance 80,000Fmg + VAT 20%/day.

Hertz Tel: 22 229 61; email: somada@simicro.mg; www.madagascar-contacts.com/hertz.
4WD: 602,000Fmg/day; saloon car: 396,000Fmg/day.
Sun and Sea Tel: 22 467 33; email: sun_sea@dts.mg. 4WD (Land Rover): 470,000Fmg/day
with a driver, without petrol; Nissan: 550,000Fmg/day with a driver, without petrol.

Motorbike

This is perhaps the very best way of getting round Madagascar: fast enough to
cover a lot of ground in this large island, yet flexible enough to deal with the
terrible roads. There are a few places that rent out motorbikes.

Marko Petrovic, who used a motorbike to tour remote areas of the southeast (in
2001), found a small motorbike the most convenient because of the necessity to cross
rivers using local pirogues. The motorbike was laid across two pirogues tied together.
He says that 'brand new Yamahas, Suzukis and Hondas are very reasonably priced
and available in Tana' so buying a bike is a good option if you are staying a while.

Motorbike rental

Madagascar on Bike Tel: 22 467 33; cellphone: 33 11 381 36; email: info@madagascar-
on-bike.com; web: http://madagascar-on-bike.com. A German company supplying Honda
Transalp bikes (600cc 5h/p). Check their website for latest prices.

Mountain bike

This is an increasingly popular means of touring Madagascar. Bikes can usually be
hired in Antananarivo, Antsirabe, Taolagnaro (Fort Dauphin), Antsiranana (Diego
Suarez) and Nosy Be (the French for mountain bike is VTT). Or you can bring
your own or buy one in Antananarivo for around 600,000Fmg (about £60). You can
do a combination of bike and taxi-brousse or bike and plane, or you can set out to
cycle the whole way. Don't be overambitious; dirt roads are so rutted or sandy you
will make slow progress, and tarred roads can be dangerous from erratic drivers. See
Chapter 4, pages 96–7, for advice and information on touring by bike.

ACCOMMODATION

Hotels in Madagascar are classified by a national star system – five star being the
highest – but in my experience this indicates price, not quality. In this book I have
used three categories: A, B and C, which is based on quality as much as price. There
is a tourist tax, *vignette touristique*, of between 1,000Fmg and 3,000Fmg per person per
night. This is sometimes absorbed into the price, but is often added separately.

Outside the towns, hotels in the form of a single building are something of a
rarity. Accommodation is usually in bungalows which are often constructed of
local materials and are quiet, atmospheric and comfortable.

A word about bolsters. Visitors who are not accustomed to the ways of France
are disconcerted to find a firm, sheet-covered sausage anchored to the top of the
bed. In the better hotels you can usually find a pillow hidden away in a cupboard.
Failing that, I make my own pillow with a sweater stuffed into a T-shirt.

Breakfast is rarely included in the room price, and if it is it'll be continental
breakfast or Malagasy breakfast (just dry bread and black coffee).

What you get for your money
Category A

There are, as yet, no five-star hotels in Madagascar but the top hotels and lodges are
truly luxurious and, in the larger towns, many up to international standard. Such
hotels are usually foreign-owned. There has been a boom in hotel building during the
last few years, and there are now some very good Malagasy-owned hotels in this

category, so the difference between A and B has become somewhat blurred. Category A hotels cost between £20/US$36 and £180/US$324 for a double room (there are very few at the top price bracket). If you really want to push the boat out you can pay £308/€457/$550 for the Presidential Suite at the Colbert in Tana. The average, even for a really nice hotel, is only about £25/US$38 and many super places are a lot less.

Category B

These are often just as clean and comfortable, and most have en-suite bathrooms. There will be no TV beaming CNN into your bedroom, but you should have comfortable beds though bolsters are the norm. The hotels are often family-run and very friendly. The average price is about £15/US$27.

Category C

In early editions I described these as 'exhilaratingly dreadful at times' until a reader wrote: 'We were rather disappointed by the quality of the *Category C* hotels... We found almost all the beds comfortable, generally acceptably clean, and not one rat. We felt luxuriously cheated!' However, the following description from Rupert Parker of a hotel in Brickaville should gladden the masochistic heart, '...a conglomeration of shacks directly beneath the road bridge. The rooms are partitioned-off spaces, just large enough to hold a bed, in a larger wooden building – the partitions don't reach to the ceiling and there is only one light bulb for all the rooms – the hotel manageress controls the switch. Not only can you hear everyone's conversation and what they're up to, but when there is a new arrival, at whatever time of the night, the light comes on and wakes everyone up – that is if you've managed to ignore the rumbling and revving of trucks as they cross the bridge above you, or the banging on the gate which announces a new arrival. Suffice to say the toilet and washing facilities are non-existent.' It would be rather a shame if they've improved it in the intervening years!

Such hotels certainly give the flavour of how Madagascar used to be, and in remote areas you will still find the occasional sagging double bed and stinking hole toilet. Usually you can find the toilet by the smell, but ask for the WC ('dooble vay say'), not *toilette* which usually means shower or bathroom. In these hotels (and some B ones too) used toilet paper should not be thrown into the pan but into the box provided for it. Not very nice, but preferable to a clogged loo.

Most of the C hotels in this book are clean and excellent value, only earning the C because of their price. Almost always they are run by friendly Malagasy who will rustle up a fantastic meal. In an out-of-the-way place you will pay as little as £2.50/US$4.50 for the most basic room, though £6.50/US$12 would be more usual.

Hotely usually means a restaurant/snack bar rather than accommodation, but it's always worth asking if they have rooms.

Most B and C hotels will do your washing for you at a very reasonable price. This gives employment to local people and is an important element of responsible travel. In A hotels laundry can be disproportionately expensive!

Websites Hotels in Madagascar are increasingly having their own website. One of the best that I've used in this update (listing many hotels throughout Madagascar) is http://www.mylinea.com/masombahiny/hebergement_et_restauration/.

Camping

Until very recently Madagascar had no official campsites, although backpackers with their own tent were often allowed to camp in hotel gardens. During 2001 several campsites were set up in the south (mainly near Isalo National Park) in the expectation of vast crowds arriving for the solar eclipse. Some of these are still open for business. In addition the NGO Azafady operates several campsites in beautiful situations in the Taolagnaro (Fort Dauphin area), and some of the new national parks (Andringitra, Marojejy) are for camping only. National parks-style camping is usually on a wooden platform with a thatched roof above. Very comfortable.

Self-contained backpackers will know the wonderful sense of freedom that comes with carrying their own tent – there is all of Madagascar to explore! However, camping in rural areas that see few foreigners brings its own problems: see pages 96–7 and 148.

FOOD AND DRINK
Food

Eating well is one of the delights of Madagascar, and even the fussiest tourists are usually happy with the food. International hotels serve international food, usually with a French bias, and often do special Malagasy dishes. Lodges and smaller hotels serve local food which is almost always excellent, particularly on the coast where lobster (crayfish), shellfish and other seafood predominates. Meat lovers will enjoy the zebu steaks, although they are usually tougher than we are used to (free-range meat usually is). Outside the capital, most hotels offer a set menu (*table d'hôte* or *menu*) to their guests. This can cost as little as 30,000Fmg (£2/$3.60). At the upper end you can expect to pay 125,000Fmg (£9/US$16).

Where the menu is à la carte it is a help to have a French dictionary or phrasebook.

The national dish in Madagascar is *romazava* (pronounced 'roomazahv'), a meat and vegetable stew, spiced with ginger and containing *brèdes* (pronounced 'bread'), tasty, tongue-tingling greens. Another good local dish is *ravitoto*, shredded manioc leaves with fried beef and coconut. Volker Dorheim adds: 'If you like your food really spicy ask for *pimente verde*. If this isn't hot enough ask for *pimente malgache*.' And Sebastian Bulmer tells me that all Malagasy restaurants grind to a halt when the nation's favourite soap, *Terra Nostra*, comes on!

Independent travellers will find Chinese restaurants in every town; these are almost always good and reasonably priced. *Soupe Chinoise* is available almost everywhere, and is filling and tasty. The Malagasy eat a lot of rice, but most restaurants cater to foreign tastes by providing chips (French fries). Away from the tourist routes, however, most dishes are accompanied by a sticky mound of rice.

For a real Malagasy meal, eat in a *hotely*. These are often open-sided shacks where the menu is chalked up on a blackboard:

Henan-omby (or *Hen'omby*)	beef
Henan-borona (or *Hen'akoho*)	chicken
Henan-kisoa	pork
Henan-drano (or *Hazan-drano*)	fish

It may end with *Mazotoa homana*. This is not a dish, it means *Bon appétit*!

Along with the meat or fish and inevitable mound of rice (*vary*) comes a bowl of stock. This is spooned over the rice, or drunk as a soup.

Thirst is quenched with *ranovola* (pronounced 'ranoovool') obtained by boiling water in the pan in which the rice was cooked. It has a slight flavour of burnt rice, and since it has been boiled for several minutes it is safe to drink.

If you don't feel like a full meal, *hotelys* are a great source of snacks. Here are some of the options: *tsaramasy* (rice with beans and pork), *vary sosoa* (rice pudding), *mofo boule* (slightly sweet bread rolls), and *koba* (rice and banana, wrapped in a leaf and served in slices).

For do-it-yourself meals there is a great variety of fruit and vegetables, even in the smallest market. A selection of fruit is served in most restaurants, along with raw vegetables or *crudités*. From June to August the fruit is mostly limited to citrus and bananas, but from September there are also strawberries, mangoes, lychees, pineapples and loquats. Slices of coconut are sold everywhere, but especially on the coast where coconut milk is a popular and safe drink, and toffee-coconut nibbles are sold on the street, often wrapped in paper from school exercise books.

Madagascar's dairy industry is growing (not surprising – it was the former occupation of President Ravelomanana). There are some good, locally produced cheeses and Malagasy yoghurt is excellent and available in the smallest shops. Try the drinking yoghurt, *yaourt à boire*.

Vegetarian food

Madagascar is becoming more accustomed to *vazaha* vegetarians and with patience you can usually order meatless dishes even at small *hotelys*. *Tsy misy hena* means 'without meat'. Stuart Riddle, a vegetarian, 'had all sorts of problems, but also found some gems'. One of these was the Arinofy hotel, in Fianarantsoa, which has a separate vegetarian menu.

Drink

The most popular drink, Three Horses Beer (THB), is wonderful on a hot day. I think it's wonderful on a cold day, too. The price goes up according to the surroundings: twice as much in the Hilton as in a *hotely* and there is always a hefty deposit payable on the bottle. A newish beer is Queens, which is slightly weaker,

WILD SILK
Angus McCrae

Madagascar has a long tradition of textile weaving, of which silk appears to be one of the oldest and most important. The mulberry or Chinese silkworm, *Bombyx mori*, was first introduced from Mauritius under King Radama I in the 1820s but archaeological evidence suggests that wild silk was probably utilised well before that. Since knowledge of mulberry silk has been extant in China for some 4,500 years and of wild silk for at least 500 years more, it is tempting to think that the earliest immigrants brought the idea with them – in Indonesia, as in Madagascar, wild silk is traditionally reserved for burial shrouds. Whatever the case, Madagascar's wild silk is from the cocoons of the endemic genus *Borocera*, of the worldwide family Lasiocampidae or 'Eggar moths'. Lasiocampidae silk is otherwise known to have been made only by the ancient Greeks and the Aztecs.

Of the six currently recognised *Borocera* species, *B. cajani* (found in all regions of the island but chiefly on the central plateau) is the one most used, gathered from tapia trees in Merina and Betsileo regions. Cocoons of any species, however, might be collected if they occur in sufficient abundance, although none of the three cocoon-making species of Madagascar's 19 emperor moths (often misleadingly referred to as giant silk moths) is utilised. Unlike the mulberry silkworm, *Borocera* is not amenable to domestication and it seems that this silk must remain a fluctuating wild resource.

The caterpillars of *B. cajani* are light grey in colour. Those destined to be females grow up to 10cm in length but males are smaller. They are armed with long, black spines on the back and flanks, and when annoyed they also evert a pair and there is also Gold. Why does the Star brewery give its beer English names that the Malagasy can't pronounce? And why horses and queens when the country has few of either (and not much gold)? I don't know. Actually I do – it was to help its market abroad.

Madagascar produces its own wine in the Fianarantsoa region, and some is very good. L'azani Betsileo (*blanc* or *gris, reservé*) is recommended.

A pleasant aperitif is Maromby (the name means 'many zebu') and I have been told that Litchel, made from lychees, is good. Rum, *toaka gasy*, is very cheap and plentiful, especially in sugar-growing areas such as Nosy Be; and fermented sugar cane juice, *betsabetsa* (east coast), or fermented coconut milk, *trembo* (north), make a change. The best cocktail is *punch au coco*, with a coconut-milk base, which is a speciality of the coastal areas. Yummy!

The most popular mineral water is called Eau Vive, but other brands are now available: Olympiko and La Source. Tiko, which produces Olympiko and cartons of very good fresh juice, also make their own Cola and some nice Classico soft drinks (their lemon-lime is recommended by a reader). It's nice to be able to support a local company rather than the internationals, although Coca-Cola and other popular soft drinks such as Sprite and Fanta are available. Fresh is an agreeable shandy, and Tonic is – you guessed it – tonic water. The locally produced *limonady* sadly bears no resemblance to lemons, and Bon Bon Anglais is revolting (although I do know one *anglaise* who rather likes it!).

Caffeine-addicts have a problem. The coffee is OK if taken black, but usually only condensed milk is available. I find that one quickly regresses to childhood and surreptitiously spoons the condensed milk not into the coffee but into the

of vicious-looking rosettes of similar spines seated on a velvety blue background from two of their thoracic segments. These spines are shed and incorporated into the cocoon as it is constructed, projecting some 4mm outwards. Despite this the women spin a coarse silk from these cocoons and weave it on home looms into a highly durable fabric which resembles sacking in colour but is softer, finer and of course much more durable. The silk is carded before spinning, like cotton, wool and other fibres, and not reeled like (uniquely) mulberry silk.

Borocera caterpillars and the silk derived from them are called *landibe* ('big caterpillars') as opposed to *landikely* ('little caterpillars') for the mulberry silkworm. *Landibe* commands much the higher prices since demand for the material for burial shrouds far outstrips supply. Burial shrouds are called *lamba mena*: literally 'red cloth' although they can be of any colour, 'red' meaning power. In the past, some truly exquisite *lamba mena* of *landibe* silk were worn by royalty and others of high influence; they could wear grave cloths with impunity because they were considered immortal. Such *lambas* have been copied by entrepeneurs as high-value fashion items for the international market, thus putting further pressure on supply. Yet production remains in villagers' hands whereas mulberry silk is produced by government-backed co-operatives.

When the Malagasy were asked why they build such huge stone tombs when they are content to live in mud and wattle houses, the reply was 'But when you're dead you're dead for a lot longer than when you're alive!' Similarly, I suppose, as an ancestor you'd appreciate the most durable of clothing – a silk shroud from the *landibe*.

If you're interested in visiting silk-weaving centres see pages 204 and 163.

mouth. If you prefer unsweetened white coffee it's best to bring your own powdered milk.

The locally grown tea is very weak, the best quality being reserved for export. A nice alternative is *citronelle*, lemon-grass tea, which is widely available.

Warning If you are travelling on a prepaid packaged tour, you may be disconcerted to find that you are charged for coffee and tea along with drinks. These beverages count as 'extras' in Madagascar.

Smoking

The Malagasy are enthusiastic smokers and non-smoking restaurants, or sections in restaurants, are a rarity. Sebastian Bulmer, a smoker, reports: 'Some readers may find it helpful to be able to differentiate between genuine Marlboro Lights and the counterfeit versions that proliferate; the latter have white filters and 'five miles' written along the side of the pack.'

HANDICRAFTS AND WHAT TO BUY

You can buy just about everything in the handicrafts line in Madagascar. Most typical of the country are woodcarvings, raffia work (in amazing variety), crocheted and embroidered table-cloths and clothes, leather goods, carved zebu horn, *Antaimoro* paper (with embedded dried flowers) and so on. The choice is almost limitless, and it can all be seen in the artisans' market (Marché Artisanal) and other handicrafts markets and shops in Antananarivo and throughout the country.

In the south you can buy attractive heavy silver bracelets that are traditionally worn by men. In Tana, and the east and north (Nosy Be), you will be offered vanilla pods, peppercorns, cloves and other spices, and honey.

Do not buy products from endangered species. That includes tortoiseshell (turtle shell), snake skins (now crocodiles are farmed commercially, their skins may be sold legally), shells and coral and, of course, live animals. Butterflies are farmed commercially so buying mounted specimens is permitted. Also prohibited are endemic plants, fossils and any genuine article of funerary art. To tell turtle shell from zebu horn, hold it up to the light: turtle shell is semi-transparent.

To help stamp out the sale of endangered animal products, tourists should make their feelings – and the law – known. If, for instance, you are offered tortoise or turtle shell, tell the vendor it is *interdit*; and to push the point home you could say it is *fady* for you to buy such a thing.

The luggage weight-limit when leaving Madagascar is normally 20kg – bear this in mind when doing your shopping.

If you want to buy Malagasy craft items after your return home (to Britain) ask for a copy of Discover Madgascar's catalogue (tel: 0208 995 3529 or email: info@discovermadagascar.co.uk). In the USA, try Mad Imports (see page 153).

Semi-precious stones

Madagascar is a rewarding place for gem hunters, with citrin, tourmaline, and beryl inexpensive and easy to find. The solitaire sets using these stones are typical and most attractive. The centre for gems is traditionally Antsirabe but they are for sale in many highland towns, and now Ilakaka, the town that has sprung up at the centre of the sapphire rush, is the main hub. If you buy uncut stones bear in mind the cost of having them cut at home, and the additional expense of having them made into jewellery.

THE MUSIC OF MADAGASCAR: A BRIEF INTRODUCTION

Ian A Anderson

The music of Madagascar is like the island itself – owing many things to other parts of the world, but unique.

The Malagasy are very fond of harmony singing, varying from Polynesian style (the Merina) to almost East African on the west coast. Traditional musical instruments include the celebrated *valiha*, a member of the zither family with 21 strings stretched lengthways all around the circumference of a hollow bamboo tube (there's also a box variety called the *marovany*), the *sodina*, an end-blown flute; the *kabosy*, a small guitar with paired strings and partial frets; the *jejy voatavo* with a gourd resonator and two sets of strings on adjacent sides of the neck; the *lokanga bara*, a three-string fiddle; and a great variety of percussion instruments.

You'll also find most Western instruments, successfully adapted to local music. Visit Ambohimanga, for example, to hear one of several generations of blind accordion players. Catch one of the *hira gasy* troupes and they'll be using ancient brass instruments and clarinets. Visit a nightclub or a larger concert and a modern band such as Jaojoby, Mily Clement or Tianjama will have electric guitars, synthesisers, and kit drums and might play one of the wild Malagasy dance styles such as *salegy*, *balesa*, *watsa watsa* or *sega*. Malagasy music has also enjoyed a big explosion of outside interest in recent years. The artists who have gained the most success touring abroad since the mid '90s have been Tarika, Rajery, Jaojoby, accordeonist Regis Gizavo and guitarist D'Gary.

The local cassette market has greatly expanded in recent years, though tapes are of variable quality. There are now quite a few locally marketed CDs but again quality is an issue and many appear to be short-run CDRs. Malagasy music on record is still best purchased in Europe or North America where there is now a huge CD selection. A regularly updated Madagascar CD-ography can be found on the internet at www.frootsmag.com/content/madagascar/cdography/

The following are some currently available CDs

TARIKA: 10: Beasts, Ghosts & Dancing With History (Triloka/Artemis) *USA*
RAJERY: Volontany (Indigo/Label Bleu) *France*
JAOJOBY: Aza Arianao (Indigo /Label Bleu) *France*
REGIS GIZAVO: Samy Olombelo (Indigo /Label Bleu) *France*
D'GARY: Akata Meso (Indigo/Label Bleu) *France*
MONJA: Marovany (Cinq Planetes) *France*
VARIOUS: Tuléar Never Sleeps (Stern's/ Earthworks) *UK*
VARIOUS: Introducing Vakoka (Introducing/ World Music Network) *UK*

MUSIC

In recent years Malagasy music has become well known, with several Malagasy groups such as Tarika now touring internationally. Tarika's lead singer, Rasoanalvo Hanitrarivo (known as Hanitra) has many recordings. For more on Malagasy music see box above.

Finding good local music is a hit and miss affair when travelling. Often your best bet is to look out for posters advertising concerts. These are often put up near the *gare routière*.

COMMUNICATIONS: KEEPING IN TOUCH
Telephone
The phone service has improved enormously in the past two years. You can now buy phone cards for 25, 50, 100 and 150 units, costing from 10,000Fmg to 75,000Fmg, and use them for overseas calls from most public phone boxes (Publiphone). Only cream-coloured phones do international calls. Rates are much cheaper in the evenings after 22.00 and on Sundays.

The telephone code for Madagascar is 261 20 (+ town code + the number). Have this handy if you are asking someone from home to call you back.

Below are the phone codes for all of Madagascar (this information is repeated under the relevant town information).

Antananarivo (Tana)	22	Manakara	72
Antsirabe	44	Morondava	95
Antsiranana (Diego Suarez)	82	Moramanga	56
Farafangana	72	Nosy Be	86
Fianarantsoa	75	Sambava	88
Ile Sainte Marie	57	Taolagnaro (Fort Dauphin)	92
Mahajanga (Majunga)	62	Toamasina (Tamatave)	53
Maintirano	69	Toliara (Tuléar)	94

Cellphones
Cellphones (mobile phones) are very popular in Madagascar. Bart Snyers, a GSM engineer, sent me this useful information: 'Before we left, I learned that Madagascar has a GSM network so I was eager to find out how well it works there. I also found out that our Belgian GSM operator had a partnership with Madacom, so I would be able to use my own GSM in Madagascar. As you may know, calling with your own GSM in a foreign country is called "roaming" and is only possible if your own operator has some sort of partnership with the operator from the foreign country. It appeared to work very well. We could phone home, send/receive SMS, check our voicemail in all major cities we visited (Tana, Diego, Fianarantsoa, Antsirabe) and probably some more can be added to this list.

'Strange it works so well in a country where the *Route National* is no more than a dirt road at several places.'

Mail
The mail service is reasonably efficient; letters take about two weeks to reach Europe and a little longer to North America. Stamps are quite expensive and postcards do not always arrive (some postal workers prefer to steam off the stamps and chuck the cards). The smaller post offices often run out of stamps, but some hotels sell them.

Courier service
Colis Express hooks up with DHL. There is an office in Tana (see page 182) and in all the large towns.

Internet
Cybercafés are opening in the capital and all major towns and tourist centres. The prices vary, depending on the competition: 350Fmg per minute in Fianarantsoa, but 1,000Fmg per minute in Manakara.

MISCELLANEOUS
Tipping
I (and even *vazaha* residents) find this an impossible subject on which to give coherent advice. Yet it is the one that consistently causes anxiety in travellers. The problem is you have to balance up the expectation of the tip recipient – who is probably used to generous tippers – and the knowledge of local wages.

Some tipping is relatively simple: a service charge is added to most restaurant meals so tipping is not strictly necessary though waiters in tourist hotels now expect it. About 10% is ample. Taxi drivers should not expect a tip, though you may want to add something for exceptional service.

The most manipulative people are baggage handlers, because they usually catch you before you are wised up to Madagascar, and are masters at the disappointment act. So before you give a dollar to the doorman for carrying your bag from the taxi to the hotel lobby, bear in mind the average earnings of a Malagasy labourer. As one expat pointed out (a few years ago but it won't have changed much): 'Not many Malagasy earn more than 25,000Fmg per week (that's about £3/US$5). A good brick carrier in Tana can manage 18 bricks a time on his head and is paid 5Fmg per brick – so they have to carry 500 bricks before they earn 10 pence.' That said, a dollar is easily found (by you) and easily spent (by them) so in a stressful situation you might as well take the easy way out.

The hardest tipping question is how much to pay guides, drivers … people who have spent several days with you and given excellent service. Here I err on the generous side, because I am coming back, because the tour operator I work for needs to maintain good relations, and because these people are accustomed to generous tips. So I generally tip about 25,000–35,000Fmg a day. With devaluation, guides will expect considerably more.

Where it is essential not to over-tip is when travelling off the beaten track, where you could be setting a very dangerous precedent. It can cause problems for *vazaha* that follow who are perhaps doing research or conservation work and who cannot afford to live up to these new expectations.

Electrical equipment
The voltage in Madagascar is 220. Outlets (where they exist) take 2-pin round plugs. If you use a 3-pin fused plug plus adapter, bring a spare fuse for the plug.

Business hours
Most businesses open 08.00–12.00 and 14.00–18.00. Banks are open 08.00–16.00, and are closed weekends and the afternoon before a holiday.

Television
Posh hotels have CNN but the local station shows BBC World Service news at 09.00.

PUBLIC HOLIDAYS
The Malagasy take their holidays seriously. In every town and village there will be a parade with speeches and an air of festivity. 'New Year was celebrated throughout the night, and on New Year's Day everyone paraded their new clothes through the streets in a Malagasy version of an Easter Parade. New Year parties were held by every conceivable organisation during the next two months.' (Bryan and Eve Pinches)

Official holidays

January 1	New Year's Day
March 29	Commemoration of 1947 rebellion
Easter Monday (movable)	
May 1	Labour Day
Ascension Day (movable)	
Whit Monday (movable)	
June 26	Independence Day
August 15	Feast of the Assumption
November 1	All Saints' Day
December 25	Christmas Day
December 30	Republic Day

When these holidays fall on a Thursday, Friday will be tacked on to the weekend. Banks and other businesses often take a half-day holiday before the official holiday.

Madagascar and You

Tsihy be lambanana ny ambanilantra
'All who live under the sky are woven together like one big mat.'

Malagasy saying

RESPONSIBLE TOURISM

In recent years there has been a welcome shift of attitude among visitors to developing countries from 'What can I get out of this trip?' to 'How can I give something back?' This chapter addresses those issues, and suggests ways in which you can help this marvellous, but sometimes tragic, country.

They do things differently there

I once caught our Malagasy guide scowling at himself in the mirror. When I teased him he said: 'As a Malagasy man I smile a lot. I can see that if I want to work with tourists I must learn to frown.' He knew that the group considered him insufficiently assertive. Tolerance and the fear of causing offence is an integral part of Malagasy social relationships. So if a tourist expresses anger in a way that is entirely appropriate in his or her own culture, it may be counter-productive in Madagascar. It is deeply unsettling to the person at the receiving end who often giggles in response, thus exacerbating the situation. If you are patient, pleasant and keep your temper, your problem will be solved more quickly.

Avoid being too dogmatic in conversation (you do not have exclusivity of the truth). Make use of 'perhaps' and 'maybe'. Be excessive in your thanks. The Malagasy are very polite; we miss the nuances by not understanding the language. Body language, however, is easier to learn. For instance, 'Excuse me, may I come through?' is indicated by a stooping posture and an arm extended forward. Note how often it is used.

Part of responsible tourism is relinquishing some of our normal comforts. Consider this statistic: fuelwood demand in Madagascar has far outstripped supply. Wood and charcoal are the main sources of energy, and the chief users are city dwellers. In rural areas, tourist establishments may be the main consumers. Do you still feel that hot water is essential in your hotel?

One of the keys to responsible tourism is ensuring that as much as possible of the money you spend on your holiday remains in Madagascar. Independent travellers should try, whenever possible, to stay at small hotels run by Malagasy. Tourists on an organised tour will probably find themselves in a foreign-owned hotel, but can do their bit by buying handicrafts and donating to local charities.

Madagascar's shortcomings can be infuriating. Sometimes a little reflection reveals the reasons behind the failure to produce the expected service, but sometimes you just have to tell yourself 'Well, that's the way it is'. After all, you are not going to be able to change Madagascar, but Madagascar may change you.

TREAD SOFTLY...
Alasdair Harris – Blue Ventures

Madagascar's coastal environments comprise some of the most ecologically sensitive areas of the country. Throughout their trip visitors should be aware of the intrinsic effect that their presence and activities will have on local habitats. We encourage you to plan your holiday in a way that minimises your impact on the environment.

When trekking, try to avoid sensitive habitats and vegetation types, reducing the impact of your movement and access to and from campsites. All waste should be sorted and disposed of sensibly. In arid environments such as the southwest, freshwater use should be kept to a minimum.

In the water, swimmers, snorkellers and divers should avoid all physical contact with corals and other marine life. Divers should take care to avoid any damage to reefs, maintaining good buoyancy control at all times in order to avoid accidental contact with the reef, or stirring up bottom sediment.

In coastal hotels and restaurants, seafood is commonly caught to order, regardless of the sustainability of the catch. In some tourist areas it is not uncommon to see critically endangered species such as the humphead or Napolean wrasse served up in a restaurant kitchen. Shellfish should not be bought out of season, since this can have devastating consequences on the reproductive success of species.

The marine curios trade is equally driven by tourism, and hard as it may seem, visitors should refrain from purchasing all forms of shells that have been gleaned from reefs. In Toliara alone, almost 150 species of gastropods are exploited for the ornamental shell trade. Several of these species – notably the magnificent helmet shell and the cowries – are now threatened with extinction. Similarly, the exploitation of sea turtles is increasingly focused at the tourist market, turtle shells now fetching staggering prices in markets and *bijouteries*. After the day's catch has been brought in, it's an all-too-common sight to see the lines of gasping turtles baking slowly in the sun in fishing villages adjacent to tourist areas.

Photography

Lack of consideration when taking photos is perhaps the most common example of irresponsible tourist behaviour – one that each of us has probably been guilty of at some time. It is so easy to take a sneak photo without first establishing contact with the person, so easy to say we'll send a print of the picture and then not get round to it, so easy to stroll into a market or village thinking what a wonderful photo it will make and forgetting that you are there to experience it.

The rules are not to take people's photos without permission, and to respect an answer of 'no'. Give consideration to the offence caused by photographing the destitute. Be cautious about paying your way to a good photo; often a smile or a joke will work as well, and sets no precedent. People love to receive pictures of themselves. If you are travelling on an organised tour your guide is sure to visit that area again so can deliver the prints that you send to him. If you are travelling independently write down the addresses and honour your promise.

Philip Thomas writes: 'A Malagasy, for whom a photograph will be a highly treasured souvenir, will remember the taking of the photograph and your promise to send them a copy, a lot longer than you might. Their disappointment in those who say one thing and do another is great, so if you think you might not get it together to send the photograph then do not say that you will.'

A responsible attitude to photography is so much more fun! And it results in better pictures. It involves taking some time getting to know the subject of your proposed photo: making a purchase, perhaps, or practising your Malagasy greetings.

'PLEASE SEND ME A PHOTO'

It is not always easy to keep a promise. Of course we intend to send a print after someone posed cheerfully for the photo, but after we get home there are so many other things to do, so many addresses on torn-out pages of exercise books. I now honour my promises. Here's why.

I was checking my group in to a Nosy Be hotel when the bellboy asked if he could speak to me. He looked nervous, so suspecting a problem with the bookings I asked him to wait until everyone was in their rooms.

When we were alone he cleared his throat and recited what was obviously a carefully prepared speech: 'You are Mrs Hilary Bradt. Ten years ago you gave your business card to the lady at Sambava Voyages and she gave it to a schoolboy who wrote to you. But you were away so your mother answered the letter. She wrote many letters. My name is Murille and I am that boy. And now I want to talk to you about Janet Cross and Brian Cross and Andrew and…' There followed a list of every member of my family. As I listened, incredulous, I remembered the original letter. 'We love England strongly,' he wrote, 'especially London, Buckingham, Grantham, Dover…' I remembered passing it to my mother saying I was too busy for such a correspondence but maybe she'd like to write. She kept it up for several years, answering questions such as 'How often does Mrs Hilary go to Grantham and Dover?' and she sent a photo of the family gathering at Christmas, naming every member on the back of the photo.

This brought an indignant letter from a cousin. 'I have seen your photo. It is a very nice one. I asked Murille if he would lend it for one day only because we all study English so we must have photo of English people more to improve this language, but he refused me strongly because they are only his friends not mine…'

Murille brought out the treasured photo. It had suffered from the constant handling and tropical heat and was peeling at the edges. He wanted to trim it, he explained, 'but if I do I will have to cut off a bit of your mother's beautiful chair and I can't do that.'

Later that year I sent Murille a photo album filled with family photos. I never heard from him again – that's the way it is in Madagascar – but the story has a twist to its tail. I returned to Sambava 12 years after the original visit, and found myself addressing a classroom of eager adult students of English and their local teacher. Searching for something interesting to say, I told them about the time I was last in their town and the series of letters between Murille and my mother. And I told them about the cousin who also wrote to her. 'I think his name was Patrice,' I said. The teacher looked up. 'I'm Patrice. Yes, I remember writing to Janet Cross…'

Beggars

Whether or not to give to professional beggars is up to you. I believe that it is wrong to give to the little ragamuffin children who follow you around because it is better to give to the charities (see *How you can help*, page 149) that work with them. Actually, the same applies to all age-groups. My policy is to give to the elderly and I also single out 'beggar days' when I fill my pockets with small change and give to every beggar who looks needy and over school age. And if I make some trickster's day, so be it.

It is important to make up your mind about beggars before you hit the streets so you can avoid standing there riffling through a conspicuously fat wallet for a low-denomination bill.

The effects of tourism on local people

The impact of foreigners on the Malagasy was noted as long ago as 1669 when a visitor commented that formerly the natives were deeply respectful of white men but were changed 'by the bad examples which the Europeans have had, who glory in the sin of luxury in this country…'.

In developing countries tourism has had profound effects on the inhabitants, some good, some bad. Madagascar seems to me to be a special case – more than any other country I've visited it inspires a particular devotion and an awareness of its fragility, both environmental and cultural. Wildlife is definitely profiting from the attention given it and from the emphasis on ecotourism. For the people, however, the blessings may be very mixed: some able Malagasy have found jobs in the tourist industry, but for others the impact of tourism has meant that their cultural identity has been eroded, along with some of their dignity and integrity. Village antagonisms are heightened when one or two people gain the lion's share of tourist revenue and gifts, leading in one case to murder, and hitherto honest folk have lapsed into corruption or thievery.

Giving presents

This is a subject often discussed among experienced travellers who cannot agree on when, if ever, a present is appropriate. Most feel that giving presents is appropriate only when it is in exchange for a service. Many tourists to the developing world, however, pack sweets or pens 'for the children' as automatically as their sunglasses and insect repellent.

My repeat visits to Madagascar over the course of 28 years have shaped my own view: that giving is usually done for self-gratification rather than generosity, and that one thoughtless act can change a village irreparably. I have seen the shyly inquisitive children of small communities turn into tiresome beggars; I have seen the warm interaction between visitor and local turn into mutual hostility; I have seen intelligent, ambitious young men turn into scoundrels. What I haven't sorted out in my mind is how much this matters. Thieves and scoundrels make a good living and are probably happier than they were in their earlier state of dire poverty. Should we be imposing our cultural views on the Malagasy? I don't know.

But giving does not have to be in the form of material gifts. 'Giving something back' has a far broader meaning. We should never underestimate our value as sheer entertainment in an otherwise routine life. We can give a smile, or a greeting in Malagasy. And we can learn from people who in so many ways are richer than us. See pages 33 and 420 for more thoughts on the subject.

More and more…

Visitors who have spent some time in Madagascar and have befriended a particular family often find themselves in the 'more and more and more' trap. The foreigner begins by expressing appreciation of the friendship and hospitality he or she received by sending a gift to the family. A request for a more expensive gift follows. And another one, until the luckless *vazaha* feels that she is seen as a bottomless cornucopia of goodies. The reaction is a mixture of guilt and resentment.

Understanding the Malagasy viewpoint may help you to come to terms with these requests. You may be considered as part of the extended family, and family members often help support those who are less well-off. You will almost certainly be thought of as fabulously wealthy, so it is worth dispelling this myth by giving some prices for familiar foodstuffs at home – a kilo of rice, for instance, or a mango. Explain that you don't have servants, that you pay so much for rent, and that you have a family of your own that needs your help. Don't be afraid to say 'no' firmly.

...and the most

I know two couples, one in America and the other in Australia, who have translated their wish to help the Malagasy into airfares to their home country. This is not to be undertaken lightly – the red tape from both governments is horrendous – but is hugely rewarding for all concerned.

Off the beaten path

Travellers venturing well off the beaten path will want to do their utmost to avoid offending the local people, who are usually extremely warm and hospitable.

Unfortunately, with the many *fady* prohibitions and beliefs varying from area to area and village to village, it is impossible to know exactly how to behave, although *vazaha* and other outsiders are exempt from the consequences of infringing a local *fady*.

Sometimes, in very remote areas, Malagasy will react in sheer terror at the sight of a white person. This probably stems from their belief in *mpakafo* (pronounced 'mpakafoo'), the 'stealer of hearts'. These pale-faced beings are said to wander around at night ripping out people's hearts. So it is not surprising that rural Malagasy often do not like going out after dark – and it's a problem if you are looking for a guide. The arrival of a pale-faced being in their village is understandably upsetting. In the southeast it is the *mpangalak'aty*, the 'taker of the liver', who is feared.

Villages are governed by the *Fokonolona*, or People's Assembly. On arrival at a village you should ask for the *Président du Fokontany*. Although traditionally this was the village elder, these days it is more likely to be someone who speaks French – perhaps the schoolteacher. He will show you where you can sleep (sometimes a hut is kept free for guests, sometimes someone will be moved out for you). You will usually be provided with a meal. Now travellers have penetrated most rural areas, you will be expected to pay. If the *Président* is not available, ask for *Ray aman-dreny*, an elder.

Philip Thomas, a social anthropologist who has conducted research in the rural southeast, points out several ways that tourists may unwittingly cause offence. 'People should adopt the common courtesy of greeting the Malagasy in their own language. *Salama*, *manahoana* and *veloma* are no more difficult to say than their French equivalents.

'*Vazaha* sometimes refuse food and hospitality, putting up tents and cooking their own food. But in offering you a place to sleep and food to eat the Malagasy are showing you the kindness they extend to any visitor or stranger, and to refuse is a rejection of their hospitality and sense of humanity. You may think you are inconveniencing them, and this is true, but they would prefer that than if you keep to yourselves as though you were not people (in the widest sense) like them. It may annoy you that it is virtually impossible to get a moment away from the gaze of the

Malagasy, but you are there to look at them and their activities anyway, so why should there not be a mutual exchange? Besides, you are far more fascinating to them than they are to you, for their view of the world is not one shaped by mass education and access to international images supplied by television.

'It is perfectly acceptable to give a gift of money in return for help. Gifts of cash are not seen by the Malagasy as purchases and they themselves frequently give them. Rather, you give as a sign of your appreciation and respect. But beware of those who may try to take advantage of your position as a foreigner (and you may find these in even the remotest spot), those who play on your lack of knowledge of language and custom, and their perception of you as extremely wealthy (as of course you are by their standards).'

Valerie and John Middleton, who have travelled more adventurously and successfully in Madagascar than anyone else I know, add this advice: 'In three long visits to Madagascar we have never had a bad experience anywhere (except perhaps the traffic policeman in Toliara and the miserable police at Ivato Airport). We have, however, noted several people who have not fared so well and feel that we could possibly pass on some advice for anyone wanting to go off the beaten path.

1 To prevent misunderstanding always take a guide with you at least for communication as many isolated peoples speak only Malagasy.
2 Always introduce yourself to the local *'Président'* and explain why you are in his village or even just passing through – you will never cease to be amazed at how helpful they wish to be once your purpose is fully understood and perhaps even more importantly the authority of his backing confers a considerable degree of protection in that area (it does always help to have a purpose).
3 Always defer to his advice.
4 Find out about local *'fady'* before doing anything'.

I can vouch for the wisdom of this advice: see box below.

AN ADVENTURE IN THE SOUTH

I wanted a bit of adventure. My group and I were staying in a comfortable hotel in Anakao and had done most of the usual tourist excursions. I thought it would be interesting to explore an area of mangroves a few kilometres south which I'd heard about. Our hotel managed to get hold of an impressive open-topped army lorry and we set off in some style: nine tourists and Rija, our guide from Tana.

The track because less and less distinct and it was soon clear that the driver really didn't know where he was going – and why should he? My request was well out of the ordinary. Then we became aware of a lot of shouting and a man wearing only a loin-cloth and brandishing a spear caught up, panting and sweating. Rija translated: 'He wants to know what we're doing here. *Vazaha* don't belong here, he says, they should stay in Anakao. He wants us to go and speak to the *Président* of the village.' We headed instead for a beach, drawing up at a scene that could have come from an illustrated bible. A small group of people were gathered on the dazzling white sand. A few goats browsed on the sparse vegetation; one was being held down by a group of boys while a man performed some sort of surgery on it. A group of women were clustered round a well, watching as a child drew up buckets of water which they gave to the goats and a cow or two.

We greeted the villagers and walked along the beach to the mangroves which were as beautiful and interesting as expected. We stayed perhaps two hours, swimming, picnicking, and exploring. When we returned to our vehicle

HOW YOU CAN HELP

There are several ways in which you can make a positive contribution. By making a donation to a local project you can help the people – and the wildlife – without creating new problems. Charities based in Tana are described on pages 154 and 163. All of these welcome visitors and donations.

My initiation to my 'giving something back' favourite was over ten years ago when I met a couple of English teachers, Jill and Charlie Hadfield, who told me how they has started The Streetkids Project. Visiting a charity run by the Sisters of the Good Shepherd in Tana, they could see where a little money could go a long way. The nuns run – amongst other things – a preparatory school for the very poor. When the children are ready to go on to state school, however, the parents can't afford the £15 a year they must pay for registration, uniform and books, so the children were condemned to return to the streets as beggars. The Streetkids Project raises money to continue their education and is now administered in Britain through Money for Madagascar. See pages 150 and 163 for more information.

The organisations and charities listed below are all working with the people of Madagascar, and, by extension, habitat conservation. Most of them are very small, run by dedicated volunteers who would welcome even modest donations. Other charities work specifically for wildlife. What better way to channel your empathy for Madagascar and its problems?

UK charities assisting Madagascar
People
Andrew Lees Trust Tel: 0044207 4249256; www.andrewleestrust.org.uk. Set up in 1995, this charity helped to launch and support training at the Libanona Ecology Centre. Named after the international environmental campaigner Andrew Lees, the Trust develops social and environmental education projects in the south, specifically to increase access to information and education that empowers local populations to improve food security,

we found the entire village was waiting for us. The driver explained the situation to Rija who told us that they were not going to allow us to reboard the lorry. The spokesman for the village was a distinguished-looking man wearing a hat made, apparently, from the hump of a zebu. Apart from that he was bare-chested, as were all the other men. The air crackled with hostility. We sat down to listen to the interchange between our driver and the headman. Rija, being Merina and a woman, would not have been allowed to negotiate. For the first fifteen minutes the male villagers were very, very angry, and very eloquent. And very loud. At intervals they pointed at us accusingly. Tensions rose even higher when they suggested that we give them food and water. They pointed to the large, bulging bag we carried with us. Inside was snorkelling gear. Our driver was superb. He kept calm and distanced himself from the *vazaha*. He was only following orders, he said. After about half an hour the tension suddenly relaxed. A few smiles broke out. Hands were shaken and we made out way to the lorry.

This incident took place perhaps 15km away from one of the most popular resorts in southern Madagascar, yet it was as if we had travelled back a couple of centuries by time machine. It was indeed an adventure but I am ashamed that I let it happen. For so many years I have written about the importance of getting local approval when travelling off the beaten track in this complex island but had not heeded my own advice. How fortunate we were that we had a competent local driver who could get us out of the mess I'd got us into.

reduce poverty and manage natural resources more sustainably. Project Radio, recently shortlisted for the UNESCO international prize for rural development communications, works with a network of 16 local partners and 14 radio stations across the south to produce and broadcast vital information and educational radio programmes to isolated rural communities. A sister programme, Project Energy, has trained women in the south to build over 32,000 wood-efficient stoves that reduce domestic fuel consumption by over 50% and help reduce pressure on forest resources. Tree planting follows the stove trainings and over 1,800 trees have already started in a drought area.

Azafady Studio 7, 1a Beethoven Street, London, W10 4LG; tel: 020 8960 6629; fax: 020 8962 0126; email: mark@azafady.org, or azafady@easynet.co.uk; www.madagascar.co.uk. Works mainly in the southeast of Madagascar, aiming to break the cycle of poverty and environmental degradation so apparent in that area. Projects include tree planting and facilitation of small enterprises such as village market gardens, bee farming, basket making, and fruit drying. They fund a Health and Sanitation Programme to improve access to clean drinking water and basic healthcare. Conservation Projects include studies of the remaining littoral forest in southeast Madagascar and of endangered loggerhead turtle populations. The also run the Pioneer scheme for volunteers (see page 91).

The Dodwell Trust 16 Lanark Mansions, Pennard Road, London W12 8DT; email: dodwell@madagascar.freeserve.co.uk; www.dodwell-trust.org. A British-registered charity founded by Christina Dodwell ten years ago, running a radio project designed to help rural villagers, through the production and broadcast of a drama and magazine radio series for family health, AIDS prevention, poverty issues, and environment (similar to *The Archers* on BBC Radio). The Trust has set up 1000 listener-groups with donated wind-up/solar radios, to send back useful information and take part in programmes. In collaboration with the Ministry of Education in Tana, the Trust also sends any donated computers from UK to Madagascar, and assists with the twinning of schools in UK. The team welcome Gap-year and other UK volunteers; see page 98 or website for details. In 2004 the Trust began an initiative to build a new orphanage. The site near Tana has been obtained but the building will depend on public donations which can be made through The Dodwell Trust (who charge no fee). Just mark your envelope 'to help build the orphanage'.

Feedback Madagascar Ashfield House, by Balloch, Dunbartonshire G83 8NB ; tel/fax 01852 500657; email: jamie@feedbackmadagascar.org. Address in Madagascar: Lot IB 65 Bis Isoraka, Antananarivo 101; tel/fax: 261 20 22 638 11; email: feedback@simicro.mg. A small, but highly effective Scottish charity which bases its activities on feedback from the local Malagasy who identify and agree on development and conservation projects. These have included irrigation dams, the rebuilding of a school and hospital, the creation of a 'school reserve' near Ranomafana, a project to help communities to manage sustainably 25,000ha of rainforest in Ambohimahamasina, an agricultural training centre and the silk project near Ambalavao. Currently they are working with the Malagasy organisation Ny Tanintsika on new silk programmes, women's health, the training of family-planning providers and community health workers, social action and awareness campaigns through adult literacy programmes, support to schools on health and environment integrated activities, and villages' hygiene/toilet promotion campaigns.

Money for Madagascar LLwyncelyn Isaf, Carregsawdde, Llangadog SA19 9BY; email: theresa@mfmcar.fsnet.co.uk; www.moneyformadagascar.org. This long-established and well-run small charity funds rural health and agricultural projects and supports deprived groups in urban areas. It sends funds on a regular basis to The Streetkids Project described on page 163 and to Akany Avoko (page 154). I have found this a much easier way of making a donation than transferring the money direct to Madagascar. The staff are all volunteers and they don't even have an office, so the overheads are very low. Thus you can be confident that almost all the money you give will go direct to the

SNAKES ALIVE!
Bill Love

The 2003 trip was unforgettable! I once again contacted 'my' little school in Ankify, c/o of Le Baobab Hotel nearby, to arrange a cultural visit for my group during our stay. We visited the two-room school on the morning of November 4. Monsieur Farajao, a teacher, helped us exchange questions and answers about life in the USA and Madagascar. Everyone with me brought a half-suitcase full of school supplies, sports gear, and toys and games to donate. These went a long way, even among the 160+ school kids ranging from six to 15 years old.

As a special treat this year I also brought in a six-foot long ground boa, the largest kind of snake found in Madagascar. Our guide, Angelin Razafimanantsoa, found it the previous evening and knew I'd want to show the kids. I kept it hidden for most of the hour, saving it for the grand finale of a live *Show & Tell* style 'biology lesson'. That turned out to be the most memorable part of all!

The kids went wild when I suddenly lifted the four-inch thick snake out of an Eau Vive box on the floor. Some ran for the door while others leaped out of open windows. But soon the whole class was back crowding around to touch the tail end of the huge *do* (boa). Malagasy boas are usually very mellow, but just to be safe, I held its head up and out of reach just in case the commotion upset it. That proved to be wise because the snake quickly tired of the handling, sunk its teeth into my armpit, and held on. I shielded the bite from view and tried not to wince as I continued to smile and allow everyone to quench their curiosity. I don't think anyone realized what was actually happening, which is good because I certainly didn't want to give anyone a bad impression of this beautiful and essentially harmless local snake that was only reacting to the hundreds of hands touching it.

I've made visiting *L'Ecole Primaire Publique d'Ankify* an annual event since I always return to this magical area with my tours. Besides Madagascar's unique animals, the people are a true treasure that I proudly include in interactions as often as possible as we rove the countryside seeing and photographing nature.

Bill Love is a photographer, writer, and tour operator (www.bluechameleon.org) who regularly runs eco-tours to Madagascar. The northwest of Madagascar, including Ambanja, is his favourite stopover area. This is how he is 'giving something back' to the region.

project you want to support. Write the cheque to Money for Madagascar but enclose a note saying where you want it to be sent. MFM also provide funds for cyclone relief or other natural disasters.

Population Concern Studio 325, Highgate Studios, 53–79 Highgate Rd, London NW5 1TL; tel: 020 7241 8500; fax: 0207267 6788; email: info@populationconcern.org.uk; www.populationconcern.org.uk. 'Working for the right to reproductive heathcare worldwide.' At present this organisation, relatively new to Madagascar, is working in Toliara and Antsiranana on a variety of initiatives to improve the sexual health of young people. They also aim to reduce the incidence of teengage pregnancies.

MOSS c/o Oliver Backhouse, Forge Cottage, Main St, Kirkby Overblow, North Yorks HG3 1HF; email: obackhouse@doctors.org.uk. MOSS (Madagascan Organisation for

BLINDNESS IN MADAGASCAR
Jono Norris, Oliver and Camilla Backhouse

In 1993 the Madagascan Organisation for Saving Sight (MOSS) was set up as a registered charity aiming to improve the quality of eye healthcare in Madagascar. Work began with a survey looking at the causes of blindness and partial sight. Results, as with similar developing countries, revealed that 80% of visual impairment was either treatable or preventable by cheap, effective sustainable means. This gave us the impetus to help develop the eye programme.

One of the major causes of blindness is unoperated cataracts which number an approximate 100,000 at the present time. Recent figures are escalating, suggesting that 15,000 new cataracts are developing every year while under 5,000 are being operated on.

One of the major developments in ophthalmic healthcare has been the coordination of national services by the Lions Clubs in conjunction with the state health department and other charities creating the 'Lions Sight First Madagascar'. This has provided the country with a harmonised systematic effort to deal with eye healthcare. In the last six years the number of Malagasy ophthalmologists providing services has doubled, although there are still less than two ophthalmologists per million of population. There has been a real emphasis on Madagascar training its own doctors to provide services rather than recruiting those from overseas providing more temporary solutions. Eye doctors have been funded to travel to mainland Africa to attend teaching programmes. Public information campaigns have been to set up to highlight cataracts as a major, preventable cause of blindness, highlighting successful

Saving Sight) was set up in 1993, following a year's work by ophthalmologist Oliver Backhouse and his wife, when a survey showed that, like most other developing countries, 80% of visual impairment was either treatable or preventable by cheap, effective and sustainable means. MOSS was set up to help develop ophthalmic and general health services in Madagascar, where 300,000 people suffer blindness. MOSS is a small but very active charity with a considerable number of achievements to their credit. The charity has provided one operating microscope for use in opthalmic fieldwork and is seeking funds for a second one. See box above.

Valiha High FMS, PO Box 337, London N4 ITW; www.frootsmag.com (scroll down to the bottom of the home page). This is not a registered charity but a project to maintain the musical traditions of Madagascar, instigated by the leader of the world-acclaimed Malagasy group, Tarika. Hanitrarivo Rasoanaivo was depressed at the influence of foreign cultures on the young people of Madagascar and the violent or pornographic videos which are now their preferred entertainment. The project, set up in 1997, has been very successful. Students are forming their own *valiha* groups, but their enthusiasm for the instrument is creating its own problem – they are wearing out and need to be replaced! A small donation goes a long way towards the cost of buying the instruments, training teachers and for prizes for competitions.

Water Aid A UK-based NGO, which works to help poor communities gain access to drinking water, safe sanitation and good hygiene. In Madagascar, where the majority of the population has none of these vital services, they have been working since 1999 with local partner organisations and the national government. In the highlands they support programmes in rural parts of Antananarivo and Fianarantsoa provinces, as well as parts of Toliara and the city of Toamasina. If you would like to know more, please contact wateraidmg@dts.mg, write to BP6082, Antananarivo, or visit the website at www.wateraid.org.

operations and 'spreading the word'. Although field trips are undertaken, many people who could benefit from treatment still do not attend due to the familiar reasons of poor communication and transport, the price of medication, the fear of going to an unknown place, the reliance on local healers and poor information concerning available services. Lions and MOSS hope to continue reducing these barriers to health care and cut the numbers of needlessly blind.

MOSS itself has helped to fund various projects in the last few years. In conjunction with the Dodwell Trust, Radio Sarivolana, a radio programme, was set up to broadcast to several million listeners using soap-operas to make key messages to educate the rural populations on a wide range of issues including eye, child and reproductive health. Wind-up radios have been instrumental in enabling this project to function. Last year MOSS organised a large Malagasy Ball raising funds to buy an ophthalmic laser machine – the first of its kind in Madagascar – to improve people's vision after eye surgery.

The following true story gives the reader an idea of what these services are up against, but also illustrates the old adage that prevention is better than cure; one mother that we came across earned her income from selling carrots that she grew (a good source of vitamin A) but did not give them to her children to eat, as their stomachs were full of rice three times a day. Unfortunately four of her nine children were blind as a result of a lack of this vital vitamin. One of the achievements of MOSS was to launch a 'Vitamin A eye game' to help reduce the number of these blind children. We took out four thousand games in 2002, this has proved very popular and we hope successful.

MOSS can continue to be successful only with your kind support.

Mad Imports 262 Court St, Suite 3, Brooklyn, NY 11231; tel: 718 802 9757; email: laurel@madimports.org; www.madimports.org. A socially responsible company that imports and sells handmade art and accessories from Madagascar. The sale of these products supports community and economic development in Malagasy communities. They work with individual and collective groups of artists to import fine quality handmade art and accessories for sale in the US. This enables families to gain economic independence.

Wildlife

Conservation International (USA) 1015 18th St NW, Washington DC, 20003, USA; www.conservation.org. Very active in Madagascar. Among other projects they help fund Ampijoroa Forest Reserve.

Durrell Wildife Conservation Trust Les Augres Manor, Trinity, Jersey JE3 5BP, Channel Islands, British Isles; tel: 01534 860000; fax 01534 860001; www.durrell.org. For full details of this non-profit organisation see box on pages 76–7.

World Wide Fund for Nature Av du Mont-blanc, 1196 Gland, Switzerland (International Office); Panda House, Weyside Park, Godalming, Surrey GU7 IXR, UK; 1250 24th St NW, Washington DC 20037-1175, USA; Aires Protégées, BP738, Antananarivo 101, Madagascar. www.wwf.org

Wildlife Conservation Society www.wcs.org. A US-based organisation based at the Bronx Zoo in New York City. The main focus of WCS's programme in Madagascar is the watershed of Antongil Bay, thought to contain over 50% of all Madagascar's plant and animal species. Other WCS projects are focusing on the radiated tortoise and its spiny forest habitat in the south, and on the Sahamalaza/Radama Islands region of the northwest.

AKANY AVOKO
Simon Kirby

Located 15 minutes' drive from Ivato Airport, on the road to Mahajanga, Akany Avoko is a Children's Home caring for over 120 abandoned and impoverished children.

For 40 years Akany Avoko has fed, clothed, educated and given a secure home to orphans, street kids, children from broken families, young people with disabilities, teenage girls on remand and teenaged mums with their babies. It is run by the Malagasy Church in co-operation with the Malagasy Government and is sustained solely by charitable donations and income-generating projects within the centre itself.

As well as providing food, shelter, schooling and primary healthcare to the children who live there, Akany Avoko works to ensure that the children are capable of supporting themselves in the future and also to provide environmental education, enabling future generations of Malagasy people to help both themselves and Madagascar's precious environment.

Examples of projects currently taking place at Akany Avoko include:

- Traditional craft production and screen-printing
- Environmental education
- Organic food growing
- Solar cooking
- Recycling/fuel efficiency
- Sustainable waste and water management (eg compost toilets, biogas, rainwater collection)
- Vocational training (including cookery, dressmaking, metal and wood workshops)

Traditional dance, sports, games, and fun are also very much part of the centre's weekly routine.

Visitors are welcome to come and visit Akany Avoko, to take a look at the environmental projects in progress or to meet some of the bright and exuberant children who live there. All donations (of any size) are much needed and much appreciated. There is also a shop selling Malagasy crafts and T-shirts produced by the children.

Please contact the centre by email or phone to arrange a visit (using the details below).

Contact details
Akany Avoko, BP29 Ambohidratrimo 105, Madagascar; tel 00216 20 22 44158
Irenee Rajaona Horne: horne@wanadoo.mg
Steve and Hardy Wilkinson: akany.avoko@malagasy.com

Organisations promoting responsible tourism
Center for Responsible Tourism 1765D Le Roy, Berkeley, CA 94709, USA; www.greenpages.org. Full title: The North America Coordinating Center for Responsible Tourism (NACCRT). Advocates just travel that respects and protects cultures and environments. Focuses on non-Western world. Works to eliminate the prostituting, pornography, and trafficking of children.

Tourism Concern Stapleton House, 277–281 Holloway Rd, London N7 8HN; tel: 020 7133 3330; fax: 020 7133 3331; email: info@tourismconcern.org.uk; www.tourismconcern.org.uk. With the slogan 'Putting people back in the picture', Tourism Concern 'promotes tourism that takes account of the rights and interests of those living in the world's tourist areas'. They put pressure on governments or companies which promote harmful tourism, run meetings and conferences, publish an informative and interesting newsletter and distribute the *Community Tourism Guide* (published by Earthscan).

Finally, if on your return to Britain you want to keep connections with Madagascar, how about joining the Anglo-Malagasy Society? The London consulate (page 82) can put you in touch with the membership secretary.

Part Two

The Guide

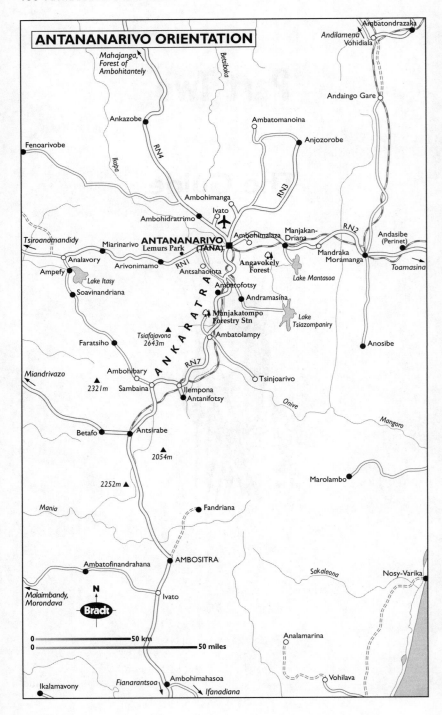

ANTANANARIVO ORIENTATION

Ambatondrazaka

Andilamena
Vohidiala

Mahajanga,
Forest of
Ambohitantely

Bestiboka

Andaingo Gare

Ankazobe

Ambatomanoina

Anjozorobe

Fenoarivobe

RN4

Ikopa

RN3

Ambohimanga

Ivato

Ambohidratrimo

Manjakan-
Driana

RN2

Andasibe
(Perinet)

Ambohimalaza

Tsiroanomandidy

ANTANANARIVO
(TANA)

Miarinarivo

Lemurs Park

Mandraka
Moramanga

Toamasina

Analavory

Arivonimamo

RN1

Antsahaointa

Angavokely
Forest

Ampefy

Lake Itasy

Lake Mantasoa

Soavinandriana

Ambatofotsy

Andramasina

Lake
Tsiazompaniry

ANKARATRA

Manjakatompo
Forestry Stn

Anosibe

Faratsiho

Tsiafajavona
2643m

Ambatolampy

Miandrivazo

Ambohibary

RN7

Tsinjoarivo

2321m

Sambaina

Ilempona
Antanifotsy

Onive

Mangoro

Betafo

Antsirabe

2054m

Marolambo

2252m

Mania

Fandriana

Ambatofinandrahana

AMBOSITRA

Sakaleona

Nosy-Varika

Malaimbandy,
Morondava

Ivato

N

Bradt

Analamarina

0   50 km
0   50 miles

Ikalamavony

Fianarantsoa

Ambohimahasoa

Vohilava

Ifanadiana

Antananarivo and Area

Looking down from the plane window as you approach Antananarivo you can see how excitingly different this country is from any of its near neighbours. Clusters of red clay houses and steepled churches stand isolated on the hilltops overlooking a mosaic of green and brown paddy fields. Old defence ditches, *tamboho*, form circles around villages or estates, and dotted in the empty countryside are the white concrete Merina tombs from where the dead will be exhumed in the *famadihana* ceremony.

Most people stay only a day or so in Tana, but there is plenty to see in the city and the surrounding Hauts Plateaux. A week would not be too long to experience the cultural, historical and natural sites which lie within a day's excursion of the capital. The Kingdom of Imerina thrived for over a century before French colonisation, so it is here that the rich and fascinating history and culture of the Merina people are best appreciated.

HISTORY

The recorded history of the Merina people (who are characterised by their Indonesian features) begins in the 1400s with a chief called Andriandraviravina. He is widely thought to have started the Merina dynasty that became the most powerful in Madagascar, eventually conquering much of the country.

Key monarchs in the rise of the Merina include Andrianjaka, who conquered a Vazimba town called Analamanga, built on a great rock thrusting above the surrounding plains. He renamed it Antananarivo and ordered his palace to be built on its highest point. With its surrounding marshland, ideal for rice production, and the security afforded by its high position, this was the perfect site for a Merina capital city.

In the 18th century there were two centres for the Merina kingdom, Antananarivo and Ambohimanga. The latter became the more important and around 1787 Ramboasalama was proclaimed king of Ambohimanga and took the name of Andrianampoinimerina. The name means 'the Prince in the Heart of Imerina' which was more than an idle boast: this king was the Malagasy counterpart of the great Peruvian Inca Tupac Yupanqui, expanding his empire as much by skilful organisation as by force, and doing it without the benefit of a written language (history seems to demonstrate that orders in triplicate are not essential to efficiency). By his death in 1810 the central plateau was firmly in control of the Merina and ably administered through a mixture of old customs and new. Each conquered territory was governed by local princes, answerable to the king, and the system of *fokonolona* (village communities) was established. From this firm foundation the new king, Radama I, was able to conquer most of the rest of the island.

Antananarivo means 'City of the Thousand', supposedly because a thousand warriors protected it. By the end of the 18th century, Andrianampoinimerina had taken Antananarivo from his rebellious kinsman and moved his base there from Ambohimanga. From that time until the French conquest in 1895 Madagascar's history centred around the royal palace or *rova*, the modest houses built for Andrianjaka and Andrianampoinimerina giving way to a splendid palace designed for Queen Ranavalona I by Jean Laborde and later clad in stone by James Cameron. The rock cliffs near the palace became known as Ampamarinana, 'the Place of the Hurling', as Christian martyrs met their fate at the command of the queen.

There was no reason for the French to move the capital elsewhere: its pleasant climate made it an agreeable place to live, and plenty of French money and planning went into the city we see today.

IVATO AIRPORT

Before describing the intricacies of arrival and departure it is worth mentioning the two restaurants at the airport. In the domestic arrivals/departure area there is a good café which serves tasty food from 06.00. The main restaurant is upstairs in the International section. It's quite smart, with waiter service and good food. As in all airports there are plenty of (expensive) souvenir shops and money-changing facilities. The Socimad Bank in International Departures gives a better rate of exchange than Bank Africa in Arrivals.

Arriving

In the Good Old Days Ivato was like the cottage of a wicked witch, seducing innocent visitors through its beguiling doors. Once inside, only the good and the brave emerged unscathed. Now (sigh) it is much the same as other international airports in the developing world. On arrival the procedure is as follows:

1 Join the correct queue: with visa, no visa.
2 Fill in the Embarkation form. This should be handed to you on the plane, but you may need to retrieve one from an official by the Immigration desk. The questions are straightforward, but be prepared to say where you'll be staying in Tana.
3 If you do not have a visa, fill in the appropriate form and have the required amount (see page 82) ready.
4 Shuffle forward in your 'queue' to be processed. When you hand in your passport watch its progress to the next official and move to the appropriate window.
5 Pick up luggage. There are trolleys to take your bags through customs. If you are carrying a video camera or something of value such as jewellery or a laptop computer you should pass through the red channel and declare it. Failure to do this may cause problems on departure. If queuing for the green 'Nothing to Declare' channel, try to get behind other tourists who are usually waved through without needing to open their bags. Luggage belonging to Malagasy arrivals is generally thoroughly searched.

Be warned that the porters at Ivato are quite aggressive. Be on your guard and, unless you need help, insist on carrying your own stuff. If you do decide to use a porter they will take advantage of the flustered new arrival's tendency to over-tip and complain vociferously if yours does not come up to expectations. A dollar is more than enough.
6 If you can fight off the porters and taxi touts for a while longer, change money at the airport. The banks are always open for international flight arrivals.

Leaving

This has now been streamlined and is an almost normal procedure. Remember that you *must* reconfirm your flight at least 72 hours before your flight departs. At this point you may be able to ask for a seat allocation.

1 Arrive at the airport at least two hours before the flight, with all or most of all your Malagasy money spent. **Remember that you cannot change your local currency back into hard currency**. The maximum you are supposed to take out with you is 25,000Fmg. The check-in counter is after you leave the main airport area (with shops), so once you have checked in there is nowhere to spend your Ariary. If you find yourself with unspent money, take it home and donate it to one of the charities listed on page 149.
2 Pick up a departure form and join the queue for the departure gate (with your luggage). When you reach the doorway show your ticket and passport, and pass through baggage security. If the X-ray machine is working you're unlikely to be asked to open your bags but have the keys ready.
3 Proceed to the check-in counter. Any orderly queue will have disintegrated by now as people compete for priority.
4 Passport control. Hand in your departure form.
5 Final passport check, hand-luggage X-ray, and you're through into the departure lounge. There are souvenir shops here (hard currency only) and a bar. It is sometimes possible to change the Malagasy money you've belatedly found in your pocket into hard currency with the ladies who supervise the (very nice) toilets.

Internal flights

The domestic building is separated from the main (international) airport by a long corridor. These flights are no-frills: there are no seat assignments – and no concept of queuing – and no meals (but drinks and sweeties). All domestic flights are no-smoking.

Lost luggage

Sometimes your luggage doesn't arrive. These days there is a relatively efficient procedure: find the lost-luggage kiosk which is open at irregular hours, fill in a form and they'll phone your hotel when the bag arrives. To be on the safe side ask for the phone number at the kiosk so you can find out if your luggage has been traced yet. If you have moved on they will usually send your bag to the nearest airport.

Transport to the city centre (12km)

There is no specific airport bus service, although one is due (so they say) in 2004. Some of the larger hotels provide courtesy buses. Otherwise official taxis will cost you about 60,000Fmg to 75,000Fmg or 80,000Fmg at night. If you walk purposefully across the car-park you will find some lurking unofficial taxis for around 40,000Fmg. Experienced travellers can go for the local bus which stops at the road junction about 100m from the airport. It costs only 1,500Fmg, and you can pay for an extra seat for your luggage. This bus takes you to the Vasakosy area behind the train station.

ANTANANARIVO (TANA) TODAY

From the right place, in the right light, Antananarivo (Tana for short) is one of the most attractive capitals in the developing world. In the evening sunshine it has the quality of a child's picture book, with brightly coloured houses stacked up the

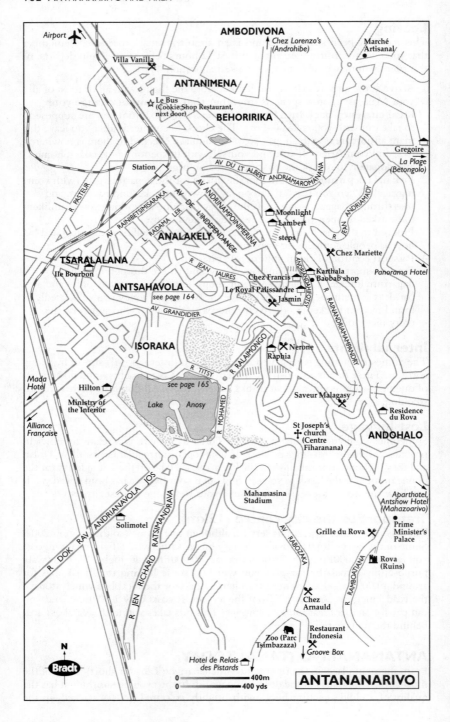

Airport

AMBODIVONA

Chez Lorenzo's
(Androhibe)

Marché
Artisanal

Villa Vanilla

ANTANIMENA

Le Bus
(Cookie Shop Restaurant,
next door)

BEHORIRIKA

Gregoire
La Plage
(Betongolo)

AV DU LT ALBERT ANDRIAMAROMANANA

Station

AV ANDRIANAMPOINIMERINA

AV DE L'INDEPENDANCE

R PASTEUR

AV RAINIBETSIMISARAKA

RADAMA LER

R JEAN ANDRIAMADY

Moonlight

Lambert

steps

Chez Mariette

ANALAKELY

TSARALALANA

Ile Bourbon

R JEAN JAURES

ANTSAHAVOLA

see page 164

AV GRANDIDIER

R ANDRIANDAHIFOTSY

R RAINANDRIAMAMPANDRY

Karthala
Baobab shop

Chez Francis

Le Royal Palissandre

Jasmin

Panorama Hotel

ISORAKA

R TITSY

R RALAIMONGO

Nerone
Raphia

Mada
Hotel

Hilton

Ministry of
the Interior

see page 165

Lake   Anosy

R MOHAMED V

Saveur Malagasy

Residence
du Rova

Alliance
Française

St Joseph's
church
(Centre
Fiharanana)

ANDOHALO

R DOK RAV ANDRIANAVOLA JOS

R JEN RICHARD RATSIMANDRAVA

Solimotel

Mahamasina
Stadium

Aparthotel,
Antshow Hotel
(Mahazoarivo)

Grille du Rova

Prime
Minister's
Palace

AV RABOZAKA

R RAMBOATIANA

Rova
(Ruins)

Chez
Arnauld

N

Bradt

Zoo (Parc
Tsimbazaza)

Restaurant
Indonesia

Groove Box

Hotel de Relais
des Pistards

0   400m
0   400 yds

ANTANANARIVO

POVERTY IN ANTANANARIVO – WHAT'S BEING DONE?

The very poor of Tana are known in French as 'les quatre mi' or 'the four mis'. This comes from the Malagasy words *miloka* ('gambling'), *mifoka* ('drugs'), *misotro* ('drinking') and *mijangajanga* ('prostitution'). Some 10% of Madagascar's population of about 14 million are estimated to live in and around the capital, over half of them below poverty level. And it can be grim. However, encouragingly, more and more local organisations are targeting specific sectors. Two that I know personally are **Akany Avoko** (see box on page 154) and the Centre Fihavanana described here.

The Sisters of the Good Shepherd, Centre Fihavanana (Soeurs du Bon Pasteur) 58 Lalana Stephani, Amparibe, 101 Antananarivo; tel: 22 299 81. They aim their well-run activities mainly at women and children. There are six sisters: Sri Lankan, French, Lebanese and Malagasy. About 180 children aged 3–12 are taught in four classes and many do well enough to get into state primary school. Undernourished babies (about 70) are fed and their mothers given training. Teenagers come to the centre to learn basic skills and handicrafts. Elderly people (about 150) come twice a month for a little food, company and care. Food is taken weekly to over 300 women, teenagers and children in prison. Finally, 72 women do beautiful embroidery at home, while caring for their families, which provides an income both for them and for the centre. A new project is housing for needy women and their children. Land has been donated and 16 simple houses built on the outskirts of Tana. Visitors to the centre can help with cash, by buying handicrafts, or by donating any unwanted clothes or medicines at the end of their holiday.

hillsides, and mauve jacarandas and purple bougainvillea against the dark blue of the winter sky. Red crown-of-thorn euphorbia stand in rows against red clay walls, rice paddies are tended right up to the edge of the city, clothes are laid out on the canal bank to dry, and zebu-carts rumble along the roads on the outskirts of town. It's all deliciously foreign and can hardly fail to impress the first-time visitor as he or she drives in from the airport. Indeed, this drive is one of the most varied and interesting in the highlands. The good impression is helped by the climate – during the dry season the sun is hot but the air pleasantly cool (the altitude is between 1,245m and 1,469m).

Sadly, for many people this wonderful first impression does not survive a closer acquaintance. Tana can seem squalid and dangerous, with conspicuous poverty, persistent beggars, and a worrying crime rate. However, in the late 1990s the then Mayor of Tana, Marc Ravalomanana (now president), launched a clean-up campaign which has had a noticeable effect. Many foreigners mourn the passing of the *zoma* (street market) but the central areas of the city are undoubtedly now cleaner and safer.

The geography of the city is both simple and confusing. It is built on two ridges which combine in a V. On the highest hill, dominating all the viewpoints, is the ruined Queen's Palace or *Rova*. Down the central valley runs a broad boulevard, Avenue de l'Indépendance (sometimes called by its Malagasy name Fahaleovantena), which terminates at the railway station. It narrows at the other end to become Rue du 26 Juin. To escape from this valley means climbing steps, if you are on foot, or driving through a tunnel if you are in a vehicle.

It is convenient to divide Tana into the two main areas most often wandered by visitors: Avenue de l'Indépendance and the side streets to its southwest (districts Analakely and Tsaralalana, or the Lower Town) and the smarter area at the top of the steps leading up from Rue du 26 Juin (districts Antaninarenina and Isoraka, or the Upper Town). Of course there are lots of other districts but most tourists will take taxis there rather than going on foot. This can be a challenging city to explore: streets are often unnamed, or change name several times within a few hundred metres, or go by two different names. When reading street names it's worth knowing that *Lalana* means street, *Arabe* is avenue, and *Kianja* is a square.

Telephone code The area code for Tana is 22.

Analakely and Tsaralalana (Lower Town)
Analakely (which means 'little forest') used to be famous for its large forest of white umbrellas, under which every product imaginable (and many unimaginable) used to be sold. Tana's *zoma* market was famous world wide. Now it has all gone (though illicit, dawn markets are still held in the side-streets) and traffic and pedestrians can move more freely.

Avenue de l'Indépendance is a broad boulevard (grassed in the centre) with shops, snackbars, restaurants and hotels up each side. If you start at the station and walk up the right-hand side you will pass the Tana Plaza and Palace hotels, the city's best bookshop (Librairie de Madagascar), one of the best restaurants (O Poivre Vert) and the Hotel de France. Continuing south you reach one of Tana's liveliest bars (Glacier) and then you're at the steps up to Antaninarenina.

This is not a street for strolling – there are too many persistent beggars and souvenir vendors. And thieves, so walk briskly. Shopwise, the north side of the

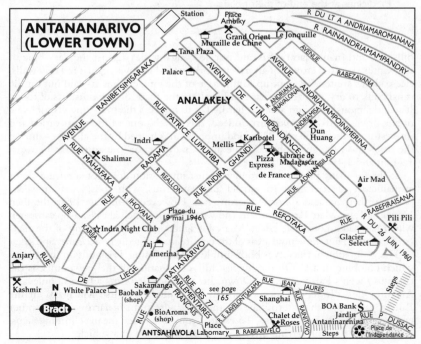

avenue is less interesting, but it does have several excellent snackbars, and the Air Madagascar office is here.

Tsaralalana is a more relaxing area of side streets to the south of Avenue de l'Indépendance (although maps do not indicate the steep climbs involved if you go too far). Walk down Rue Indira Gandhi (Rue Nice), past the shoe shop Aigle d'Or and the Mellis Hotel to the cumbersomely named Place du 19 Mai 1946. Beyond it is the Hotel Taj and the very popular Sakamanga Hotel/Restaurant. The excellent Baobab souvenir shop is here, as is BioAroma, which sells beauty products and herbal remedies. To avoid a steep (rather dull) climb to Isoraka you can then double back on one of the parallel streets to Avenue de l'Indépendance.

Antaninarenina and Isoraka (Upper Town)

This is the Islington of Tana; or the Greenwich Village. Here are the jewellers, the art shops and craft boutiques, the atmospheric hotels, the inexpensive guesthouses, and a terrific but little-known museum. There is also a rose garden where, in October, the jacaranda trees drip their nectar on to the heads below. I love this area. There is no feeling of menace here (which is not to say crime doesn't exist) so this is the district for gentle strolling.

Start at the bottom of the steps by the Select Hotel on Avenue de l'Indépendance and as you climb up, marvel that so many men can make a living selling rubber stamps. Visit the shopping arcade on the right, near the bottom of the steps, and check out some of the best postcards in Tana. At the top of the steps is Place de l'Indépendance, and Jardin Antaninarenina with its jacarandas and rose bushes. And benches. Nearby is Le Buffet du Jardin where you can sip a fruit juice in the sun. Other landmarks are the Hotel du Louvre and the Shoprite supermarket. Turn left at the Maison and you come to the post office where, if you go through a side door to the philatelic counter, you can buy special-issue Malagasy stamps. If you feel like a coffee, cross the road to the Colbert. The streetside bar/café is where conservationists and other expats meet to discuss their latest challenges.

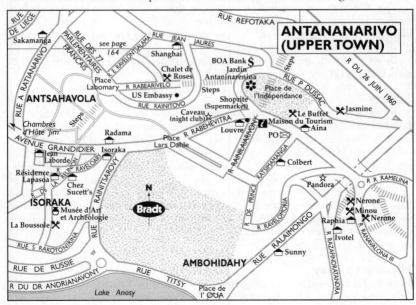

Now it's time to explore Isoraka. A 30-minute walk will show you the main sights. Start up Rue Rabehevitra, past the Radama Hotel and the good-value Isoraka Hotel. Turn left and you'll pass first the very nice little restaurant, Chez Sucette's, then a cobbler's shop with a group of men sitting outside chatting and stitching. If you have anything that needs repairing, this is the place. On a corner is the small and friendly Résidence Lapasoa. At this point look out for a bronze 'tree' hung with clay pots. This marks the Musée d'Art et Archéologie, which is a super little museum with changing exhibits. Alas, it is closed at weekends.

On the way back, drop in at one of Tana's best craft shops, Galerie Yerden on Rue Dr Villette, then pick whatever street you fancy to get you back to Place de l'Indépendance.

Getting around

Traffic jams and pollution are a major problem in Tana. Since 1989 the number of cars has increased from 43,000 to 150,000 in 2000: 882 vehicles per kilometre or one vehicle for every metre of road. It therefore makes sense to avoid vehicular transport when possible. Get to know the city on foot during the day (but carry nothing of value); use taxis for long distances, unknown destinations, and always at night.

Taxis are cream-coloured so easily recognisable. Tough bargainers will pay about 6,000Fmg for a short trip but most *vazaha* end up paying around 12,000Fmg. 25,000–30,000Fmg is not unusual. Prices are much higher after dark. Taxis do not have meters so agree on the price before you get in. Expect to pay more than the locals, but avoid the exorbitant vazaha price charged by the taxis serving the big hotels. Battered old vehicles which wouldn't dare go near a hotel will be cheaper and you have the extra bonus of watching the street go by through the hole in the floor, or being pushed by helpful locals when the vehicle breaks down or runs out of petrol. The taxis that wait outside posh hotels like the Colbert are more expensive but also more reliable than those cruising the streets.

The advantage of not having meters is that if the driver gets lost (which frequently happens) you will not pay any more for the extra journey. In my experience Tana taxi drivers are honest and helpful and can be trusted to get you to your destination – eventually. They will also pick you up at an agreed time.

Buses are much cheaper, but sorting out the destinations and districts can be difficult. A good map of Tana is helpful here.

Safety

Sadly, robbery has become quite common in Tana. Leave your valuables in the hotel (preferably in a safe deposit or locked in your bag) and carry as little as possible. Avenue de l'Indépendance seems particularly risky. One scam is the 'Ballet of the Hats'. Kids carrying wide-brimmed straw hats encircle you and, using the hats to obscure your view, work through your pockets, money-belt, neck-pouch or whatever. If you can manage to carry nothing at all – no watch, no camera, no money… not even a paper tissue in your pocket – you will bring back the best souvenirs: memories. But few people (myself included) heed this advice, so just be on your guard and never wander around with something like a passport or your airline tickets which you really can't afford to lose (but see *Passports and IDs* on page 121).

Where to stay

New hotels and restaurants are opening all the time in Tana. This selection is by no means complete – be adventurous and find your own!

ALL'S WELL...
Janice Booth

Airline incompetence caused me to arrive in Madagascar minus my luggage – so I went off to the Shoprite supermarket, down in the Faravohitra area near Avenue de l'Indépendance, and then to a nearby street market, to replace basic items. It was good to be back in Tana and the time passed quickly; afternoon sunlight soon turned to dusk.

The theft was carried out with copybook slickness. A hand reached out silently from the deepening shadows and tugged at my small wrist purse, which I had wedged (I thought) securely under my arm. I clutched it with both hands, but the thief was strong – gradually my fingers lost their grip. I chased after him, shouting (in French) 'Stop thief! That man in red! Stop him!' Malagasy passers-by turned and stared – but he ran too fast for them to react. They stopped me from pursuing him up the narrow Escalier Rahoerason, warning me anxiously that it wasn't safe.

The catastrophe was that the bag contained my passport, which I was carrying only because the receptionist had handed it to me just as I was leaving the hotel and I hadn't bothered to take it back to my room.

Luckily I was with an efficient tour company, Za Tours. The director's husband took me to the main police station. He translated for me during the lengthy questioning (no-one seemed to speak much French or English); then we waited while an official typed out a formal 'declaration' in triplicate, with two fingers, on an ancient manual typewriter. If you lose your passport, this 'declaration' is vital – it gives temporary proof of identity and backs up insurance claims.

Next morning, after completing the necessary forms at the British Embassy (for a temporary Travel Document to get me back to Britain I needed 300,000Fmg plus two passport photos), I went to the offices of the newspaper Midi to insert an advertisement, giving Za Tours' phone number and offering an unspecified 'reward' for the passport's return. I also asked a journalist to interview me for the next day's edition. Then, one of Za Tours' Malagasy staff came with me to the area where I'd been robbed, to talk to the street vendors. He wrote out a short notice in Malagasy, giving details of the theft and Za Tours' phone number – I had several photocopies made and friendly stallholders agreed to display them.

I rejoined the tour group and continued my trip. Ten days later when we returned to Tana there was no news. I was in Za Tours' office collecting my return air ticket when the phone rang. The director answered it. Amazed, she told me: 'It's a man who says he's found your passport!'

Her driver rattled me off across Tana in a 4WD and located a small mechanic's workshop. Inside, an oil-stained Chinaman wiped his hands on a rag and greeted me with great dignity. My passport was in his safe. He said he had found it in the street, not far from where I'd been robbed, and accepted the reward with just the right level of reluctance.

For security reasons the British Embassy had cancelled the passport's validity, so I phoned to get it re-activated. And tucked it lovingly away into a secure, concealed, inside pocket, well protected from thieving fingers!

Note that the top-range hotels charge a tourist tax of around 2,000Fmg.

Category A
Upper town
Hotel Colbert Rue Printsy Ratsimamanga, Antaninarenina; tel: 22 202 02; fax: 22 340 12 or 22 254 97; email: colbert@dts.mg or colbert@simicro.mg; www.madagascar-guide.com/colbert. Total of 140 rooms. The main hotel has standard, comfortable accommodation and a new annexe caters for the luxury end of the market. These rooms, almost embarrassingly opulent, are the best in Tana. Indoor pool, sauna, fitness centre, business centre, casino. Very French. Recommended for its good location, nice atmosphere and excellent food. Rooms: €457 (for the presidential suite) to €145 in the annexe; €163–174 in the main hotel. Continental breakfast €9. Most credit cards accepted. Transfer from the airport €7 per person.

Hotel du Louvre 4, Place P Tsiranana, Antaninarenina; tel: 22 390 00; fax: 22 640 40; email: hoteldulouvre@simicro.mg; www.hotel-du-louvre.com. 60 air-conditioned rooms. Convenient, safe location, comfortable, well-run, with a pleasant, small bar and good restaurant. Internet facilities. €53 single, €60 double, €85 de luxe. Breakfast buffet: 40,000Fmg. Airport transfer 100,000Fmg (nights) and 75,000Fmg (day).

Radama Hotel 22 Av Ramanantsoa, Isoraka; tel: 22 319 27; fax: 22 353 23; email: radama@simicro.mg; www.madonline.com/voyages/radama. A very nice small (16 rooms) hotel in a great location. Rooms vary, so hold out for a good one with a view. Ideal for business people (there is a conference room) or independent travellers. No lift (elevator). Most credit cards accepted. From €46 (double room to studio apartment); breakfast €4.

Lower town
Hilton Hotel Rue Pierre Stibbe, Anosy; tel: 22 260 60; fax: 22 260 51; email: sales_madagascar@hilton.com. On the western side of Lake Anosy. One of Tana's skyscrapers (as you'd expect), with 170 rooms from €170 to €410. Lovely views from the upper floors. Its advantages are the offices and shops in the building, including a cybercafé, a reliable cash machine, and the swimming pool. In the pleasantly hot sun of the dry season this is a real bonus. It is some way from the centre of town (though the walk in is enjoyable). Most credit cards are accepted. Free airport transfers.

Hotel Le Royal Palissandre 13 Rue Andriandahifotsy (shown on some maps as Rue Romain Desfossés), Faravohitra; tel: 22 326 14 and 22 605 60; fax: 22 326 24; email: HotelPalissandre@simicro.mg. A recommended hotel with all comforts, good food, lovely views and a pleasant location within walking distance of the centre of town. Rooms: €90 double with breakfast, €80 single; meal €15. There's a bar and a meeting room. Transfer from the airport is 125,000Fmg (nights) and 115,000Fmg (day).

Palace Hotel 8 Av de l'Indépendance; tel: 22 256 63; fax: 22 339 43; email: hdf_tana@dts.com. 25 rooms, varying in size, the largest being studio apartments. Owned by Hotel de France, this is a smart hotel at the lower end of the avenue. No restaurant, but a short walk to the Tana Plaza. Rooms €60–110, breakfast €6. This hotel is threatened with closure in 2004.

Tana Plaza 2 Av de l'Indépendance (near the station); tel: 22 662 60 and 22 218 65; fax: 22 642 19; email: hdf_tana@dts.mg. An upmarket hotel with 75 small but good rooms (the ones facing the street are noisy). Good restaurant. Rooms €60. Airport transfer 100,000Fmg.

Hotel de France 34 Av de l'Indépendance; tel: 22 202 93 or 213 04; fax: 201 18; email: hdf_tana@dts.mg. A very pleasant hotel with 30 large rooms, a convenient location and very good food. Internet facilities. Double room €60, breakfast €6.

Outskirts

Aparthotel (Radama House) Route d'Ambohipo, Ambatoroka; tel: 22 334 71/22249 84; fax: 22 334 94; email: radama.house@wanadoo.mg; www.radamahouse.com. Caters mainly for the business traveller, with apartments that can be taken for a week, as well as hotel rooms. Secure parking. Prices (per day) vary from 375,000Fmg for an apartment (two people) to 200,000Fmg for a room with en-suite shower. The excellent Restaurant Tranovola is here.

Antshow Not so much a hotel, more a total Malagasy experience. See page 179.

Chez Lorenzo's Lot II 35 N Androhibe; tel: 22 427 76; fax: 22 421 76; email: lorenzo@wanadoo.mg. Five comfortable rooms, 243,000Fmg with breakfast, tax included. One room has satellite TV and costs 363,000Fmg (including breakfast and tax).

Hotel Panorama Route D' Andrainarivo, BP756 Antananarivo; tel: 22 412 44; fax: 22 412 47; email: panorama@dts.mg. Double or twin 363,000Fmg. The restaurant serves international and Malagasy food.

Hotel Gregoire Lot II M 53 Ter Mahavoky, Besarety; tel: 22 222 66, fax: 22 292 71; email: gregoire@bow.dts.mg. Single 203,000Fmg with TV and safe; double 253,000Fmg. Central heating. Good restaurant.

Category B
Upper town

Hotel Raphia Rue Ranavalona III, Ambatonakanga; tel: 22 253 13; email: hotelraphia@wanadoo.mg. A nice hotel with 11 rooms and a garden. From the terrace on the 4th floor there are lovely views over Lake Anosy. 110,000Fmg (shared bathroom). Also a bungalow with bathroom for 146,000Fmg. Airport transfers 60,000Fmg.

Hotel Aina 17 Rue Ratsimilaho; tel: 22 630 51; email: ainahtl@dts.mg. Just beyond the Colbert. No restaurant 'but with the Colbert just around the corner, who cares?' Recommended as efficient and good value. 182,000Fmg. Breakfast: 18,000Fmg.

Résidence Lapasoa 15 Rue de la Réunion, Isoraka; tel: 22 611 40, cellphone: 032 0761 140; fax: 22 281 54; email: dina.lapasoa@malagasy.com. A friendly little B&B with 7 rooms in a nice part of town, ideal for lone travellers. 225,000Fmg single, 240,000Fmg double, breakfast: 20,000Fmg.

Hotel Le Jean Laborde 3 Rue de Russie, Isoraka; tel: 22 330 45; fax: 22 327 94; email: labordehotel@hotmail.com. Rooms vary in price from 80,000Fmg (shared bathroom) to 205,000Fmg (suite). This hotel went through a bad patch but is now recommended, especially the restaurant.

Hotel Restaurant Chez Francis Rue Andriandahifotsy (a little way up the hill from the Royal Palissandre); tel/fax: 22 613 65; email: chezfrancis@vaniala.com. 12 rooms with shower. 2 clean WCs on each landing. A super little place in a good location with lovely views over Tana from the back rooms (could be noisy at the front).107,000Fmg double, 150,000Fmg treble. Breakfast is 15,000Fmg.

Lower town

Karibotel Av de l'Indépendance; tel: 22 665 54 or 22 629 31; cellphone: 033 1166 554 fax: 22 629 32; email: karibotel@dts.mg; web: http://takelaka.dts.mg/karibotel. Two blocks down from Tana Plaza. Clean, safe, comfortable. Credit cards accepted. From 250,000Fmg to 295,000Fmg with TV, phone, bathroom and toilet.

La Muraille de Chine 1 Av de l'Indépendance; tel: 22 281 41 or 22 230 13; fax: 22 628 82; email: murchine@dts.mg. One of Tana's longest-established hotels, with a restaurant specialising in Chinese food. It also has its own travel agency, Montana Voyage. Rooms 125,000Fmg to 195,000Fmg, all en suite.

Ivotel BP816, Ambohidahy (near Lake Anosy); tel: 22 227 16; fax: 22 249 29; email: ivotel@dts.mg. 20 simple but comfortable rooms including five studio apartments. Good restaurant, friendly service, reliable hot water. Standard room 253,000Fmg, suite 353,000Fmg.

White Palace Hotel 101 Rue de Liège, Tsaralalana; tel:22 664 59 or 22 669 98; fax 22 602 98. A mid-range hotel conveniently located in the lower town but some rooms reportedly damp in wet weather. Studio rooms with cooking facilities 263,000Fmg, double/twin rooms with en-suite bathroom, 198,000Fmg, small rooms 153,000Fmg. Breakfast 12,500–32,500Fmg

Indri Hotel 15 Rue Radama, Tsaralalana (11/2 blocks from Av de l'indépendance); tel/fax: 22 209 22. A comfortable, friendly, medium-sized hotel in a convenient location with a lively cocktail bar. Low season rates (January to July): spacious room: 165,000Fmg, standard room: 135,000Fmg or 105,000Fmg. Continental breakfast 20,000Fmg.

Hotel Mellis Rue Indira Gandhi; tel: 22 234 25 or 22 660 70; fax: 22 626 60; email: htmellis@wanadoo.mg; www.hotel-mellis.com. A perennial favourite in a convenient location. Rooms from 95,000 to 275,000Fmg.

Taj Hotel 69 Rue de Liège, Tsaralalana (near Place du 19 Mai 1946); tel: 22 624 09/10; fax: 22 331 34; email: taj@dts.mg. Comfortable rooms with hot water. 160,000Fmg single/double. Good restaurant. However, here is a reader's warning: 'The red-light district seems to be right across the street – with upwards of 20 prostitutes hanging out all night long. Sadly, we saw several expats bringing the women into the Taj. So if sex tourism isn't your bag, you might want to stay elsewhere.'

Hotel Anjary Rue Razafimahandry and Dr Ranaivo, Tsaralalana; tel: 22 244 09; fax: 22 234 18; email: anjari@wanadoo.mg. Clean, large, secure, friendly. Reliable hot water. The rooms on the 4th floor are best but avoid those facing the (noisy) street. 153,000Fmg double with shower. Plus (treat yourself!) an hour's massage for 50,000Fmg.

Ile Bourbon 12 Rue Benyowski, Tsaralalana; tel: 22 279 42; fax: 22 624 96. Room is 115,000Fmg or 125,000Fmg (double), breakfast 24,000Fmg.

Shalimar, 5 Rue Mahafaka, Tsaralalàna; tel: 22 260 70; fax: 22 689 95; email: yascom@dts.mg. 23 rooms from 150,000Fmg to 200,000Fmg; meals 27,500–35,000Fmg.

Sakamanga Rue A Ratianarivo; tel: 22 358 09/22 640 59; fax: 22 245 87; email: saka@malagasy.com. 10 rooms, of varying size and price, all with en-suite bathrooms. A lovely small hotel with beautiful hardwood floors, stairs and bar, and interesting historic photos on the walls. French run. Usually full. 145,000–220,000Fmg. There is an excellent, lively French restaurant, also heavily booked. 'By far the most best value and most atmospheric hotel in Tana. Definitely worth booking in advance.' (S Bulmer).

Sunny Hotel Rue Ralaimongo (northeast side of Lake Anosy); tel: 22 263 04; fax: 22 290 78; email: sunny@dts.mg. A good location (though not sunny) handy for both lower and upper town; friendly staff, good food. 16 rooms: 14 standard and 2 suites: €50 and €70 respectively. Includes breakfast.

Outskirts

Solimotel BP3850 Anosy; tel: 22 250 40. Room is from 155,000Fmg to 190,000Fmg, additional bed is 45,000Fmg. Good restaurant serving European and Malagasy food.

La Karthala 48 Rue Andriandahifotsy; tel: 22 248 95; fax: 22 272 67. Not as conveniently located as some, but the chance to be at home with a Malagasy family. Madame Rafalimanana speaks good English. Rooms 120,000Fmg.

Hotel Shanghai 4 Rue Rainitovo, Antsahavola (near the US Embassy); tel: 22 314 72 or 22 675 13; fax: 22 315 61; email: shangai@malagasy.com. Room rates are highly competitive, with a double room at 125,000Fmg. Hot water. A good breakfast costs 17,500Fmg.

Le Relais des Pistards BP3550, Rue Fernand Kasanga (same road as Tsimbazaza), about 1km beyond the zoo; tel: 22 291 34; fax: 22 629 56; email: pistards@simicro.mg. A friendly, family-style hotel run by Florent and Jocelyn Colney. Pleasant communal dining room, and excellent cooking. Florent Colney is an avid mountain biker, so a stay here is a must for those planning to cycle in Madagascar. His advice will be invaluable. 95,000Fmg double, 65,000Fmg single; double suite 125,000Fmg, single suite 101,000Fmg. Price includes breakfast.

Résidence du Rova Lot VN 3 A Place Ratsimandrava, Ambohijatovo; tel: 22 341 46; fax: 22 239 12; email: cmdmtnr@dts.mg. 10 rooms for €56–75. Secure garage for €3 per day.

Mada Hotel: Andavamamba (opposite the Alliance Française); tel: 22 552 08; fax: 22 615 45; email: miramada@wanadoo.mg. 16 rooms with en-suite bathrooms and TV. Double (with extra bed) 153,000Fmg; twin 128,000Fmg and regular double 103,000Fmg.

Category C

Hotel Isoraka 11 Av Gal Ramanantsoa, Ambatonilita; tel: 22 355 81; fax: 22 658 54; cellphone: 032 0218 121. One of the few budget hotels in the Upper Town. Clean, with hot water. Communal bathroom. Extremely friendly and helpful, but little English spoken; also very noisy. Offers airport transfers (60,000Fmg), snack bar and laundry service. 55,000Fmg (single), 75,000–85,000Fmg (double).

Moonlight Hotel Rue Andriandahifotsy, just beyond the steps to the Lambert. 'What a find! Very cheap, clean, comfortable, hot showers and helpful English-speaking staff" (Stuart Riddle). 45,000Fmg single.

Select Hotel Av de l'Indépendance; cellphone: 032 414 005 or 033 1284 531. An ugly tower block, but conveniently located near the steps to the Upper Town. Rooms 97,000Fmg with en-suite bathrooms.

Hotel Glacier 46 Av de l'Indépendance; tel: 22 202 60 or 22 291 04; fax: 22 203 32; email: hotel.glacier@simicro.mg. One of the oldest – and shabbiest – hotels in Tana, but it is conveniently located, has a lively bar (full of prostitutes) and excellent music with *salegy* bands from all over Madagascar. Singles 140,000Fmg with breakfast, doubles 150,000Fmg.

Hotel Lambert Tel: 22 229 92. Up the opposite flight of stairs to those that lead to Place de l'Indépendance. Basic, clean, convenient. Currently 16 rooms but with plans to extend. Good value and popular, but be prepared to climb a lot of stairs! 40,000–70,000Fmg and 80,000–90,000Fmg. Breakfast 10,000Fmg, meals 10,000 to 18,000Fmg.

Chambres d'Hôte 'Jim' At intersection of Rues Grandidier and Andrianary; tel: 22 374 37. New, clean, with balconies offering sunset views. En-suite showers, shared toilet. About 80,000Fmg. Only 4 rooms so phone first.

Bed and breakfast

Villa Soamahatony BP11044, Route Digue, Antananarivo 101; tel: 22 585 18; cellphone: 033 1103 337; email: soamahatony@wanadoo.mg. Stay *en famille* with Sahondra and Daniel Dartiguepeyrou, a French-Malagasy couple. Their villa, set in 2ha of grounds, is in Ankadivory (Ankadivory – Ambohijanahary – Ambohibao – Antehiroky), ten minutes by car from Ivato Airport. With advance notice they will pick you up from the airport and arrange car rental for short excursions. See their website: http://takelaka.dts.mg/soamahatony. 'A fantastic experience. The food was fabulous and it was great to stay with such a knowledgeable and friendly family. The hosts are the pulse of Madagascar...' (L Brandstetter). Three rooms with shared facilities; email them for the rates.

Soamiandry Sarl Antananarivo; tel: 22 444 54. (7 rooms) Family run (so book ahead). 'Joshua and Fara try to do everything for you; it's one of those places you remember.' Garden, swimming pool. €15 double, breakfast €2.

Country View Guest House BP46 Ambohidratrimo; tel: 22 582 78; email: janocki@mweb.co.za. A new South African owned guesthouse 15 minutes from Ivato. Comfortable, hospitable and friendly. There are 6 rooms: with shared bathroom US$28, with balcony and shared bathroom $32, en-suite bedroom $36, en suite with balcony $40, self-contained unit with kitchen $42. English breakfast $5, a 3-course dinner is $8. Airport transfers $5 per passenger or $3 pp if sharing. TV, computer links, fax and email facilities available.

Accommodation near the airport

It can take 45 minutes to get to the airport from the centre of town, so staying nearby is a sensible option, especially when you have an early morning flight.

Mahavelo Near Club du Car, Ivato; cellphone: 032 0772 068; email: hotelmahavelo@yahoo.fr. About 20 comfortable rooms for 175,000Fmg (twin) and a large dining hall. Breakfast 15,000Fmg. 'The restaurant is superb, with a new French chef.' (RP). Airport transfers 40,000Fmg.

Résidence Tanikely BP31 Ivato 105; tel: 22 453 96, cellphone: 033 1103 535; fax: 22 453 97. 2 bungalows, 4 rooms. French-owned, comfortable self-contained units, with cooking facilities, set in a pleasant garden with a swimming pool. Ideal for families. 300,000Fmg double.

Hotel Restaurant Farihy ME 475 Mandrosoa, Ivato; tel: 22 580 76, cellphone: 032 4026 331; fax: 22 307 74. A very pleasant place with rooms or bungalows. 175,000Fmg per bungalow (twin or double), or 150,000Fmg per room; continental breakfast 12,500Fmg; American breakfast 25,000Fmg.

Sifaka Auberge Lot 152 A Antanetibe, Antehiroka, Ivato, Antananarivo (near Toyota); tel: 22 481 32; fax: 22 441 74; email: sifaka.auberge@dts.mg. 8 rooms, double with bathrooom and toilet is 200,000Fmg and twin with shared facilities 175,000Fmg. Breakfast from 20,000Fmg.

Hotel Ivato Lot K6 Imotro, Ivato; tel/fax: 22 445 10 or 22 743 05, cellphone: 033 1101 463; email: ivatohotel@dts.mg. Friendly, clean, hot showers. 105,000Fmg double or twin; 135,000Fmg triple; family room is 175,000Fmg. The restaurant (good) is closed on Tuesdays.

Auberge du Cheval Blanc BP23, Ivato; tel: 22 446 46; email: Chevalblanc@dts.mg. Rooms 110,000Fmg single/double. Restaurant. MasterCard and Visa accepted.

Hotel/Restaurant Auberge d'Alsace Route d'Ivato 105 Mandrosoa; tel: 22 446 56; email: synorosoa@yahoo.fr. Large rooms with desk, en-suite large bathrooms. Good restaurant. 85,000Fmg per room; additional bed 20,000Fmg. Breakfast 12,500Fmg. This hotel also arranges car-hire, working with the agency Pro-car.

Le Manoir Rouge Tel: 22 441 04; fax: 22 482 44. Rooms from 40,000Fmg (shared bathroom) to 75,000Fmg (en suite) and 95,000Fmg (bungalow). Camping permitted. Good food. Cybercafé. Recommended.

Tonga Soa Mandrosoa; cellphone: 032 0218 111. This very pleasant place is only five minutes from the airport. It started life as a restaurant (see *Where to eat*) but now has several rooms with more being added.

Motel Au Transit BP5260 Antanetibe, Ivato, on the way to the airport; cellphone: 033 1133 831. Double with toilet but cold water is 52,000Fmg. Bungalow twin or double with facilities and hot water is 62,000Fmg. Family room (a double and a single) is 157,000Fmg with toilet and a bath. Additional bed is 10,000Fmg. Breakfast costs 10,000Fmg.

Where to eat
Hotel restaurants

Most of the better hotels serve good food. Expats and Malagasy professionals favour the **Colbert**. The 'all you can eat' Sunday buffet is good value (but beware of the health risks of eating cold buffets). There are two restaurants at the Colbert; the Taverne is the smartest and imposes a dress code on its diners. The food and service are excellent – this is the place to go for that special treat. Phone 22 202 02 for reservations. Bring your French dictionary – menus are not translated. The bakery next door is very popular with homesick *vazaha*. 'It has a greater variety of pastries than I've ever seen and real ice-creams in cones.'

The **Hilton** does a whole series of buffets which in the past were very good; standards seem to have declined recently, however. A better bet is the **Tana Plaza** which has an excellent restaurant with live music (traditional) in the bar. On Av de l'Indépendance there is the popular **O! Poivre Vert**, next to the Hotel de France, and a short walk away is the **Sakamanga** restaurant: crowded and lively, with excellent food. It also has internet facilities. Book ahead: tel: 22 358 09. 'It's best to arrive at around 7.30… the food is fantastic and the ambience very pleasant.' (W Applequist)

The restaurant at **Hotel Jean Laborde** has 'the best food I had in Madagascar' (S Gibson) and the Indian restaurant on the 7th floor of the **Anjary Hotel** is recommended for the good food and super views (no alcohol). **Kudeta** (tel: 22 281 54), owned by the Residence Lapasoa, is recommended for its European food.

Upper- and middle-range restaurants

Restaurant Tranovola Route d'Ambohipo, Ambatoroka; tel: 22 334 71/22 249 84; fax: 22 334 94; email: radama.house@wanadoo.mg. Opened only in 2003, this is the place to go for an end-of-the-trip treat. Superb – and unusual – Malagasy cooking, beautifully presented. The manager, Elyane Rahonintsoa, ensures that this is an evening to remember.

Villa Vanille Pl Antanimena; tel: 22 205 15. A fine old Tana house five minutes by taxi from Tana Plaza, specialising in Creole food. Music (traditional and jazz) every evening. 'Fabulous – it was so good we had to go back. They also have Malagasy art for sale.' (D Simon)

Au Grille du Rova About 100m down from the ruins of the Queen's Palace; tel: 22 627 24; fax: 22 622 13; email: malagasy@dts.mg. Excellent food, eaten indoors or outside, with a view over the city: about 35,000Fmg. Open from 10am to 10pm every day. Traditional Malagasy music every Sunday, from midday to sunset. Good English spoken. Recommended.

La Table d'Hote de Mariette (Chez Mariette) 11 Rue Geoge V, Faravohitra; tel: 22 216 02; fax: 22 277 19; www.sinergic.mg. Beautifully prepared and served Malagasy food. European food also available.

Nerone 28 Rue Ratsimilaho, Ambatonakanga; tel: 22 231 18; email: smietana@dts.mg. A small, upmarket Italian restaurant offering a variety of à la carte dishes and Italian wines.

La Boussole 21 Rue de Dr Villette, Isoraka; tel: 22 358 10; email: cportugal@netclub.mg or labousoule@netclub.mg. A stylish French restaurant with excellent food, a cosy bar and a charming patio for outdoor dining. Especially lively on Friday nights.

La Jonquille 7 Rue Rabezavana, Soarano; tel: 22 206 37. Good, imaginative menu, mainly Chinese. Especially good for seafood. Reasonable prices.

Restaurant Jasmin 8 Rue Paul-Dussac; tel: 22 342 96. Good Chinese food.

Chez Arnaud Rue Rabozaka (the road leading from Mahamasina stadium to the zoo); tel 22 631 59. 'Without doubt the best pizza in town!' Also a good French menu and pasta dishes. Quite pricey, however.

Tonga Soa Mandrosoa (about 2km from Ivato Airport); tel: 22 442 88. A small, intimate restaurant run by Ninah and husband (and chef) Patrick. 'This is the most pleasant little restaurant I know in Tana and a wonderful place to go for a quiet evening meal or on the way to the airport. The menu is not as extensive as some (because Patrick will use only fresh ingredients) but the food is the best in Tana' (Nick Garbutt) There is another reason to visit: 'The lush gardens are well planted with trees, shrubs and flowers that attract a wide variety of birdlife and there are also upwards of 50 jewel chameleons here. They lay their eggs at the edges of the car-park!'

Le Grand Orient Tel: 22 202 88. Round the corner from the railways station. One of Tana's long-established restaurants. Chinese, fairly expensive, but an extensive menu, nice atmosphere and piano music every night.

El Pili Pili Analakely (opposite Hotel Le Glacier); tel: 22 556 14. A popular restaurant with local people because of the low prices and good pizzas. Open daily from 09.00 to midnight.

Le Palanquin Pk 12 Route d'Ivato (on the way to the airport, on the right-hand side, before Aero Pizza); tel: 22 485 84. Recommended by resident John Pitterle for 'their good food (mainly Chinese) and good service. The atmosphere is very nice too.'

Pizza Express Galerie Kamoula 26, Avenue de l'Indépendance; tel: 310 30 or 228 18. Opens from Monday to Sunday until 23.00. Good pizzas!

La Saveur Malagasy Ambatovinaky; tel: 22 613 91. Malagasy food, open from 10.00 to 22.30, closed on Sundays.

Aéro Pizza On the way to the airport; tel: 22 482 91, cellphone: 033 1118 500. Pizza!

Dun Huang Analakely, near Shoprite. Good Chinese food, large portions. Meals from 30,000Fmg.

Minou Rue Ratsimilaho, Ambatonakanga; tel: 22 288 62. A very good budget restaurant with inexpensive, tasty food.

Budget restaurants

Restaurant Chez Sucett's 23 Rue Raveloary, Isoraka; tel: 22 261 00; www.chezSucett's@yahoo.fr. A pleasant small restaurant in a safe area, serving excellent food. Universally praised. About 25,000Fmg for a meal.

Le Café du Parc Down the road to Tsimbazaza.

Restaurant Indonesia Directly across from the zoo entrance. Surprisingly, this is the only Indonesian restaurant in Madagascar. Recommended.

Chalet des Roses 13 Rue Rabary Antsahavola (in the centre of town, opposite the American Embassy); tel: 22 642 33; email: roses@simicro.mg. 'Delicious, clean and affordable.'

Kashmir 5–7 Rue Dr Ranaivo (opposite Anjary Hotel). Muslim, very good and reasonably priced food.

Shalimar 5 Rue Mahafaka, Tsaralalana; tel: 22 260 70. Good curries and a selection of vegetarian dishes.

Le Muguet A cheap and cheerful Chinese restaurant at the bottom of the steps leading to the Lambert Hotel.

Murraille de Chine Av de l'Indépendance, near the station. Good, reasonably priced Chinese food.

Restaurant aux Douze Corbeilles On the steps up to Antaninarenina. A Malagasy-run, non-smoking restaurant (quite a rarity!). Excellent food at very reasonable prices.

Snack bars

Le Buffet du Jardin Pl de l'Indépendance. This fast-food restaurant is a convenient place for lunch, a beer or coffee, with pleasant outdoor tables. Ideal for people-watching and meeting other travellers or foreigners living in Madagascar. The food is mediocre, however.

Pandora 1 Rue Rabobalahy Antaninarenina; tel: 22 37748. Pizzas, hamburgers… Opens from 18.30 until dawn.

Mad' delices Avenue Grandidier Isoraka (opposite Hotel Isoraka); tel: 22 266 41, cellphone: 032 0254 673. 'They have very good pizzas, a selection of Malagasy food, luscious pastries and ice-cream. Service is friendly and helpful, and the restaurant is bright and spotless! They also do a really good breakfast. We liked it so much we ate almost every meal there.' (Heather Bomsta). 'The "pudding" is absolutely heavenous!' (S Riddle)

The Cookie Shop Antanimena, next to Le Bus nightclub. American style coffee, muffins and bagels, for homesick *vazahas*. English spoken!

Macadam 4 Rue de la Réunion, Isoraka. Recommended for burgers. Open 08.00–16.00.

Avenue de l'Indépendance has a growing number of eateries: **Tropique** (good pastries and ice-cream), **Honey** (very good for breakfast and ice-cream, but closed at weekends), **Solimar** for tamarind juice, and **Le Croissanterie** for fresh fruit juice. Also **Bouffe Rapide** and **La Potinerie** (near Air Mad). In the Upper Town both the **Patisserie Suisse** (Rue Rabehevitra) and the **Patisserie Colbert** do good pastries and teas. Patisserie Suisse serves a delicious range of cakes and tarts, but closes at midday for up to three hours.

Nightlife

Papillon at the Hilton is a popular nightclub. Also **Le Caveau** (4, Rue Jeneraly Rabehevitra, Antaninarenina; tel: 22 343 93) and the **Indra** nightclub in Tsaralalana are recommended.

Bars and discos include **Le bus** in Antanimena (tel: 22 691 00). **La Plage** in Betongolo (cellphone: 032 0465 366 or 033 1206 718 or 22 596 47) opens from Thursday to Saturday; upstairs is 'exotic cabaret' and on the ground floor is international music. **Pandora** (1 Rue Rabobalahy, Antaninarenina, tel: 22 377 48) has a tropical atmosphere.

Another option is the **Groove Box**, near Tsimbazaza, which draws the crowds. A live band plays jazz on Thursday, international music on Fridays, and dance music on Saturdays.

Finally, it's worth having a drink at the **Hotel Glacier**, on Avenue de l'Indépendance, to admire the wonderful 1930s' decor and to observe the more disreputable side of Tana's nightlife!

Entertainment

If you are in Tana for a while, buy a local paper to see what's on or keep an eye out for posters advertising special shows or events. Or drop into the Centre Albert Camus on Av de l'Indépendance to pick up a programme for concerts and films.

For a truly Malagasy experience go to a performance of *hira gasy* (pronounced 'heera gash'). See box on page 176. There are regular Sunday performances at Andavamamba, in the front yard of a grey concrete three-storey house set back off the street that goes past Alliance Français. A few Malagasy flags fly above the high, red brick wall and the entrance is via a footpath (not signposted). It starts at 10.00 and finishes around 16.00. Tickets cost 4,000Fmg. Part of the seating is under a tarpaulin canopy and the rest is in the open. It's an exciting and amusing day out – have plenty of small denomination notes ready to support the best performers. There are food stalls with drinks. If you miss the Andavamamba *hira gasy* you can arrange to see a performance at Akany Avoko (see page 154).

Any entertainment that allows you to join a Malagasy audience will be worth the entrance fee.

Films are dubbed into French.

WHAT TO SEE AND DO

As if to emphasise how different it is to other capitals, Tana has relatively little in the way of conventional sightseeing, and even less since the Queen's Palace (*Rova*) burned down. However, there's quite enough to keep you occupied for a few days.

La Maison du Tourisme in theory produces printed lists of hotels, tour operators, car-hire companies etc, and sells good quality T-shirts, handicrafts and postcards. In practice they have little to offer. They may have maps, but better quality ones can be bought in bookshops. Open from 08.00 to 16.00, but they are sometimes open until 18.00. Closed on Sundays. They are located at 3 Rue Elysé

HIRA GASY

A visit to a session of *hira gasy* provides a taste of genuine Malagasy folklore – performed for the locals, not for tourists.

In the British magazine *Folk Roots* Jo Shinner describes a *hira gasy*: 'It is a very strange, very exciting affair: a mixture of opera, dance and Speaker's Corner bound together with a sense of competition.

'The performance takes place between two competing troupes of singers and musicians on a central square stage. It's an all day event so the audience packs in early, tea and peanut vendors picking their way through the throng. Audience participation is an integral part – the best troupe is gauged by the crowd's response. Throughout the day performers come into the crowd to receive small coins offered in appreciation.

'The most immediate surprise is the costumes. The men enter wearing 19th-century French, red, military frock-coats and the women are clad in evening dress from the same period. Traditional *lamba* are carefully arranged around their shoulders, and the men wear straw Malagasy hats. The musicians play French military drums, fanfare trumpets, flutes, violins and clarinets. The effect is bizarre rather than beautiful.

'The *hira gasy* is in four parts. First there are the introductory speeches or *kabary*. Each troupe elects a speaker who is usually a respected elder. His skill is paramount to a troupe. He begins with a long, ferociously fast, convoluted speech excusing himself and his inadequacy before the audience, ancestors, his troupe, his mother, God, his oxen, his rice fields and so on – and on! Then follows another speech glorifying God, and then a greeting largely made up of proverbs.

'The *hira gasy* pivots around a tale of everyday life, such as the dire consequences of laziness or excessive drinking, is packed with wit, morals and proverbs and offers advice, criticism and possible solutions. The performers align themselves along two sides of the square at a time to address different parts of the audience. They sing in harsh harmony, illustrating their words with fluttering hand movements and expressive gestures, egged on by the uproarious crowd's appreciation. Then it is the dancers' turn. The tempo increases and becomes more rhythmic as two young boys take to the floor with a synchronised display of acrobatic dancing that nowadays often takes its influence from karate.'

Ravelontsalama, Ambatomena (near the French Embassy); tel: 22 351 78; fax: 22 558 17; email: mtm@simicro.mg; www.madagascar-tourisme.com.

Rova

For over a century the Queen's Palace, or *Rova*, the spiritual centre of the Merina people, dominated the skyline of Tana. In 1995 it was destroyed by fire – an act of arson unprecedented in Madagascar's history.

The ruin still dominates the skyline – in some ways more dramatically than before – and it should soon be open to visitors again. It is anyway worth the walk up to the palace for the view and to imagine its former grandeur.

Prime Minister's Palace (Musée d'Andafiavaratra)

This former residence of Rainilaiarivony (he who married three queens) has been painstakingly restored and now houses the few precious items that were saved from the *rova* fire. It was built in 1872 by the British architect William Pool. After independence it became in turn an army barracks, law courts, a school of fine arts, the presidential palace and (again) the prime minister's palace. It was burned in 1975. The museum is open from 10.00 to 17.00. Closed Mondays. Entry fee 25,000Fmg.

Tsimbazaza

This comprises a museum (natural history and ethnology), botanical garden and zoo exhibiting – with a few exceptions – only Malagasy species.

The zoo and botanical garden

Until 1999 Tsimbazaza (pronounced 'Tsimbazaz', and meaning 'Where Children are Forbidden', dating from when it was a sacred site) was the centre for the Madagascar Fauna Group, an international consortium of zoos and universities working together to help conserve Madagascar's wildlife. Sadly, the group has withdrawn its financial support, tired of the interminable struggle to bring the zoo up to Western standards (it still supports Ivoloina; see page 307). This is disheartening, but gives us a chance to step back and consider the importance of Tsimbazaza to the local people. They *love* coming here, and put on their best clothes for the occasion. The chief attraction is the ostrich! And why not? An ostrich is a far more extraordinary animal to a Malagasy child than a lemur.

If you go (and you won't see such a comprehensive collection of Malagasy fauna at any other zoo) avoid tipping the 'guides' who should be looking after the animals not trailing after tourists, and hope that the authorities find a compromise between what we in the West expect a good zoo to be, and how the locals want it. A neat example of the difference between the American and the Malagasy view of animal management and life in general was the argument some years ago over a project to have a free-ranging group of lemurs in the park. There was no problem agreeing on the desirability and visitor appeal of this, the conflict was about the components of the group. The American coordinator insisted on single-sex lemurs ('One thing we do *not* want are babies when we have a surplus of lemurs') whilst the Malagasy were holding out for a proper family unit: mother, father and children, because that's what happiness is all about.

Among the animals on display in the zoo are four aye-ayes. Arrangements may be made to visit them after dark when they are active, for a fee of 50,000Fmg per person.

The botanical garden is spacious and well laid out, and its selection of Malagasy endemics is being improved with the help of advisers from Kew (UK) and the Missouri Botanical Garden (USA).There's a new and interesting palm garden. The botanical area provides a sanctuary for numerous birds – indeed, this is an excellent place for birders – including a huge colony of egrets. There are also some reproduction Sakalava graves.

The museum (Musée Académie Malgache)

This is an excellent museum for gaining an understanding of Madagascar's prehistoric natural history and the traditions and way of life of its inhabitants. Skeletons of now extinct animals, including several species of giant lemur and the famous 'elephant bird', provide a fascinating glimpse of the Madagascar fauna which the first humans helped to extinction (explanations in French only). There are also displays of stuffed animals, but the efforts of the taxidermist have left little to likeness and a lot to the imagination. It's worth taking a close look at the aye-aye, however, to study its remarkable hands.

The room housing the ethnological exhibits has been modernised, with clear explanations of the customs and handicrafts of the different ethnic groups.

THE MARTYR MEMORIAL CHURCHES
Dr G W Milledge

My grandfather, James Sibree, a civil engineer from Hull, was appointed by the London Missionary Society in 1863 to build four memorial churches to commemorate the Malagasy Christians put to death by order of Queen Ranavalona I during the period 1837 to her death in 1861. The sites, mainly within easy walking distance of the palace, were associated with the execution or imprisonment of the martyrs. Mr William Ellis of the London Mission had noted that the sites were suitable for church building, thought of the memorial churches and petitioned King Radama II for the sites to be reserved. This was granted. He also petitioned the mission board who agreed to raise funds in England.

Mention should be made of the difficulties and delays in starting to build large stone churches; quarry men, masons and carpenters all had to be trained. Stone was readily available but other materials were difficult to obtain. Workmen often departed for family functions, government work or military service, and work was held up for weeks. As the spire of Ambatonakangar rose to heights unknown in Malagasy buildings, wives of his workmen pleaded with James Sibree not to ask their husbands to go up to such dangerous heights.

Ambatonakanga is situated at the meeting of five roads in an area given on the map as Ambohidahy. The first church in Madagascar was on this site: a low, dark, mud brick building in which Christians were imprisoned, often in chains before, in many cases, being led out to execution. The first printing press was also on this site and the first Malagasy Bibles were printed here. The present church, opened in 1867, follows the Early English style, with 'Norman' arches. It was the first stone building in Madagascar.

Ambohipotsy is on a commanding site at the southern end of the ridge beyond the Queen's Palace. Its slender spire can be seen for miles around the surrounding plain. On this site the first martyr, a young woman called Rasalama, was speared to death in 1837. Later 11 other Christians suffered the same fate.

Faravohitra Church is on the northern side of the city ridge, built where four Christians of the nobility were burnt to death on March 28 1849. Though not as fine a site as Ambohipotsy, it also commands good views.

Ampamarinana Church is a short way below the Palace on the west side of the ridge on the summit of 'The Place of the Hurling' from where prisoners were thrown to their deaths. Fourteen Christians were killed here on the same day in 1849.

So the four churches stand on historic sites as a memorial to those brave martyrs for their faith, and witness to the interest and concern of Christians in Britain for their fellows in Madagascar.

The late Dr Milledge travelled to Madagascar at the age of 88 to visit the place where he was born. Throughout the trip he was honoured as a descendant of James Sibree, one of Madagascar's major benefactors and perhaps the greatest writer the island has inspired.

Practicalities

Tsimbazaza is about 4km from the city centre. There are buses from Avenue de l'Indépendance (number 15), but it is easier to take a taxi there and bus back. It is open every day from 09.00 to 17.00. For tourists the entrance fee is 50,000Fmg (20,000Fmg for children aged 6 to 12). This fee goes towards the upkeep of the park, so watch out that a used ticket is not reissued. Sundays are always very busy, so don't anticipate peace and quiet then.

There is a souvenir shop with a good selection of high-quality T-shirts and postcards, but no restaurant or snack bar. And the toilets are difficult to find (ask at the shop).

Flower market

A colourful flower market is held at the northwestern edge of Lake Anosy. There's something happening here each day but on Sundays it's buzzing and well worth a visit, not only for the flowers but for the colony of white egrets nesting in the trees.

Museum of Art and Archaeology

This lovely little museum is described under *Isoraka* (page 166). The hours are 09.00-17.00. Closed at weekends.

Antshow

This Malagasy Arts and Cultural Centre is the brainchild of Hanitrarivo Rasoanaivo, the lead singer of Tarika, who also founded the charity Valiha High (see page 152). It comprises a large exhibition space, a performance area, the first professional music studio in Madagascar, and a restaurant serving Malagasy food. Five rooms provide luxury accommodation. 'Great home-cooked food and all the local music you could wish for, playing live downstairs. A really superb place to stay.' (K Harvey) Androndra is about 20 minutes southeast of the city centre. Tel: 22 56 547, cellphone: 033 1125 868; email: hmblanche@simicro.mg; www.frootsmag.com/antshow.

SHOPPING
The handicrafts markets

The *Marché Artisanal*, which is best reached by taxi, shows the enormous range and quality of Malagasy handicrafts. Most noteworthy is the embroidery and basketry, woodcarving, minerals, leatherwork (stiff cowhide, not soft leather) and the unique *Antaimoro* paper embedded with pressed flowers. The market is held in the Andravoahangy region of town. This is to the right of the station (as you face it) northeast on Rue Albertini. Open 09.00–17.00, except Sunday. Beware of pickpockets.

This market has now been superseded (in popularity) by the more accessible one (also the *Marché Artisanal*) in district 67 (a major bus stop when approaching the city from the airport). It is open only on Thursdays and Fridays. 'This was the best find: crafts and everything else sold by the makers at rock-bottom prices but minus the craft market haggling, I was happiest here assured the Fmg was received by the makers who were lovely to chat to and gave unsolicited discounts.' (Lorna Gillespie)

Serious shopping

The best-quality goods are sold in specialist shops. In the centre of town, within walking distance of most hotels, is the excellent **Baobab** company. Their two shops, one near the Hotel Palissandre and the other (better, I think) near the Hotel

Sakamanga, sell a wonderful variety of high-quality goods and T-shirts. The specialist shop, **La Tee-shirTerie**, is nearby and, as you would expect, has an excellent selection of T-shirts. **Galerie Yerden** in Isoraka (see page 166) has a huge variety of quality products. An excellent place for wood crafts is **Viva Home** at 23 Rue Ramelina, Antaninarenina, not far from the Colbert; tel: 22 692 71. **Gasyk' Art** has a nice variety of crafts with a showroom at Ivato Airport. The shop is at 62B Talatamaty, on the way to the airport; tel: 22 447 53; email: gasykart@simicro.mg. Another craft shop is **Just' Original**, near the Raphia Hotel in Ambatonakanga. **Sandra Boutique** is in the same area.

There's a good art gallery, **La Flamant Rose**, at 45–47 Avenue de l'Indépendance, Analakely Espace Rarihasina; tel: 22 557 76, cellphone: 032 0235 419; email: flamant.rose@simicro.mg.

Further from town is **Galerie Le Bivouac**, Antsofinondry – on the road to Ambohimanga – which sells beautiful painted silk items, woodcarvings and other handicrafts of a high quality; tel: 22 429 50, email: bivouac@dts.mg. This is also a good place for lunch: Restaurant le Bivouac. Nearby is the **Atelier Jacaranda** which specialises in batik. The quality here is excellent and the prices low. The Jacaranda workshop is next to Le Bivouac (worth visiting if you have time), but sales are made from the gallery 1km down the road, on the other side of the canal. Nearer the centre of town, though still a taxi ride away, is **Lisy Art Gallery** on the Route de Mausolée opposite the Cercle Mess de la Police, and near the Hotel Panorama; tel: 22 277 33, cellphone: 032 0244 416; email: lisy@dts.mg. This is one of the least expensive shops in Tana; open Monday–Friday, 08.30–18.00, Saturday 08.30–12.30, and 14.00–18.00.

For exquisite (and consequently expensive) **weavings** based on traditional *lamba* designs contact British resident Simon Peers; tel: 22 295 02; fax: 22 319 56 for an appointment.

On the way to the airport, not far from the *Marché Artisanal*, there are two small family enterprises run by people from Ambalavao who make **Antaimoro paper** (see page 219). Look for a small green building on the right. The first one is called Sataria (ask for Tsaramila or Rasoa) and for the other ask for Mr Mandrosomana (cellphone: 033 1138 658 or 033 1156 234).

BioAroma, at 51 Av Gen Ramanantsoa (tel/fax: 22 545 57 or 22 326 30; www.madashop.com), up the hill from the Hotel Sakamanga, has a huge selection of their own brand of natural remedies, essential oils, cosmetics and other beauty products. You can also have aromatherapy, a manicure or a massage here. It's all quite clinical with assistants dressed in white coats. They are open weekdays and Sunday mornings. An alternative for beauty products made from Malagasy plants, look for the trade name Phytoline; there is a good selection at the Hilton shop and in the airport departure lounge.

If you have money to spend and are interested in boats, Jenny Roberts recommends a visit to **Le Village Sarl** (Lot 36F, Ambohibao; tel: 22 451 97; www.madagascar-contacts.com/village, email: village@dts.mg) on the left-hand side on the way to the airport. 'The manager, Herve Scrive, employs and has trained 54 local people. They make around 30 different scale model boats, some historic (the *Mayflower*, the *Bounty*) based on the original drawings for the boats. Prices range from €115 to €1,507 for a 120cm model of the *Victory*. They can be shipped home but this is very pricey I believe. We chose to have it packed so that we could get it back on the plane/s with us.' If you do this, get a duplicate receipt from Le Village; you may need to show it at the airport on departure. Open from 07.00 to 17.00 Monday to Saturday, and by appointment on Sundays.

If you make it here, then pay a visit to **Artisanat Aina**, also in Ambohibao on the opposite side of the road. They make Antaimoro paper here (and you can watch the process) and also raffia-work and other crafts. Cellphone: 033 1107 616; email: aina.sarl@dts.mg; www.ainasarl.com.

Charity outlets

If you want both quality and the pleasure of 'giving something back' do your shopping at one of the centres that provide work and hope for the disadvantaged girls and women of Tana. **Akany Avoko** (see page 154) sells a range of handicrafts at its heart-warming Half Way House. Phone 22 441 58 to book a visit.

My favourite place is the **Centre Fihavanana** (see page 163) in Mahamasina, near the stadium, which is run by the Sisters of the Good Shepherd. The centre is in a building set back from the road to the right of an orange-painted church. Ask the taxi driver to take you to the Eglise St Joseph. The women here work to a very high standard, producing beautiful embroidery and greetings cards. The centre is always in need of funds to continue their admirable work with the very poor, and a visit will warm the most resilient of hearts. Judith Cadigan writes: 'We are so glad you suggested visiting the Soeurs du Bon Pasteur in Tana. We bought lots of embroidered linens and were shown around the school, shook hands with what felt like most of the 200 children there, were serenaded by one of the classes, and were altogether greatly impressed by what the nuns are doing. We waited to go there until almost our last day, so that we could take along unused antibiotics, and they were indeed glad to have them. Since I do some embroidery myself, I have a good deal of leftover thread; I asked if they'd like me to send it to them and they sounded as though they'd love it, so I have just sent off a package to them. They use DMC thread.' Most of the sisters speak English. For an appointment phone Sister Lucy or Sister Janet on 22 299 81.

Supermarkets

Most supermarkets sell handicrafts, but you can also try some other locally produced goodies such as chocolate (Chocolat Robert is excellent!) and wine. Both are available from the **Shoprite** supermarket, beneath the Hotel du Louvre in the Upper Town. There is another branch at the lower end of Avenue de l'Indépendance (but avoid this area after dark). Other Shoprites are at Talatamaty on the way to Ivato Airport, near the Hilton Hotel, in a big glass building called Fiaro, and at Ambodivona on the way to the *gares routière* serving the east, north and northwest of the country. The latter has a nice T-shirt shop and a restaurant. A cheaper supermarket is **Score Jumbo**. This is one of the best places to buy T-shirts. There are stores on the way to the airport, at Ankorondrano, on Rue Ravoninahitriniarivo near the Air France office, and in Tanjombato in the south part of the city on the way to Antsirabe.

Maps

A large selection of maps (and also old photo prints) can be bought at the **Institut National de Géodésie et Cartographie** (its long Malagasy name is shortened to FTM), Rue Dama-Ntsoha RJB, Ambanidia (tel: 22 229 35). Hours 07.30–16.00. They produce a series of 12 maps, scale 1:500,000, covering each region of Madagascar. The staff are pleasant and helpful. FTM maps of the more popular tourist areas can usually be bought in bookshops in the town centre – where you can also buy good maps of Tana.

Bookshops

The best bookshop is **Librairie de Madagascar**, on Avenue de l'Indépendance. Also recommended is **Librairie Md Paoly**, a small Catholic bookshop opposite Hotel Mellis.

Photography

Reliable print film can be purchased and processed in Tana. There are two shops on Avenue de l'Indépendance. There is a useful arcade half-way up the main steps (look for the Kodak sign). This shop also does passport photos.

MEDIA AND COMMUNICATION

Couriers

Colis Express 11, Rue Randrianary Ratianarivo, Ampasamadinika; tel: 22 272 42. The main office is in Andrefan' Ambohijanahary LOT 3 E 54 bis, tel: 22 623 05 or 22 557 42.
Midex Madagascar Located at the Auximad office, 18 Rue J J Rabearivelo, Antsahavola; tel: 22 225 02; fax: 22 310 98; email: auximad@dts.mg. Also in Antanimena tel: 22 259 24/ 22 306 70.

Cybercafés

Most of post offices and the bigger hotels have internet facilities. There is a cheaper cybercafé on the same road as the post office, near the Colbert. In the same area is Simicro (tel: 22 656 60); turn right out of the Colbert, go round the corner, and Simicro is about 20m further, on the same side of the road. 1,500Fmg for 15min. In the Lower Town there's an internet café near the Hotel Sakamanga.

Newspapers and magazines

Good news! Madagascar now has its own English-language newspaper: *Madagascar News*, published by the English Speaking Union.

The main daily newspapers are the *Madagascar Tribune* (in French) which tends to follow the government line and is relatively upmarket, and *Midi Madagasikara* (in French and Malagasy), the paper with the highest circulation but little international news. *Express* is a daily newspaper in French and Malagasy, read mainly by intellectuals. *Dans les Média Demain* is an independent weekly magazine, and *Revue de l'Océan Indien – Madagascar* appears monthly.

Post office

The main post office is opposite the Hotel Colbert. There is a separate philately section where you can buy attractive stamps. The post office is open 24 hours a day for outgoing phone calls – useful in an emergency, and much cheaper than phoning from a hotel. Post offices in Analakely and Antaninarenina have internet facilities (called cyberpaositra) for 1,500Fmg for 15 minutes.

MEDICAL EMERGENCIES

Clinics (private)

MM 24 X 24 Mpitsabo Mikambana, Route de l'Université, tel: 22 235 55; email: mm24@wanadoo.mg. Inexpensive and very good.
Espace Medical Tel:22 625 66; email: esmed@dts.mg. Provides a complete medical service including evacuation (see below) and a clinical laboratory.

Private hospitals

Clinique des Soeurs Ankadifotsy; tel: 22 235 54/22 695 20; fax: 22 230 95. Its main English-speaking doctor is Dr Louis Razafinarivo.
Polyclinique d'Ilafy Tel: 22 425 66 or 22 425 69. Similar quality.

Military hospital

Le Centre Hospitalier Tel: 22 397 53. All facilities such as medical consultation, dentistry, X-ray and surgery, clinical laboratory, etc. The cost of hospitalisation is as low as 25,000Fmg (£7/€10) per day for a bed but 'luxury' is 325,000Fmg. Intensive care: 100,000Fmg per day; cardiac intensive care: 150,000Fmg. 'This hospital is the most set up for emergencies and accidents. As with most hospitals in Madagascar you will need someone to stay with the patient all the time and act as the nurse and gopher.' (R Conway)

Emergency evacuation
Espace Medical 65 Rue Pasteur Rabary, Antsahabe; tel: 22 625 66; email: esmed@dts.mg. Director: Dr Arilaza Razafimahaleo. Ambulance with equipment and doctor or simple ambulance. Helicopter also available.

Dentist
Dr Mariane Ottoni Tel : 22 529 70.

Pharmacies
Pharmacie Principal Rte de Hydrocarbures (opposite the big 'Digital' building) Ankorondrano; tel: 22 533 93 or 22 439 15; email: pharm.s@dts.mg. The largest pharmacy in the city.

For normal requirements the pharmacy opposite the post office in Upper Town has most things.

MISCELLANEOUS
Airline offices
Air Madagascar 31 Av de l'Indépendance; tel: 22 222 22. Hours: 07.30–11.00, 14.30–17.00.
Air France Tour Zital 2nd floor, route des Hydrocarbures, Ankorondrano; tel: 23 230 01 or 23 230 41, booking phone 23 230 23; fax : 23 230 41
Interair The office is at the Hilton Hotel; tel: 22 224 06/22 224 52; fax: 22 624 21
Air Austral Immeuble Marbour Antsahavola; tel: 22 359 90
Corsair 1 Rue Rainitovo, Antsahavola; tel: 22 633 36; fax: 22 626 76
Air Mauritius Immeuble Marbour Antsahavola; tel: 22 359 90

Bank and emergency funds
There are now ATMs in Tana, the most convenient being at the Hilton. They don't always work so cannot be relied on. The BOA bank next to the **Shoprite** supermarket will let you draw up to US$200 a day on American Express or MasterCard. Banking hours: 08.00–15.00. Closed on Saturdays. There's a Western Union office on Lalana Generaly Rabehevitra, in Antaninarenina. The American Express office is in the Hilton Hotel.

Cash machines
You can use your credit card to get cash at the following banks (see page 126 for more information).

UCB Antsahavola, near the American Embassy. Accepts Mastercard.
BFV 14 Rue General Rabehevitra, Antaninarenina.
Hilton Hotel

Computer/mobile phone supplies
Concept 12 Rue Ramahazomanana (near the medical school); tel: 22 260 98; they also have a branch in Analakely, near the Ambondrona steps; tel: 22 060 98.
MMC Route Circulaire, Manakambahiny; tel: 22 661 56. English spoken.

Embassies

UK Lot II I 164 ter, Alarobia Amboniloha (BP167), 101 Antananarivo; tel: 22 493 78/22 493 79/22 493 80; fax: 22 493 81; ukembant@simicro.mg
USA Antsahavola (BP620); tel: 22 200 89/22 212 57. For visa/passport business it is open Mondays, Wednesdays and Fridays.
France Rue Jean Jaurès (BP204); tel: 22 237 00/22 200 08.
Germany Route Circulaire (BP516); tel: 22 238 02.
Italy Rue Pasteur Rabary, Ankadivato (BP16); tel: 22 212 17.

English-speaking Union

Chairman: Dr Hary Jeannoda, 16, Residence des Professeur, Nanankanbahiny, Antananarivo 101. Tel: (261 20) 22 30 840; email: vhjeannoda@univantananarivo.mg.

Fixers

A local guide/fixer can take a lot of hassle out of planning an independent trip, but bear in mind that anyone recommended here will charge more than newcomers whom you have found yourself!

Pierre (S Pierrot Patrick) Lot VT 62E, Ambohibato, Ambohipo, Antananarivo 101; tel: 22 295 52, cellphone: 032 0222 868. Pierrot often meets international flights and will identify himself.
Henri Serge Razafison Lot 1384 Cité 67Ha, Antananarivo 101; tel: 22 341 90.
Christophe Andriamampionona Tel: 22 445 08. 'Very knowledgeable.'

Vehicle hire

Full details on hiring a car or motorbike are given in *Chapter 6*. If you are dealing with a Tana travel agent they will also be able to arrange car hire. Large hotels will also have car-hire agencies.

Quite a few visitors find their own driver, rather than hiring a car and driver through an agency. Marja and Wim, from the Netherlands, have used the same driver for both their trips to Madagascar: **Justin Randrianarison**; tel: 22 472 46, cellphone: 032 0753 219. 'He owns a 1989 (but looks brand new) Peugeot 505 and works independently. He lives 10km outside Tana on the way to Antsirabe and is a very pleasant and reliable person, a good driver and speaks some English.'

Laurel Brandstetter recommends **Jean Claude**. 'He speaks English, French, German and Malagasy and he and his partner have a very comfortable vehicle. We hired him and his car from Tana to Ranohira (Isalo) and had a great experience. JC knew just what hotels and restaurants to take us to and was friendly, helpful and knowledgeable.' He can be contacted through Villa Soamahatony (see page 171) or by phoning cellphone 032 0775 080.

Information and permits for nature reserves

ANGAP Main office: BP1424, Ambatobe (near the Lycée Français d' Antananarivo and SNGF : Silo National des Graines Forestières); tel: 22 415 38. There's a more conveniently located branch office in the tour operator Océane Aventures, 22, Rue Andrianary Ratianarivo, Ampasamadinika; tel: 22 312 10; fax: 22 312 22. Open Monday to Friday, 08.00–12.00, 14.00–18.00. ANGAP is the organisation responsible for the administration of almost all the protected areas of Madagascar. Permits (50,000Fmg) for the national parks and reserves may be purchased here, although they are now available at the town serving each reserve. It is worth visiting the Tana office, however, for the latest information on the reserves, and to purchase a National Park Passport. These cost 20,000Fmg. With the passport you are entitled to a discount if you are visiting several parks/reserves. For

instance, visit the six most popular places (Montagne d'Ambre, Ankarana, Masoala, Andasibe-Mantadia, Ranomafana, and Isalo) for the price of four: 130,000Fmg; two national parks cost 75,000Fmg and three 115,000Fmg. There is also an excellent reference library adjacent to the main office.
WWF BP4373; tel: 22 255 41.

Visa extension
A visa extension can be obtained overnight from the Ministry of the Interior near the Hilton Hotel (see page 82).

Church services
Anglican (contact tel: 22 262 68): Cathedral St Laurent, Ambohimanoro; 09.00 service each Sunday.
Roman Catholic (tel: 22 278 30): three churches have services in Malagasy, and three in French. Phone for details.

Golf course
There is a good golf course, the **Club de Golf de Rova** at Ambohidratrimo, 20km from town on the road to Mahajanga. It is open to visitors except at the weekend. Good meals are served at the club house and the Wednesday buffet is particularly recommended.

For more on golf in Madagascar contact **Golf Travel Madagascar**, 17 Rue Ny Zasindriandiky, Antanimena (BP178, Antananarivo 101); email: golf.tr@dts.mg.

EXCURSIONS
Bus stations (*gares routières*)
The *gares routières* for taxi-brousses are on the outskirts of the city at the appropriate road junctions. Fasan'ny karana, on the road to the airport, is the *gares routière* serving the south, southeast and southwest of the country. Gare de l'Ouest, Anosibe (Lalana Pastora Rahajason on the far side of Lac Anosy) serves the west and Gare du Nord (at Andravoahangy, behind the Artisan's market) takes care of the north (at the time of writing this is closed for renovation).

Northeast and east of Antananarivo
Ambohimanga
Lying 21km northeast of Antananarivo, accessed on RN3, Ambohimanga (pronounced 'Ambooimanga'), meaning the 'blue hill', was for a long time forbidden to Europeans. From here began the line of kings and queens who were to unite Madagascar into one country, and it was here that they returned for rest and relaxation among the tree-covered slopes of this hill-top village. These days tourists find the same tranquillity and spirit of reverence and this recently named World Heritage Site is highly recommended as an easy day's trip.

Ambohimanga has seven gates, though some are all but lost among the thick vegetation. By one of the most spectacular, through which you enter the village, is an enormous stone disc which was formerly rolled in front of the gateway each night. Above the gateway is a thatched-roof sentry post and to the right is a bizarre Chinese pagoda (don't ask me what or why...). The entrance area has recently been 'developed' – for no obvious reason. There are some useful small shops here selling drinks and snacks.

Climbing up the stairs towards the compound you pass some handicrafts stalls with a variety of unique and appealing souvenirs, and in the courtyard are two huge fig trees providing shade for a picnic.

Ambohimanga still retains its spiritual significance for the Malagasy people. On the slope to the left of the door to the compound (where you must pay a 35,000Fmg fee) is a sacrificial stone. Melted candle-wax and traces of blood show that it is still used for offerings, particularly in cases of infertility. Rituals involving the placing of seven small stones in the 'male' or 'female' hole will ensure the birth of a baby boy or girl.

The hours are 09.00–11.00, 14.00–17.00 (closed Mondays).

Inside the compound

The centre-piece here is the wooden house of the great king Andrianampoinimerina (1787–1810). The simple one-roomed building is interesting for the insight it gives into everyday (royal) life of that era. There is a display of cooking utensils (and the stones that surrounded the cooking fire) and weapons, and the two beds – the top one for the king and the lower for one of his 12 wives. The roof is supported by a ten-metre rosewood pole. A visit here can be full of surprises: 'Remember this is not a museum, it is the king's palace: he is there. On all my visits there were always several people asking the king for favours. On one memorable occasion I entered his hut to find what seemed like a party in full flow. A man had been possessed by the spirit of a king from the south, and he had come to the palace to greet, and be greeted by, King Andrianampoinimerina. The man had gone into a trance and a group of mediums were assisting him. They had found an accordion player and the man was dancing to get the king's attention. We were spellbound by all this, but the Malagasy visitors totally ignored what was going on and continued to look round the hut as though nothing was happening!' (Alistair Marshall)

Andrianampoinimerina's son, Radama, with British help, went a long way to achieving his father's ambition to expand his kingdom to the sea. His wife succeeded him as Queen Ranavalona. Three more queens followed and, although the capital had, by that time, been moved to Antananarivo, they built themselves elegant summer houses next to Andrianampoinimerina's simple royal home. These have been renovated and provide a fascinating glimpse of the strong influence of the British during those times, with very European décor and several gifts sent to the monarchs by Queen Victoria. French influence is evident too: there are two cannons forged in Jean Laborde's Mantasoa iron foundry. Here also is the small summerhouse belonging to Prime Minister Rainilaiarivony. Understandably cautious about being overheard (he wielded more power than the queens he married) he chose an open design with glazed windows so that spies could be spied first.

Also within the compound is a mundane-looking concrete pool (the concrete is a recent addition) which was used by the queens for ritual bathing and had to be filled, so they say, by 70 virgins, and a corral where zebu were sacrificed. An enclosing wall built in 1787, and faced with a rock-hard mixture of sand and egg, completes the tour.

From a high point above the bath you can get a superb view of the Haut Plateau and Tana in the distance, and on an adjacent hill the white mausoleum of the king's *ombiasy*.

Getting there

Ambohimanga is reached on a good road by private taxi or bus/taxi-brousse. The latter takes about 30 minutes and is cheap. To return to Tana, go to the square below the entrance where the taxi-brousses wait for passengers.

Where to eat

Ambohimanga is an ideal place for a picnic, and there is a nice restaurant (tables in the garden) off the palace courtyard. Meals are reasonably priced and there is live music at weekends.

Domaine de Croix Vallon (Anjozorobe)

If you continue northeast along RN3 to Anjozorobe, you will find this private reserve which is owned by the tour operator Boogie Pilgrim. This comprises 2,500ha of the Anjozorobe Forest Corridor, one of the last vestiges of dense rainforest in the *haut plateau*. The forest covers 66,500ha and stretches for over 80km. Ten species of lemur are found here including indri and diademed sifaka. It is also rich in birdlife (82 recorded species). The reserve itself has a variety of hiking trails and a mountain-bike track. Boogie Pilgrim is working with local communities to demonstrate the benefits of conservation through the private sector.

Soa Camp is 10km from the reserve, along a track to the right shortly before Anjozorobe. It has four igloo tents each with twin beds, a rustic shower (but hot water) and a chemical toilet. Malagasy meals are provided. Boogie Pilgrim offers a day package (entry fee, guided walk in the forest, lunch at Soa Camp) for 80,000Fmg (16,000ariary) or 24 hours (accommodation with breakfast and lunch plus one visit to the forest) for 147,500Fmg (17,800ariary). Further information: tel: 22 530 70; email: contact@boogie-pilgrim.net; www.boogie-pilgrim.net.

Ambohimalaza (La Nécropole Royale)

Off RN2 which leads to Toamasina is a remarkable cemetery. Ambohimalaza was one of the 12 sacred hills of King Andrianampoinimerina, and only the Merina aristocracy are buried here. Their tombs are topped by a *tranomanara* or 'cold house' resembling a little chalet, which indicates that the deceased was of royal blood, as does the red colour of some of the tombs. Nearby are the tiny graves of uncircumcised children who are not allowed to be buried in the family tombs. Around the perimeter you can see the remains of the deep moat and traces of a retaining wall. There is even one of those huge circular stones for closing off the entrance.

The whole area is resonant with atmosphere. Rupert Parker writes: 'It's difficult not to feel the presence of the ancestors of the royal family. My camera certainly felt them and gave up the ghost in the middle of the film – back in the UK they said it couldn't be fixed and my Malagasy friends gleefully pointed out that the ancestors had had their revenge. They also stole a shoe from one of my young nephews – that was his excuse anyway!'

Getting there

The easiest way is by private taxi, but taxi-brousses run every day except Sunday from Ampasampito, on the east of Tana to the village of Ambohimalaza, then it's a 2km walk to the site.

Lake Mantasoa

Some 70km east of Antananarivo is Mantasoa (pronounced Manta*soo*) where in the 19th century Madagascar had its first taste of industrialisation. Indeed, historians now claim that industrial output was greater then than it ever was during the colonial period. It was thanks to Jean Laborde that a whole range of industries was started, including an iron foundry which enabled Madagascar to become more or less self-sufficient in swords, guns and gunpowder, thereby increasing the power of the central government. Jean Laborde was soon highly influential at court and he built a country residence for the queen at Mantasoa.

Many of the buildings remain, and a day's visit to Mantasoa is most rewarding. A stay of a few days would be even better, to give you a chance to walk the quiet, leafy tracks and enjoy the unspoilt small village.

THE TWO-MAN INDUSTRIAL REVOLUTION

Technology was largely introduced to Madagascar by two remarkable Europeans: James Cameron, a Scot, and Jean Laborde, a Frenchman.

James Cameron arrived in Madagascar in 1826 during the country's 'British' phase when the London Missionary Society (LMS) had attempted to set up local craftsmen to produce goods in wood, metal, leather and cotton. Cameron was only 26 when he came to Madagascar but was already skilled as a carpenter and weaver, with wide knowledge of other subjects which he was later to put to use in his adopted land: physics, chemistry, mathematics, architecture and astronomy. Cameron seemed able to turn his hand to almost anything mechanical. Among his achievements were the successful installation and running of Madagascar's first printing press (by studying the manual – the printer sent out with the press had died with unseemly haste), a reservoir (now Lac Anosy) and aqueduct, and the production of bricks.

Cameron's success in making soap from local materials ensured his royal favour after King Radama died and the xenophobic Queen Ranavalona came to power. But when Christian practice and teaching were forbidden in 1835, Cameron left with the other missionaries and went to work in South Africa.

He returned in 1863 when the missionaries were once more welcome in Madagascar, to oversee the building of stone churches, a hospital, and the stone exterior to the *rova* or Queen's palace in Antananarivo.

Jean Laborde was even more of a 'renaissance man'. The son of a blacksmith, Laborde was shipwrecked off the east coast of Madagascar in 1831. Queen Ranavalona, no doubt pleased to find a less godly European, asked him to manufacture muskets and gunpowder, and he soon filled the gap left by the departure of Cameron and the other artisan-missionaries. Laborde's initiative and inventiveness were amazing: in a huge industrial complex built by forced labour, he produced munitions and arms, bricks and tiles, pottery, glass and porcelain, silk, soap, candles, cement, dyes, sugar, rum ... in fact just about everything a thriving country in the 19th century needed. He ran a farm which experimented with suitable crops and animals, and a country estate for the Merina royalty and aristocracy to enjoy such novelties as firework displays. And he built the original Queen's Palace in wood (in 1839), which was later enclosed in stone by Cameron.

So successful was Laborde in making Madagascar self-sufficient, that foreign trade was discontinued and foreigners – with the exception of Laborde – expelled. He remained in the queen's favour until 1857 when he was expelled because of involvement in a plot to replace the queen by her son. The 1,200 workmen who had laboured without pay in the foundries of Mantasoa rose up and destroyed everything – tools, machinery and buildings. The factories were never rebuilt, and Madagascar's Industrial Revolution came to an abrupt end.

He returned in 1861 and became French consul, dying in 1878. A dispute over his inheritance was one of the pretexts used by the French to justify the 1883–85 war.

Getting there

Mantasoa can be reached by taxi-brousse from Tana. The village and its attractions are quite spread out, but it is a very pleasant area for walking.

What to see

Beside the school playing field is a chimney, once part of the china factory. The cannon factory still stands and part of it is lived in, and the large furnace of the foundry remains. All are signposted and fascinating to see; you can just imagine the effort that was required to get them built.

Jean Laborde is buried in the cemetery outside the village, along with 12 French soldiers; there is an imposing mausoleum with a strikingly phallic monument.

The very active *Les Amis de Jean Laborde* have started developing the area for tourism. If you have a special interest in this fascinating man you can phone them on 42 402 97 or email: topoi@dts.mg.

The first project has been to restore Laborde's house which is now a very interesting museum set in a lovely garden. All the labels are in French but a guide may be available to translate. It is worth making the effort to follow Laborde's remarkable story and achievements (see box).

Where to stay/eat

Domaine de l'Ermitage BP16, Mantasoa; tel: 42 660 54. The rooms are so-so but the meals and old-fashioned atmosphere make it well worth a stay. Room with a shower is 200,000Fmg, with bath 250,000Fmg. Meals are 55,000Fmg, 65,000Fmg on Saturday nights. The Sunday buffet is excellent value for 85,000Fmg with a small band playing songs from the 1950s, and breakfast is 25,000Fmg. The Ermitage is set up as a country club and offers all sorts of recreational activities such as riding, tennis, boating on the lake, country walks etc.

Motel le Chalet/ Le Chalet Suisse BP12, Mantasoa; tel: 42 660 95. The Swiss owner, Mme Verpillot, seems to have been around since Jean Laborde's day and has now handed over the running of the place to her son Adrian. There are five bungalows costing between 95,000Fmg and 165,000Fmg and a restaurant serving good food. Meals (which must be eaten there) cost 45,000Fmg (60,000Fmg Sunday lunch). The walk here from the taxi-brousse drop-off point is a pleasant 1½ hours.

Angavokely Station Forestière

Clare and Johann Herman recommend this day trip from Tana. 'At Carion, 30km from Tana on the RN2, you follow the track to Angavokely which takes about 30 minutes down a rutted track which had once been cobbled. It ends at an extraordinary turreted barrier which will be opened after you have applied at the offices a ten-minute walk away. They are located in a large set of buildings amongst a defunct sawmill. A permit costs 20,000Fmg. Faded direction signs and a map indicate the way to the arboretum with picnic tables and parasols, and you can camp. Mt Angavokely is a fair climb up past the eucalyptus plantation and takes about 30 minutes. Thoughtfully, steps with railings are built in the rock face so that you can enjoy the splendid views from the top of the Ankaratra mountains and Lake Mantasoa. A wide track leads back down through the arboretum to the offices.'

Northwest and west of Antananarivo
The forest of Ambohitantely

The name means 'Where Honey is Found' and is pronounced 'Ambweetontel'. This is the last remnant of natural forest in the province of Ankazobe and there are hopes that it will become a protected area. This report (written a few years ago) is by Dr Graham Noble and Sandra Baron of South Africa. 'It takes at least 2½ hours to get to the forest which lies 150km northwest of Tana off the road to Mahajanga. The access village is Ararazana. The forest is 10km from the road and you do not see a tree until you reach the site.

'Estimates of its size vary from 1,400 to 3,000ha. It is surrounded by a barrier of burnt trees, but as you go two metres into the forest the leaf-litter is already 10–15cm deep. There is a network of paths through the forest. The University of Antananarivo has a right to a part of it as a study site and refers to that section as the Botanical Garden. The forestry director is very keen to receive tourists into the area for day walks and will also organise provisions for overnight stays. Good birding and lots of orchids.'

Derek Schuurman adds: 'This is actually a very beautiful little rainforest, with rufous mouse lemurs and common brown lemurs as well as tenrecs. Birds found there include the Madagascar blue pigeon, long-billed greenbul, forest rock thrush, blue vanga and, en route, the Réunion harrier.' However, he adds that it is really worth visiting only if you are driving north to Mahajanga and so pass nearby. You will see nothing here that can't be found (more easily) in Andasibe-Mantadia.

Check with ANGAP on the current status of the forest (and to buy a permit), and make a further visit to the Direction des Eaux et Forêts in Ankazobe, 106km from Tana. Because of a problem with bandits in the area, you are advised to check with the Eaux et Forêts people about where to stay/camp, and always travel with a reliable guide.

Lemurs Park

This large zoo makes a good day trip from Tana for those on a quick visit who are not able to see lemurs in their natural habitat. Six species of lemur live free in the 4ha park; many of them are confiscated pets, and this is the first step towards rehabilitation. Feeding times are 09.00, 12.00, 14.00 and 16.00; if you can visit just before these times the lemurs will be more active. The park is 22km west of Tana, on the road to Arivonimamo (RN1). The entrance is on the right and clearly signposted. The entry fee is 25,000Fmg. There is a good restaurant here (but it doesn't open until noon) plus a giftshop. Open 10.00 to 16.00, closed on Mondays. Contact details: tel: 22 234 36, cellphone: 033 1172 890; email: info-lemurs@lemurspark.com; www.lemurspark.com.

Lake Itasy area
Derek Schuurman

Approximately 2½–3 hours' drive west of the capital, **Ampefy** makes for a good location if you have a day or two to spare in the highlands and want to sample some local highlands' culture as well as seeing some unusual geological /geographical features.

Lalaina Ramaroson of Za Tour and I set off with a 4WD vehicle (essential if you want to see the geysers) in the early morning. One of the first things I noticed, on the western outskirts of Antananarivo, are some marvellous examples of Merina tombs. About 40km further along the RN1 road, we stopped by at the farmers' market at **Mangatary**, which takes place on Thursdays. The local farmers sell produce from their colourful zebu-drawn wagons.

Another noticeable feature of this part of the highlands is the groves of tapia trees, much like around Isalo but seemingly even more extensive.

Lake Itasy

This is a popular weekend retreat with Malagasy families from Antananarivo with a good lakeside hotel, Hotel Kavitaha, in a lovely tranquil setting. The

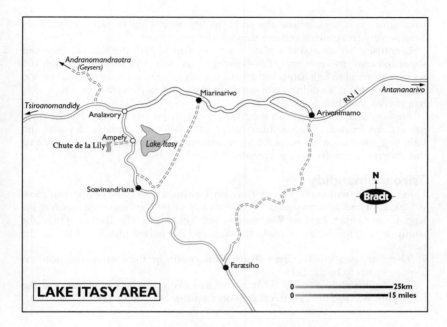

Andranomandraotra
(Geysers)

Tsiroanomandidy

Analavory

Miarinarivo

RN 1

Antananarivo

Arivonimamo

Ampefy
Chute de la Lily

Lake Itasy

N

Bradt

Soavinandriana

Faratsiho

LAKE ITASY AREA

0 —————————— 25km
0 —————————— 15 miles

restaurant (good food, tilapia a speciality) overlooks the lake which is fed by the Lily River; the setting is serene and relaxing. On the far side of the lake (opposite the restaurant) at some waterfalls is a boulder marked by a Malagasy flag. This is a small shrine where people place sacrificial offerings while praying for blessings.

There are two notable excursions from the hotel, the Chute de la Lily and the Geysers of Andanomandraotra.

Where to stay
Hotel Kavitaha Tel 48 840 04; email: bicrakotomavo@wanadoo.mg. 21 neat rooms: seven triple, 14 twin or double; 175,000Fmg per room (195,000Fmg for a family room). Breakfast is 20,000Fmg and meals are 45–60,000Fmg. The hotel offers a range of activities and facilities (pedalos, kayaks, pirogues, table tennis, fishing, etc) and is ideal for families. The hotel is reached by driving due west of Tana on RN1 until **Analavory** (approx 2½ hrs). Then turn left to Ampefy and the Kavitaha Hotel.

Chute de la Lily
This large and impressive waterfall is 7km from the hotel. It's a good idea to do this excursion with a Malagasy guide familiar with the back roads and how to get into and out of the waterfall area. There is a lively village here and at the falls a tiny stall where residents sell some simple crafts.

The Geysers of Andanomandraotra
Getting here is a challenge. Four kilometres from Analavory town is a turn-off to Andranomandraotra, the place where the geysers are located. The distance from the turn-off to the geysers is only 8km but, on a frightening 'road', covering that 8km took us about an hour, one way.

You drive through picturesque, typical highlands scenery with grass-covered hills, flowery meadows and more plantations of pawpaw than I have ever seen. You pass through villages where the residents are incredibly friendly, most likely because very few tourists venture through these parts.

Eventually, we arrived at a place where we had to park the vehicle, leave our shoes and cross two extremely fast-flowing rivers. The river beds were rough and rocky, so we had to link hands and form a human chain to get across. So strong was the current that if we didn't form the chain, we could easily have been swept away had anyone lost their foothold.

Anyhow, after crossing both the rivers, you arrive at the place where the three geysers are located. The combination of pale, off-white mineral deposits and bubbling, spouting water make for quite a spectacle but it must be emphasised that this excursion is really not for everyone.

Tsiroanomandidy

Lying about 200km to the west of Tana, on a surfaced road (four hours), this town is a pleasant and attractive place to spend a day or two. Its main attraction is the large cattle market, held on Wednesdays and Thursdays. The Bara people of the south drive huge herds of cattle through the Bongolava plateau to sell at the market.

There are two hotels. **Chez Marcelline**, north of the market and near the airport, seems to be the better.

Tsiroanomandidy is linked to Maintirano and Mahajanga by Twin Otter, and also to Morondava. You can also travel west on the River Manambolo (see *Chapter 16*).

HAINTENY

Consider, children, the conditions here on earth:
The trees grow, but not unceasingly,
For if they grew unceasingly, they would reach the sky.
Not only this,
but there is a time for their growing,
a time for their becoming old,
and a time for their breaking.
So it is, too, for man: there is a time for youth,
a time for old age,
a time for good,
a time for evil,
and a time for death.

The Highlands South of Tana

Many visitors drive the full length of Route Nationale 7 (RN7) to Toliara, either by hired car or by public transport. It is a delightful journey, providing an excellent overview of the *Hauts Plateaux* and Merina and Betsileo culture, as well as spectacular scenery, especially around Fianarantsoa.

FROM TANA TO ANTSIRABE

It takes about three hours to drive to Antsirabe non-stop. But there are numerous suggested pauses and diversions so most people take the best part of a day to do the 170km. The photo-opportunities are terrific – all along this stretch of road you will see Merina tombs, and can watch the labour-intensive cultivation of rice paddies.

About 15km from Tana look out for a huge, white replica of the *rova* (as it was before it burned) across the paddy fields on the right. This was ex-President Ratsiraka's palace, funded by North Korea.

Ambatofotsy

An interesting diversion for those with their own vehicle is this lakeside resort some 20km south of Tana. There's a small nature park here with around 160 plant species, a few lemurs and one or two snakes and other reptiles. There is also a museum. The entrance fee is 25,000Fmg. Accommodation is available at the hotel/restaurant **Le Carat**, tel: 22 297 80 or 030 23 812 22. There are 19 bungalows costing from 92,000Fmg to 232,000Fmg; meals cost 50,000Fmg.

DISTANCES IN KILOMETRES

Antananarivo–Ambatolampy	70km
Antananarivo–Ampefy	135km
Antananarivo–Antsirabe	170km
Antananarivo–Ambositra	330km
Antananarivo–Fianarantsoa	408km
Antsirabe–Ambositra	70km
Antsirabe–Fianarantsoa	240km
Antsirabe–Miandrivazo	225km
Antsirabe–Ihosy	138km
Ambositra–Ranomafana	331km
Fianarantsoa–Mananjary	204km
Fianarantsoa–Manakara	264km
Fianarantsoa–Ihosy	206km

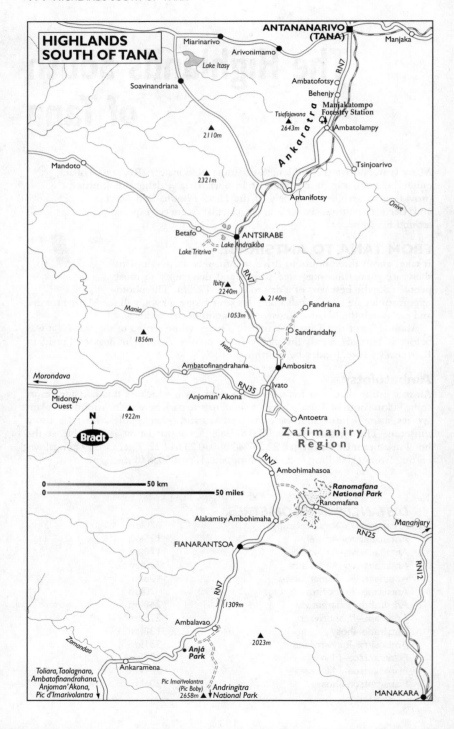

FROM TANA TO ANTSIRABE 195

Ambatolampy and region

Ambatolampy lies some two hours/68km from Tana and has a colourful market as well as a very good hotel/restaurant. It is also the starting point for two interesting excursions to Tsinjoarivo, with its summer *rova*, and the forestry station of Manjakatompo.

South of the town, near the Manja Ranch, is an insectarium set up by a Frenchman, Jean-Baptiste Cornet (admission about 25,000Fmg). He is hoping to use the revenue to provide financial support to entomology students.

Telephone code The area code for Ambatolampy is 42.

Where to stay/eat
Hotel au Rendez-vous des Pecheurs Tel: 42 492 04. 8 rooms, Albanian-owned and renowned for its excellent food (meals are 65,000Fmg). This is a popular stop for tour buses travelling south so it can be crowded at lunchtime. The rooms are simple but comfortable, mostly with shared bathrooms (with a big bathtub) and hot water; some have en-suite WC. 75,000Fmg (single), 100,000Fmg (double), 125,000Fmg (triple).
Manja Ranch BP36, Ambatolampy 104; tel: 42 492 34; email: ManjaRanch@hotmail.com. Rooms (shared bathrooms, unreliable water) are about 50,000Fmg, but two new bungalows have en-suite bathrooms for 75,000Fmg. Breakfast is 15,000Fmg. Camping: 10,000Fmg or free if you eat at the ranch. Good meals for 40,000Fmg. About 2km south of Ambatolampy and owned by Doug Cook, an American, and his Malagasy wife Bijou. Horses and bikes for hire.

Tsinjoarivo

From Ambatolampy a road leads southeast to Tsinjoarivo. Johan and Clare Hermans write: 'Check conditions before setting out; although only about 50km it takes a good three to four hours by car and is not an all-weather road (there is an alternative road on higher ground which bypasses some of the boggiest stretches of the main road). The journey is worthwhile for the series of waterfalls and the *rova* of Queen Rasoherina; in her time it took three days to get there from Tana by palanquin. There is a guardian who will show you round the buildings, one for the queen with the remains of some fine wooden carving from her bed, and others for the prime minister, the chancellor and the guard. Situated on a promontory overlooking the falls, the site has spectacular views and an incredible atmosphere. There are stone steps down from the *rova* to the viewpoint at the falls, complete with spray.'

Manjakatompo Forestry Station

A road leads west and then north from Ambatolampy to Manjakatompo, an hour's drive (17km). 'The road passes through aluminium smelting villages – worth a stop to watch them making cutlery and cooking pots. Permits for the Manjakatompo Forest are obtainable at the gate: 20,000Fmg. Guides not obligatory (ours was not worth the money). Well signposted walks, sights include a small waterfall, and an interesting lichen forest with two royal tombs, circa 1810 near the encampment. It is a four-hour hike to Tsiafajavona, tallest peak of the Andringitra range.' (Johan and Clare Hermans)

Merina tombs

About 15 minutes beyond Ambatolampy are some fine painted Merina tombs. These are on both sides of the road, but the most accessible are on the right.

Hotel Antsaha

If you have your own transport and want to stay away from cities, this hotel (tel: 44 050 02; email: antsaha@tonga-soa.zzn.com) some 19km north of Antsirabe is a good option. 14 bungalows with hot water, two with kitchens. 150,000Fmg; breakfast 25,000Fmg.

ANTSIRABE

Antsirabe lies 170km south of Antananarivo at 1,500m. It was founded in 1872 by Norwegian missionaries attracted by the cool climate and the healing properties of the thermal springs. The name means 'The Place of Much Salt'.

This is an elegant city, and with its top-class hotels and interesting excursions merits a stay of a few days. A broad avenue links the handsome (though now unused) railway station with the amazing Hotel des Thermes; at the station end is a monolith depicting Madagascar's 18 main ethnic groups.

Antsirabe is the agricultural and industrial centre of Madagascar, best known as the centre for beer. You can smell the Star Brewery as you enter the town.

This is the *pousse-pousse* capital of Madagascar. There are hundreds, perhaps thousands of them. The drivers are insistent that you avail yourself of a ride, and why not? But be very firm about the price. Now that lots of tourists come to Antsirabe, the drivers have found they can make a dollar just by posing for pictures. To actually have to run somewhere towing a large *vazaha* for the same price must seem very unfair.

On a promontory overlooking the baths stands the Hotel des Thermes: an amazing building in both size and architectural style. There is nothing else like it in Madagascar – it would not be out of place along the French Riviera and is set in equally elegant gardens (see *Where to stay*).

If you are travelling between May and September you will need a sweater in the evening. It gets quite cold.

Telephone code The area code for Antsirabe is 44.

Getting there and away
By rail
The passenger train from Tana may be re-established by the time you read this. Check at the station in Tana.

By road
Antsirabe is generously served by buses and taxi-brousses. These leave from Fasan'ny Karana in Tana, the journey taking about three hours. Continuing south to Ambositra takes two hours and costs 7,000Fmg. Travelling from Antsirabe to Fianarantsoa (non-stop) by private car takes five hours.

Note that there are two taxi-brousse stations in Antsirabe – one in the north of the town and one in the south.

Where to stay
A special feature of Antsirabe are the private guesthouses. These offer a friendly and economical alternative to hotels.

Category A
Avana Hotel (formerly Aida) Tel:44 492 98; email: avanahotel2000@yahoo.fr. A large hotel on the northern side of town, near the taxi-brousse station. Comfortable, and competitively priced. 173,000Fmg (double room or twin with continental breakfast), or

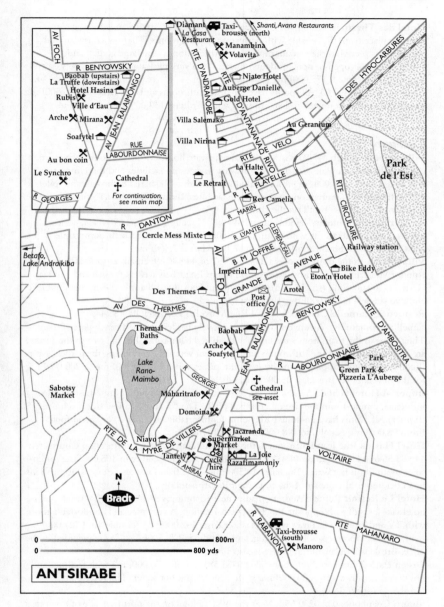

The map shows the following labels:

Diamant
La Casa Restaurant
Taxi-brousse (north)
Shanti, Avana Restaurants
Manambina
Volavita
AV FOCH
RTE D'ANDRANOBE
R BENYOWSKY
Baobab (upstairs)
La Truffe (downstairs)
Hotel Hasina
Rubis
Ville d'Eau
Arche
Mirana
AV JEAN RALAIMONGO
Soafytel
RUE LABOURDONNAISE
Au bon coin
Le Synchro
R GEORGES V
Cathedral
For continuation, see main map
Njato Hotel
Auberge Danielle
Gold Hotel
Villa Salemako
RTE D'ANTANANARIVO
Au Geranium
Villa Nirina
RTE DE VELO
La Halte
FLAYELLE
Le Retrait
R H
Res Camelia
R MARIN
R DANTON
Cercle Mess Mixte
R LYANTEY
B M JOFFRE
CLEMENCEAU
RTE CIRCULAIRE
Park de l'Est
R DES HYPOCARBURES
Railway station
Imperial
AVENUE
Bike Eddy
Eton'n Hotel
Betafo, Lake Andraikiba
AV FOCH
GRANDE
Arotel
Des Thermes
Post office
AV DES THERMES
Thermal Baths
Baobab
Arche
Soafytel
R GEORGES V
Cathedral see inset
R BENYOWSKY
RTE D'AMBOSITRA
LABOURDONNAISE
Park
Green Park & Pizzeria L'Auberge
Lake Rano-Maimbo
Sabotsy Market
Maharitrafo
AV JEAN RALAIMONGO
Domoina
Niavo
RTE DE LA MYRE DE VILLERS
Tantely
Cycle hire
Jacaranda
Supermarket
Market
La Joie
Razafimamonjy
R VOLTAIRE
N
Bradt
R AMIRAL MIOT
R RABANONA
Taxi-brousse (south)
Manoro
RTE MAHANARO
0 _____ 800m
0 _____ 800 yds
ANTSIRABE

303,000Fmg (suite), additional bed is 45,000Fmg per night, radiator 40,000Fmg per night. Meals are 60,000Fmg.

Arotel Rue Ralaimongo, Antsirabe 110; tel:44 481 20, 44 485 73, or 44 485 74; fax: 44 491 49; email: arotel.inn@dts.mg. 39 rooms, 6 suites, 2 apartments. Twin or double rooms for €38, apartment €44. Continental breakfast €4, and main meals €8.50. A well-situated, comfortable hotel. Luxurious full-sized bathtubs. Good food. There is a lovely secluded garden at the back with a swimming pool that is open to non-residents at 4,000Fmg.

Hotel des Thermes Tel: 44 487 61/2; fax 44 492 02; email: sht@wandadoo.mg. An amazing place from the outside with perfectly adequate rooms. There is a cosy bar and good food is served in the restaurant. In the warmer months the large garden and swimming pool (open to non-residents) makes this a very pleasant place to relax. Visa and MasterCard accepted. 175,000Fmg (double).

La Casa Tel: 44 492 03. All rooms have en-suite bathrooms and TV. Breakfast 16,500Fmg. Comfortable, but 'you need to like brown if you stay here'.137,000Fmg (double) to 275,000Fmg (suite).

Category B

Villa Salemako Tel: 44 495 88. A good-value private home with five rooms for visitors, run by Julia-Brigitte Rakotonarivo. Rooms vary in size and facilities and therefore price. The range is from 75,000Fmg for a small double room with shared bathroom and toilet, to 100,000Fmg for a family room with en-suite facilities. Beautiful garden. To find the house look for the Malagasy motif on the chimney.

Au Geranium Route du Velodrome; tel: 44 497 31; cellphone: 032 0704 544. 8 nice rooms, double 55,000Fmg with bathroom, 50,000Fmg for a shared bathroom; triple 65,000Fmg (shared bathroom). Continental breakfast is 7,500Fmg.

Villa Nirina Route d'Andranobe; tel: 44 485 97 or 44 486 69; email: zanoa@blueline.mg. Run by Mrs Zanoa Rasanjison, who speaks fluent English as well as French and survival German. 100,000Fmg (single), 120,000Fmg (double or twin). Family room (one double and two singles) is 180,000Fmg. Breakfast included .

Residence Camelia One block east of Rue Marechal Foch; tel: 44 488 44; email: camellia@simicro.mg. A converted villa set in lovely gardens in the French part of town. The rooms in the main house are small, with shared bathrooms, but the two in the annexe are spacious with en-suite bathrooms and their own veranda overlooking the garden. More (luxury) accommodation is being built. Room prices vary from 70,000Fmg to 200,000Fmg for the new annexe. Breakfast 25,000Fmg.

Imperial Hotel Grande Av; tel: 44 483 33. 'Soulless oriental with definite Eastern Bloc influence; dining-room the size of a football pitch. The "casino" is a few slot machines.' (S Bulmer) All rooms have en-suite bathrooms. Comfortable but noisy. Very good food. From 98,000Fmg (single) to 148,000Fmg (family room).

Hotel Hasina Rue Jean Ralaimongo, the same building as the furniture shop Courts; tel: 44 485 56 or 44 487 13; fax: 44 483 55. Double 100,000Fmg and twin 105,000Fmg for en-suite rooms with hot water. Breakfast 10,500Fmg, with fruit juice an extra 2,500Fmg. This hotel belongs to the owner of the restaurant Razafimamonjy.

Hotel Le Retrait Route d'Andranomadio, near Kisomby; tel: 44 050 29. To reach the hotel take a small path opposite the Total petrol station. A very nice and comfortable room with TV and en-suite facilities with hot water costs 102,000Fmg (double) and 127,000Fmg twin. A family room costs 153,000Fmg, and a studio is 178,500Fmg. Tax is included in the price. Breakfast is available and there is also a bar.

Green Park Tsarasaotra; cellphone: 032 0753 581. Double 70,000Fmg with facilities and hot water. Family room is 80,000Fmg with facilities and hot water. The restaurant L'Auberge is next door.

Shanti Cellphone: 032 0230 552. Near the Avana Hotel on the northern side of town near the taxi-brousse station. This is an Indian hotel with restaurant; Family room is 75,000Fmg; double 60,000Fmg with bathroom and toilet.

Category C

Hotel Diamant 110 Route d'Andranobe; tel: 44 494 40; fax: 44 493 72; email: diamant@madawel.com; www.madawel.com. A well-established, medium-sized hotel offering a good selection of rooms. Prices vary according to quality: 49,000Fmg, 74,000Fmg and 94,000Fmg, with a new room with TV, phone and bathroom costing between 129,000Fmg and 179,000Fmg. Breakfast 9,000Fmg; American breakfast 15,000Fmg. Meals from 18,000Fmg to 25,000Fmg; a Malagasy meal costs 10,000Fmg. Internet facilities (English keyboard) for 100Fmg/min.

Hotel Soafytel Tel: 44 480 55. This hotel has slipped from B to C because it needs renovating, but it has hot water and it's cheap! Low-season price for an en-suite room is 90,000Fmg. Family room 85,000Fmg. A standard double room with en-suite bathroom but shared toilet is 60,000Fmg.

Hotel Kabary Near the railway station. Tel: 44 496 07; email: kabary110@yahoo.fr. Rooms between 55,000Fmg and 65,000Fmg, shared bathroom. Serves good breakfasts, has live music at night, friendly staff. 'A very hip, cheerful place.' (DF)

Hotel Niavo (The full name is Hotel/Restaurant Fitsangantsanganana Niavo!) Rue Rakotondrainibe Daniel; tel: 44 484 67. En-suite rooms from 25,000Fmg to 80,000Fmg. 'The only poor-quality hotel I stayed in. But its location is good, being close to the market and the southern taxi-brousse station. Double room, shared facilities. En-suite rooms from 50,000Fmg. Cockroaches included in the price.' (Stuart Riddle)

Hotel Le Nouveau Baobab Tel: 44 483 93. Single 37,000Fmg, double 47,000Fmg; with bathroom 52,000Fmg, room with TV but shared toilet 72,000Fmg, while en-suite bathroom and TV is 82,000Fmg.

Hotel Bike Eddy (Buffet de la De Gare) Tel: 44 495 91. Near the station and very cheap: 35,000Fmg (shared facilities).

Volavita Route D'Antananarivo; tel: 44 488 64; fax: 44 489 60; email: volavita@blueline.mg. A simple room with bathroom but outside toilet is very cheap: 30,000Fmg. A triple room (bathroom but outside toilet) is 50,000Fmg, and a four-person room with en-suite bathroom and hot water is 65,000Fmg; family room 70,000Fmg. There's an extra charge of 15,000Fmg for a TV in the room. This hotel also has more comfortable rooms for 75,000Fmg and 100,000Fmg.

Njato Hotel Located near Diamant Hotel on the left of the petrol station as you enter from Tana, this is a very simple hotel, 25,000Fmg shared bathroom and 40,000Fmg with bathroom.

Gold Hotel Cellphone: 032 0208 017. Near Villa Nirina, another simple hotel, Rooms from 25,000Fmg to 70,000Fmg shared bathroom.

Cercle Mess Mixte Tel: 44 483 66. Double with toilet, wash-basin but shared bathroom with hot water is 45,000Fmg. 3 single beds or one double and one single with bathroom and toilet is 65,000Fmg or 75,000Fmg with TV. A basic breakfast is about 4,000Fmg.

Hotel Rubis Rue Stavengere. Another very simple hotel behind Soafytel; rooms between 25,000Fmg and 35,000Fmg.

Hotel Restaurant Le Synchro Tel: 030 44 863 18; the hotel is reached via a path in front of the Cathedral (about 500m). Rooms with shared facilities are 35,000Fmg, 45,000Fmg or 50,000Fmg; breakfast is 8,000Fmg.

Guest House Maharitrafo Rue Rakotondraibe Daniel; cellphone: 033 1203 947; email: maharitrafo@hotmail.com. Double is 45,000Fmg, triple is 60,000Fmg with shared bathroom with hot water. Next door is a snackbar and restaurant.

Hotel Restaurant Domoina Rue Kleber Antsenakely; tel: 44 495 16. Another simple hotel costing from 30,000Fmg to 50,000Fmg for rooms with shared bathroom. Breakfast is 3,000Fmg.

Hotel Restaurant Tantely In front of Ex-Pharmacie d'Ampatana; tel: 44 491 37. One double and one single bed is 60,000Fmg, whilst a double is 35,000Fmg. Breakfast is 5,000Fmg or 6,000Fmg.

Manoro Hotel Ambavahadimangatsiaka; tel: 44 480 47. Room: 56,000Fmg, 61,000Fmg, 76,000Fmg with facilities and hot water. Breakfast is 7,500Fmg and continental breakfast 12,500Fmg.

La Joie Rue Duplex; cellphone: 033 1147 423. Room from 35,000Fmg to 90,000Fmg with wash-basin and bidet but shared toilet and bathroom with hot water. Breakfast 6,000–10,000Fmg.

Ville D' Eau (guesthouse) Near Mirana (formerly Helena Patisserie); tel: 44 499 70. Double or twin room with shared bathroom (hot water) and toilet from 30,000Fmg to 64,000Fmg. Double or twin with bathroom is 74,000Fmg with hot water. Breakfast is between 3,000Fmg and 12,500Fmg.

Eton'n Hotel Opposite the railway station; tel: 030 44 862 67. Rooms are 60,000Fmg and 70,000Fmg with bathroom and hot water. Order ahead if you want breakfast.

Space Hotel Near Avana Hotel, a very simple place on the northern side of town, near the taxi-brousse station. Double 30,000Fmg with cold water but 50,000Fmg with hot water.

Where to eat

Arche Rue Stavanger; cellphone: 032 02 479 25. 'On a little street leading from Av Foch to Av Jean Ralaimongo. Small, French-owned, good food, live music in the evenings, good atmosphere.' (S Bulmer)

Bar-Restaurant Razafimamonjy Antsenankely; tel: 483 53. Opposite the market on Av de l'Indépendance. Once highly praised but, in the opinion of one reader, no longer what it was. 'It has a very restrictive menu and service that was so bad I nearly left without paying.' Mainly Chinese; reasonable prices.

Restaurant Manambina Route d' Antananarivo. Tel: 44 493 02, cellphone: 032 0779 043. Malagasy, French, Chinese and vegetarian dishes. Closed Mondays.

Auberge Danielle Roughly opposite the Hotel Diamant. This little *hotely* serves well-prepared, cheap meals.

Salon de Thé Moderne A pleasant snack bar opposite the Pharmacie Mahasoa.

Mirana (formerly Helena Patisserie). Tel: 44 491 81, cellphone: 033 1119 987. Opposite the BNI Bank. Good for breakfast and take-away meals. 'Pizza, quiche, and the first apple turnovers I've tasted in Madagascar; OK, so they were made from strawberries but one can't be too fussy when travelling!' (F Kerridge)

La Truffe A new restaurant in the vicinity of the station in the same building as Hotel Baobab (downstairs) next to Hotel Hasina.

Jacaranda Antsenankely, in front of restaurant Razafimamonjy; tel: 44 484 56.

Au Bon Coin Opposite the cathedral, same ownership as Le Nouveau Baobab Hotel. Malagasy and Chinese food.

Nightlife

Tahiti nightclub At the Hotel Diamant. 'Worth a visit.' (SB)

Bicycle hire

In the first street (south) behind the daily market is a **bicycle hire** shop. Good mountain bikes for about 50,000Fmg per day. Bikes can also be hired outside the Hotel des Thermes. The best option, however, is find Jean Noel at the restaurant Arche. 'He has a stack of good bikes which he hires out for just 25,000Fmg a day. He provided a good map and even gave me a puncture repair kit and tools for no extra cost. A lovely bloke!' (Stuart Riddle). Jean Noel, who can also organise excursions on foot, bike or car, can be contacted on cellphone 032 02 176 05, email: rabemananjaram@yahoo.fr.

What to see and do

Saturday is **market** day in Antsirabe, an echo of Tana before they abolished the *zoma* but with an even greater cross-section of activities. It's enclosed in a walled area of the city on the hill before the road to Lake Tritriva. 'The entire back wall of the market is a row of open barber stalls. Each has a small mirror, a chair and a little peg for one's hat. There are a few local gambling places nearby, too. They're hard to find, and the stakes can get pretty high.' (Maggie Rush).

It is worth paying a visit to the **thermal baths** (*thermes*). There is a wonderfully hot swimming pool full of laughing brown faces that laugh even harder at the sight of a *vazaha*. But it's friendly laughter. You can also take a none-too-clean, 4,000Fmg private bath here (but there's a 20-minute limit) and have a massage. Open to the public only in the morning.

Excursions from Antsirabe
Lake Andraikiba
This large lake 7km west of Antsirabe is often overlooked in favour of the more spectacular Lake Tritriva. 'One of the few moments when you stepped back into another world. Very laid back, very few people. Tranquil and picturesque.' (Volker Dornheim)

Taxi-brousses heading for Betafo pass close to the lake, or you can go by hired bicycle. **Hotel Dera** overlooks the lake. Cellphone: 032 0465 848. Chalets 80,000Fmg.

Lake Tritriva
The name comes from *tritry* – the Malagasy word for the ridge on the back of a chameleon (!) – and *iva*, deep. And this emerald-green crater lake is indeed deep – 80m, some say. It is reached by continuing past Lake Andraikiba for 12km on a rough, steep road (4WD only) past small villages of waving kids. You will notice that these villages are relatively prosperous-looking for Madagascar – they grow the barley for the Star Brewery.

Apart from the sheer beauty of Lake Tritriva (the best light for photography is in the morning), there are all sorts of interesting features. The water level rises in the dry season and debris thrown into the lake has reappeared down in the valley, supporting the theory of underground water channels.

Look across the lake and you'll see two thorn trees growing on a ledge above the water with intertwined branches. Legend says that these are two lovers, forbidden to marry by their parents, who drowned themselves in Tritriva. When the branches are cut, so they say, blood, not sap, oozes out. You can walk right round the lake for impressive views of it and the surrounding countryside.

The local people have not been slow to realise the financial potential of groups of *vazahas* corralled at the top of a hill. There is an 'entrance charge' of 10,000Fmg, and once through the gate don't think you will be alone at the lake.

Getting to Tritriva without a 4WD vehicle is difficult. The best ways are to take a bus to Lake Andraikiba and then walk or to rent a bike and make it a day trip. If you are self-sufficient you can stay in the village of Belazao, midway between the two lakes (no hotel), or camp at the lake.

Betafo
About 22km west of Antsirabe, off the tarred road that goes as far as Morondava, lies Betafo, a town with typical highlands red-brick churches and houses. Dotted among the houses are *vatolahy*, standing stones erected to commemorate warrior chieftains. A visit here is recommended. It is not on the normal tourist circuit, and gives you an excellent insight into Merina small-town activities. Monday is market day. There is no hotel in Betafo but you should be able to find a room by asking around.

At one end of the town is the crater lake, Tatamarina. From there it is a walk of about 3km to the Antafofo waterfalls among beautiful views of rice fields and volcanic hills. You will need to find someone to show you the way. 'It's very inviting for a swim but they told me there are ghosts in the pool under the falls. If you go swimming they will pull at your legs and pull you to the bottom.' (Luc Selleslagh)

On the outskirts of Betafo there are hot springs, where for a few francs you can have a hot bath with no time limit.

CONTINUING SOUTH ON RN7

Leaving Antsirabe you continue to pass through typical highland scenery of rice paddies and low hills.

An interesting sidetrip from this stretch is to Mt Ibity. Valerie Middleton writes: 'About 15km south of Antsirabe on the RN7 a large white sign points westwards to the "Holcim Cement Works". This good dirt road can be followed to the village of Ibity opposite the works, above which rears Mount Ibity. This mainly quartzite massif provides excellent walking opportunities as it naturally has few trees, thus allowing panoramic views from almost any point. Many small footpaths cross and circumnavigate the hills (about 10 hours, all between 1,600m and 1,900m). Unusual caves formed in quartzite can also be visited (a six-hour round trip to 2,000m). Large rounded boulders dominate the lower slopes whilst highly eroded blocks create a wilderness higher up. The flora is particularly fascinating and includes many endemics to be found only on the quartzite of Mount Ibity. Small quarries for semi-precious stones scar the mountain and the surrounding hills – we visited several including tourmaline, rose quartz and talc. The best access is to turn left immediately before the village, go past a new church and then fork right on a rough track up to the house man in charge of the communications dish and antennae. His son is a good guide.'

About 2½ hours (70km) after leaving Antsirabe you reach Ambositra.

AMBOSITRA

Ambositra (pronounced 'Amboostr') is the centre of Madagascar's woodcarving industry. Even the houses have ornately carved wooden balconies and shutters. There is an abundant choice of carved figures and marquetry, in several shops, and the quality is improving, although there are occasional lapses into pseudo-Africana. Most of the stores selling woodcarving and other handicrafts are on the street that runs past the Grand Hotel.

The best woodcarving shop (and workshop) is Chez Victor, opposite the Grand Hotel. It has a huge selection at very reasonable prices. Clare Hermans recommends 'Mr Randrianasolo's workshop at Ilaka Centre, just north of Ambositra. He has 25 apprentices working for him and has some artefacts that are different from the usual run-of-the-mill stuff.'

'Some of the best cheese in Madagascar is made by the cloistered nuns at the Benedictine convent. The chapel and convent are architecturally stunning. Stepping into the courtyard feels like you've wandered into 17th-century France. The convent is on the road leading down from the post office.' (Mark Shehinian)

The people of Ambositra have a reputation among highlanders for being friendly and talkative. However, several readers have complained that this town has more persistent beggars than anywhere else in Madagascar. Probably because it's small, and many tour groups stop here.

Telephone code The area code for Ambositra is 47.

Where to stay

Prestige Andrefan' i Vinani, Ambositra; tel: 47 711 35. Seven large, comfortable rooms with shared bathrooms. 35,000Fmg (single), 55,000–95,000Fmg (double). 'A beautiful, charming auberge. The owner, Francis Rakotonisa, couldn't have been more thoughtful and helpful.' (Sharon Giarratana) Reserve ahead as rooms are often booked, especially on weekends.

Hotel Violette Tel: 47 710 84. In Madiolahatra, slightly north of town. 112,000Fmg (double), 92,000Fmg (single). There are four bungalows 100m away for 120,000Fmg. Popular with tour groups.

Hotel Mania Malagasy-owned, in the centre of town. 11 en-suite rooms. 91,000–101,000Fmg. 'The entrance is pedestrian only via a gate off the main street, locked at night so you have to ring the bell to get in.' The owners can organise tours to Zafimaniry villages, and also rent out bicycles.

La Source Tel: 47 711 96. Opposite Le Tropical, in the centre of town. 60,000Fmg for double room with shared bathroom and toilet. 'Seedy and run-down. Don't sleep here unless your only other option is sleeping in the street.'

Le Relais des Tropiques (Formerly Le Tropical) Tel: 47 711 26. Seven simple rooms (shared facilities), most with multiple beds. 60,000Fmg with shared shower and toilet, or 100,000Fmg en suite. 'Ask for the cool, artsy, sky-lit room outside the main building' (MS). French-Malagasy owned, this used to be the best accommodation in Ambositra. Now a bit run-down, but the owners seem to be remodelling.

Grand Hotel This non-grand hotel has been around a long time and has a loyal clientele among frequent Mad travellers. It's a beautiful old building: 'very woody' as one enthusiast described it. There are a few rooms with en-suite bathrooms for 85,000Fmg; others with a basin, bidet and screen are 50,000Fmg. Good value.

Where to eat

Hotely ny Tanamasoandro Good and cheap. Also has rooms.

Hotely Gasy 'The best restaurant on our entire trip.' Amazing Scottish décor, huge portions.

Restaurant Oasis Mid-range restaurant with nice seating upstairs and tasty food. Near the Bank of Africa.

Guide services

There are a few guide services in Ambositra that take tourists out to nearby Betsileo villages.

Maison de Guide 'Tsangatsanga'; tel: 47 714 48 (across from Hotel Prestige). Hery, a friendly guide there who speaks French and a little English, takes people on tours of Soatanana. He can recommend other guides who speak good English.

Internet café

If you need an internet fix, there is an internet café, ambositra@net (which occasionally has snacks and drinks, too) down the hill from the post office towards the Benedictine monastery. It charges 750Fmg/minute for connection time.

PLACES OF INTEREST NEAR AMBOSITRA
Royal Palace

On a hill east of Ambositra is a ruined royal palace. It takes about 1½ hours to walk up (there's no shortage of guides to show you the way). 'At the palace an official guide introduced himself. The "palace" used to consist of two houses, but one recently burned down. There are still two flagpoles, two tombs and a rock on which the king stood to make his speeches. There is a small museum which contains the story of the place in some detail. There's a brilliant view of the surrounding hills and valley.' (Volker Dornheim)

Silk-weaving village

Two Peace Corps volunteers, Mark Shahinian and Kyley Schmidt, have written to me about their work with the silk-weavers of **Soatanana**, a village about 32km from Ambositra. 'The village is nestled in picturesque rice paddies surrounded by granite peaks. The scenery alone is worth the trip. Soatanana is a traditional highlands village with rice farming and ox-cart building, but what makes it outstanding is its silk-cloth production. We are working to help these women develop a sustainable business based on their weaving. The Soatanana weavers make the finest cloth we've seen in Madagascar and concentrate on the *landy be* or wild *Borocera* silk found only in Madagascar (see page 136). They've just formed a co-operative and are starting to pick up commercial buyers from the US and Europe.

'The trip to Soatanana can be made in an hour in private transport. A 4WD can bring you right into Soatanana all year round – a 2WD can get to within 4km in the rainy season. The best option is to find one of the many guide services in Ambositra or to hire a taxi to take you directly there (about 100,000Fmg round trip). To get there first go 12km south from Ambositra on RN7 and take paved RN35 15km west to Anjoman' Akona. Then ask for directions to Soatanana – you will need to take the dirt road that goes to Ambohimahazo. If taking public transport, take a taxi-brousse from Ambositra to Anjoman' Akona (7,500Fmg) or Ambohimahazo (10,000Fmg). Ask for directions to Soatanana from there. When you get there you can see the weavers in action as well as purchase the cloth they weave.'

Readers with a special interest in textiles can email Kyley or Mark before their visit: kyleyschmidt@yahoo.com or Markshahinian2@yahoo.com.

Ambatofinandrahana

Mark and Kyley have provided this information for those wishing to see more of the area: 'If you continue on RN35 west past Anjoman' Akona, 50km down the paved road is Ambatofinandrahana ('Place Where Stone is Cut'). Much of Madagascar's marble and granite is cut and processed here in a factory 3km south of town. Some of the stone is quarried 5km from the factory, but most comes on flatbed trucks from the hinterlands west of 'Ambato' as the locals call it. MAGRAMA is the name of the factory and they are happy to give free tours. The finished stone is sold to wealthy Tana residents and some is exported to Europe.

'Just north of Ambato (5km on a dirt road) are some wonderful hot springs. Buildings put up by the French have fallen into disrepair and now look like Roman ruins, lending the place a charming sense of disorientation. Go in the early morning, when the air is cool and the water is clean. Ask anybody in town how to get to the "ranomafana".

'There is one tourist hotel in Ambato – the **Hotel du Marbre**. The rooms are nice, and the hotel has a garden full of native plants. Doubles with shower and toilet down the hall cost 75,000Fmg.'

Sandrandahy and Fandriana

A rough road northeast of Ambositra leads to Fandriana, well known for its raffia work, hats and so on. It takes about 1½ hours to cover the 45km from Amositra. Roughly halfway is Sandrandahy which holds a huge Wednesday market. This is also a silk weaving centre, where exquisite *lambas* are made.

RICE

The Malagasy have an almost mystical attachment to rice. King Andrianampoinimerina declared: 'Rice and I are one,' and loyalty to the Merina king was symbolised by industry in the rice paddies.

Today the Betsileo are masters of rice cultivation (they manage three harvests a year, not the normal two) and their neat terraces are a distinctive part of the scenery of the central highlands. However, rice is grown throughout the island, either in irrigated paddies or as 'hill rice' watered by the rain. Rice production is labour-intensive. First the ground must be prepared for the seeds. Often this is done by chasing zebu cattle round and round to break and soften the clods – a muddy, sticky job, but evidently great fun for the boys who do it. Seeds are germinated in a small plot and replanted in the irrigated paddies when half grown. In October and November you will see groups of women bent over in knee-deep water, performing this back-breaking work.

The Malagasy eat rice three times a day, the annual consumption being 135kg per person (about a pound of rice per day!) although this is declining because of the availability of other foods and reduced productivity. Rice marketing was nationalised in 1976, but this resulted in such a dramatic drop in the amount of rice reaching the open market that restrictions were lifted in 1984. By that time it was too late to reverse the decline in productivity, which was mainly due to the decay of irrigation works. Despite a steady increase in acreage at the expense of the precious forest, production is continuing to fall.

Small farmers grow rice only for their own consumption but are forced to sell part of their crop for instant cash. Richer families in the community store this grain and sell it back at a profit later. To solve this small-scale exploitation, village co-operatives have been set up to buy rice and sell it back to the farmer at an agreed price, or at a profit to outsiders if any is left over.

Zafimaniry villages

The Zafimaniry people follow a traditional way of life in the forests southeast of Ambositra. This is not an area to attempt without an experienced guide, however. The danger is not so much in getting lost, but in the detrimental effects uncontrolled tourism has already had on the villagers nearest the road. Perhaps because of this, few people seem to visit these days and I have no recent reports on the area.

Guided tours of the Zafimaniry countryside are advertised in hotels in Ambositra or Fianar (the Tsara Guest House, for instance). Dany and Sahondra, a French-Malagasy couple running Villa Soamahatony, a B&B in Tana (see page 171) do trekking trips there and are extremely knowledgeable. Contact them by email: soamahatony@wanadoo.mg.

SOUTH FROM AMBOSITRA ON RN7

From Ambositra, the scenery becomes increasingly spectacular. You now pass remnants of the western limit of the rainforest (being systematically destroyed). The road runs up and down steep hills, past neat Betsileo rice paddies interspersed with eucalyptus and pine groves. The steepest climb comes about two hours after Ambositra, when the vehicle labours up an endlessly curving road, through thick forests of introduced pine, and reaches the top where stalls selling oranges, honey or baskets provide an excuse for a break. Then it's down through more forest, on

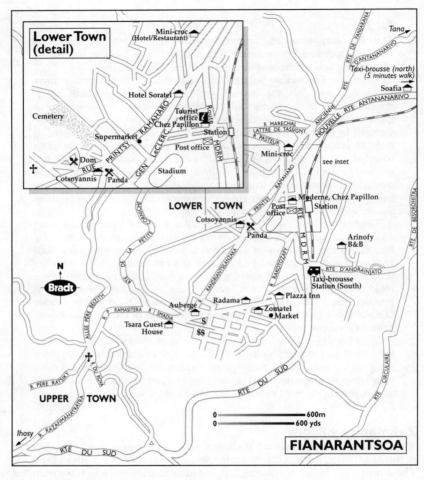

a very poor stretch of road, to **Ambohimahasoa**. Hotel Nirina serves good snacks. Leaving Ambohimahasoa you pass more forests, then open country, rice paddies and houses as you begin the approach to Fianarantsoa.

FIANARANTSOA

The name means 'Place of Good Learning'. Fianarantsoa (Fianar for short) was founded in 1830 as the administrative capital of Betsileo. It is one of the more attractive Malagasy towns, built on a hill like a small-scale Antananarivo. Fianar is an ideal base from which to do a variety of excursions (organised by the excellent Tsara Guest House): Andringitra, Ranomafana and even Isalo are within easy(ish) reach.

There is quite a contrast between the quite attractive Upper Town (old town) and the dreary Lower Town. It's worth making a trip to the Upper Town for its narrow winding streets and plethora of churches. There are good views, especially in the early morning when the mist is curling up from the valley.

Telephone code The area code for Fianar is 75.

Getting there and away
By road
For a tranquil journey the company KOFIAM, which operates buses between Fianar and Tana with a lunch stop in Ambositra, has been recommended. There is also the Jumbobus which runs between Tana and Toliara. Taxi-brousses can be very slow, taking from six to ten hours from Tana (40,000Fmg). The northern taxi-brousse depot is 20 minutes walk north from the train station.

For the onward journey to Toliara, a taxi-brousse takes from nine to 14 hours.

By rail
See page 211.

By air
Air Mad supposedly has twice-weekly Twin Otter flights to Fianar, currently on Wednesdays and Sundays. The latter is the more reliable.

Where to stay
Category A
Tsara Guest House Ambatolahikosoa (New Town); tel: 75 502 06; fax: 75 512 09; email: tsaraguest@dts.mg; www.tsaraguest.com. For over a decade the Tsara has been the most popular *vazaha* place in Madagascar, universally praised by readers. It is located in an old house that began life as a church, with a terrace from which you have a wonderful view of the town, and a garden for relaxing. The owners, Jim Heritsialonina and his Swiss wife Natalie, deserve their success – they have worked unstintingly to provide all the comforts and atmosphere that travellers desire. Excellent restaurant. Wide variety of tours offered. The profits from this place go to support a small school at the edge of the rainforest. The best rooms, with beautiful views over the rice paddies and en-suite bathrooms, are 280,000Fmg; those in the main house (shared bathrooms) are 100,000Fmg. Visa and MasterCard accepted.
Zomatel Place du Zoma; tel: 75 507 97; fax: 75 513 76; email: zomatel@zomatel-madagascar.com or zomatel@altern.org; www.zomatel-madagascar.com. A new, comfortable but rather characterless upmarket hotel near the market. TV, en-suite bathroom, minibar, air conditioning, etc. Good restaurant. Secure parking, internet café. 'The only problem is that most rooms have windows that open directly on to the corridor. There are some that open onto the road, with excellent views over town, so ask for those.'

MY COPYBOOK
The children of Fianar have learned (from whom?) an irresistible method of getting money – and more – from tourists. When my group met for dinner each had a similar story and each (including myself) was charmed by it. A little boy came up to me in the street and said, in impeccable English: 'Excuse me, I wonder if you would be willing to buy these cards I have made. I shall use the money to buy a copybook for school. I also collect foreign coins. Perhaps you have one for me?' I asked his age (12) and a few questions about his family. Each question was answered courteously and in the same fluent English. I gladly bought some of his nicely-drawn cards and found a shiny English penny for him.

Every town in Madagascar has its child beggars, but only Fianar seems to have these courteous, well-educated ones. I would love to know who taught them that courtesy succeeds better than aggression.

(SC) 25 double bedrooms at 150,000Fmg, 4 single rooms at 95,000Fmg and 3 family rooms (1 double and 2 single beds) at 225,000Fmg. 2 suites at 300,000Fmg. Tourist tax 3,500Fmg per night.

Hotel Soratel (Sorako Hotel) Immeuble SORAKA, Ampazambazaha; tel: 75 516 66; fax: 75 516 78; email: info@soratel.com; www.soratel.com. Located near the train and taxi-brousse station, this hotel delights some: 'Double rooms with wonderful huge bath, hot water, minibar, fridge stocked with cold drinks; extremely helpful, friendly staff.' (DF) but others are more cautious: 'Rooms are nice but overlook a busy road of shops and can be overlooked by the opposite building when the curtains are open! The hotel has an indoor car-park but no restaurant (only a coffee shop).' (SC) 26 rooms, 120,000–170,000Fmg including breakfast.

Hotel Soafia Tel/fax: 75 503 53 or 75 513 13; email: soafia.hot@wanadoo.mg; www.sofia.com. This large hotel (83 rooms) has all sorts of unusual features. 'Looks like a cross between Disneyworld, a Chinese temple and a gigantic doll's house' (J Hadfield). 'A veritable rabbit warren ... walking around the spartan corridors made me feel I was going to round a corner and meet Jack Nicholson wielding an axe! A bizarre place' (Jerry Vive). 'Bathroom windows opening onto the corridor I thought a particularly interesting touch ... faded grandeur. Definitely one for those who fancy something a bit different.' (S Bulmer) Though it has its loyal friends, not many people like this hotel but all and sundry praise its patisserie which sells wonderful bread, croissants and pastries, and there are all sorts of useful goodies for sale in the shop such as phone cards and stamps. The photo shop next door sells very high quality postcards. Rates: studio is 150,000Fmg, double with bath is 135,000Fmg and double with shower costs 125,000Fmg.

Category B
Hotel Mahamanina Route d'Andriamboasary; tel: 75 521 11 or 75 502 50; email: daday@malagasy.com; www.fianarantsoa.com. Very pleasant rooms, many studios, with good views from the balcony. Excellent restaurant. Rates: ground floor, en-suite double 75,500Fmg, double (shared toilet) 70,500Fmg , family room 86,500Fmg. First floor, en-suite double 86,500Fmg, double (shared toilet) 71,500Fmg, and family room is 116,500Fmg or 126,000Fmg. Breakfast is included in the rates.

Auberge Betania BP1188, 301 Fianarantsoa; tel: 75 520 79. Located near the crossroads,150m down the hill from the Tsara. There is no sign, but the entrance is above a stairway to the right of a bookshop. A Norwegian reader raves about this private home that has just four single rooms and one double, with a shared bathroom and (separate) toilet. The couple who own it, Mamy and Hasina Randriamahazo, double as guide and driver and can take you anywhere in the country. This sounds an ideal place for a solo traveller. 'Hasina is the always-helping (with a smile) lady that solves the problems before we know they are happening.' Rooms are 55,000Fmg single, 65,000Fmg double. Breakfast: 20,000Fmg, dinner 40,000Fmg.

Arinofy Hotel Tel: 75 508 38. This place goes from strength to strength. 'I'd say without a doubt that the Arinofy was the nicest hotel I stayed in in all the country' (Leo Barasi, who used only *Category C* hotels). 'Hot showers, clean toilets, comfy clean rooms, good, friendly multilingual service.' Stuart Riddle was equally ecstatic: 'A wonderful welcome, clean, pleasant rooms, a nice garden and the most amazing restaurant! They actually had a whole vegetarian section on their menu. The food was top quality and served with a huge smile.' An en-suite twin-bedded room is 75,000Fmg or 65,000Fmg with shared facilities and a four-bunk one considerably less. You can eat in a communal dining room and there is a laundry service. Camping is also permitted in the garden, either with your own tent (25,000Fmg) or using one supplied by the hotel (40,000Fmg).

Hotel Chez Papillon Tel: 75 500 03 or 75 508 15; fax: 75 518 76. Near the station, so very handy for catching the early train. 12 rooms, Double 60,000Fmg. family room for 3 people is 100,000Fmg and family room for two people is 70,000Fmg.

Hotel Cotsoyannis 4 Rue de Prince Ramaharo; tel: 75 514 72; fax:75 514 86. This long-established hotel has been improved by a recent extension: pleasant rooms with en-suite bathrooms, good views. Good pizzas served in the restaurant. Low season (Jan–Feb) double, twin or single costs 100,000Fmg; high season (March–Dec) double, twin or single costs 120,000Fmg. Breakfast 25,000Fmg and meals cost 60,000Fmg.

Lac Hotel Sahambavy; tel: 75 518 73; fax: 75 519 06; email: lachotel@vitelcom.mg. A set of bungalows in a quiet, lakeside location. 105,000–123,000Fmg (family bungalow). Very friendly (no English spoken).

Mini Croq Hotel-Restaurant Tel: 75 505 87; email: minicroq.hotel@dts.mg. A popular restaurant now offering a few rooms. Double with toilet 76,500Fmg, en-suite twin 81,000Fmg, en-suite family room 121,500Fmg plus other variations ranging from 51,000Fmg to 61, 500Fmg. 'To locate it follow the road from the service station up the hill one block; it is near the large pharmacy on the top of the hill. Off-street, secure parking, clean, bright and cheerful.' (L Gillespie)

Plazza Inn Tel: 75 515 72. Rooms between 75,000Fmg and 190,000Fmg. Breakfast 12,000Fmg to 18,000Fmg.

Tombotsoa Tel: 75 514 05. Behind the municipal stadium, next to the Western Union office. Double room 125,000Fmg, but a more comfortable room is 150,000Fmg. Triple is 175,000Fmg, and single 85,000Fmg. Continental breakfast is 12,000Fmg.

Category C

Vatolahotel Next door to the Tsara. Family-run with simple but clean rooms for 40,000Fmg. Good food. 'The owner is very accommodating to vegetarians and will make great meals to order, with advance notice' (Tom Voth).

Notre Dame de Cenacle, Maison d'Accueil Tel: 75 514 23. 'These nuns in Talatamaty have rooms for 20,000Fmg and dormitories for 15,000Fmg; clean, quite and pleasant, but there is a 10pm curfew. They also serve meals.' (SC).

Raza Hotel Tel: 75 519 15. Double rooms for 61,000Fmg.

La Ruche d'Or Tel: 75 506 14. Rooms are between 40,000Fmg and 75,000Fmg.

CAPR Tsinzoezaka Upper town. Rooms for a similar price.

Hotel Rova Behind the Zoma market. Four rooms at around 50,000 Fmg.

Nouvelle Hotel (Ambalapaiso ambany) opposite the Philips store.

Hotel Espoir Near the Interphoto shop, between Ampazambazaha and Antarandolo.

Where to eat

Chez Nirina Across the road from, and just down from, the Fianarantsoa hospital in Tambohobe. Great hospitality, great food, good atmosphere.

Chez Papillon Tel: 75 500 03. Back in the 1980s and 1990s this restaurant basked in its reputation of being the best restaurant in Madagascar. Now there are many better places, but the service is good and English is spoken. Its breakfasts are particularly recommended.

Gosena Up the hill from the Tsara Hotel on the old road to the old town. 'A charming, well-lit, family-owned place specialising in Vietnamese soups, sandwiches and pastries. Prices were very reasonable and it was filled with Malagasy families. Great food and, as an added bonus, it's no smoking!' (Tom Voth)

Panda Across the street from the Hotel Cotsoyannis. Very good Chinese meals, and game dishes (bat, frog and pigeon, according to one reader!) for around 35,000Fmg and attractive décor.

Estmill Grill Directly behind the Hotel Sofatel on Rte MDRM. 'Absolutely fantastic! I had the *romozava*. A slightly up-scale locals' joint.'

Resto Blue Very good, inexpensive food. Friendly.

Tiki dairy shop Across from the train station. Great yoghurt and cheese.

L'Ancre d'Or Ampazambazaha, across the road from the Soratel, near the fruit market.
Zomatel Excellent pizzas and ice-cream.
Mahavantana Antsororokavo. Malagasy, Chinese and European dishes.

Internet café
Chez Dom Opposite the Panda Restaurant. Only one computer, but if you need to wait there are tasty foot-long sandwiches for 9,000Fmg, and good burgers.

There are also internet facilities at the post office, L'Ancre d'Or, Zomatel, and in the many *Espatel* places around town.

Nightlife
Moulin Rouge 'A fantastic nightclub on the outskirts of town. The place to be at the weekend. Varied music: Malagasy, African, Reggae, funny Euro-pop disco.'
Soafia Dance For a hot sweaty experience, slightly more upmarket than the Moulin Rouge.
Chez Tantine By the (former) taxi-brousse station. Very Malagasy and fun.
L'Ancre d'Or Ampazambazaha, opposite the Soratel. This popular bar will soon be opening a cabaret.

What to see and do
This is a good town for strolling around. Take your time to explore the Upper Town and then visit the market. This is best on Friday, so is called *zoma* (which means Friday). When walking check out the telegraph wires – they are festooned with the webs of *nephila* spiders!

A couple of readers have recommended an Antaimoro paper-making business run by Maurice Razafimahaleo. 'This is a family concern and they are most happy to show you the process. The prices are very reasonable and the product more interesting than most.' From the old taxi-brousse station follow the signs to Arinofy hotel, go over the bridge and take the road to your right following the power lines. It's a bit of a climb so don't give up! Go past the Gendarmerie, turn right at the top of the hill and the house is on the left, just past the communal water tap. You will see the paper drying on frames.

Guide/tour operator
MARAO de Fianar Cellphone: 032 0406 495; email: aurelienmada@yahoo.fr. Highly praised by a reader as being extremely reliable and professional. He will organise any trip in the Fianar area: Andringitra, Ranomafana and Isalo among others.
La Maison des Guides Tel: 75 517 30. This is a new initiative of the Association 'Coeur Malgache', for professionally-trained guides specialising in mountain treks.

Excursions
Sahambavy Tea Estate Tel: 75 521 91 or 75 511 56. The estate is situated on one side of a very pretty valley beside Lake Sahambavy, 25km by road from Fianar, or by rail to the Sahambavy station on the way to Manakara. Around 75% of the tea is exported to Kenya and the rest is for local consumption in Madagascar. The plantation is now under Greek/Mauritian management (all the packaging comes from Mauritius). Tours demonstrate the process from picking to packaging. Opening hours: 07.30–15.30; price: 25,000Fmg for a guided tour and tasting.

The *Micheline* If you really want to push the boat – or rather the train – out in Fianar, you can hire the *Micheline*, a white 'bus' which runs on railway tracks. The *Micheline* is based in Fianar and can be hired for 1,500,000Fmg per day (about £100 at today's exchange rate). More information from 75 513 54 (the railway station in Fianar).

Train to Manakara

This line was privatised in 2000 which ended decades of deterioration. It leaves for Manakara on Sundays at 07.00 and the spectacular journey takes ten hours. The ticket office opens at 06.00 and you should get there shortly after it opens to secure the best seats. Ticket prices are 60,000Fmg first class and 40,000Fmg second class.

In the relatively recent past the163km trip had taken up to 48 hours, with sometimes one or two nights spent on the stationary train. This state of affairs could return, of course (as any Briton knows, privatising the railway does not guarantee punctuality!) but the future of this lovely railway looks rosy. There has been substantial investment by USAID and LDI, donations by a Swiss railway company, and even the King of Thailand got involved with advice on an erosion-preventing plant. There is, however, a downside. The popularity of the railway means that it is now very overcrowded, even in first class. Stuart Riddle recommends arriving just before departure and standing by the open doors for the whole journey (you can sit on the step if you get tired), 'That way you will not only get the best views but will avoid the smell from the toilet which pervades the carriages.' Stuart also points out that the windows are partially tinted, making it impossible to see the spectacular view from your seat..

You can buy a nice little booklet, produced by the ADI-FCE (railway users' association), which describes the history of this railway, the villages on the way, and various statistics about the line (it was constructed between 1926 and 1936, there are 67 bridges and 48 tunnels, the longest of which is 1,072m long). The train stops frequently, for ten minutes at a time, allowing ample time for photography and for buying fruit, snacks or drinks from vendors. 'Most of all it is the people on the railway stations and in the villages that make this trip unforgettable, and as a bonus the landscape is beautiful…and as you near Manakara the railway crosses the airport runway! One last comment: on arriving at Manakara one should be prepared to deal with at least 100 pousse-pousse men waiting for you at the railway station.' (Marja van Ipenburg) 'We went 2nd class and shared the journey with an assortment of poultry and, as we neared the coast, a truly extraordinary quantity of manioc….I spent most of the time on my feet staring out of the window in fact, it was fascinating watching the scenery and produce change as we progressed and many fellow passengers seemed to enjoy the journey in the same way…travelling past the windsock and across the runway to draw into the railway station, then finding a beachside *chambre* made it a lovely day.' (FRB) 'The train journey was one of the highlights of the trip. At the rear of the train was a flat, open transport carriage on which we were able to sit for part of the journey, enabling us to get uninterrupted views to both the left and the right. Whilst both classes of the train were totally packed there were only five people sitting on this. It is an opportunity to get some fantastic photographs and the speed at which the train travels means that there is very little danger.' (S Bulmer)

RANOMAFANA

The name Ranomafana means 'hot water' and it was the waters, not the lemurs, which drew visitors in the colonial days and financed the building of the once-elegant Hotel Station Thermale de Ranomafana.

These days the baths are often ignored by visitors anxious to visit the Ranomafana National Park which was created in 1991. This hitherto unprotected fragment of mid-altitude rainforest first came to world attention with the discovery of the golden bamboo lemur in 1986 and is particularly rich in wildlife.

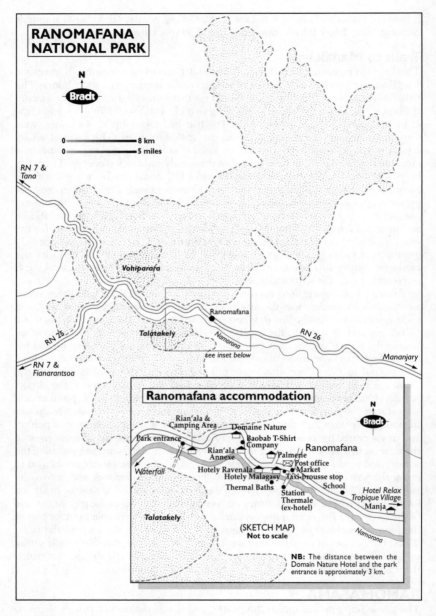

Ranomafana has experienced a welcome explosion of accommodation in recent years (for nearly a decade after it opened there was just one, dire hotel) so now pleases almost everyone. I have always loved it! First you have the marvellously scenic drive down, with the dry highland vegetation giving way to greenery and flowers. Then there are the views of the tumbling waters of the Namorona River, and the relief when the hillsides become that lovely unbroken, knobbly green of virgin forest and you know you are near the reserve. Hidden in these trees are 12 species of lemur: diademed (Milne-Edwards) sifaka, red-bellied brown lemur, red-fronted lemur, black-and-white ruffed lemur and three species of bamboo lemur. At night you can add mouse lemur, woolly lemur (avahi), lepilemur, greater dwarf lemur, and even aye-aye. Then there are the birds: more than 100 species with 36 endemic. And the reptiles. And the butterflies and other insects. Even if you saw no wildlife, there is enough variety in the vegetation and scenery, and enough pleasure in walking the well-constructed trails, to make a visit worthwhile. And – I nearly forgot – in the warm summer months you can swim in the cold, clear water of the Namorona while a malachite kingfisher darts overhead. Some negative things: the trails are steep and arduous, the guides are well below the Périnet standard, it often rains and there are leeches.

Getting there and away

In your own transport the journey is about three hours from Fianar or four hours from Ambositra. Although on maps two access roads are shown, the one from Ambohimasoa (via Vohiparara) is impassable. The only road is in a terrible condition with huge potholes and deep furrows in the mud. It starts at Alakamisy Ambohimaha, about 26km north of Fianar. I have been told that foreign aid has been provided to repair the road over the next few years. I hardly dare believe it.

Public transport can be a problem since it is so often full. The trick is to leave Fianar early in the morning: be at the *gare routière* at 06.00 to ensure a good seat. At least two taxi-brousses leave between 07.00 and 09.00. There are also taxi-brousses in the afternoon. Because of the current state of the road the 40km journey can take up to five hours.

Where to stay
Category A

Centrest Sejour Tel: 75 523 02 (ex 13) or 75 513 47 (ex 13). Beyond the museum, on the left as you enter Ranomafana. Very pleasant thatched bungalows with en-suite bathrooms. Well run, with a good restaurant. 180,000Fmg single, 195,000Fmg double, and 225,000Fmg triple. Breakfast is 7,500Fmg and meals are 50,000Fmg.

Iary Hotel Located near the village of Ranomafana. Rooms with a private bathroom and hot water are 120,000Fmg. Breakfast is 15,000Fmg and meals are 50,000Fmg.

Category B

Hotel Domaine Nature A very well-managed, friendly and popular hotel with 14 bungalows (en-suite bathrooms) overlooking the river, halfway between the village and the park, and some new (cheaper) ones on the hillside on the other side of the road with shared facilities. 185,000Fmg (double), 240,000Fmg triple; breakfast 30,000Fmg, dinner 60,000Fmg, picnic 30,000Fmg. Bookings (Tana) through Destinations Mada; tel: 22 310 72, fax: 22 310 67.

Category C

Rian'ala Dormitory accommodation near the park entrance for only 28,000Fmg. Meals around 18,000Fmg. The food is excellent, and the moths 'the size of frisbees' which are attracted to the lamps are an added bonus! Staying here is convenient for the park but quite isolated. However, without your own transport this is by far the most convenient option, particularly if you want to do a night walk. Ask the taxi-brousse driver to stop at the park entrance.

Rian'ala Annexe Three rooms with hot water: 65,000Fmg (double), 90,000Fmg (triple).Good value accommodation opposite the museum.

La Palmerie (Gîte Jardin) Reservations (Tana) tel: 22 223 51 or cellphone: 033 1146096. Double rooms for 50,000Fmg. Breakfast in the lovely garden for 7,500–15,000Fmg. In town, opposite the *navette* stop for transport to the park (if it's running). Recommended.
Hotely Ravenala 10 rooms, all 30,000Fmg; breakfast 7,500Fmg; lunch and dinner from 5,000Fmg (Malagasy cooking), more for something fancy. Located opposite the museum. Basic, funky, very friendly, beautiful views, good food.
Hotel Manja 10 bungalows and some rooms. 60,000Fmg (bungalows), 60,000Fmg to 180,000Fmg for rooms, depending on facilities. On the road to Mananjary (RN26), 5 minutes' walk east along the river. The food here is excellent, a good range of Malagasy and Western standards to suit any budget from 6,000Fmg up, plus tasty cocktails. 'One of those places that made me consider tearing up my return airline ticket and staying forever!' says reader Bradley Rink.

Out of town
For those with their own transport there are a couple of quiet hotels on the way to Mananjary which are recommended.

Hotel Relax 5km from Ranomafana. 120,000–130,000Fmg. It, and its restaurant, Le Terrace, are highly recommended. 'Lovely setting, away from the bustle of Ranomafana.'
Tropique Village 180,000–250,000Fmg. A new (2001) upmarket hotel in Mahatsynosorano, about 9km from Ranomafana.

Camping
There is a very good campsite at the park entrance: 10,000Fmg per person with your own tent, or you can rent a large one for 15,000Fmg a night and pay an additional 10,000Fmg per person. There are six covered tent sites, with open-sided A-frame thatched shelters giving shade as well as protection from the rain, and one centrally located covered picnic table. There are basic toilets and showers, a tap provides drinking water and there is a bungalow with kitchen facilities. There is no food available here, although Rian'ala dormitory is right next door and there's a charming 'snack bar' for beer and biscuits close by. Or you can walk (45 mins) or get transport to Ranomafana village where there are groceries and some nice *hotelys*.

This campsite was built by the villagers and is run by ANGAP; the money goes directly to the community.

Where to eat
Chez Roger (Tsilavintsoa) Just up the road from the taxi-brousse stop. 'It has great food for about 15,000Fmg, including Malagasy specialities such as *Ravitoto sy hena kisoa* (pork and crushed casava leaves) and *akoho rony sy sakamalao* (chicken soup and ginger) and also spaghetti and so on. Amazing homemade ice-cream and crepes.' (Julia Jones) Roger is friendly, knowledgeable, speaks English and is also the current Mayor of Ranomafana.
Resto Bamboo Between the post office and the museum. Good food, convenient location.
Hotely Malagasy In the village, serving 'the best value food in Madagascar'.

Three *hotelys* opposite the market serve basic, but tasty food for 5,000–6,000Fmg.

Ranomafana and conservation
The Ranomafana National Park Project, set up by Dr Patricia Wright, established a large range of activities, from education and health-care for the villagers on the periphery of the park, and an ecological monitoring team that works at several sites within the park. ANGAP and NGOs have continued this good work. The national park is one of the country's flagship conservation projects, with the involvement of the local communities playing an important role.

Much scientific research takes place in the park and there have been some clashes between researchers and tourists. Tourists have been known to push researchers aside in order to get a better photo, and to encourage guides to shake or bang on trees to persuade a lemur to move. It goes without saying that this is irresponsible behaviour and is counter-productive since some researchers withhold information on the whereabouts of the rarer lemurs for fear of being disturbed in their work.

A world-class research station near the park entrance (the **Centre Valbio**) was completed in 2003 under the initiative of an international consortium from countries including Finland and Italy, along with UNESCO and Stony Brook University, New York. This new facility brings great possibilities for research and development in the area.

Visiting the national park
Getting there from your hotel
The entrance to the park is some 6km west of the now defunct Hotel Station Thermale, on the main road. A *navette* (minibus) run by ANGAP has recently broken down and was out of service at the time of writing. When running it leaves Ranomafana village at 07.00 to take visitors and guides up to the park entrance. It returns at 16.00 and costs 5,000Fmg. If there is no bus, don't despair. 'I think the views *of* the park are far more spectacular than in the park,' says Stuart Riddle, who loved the 80 minutes it took him to walk up the hill to the park entrance.

Permits and guides
Permits (50,000Fmg) are obtainable from the National Park Office. You are not allowed into the park without a guide. Most speak only French, but they usually know the animals' names in English. There are some knowledgeable guides in Ranomafana, but the standard is still far removed from the courteous, informative guides of Périnet. This is now the only popular national park which provokes readers to complain regularly about the laziness and even rudeness of their guides. One exception is Angelin, '…a joy to spend time with, his English was excellent and his knowledge remarkable.' (SR)

The official fees are posted at the park entrance: currently 125,000Fmg for a long day tour and 75,000Fmg for a night visit. Groups of more than four must have two guides. Try to check the posted rate before hiring a guide, and confirm your intentions – and interests – with him or her before you set out. Guides will expect a tip in addition to the set fee.

In the forest
The paths in the forest have been improved in recent years. There are standard routes, most taking a few hours, but if you are fit you should opt for the longer tours taking 6–8 hours. You will see primary forest, where the vines are thicker, the trees bigger and it will be quieter. Even for the shorter walks you need to be reasonably fit – the paths are moderate to steep, and sometimes slippery. Your guide will assume that it is lemurs you have come to see; so, unless you stress that you are interested in other aspects such as botany or insects, he will tend to concentrate on mammals and birds. If you are keen on chameleons try and arrange a night-walk. You are most likely to see red-fronted brown lemurs, grey bamboo lemurs and the rarer red-bellied lemur. Greater bamboo lemur and even the star attraction, golden bamboo lemur are now fairly frequently seen. The most memorable of the easily found lemurs is a subspecies of the diademed sifaka, Milne-Edwards' sifaka. Unlike the more familiar Verreaux's sifaka from the dry forests of the south, which is largely white, this is dark brown with cream-coloured sides.

A DAY IN THE LIFE OF A RESEARCH ASSISTANT
Alex Hall

It's usually dark when I wake up, and pre-empting the alarm clock makes the first few minutes of a day a bit more bearable. The darkness here is real pitch-black bumping-into-things darkness since there are no lights for miles and the thick canopy blocks out the moonlight. Sleeping in a tent in a place like this is conducive to the heaviest kind of sleep; I like to imagine myself as a tiny invisible dot on the map buried under the forest. That said, cacophonous insects and other nocturnal species are a rhythmic reminder that I'm just one of millions of animals out here, although the others aren't encased in Goretex.

After heaving down coffee, rice and eggs I set off on the trails to find the animals. The brisk walk quickly shakes off the last wisps of sleep and the day's data collection gets underway. I follow red-bellied lemurs and record their activities, as well as collecting their poo to test for a stress hormone called cortisol. I'm a research assistant for an American scientist working in conjunction with the Institute for the Conservation of Tropical Environments. We work with a Malagasy student too and are basically looking at the difference in the stress levels of lemurs between primary and secondary forest.

Sometimes I go hurtling down mud-slicked slopes and tramping over rotting tree stumps just trying to keep up with them. These lemurs keep rather odd hours though so if they decide to curl up and sleep for a few hours I just sit and wait. It's a great place to daydream, although sitting out in the rain can wear a bit thin. An unusual centipede, a geriatric chameleon or a boa constrictor could all add interest to an ordinary day. Even the leeches are painless, although they do find their way into the most personal of places.

I learned most about the forest from the Malagasy research guides. Their vast collective knowledge is particularly indispensable since almost everything in Madagascar is unique to the island. We spend a lot of free moments swapping language lessons and although English is harder to learn than Malagasy I seem to be lagging quite a bit. Rainforest humour tends to be rather slapstick and I think it makes for better relations that I fall over a lot.

I work at two sites and sometimes bump into tourists on the trails around Talatakely. I have never encountered any irresponsible tourism at Ranomafana, maybe because anyone willing to make the trip has an interest in wildlife anyway. With a new world-class research station, the Centre Valbio, there are more scientists and research staff here too. It's quite a contrast to the gentle isolation at the Vatohranana camp. When research is done for the day I might wash in the river or just read for a bit; solitude is never hard to find. If it's still light it's great to explore a stretch of the river, there are some astonishing waterfalls that people very rarely see. Jumping through rapids and edging over slippery platforms is childishly satisfying.

It's hard to stay up after eight o'clock when it's so dark and the rain is pattering down on the tarpaulin. I find it restorative to walk into Ranomafana on a Saturday, the hot water at the baths relaxes the muscles and a cold THB does the rest. I teach English classes sometimes too and the people here are great to work with, certainly less demanding than the animals. Even though I can try, I'll never really know how things work on an island like this.

A delightful walk is to the *Cascade* of the River Namorona. If the circular route is taken it is quite strenuous, with a long steep descent to the waterfall. This is a dramatic and beautiful place and it's worth lingering to watch for kingfishers. A hydro-electric scheme diverts some of the water plunging over the cliffs, but this is not intrusive. The walk back, along the river, is outside the park boundary so gives you a chance to see small farming communities. Another waterfall, *Le Petite Cascade*, is hidden in the forest. A long ribbon of water falls into a deep pool which provides a chilly but invigorating swim (so bring your swimsuit). Allow three hours round trip for this excursion.

Another trail system has been established on flatter ground at Vohiparara, near the boundary of the park, 12km west of Ranomafana on the main road. It only takes about three hours to do all the trails here with a guide. 'Vohiparara is good for birders. Among many others you may see the brown emutail, Madagascar snipe, Meller's duck and the extremely rare slender-billed flufftail. The song of the cryptic warbler was first recorded here in 1987.' (Derek Schuurman) According to Nick Garbutt this is also the best place for the rufous-headed ground-roller and yellow-bellied sunbird-asity.

A new path has recently been opened in *Parcelle II*, back up the road past the falls and in a boggier area of the reserve. 'The forest there is more varied and wetter with a lower canopy. We saw some Milne-Edwards' sifakas quite easily. We also arranged a half-day walk in another part of the forest through the official guide. Starting at the village of Ambatolahy, we hiked up behind the village into the reserve accompanied by a local guide-villager. The track followed ridges and criss-crossed streams. A nice example of how money is going from the visitors to the locals directly.' (Clare & Johan Hermans)

ANGAP are planning an even more ambitious (and exciting-sounding) two-day circuit with a night camped at the village of Bevohajo. This community is near a spectacular waterfall and perform the traditional *tombolo* dance of the local Tanala people. Enquire at the ANGAP office for information.

A nocturnal visit to Belle Vue, a popular viewpoint, is now an established part of all tours. A viewing platform and shelter have been built here and the steep paths have been made as safe as possible, but even so negotiating them by torchlight can be tricky. Try to arrive early. By dusk there may be as many as 50 people with cameras at the ready waiting for the mouse lemurs, red-bellied lemurs and civet (fanaloka) to arrive for their supper. Which they do, with clockwork regularity. The animals seem oblivious to the flashes of cameras, outstretched hands and squeals of delight, and are certainly appreciative of this effortless meal. Everyone leaves happy, including the 'wild'life, so it seems snooty to be disapproving. And you won't get a better chance of getting a close-up view of mouse lemurs and fanaloka in Madagascar.

Museum/gift shop

This is part of the Ranomafana National Park Project to improve visitor understanding of the area. This is an interesting museum and the handicrafts for sale are of a high standard including beautifully embroidered T-shirts.

Thermal baths

These are close to the former Station Thermale hotel. It costs only 5,000Fmg for a wonderful warm swim in the pool or 2,500Fmg for a private bath ('in a grotty little room where the door doesn't close all the way'). You can even have a massage for 25,000Fmg. Open 08.00–16.30; closed Wednesday afternoons for cleaning. On Thursday to Saturday nights you can have a nocturnal swim with poolside beers and barbecue.

The road to Manakara

The journey by car takes about five hours, passing several interesting small towns, all of which have shops and *hotelys*. This road would repay a more leisurely journey on foot or by bike. Bjørn Donnis points out that after Irondo, as you near the coast, the landscape becomes bone-dry – quite unexpected in the 'eastern rainforest'. This is due (you guessed it) to deforestation and overgrazing. Manakara and other eastern towns are covered in *Chapter 13*.

CONTINUING SOUTH ON RN7

The next leg of the journey, to Ihosy, is 206km. Coming from Fianar the landscape is a fine blend of vineyards and terraced rice paddies (the Betsileo are acknowledged masters of rice cultivation), then after 20km a giant rock formation seems almost to hold the road in its grasp. Its name is, appropriately, *Tanan'Andriamanitra*, or 'Hand of God'. From here to Ihosy is arguably the finest mountain scenery in Madagascar. Reader Bishop Brock who cycled the route writes: 'Those three days were the most rewarding of my career as a bicycle tourist. I pity people who only pass through that magnificent landscape jammed inside a taxi-brousse.'

It is worth noting that taxi-brousses from the north continue south in the afternoon. This may be the best time to get a place if you're pushed for time.

AMBALAVAO

Some 56km southwest of Fianarantsoa is my favourite town, Ambalavao. The road drops steeply down to the town providing excellent views across the landscape. RN7 does not pass through the attractive part of Ambalavao, and I strongly urge people to stop here for a few hours or at least to amble through the car-less streets which are thronged with people, and take in the once-grand houses with their pillars, carved balconies, and steep, red-tiled roofs. If travelling south this is the last time you'll see typical highland architecture.

Getting there and away

Although Ambalavao is on RN7, southward-bound travellers may prefer to make it an excursion from Fianarantsoa, since vehicles heading to Ihosy and beyond will have filled up with passengers in Fianar.

Where to stay

Hotel Snackbar Aux Bougainvillées BP14, Ambalavao 308; tel: 75 340 01. Adjacent to the Antaimoro paper shop. 16 bungalows with en-suite bathrooms and solar-powered hot water, seven rooms with cold water and shared toilet and shower. Clean and comfortable. Pleasant restaurant serving huge portions of good, plain food. Bungalows 106,000Fmg, rooms with shared facilities 70,000Fmg.
Stop Hotel Five double rooms with communal WC and washing facilities. Basic but adequate.
Chez Notre Similar in price and quality to Stop Hotel. Their sign proudly announces they have sheets and curtains.

Camping

If you have a tent you can camp at Ankazondandy.

What to see
Antaimoro paper

Ambalavao is the original home of the famous Malagasy 'Antaimoro' paper. This papyrus-type paper impregnated with dried flowers is sold throughout the island as wall-hangings and lampshades. The people in this area are Betsileo, but paper-making in the area copies the coastal Antaimoro tradition which goes back to the Muslim immigrants who wrote verses from the Koran on this paper. This Arabic script was the only form of writing known in Madagascar before the LMS developed a written Malagasy language nearly 500 years later using the Roman alphabet.

Antaimoro paper is traditionally made from the bark of the *avoha* tree from the eastern forests, but sisal paste is now sometimes used. After the bark is pounded and softened in water it is smoothed on to linen trays to dry in the sun. While still tacky, dried flowers are pressed into it and brushed over with a thin solution of the liquid bark to hold them in place.

The open-air 'factory' (more flowerbeds than buildings) where all this happens is to the left of the town in the same compound as the Hotel Bougainvillées and is well worth a visit. It is fascinating to see the step-by-step process, and you get a good tour. A shop sells the finished product at reasonable prices. For information on the paper-making process, Anja Park (see below) and other places of interest in the area, ask for Adrien.

Excursions from Ambalavao
Soavita winery
This place offers free tours on weekdays when you can be shown the various stages of winemaking by one of the workers, followed by a tasting. This may (sadly for lovers of eccentricity) have been modernised since Debbie Fellner visited a few years ago. 'We stopped at Soavita, 3km from Ambalavao, in hopes of touring the winery. Silly us expecting to find something organised! We wandered around the property until we found what appeared to be the front entrance. A few young men were playing soccer nearby in the cleared vineyards. After an hour or so, one of the men came to unlock the factory doors and led us into the cellars. He proceeded to give us a "tour" of sorts in Mala-French-Charades. He scooped out glassfuls of wine from various ageing vats for us to taste (then poured the remaining wine back into the vats!), showed us the labelling process (an old, toothless woman slapping labels on wine bottles with coconut paste) and showed off the 'high-tech' cork-insertion apparatus. It was the best wine tour I've ever been on, even if I only understood a fraction of what was going on.'

Silk weaving
Initially run by the charity Feedback Madagascar, the CCD Namana silk-weaving project encourages the development of this ancient Malagasy craft. It is based at Ankazondandy, about 3km south of Ambalavao. A second project, NathOcean, also work with silk but specialise in embroidery.

If you would like to see either project (weekdays only) you can either just turn up or ask for directions from the Hotel Bougainvillées in Ambalavao.

Cattle market
Held Mondays and Thursdays on the outskirts of town. It gets going at about 3am, so you need to be an early riser! The herdsmen take a month to walk the zebu to Tana, and you'll see these large herds on the road. Look out for yellow eartags: this is a 'zebu passport' giving the owner the right to take his cattle across regional boundaries.

Anjà Park
About 15km south of Ambalavao is a new, community-run park which offers superb scenery, intriguing plants adapted to the dry southern climate, some interesting Betsileo history and several troops of cheeky ring-tailed lemurs.

ZEBU

The humpbacked cattle, zebu, which nearly outnumber the country's human population, produce a relatively low yield in milk and meat. These animals are near-sacred and generally are not eaten by the Malagasy other than at ceremonies of social or religious significance. Zebu are said to have originated from northeast India, eventually spreading as far as Egypt and then down to Ethiopia and other parts of East Africa. It is not known how they were introduced to Madagascar but they are a symbol of wealth and status as well as being used for burden.

Zebu come in a variety of colours, the most sought-after being the *omby volavita*, which is chestnut with a white spot on the head. There are 80 words in the Malagasy language to describe the physical attributes of zebu, in particular the colour, horns and hump.

In the south, zebu meat is always served at funerals, and among certain southern tribes the cattle are used as marriage settlements, as is done in Africa. Whenever there is a traditional ritual or ceremony, zebu are sacrificed, the heads being given to the highest ranking members of the community. Blood is smeared on participants as it is believed to have purification properties, and the fat from the hump of the cattle is used as an ingredient for incense. I have seen a Vezo village elder wearing a domed hat apparently made from a zebu hump. Zebu milk is an important part of the diet among the Antandroy; it is fady for women to milk the cows but it is they who sell the curdled milk in the market.

Tourists in the south will see large herds of zebu being driven to market, a journey that may take several days. All cattle crossing regional borders must wear a 'zebu passport' in the form of yellow ear-tags. Cattle-rustling is now a major problem. Whereas before it was mainly confined to the Bara, as an initiation into manhood, it is now organised by large, Mafia-like gangs. In former times the punishment matched the crime: a fine of ten zebu would have to be paid by the thief, five for the family from whom the cattle were stolen and five for the king.

To the rural Malagasy a herd of zebu is as symbolic of prosperity as is a new car or a large house in our culture. Government aid programmes must take this into account; for instance improved rice yields will indirectly lead to more environmental degradation by providing more money to buy more zebu. The French colonial government thought they had an answer: they introduced a tax on each animal. However, local politicians were quick to point out that since Malagasy women had always been exempt from taxation, the same rule should apply to cows!

The local people have long recognised the tourist potential here but it is only in the last few years that they have organised themselves into gaining some income from it. The region is sacred to the Betsileo: their ancestors are buried here and it has always been *fady* to hunt the lemurs. The caves have provided a useful sanctuary in times of trouble, and were inhabited up to around 100 years ago.

The reserve covers 8ha, and is home to about 300 ring-tails. Given the health problems affecting the lemurs of Berenty (see page 275) this park provides a worthwhile alternative for tourists wanting a lemur fix and to benefit the local people. It costs 25,000Fmg to visit the park where you are provided with a guide (80,000Fmg for a group of eight). The well-maintained trail winds past some impressive rocks topped by waiting lemurs, to a sacred cliff where there is an apparently inaccessible tomb high in the rock face. The tour takes one to two hours.

Adrien at the Hotel Bougainvillées (tel: 75 340 01) organises visits from Ambalavao. You can also try emailing apmm-fia@vitelcom.mg or check the website www.madagascar-mountain.org

Beyond Ambalavao on RN7

The scenery beyond Ambalavao is marvellous. Huge granite domes of rock dominate the grassy plains. The most striking one, with twin rock towers, is called *Varavarana Ny Atsimo*, the 'Door to the South' by the pass of the same name. Beyond is the 'Bonnet de l'Evêque' (Bishop's Hat, but it looks more like a cottage loaf to me), and a huge lump of granite shaped like an upturned boat, with its side gouged out into an amphitheatre; streams run into the lush vegetation at its base.

You will notice that not only the scenery but the villages are different. These Bara houses are solidly constructed out of red earth (no elegant Merina pillars here) with small windows. Bunches of maize are often suspended from the roof to dry in the sun.

Shortly after Ambalavao you start to see your first tombs – some painted with scenes from the life of the deceased.

The next town of importance is Ihosy, described in *Chapter 10*.

ANDRINGITRA MOUNTAINS

These spectacular granite peaks and domes have entranced me since I first travelled the length of RN7, so I am thrilled that they can now form the focus for a trekking holiday. The wonderful Andringitra National Park does not cover the entire area – there are other lodges and camps on the outskirts of the park which offer equally good scenery.

Where to stay/eat

Tsara Camp Owned by Boogie Pilgrim, this tented camp is located outside the park's boundaries on the northwest side of the range. The approach road is an unsignposted track off the RN7 before the village of Tanambao, 37km south of Ambalavao; in all it takes about two hours from the main road. It is not an all-weather track and so the camp closes in the rainy season for three months. The camp consists of ten large tents under thatched shelters, set in a spectacular plain bounded by the Andringitra Massif to the east. It is a hybrid between safari and basic camping with wooden floors to the canvas tents. Each tent has its own bathroom with hot water, hand-basin and chemical toilets.The eating area is in a bigger tent serving simple Malagasy food. There's a refrigerator, so cold drinks are available. Although the main trekking routes of the national park are not easily accessible from here, they can be arranged. For the less energetic there is a half-day walk to the private reserve in the Tsaranoro Valley to see ring-tailed lemurs (30,000Fmg). This walk can be extended to a tough all-day hike up the hill the locals call the Chameleon, 1,500m. Rates at Tsara (full-board only) are €55 a day. For more information email: contact@boogie-pilgrim.net.

Camp Catta Up the road from Tsara Camp, this place has established itself as a centre for climbing and paragliding (note that technical climbing is not allowed in the national park). There are basic brick-built huts and a generator – and lots of ring-tailed lemurs, as the name implies. Arrangements to stay here can be made through the Cotsoyannis Hotel in Fianar; email: campcatta@campcatta.com; www.campcatta.com.

Le Gîte If you want to sleep under a roof rather than in a tent, the gîte near Ambolamandary, 7km from the park entrance, is very comfortable. It costs 60,000Fmg for a shared room and facilities (cold water, though). However, this is an hour's drive from the

THE RING-TAILED LEMURS OF ANDRINGITRA

When researchers first started investigating the fauna of Andringitra, in the early 1990s, they thought they'd found a sub-species of *Lemur catta*. The lemurs here look different from those in the southern spiny desert and gallery forest of Berenty. They appear slightly larger, their fur is thicker, and the colours seem more dramatic: a chestnut back, rather than grey-brown, with whiter whites and blacker blacks. And their behaviour is different. In the absence of trees these lemurs leap from rock to rock with great agility, often on their back legs like sifakas. It is now known that this variation is simply an adaptation to their cold, treeless environment, so the lemurs of Andringitra are an ecotype, not a sub-species.

trail system so cuts into the day's hiking. You need to bring your own food, but there is a cook at the gîte to prepare it for you. Book through the WWF in Ambalavao, tel: 75 340 81.

A new gîte has been built a little further away from the park entrance, which will have a restaurant.

Camping

There are four campsites, the most popular of which is Belambo, (1,550m) in a wooded area close to the Zomandao River. There is a cooking hut with enough seats for a small group, level places for tents, and a long-drop toilet. When I was there in 2003 it lacked an outside picnic table (or rather the table was there but no seats) but this will no doubt be rectified.

Andringitra National Park

Created in 1999, this park protects the flora and fauna around Madagascar's second highest peak. The former Pic Boby, 2,658m, has been renamed Pic d'Imarivolanitra, which means 'Close to the Sky': poetic but not half as easy for *vazahas* to remember. Andringitra (pronounced 'Andringtra') has some wildlife, but landscape, vegetation and trekking are the chief attractions. And what attractions! I would put Diavolana (see below) in the top ten of all mountain walks that I have done: the combination of granite peaks and gneiss formations, endemic succulent plants and ring-tailed lemurs (though at a distance) makes this an utterly different – and utterly marvellous – walking experience. Each circuit covers different terrain, from forest and waterfalls to the frosty peak of Imarivolanitra. In the warmer, wet season the meadows are carpeted with flowers, including 30 species of terrestrial orchid.

The WWF and ANGAP must be commended for the care they have taken in creating the trails which are beautifully engineered through difficult terrain to make them as safe and easy as possible. Although the trail system covers a variety of ecosystems, the park also protects an area of montane rainforest in the east which is closed to visitors. This provides a sanctuary for such rare species as golden and greater bamboo lemurs.

Local guides

The guides are well trained and knowledgeable, particularly on the medicinal use of plants, though few speak English. 'Our English-Malagasy dictionary was the key to our interaction with the local guides and porters. Each night, we'd teach each other words from our surroundings – rain, thunder, lightning, mountains, waterfalls. A deck of playing cards was also a great icebreaker. One night, the six of us sat around the campfire playing blackjack and chewing bubble gum. The

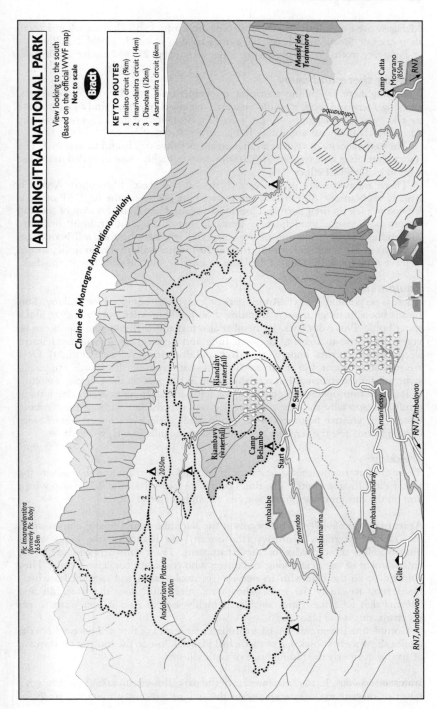

ANDRINGITRA NATIONAL PARK

View looking to the south
(Based on the official WWF map)
Not to scale

Bradt

KEY TO ROUTES
1 Imaitso circuit (9km)
2 Imarivolanitra circuit (14km)
3 Diavolana (12km)
4 Asaramanitra circuit (6km)

Massif de
Tsaranoro

Camp Catta
Morarano
(850m)
RN7

Sahanambo

Chaîne de Montagne Ampiadianombilahy

Pic Imarivolanitra
(formerly Pic Boby)
2658m

Andohariana Plateau
2000m

2050m

Riandahy
(waterfall)

Riambavy
(waterfall)

Camp
Belambo

Start

Start

Ambalabe

Ananifotsy

Zomandoo

Ambalamarina

Ambalamanandray

RN7, Ambalavao

Gîte

RN7, Ambalavao

RN7, Ambalavao

Malagasy are quick learners when it comes to cards! I still chuckle when I recall their cries of "heet!" and "boosted!" as they tried to score 21.' (Debbie Fellner)

Fees vary from 35,000Fmg for the longer circuits to 25,000Fmg for a half day.

Getting there and away

Travelling here by public transport is problematic but for true backpackers, carrying a tent and food, it would be worth the effort. You may find a taxi-brousse to take you at least part of the way, but be prepared for a lot of walking. Alternatively hire a car and driver in Fianar.

The vast majority of visitors arrange an all-inclusive trip from Fianarantsoa. The Tsara Hotel uses Lola (tel/fax: 75 520 80) who was highly recommended in the last edition by Debbie Fellner.

There are two entry points, east (Namoly) and west (Morarano). Access is usually via Namoly. All visitors need to go to the *gîte* where the ANGAP office is located to pick up their permit, a journey of around two hours. A map of the trail system and visitor guidelines is available here. It's another hour or more (depending on the condition of the road, and whether the four toll booths are manned) to the parking area and a further 20-minute walk to the campsite, so aim to leave Ambalavao by 14.00 at the latest to avoid setting up your tent in the dark.

Equipment

There is no point in going to Andringitra unless you are equipped for walking. This means boots or tough trainers (running shoes), hiking poles, good raingear, and a water bottle. Plus a day pack. Remember also that at this altitude the nights can be very cold (close to freezing between June and September) so you need warm sleeping bags, thermal underwear, gloves, and thick socks (to wear at night). Days are pleasantly warm, but it can rain – hard – at any time. It's worth bringing a swimsuit for the freezing (but refreshing) dip in the pool on the Diavolana circuit.

If a local tour operator is providing the tents and sleeping mats, do check them carefully, especially the mats. We were given airbeds, but without their rubber bungs. The creative members of the group made their own stoppers out of twigs (which failed) and the sensible resorted to sleeping pills (which worked).

Trekking

There are four main circuits: Asaramanitra, Imaitso, Diavolana and the route to the top of Pic d'Imarivolanitra. The times below are taken from the WWF map which errs on the cautious side. Fit people can cut an hour or so off.

Asaramanitra *6km/4hrs.* This begins at the Belambo campsite and climbs up to two sacred waterfalls, Riambavy (the queen) and Riandahy (the king) which plunge 250m off the edge of the escarpment. These falls are said to be the embodiment of an ancient king and queen who could not conceive a child. They climbed up to the falls with an *ombiasy* (spiritual healer) and sacrificed a white-faced zebu to satisfy the gods. They were successful: now the waterfalls and streams that feed them are considered highly sacred. And if you want to get pregnant, this is the place to go.

Completing the circuit you pass through a large area of forest. This is where the guides show their knowledge of medicinal plants. Close to the campsite is the cave of Ijajofo, formerly the hiding place of cattle thieves.

Imaitso *9km/4hrs.* In the extreme east of the park, this circuit takes you through a remnant of primary forest clinging to the side of a mountain and too steep for cultivation. Below are the ricefields of the local communities. There are some lovely views and the possibility of seeing lemurs (five species) in the forest.

Diavolana *12km/10hrs* This is the real Andringitra – a close-up experience of the granite peaks and escarpments that have intrigued me for so many years. It's a tough walk, but our group of varying fitness did it in about seven hours including a lunch break. There's an altitude gain of 500m, but you hardly notice, so beautiful is the scenery. Leaving the campsite you walk up through forest to the junction of the trail to Pic d'Imarivolanitra. You soon cross the heads of the two sacred waterfalls and, if you're feeling courageous, you can swim in the icy pools. The trail then passes through tall, heather-like shrubs (*Phillipia* spp) and up towards the escarpment. The next stretch resembles a giant rock garden with colourful mosses and lichens decorating the boulders, succulents (*Crassulaceae*) nestling at their feet, and masses of daisy-like *Helichrysum* flowers. Wonderful!

A viewpoint looks over the slabs of granite near Camp Catta. Here you may see the characteristic Andringitra ring-tailed lemurs (see box on page 222) leaping around the rocks. A trail leads to the Mororano (western) entrance to the park (17km), but to complete the circuit you descend steeply – stopping at intervals to admire the view – to the forest and campsite. It was on this final stretch that our guide found a highland streaked tenrec – perhaps the most enchanting of all Madagascar's tenrecs.

Pic d'Imarivolanitra (Pic Boby) *14km (one way)*. This trek is usually done in two or three days so needs advance planning so porters are available to carry the tents and food. This is the ultimate Andringitra, with stunning views and all the high-altitude flora described above.

HAINTENY

Destiny is a chameleon at the top of a tree:
a child simply whistles and it changes colour.
The lake did not want to create mud,
but if the water is stirred it appears.
There are many trees,
but it is the sugar-cane that is sweet.
There are many grasshoppers,
but it is the ambolo that has beautiful colours.
There are many people,
but it is in you that my spirit reposes.

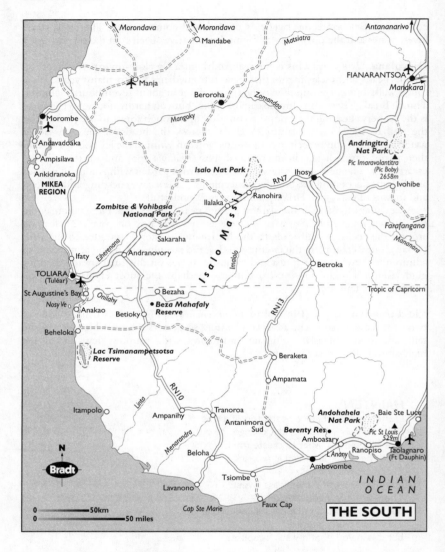

THE SOUTH

HAINTENY

Reflect on regrets, Andriamatoa.
They do not look in at the door to be told 'enter!'
They do not sit to be told 'May I pass?'
They do not advise beforehand,
but they reproach afterward.
They are not driven along like sheep,
but they come following like dogs;
they swing behind like a sheep's tail.

The South

This is the most exotic and the most famous part of Madagascar, the region of 'spiny desert' where weird cactus-like trees wave their thorny fingers in the sky, where pieces of 'elephant bird' shell may still be found, and where the Mahafaly tribe erect their intriguing and often entertaining *aloalo* stelae above the graves. Here also are some of the country's most popular national parks and reserves, as well its best beaches and coral reefs. No wonder the south features on almost all tour itineraries.

BACKGROUND INFORMATION
History
Europeans have been coming to this area for a long time. Perhaps the earliest were a group of 600 shipwrecked Portuguese sailors in 1527. Later, when sailors were deliberately landing in Madagascar during the days of the spice trade in the 16th and 17th centuries, St Augustine's Bay, south of the modern town of Toliara (Tuléar), became a favoured destination. They came for reprovisioning – Dutch and British – trading silver and beads for meat and fruit. One Englishman, Walter Hamond, was so overcome with the delights of Madagascar and the Malagasy, 'the happiest people in the world', that fired by his enthusiasm the British attempted to establish a colony at St Augustine's Bay. It was not a success. The original 140 settlers were soon whittled down to 60 through disease and murder by the local tribesmen who became less happy when they found their favourite beads were not available for trade and that these *vazaha* showed no sign of going away. The colonists left in 1646. Fifty years later St Augustine was a haven for pirates.

The people today
Several ethnic groups live in the south: the Vezo (fishermen), Mikea and Masikoro (pastoralists) are subclans of the Sakalava. The Mahafaly, Antanosy, Antandroy and Bara all have their homes in the interior. These southern Malagasy are tough, dark-skinned people, with African features, accustomed to the hardship of living in a region where rain seldom falls and finding water and grazing for their large herds of zebu is a constant challenge. The **Bara** are particularly known for their association with cattle – this warlike tribe resisted Merina rule and were never really subdued until French colonial times. Cattle rustling is a time-honoured custom – a Bara does not achieve manhood until he has stolen a few of his neighbour's cows.

In contrast to the highland people, who go in for second burial and whose tombs are the collective homes of ancestors, those in the south (with the exception of the Bara) commemorate the recently dead. There is more opportunity to be remembered as an individual here, and a **Mahafaly** or **Masikoro** man who has lived eventfully, and died rich, will have the highlights of his life perpetuated in the form of wooden carvings (*aloalo*) and colourful paintings adorning his tomb.

DISTANCES IN KILOMETRES

Ihosy–Toliara	327km
Ihosy–Taolagnaro	506km
Ihosy–Betroka	132km
Ihosy–Ranohira	75km
Ranohira–Toliara	244km
Toliara–Anakao	50km
Toliara–Andavadoaka	325km
Toliara–Andranovory	70km
Toliara–Ejeda	304km
Toliara–Bezaha	125km
Toliara–Ampanihy	290km
Toliara–Bevoay	206km
Toliara–Morombe	284km
Bezaha–Ampanihy	195km
Bezaha–Ejeda	145km
Betroka–Ihosy	132km
Ampanihy–Berenty	267km
Ampanihy–Taolagnaro	334km
Taolagnaro–Betroka	374km
Taolagnaro–Manantenina	110km
Taolagnaro–Amboasary	110km
Taolagnaro–Ambovombe	145km
Ambovombe–Tsiombe	67km
Tsiombe–Faux Cap	30km
Tsiombe–Lavanono	92km
Faux Cap–Cap Sainte Marie	40km
Lavanono–Androka	250km
Androka–Itampolo	61km
Itampolo–Anakao	134km

Formerly the *aloalo* were of more spiritual significance; but just as we, in our culture, have tended to bring an element of humour and realism into religion, so have the Malagasy. As John Mack says (in *Island of Ancestors*), 'Aloalo have become obituary announcements when formerly they were notices of rebirth.'

Antandroy tombs may be equally colourful. They are large and rectangular (the more important the person the bigger his tomb) and, like those of the Mahafaly, topped with zebu skulls left over from the funeral feast. A very rich man may have over 100 skulls on his grave. They usually have 'male and female' standing stones (or, in modern tombs, cement towers) at each side. Modern tombs may be brightly painted with geometric patterns or imaginative paintings (unlike those of the Mahafaly these do not represent scenes from the life of the deceased).

In Antandroy country, burial sometimes takes place several months after the day of death, which will be commemorated by the sacrifice of cattle and ritual mourning or wailing. A few days later the body is placed in the coffin – and more zebu are sacrificed. Meanwhile finishing touches will be made to the tomb, before the internment ceremony which takes place over two days or more. The tomb is finally filled in with stones, and topped with the horns of the sacrificed zebu. Then the house of the deceased is burnt to the ground. The burial ceremonies over, the family will not go near the tomb again.

The **Antanosy** have upright stones, cement obelisks or beautifully carved wooden memorials. These, however, are not over the graves themselves but in a sacred and secret place elsewhere.

Getting around

Road travel in the south can be a challenging affair, but some of the roads are being improved, and most of RN7 to Toliara (Tuléar) is now paved. Apart from this and the road between Taolagnaro (Fort Dauphin) and Ambovombe, the 'roads' that link other important towns are terrible, so most people prefer to fly. In addition to the regular flights to the main towns of Taolagnaro and Toliara there are occasional small planes to Ampanihy, Bekily and Betioky as well as Ihosy. Check the current schedule with Air Mad.

IHOSY

Pronounced 'Ee-oosh', this small town is the capital of the Bara tribe. It is about five hours from Fianar by taxi-brousse and lies a few kilometres north of the junction for Toliara and Taolagnaro. The road to the former is good; to the latter, bad. A now impassable road also runs from Ihosy to Farafangana, on the east coast.

It is a medium-sized town which had its moment of glory in June 2001, when it was one of Madagascar's eclipse centres. Now it feeds and accommodates those travelling south on RN7, and there is a good selection of small *hotelys* serving lunch. Those staying longer can ask for the services of Alexandre Ralainandrasana, who is a *Guide Touristique Regional* with an office at Lot IM14 Andrefantsena, Ihosy. This is on the right on the road towards Toliara.

Telephone code The area code for Ihosy is 75.

Where to stay

Zaha Motel Tel: 75 740 83. Pleasant, comfortable bungalows, with en-suite bathrooms with cold water (hot if you ask them to turn on the gas heater). 90,000Fmg.
Eva Hotel/Restaurant Originally a restaurant built in anticipation of eclipse visitors in 2001, this now has four pleasant rooms and is probably the best of the cheaper options. It is quite a walk from the centre of town, however – about 400m down the road to Toliara (on the right-hand side; the restaurant serves very good Chinese and Malagasy food).
Relais Bara Basic but adequate
Hotel Revaka About 400m from the taxi-brousse station, on the road from Fianar. There is road parking here and camping is permitted in the garden.

Where to eat

Nirina Hotel In the centre of town, a typical local restaurant serving good Malagasy dishes.

In town there is a nice little square of open-sided *hotelys* serving good Malagasy food.

FROM IHOSY TO FARAFANGANA

This road (which looks promising on the map) has been impassable by car for over 20 years. From Ihosy it is possible to go as far as **Ivohibe** and from Farafangana you can get to Vondrozo by 4WD. However, between Ivohibe and Vondrozo all the bridges have collapsed and the road has become overgrown with trees, making it difficult even for a motorbike.

FROM IHOSY TO TAOLAGNARO (FORT DAUPHIN)

RN13 is in very poor condition. Adventurous travellers with a strong pair of legs or, better, a mountain bike, will enjoy the complete lack of tourist development. Nowadays anyone driving to Taolagnaro takes the better road via Andranovory. I have had no information about the route for several years and would love to hear from anyone who's done it.

The first town is **Betroka**, then **Beraketa.** Eventually you reach Ambovombe and the paved road to Taolagnaro.

FROM IHOSY TO TOLIARA (TULEAR)

After leaving Ihosy, RN7 gives up its rather impressive asphalt and fragments into numerous sandy tracks across the Horombe Plateau. This final unpaved stretch is one of the government's road-building priorities, so may well have been surfaced by the time you read this. It currently takes about two hours to cross these monotonous grasslands. Boring for some, fascinating in its emptiness and glimpses of the traditional way of life for others. Wendy Applequist from the Missouri Botanical Garden who visited in the wet season was enchanted: 'The Horombe Plateau will forever top my list for the most beautiful places in the world. We stopped several times to look at some of the few trees there. It's all red quartz sand and whistling winds, with wonderful plants and fungi that you will miss unless you get down on your knees to look.'

As you approach Ranohira, *Medemia* palms enliven the scenery. Henk Beentje of Kew Gardens writes: 'The palms are properly called *Bismarckia*, but the French didn't like the most common palm in one of their colonies to be called after a German so changed the name, quite illegally according to the Code of Botanical Nomenclature!'

RANOHIRA AND ISALO NATIONAL PARK

The small town of Ranohira lies 75km south of Ihosy ($2\frac{1}{2}$ to 3 hours) and is the base for visiting the popular Isalo National Park. It is also the nearest established town to Ilakaka, the new settlement that is the base for the sapphire trade, which has transformed it from a sleepy little town to a bustling commercial centre.

Getting there and away

Getting to Ranohira is usually no problem. If leaving from Toliara note that the taxi-brousses and buses depart early in the morning, so it is best to book your seat the night before. Continuing south can be a problem since taxi-brousses are usually full by the time they arrive in Ranohira. If time is short it's worth considering hiring a car and driver in Toliara to make this excursion.

Where to stay
Category A
Relais de la Reine BP01, 313 Ranohira; www.3dmadagascar.com/relaisdelareine. Bookings through Madagascar Discovery Agency in Tana; tel: 22 336 23; 22 351 65; fax: 22 351 67; email: mda@wanadoo.mg. This lovely French-run hotel is not in Ranohira but at Soarano, 9km further south on the edge of the park. It has been thoughtfully designed to blend as much as possible into the surrounding 40ha of landscape and is one of the nicest hotels in Madagascar. There are blocks of six rooms grouped round a courtyard (37 in total) and solar panels provide hot water. The water is drawn from their own stream and fans cool the rooms in the hot season. There is also a swimming pool and tennis court. The hotel has an equestrian club with good-quality horses and can organise riding tours in Isalo, from an hour or a half day to treks of several days; €14 an hour, €45 half day, €75 full day.

Car transfers can be arranged from Toliara, and the hotel even has a landing strip if you decide to splash out and book their private plane. A twin-bedded room with bathroom costs €60, breakfast is €4, and a main meal costs €11.

Category B

Motel d'Isalo Tel: 22 330 82. The first hotel as you approach the town from the north. 50 rooms. Nice bungalows, solar heating, but some way from the centre of town so inconvenient for independent travellers. Suitable for groups – who love it. 125,000–150,000Fmg.

Hotel Orchidée d'Isalo Tel: 75 801 78. Located in the centre of the village. 39 rooms. Recent independent travellers have complained about slow service and general unhelpfulness, but this may have changed by the time you read this. Tour operators consider it the best option in town for groups. There are some new rooms for 188,100Fmg, and the old rooms are 100,100Fmg with hot water and fan, and 78,100Fmg with cold water. Meals are 40,000Fmg and breakfast 15,000Fmg.

Isalo Ranch BP3, 313 Ranohira. A group of 18 bungalows, a few kilometres south of Ranohira. Some have en-suite bathrooms, others shared facilities, but all have solar-powered hot water. Double with en-suite bathroom: 125,000Fmg; family bungalow (sleeping 4) 140,000Fmg; bungalows, double, shared facilities 80,000Fmg. The food is reportedly very good. Transport is provided to and from the National Park.

Hotel les Joyeux Lémuriens Tel: 22 536 64; cellphone: 032 0260 350. 20 rooms. Once the most popular backpacker hotel in Ranohira, but now quite pricey. From 165,000–220,000Fmg. Breakfast 20,000Fmg, mail meals 45,000Fmg.

Category C

Hotel Berny Tel: 75 801 76; fax: 20 94 419 20. 19 rooms of varying quality and price. Very friendly, centrally located next to the ANGAP office; English spoken. 80,000–100,000Fmg; meals 6,000–20,000Fmg.

Momo Trek 19 Bara-style huts next to the ANGAP office. Simple but clean. 'Momo is a former guide; he is genuine and can help you with anything you could possibly need in Ranohira. He and his family are great people and know the value of good service.' (Alex Hall) 'The restaurant had good food and was great fun. We stayed up late dancing, drinking, eating and chatting with Momo who speaks good English.' (L Brandstetter) Bungalows are 75,000–140,000Fmg; camping 7,500Fmg. Meals are 40,000Fmg.

Les Toiles de L'Isalo Tel: 22 245 34. Single: 100,000Fmg, double 125,000Fmg, triple 150,000Fmg; breakfast is included.

Isalo National Park

The combination of sandstone rocks (cut by deep canyons and eroded into weird shapes), rare endemic plants and dry weather (between June and August rain is almost unknown) makes this park particularly rewarding. For botanists there is *Pachypodium rosulatum* or elephant's foot – a bulbous rock-clinging plant – and a native species of aloe, *Aloe isaloensis*; and for lemur-lovers there are sifakas, brown lemurs and ring-tails. Isalo is also sacred to the Bara tribe. For hundreds of years the Bara have used caves in the canyon walls as burial sites.

Tourists who do not wish to hike (and this should not be undertaken lightly – it can be very hot) or to pay the park fee have various options. Simply driving past the sandstone formations which can be seen from the road is exciting enough. Another popular visit – perhaps too popular at times – is to La Fenêtre, a natural rock formation providing a window to the setting sun. Walk behind the rocks for the proper Isalo feeling of space and tranquillity.

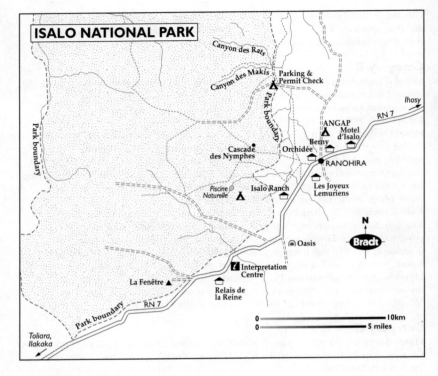

Permits and guides

For an excursion in the park you will need a permit (50,000Fmg) which must be purchased at the ANGAP office in Ranohira, next to Hotel Berny. You must take an accredited guide with you. The park authorities have worked hard at rewarding the best guides by giving them a star rating which is posted outside their office. Charges (standard for most parks) are posted on the wall of the office. Prices depend on the length of tour: 50,000Fmg for a minimum of three people for the Namaza canyon or the Piscine Naturelle, or 60,000Fmg for the Canyon des Makis. For a full day combining two or more of these it's 110,000Fmg for a minimum of three people.

Schematic maps of the park are available from ANGAP.

Isalo Interpretation Centre (Maison de l'Isalo)

Well worth a visit to learn more about the people who live around the park, as well as the wildlife in the national park itself. 'The most sophisticated I saw in Madagascar, with commentary in Malagasy, French and English throughout, modern interpretation boards and interactive displays.' The only negative is that it is poorly located some way south of the town.

Hiking in the park

There are several established circuits, with campsites, and most guides are reluctant to deviate from these. No matter, they provide all the Isalo specials of lemurs, cool leafy canyons, and hot, dry plains with those extraordinary rock formations and accompanying succulent plants.

Circuit Namaza This has you following a stream (some scrambling) up a leafy canyon to the Cascade des Nymphes. The walk takes 30-45 minutes, and you are rewarded at the end with a refreshing swim in surprisingly cold water. The pool is very deep, and you need to swim to see the waterfall and the imposing, fern-fringed black cliffs which almost hide the sky.

The campsite here is regularly visited by ring-tailed and brown lemurs. Hoopoes are also frequently seen. A lovely place.

Canyon des Makis (Canyon des Singes) This is 17km from Ranohira, accessible by a rough track (4WD only – or on foot). At the canyon a path goes over rocks and along the edge of the tumbling river; there are pools into which you can fling yourself at intervals and, at the top, a small waterfall under which to have a shower. The sheer rocks hung with luxuriant ferns broaden out to provide views of the bare mountain behind, and trees and palms provide shade for a picnic. It is as beautiful and refreshing as Namaza with the added bonus of a troop of sifakas near the canyon entrance.

Piscine Naturelle This is justifiably the most popular destination for hikers in Isalo, so can be crowded. As the name implies, this is a natural swimming pool. Fringed with palm trees and constantly filled by a waterfall, it is both stunningly beautiful and wonderful for swimming, having been unobtrusively improved so that getting in and out of the water is easy. There is also an open-sided shelter where Benson's rock thrushes flirt with bathers.

The nearby campsite has a flush (!) toilet and a shower.

With the help of a vehicle you can do one of the canyons and the Piscine in one day with the option of a long (about 18km) walk across the Isalo Plateau. This is hot and arduous, but well worth it for the views and plants (specially *pachypodium*).

Budget travellers with only a day in hand should opt for the Piscine Naturelle. It is less distance to walk (6km/2hrs each way, if the shortest route is taken); and it provides good viewpoints with a wonderfully cool swim at the end. 'First you have a fairly steep ascent and after about 10 to 20 minutes you get on to a rocky plateau with just a little bit of bushy vegetation left and right of the path between the rocks plus the odd tree. The rock formations have been given names by the guides: The Turtle, The African Woman, The Skull and The Crocodile.

'After walking for about 20 minutes on this plateau, you arrive at a point where your guide will make you climb up a rock (very easy) and suddenly you overlook a valley which is rocky and barren except for a line of green through its middle that indicates the flow of the stream. Take a few minutes break and enjoy! From here it's about 20 minutes or so to some rocks and suddenly you are a few metres above the pool. Getting down to the pool is like going through one of the glass houses in Kew Gardens, only you can walk between the plants and it's much bigger.' (Volker Dornheim)

Those with a vehicle can drive along a track (with one ford) from Ranohira for 30 minutes to the base of the rocks where the hiking trail starts. From there it is about 90 minutes to the pool. Most of the better hotels in Ranohira can provide vehicles.

Fit hikers can walk from Ranohira to the Canyon des Makis or Namaza (9km/3hrs each way). You start from the church, striding across a flat plain with the canyons tantalisingly in view the whole time. The hot sun should be taken very seriously: carry two litres of water (and purifying tablets for the canyon water), wear a hat and apply liberal quantities of sunscreen. The contrast between the space and yellowness of the plain and the ferny green of the canyon makes the effort well worthwhile.

For the real Isalo experience you should trek for a few days. The combined Piscine/Canyon des Makis circuit is the most popular and usually done in three days. The first day to the campsite at the swimming pool is only two or three hours, then five or six rugged hours the next day to the canyon. It is then a three-hour walk back to Ranohira.

The less visited parts of the park are even more rewarding, but it is not easy to find a guide willing to take you away from the beaten track.

Beyond the park

Those with a 4WD vehicle can explore some of the dirt roads bordering the national park. 'We got a guide from the park office in Ranohira and went up a dirt road west of the park towards the valley of the Malio River. In a small forest patch we rediscovered a liana previously known from only two 40- to 50-year-old collections. This is an interesting piece of forest... When you hit sand you have to park and walk through dense, liana-filled jungle with gigantic butterflies flitting through the gloom. Our guide told us that when he was a boy, they used to roast and eat the huge spiders that spin webs across the trail to catch *vazaha*. "But that was when I was a boy," he said while I was gagging. "I wouldn't do that now, of

GEMSTONES

Tim Ireland

As a geologist and a gemologist I spent a good part of my trip explaining to other travellers how the gemstones occur, why they occur where they do, and what the significance of the local geology is. It seems appropriate to describe that here to future readers.

The crystalline rocks that comprise most of Madagascar are similar in age and type to those of southern India and Sri Lanka in which gemstones are also abundant. Broadly these are termed 'high grade metamorphic' rocks, alluding to the fact that they have been changed dramatically, through recrystallisation without complete melting, from some precursor rocktype. The current mineralogy and texture of the rocks indicates the conditions under which recrystallisation occurred; the entire region has been exhumed from an original depth of 10-30km, and cooled from an original temperature of around 700°C. This is not to say that the rocks were that distance below their present position, but rather that they were somewhere in the core of an ancient collisional mountain belt not unlike the Himalaya. Erosion has stripped material from those ancient mountains to expose their crystalline interiors, and at the same time the land has flexed upward in response. These processes have combined to leave rocks at the surface today that formed under the weight of tens of kilometres of other rock.

The younger flat-lying rocks of the west are made up largely of marine sediments that lap on to this crystalline core of Madagascar. Within the massive volume of rock, worn down over the millennia, gemstones formed only in comparatively minute units in which certain chemical and physical conditions prevailed for sufficient time. As erosion slowly dismantled the mountains, it first uncovered, and then destroyed the gem-bearing units of rock. As precious stones by their nature are dense and physically durable, they collected in major course … because they're endemic!" I thought this was a young man who had a real future in science.' (Wendy Applequist)

Ilakaka

This extraordinary settlement has sprung up within the last few years as the centre of the sapphire trade. Tour buses now drive straight through with the windows closed for fear of bandits. However, providing you are sensible over security it is worth a visit for the Wild West atmosphere. There is, perhaps, nowhere else like it in the world: savour it while you can, in a couple of years it will probably be a ghost town. When I passed through in 2003 it was humming with life and full of swaggering men with guns on their hips. Every other shop has the word *Saphir* above its doorway, and the quantity of high-priced consumer goods for sale is remarkable. There are plenty of restaurants and hotels, if you decide to stay.

CONTINUING SOUTH

The drive from Isalo to Toliara (244km) takes a minimum of four hours.

The sapphire rush is moving south and you will pass the temporary grass huts and piles of earth dug by fortune seekers for many kilometres. Other smaller versions of Ilakaka are springing up along this route. Eventually the rugged mountains give way to grasslands, and following the rains there are many flowers

river channel deposits adjacent to the weathering mountains while other components of the rock were more completely broken down. As finer, lighter particles, these were carried further by the rivers to be deposited further downstream or even reach the sea. There are few in-situ occurrences of the true precious stones (sapphire, ruby etc) in Madagascar, and the majority of mining involves searching for and chasing the old river channel deposits.

To retrieve the gemstones in Ilakaka, an exploratory shaft is sunk until the miners recognise a particular combination of rocktypes in the boulders of the gravel; certain rocks were being shed from the mountains and accumulated in the gravels contemporaneously with deposition of the gemstones. At this stage a few bags of gravel are washed and, if the results are good, a pit is sunk on the site down to the level of the rich gravel layer. The numbers quoted to me by one miner testify to astonishing richness of the good gravel at Ilakaka. Just half a dozen bags of gravel from an exploratory hole might yield 20 million francs worth of sapphires. The catch is that that payload layer is often around 15m deep, yet only 1m thick, and that demands a very large hole for a small yield. Curiously, the government has precluded the use of heavy machinery by Malagasy people, while outsiders are free to mine in whatever fashion they wish. So while small syndicates of Malagasy miners break their backs shifting dirt with shovels, Thai and Sri Lankan miners use earth-moving equipment to dig the efficient way. Money floods out of Madagascar by way of gemstones at a rate beyond anyone's wildest dreams – incalculable because of the shady nature of the industry. At the end of the day, a few thousand Malagasy are securely employed in Ilakaka for the duration of the rush (two years, ten years, 100 years?), while a small number of foreigners make enough to retire in style several times over. The smartest Malagasy I met at Ilakaka weren't digging stones…they were providing security to the foreign buyers with their suitcases of money and their pockets of jewels.

– the large white *Crinum firmifolium* and the Madagascar periwinkle – but in the dry season it's quite monotonous. The next town of importance is **Sakaraha**, which has been transformed into another sapphire centre. There are places to stay here if you want to spend some time in Zombitse National Park.

Warning The police roadblocks along RN7 give plenty of scope for corrupt officers to hassle drivers (and passengers) of private vehicles. 'Closer to Tuléar it was much scarier, particularly since we were two women alone. The police got inside the car with us and demanded rides to a nearby town plus pay-offs.' (L Brandstetter)

Zombitse and Vohibasia National Park

Zombitse is a stark example of the effects of deforestation. Years of continuous felling have turned the surrounding areas into an arid moonscape and what remains is an isolated pocket of forest. Thankfully, this enclave is now protected. The park covers 21,500ha, straddling RN7 some 25km northeast of Sakaraha. It is an important example of a boundary zone between the western and southern domains of vegetation and so has a high level of biodiversity.

Zombitse is of major significance to birdwatchers as it offers the chance to glimpse one of Madagascar's rarest endemics, Appert's greenbul, which is confined to this forest. Many other species, like cuckoo roller and giant coua, may also be seen.

There is now a park office (on the southern side of RN7) and official guides to take you along the good paths and circuit trails. It takes just over an hour to reach the park from Isalo or two to three hours from Toliara, so serious birdwatchers should leave as early as possible in the morning to avoid the heat, or stay in Sakaraha.

'In the dry season the forest initially gives the impression of being rather lifeless. This is deceptive. Whilst looking for the greenbul is often the priority, I've seen plenty of other remarkable species. Verreaux's sifakas are regularly seen (even in trees by the road) and red-tailed lepilemurs are common (the guides often know their sleep sites). Reptiles like the spectacular, locally endemic Standing's day gecko can be found resting on trunks. On one very lucky occasion, I even encountered a pair of courting/mating fosas in a tree!' (Nick Garbutt)

Beyond Sakara you will start to see painted tombs, some with *aloalo,* near the road. Be wary of taking photographs, however. Some locals have become adept at materialising out of nowhere and demanding payment. As you get closer to Toliara you'll see your first baobabs and pass through a cotton-growing region. Look out for the enormous nests of hammerkop birds in roadside trees.

About two hours from Sakaraha is the small village of **Andranovory** which has a colourful Sunday market. Another hour and Toliara's table mountain, La Table, comes into view on the right; half an hour later you pass the airport and head for the town.

TOLIARA (TULEAR)

The pronunciation of the French, Tuléar, and the Malagasy names is the same: 'toolee-ar'. Toliara's history is centred on St Augustine's Bay, described at the beginning of this chapter, although the name of the town is thought to derive from an encounter with one of those early sailors who asked a local inhabitant where he might moor his boat. The Malagasy replied: *toly eroa,* 'mooring down there'. The town itself is relatively modern – 1895 – and was designed by an uninspired French architect. His tree planting was more successfully aesthetic, and the shady tamarind trees, *kily*, give welcome respite from the blazing sun.

There are three good reasons to visit Toliara: the rich marine life with good snorkelling and diving, the Mahafaly and Masikoro tombs and a museum which puts it all in context, and the remarkable spiny bush in places north and south of the town (although this is being destroyed at an alarming rate).

The beaches north and south of the town have fine white sand, and this whole area is opening up to tourism (fortunately the poor or non-existent roads are an effective deterrent to overdevelopment). Beyond the sandy beaches is an extensive coral reef. In recent years, however, this has suffered from coral bleaching and is not longer particularly rewarding for snorkellers. Toliara itself, regrettably, has no beach, just mangroves and mud flats.

Telephone code The area code for Toliara is 94.

Warnings In the cool season (May to October) the nights in Toliara are very cold. The cheaper hotels rarely supply enough blankets. Businesses close between 12.00 and 15.00; banks are closed from 11.30-14.00.

Getting there and away
By road
Route Nationale 7 (RN7) is served by a variety of quite comfortable vehicles. Expect to pay around 125,000Fmg for a proper bus. Cheaper taxi-brousses leave the Gare du Sud in Tana at about 15.00. The trip is advertised as taking 24 hours, but journeys of 18 hours to 35 hours have been known.

By air
There are daily flights from Tana and Taolagnaro, but in the high season these tend to be fully booked. However, it's always worth going to the airport, whatever they say in the office.

Getting around
Distances are quite large, but pousse-pousses are plentiful. Expect to pay roughly 2,500Fmg but make sure you have the right change. Don't grudge paying more – a pousse-pousse driver's life is not easy, and they are a friendly bunch. Taxis are plentiful. The going rate is 5,000Fmg for any trip (except the airport which is 25,000Fmg). However, if you stop anywhere – even briefly – en route you will be charged for two trips.

Car hire
New Horizon Bd Gallieni, about 200m east of the post office; tel/fax: 94 427 73. Italian owner Guiseppe (Jimmy) Castelluccio rents out reliable 4WD vehicles.

Where to stay
Most visitors spending any time in the Toliara area stay at the beach resorts (see pages 243–54) but there are some good-value hotels in or near the town.

Category A
Motel Le Capricorne Tel: 94 426 20; fax: 94 431 66; email: motel.capricorne@wanadoo.mg or capric@dts.mg. 10 rooms. About 2km from the town centre on RN7. Considered the best of the Toliara hotels. It has a lovely garden and is well run with a good restaurant. Single: €51, double €55. Prices include breakfast. Meals are €10.
Hotel Plazza Cellphone: 032 0249 214. One of Toliara's oldest hotels and the best located

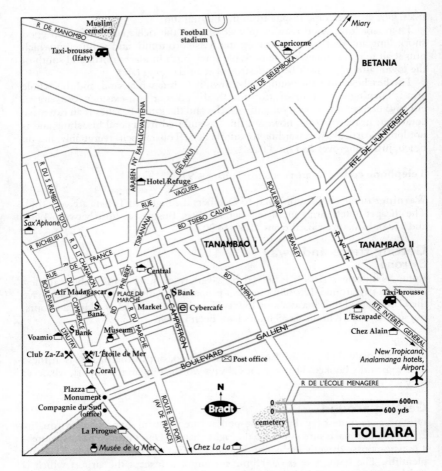

R DE MANOMBO · Muslim cemetery · Football stadium · Miary · Taxi-brousse (Ifaty) · Capricorne · AV DE BELEMBOKA · BETANIA · ARABEN IVY FAHALEOVANTENA · (DELAVAU) · RTE DE L'UNIVERSITÉ · Hotel Refuge · VAGUIER · R DU S KAMBETTE TOTO · RUE · BOULEVARD · BD TSIEBO CALVIN · Sax'Aphone · R. RICHELIEU · R D L'I CHANARON · RUE DE FRANCE · TSIRANANA · TANAMBAO I · BRANLEY · R N 14 · TANAMBAO II · RUE DU · BD · R DU COMMERCE · PLACE DU MARCHÉ · PHILBERT · Central · BD CAMPAN · Taxi-brousse · Air Madagascar · R G CAMPISTRON · Bank · Market · Cybercafé · RTE INTERET GENERAL · L'Escapade · BOULEVARD · L'ALITA · Bank · Museum · GALLIENI · Chez Alain · Voamio · Bank · Club Za-Za · L'Étoile de Mer · New Tropicana, Analamanga hotels, Airport · Le Corail · BOULEVARD · Post office · Plazza Monument · ROUTE DU PORT (AV DE FRANCE) · R DE L'ÉCOLE MENAGERE · Compagnie du Sud (office) · N · Bradt · cemetery · 0 — 600m · 0 — 600 yds · La Pirogue · Musée de la Mer · Chez La La · **TOLIARA**

in spacious gardens facing the sea. 21 rooms; recently refurbished. Some rooms have air-conditioning.. 130,000–210,000Fmg. Meals 50,000Fmg. Accepts Visa and MasterCard.
Hotel Paletuvier Tel: 94 440 39. A good hotel with 14 rooms opposite L'Etoile de Mer restaurant. 130,000Fmg double, 150,000Fmg triple.
Le Sax'Aphone Villa Soarimanga, Besakoa, (on the western outskirts of Toliara, opposite a school); tel: 94 440 88, cellphone: 032 0223 744; email: sax.aphone@simicro.mg. Four bungalows, and three rooms (total capacity 19 guests). A wonderful guesthouse run by the charismatic Alain and Michèle Bonard, who named it after a jazz club they used to run in Montpellier. They speak French, English and German. This is more like a private home than a hotel, and is a perfect place for solo travellers. There's a lovely common room, and the bar/restaurant serves excellent meals and has a great atmosphere. Rooms 75,000–95,000Fmg, bungalows 135,000Fmg.
Chez Alain BP89; tel: 94 415 27; email: c.alain@wanadoo.mg; www.chez-alain.net. Deservedly one of the most popular *vazaha* hotels in Madagascar, with 21 rooms to suit almost every budget. Well run, friendly, excellent food (huge portions!). Mountain bikes for hire. The diving centre L'Ancre Bleue is based here. From 70,000Fmg (double room with shared toilet) to 350,000Fmg (suite). Breakfast 18,000Fmg.

Category B

L'Escapade A new hotel in a good location at the eastern end of Blvd Gallieni. 10 rooms round a courtyard plus bungalows with fans. Pool table. 75,000Fmg.

Hotel Lavasoa Tel: 94 418 39. Nine basic rooms, some en suite, in a quiet street. Pleasant garden. 35,000–40,000Fmg.

Le Refuge Tel 94 423 28; fax: 94 425 94. 11 rooms. A very pleasant medium-priced hotel near the centre of town. Swimming pool (though to use it costs an extra 10,000Fmg). En-suite double with fan is 80,000Fmg, triple is 90,000Fmg, and a family room costs 105,000Fmg. Air-conditioning 105,000Fmg. American breakfast costs 18,000Fmg and continental breakfast is 14,000Fmg.

Hotel Central Bang in the centre of town, so convenient for the market and museum. Hot water and en-suite WC for 75,000Fmg, or shared facilities for 35,000Fmg. Recommended.

Le Pousse-Pousse Rue de l'Eglise; 60,000Fmg. Two minutes from the market square, this is a friendly, French-owned hotel. Rooms are very clean, with a shower and sink. 'The only disadvantage is the tin roof. There's a central courtyard, a good bar and the best peppered zebu steak with chips in all of Madagascar.' (D Simon)

New Tropicana Cellphone: 032 04 478 59. Near the airport.

PET LEMURS

Several hotels in the Toliara region keep pet lemurs. The pathetic sight of these animals in cramped cages or tied by a cord around their loins upsets all visitors. Here's a report from a South African tour leader who decided that action speaks louder than words.

'The hotel has a cage with three ringtails. I was shocked to see this and so were the clients so we designed this bold plan to liberate the lemurs. It was working like clockwork. Our transport was waiting and I had the clients in position. The manager, cooks, and receptionist all duly entertained by their barrage of questions as I slinked through the back and opened the cage door just enough to let the ringies out. Then we all casually made our way to the truck. I peeped over my shoulder and saw the lemurs come out, stand up and sniff the air – that sweet scent of freedom – and then the Helsinki Syndrome kicked in and they made a bee-line for the kitchen window. We drove off to screams and pots and pans clanging. I laughed but wanted to cry. Bloody idiots. Now I understand why they are "pre-simians".'

So what should we do in these circumstances? As this story demonstrates, you cannot 'liberate' an animal accustomed to captivity. It will literally not know what to do with itself and will return to its cage. The solution, as always in Madagascar, is more complicated than it seems. The reason these adorable animals are kept caged or tied is that as they grew from charming babies into assertive adults they started biting the hand that fed them.

'So what can we do?' a hotelier in Toliara asked me, her hands thrown wide in Gallic gesture. 'A kid brings us a little baby lemur and says that the mother is dead and do we want to buy it? I say yes because I think I will treat it more kindly than the kid. Maybe I shouldn't … because then he started biting my guests so now I have to keep him tied up.' For more on this tricky subject read about Little Madi on page 306.

Category C
Arboretum d'Antsokay The Arboretum (see page 242) has five basic bungalows (cold water, shared toilet). Perfect for those who want to see the birds and other wildlife in the early morning. 50,000Fmg.

Chez La La On the Route du Port opposite the departure point for boats to Anakao. Probably the best bet in this category. Great location, inexpensive and comfortable. Pleasant bar and very friendly staff.

La Pirogue Tel: 94 415 37. 57,000Fmg double with fan; 57,000Fmg double with en-suite bathroom and hot water. Very noisy. 'Don't stay there unless you have to. For animal lovers they have boisterous dogs, swarms of mosquitoes and four-inch cockroaches.' (Alex Hall)

L'Hotel Analamanga Tel/fax: 94 415 47. Double room 50,000Fmg, bungalow 40,000Fmg. Located on the outskirts of Toliara as you arrive on RN7. Some rooms plus five neat, small bungalows on stilts; clean communal bathrooms. Nice quiet setting out of town, cool under trees, but within easy walking distance of town.

Where to eat
L'Etoile de Mer Tel: 94 428 07. This unpretentious restaurant located in a wooden building on the seafront, between the Plazza Hotel and the Voamio, has maintained its high standards since I first visited Toliara in 1982, and deserves its success. It specialises in seafood.

Le Jardin A restaurant near the Hotel Central has earned rave reviews from several readers. 'The best pizza in Madagascar, a range of tasty salads, freshly squeezed orange juice…'

Gelateria Next door to Le Jardin. 'The best ice-cream and the best coffee in town.'

Club Za Za Serves particularly good fish.

Zanzibar Route de L'Ecole Menagere Serves huge pizza, and has a friendly atmosphere.

Corto Maltese 'Small, French-owned, good food. In town: hotel or pousse-pousse driver should know where it is.' (SB)

La Bernique 'Opposite Monument. French-owned bar with snacks and the most comprehensive collection of malt whiskies I found in Madagascar. Well worth several visits!' (SB)

Nightlife
Za Za Club One of two nightclubs in Toliara, has been popular for years but has had poor reports recently. 'The music is a poor cross between Western and *gasy*. Most clientele are young local girls looking out for *vazaha* men. However, it is possible to sit away from the loud music to have a conversation as there is loads of room.' (TS) 'The "dancing competitions" are open to *vazaha* and you can put your name down on the night!' (SB)

Club Mozambique Just down the road from Za Za. Much smaller and more friendly and has free entry. Music the same, and clientele the same. .

Internet facilities
Internet Café Rue du Commerce.

Cyber Café Bd Philbert Tsiranana next door to Credit Lyonnais Bank.

Cybersport Ganivala Below Hotel Central. Good internet with friendly staff.

Money change
Socimad Corner of Rue Père Joseph Castan and Rue de l'Eglise; tel: 94 216 91. Fast and efficient.

Shopping
Befana Boutique Sells a range of good-quality local crafts, run on a co-operative basis.

Craft market The main craft area is towards the end of Bd Gallieni near the monument.

Natur'ant Déco Essential oils and herbal remedies.

Medical clinic

Clinique St Luc Tel: 94 422 47 or 320 229 451; email: cliniquesaint-luc@dts.mg. Dr Rasolonjatovo. A private clinic that can handle most medical problems. Note, however, that it does not have oxygen for diving emergencies.

CHR (Centre Hôpital Regional) Tel: 94 418 55; Dr Valikara, director. Located in Tsenengea. This is the main hospital for the southwest, and can handle serious emergencies (including diving mishaps). The standard of hygiene is not as good as Clinique St Luc, however.

Watersports
Diving and snorkelling

For many people the main reason to visit Toliara is for the coral reefs. The WWF recognises the importance of these in developing ecotourism in the area and a conservation programme is under way, centred at the University of Toliara. The goal of the project is 'to ensure that the coral reefs and coastal zone are effectively conserved through the establishment of a multiple-use marine park and sustainable economic development'. Certainly there is potential for marine ecotourism, although dead or dying coral is disturbingly evident and many areas which were impressive five years ago are unrecognisable now. See boxes on pages 266 and 436–7 for information on marine conservation. The following is a summary of diving centres in the Toliara region.

Deep Sea Club BP158, Toliara; tel: 94 426 20
Bamboo Club BP47, Toliara; tel: 94 427 17
Club Nautique (Dunes Hotel); tel: 94 339 00
Club Nautique (Lakana Vezo Hotel); tel: 94 426 20
Gipsy Club (Hotel Nautilus); tel: 94 418 74; email: nautilus@simicro.mg
L'Ancre Bleue (Hotel Chez Alain); tel: 94 415 27; email: chez.alain@simicro.mg
The Grand Blu (Mangily); hotel and dive club
Alizee Dive In Hotel Safari Vezo, Anakao

Sailing

Location Catamaran (tel: 94 433 17) organise catamaran trips to the Barren Islands, Belo Sur Mer, Andavadoka, Ifaty, Anakao and Itampolo.

Surfing

Toliara, Anakao and Lavanono are all places served by the surfing project set up by Yves Jousseaume in Taolagnaro. See also box on page 242.

Warning Sea-urchins are a problem in the shallows off many of the beaches around Toliara. Be very careful not to touch them and wear some form of foot protection when swimming or snorkelling (see pages 252–3 for first-aid advice).

Sightseeing and excursions
In town

Toliara has more 'official' sightseeing than most Malagasy towns. Some places are worth the trip, others are not. In town the most interesting place to visit is the small **museum** on Boulevard Philbert Tsiranana, run by the University of Toliara. The entry fee is 25,000Fmg. There are some remarkable exhibits, including a Mikea mask (genuine masks are rare in Madagascar) with real human teeth. These are well-displayed and labelled in Malagasy and French, and include some Sakalava erotic tomb sculptures. Marine enthusiasts should visit the **Musée de la Mer**, also run by the university, on Route de la Porte (tel: 94 41 612). The main attraction

SURFING IN SOUTHWEST MADAGASCAR
Bruce Harris

As far a surfing goes, my advice to avid surfers would be to head straight to Toliara and organise a guide to show you round the many quality offshore reef breaks in the area. This region definitely has the best surf in the country. It is exposed to the southwest groundswells that sweep up past South Africa and has spots that work in different winds. I wouldn't stay based in Toliara though, but head either to Ifaty or Anakao.

The main hitch with surfing in the southwest is the locations of the breaks – most are at least 1km offshore. You need a boat to access these breaks and, more importantly, you need a guide to show you where they are. Probably the best man for this job is Tony Adkins, a South African. Tony runs 'no frills' tours on his catamaran The Hoonos for around €50 a day. The facilities are basic, but he knows his way around. Tony can be contacted through the Bafana Boutique in Toliara, tel: (261 20) 94 433 17.

The following Tana-based adventure travel company runs surfing tours:

Mada Surfari Travel & Tours B2, Galerie ZOOM, Ankorondrano (BP 8323), 101 Antananarivo. Tel/fax: (261 20) 22 318 46 or 22 246 33; cellphone: 032 02 411 76 or 033 02 411 76; email: fredralaimi@mada-surfari.com, infos@mada-surfari.com; web: www.mada-surfari.com. The company is managed by a Malagasy surfer, Fred Ralaimihoatra.

There is also surf on the east coast of the island, especially north of Toamasina, where the coastline starts to become a bit more irregular. I only spent a couple of days in the east, at Mahambo. There is plenty of surfing potential here and, I suspect, even more further north.

For more on Bruce's trip check out his website: http://mada.moreorless.au.com/

here is a coelacanth – the only one now on view in Madagascar. 'Fascinating collection of crustacia and a couple of unexpected oddities. The coelacanth looks rather unwell.' (S Bulmer) Entrance 25,000Fmg.

The **market** is lively and interesting. This is one of the best places in all of Madagascar for *lambas*. You can also find the mohair rugs that are made in Ampanihy, a terrific selection of herbal remedies (*fanafody*), and a wide range of fruit. The best place for **handicrafts** are the stalls towards the Monument end of Boulevard Galieni.

Day excursions from Toliara
Arboretum d'Antsokay

This botanical garden should not be missed by anyone with an interest in the flora – and its accompanying fauna – of the southwest. It was established in 1980 by the Swiss-born botanist Hermann Pétignat who died in 2000. There are nearly 900 species of plant here, 90% of which are endemic to the region. Around 80% have medicinal qualities.

The Arboretum lies 12km from Toliara, just north of the track to La Mangrove hotel and St Augustine on RN7. It is clearly signposted. A trained guide takes you on a two-hour tour of the 'improved' area (7ha) of the 50ha arboretum. Here you will see the rare plants nurtured by the late M Pétignat, including 100 species of euphorbia and 60 species of kalenchoe. You will also see an abundance of birds and reptiles. Indeed, with the spiny forest fast disappearing from the southwest, this is one of the best places in the region for birders.

Entry (with the tour) costs 25,000Fmg. Try to arrive as early as possible in the morning to miss the heat of the day. Or, better, stay overnight in one of the basic bungalows. Excellent meals are served at the Auberge de la Table. Contact details for the arboretum: andry.petignat@caramail.com.

Tombs

The most spectacular tombs within easy reach of the town are those of the Masikoro, a sub-division of the Sakalava. This small tribe is probably of African origin, and there is speculation that the name comes from *mashokora* which, in parts of Tanzania, means scrub forest. There are also Mahafaly and Bara tombs in the area.

The tombs are off RN7 a little over an hour from Toliara, and are clearly visible on the right. There are several large, rectangular tombs, flamboyantly painted with scenes from the distinguished military life of the deceased, with a few mermaids and Rambos thrown in for good measure. Oh, and a scene from *Titanic*. These are known as the **Tombs of Andranovory**.

Another tomb, on the outskirts of town beyond the university, is **King Baba's Tomb**. This is set in a grove of Didierea trees and is interesting more for the somewhat bizarre funerary objects (an urn and a huge, cracked bell) displayed there and its spiritual significance to the local people (you may only approach barefoot) than for any aesthetic value. This King Baba, who seems to have died about 100 years ago, was presumably a descendant of one of the Masikoro kings of Baba mentioned in British naval accounts of the 18th century. These kings used to trade with English ships calling at St Augustine's Bay and gave their family and courtiers English names such as the Prince of Wales and the Duke of Cumberland. On the way to King Baba's Tomb you may visit a little fenced-off park of banyan trees, all descending from one 'parent'. This is known as 'the sacred grove' and in theory would be a place for peaceful contemplation, but the hordes of tourist-aware children are a deterrent.

Tour operators

Most excursions can be made by taxi but for something more ambitious where a guide is advisable the following tour operators are recommended.

Air Fort Services BP1029; tel: 94 426 84, cellphone: 032 0439 632.
Compagnie du Sud Mahavatse 2, Toliara. Tel: 94 437 21, cellphone: 032 0462 409 (mobile); email: contacts@compagniedusud.com; www.compagniedusud.com. Run day excursions to Anakao, Nosy Ve, and Sarondrano and also further afield to Tsimanampetsotsa and region.

Adventure tours

Trajectoire BP283, Toliara 601; tel/fax: 94 433 00; email: trajectoire@simicro.mg. Run by Bernard Forgeau, who owns a secluded hotel in Madiorano (see page 248). He runs small group adventure tours throughout remote areas of the southwest, including the Makay massif by motorbike and the descent of the Mangoky River by canoe.

BEACH RESORTS NORTH OF TOLIARA
Ifaty and Mangily

Ifaty and Mangily to its north have now merged into one area offering sand, sea and snorkelling, plus beach bungalows. Ifaty/Mangily lies only 27km north of

Toliara, but the road is terrible. This is the consequence of deforestation: with all the trees gone, there is nothing to hold the sandy topsoil, and no repair is going to last more than a few months.

Warnings Cell phones often don't work in Ifaty, so hotel radios are the only means of contacting the outside world. There are no money-changing facilities. When selecting a hotel, bear in mind that only those in the north of Ifaty/Mangily have sandy beaches. Mosquitoes are a problem in Ifaty, especially at dusk.

Getting there and away
Because of the bad road it can take as much as three hours by taxi-brousse. The normal price is 10,000Fmg but *vazaha* will be charged 25,000Fmg. Hotels charge as much as 80,000Fmg for a transfer. Taxi-brousses for Toliara leave from opposite Chez Alex twice a day, in the early morning and around 13.00.

Where to stay/eat
Note that the hotels and beach bungalows are strung out over a long area. The cheaper ones are in the village itself, which has some food stalls selling grilled fish and some vegetables.

Category A
Hotel Paradisier Tel: 94 429 14 or 22 336 23 (their agent in Tana); email: paradisier@paradisier.com. The most expensive hotel in Ifaty, with a luxury suite. 'Staff friendly and obliging, bungalows very comfy with huge mozzie net and coil provided. Veranda with cooling sea breezes. Food good, too.' 21 bungalows (fans, but no air conditioning) for €56; meals are €11, breakfast €4. 'There is very nice littoral forest surrounding the hotel with good birdwatching (couas, vangas etc) and there is also good reptile hunting, particularly after dark – I've found Dumeril's boa, *Paroedura* gecko and chameleons (*Furcifer antimena*).' (Nick Garbutt)
Nautilus Tel: 94 418 74, cellphone: 032 0741 874; email: nautilus@simicro.mg. 17 air-conditioned bungalows near Lakana Vezo. An upmarket hotel on a nice beach. Excellent restaurant, especially for seafood (€11 main meal, €6 for breakfast). Double room €51 air-conditioned or €41 with fan. The Gipsy Club diving centre is located here.
Hotel Lakana Vezo Book through the Capricorne Hotel, Toliara; tel: 94 426 20; email: capric@dts.mg. One of the best hotels in Ifaty; one hour's walk south of the Dunes Hotel. 10 bungalows; studio with TV and minibar 256,000Fmg single, 281,000 double; bungalows 186Fmg single, 211,000Fmg double; single room 196,000Fmg or 221,000Fmg double. Meals: 60,000Fmg, breakfast 25,000Fmg. The Club Nautique is probably the best in Ifaty, run very professionally by Denis and Natalie Guillamot. A wide variety of activities are available, though snorkelling and scuba-diving are favourites. The hotel also offers powerboat excursions to Nosy Ve and Anakao.
Hotel de la Saline BP456; tel: 94 417 03; fax: 94 413 84; email: hotel.de.la.saline@dts.mg. 10 two-person bungalows, 5 with air-conditioning (213,000Fmg); family bungalow for 475,000Fmg. Breakfast is 16,000Fmg and a main meal 55,000Fmg. Facing the salt pans, rather than the beach, this French-managed hotel has a particularly good dining-room, with terrific views over the lagoon and superb food.

Category B
Dunes Hotel Tel: 94 439 00; cellphone: 032 0465 859; email: gino@dts.mg. In the southern part of Ifaty (rocky beach) bordering Mangily, this is a set of concrete bungalows with two adjoining bedrooms: 62 rooms in all. 'Quiet, wonderful staff, good food, lots of

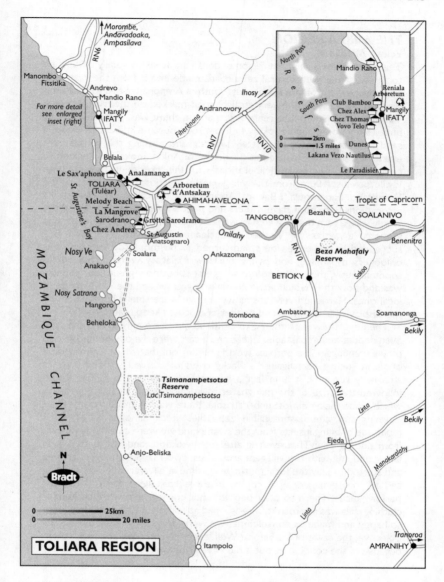

TOLIARA REGION

birds and butterflies in the garden.' (S Gibson). The Club Nautique des Dunes is located here: snorkelling 66,000Fmg, whale-watching 90,000Fmg. 78,000–90,000Fmg per bungalow depending on the season. Breakfast 21,000Fmg, meals: 54,000Fmg; buffet on Sundays and holidays 60,000Fmg. Transport from Toliara 66,000Fmg.

Hotel/Club Bamboo Tel: 94 427 17; cellphone: 032 761 294 355. 23 bungalows; good value, but rather hot in summer. 165,000–250,000Fmg. There's a diving club (but more geared to snorkelling) – 40,000Fmg for snorkelling trips. For bookings enquire at the Bamboo shop opposite the Hotel Central in town. Their transfers cost 75,000Fmg (from the airport). There are varying levels of enthusiasm from readers for the meals and service but

THE MIKEA REGION
Valerie Middleton

This is a vast, low-lying, hot region of dense dry forest, virtually untouched to the west but with several zebu roads made into it from the east. Our objective was the Safora Plateau just south of Amponanga and to reach this we decided to see if the very straight road marked on the map between Vorehey and Ankidranoka really was that straight. It was, and all went well until 15km from Ankidranoka when the road became sufficiently deep in sand to necessitate us alternately walking and pushing the vehicle. We eventually arrived exhausted at the village of Ankidranoka and decided to camp nearby. Our usual deliberations with the 'Président' turned up an idyllic site just 100m from the village and water just on the edge of the Helodrano Fanemotra ('Bay of Assassins' – so called because of its associations with both slave traders and pirates). As is normal we had the whole village turn out to watch as we set up camp, generally from less than a metre away as we washed and cleaned ourselves. We eventually succeeded in our endeavours and turned to be more sociable with our onlookers by smiling and saying our few Malagasy words. Then, quite spontaneously, they all burst into song first about how great their country was and how they would strive to make it greater and then a selection of local ones. Hardened veterans as we are we were totally dumbstruck by this display of friendliness and neither of us could keep tears away!

The next day we attempted to continue our drive only to find the sand even deeper and impassable. Zebus and a cart were the obvious answer so off we went again. It is perhaps worth pointing out that whilst a photograph of us in such a cart against a background of tropical splendour looks amazingly romantic it is in fact a horrendous way to travel. Our route followed the edge of the mangroves, disturbing decomposing vegetation which made the air almost unbreathable, there was no shade from the late morning sun, the unsquashable zebu flies stuck all over us as did a multitude of biting insects from the swamp and we were constantly thrown from side to side! That evening after our exertions and just as dusk was falling and still with the villagers around us, two mandolin players arrived and started to play the local music. In no time at all everyone was swaying and all the teenagers with combs in there hair were giving their best performances! These so poor people – not one of them wore an item of clothing that was not torn to shreds – had absolutely nothing yet they were so happy and made us so welcome, we were definitely humbled. And our objective, the caves of the Safora? Well, even the zebu couldn't reach them because of the conditions, but it didn't really matter!

Volker Dornheim loved it: 'Very nice, simple bungalows with toilets and showers, three bordering the beach. A little army of employees makes sure the place is clean and tidy. Small swimming pool. Very good food, especially the fish (55,000Fmg). We thought the setting was much better than the other places and the bamboo huts blend in to the environment.' **Hotel Vovo Telo** Tel: 94 439 69 (Toliara), cellphone: 032 0262 148; email: hotelvovoleto@simicro.mg; www.hotel-vovotelo.com. 12 bungalows for all budgets north of the Dunes Hotel. Highly praised by all that stay there. Excellent (but fairly expensive) food, and local dancing once a week. Also a noisy nightclub. Rooms and bungalows range from 110,000Fmg to 250,000Fmg. Breakfast 15,000Fmg.

Mangily Hotel Tel: 94 42197, cellphone: 032 0219 765 or 032 0255 428; fax: 94 414 19; email: mangilyhotel@hotmail.com. Next to the Vovo Telo. Bungalows right on the beach with shower and WC: 150,000Fmg per person (double). Only breakfast served (but the Vovo Telo has a good restaurant). 'Fabulous place, natural materials, superb view, grounds and food. Very clean.'

Category C
Chez Alex Beachfront bungalows with shared toilet and shower block. Very good value at 10,000Fmg. There's a reasonable restaurant: 35,000Fmg for two courses. The hotel has its own diving centre and will take guests in a pirogue to the reef for snorkelling (30,000Fmg). 'Friday and Saturday nights are party nights at Chez Alex. Either join in or wear earplugs.' (C Bulmer)

Chez Thomas Another cheap, basic, friendly place though not as well located as Chez Alex. Good meals for 25,000Fmg. 10,000Fmg per bungalow.

Chez Daniel Email: bigorno@malagasy.com. Just north of Vovo Telo. 'Three comfortable bungalows for 70,000Fmg each with electricity and occasional hot water. The *patron* is a friendly Frenchman whose Malagasy wife will provide breakfast on the terrace if required. Laid-back atmosphere. No English spoken.' (S Bulmer)

Restaurant
Jocelyn In the village behind Vovo Telo and the now-closed Mora Mora. 'Small and relaxed with a menu that changes almost daily according to the catch.' (SB)

Birding in the spiny forest
Ifaty is a popular place for birdwatchers, having a fast-dwindling area of spiny forest where some of the southern endemics can be seen. The best guides are undoubtedly Mosa, his son Freddie and his father Masindraka who have, to the relief of birding groups, returned to Ifaty after an unsuccessful venture into sapphire mining. Hotels know where to find them (normally the local bar), or provide someone who knows the way.

Tom Gray writes: 'The spiny forest is amazing and very easy to find. Local villagers offer their services as guides but are not really necessary and most know very little about the wildlife and plants. The **Reniala Arboretum**, signposted from the main road about 500m north of Mangily, is easily reachable on foot (see map). This outstanding *Reserve Ornithologique et Botanique* is a small area (45ha) of protected spiny forest offering guided tours for birders, naturalists and interested tourists. A 2–3 hour tour cost 30,000–40,000Fmg and an early morning visit more or less guarantees long-tailed ground roller and subdesert mesite. Guides, who live at the reserve and can be arranged on arrival, are excellent at locating these two species and are also knowledgeable about the area's unique flora. In addition to birds there are many baobabs (including a massive 1,000-year-old one), Didierea and Euphorbia. A visit here is highly recommended for anyone visiting Ifaty. As one of the only protected areas of spiny forest around Toliara and probably the only reserve protecting long-tailed ground roller it deserves to succeed.' Contact details: Tel 94 20 41 756; email: reniala-mada@dts.mg; www.reniala-madagascar.com. Opening times: summer: 08.00–18.00, winter 07.30–17.30. Birding is best from 05.30 to 10.00 and again from 16.30 on.

Keen birders can stay at the reserve in traditional bungalows with shower: 75,000Fmg including breakfast. Lunch and dinner must be ordered in advance. Camping is 25,000Fmg per tent per night (tent included).

THE SPINY FOREST
Dr Jim Bond
There are two distinct types of spiny forest vegetation now recognised (Du Puy & Moat 1996): 'spiny-forest-on-sand' (eg: at Ifaty, Mikea Forest) and 'spiny-forest-on-limestone' (eg: Mahafaly Plateau).

Superficially and to the untrained eye, there may not appear to be any obvious difference – they both have the characteristic dominance of Didiereaceae and woody tree euphorbias. However, at the species level there is – a slide taken of 'spiny forest' in the south near Berenty, for example, will have almost none of the species in common with one taken in the southwest at Ifaty. Where at the former there would be *Alluaudia procera* as the dominant 'octopus tree', at the latter it would be *Didiera madagascariensis*. Similarly, *Euphorbia e. enterophora* and *E. stenoclada*, or *Adansonia za* and *A. fony* respectively... the difference goes right down through to the creepers and undergrowth layers is clearly soil dependent.

This is yet another reason why conservation of sustainable populations is such an important priority, even in a relatively intact area like the Mikea Forest, with its own varying vegetation zones – it is literally unique.

Madiorano
This village a few kilometres north of Ifaty offers a more peaceful setting.

La Mira Cellphone: 032 0262 144. 8 rooms from 125,000Fmg to 250,000Fmg; meals 75,000Fmg and breakfast 15,000Fmg.
Chez Bernard 'Ideal for the discerning independent traveller – no tour groups. Five peaceful, comfortable bungalows for about 130,000Fmg (full board) near a quiet stretch of beach. Not far to walk to PK32 (the road). Excellent food, huge portions. Rustic douche facilities. Bernard Forgeau is a very pleasant and interesting Breton bush-hand and explorer.' He can be contacted through Trajectoire (see page 244) in Toliara.' (Jim Bond)

NORTH TO MOROMBE AND MORONDAVA
The daily taxi-brousse leaves Toliara at 07.00, the trip takes roughly 14–20 hours during dry season and can be pretty uncomfortable. Tom Savage (Blue Ventures) warns: 'Do not attempt this journey during the rainy season. It took us 3½ days to complete the 240km journey!' A more comfortable option may be to take the transport offered by Lakana Vezo to service their bungalow complex in Morombe. More information – on the bungalows as well as the transport – from Lakana Vezo in Ifaty.

There are flights between Toliara and Morondava via Morombe. Toliara to Morombe by plane costs 450,000Fmg.

THE ONILAHY REGION
Two correspondents have raved about this unspoiled area northeast of Toliara. Valerie Middleton writes: 'By turning right some 17km from Toliara on the RN7 it is possible to reach the Onilahy River at a point where virtually every salad and vegetable crop known is grown on the rich sediments. If the rough road is followed eastwards the attractively situated village of Tolikisy is reached (not Tokilisy as shown on maps). A meeting with the village *président* may elicit an invitation to camp up the delightful Atsodroka Valley at the entrance to the

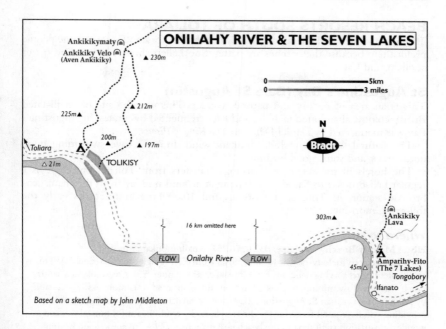

ONILAHY RIVER & THE SEVEN LAKES

Ankikikymaty
Ankikiky Velo
(Aven Ankikiky)
▲ 230m

0 ═══════ 5km
0 ═══════ 3 miles

225m▲

▲ 212m

N

Bradt

200m
▲

▲ 197m

Toliara

△ 21m

TOLIKISY

16 km omitted here

303m▲

Ankikiky
Lava

◁ FLOW   Onilahy River   ◁ FLOW

45m△   Amparihy-Fito
(The 7 Lakes)
Tongobory

Ifanato

Based on a sketch map by John Middleton

village. Small cliffs and exotic trees like moringa and banyans dominate the hillsides. The many ring-tailed lemurs may also keep you awake at night with their continuous screaming! From the head of the valley a local guide, again with the good grace of the *président*, can take you on a 7km trip on to the plateau to visit the chasm of Ankikiky Velo. This is well worth the effort and measures around 80m in diameter and 60m in depth. A further 15 minutes away is the new village of Ankikymaty where another cave of impressive dimensions can be descended to nearly 90m in an enormous passage. This Ankikiky Plateau region was, until a couple of years ago, rich in forest cover and wildlife. There is now an exodus of people from Toliara wanting to cultivate this very poor and stony land. The forest now remains good only at the edge of the plateau and on the steep riverside slopes.

'Continuing upriver from Tolikisy the scenery becomes quite dramatic until about 2km before Ifanato a crystal-clear stream gushes beneath the road. There is a place to park here and by following the footpath on the left for 50m a superb flat campsite can be found above the first of the "Seven Lakes". These lakes are of a beautiful blue colour and are connected by yellow to orange tufa cascades and waterfalls extending for over 700m. This tufa is relatively soft and it is best to try to avoid walking on it where possible. Apart from the first lake upon which there is a *fady*, swimming can be done in most of them. The surrounding gallery forest is superb. There are more lakes further upstream but these are very difficult to get to and are not so beautiful. It is, however, possible to follow a zebu trail into the mountains where there is yet another vertical shaft known as Ankikiky lava. Ifanato, a couple of kilometres further on, has a couple of reasonable restaurants including one run by a Frenchman but to follow the road further into Tongobory is extremely difficult if not currently impassable. The "Sept Lacs" were apparently a very popular destination in the French colonial period.'

BEACH RESORTS SOUTH OF TOLIARA

The resorts south of Toliara now almost match Ifaty for comfort and some people prefer them because the beaches are better. Snorkellers, however, will find better coral around Ifaty.

St Augustine's Bay (Baie St Augustin)

This is an area of history and natural wonders. This was the site of an ill-fated British colony, abandoned in 1646, and later frequented by pirates. St Augustine's Bay was mentioned by Daniel Defoe in *The King of Pirates*.

The natural wonders include dramatic sand dunes, a cave swimming pool, bottle trees, and some good birding.

The hotels in the region will arrange transfers from Toliara, but there is a regular taxi-brousse to Sarodrano, leaving at around midday from the main taxi-brousse station in Toliara. It costs around 10,000Fmg and returns early the following morning.

Where to stay

Hotel Melody Beach Cellphone: 032 0216 757; email: moukar@dts.mg; www.ifrance.com/melody-beach. 15 bungalows from €24 (single) to €32 (double). This is an excellent hotel serving delicious food (breakfast €3; dinner €8). Overlooking a sandy beach with good swimming, it is just 5km from the main road so is more easily accessible by public transport than St Augustine's Bay itself or Anakao. It is easy enough to walk in providing you have good footwear for the rough, rocky road. 'Beautiful bungalows and a wonderful situation right next to the beach and mangroves, close to some good birding habitat and a Ringtail lemur roost.' (D Paine)

La Mangrove Tel: 94 415 27 (Toliara); email: c.alain@wanadoo.mg; www.chez-alain.net. 8km from RN7 (the turn-off is signposted). Under the same ownership as Chez Alain in Toliara. Ten bungalows for 80,000–100,000Fmg, depending on whether they have en-suite WC or shared. Good meals at 50,000Fmg. There's no beach, but a rocky access to the sea for swimming. This is a diving centre, and boat excursions to Nosy Ve and Anakao can be arranged. Bookings and transfers (40,000Fmg) through Chez Alain. If you want to hike it, avoid the heat of the day and keep to the road; the whole area is laced with confusing tracks.

Chez Andrea An Italian-owned hotel near Sarodrano. Thoughtfully designed, very friendly, excellent food and service. Book through Boogie Pilgrim in Tana.

Excursions

Grotte Sarodrano

Under a rocky overhang is a deep pool of clear blue water. Swimmers will find the top layer of water warm is only mildly salty, while the cooler lower layer is saline. Fresh water flows from the mountain into the pool, on top of the warmer, heavier layer of salt water from the sea. You may find yourself paying a local 5,000Fmg to go to the pool. Grotte Sarodrano is a 4km walk south from La Mangrove Hotel (along an easy road). Kids with pirogues hang around there to take you back for about 30,000Fmg. Well worth it!

Birding

Tom Gray reports: 'Interesting spiny forest slightly different to that at Ifaty with good, relaxed birding (considerably cooler than Ifaty) either side of the road towards St Augustin. A pleasant place for a couple of days' relaxing. Verreaux's coua relatively easy to find in the spiny forest south of Sarondrano plus subdesert brush warbler and green-capped coua. Offshore lots of waders and terns plus Humblot's heron.'

Lemur cave

About 15 minutes' walk from the Hotel Melody Beach is a cave where ring-tailed lemurs spend the night. The best (only) time to see them is late afternoon, but they are quite shy.

ANAKAO AND REGION
Anakao

Anakao is a pretty little Vezo fishing village with colourful boats drawn up on the sands. Several new hotels, catering for most budgets (but not luxury), have opened in recent years so it now competes with Ifaty for tourists looking for a beach with snorkelling and some birdwatching within reach of Toliara. Sadly, the coral around Anakao has suffered from bleaching and the snorkelling is no longer very rewarding (although I'm told that the diving is still excellent). It has several advantages over its rival: isolation (Anakao is accessible only by boat or a very rough track), a better beach, and the nearby island of Nosy Ve which has fine white sand and a breeding colony of red-tailed tropic birds.

Anakao is accessible from Toliara via a 50km dirt road, or by boat. All the hotels provide a transfer service, either by sea, or a combination of road and sea.

Tourism here has created some of the most persistent child beggars in Madagascar. They provide a reminder of the futility of giving sweets or small presents to children. This was a practice fostered by the guests of the one hotel several years ago but has only served to widen the gap between visitor and local. If you have the patience to engage with these kids by playing games, practising your Malagasy, or even just being quietly firm rather than irate you are making a genuine contribution to their welfare.

Where to stay

Note that fresh water is a problem in Anakao – there is not enough of it.

Prince Anakao Tel: 94 439 57; email: anakao@simicro.mg. With 27 bungalows, this is one of only two hotels in Anakao able to take groups. Comfortable bungalows but no mosquito nets and mozzies are a problem here. No hot water. Good food. €24 half-board. Rooms 120,000–175,000Fmg. Meals 45,000Fmg. Tranfers (by sea and truck) €20.

Bivouac Lalandaka (Chez Monica) Cellphone: 032 0434 142 (Toliara office) or 032 0227 520 (Anakao); email: monicanakao@wanadoo.mg. An informal, friendly place run by the exuberant Swiss owner, Monica Zanantsoa. Six bungalows with bucket showers (water can be heated on request) and shared toilets but three more bungalows with en-suite facilities are being built. Good food with bread

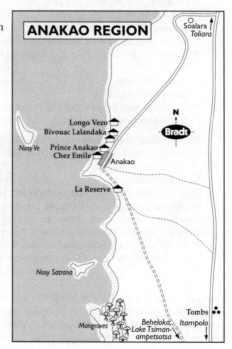

MARINE BEASTIES

Rob Conway and Jane Wilson-Howarth

One of the main reasons that people enjoy snorkelling and diving is the contact with marine species within their natural habitats, and Madagascar has one of the most beautiful and diverse marine environments within the western Indian Ocean. But there is a negative side – not all these creatures are harmless. Most injuries from marine creatures are due to inexperienced snorkellers and divers, unfamiliarity with the local environment, or self defence on the part of the animal. Depending on the type of injury, the first aid treatment will differ. Below are some of the marine nasties that you may encounter in Madagascar and the first aid measures should you get hurt.

Sea-urchins

The most common injury to swimmers and snorkellers is from sea-urchins, often from stepping on an urchin or part of an urchin. Such injuries are painful but not dangerous. Treat by washing the wound and then remove as many of the spines as possible with tweezers or, if little bits remain in your sole and you have nothing else, use a toothpick or similar; the wound will not heal until all the bits are out.

Ray, scorpionfish, lionfish, and stonefish stings

Symptoms include immediate pain, laceration, nausea, vomiting, shock, swelling and occasionally collapse. First-aid treatment should include:

- Immerse wound in non-scalding hot water (43.3–45°C) for 30–90 minutes. The stung body part will be so painful that you won't be able to tell whether the water is too hot, therefore use a non-stung hand to check that the water isn't likely to scald.
- Repeat the immersion if pain recurs; it may be necessary to top up the water. But remove affected limb from the water before doing so.
- Remove any visible pieces of the stinger and irrigate vigorously with fresh water.
- Once the worst of the pain has subsided try to find someone to clean and dress the wound.
- Over the next several days look out for spreading redness, throbbing and/or fever; these symptoms imply infection which will need antibiotic treatment.

This situation is one where good first aid is probably going to be better for the patient than anything that will be offered by doctors.

Sea snakes

The beautiful *Pelamis platurus* spends most of its life out at sea but they are occasionally encountered around the coasts of Madagascar. Sea snake venom is one of the most potent known to man. Fortunately for us they are usually timid, sluggish creatures that avoid humans. You are unlikely to be bitten unless you tease or handle one, or if you go close to a mating bundle of sea snakes – they resent disturbance of their orgy. If you are unfortunate enough to be bitten by a sea snake

baked in a solar oven. This is arguably the best diving centre of Anakao. Other watersports include kite-surfing and pirogue trips with the local Vezo who benefit from projects funded by the hotel. Bungalows 102,000Fmg–162,000Fmg.

Longo Vezo Tel/fax: 94 437 64, cellphone: 032 0263 123; email: longovezo@simicro.mg.

the following symptoms may occur: stiffness and aching, respiratory distress, difficulty swallowing or speaking or weakness. First aid treatment is as follows:

- Apply pressure bandage and immobilise limb.
- Seek medical attention.
- *Do not* use suction technique.

Cone shells
Cone shells are beautiful shells that contain a dart-like projection at the front of them. *Do not touch* as they can deliver a painful and potentially deadly sting. If stung:

- Apply pressure bandage and immobilise limb.
- Seek medical attention.

Stings from fire coral, anemone, hydroid or jelly fish
Anemones are beautiful creatures that live amongst the coral and have stinging tentacles. Often small clown fish will live amongst these tentacles, protected by a mucous layer on their skin. Brushing against any coral will give a nasty abrasion which is inflamed and slow to heal. Fire coral looks like coral, but on closer examination there are fine stinging cells. Hydroids are small marine creatures, looking like plants, that again have stinging cells on their outer surface. Jelly fish are commonly encountered whilst diving or swimming in tropical waters and often do not sting; they may cause minor skin irritation.
If stung by any of these:

- Rinse with *seawater*. Do not use freshwater.
- If the stinger was a box jellyfish there will be characteristic cross-hatched tentacle-prints on the skin surface and irrigation with vinegar will inactivate the stingers. Vinegar actually makes things worse if the jellyfish is a Portuguese man-of-war but most stings are mild and the following treatments suffice.
- Shave off area with credit card to remove stinging cells, being very careful not to sting yourself.
- Apply hydrocortisone cream to reduce inflammation.
- If collapse occurs, offer cardio-pulmonary resuscitation since the severe effects of the venom fade quite quickly. Next get medical help as soon as you can.

Bites
Most marine animals are not interested in human beings. The majority of bites are in self defence. The primary concern for the first aider is to control bleeding and minimise the risk of infection. Sharks and moray eels are the two animals that could attack swimmers or divers on the reef, as well as titan trigger fish during nesting season; the titan is up to 75cm long and will defend her nest ferociously.

- Control bleeding by applying firm bandages or strips of cloth.
- Clean wound and flood with lots of water to minimise infection.
- Seek medical advice.

A good diving centre as well as comfortable bungalows. Double 90,000Fmg (shared facilities) or 120,000Fmg en suite.
Safari Vezo Tel/fax: 94 413 81, cellphone: 032 0263 887. For years this was the only hotel in Anakao and it has stood the test of time. 23 comfortable bungalows, but next to Anakao

village so child beggars can be a problem. There is a good boutique, and the Club Nautique is an excellent diving centre. Bungalows sleeping four are 160,000Fmg/€25, and doubles are 120,000Fmg/€19. Breakfast costs 25,000Fmg and lunch/dinner 65,000Fmg. Transfers from Toliara: 220,000Fmg round trip.

Chez Emile Six cheap and cheerful bungalows close to the village. Bucket showers and shared (squat) toilet. Very friendly, with a bar that is popular with the locals. Emile and his wife have a little shop which sells snacks and a limited selection of postcards. Bungalows: 40,000Fmg.

Hotel La Reserve Cellphone: 032 0214 155 or 02 09 443 717; email: quad@dts.mg. 110,000Fmg. Six simple bungalows with shower and WC a few kilometres south of Anakao village so mercifully free from hassle. Owner-managed (French) with excellent food. This would be my choice for a bit of quiet relaxation.

Where to eat
Chez Madame Coco Near Chez Emile; good food, nice ambience.

Excursions
The 'Aquarium'
This area of protected shallow reef was once popular with snorkellers but has suffered badly from coral bleaching. Divers still find it rewarding, however, and there's the added attraction of meeting Romeo, an inquisitive grouper. There is also Juliet, a conger eel.

Diving
With dead coral reducing the attraction of shallow reef for snorkellers, the emphasis has switched to diving, and Anakao has two excellent diving centres at Chez Monique and Safari Vezo and Longo Vezo. All will do a 'baptism' dive for beginners. The best months for diving are between April and December when the water is clear of river sediment. The highlight, for some, is diving with whales (between June and October). Diving centres charge about 240,000Fmg for beginners and 225,000Fmg for certified divers.

Tombs, wildlife and aepyornis eggshells
A day spent exploring on foot is rewarding. Take the track behind the village heading south. On the outskirts of Anakao you will find some interesting tombs – one has a satellite dish on the roof to provide eternal entertainment for the ancestors – and will then come to a small peninsula jutting into the sea. This is being developed as an extension of Anakao, but it is still possible to find fragments of eggshell from the long-extinct *aepyornis*. Please keep your collecting instincts under control so that others can enjoy this extraordinary glimpse of the past. Bear in mind also that it is illegal to take these eggshells out of the country.

Shortly after the peninsula you will come to the excellent little hotel La Reserve, so you can break for lunch or a drink.

Continuing south, once you are well clear of population areas you should start to see wildlife. Tortoises are quite common along with other reptiles such as chameleons, day geckos, and other lizards. There are some wonderful didierea trees here as well. Wildlife is much more visible in the wet season.

Three bays south of Anakao is a large area of mangroves with accompanying wildlife and some lovely peaceful beaches. But you are now straying well outside the *vazaha* region and should be careful not to upset the locals (see box on page 148).

Nosy Ve and Nosy Satrana

Nosy Ve (the name means 'Is There an Island?'!) lies 3km west of Anakao, and is a sacred site for the Vezo people. It has a long history of European domination: the first landing was by a Dutchman in 1595, and Nosy Ve was officially taken over by the French in 1888 before their conquest of the mainland although it is hard to see why: it is a flat, scrub-covered little island.

What makes Nosy Ve special to modern-day invaders is the tranquillity of its white, shell-strewn beach, the snorkelling on its fringing reefs and the breeding colony of red-tailed tropic-birds. They breed year-round so you can be sure of seeing them at their nest sites under bushes at the southern tip of the island, as well as flying overhead: a thrilling sight.

Camping is not allowed on the island, and visits are dependent for their success on wind and tide (strong wind makes snorkelling difficult; high tide is equally unrewarding for snorkellers and beach-combers). For this reason a visit with a Vezo fisherman using pirogues which can land at low tide are often more successful that those using a large motorboat. With little natural shade on the island, make sure your boatman erects a sail on the beach to provide respite from the burning sun.

The island is illegally exploited by the local Vezo people but they do not harm the tropic-birds, the result of a *fady* originating in a great fire which destroyed much of the island's vegetation – except for the tropic-bird colony and the ancestors' tombs. Another (fortunate) *fady* is against defecating on the beach. A boy angered an ancestor and went missing for doing just that. Tourists should also respect the ancestors and keep away from the tombs.

Nearby Nosy Satrana is a peaceful small island with some ancient tamarind trees. It offers excellent diving, good snorkelling but no tropic-birds.

A day's excursion to Nosy Ve, with snorkelling equipment provided, will cost between 35,000Fmg pp using a sailing pirogue and 150,000Fmg for a day excursion with a picnic provided.

LAKE TSIMANAMPETSOTSA

The large, shallow soda lake (pronounced 'Tsimanampetsots') is the focal point for this terrific reserve of 45,604ha which is now being developed for tourism. It lies about 40km south of Anakao, down a very bad road, so is only just manageable as a day trip. It's better to stay at Beheloka (see below) and enjoy the reserve and its birds in the cool of the day. The lake is renowned for its waterfowl, notably flamingos, and other rare endemic birds including the Madagascar plover (*Charadrius thoracicus*), but the spiny forest is wonderful as well. There are two quite extraordinary baobabs and also a magnificent banyan tree with its aerial roots hugging the side of a cliff face to find purchase in the soil some 20 metres below. An extraordinary sight. The emblem of the reserve is the very rare Grandidier's mongoose (*Galidictis grandidieri*).

At the time of writing you need to be pretty fit to cope with the long, hot walk by the lake and through the forest (a shorter, circular route is being planned). Bring at least two litres of water and water-purifying tablets so you can top up from the rather dubious looking well near the campsite. The lake, with its greater and lesser flamingos, is starkly beautiful, but the dry forest is interesting at every step. You will be taken to Mitoho Cave (a sacred site) where a rare endemic species of blind fish, *Typhleotris madagascariensis*, is easily seen.

The usual park fee must be paid at the ANGAP office a couple of kilometres from the park entrance. You pick up your guide (fee 15,000Fmg) here as well.

Getting there and away

Tsimanampetsotsa is not accessible by public transport. You need your own vehicle or to sign up for a tour from one of the hotels in Anakao, with Chez Alain, or with the tour operator Compagnie du Sud in Toliara.

Where to stay

La Canne à Sucre (Chez Barnard) Beheloka; tel: 94 437 21 or cellphone: 032 0462 409. Bookings can be made through Chez Alain or Compagnie du Sud. Beheloka is the nearest settlement to Tsimanampetsotsa, but it is still about an hour's drive from the reserve. However Chez Bernard merits a stay of a couple of days so you can enjoy the beach and relax before the long walk in the reserve. Bernard is a friendly Frenchman whose little hotel can sleep 16 people. The rooms and bungalows are very simple but clean and comfortable, and the food is good. Rooms in the main building cost 85,000–110,000Fmg, while bungalows are 130,000Fmg.

Camping

There are two camping areas in the reserve (water, but no other facilities) which are ideal for birders or other naturalists who want to see this extraordinary place when it's still cool enough to enjoy the flora and fauna at leisure.

CONTINUING SOUTH

The far south is gradually being developed and you can drive on a barely motorable, sandy road until you join RN10, which links Toliara with Taolagnaro. The beaches is this region are littered with fragments of *aepyornis* eggshell. Intrepid drivers with a 4WD can continue to the very tip of Madagascar, to Cap Sainte Marie (see page 259).

Itampolo

This small town, about 150km south of Toliara, is said by some to have the most beautiful beach in Madagascar with pinkish-coloured sand. 'An interesting excursion can be made to a cenote (a vertically sided collapsed doline floored by a lake whose surface is at the local water table). This is situated barely 3km south of Itampalo and is just 50m east of the road. It is locally known as *Vintana* and measures around 35m in diameter and is 5m to the water surface at its lowest point. The water, of course, is bottomless! Following the now impassable road to Ejeda onto the plateau with its varied succulent flora and caves can make another interesting excursion.' (VM)

Where to stay

Hotel Sud Sud . Under the same ownership as Chez Alain: tel: 94 415 27 (Toliara); email: c.alain@wanadoo.mg; www.chez-alain.net or www.chez.com/photovoyage/itampolo.html. 4 simple but comfortable bungalows, plus 3 smaller rooms above the restaurant (good food). 75,000–140,000Fmg. Breakfast 18,000Fmg; meals 55,000Fmg. Camping for 15,000Fmg per person.

Lavanono

This is the surfing capital of Madagascar. See page 242.

BEZA MAHAFALY SPECIAL RESERVE

This reserve is the model for the WWF's integrated conservation and development efforts. It was established at the request of local people who volunteered to give up using part of the forest. In return they have been helped with a variety of social and agricultural projects; for example by the provision of a school and the building of irrigation channels. Many research projects take place there. The goal has always been to integrate conservation and rural development projects around the reserve, and to support the sustainable use of natural resources.

The reserve protects two distinct types of forest: spiny forest and gallery (riverine) forest. In this it mirrors Berenty, but there the comparison ends. Tourism is not discouraged, but at present the Malagasy locals and researchers come first. This is an enormously rewarding place for the serious naturalist, however. In addition to lemurs, the forest has four species of tenrec including the rare large-eared one, *Echinops telfairi*, three species of carnivores including the fosa, and lots of reptiles. About 90 species of birds have been recorded.

Practical information

Beza Mahafaly is 35km north of Betioky along a very rough road. To get there you need a 4WD vehicle, a zebu cart, a bicycle or a strong pair of legs. Its inaccessibility discourages all but the most persistent traveller. If you fit this category enquire at ANGAP before you make the trip. You may need to bring a guide from Betioky: it is not easy to find your way since the road has many branches.

THE ROAD TO TAOLAGNARO (FORT DAUPHIN)

A taxi-brousse from Toliara to Taolagnaro takes two to three days. It's a shame to pass straight through such an exciting area, however. Much more interesting is to rent a vehicle and driver, or to do the trip by taxi-brousse in stages, staying at Betioky, Ampanihy and Beloha or Ambovombe, or – most interesting of all – by a combination of walking and whatever transport comes along, taking pot luck on where you'll spend the night.

Bezaha

A side trip to this town, which lies east of the road to Betioky, is worth it if you have your own vehicle: 'A road full of botanical and scenic wonders' and there are some good Mahafaly tombs along the road.

Betioky to Ampanihy

Betioky is a day's taxi-brousse ride from Toliara but on the 'single worst road that I have ever seen in my life.' (WA) Recent reports suggest that there is no longer a tolerable hotel in Betioky but I have not checked this out personally.

Some 20km south of Betioky is the small village of **Ambatry**. Next comes **Ejeda**, about 2½ hours from Betioky on a reasonable dirt road. Ejeda to Ampanihy takes about five hours by truck on a very bad, rocky road. All along this road you should see Mahafaly tombs.

Ampanihy

The name means 'the Place of Bats', but it is now the place of the goats. The weaving of mohair carpets was a thriving business in the 1970s and 1980s but the careless cross-breeding of the Angora goats reduced the quality of the wool until the industry collapsed. In 1994 a Frenchman, Eric Mallet, built a new carpet factory and trained local women to work the looms. The wool, however, was imported from France and New Zealand. Thanks to EU funding, 1999 saw the first pure-bred angora goats born in Ampanihy for decades and the industry seems set for a good future. These rugs are very beautiful, incorporating traditional Mahafaly motifs. Only natural colours and vegetable dyes are used. In 2003 a best-quality rug cost 200,000Fmg.

Where to stay/eat

Hotel Angora This is now the only hotel in town but praised by Bob and Sue Cushman who found themselves accidentally in Ampanihy. 'Even after 9pm they fed us, then walked us to our beds [the bungalows are two blocks from the restaurant]. Rooms each had a shower and toilet, separated from the room by a shower curtain. There was a mosquito coil and a packet of US Aid supplied condoms (which we left for the next guests). Next day the rug sales women arrived and I have three magnificent samples of beautiful work.' Camping is allowed in the grounds here.

Ampanihy to Ambovombe

After Ampanihy you enter Antandroy country and will understand why they are called 'people of the thorns' (Androy means 'The Land of Thorns'). The road deteriorates (if you thought that possible) as you make your way to **Tranoroa** (the name means 'Two Houses') in about five hours. This is one of the main weaving towns in the south. Another five hours and you approach Beloha on an improving road (much favoured by tortoises, which thrive in the area since it is *fady* to eat them) and with tombs all around.

Beloha is probably the best place to spend the night on this leg of the journey. Take a look at the new Catholic church with its beautiful stained glass, made by a local craftsman. This is also the departure point for the coastal village of Lavanono.

Between Beloha and Tsiombe is the most interesting stretch of the entire journey. There are baobabs, tortoises (sadly it is not *fady* for the local Antanosoy to eat them) and tombs about 33km before **Tsiombe**. 'If "be" means "big" then "Tsiom" must mean "cockroach"!' Luc Selleslagh had reservations about his hotel, but there *is* a choice of simple *hotelys*. Two roads lead from here to Faux Cap and Cap Sainte Marie.

From Tsiombe it is 67km to Ambovombe. The next place you come to is **Ambondra**, the main centre for weaving in the region. Here you may be able to buy woven cloth from the makers. You are now not far from Ambovombe and the main tourist beat.

Ambovombe to Amboasary and Taolagnaro

With the end in sight, most travellers prefer to push on to Taolagnaro, but there are several hotels in **Ambovombe**: the **Relais des Androy** (no running water; good food), the **Oasis** (running water), and the Fanantenana (very basic, but cheap). Ambovombe has a good Monday market. This town is interesting as a centre for sustainable development projects overseen by the Peace Corps, involving the local people. At their request, for example, the town now has 20 new wells.

About 30km from Ambovombe is Ambosoary, the village that marks the turn-off to Berenty. If you decide to drop in to Berenty, thus saving the very high transfer fee from Taolagnaro (Fort Dauphin), think again. Transport from Taolagnaro is part of the package and you may not be admitted on your own (although with your own car this is less of a problem). From Amboasary to Taolagnaro is less than two hours on a paved road.

Amboasary

This thriving town with a bustling market makes a worthwhile stop if you are visiting Lake Anony or Amboasary Sud. Don't stay too long, though: 'Without charm, like a Mexican border town and full of street kids.'

Where to stay/eat

Hotel-Restaurant Mandrare A complex of small bungalows constructed from *Alluaudia procera* [ouch!].

THE FAR SOUTH

Adventurous travellers are increasingly seeking out the extreme southwest which is, as yet, relatively untouched by tourism. The coastal village of Lavanono has been recommended by several tough travellers, and the whole area is worth investigating.

This is a good area to see humpback whales; between September and November they can be observed quite close to shore with their calves.

Lavanono

The 'road' to this lovely place runs from Beloha via Tranovaho. Access is difficult without your own 4WD, but worth the effort, both for the surfing and the friendliness of the people.

Where to stay

Chez Gigi Rupert Parker writes: 'Gigi is from Reunion but all profits are ploughed back into the village. It's a very beautiful spot: nicely constructed, right by the sea with good surfing close by. The bungalows are simple but cosy and food is good – lobster is a mainstay. Prices are reasonable'.

For camping, Bruce Harris suggests you contact Miandrisoa Melanethon: 'He can provide a place to camp and is a prince of hospitality. His cell phone number is 032 02 266 or 033 12 699 03.'

Cap Sainte Marie

Cap Sainte Marie is the southernmost tip of Madagascar and is as spectacular as its neighbours, with high sandstone cliffs and dwarf plants resembling a rock garden. Some years ago Andrew Cook walked here from Lavanono (a distance of 30km which took him two days). The Cape can also be accessed by 4WD. Note that since Cap Sainte Marie is a reserve, a permit must be purchased, and this is best arranged in Tana. Bill Love, who drove this route in 2003, has this comment: 'I should mention that the heaviest occurrence of radiated tortoises was between Lavanona and Cap St. Marie – we counted 110 just on the coastal road in about two hours' drive. On the drive out to the lighthouse at Cap St Marie, we literally had to move them off the two-track dirt road many times. The "road" was so narrow in places where the prickly pear cactus had grown up that we had to frequently back up hundreds of feet to find places wide enough to open the 4WD's doors, get out, and shove torts into "holes" in the wall of cactus. The cactus was scraping the car mirrors often as we drove; a man on an open ox-cart would get flayed alive unless he sat in the exact centre of his cart.'

Where to stay

Chez Gigi This hotel in Lavanona, just west of Cap Ste Marie, is recommended by Rupert Parker: 'Gigi is from Réunion but all profits are ploughed back into the village. It's a very beautiful spot: nicely constructed, right by the sea with good surfing close by. The bungalows are simple but cosy and food is good – lobster is a mainstay. Difficult to get to without a 4WD, though. Prices are reasonable.'

Faux Cap

I made my first visit to this dramatic, lonely place in 1997, and then predicted that it would soon be developed for tourism. This hasn't happened yet, but with the recent improvement of the road it has become more accessible so it is only a question of time.

Faux Cap is a small community, isolated from the outside world not only by the poor roads, but by wild seas and a treacherous coral reef. The huge, shifting sand-dunes are littered with fragments of *aepyornis* shell. It is an extraordinary place which is worth making a considerable effort to visit.

Getting there and away
The starting point for a trip to Faux Cap is Tsiombe. Stay at one of the *hotelys* and ask around for ongoing transport. With your own 4WD the 30km journey should take about 3½ hours. If you decide to hike, be prepared to carry all that you need. There is a good chance that you will catch a lift, however. The village at Faux Cap is called Betanty.

Where to stay/eat
Hotel Cactus 18 basic bungalows. No running water or electricity but beautifully located and run by the very friendly Marie Zela. Good food with huge portions. A great place to relax for a few days.
Libertalia Contact through Xavier and Henriette Chabanis, quartier Amparihy, BP89, Fort Dauphin 614; tel: 92 211 13; email: madalibertalia@yahoo.fr. 5 new bungalows with solar power. 'Beautiful locale, stone buildings, good food, cold beer, and a wind that didn't stop.' (B & S Cushman).

FROM CAP SAINTE MARIE TO ITAMPOLO
The following account was sent by intrepid Madexplorers, John and Valerie Middleton. 'It is possible to follow this very southerly route in a 4WD, for those with an adventurous mind and good navigational skills, all within a long day. A stay at Lavanono is to be recommended as apart from the situation and friendly villagers it involves a spectacular descent from the plateau. Once back on the plateau we set a GPS course for the Erea Gorge of the Menarandra River, this keeping us between three and eight kilometres from the sea. A confusion of dead- end tracks and a sparse population plus having to remove 100+ football-sized reticulated tortoises from the road slowed us considerably. The dry riverbed of the Menarandra is rather like crossing a desert and the track on the far side not obvious. From the gorge the route continues with equal interest via Bevolava West, Soadona and the Linta River and finally to Itampolo.'

TAOLAGNARO (FORT DAUPHIN)
History
The remains of two forts can still be seen in or near this town on the extreme southeast tip of Madagascar: Fort Flacourt built in 1643; and one that dates from 1504, and thus the oldest building in the country, which was erected by shipwrecked Portuguese sailors. This ill-fated group of 80 reluctant colonists stayed about 15 years before falling foul of the local tribes. The survivors of the massacre fled to the surrounding countryside where disease and hostile natives finished them off.

A French expedition, organised in 1642 by the Société Française de l'Orient and led by Sieur Pronis, had instructions to 'found colonies and commerce in Madagascar and to take possession of it in the name of His Most Christian Majesty'. An early settlement at the Bay of Sainte Luce was soon abandoned in favour of a healthier peninsula to the south, and a fort was built and named after the Dauphin (later Louis XIV) in 1643. At first the Antanosy were quite keen on the commerce part of the deal but were less enthusiastic about losing their land. The heavily defended fort survived only by use of force and with many casualties from both sides. The French finally abandoned the place in 1674, but their 30-year occupation formed one of the foundations of the later claim to the island as a French colony. During this period the first published work on Madagascar was written by Pronis's successor, Etienne de Flacourt. His *Histoire de la Grande Île de Madagascar* brought the island's amazing flora and fauna to the attention of European naturalists, and is still used as a valuable historical source book.

Taolagnaro/Fort Dauphin today

The town itself is unattractive, but it is the most beautifully located of all popular destinations in Madagascar. Built on a small peninsula, the town is bordered on three sides by beaches and breakers and backed by high green mountains which dwindle into spiny forest to the west. One eye-catching feature of the bay is the shipwrecks. A romantic imagination associates these with pirates or wreckers of a bygone era. In fact they are 'all unfortunate insurance scams with boats that should have been out of use years ago'. Pity!

More geared to tourism than any other Malagasy mainland town, Taolagnaro is a very lively place offering a variety of restaurants and nightlife, as well as exceptionally interesting excursions and some fine beaches. Independent travellers would do well to plan a stay of a few days here.

Most people (myself included) still use the French name, Fort Dauphin, but to be consistent with the rest of the book I shall stick to Taolagnaro in the text.

I am grateful to Brett Massoud, of Azafady (see page 150) for much of the original information here, and to Yvonne Orengo of the Andrew Lees Trust (see page 149) for 2004 updates.

Telephone code The area code for Taolagnaro is 92.
Warnings Taolagnaro is prone to strong winds in September and much of October. Muggings and sexual assaults have been reported on some of the beaches.

Getting there and away
By road
The overland route from Tana (bypassing Toliara) is reportedly best done with the companies Sonatra or Tata which operate three times a week from the taxi-brousse station on the far side of Lake Anosy. These buses go via Ihosy, Betroka and Ambovombe. You should book your seat as far in advance as possible. For the journey overland from Toliara, see page 257.

By air
There are flights to Taolagnaro from Tana and Toliara every day (but check the latest Air Mad schedule). The current price (one way) is the equivalent of £74.60 including tax. Sit on the right for the best views of Taolagnaro's mountains and bays. Flights are usually heavily booked. Airport transfers from the de Heaulme hotels are expensive. Take a taxi (fixed rate) for the 4km ride into town.

Where to stay
Much of Taolagnaro belongs to M Jean de Heaulme, the owner of Berenty Reserve. His hotels are the Dauphin and the Miramar, with a new one being built. You are expected to stay in one of these if you want to visit Berenty.

Category A
Hotels Le Dauphin and Le Galion PO Box 54; tel: 92 212 38. The Dauphin is the main hotel and Galion its annexe. Meals are taken in the Dauphin which has a lovely garden. Prices are €48 single or double, plus breakfast: €4.50. A new de Heaulme hotel is being built next to the Dauphin, which is likely to be a higher standard (and more expensive).

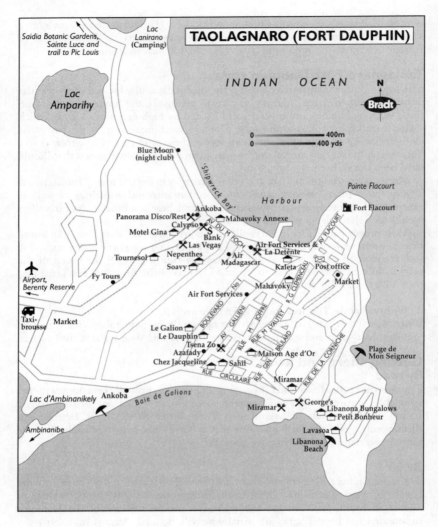

TAOLAGNARO (FORT DAUPHIN)

Hotel Miramar Tel: 92 211 54. Nicely situated on the cliff road overlooking Libanona Beach. There are a limited number of rooms costing the same as the Dauphin, through which bookings must be made. Double or twin rooms are €48. About 50m down the road is its restaurant, one of the best in Taolagnaro, superbly located on a promontory with wonderful views over two beaches; a rough walk in the dark (bring a torch). Meals: 55,000Fmg.

Category B

Hotel Lavasoa BP329, Taolagnaro 614; tel/fax : 20 92 211 75; email: lavasoa@fortnet.net; web: http://lavasoa.free.fr. Five bungalows, each with en-suite bathroom and wooden balcony overlooking Libanona Beach. Anne and Eric Marmorat, the owners, go out of their way to look after their guests, and Lavasoa is considered by one British tour operator to be the best hotel in Taolagnaro. Rates: €30 (double), €35 (triple) B&B. Note that there is no restaurant, but a picnic lunch will be prepared for €7. There is also a small breakfast bar overlooking the beach which can serve fried eggs, sandwiches and beer! Excursions to hard-to-reach places such as Andohahela: 4WD with driver €100 per day. Transfer to airport €5pp.,

Petit Bonheur BP210; tel: 92 211 56/212 74. Bungalows 80,000Fmg or rooms at 100,000Fmg. Another very friendly hotel on Libanona beach. Single/double rooms with a shared shower, and bungalows. The hotel runs tours in 4WD vehicles, including Le Grand Sud (Cap Ste Marie and Faux Cap). They also operate boat trips to Lokaro (see *Excursions*).

Hotel Kaleta BP70; tel: 92 212 87; fax: 92 213 84. Rooms 240,000Fmg (for rooms facing the sea) or 160,000Fmg. En-suite bathrooms. A 32-room hotel in the centre of town. Airport transfer 10,000Fmg.

Motel Gina BP107; tel: 92 212 66; fax: 92 217 24. Pleasant bungalows with en-suite bathrooms on the outskirts of town, ranging from 80,000–220,000Fmg, depending on the season. Excellent restaurant. Unlike many other hotels, the Gina accepts Visa credit cards. Bike hire and excursions offered. An annexe has opened across the road.

Hotel Panorama Situated behind the Panorama disco, above Shipwreck Bay. 62,000Fmg double with en-suite shower. Also bungalows with a sea view.

Hotel Nepenthes New bungalows, hotel and restaurant set in quiet spacious grounds in Ampasikabo on the road that leads to the WWF. Rooms 70,000Fmg per night (single) or a bungalow for 4 at 120,000Fmg. Plus 1,000Fmg tax.

Soavy Hotel Down the road from Nepenthes, providing similar accommodation and restaurant. Pleasant surroundings. Prices from 35,000Fmg per night (single), 50,000Fmg (double) and 60,000–70,000Fmg for a bungalow.

Tournasol (See under *Where to eat*). 10 new rooms for 75,000Fmg.

Category C

Libanona Bungalows BP70; tel: 92 213 78; fax: 92 213 84. Its location vies with the Miramar as the best in Taolagnaro, but the bungalows vary in quality. 100,000Fmg. Breakfast 17,000Fmg, dinner 40,000Fmg. This hotel has been struggling since *La Crise* and may now be closed.

Hotel Mahavoky Annexe Most rooms have a balcony with dramatic views of the shipwrecks in the bay. Nice friendly manager and staff, and centrally located.

Hotel Mahavoky Tel: 92 213 32. Situated in the town centre opposite the Catholic cathedral. Inexpensive rooms with communal (outside) shower and WC. Occupies an old missionary school which gives added interest. There's a helpful, English-speaking manager. The former good restaurant is closed.

Maison Age d'Or A popular hotel with backpackers because of its hugely hospitable owner, Krishna Hasimboto. 6 rooms, all but one with shared bathroom. Bring your own mosquito net. The Age d'Or is best reached via the Kaleta Hotel bus from the airport.

Chez Anita 50m from the Age d'Or. Rooms for 37,000–42,000Fmg. Good food. Recently they have expanded the dining room and added a table on a 2nd floor terrace.

Hotel Chez Jacqueline Tel: 92 211 26. A family-run hotel in Bezarikely (the cliff road) in a nice location beyond the Miramar Restaurant (Ampasimasay). Good value at 50,000Fmg for 4 clean rooms with en-suite bathroom.

Sahil Hotel Indian-owned and immaculate. 65,000Fmg for double room with telephone, en-suite shower and hot water. Recommended. The food is very good, no alcohol served.

Libanona Ecology Centre bungalows Mark Fenn writes: 'We also have several guest bungalows complete with kitchen facilities. These bungalows are especially handy for people with small children or school groups (for which we can organise meals). We are not in the tourism business but it helps us to pay bills and upkeep on the buildings. The bungalows are simple, yet are older and have character. They are also situated on a peninsula with breathtaking ocean views (and whale-watching from July to November). People should contact us in advance via email: libanonaecology@hotmail.com, or phone 92 212 42.'

Camping
Azafady have set up several campsites in the beautiful area to the northeast. The nearest one to the town is Lake Lanirano, 2km away from Taolagnaro. See page 269.

Where to eat
In Taolagnaro eating is taken seriously. All the *Category A* hotels serve very good food with an emphasis on *fruits de la mer*. If you are dining away from your hotel, the following are recommended:

Serious eating
Miramar A contender for one of the best restaurants in Madagascar. Go for lunch, so you can enjoy the marvellous view. Not cheap, but worth every penny.

Gina's Restaurant (Motel Gina) Again, not cheap but excellent food.

Restaurant Las Vegas Opposite Motel Gina. A lively and deservedly popular place run by Gabriella. 'The only place to eat, drink and meet people. Happy, friendly atmosphere, cheap tasty food. A brilliant place – I miss it and everyone there!' (Ania Dudziec)

Tournasol Tel: 216 71. 'A newish restaurant offering a bright, clean and crisp atmosphere, good food and service. Often has calamari on the menu when no-one else in town does! Situated just up from the Gina Motel and Las Vegas restaurant, with garden. About 70,000Fmg for three courses.' (YO)

George's Beach Restaurant 'A circular restaurant looking across the Libanona Bay and boasting excellent cuisine. You can order lunch, or dinner in advance (advisable, but not essential), bathe in the sea and return an hour later for a fresh chilled fruit juice before your meal. Approx 55,000Fmg for three courses.' (YO) Get there by 19.00 in case they close the kitchen early.

Restaurant Pub Bar Calypso A slick-looking restaurant opposite the Panorama. It has a very well-equipped cocktail bar, a nice terrace plus indoor seating, and good but slow-to-arrive food. They also do cabaret evenings with live music.

Snacks
Mahavoky Escale Buvette Near the Panorama disco. 'Claude and his wife Mamanina always are hospitable and friendly for those who want to get to know the locals better.' (Mark Fenn)

Tsena Haja This little family-run bar is recommended for a quick pre-dinner snack. It is in Bazarikely on the steep road that leads down to Avenue Gallieni. Service is quick, the place is always busy, and the snacks are good.

La Recreat Beer, coffee and light meals. Very nice outdoor café almost opposite the BFV bank. Friendly service and excellent *Mi Sao* and sandwiches.

Nightlife
Panorama Disco This is very popular with the locals. On the road to the airport, not far from Motel Gina, it is open every night except Mondays and used to be enjoyed by *vazaha*. But a recent traveller reports: '...resembles a building site, seedy, very assertive prostitutes of both sexes – can be intimidating for females'. Some still enjoy it, however. 'Much of its appeal is in its location, perched on the edge of the bay. When you get too hot and sweaty from dancing you can take a stroll outside to cool off in the ocean breeze and watch the waves roll in.' (RM) Panorama now has a new restaurant, La Terrace, facing the sea.

The Blue Moon on the far side of the port, Blue Moon provides a welcome new alternative for nightlife in Taolagnaro, with varied entertainment from local live Malagasy bands every week-end, to a full-scale pool table, and the fastest food you can find in the south – burgers, pizza and fries alongside the more traditional Malagasy samosas and brochettes. With views over the bay of Fort Dauphin and a friendly staff, it offers an enjoyable, relaxed evening out.' (YO)

Shopping

Taolagnaro has some distinctive local crafts. Most typical are the heavy (and expensive) silver bracelets worn traditionally by men. These are often offered for sale outside the main hotels. The best souvenir shop in town is **Au Bout du Monde** boutique, on the left-hand side of the road to the airport.

If you go to Libanona Beach you will be offered shells or necklaces for sale by charming local girls who have expertly sussed out the guilt factor prevalent in most *vazaha* dealings. When you refuse to buy their goods they insist on giving you a simple shell necklace as a gift. There are no strings attached – they know that the next day you will be prepared to buy anything!

Vehicle hire/tour operators

Air Fort Services Located on Av Gallieni. Postal address: BP159; tel: 92 212 24; email: air.fort@wanadoo.mg. The main tour operator in the region. They hire out vehicles (from cars to buses, but no longer do bicycles) and even small planes, as well as offering a variety of tours. This company owns the private reserve of Nahampona (see page 267). They also do plane reservations.

Safari Laka Tel: 92 212 66. Situated in the Hotel Gina, and offering adventure trips ranging from mountain biking to trekking and canoeing.

Fy Tours Tel/fax: 92 216 31. On the road between Tanambao market and the Gina. 'They can organise just about any tour you could imagine and we have found them to be highly competitive price-wise.' (BM) Fy also rent out 4WD vehicles (with driver).

Bike hire Opposite the BFV Bank and next door to La Recreat Restaurant (and with the same proprietor) is a motorbike and bicycle hire business (with no name). Motorbikes in general in Fort Dauphin are around 250,000Fmg per day and bicycles are between 25,000Fmg and 50,000Fmg per day.

Watersports

Base Nautique Vinanibe Tel: 92 211 32; www.perso.wanadoo.fr/madafunboard/. This watersports club is situated 8km from Taolagnaro in Ambinambibe, on the shores of Lake Vinanibe. The club offers windsurfing and waterskiing, paddle boats and sun loungers with a view over the lake. Accommodation and restaurant.

Ankoba Sports Based in two locations, one (their office) is in the same building as the Panorama disco, and the other (their beach bar) is on the beach at the Baie de Galions. 'They hire everything that you could need for a water based holiday, from a surfboard (75,000Fmg per day or 25,000Fmg per hour) to a motorboat (700,000Fmg per day for the biggest and 350,000Fmg for the smallest, both including petrol and skipper) and at their beach location they have a really wonderful tree-fringed hideaway with direct beach access. There they serve cold drinks, hire windsurfers, surfboards, snorkelling and diving gear etc. This beach near Ankoba and heading south to Ambinanibe is much more popular with tourists these days as you can usually avoid the shell necklace sellers, it is much quieter in general, it is clean, and the water is shallow for safe frolicking.' (BM)

Surfing

With some of the most superb coastline of the Indian Ocean, the south of Madagascar offers fantastic and, as yet, relatively unexplored surfing opportunities. A local surfing project has been set up in the bay of Monseigneur, on the other side from Libanona beach, to help develop a surf school for

SNORKELLING AND DIVING IN LOKARO

Alasdair Harris

The spectacularly beautiful Baie de Lokaro lies some 20km north of Fort Dauphin. Visitors to this remote tropical paradise cannot fail to be struck by the stunning scenery of the region: pristine littoral and tropical forests, rushing streams, meandering rivers and palm-fringed, emerald lakes. All these stretch from the mountains on the horizon down to the long stretches of fine white sand that fringe the shore. Exposed rocky islets protect the bay's turquoise waters from the wild ocean beyond, and help explain why Lokaro boasts the only substantial coral habitat in the southeast of Madagascar – in fact the only coral habitat south of Toamasina, some 500km further north.

The coral can be found in an idyllic lagoon sheltered by one of the bay's islands. This offers great snorkelling opportunities and can be reached from Lokaro's main beach. Travel to the northern point of the beach and head out a few hundred metres across the sandy spit that connects the beach with Lokaro Island, a favourite haunt for local fishermen. At various times of year the spit is partially covered by the sea, but the water depth is never so great that the journey cannot be made on foot. The lagoon itself is situated between the two rocky outcrops that make up Lokaro Island.

A short swim out into the shallow lagoon is sufficient to see the thriving colourful communities of coral, fish and invertebrates. At least two species of sea turtle are known to use the lagoon's beach as a regular nesting ground. Visitors to the area should respect the uniqueness of the habitat, by exercising caution when swimming in order to avoid damaging the fragile coral, and also when walking on the beach to avoid disturbing turtle nests.

For those wanting to dive, primitive (but adequate) scuba equipment and dive boats can be hired at Ankoba Sports in Fort Dauphin, although with no up-to-date diving facilities available in the town, most diving visitors opt to bring their own equipment. No public boat services run north from Taolagnaro, and the cost of hiring a powerboat to visit Lokaro (approximately 1½ hours each way) remains high, at around US$75 per day.

In addition to Lokaro, other smaller patch reefs can be found on the coast closer to Taolagnaro, the best of these being between Taolagnaro and Lokaro, running along the more sheltered sections of the southern side of Evatraha Point, west of the lighthouse. However, owing to the dangerous and unpredictable swells and currents in the area, diving here should be attempted only from the safety of a boat, and not from shore. Diving in these more exposed waters offers excellent opportunities for viewing larger pelagic species such as barracuda, kingfish, trevallies and sharks. In addition to being ideally situated for viewing humpback whale migrations, the region also offers rare sightings of schooling hammerhead sharks.

EUCARE (Edinburgh University Coral Awareness and Research Expeditions) organises teams of divers working with local personnel to survey and chart unexplored coral reefs around Madagascar and the Western Indian Ocean (www.eucarenet.com).

Malagasy youngsters and launch the first surf federation on the island (Surf Development Federation – SDF). The organiser, Yves Jousseaume, has been training young Malagasy surfers for several years. At the time of writing he is in France, but local surfers will show you the best 'surf spots' along the southern coastline. At the end of their trip Surfers are invited to leave boards, wetsuits or any other surf equipment, which helps to support the school and the training of these local children.

For information phone 92 217 54.

Sightseeing and excursions
In and around town

Taolagnaro offers a choice of beach or mountain. The best easy-to-reach beach is **Libanona**, with excellent swimming (but beware the strong current) and superb tide-pools. Admirers of the weird and wonderful can spend many hours poking around at low tide. The pools to the left of the beach (as you face the sea) seem to be the best. Look out for a bizarre, frilly nudibranch or sea-hare, anemones and other extraordinary invertebrates, as well as beautiful little fish. Locals recommend that you visit in groups because of the danger of muggings. There is another beach below the Hotel Dauphin, but this is dirty (turdy) and there have also been muggings there.

Pic Louis, the mountain that dominates the town, is a straightforward though strenuous (and hot) climb up a good path and offers nice views. The trail starts opposite SIFOR, the sisal factory about 3km along the road to Lanirano. It takes 1½–2 hours to get to the summit, so allow at least a half day to get up there and back – or better still take a picnic. The view from the top is spectacular: on a clear day you can see as far as Baie Sainte Luce. Apart from birds there is not much wildlife to be seen, though Nick Garbutt reports: 'I was once up there with a group when someone called out "Oh look, a monkey!" A grey bamboo lemur leapt over the rocks and into the nearby bushes.'

Another arm of the de Heaulme empire is the **Saidia Botanical Gardens**, situated about 16km out of town towards Sainte Luce. Clare Hermans reports: 'A private garden complete with crocodile pen. Planting of local flora has been attempted and the trees have been untouched for 30 years. It may soon be the only place to see the local flora if the rate of cutting and burning continues. There are a few lemurs on islands in the lake – apparently an overspill from Berenty where some over-habituated ones had become aggressive.'

Day trips

There are numerous places to visit as a day trip in this beautiful part of Madagascar. If you haven't a car you will probably need to join an organised tour, though the energetic could reach most places by hired bike.

Portuguese Fort (Île aux Portuguais)

The tour to the old fort, built in 1504, involves a pirogue ride up the River Vinanibe, about 6km from Taolagnaro, and then a short walk to the sturdy-looking stone fortress (the walls are 1m thick) set in zebu-grazed parkland. This is the oldest building in Madagascar, and worth a visit for the beautiful surroundings.

Réserve de Nahampoana

This is an easily accessible zoo cum reserve owned by Air Fort Services (see page 265). The 67ha park is just 7km (15mins) from Taolagnaro, on the way to Sainte Luce. It provides the usual tame lemurs (both local species and introduced), reptiles

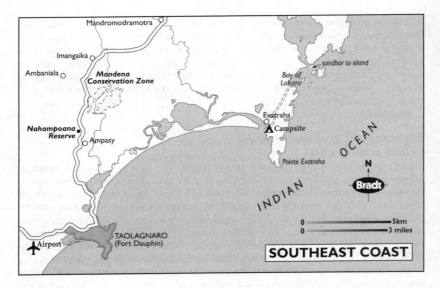

(again, some chameleon species do not really belong here) and regional vegetation. The price for a permit and guide is €10, and €9 for a picnic lunch. This is the ideal lemur-fix for those on a tight budget. 'This is always a big hit and I try to set aside five hours for a visit. Although it is an artificial set-up (botanical garden) the lemurs are in top condition and very, very charming.' (M Burger, tour leader)

Further afield
Baie Sainte Luce (Manafiafy)
About 65km northeast of Taolagnaro is the beautiful and historically interesting bay where the French colonists of 1638 first landed. There is a superb beach and a protected area of humid coastal forest here, owned by M de Heaulme, and also some bungalows (usual de Heaulme price). It is possible to reach Manafiafy by taxi-brousse but most people will opt for the organised tour run by Air Fort Services, among others.

Evatraha
This is a very attractive coastal village to the north of Taolagnaro, situated on the mouth of a small river just south of Lokaro. Day trips here, by boat, can be organised through many tour operators, or a longer stay through the operator Tour Laka, based at the Mahavoky Annexe, and run by Fy. 'He has two beautiful bungalows on the lake edge at Evatraha, a fast boat to get you there, and great staff at the bungalows to look after you. They can arrange for fish or lobsters to be delivered by fishermen, and the prices are very reasonable. The bungalows (each with double bed only but en-suite bathroom) are 35,000Fmg per night. The boat trip is about 500,000Fmg for the return journey and easily handles a group of four plus baggage. Some captive lemurs detract from the experience.' (BM) There is also the Azafady campsite here (see opposite page).

Security warning Serious sexual assaults, violent robbery and a rape have occurred on the beach between Taolagnaro and Evatraha in the last few years. It is inadvisable to walk to Evatraha without a Malagasy guide or at the very least in a group.

Lokaro

The isolated Bay of Lokaro is perhaps the most beautiful spot on the southeast coast. Alasdair Harris and his team of underwater researchers spent six weeks there studying the coral reef, and his report (see box on page 266) makes mouth-watering reading. Most visitors can see Lokaro only as part of a day's excursion, but Al makes a strong case for spending more time there, which is no problem if you stay at Evatraha (camping or bungalows). There is no public transport to either Lokaro or Evatraha, but Evatraha can be reached from Taolagnaro either by pirogue (a peaceful sail downriver), by road in a sturdy 4WD or mountain bike, or on foot – a three-hour, 10km walk along the beach running north from Taolagnaro. Four-wheel-drive vehicles can be rented in Taolagnaro for around US$80 per day (journey time around two hours). From Evatraha, it is an hour's walk through hills and forest to the beach at Lokaro.

The essential requirement for a stay of a few days is self-sufficiency. Preferably you should have your own tent, stove and supplies – although you can buy almost everything you need in Evatraha, from eggs to beer and bottled water 'and plenty of the best shellfish I've ever tasted'. If you organise your stay through Azafady (see page 150) the logistics will be taken care of.

In conclusion Al writes: 'The best way by far [to reach Lokaro] is to stroll up on the spectacularly long beach that heads out north of Fort Dauphin [but do heed the security warning above]. It's an awesome stretch of fine white sand with enormous breakers crashing down every few seconds. As for campsites, there are some of the most mind-bendingly beautiful spots I've ever visited that would be just perfect to pitch a tent. Or try getting a pirogue there and then walking back – the silent sail down the meandering river through the forest to Evatraha is not to be missed. It makes you feel as though you're in a Conrad novel set in southern Madagascar.' Makes you ache to do it, doesn't it?

Accommodation

Camp Pirate This is a campsite run by the Hotel Lavasoa (see page 262). The 'camp' consists of very simple bungalows with mosquito nets. Communal toilet/shower. An open-air restaurant serves fresh seafood. Lavasoa can take you via the inland waterways on their zodiac and the campsite is fully equipped and very peaceful – perfect for those who don't want the bother of bringing tents and equipment from Fort Dauphin. It costs €35 round trip for transport; rooms start at €15 per night.

Azafady campsites

The following information is provided by the organisation Azafady. Their campsites give you the chance of staying in some of Madagascar's most beautiful places and helping out in a community project (if you want). 'Prices vary according to whether you are a student, a researcher or a tourist, and we welcome enquiries at our main office in Avenue Gallieni in Fort Dauphin or by email to azafady@fortnet.net.'

Lake Lanirano A lakefront site 2km from Fort Dauphin, with full kitchen facilities and a huge dining/recreation room in a large stone house. Showers and toilets are provided and the house has mains electricity. The Lanirano site is home to several Azafady projects, and campers can witness or volunteer to assist with the conservation tree nursery, the medicinal plants garden, or can learn to build bee-hives or solar fruit dryers through the 'sustainable livelihoods' training programmes. The site, close to the foot of Pic St Louis, and local dugout canoes can be hired and paddled through the many kilometres of lakes and rivers that lead you to Evatraha.

Evatraha An 11ha site a couple of minutes' walk from the village, with two bungalows, each sleeping three or four, and sufficient space for up to 50 campers easily. Camp-fire, an outdoor shower room, an outdoor (covered) cooking room, and clean latrines. All catering equipment is provided. An ideal base for exploring Lokaro.

Evatraha Beach Camp About 1km from the village, near a white-sand beach. An excellent place for observing the activities of local fishermen, but large enough for privacy too. No facilities (except a latrine toilet) and all equipment (including water) must be carried to the site. Catering equipment can be provided.

Sainte Luce Forest Camps Sainte Luce is about 70km by road from Fort Dauphin. Both camps are 3–4km walk from the village, and are convenient for biological research or hiking in the littoral forests. Camp S9 Limit is on the border of the forest closest to the village (suitable for up to 30 campers), and the other camp, Camp S9 Central, is an easy 15-minute hike into the forest. In both cases wildlife is abundant: Camp S9 Central has a habituated troop of collared brown lemurs, and three other species of lemur are present. Both of these camps are based inside locally protected forest,and are therefore simple and relatively undeveloped. All Sainte Luce forest camps are managed between Azafady and the local forest management committee (VOI) and revenue raised from campers here goes directly to the committee to help fund ongoing conservation activity.

Sainte Luce Beach Mission Situated on a 60ha headland, the site of a former missionary school, about 3–4 km from the forest camps. It is fringed by coconut palms, and is two minutes' walk into the beautiful and totally traditional Antanosy village of Manafiafy (Sainte Luce). At present only camping may be available, though you can enquire about rooms in the102-year-old ex-missionary house which is being restored. Facilities include shower rooms and toilets at the campsite and a separate kitchen/dining house. This is the second base for village development activities and plenty of work is available for groups or individuals ready to participate in community projects.

Spiny Forest or Rain Forest Camping Azafady can arrange camping for groups in several other places where we currently have no facilities but are still well known because of our community projects. We highly recommend the stunning rainforest at Farafara Vatambe (40km north of Fort Dauphin) for incredible waterfalls, magnificent primary forests and palm jungles. The site can be reached by car but we recommend the adventurous hike through villages, across (and in) rivers, past waterfalls and along the side of the mountain forests, from Belavenoka to Vatambe. Spiny forest camping can be arranged in several sites, all with intact forest, for those with an interest in dry forest. Please contact us for further details.

THE WILDLIFE RESERVES

The southeast of Madagascar gives the best opportunity in all of Madagascar for wildlife viewing to suit all budgets and all levels of energy. Whilst Berenty is rightly world famous, adventurous visitors should give equal consideration to Andohahela, whilst those on a tight budget can consider the Mandena Conservation Zone.

Berenty Private Reserve

This is the key destination of most package tours and I've never known a visitor who hasn't loved Berenty (well, there was one…). The combination of tame lemurs, comfortable accommodation and the tranquillity of the forest trails makes this *the* Madagascar memory for many people. The danger is that Berenty is already becoming overcrowded, and too many groups bring problems. Fortunately, there is only a limited amount of accommodation, so if you can arrange to spend a night or two you can still have the reserve to yourself in the magic hours of dawn and dusk.

Visits to the reserve must be organised through the Hotel Dauphin (or the Capricorne in Toliara). Accommodation is on half-board basis, €64 single, €80.5 double. Meals are €11.

The road to Berenty

The reserve lies some 80km to the west of Taolagnaro, amid a vast sisal plantation, and the drive there is part of the experience. For the first half of the journey the skyline is rugged green mountains, often backed by menacing grey clouds or obscured by rain. Traveller's trees (*ravenala*) dot the landscape, and near Ranopiso is a grove of the very rare triangular palm, *Neodypsis decary*. (To see an example close up, wait until you arrive in Berenty where there is one near the entrance gate.)

Your first stop used to be a visit to some **pitcher plants** – *Nepenthes madagascariensis* – whose nearest relatives are in Asia. Sadly, this area has been destroyed by fire.

An optional stop before reaching the spiny forest is at an **Antanosy 'tomb'** (actually the dead are buried elsewhere) known as the Tomb of Ranonda. It was carved by the renowned sculptor Fiasia. The artistry of this unpainted wooden memorial is of a very high standard though the carvings are deteriorating in the frequently wet weather. There's a girl carrying the Christian emblems of Bible and cross; someone losing a leg to a crocodile; and the most famous piece, a boatload of people who are said to have died in a pirogue accident. On the far side there used to be a charming herd of zebu, portrayed with unusual liveliness (a cow turns her head to lick her suckling calf). In 1990 the cow and her calf were ripped away by thieves. To add to the poignancy, a row of cattle skulls indicate the zebu that had to be sacrificed to counteract this sacrilege. One hopes the revenge of the Ancestors was terrible.

The very reasonable response by the villagers to this desecration has been to fence off the tombs, which can now be viewed only through binoculars.

In the area are other memorials, but without carvings. These cenotaphs commemorate those buried in a communal tomb or where the body could not be recovered, and look like clusters of missiles lurking in the forest.

Shortly after **Ranopiso**, and the turn-off to Andohahela National Park, there is a dramatic change in the scenery: within a few kilometres the hills flatten and disappear, the clouds clear, and the bizarre fingers of *Didierea* and *Alluaudia* appear on the skyline, interspersed with the bulky trunks of baobabs. You are entering the spiny forest, making the transition from the Eastern Domain to the Southern Domain. If you are on a Berenty tour your guide will identify some of the flora. If on your own, turn to page 45.

The exhilaration of driving through the spiny forest is dampened by the sight of all the **charcoal sellers** waiting by their sacks of ex-*Alluaudia*. These marvellous trees are being cut down at an alarming rate by people who have no other means of support. While condemning the practice, give uneasy thought to the fact that your sumptuous meals in Berenty will be cooked on stoves fuelled with locally produced charcoal. And that it is city-dwellers who consume the most charcoal in Madagascar: on average two sacks a month.

One enterprising community sells **woodcarvings** of subjects that are always hard to find in Madagascar: the local fauna. These are carved from a lightweight *Burseraceae* wood known locally as *daro*. For a dollar or so you can buy primitive but delightful lemurs, tortoises and chameleons – a world better than the pseudo-African carvings found elsewhere.

If you pass through the village of **Ankaraneno** (25km from Taolagnaro) on a Thursday, do stop for the zebu market. Fascinating.

Amboasary, which also has a terrific market, is the last town before the bridge across the River Mandrare and the turn-off to Berenty. The rutted red road takes you past acres of sisal and some lonely looking baobabs, to the entrance of the reserve.

The reserve

The name means 'Big Eel' but Berenty is famous for its population of ring-tailed lemurs and sifakas. Henri de Heaulme and now his son Jean have made this one of the best-studied 260ha of forest in Madagascar. Although in the arid south, its location along the River Mandrare ensures a well-watered habitat (gallery or riverine forest) for the large variety of animals that live there. The forest is divided into two sections, Malaza (the section near the tourist bungalows) and Ankoba to its northwest.

The joy of Berenty is the selection of broad forest trails that allow safe wandering on your own, including nocturnal jaunts. Remember, many creatures are active only at night and are easy to spot with a torch/flashight; also the eyes of moths and spiders shine red, and all sorts of other arthropods and reptiles can be seen easily. A dusk visit (with a guide) to the reserve's area of spiny forest is a must: you'll observe mouse lemurs, but just seeing those weird, giant trees in silhouette and hearing the silence is a magical experience.

Next day get up at dawn; you can do your best birdwatching, see the sifakas opening their arms to the sun, and enjoy the coolness of the forest before going in to breakfast.

Berenty wildlife: an overview

Lemurs are what most people come here for, and seeing the following species is guaranteed: brown lemur, ring-tailed lemur and sifaka. The lemurs here have not been hunted for seventy years, so they trust people. They were fed bananas by tourists in the 1980s and '90s, but this is no longer allowed. Disappointed that an outstretched hand no longer offers food, they will try to sneak into your cabin to find it for themselves. **Ring-tailed lemurs** have an air of swaggering arrogance, are as at home on the ground as in trees, and are highly photogenic with their grey, black and white markings and waving striped tails. These fluffy tails play an important part in communication and act as benign weapons against neighbouring troops which might have designs on their territory. Male ring-tailed lemurs indulge in 'stink fights' when they scent their tails with the musk secreted from wrist and anal glands and wave them in their neighbours' faces. The opponent retreats or else waits his turn and then waves back. They also rub their genital glands on the trunks of trees and males score the bark with their wrist-spur to scent-mark their territory.

There are approximately 500 ring-tailed lemurs in Berenty, and the population has stayed remarkably stable considering that only about a quarter of the babies survive to adulthood. The females, which are wholly dominant over the males, are receptive to mating for only a week or so in April/May, so there is plenty of competition amongst the males for this once-a-year treat (April is also the best time to observe 'stink-fighting' among males). The young are born in September and at first cling to their mother's belly, later climbing on to her back and riding jockey-style. Ring-tails eat flowers, fruit and insects – and the occasional chameleon.

Attractive though the ring-tails are, no lemur can compete with the **Verreaux's sifaka** for soft-toy cuddliness, with its creamy white fur, brown cap, and black face. Sifaka belong to the same family of lemur as the indri (seen in Andasibe/Périnet). The species here is *Propithecus verreauxi verreauxi* and there are

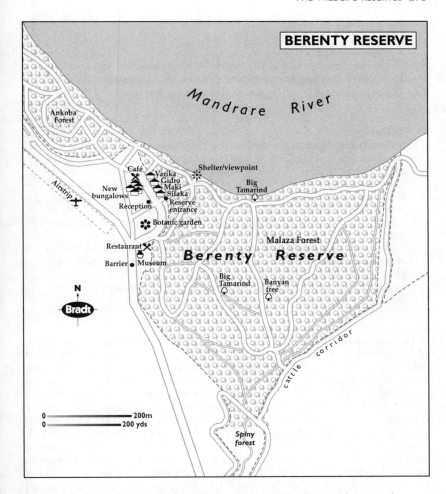

about 300 of them in the reserve. Unlike the ring-tails, they rarely come down to the ground but when they do the length of their legs in comparison with their short arms necessitates a comical form of locomotion: they stand upright and jump with their feet together like competitors in a sack race. The best places to see them do this are on the trail to the left at the river and across the road by the aeroplane hangar near the restaurant and museum. Sifaka troop boundaries do not change, so your guide will know where to find the animals. The young are born in July. Like the ring-tails, sifaka make a speciality of sunbathing – spreading their arms to the morning rays from the top of their trees. They feed primarily on leaves and tamarind fruit so are not interested in tourist-proffered bananas.

The **red-front brown lemurs** (*Eulemur fulvus rufus*) were introduced from the west and are now well established and almost as tame as the ring-tails. These are the only sexually dimorphic lemurs in Berenty – in other words you can tell the males from the females by their colour: males have a fluffy orange cap; females' heads are greyish and bodies are a more chestnut brown than the males. Both sexes have long, black noses and white 'eyebrows'.

SISAL

This crop was introduced to Madagascar in the inter-war years, with the first exports taking place in 1922 when 42 tons were sent to France. By 1938, 2,537 tons were exported and 3,500ha of sisal were planted in the Tuléar and Fort Dauphin region. By 1950 production reached 3,080 tons. In 1952 a synthetic substitute was developed in the US and the market dropped. The French government stepped in with subsidies and bought 10,000 tons.

The Tuléar plantations were closed in 1958 leaving only the de Heaulme plantations in Fort Dauphin. In 1960 these covered 16,000ha, and by the mid 1990s 30,000ha of endemic spiny forest (that's about 100 square miles!) had been cleared to make way for the crop, with plantations under the ownership of six different companies. Workers earn 160,000Fmg per month (1999 figure). There is no sick pay or pension provision. The de Heaulme plantation alone employs 15,000 people who cut 300,000 leaves per day.

And here's something to think about: in the late 1990s there has been a resurgence of demand for sisal, with exports predicted to reach 5,000 tons by the year 2005, putting more spiny forest at risk. Why? Because we 'green' consumers in the EU are demanding biodegradable packaging. What is the best biodegradable substance? Sisal!

Berenty happens to be the perfect place to observe one of the unique aspects of lemur behaviour: female dominance. Ring-tails and sifaka males are always submissive to females, while brown lemurs are much less so. Alison Jolly, who has written so absorbingly about Berenty in her recent book *Lords and Lemurs* (see page 454) says 'I have seen a male brown lemur at Berenty throw a female out of a tree, which scandalized me as a ringtail watcher.' Dr Jolly adds: 'Female dominance is very odd among primates and other mammals. Of over 300 primate species, only the 30 plus species of lemurs tend toward female dominance as a group. No monkeys or apes show the 100% full-time chivalry of many lemur males. I call it chivalry rather than wimpishness, because males fight and wound each other, and could certainly fight females if they chose – but it is built-in that they don't confront females. There are half a dozen scientific theories about why female dominance and male submission evolved to be so widespread in lemurs. None of them is quite convincing so it remains an evolutionary mystery.'

There are other lemurs which, being nocturnal, are harder to spot although the **lepilemur** (white-footed sportive lemur) can be seen peering out of its hollow tree nest during the day. **Grey mouse lemurs** (*Microcebus murinus*) may be glimpsed in the beam of a flashlight, especially in the area of spiny forest near the reserve, a popular destination for night walks.

Apart from lemurs there are other striking mammals. **Fruit bats** or flying foxes live in noisy groups on 'bat trees' in one part of the forest. You are not permitted to approach closely but you will still have a rewarding view of these appealing animals.

Birdwatching is rewarding in Berenty, and even better in Bealoka ('Place of much shade') beyond the sisal factory. Nearly 100 species have been recorded. You are likely to see several families unique to Madagascar, including the hook-billed vanga, and two handsome species of couas – the crested coua and the giant coua which have dramatic blue face-markings. The cuckoo-like coucal is common, as

Above Black-and-white ruffed lemur (*Varecia variegata*), eastern Madagascar (HB)

Right Ring-tailed lemur, *Lemur catta*, on an *aloalo* (Mahafaly tomb carving), Berenty (NG)

Above 'Little Madi' (see page 306) (HB)

Above Fosa (*Cryptoprocta ferox*), western Madagascar (NG)

Below Highland streaked tenrec (*Hemicentetes nigriceps*), Andringitra (PH)

are grey-headed lovebirds and the beautiful paradise flycatcher with its long tail feathers. These birds come in two colour phases: chestnut brown, and black and white. Two-thirds of the Berenty paradise flycatchers are black and white. If you visit from mid-October to May you will see a variety of migrant birds from southeast Africa: broad-billed roller, Malagasy lesser cuckoo and lots of waders (sanderlings, greenshank, sandpiper, white-throated plover).

Then there are the **reptiles**. Although Berenty's chameleons are somewhat drab-coloured (two species are found here, *Furcifer verrucosus*, or warty chameleon, and *Furcifer lateralis*, often called jewel chameleon but in Berenty most un-gem like), they are plentiful. There is also a good chance of seeing Dumeril's boa (a huge, placid snake). In captivity there is a sulky-looking crocodile (its companion escaped after its enclosure was damaged in a cyclone) and some happy radiated and spider tortoises.

Finally, don't forget the **insects**. One of my favourite activities in Berenty is visiting the 'cockroach tree', a large tamarind on the left of the main trail to the river. This is pockmarked with small holes, and if you visit at night and shine your torch into the holes, you will see pairs of antennae waving at you. These belong to giant hissing cockroaches. If you are able to catch one of these 6cm insects it will give a loud, indignant hiss. (I have kept them as pets in England; they brought me endless enjoyment!) Another equally entertaining insect is the ant-lion (see box on page 52). Look for their conical holes on the sandy paths, then find an ant as a drop-in gift.

Berenty has been welcoming tourists longer than any other place in Madagascar, and all who fall in love with it will want to do what they can to preserve it and its inhabitants. The ban on feeding the lemurs is a sensible conservation measure. As long as visitors continue to behave responsibly they will be allowed to wander in the forest unaccompanied – a real treat for those who value solitude and the time to sit quietly and observe this unique piece of nature. However, don't miss out on the tours with the excellent English-speaking guides, who will greatly increase your knowledge and understanding. Their fee is paid by the reserve but a tip is appropriate.

Where to stay/eat

There are 12 bungalows (sleep two, comfortable, fairly reliable hot water) and six older buildings with pairs of twin rooms. Accommodation is also available in Ankoba. Generators are switched off at 22.00, after which there is no electricity. Without the electric fans it can get very hot. Rooms are screened, but in the older bungalows you should burn a mosquito coil (provided).

There is a snack bar near the bungalows where breakfast is served, and the bar/restaurant (near the museum) offers good fixed-menu meals, and cool outdoor seats for your pre-dinner drink. Near the restaurant is quite a good souvenir shop.

An efficient and reasonable laundry service is available – ask at Reception.

THE BALD LEMURS OF BERENTY
Alison Jolly

Some ring-tailed lemurs in troops near Berenty cafeteria go nearly bald during the dry season, but grow their fur back in the wet season. This is not a contagious disease or anything to do with tourism. It is probably the result of feeding on *leucaena*, a toxic introduced tree. If you see a team of veterinarians among the tourists, ask them for the latest information! Meanwhile lemurs in the rest of the forest away from the *leucaena* areas are as furry as ever.

Excursions

Tourists staying more than a day should take the two excursions offered. The area of **spiny forest** here is superb (though hot) and may be your only chance to see mature *Alluaudia* trees. Some tower over 15m – an extraordinary sight. A visit to the **sisal factory** may sound boring but is, in fact, fascinating – and, for some, disturbing. On the natural-history front, this used to be one of the best places in Madagascar to see and photograph the enormous *Nephila* spiders on their golden webs. On my last visit I was horrified to find that my beloved spiders had been cleared away; however, I have faith that *Nephila* persistence will overcome this temporary setback.

Museum of the Androy

This is undoubtedly the best ethnological museum in Madagascar, and if your interest in the region extends beyond the wildlife, you should allow at least an hour here. Several of the rooms are given over to an explanation (in English and French) of the traditional practices of the Antandroy people, illustrated by excellent photos. There are some beautiful examples of handicrafts and a small but interesting natural history section including a complete *aepyornis* egg. This museum should be seen in conjunction with the replica Antandroy 'village' near the botanical garden, where you can step inside a small house, very similar to those you pass on the road to Berenty.

All credit to M de Heaulme for celebrating the lives of the human inhabitants of the region in this way. Don't miss this opportunity to learn more about the People of the Thorns.

Mandena Conservation Zone

This reserve was established by QMM (see box) to protect 230ha of rare littoral forest in the region that is the centre of their controversial ilmenite mining project. The conservation area includes 160ha of the least degraded fragments of forest and 60ha of wetlands. Twenty-two species of flora are endemic to this region, with about 200 species of large trees. Littoral forest is similar to coastal rainforest, but with a 2% or 3% difference. In 2001 a troop of brown collared lemurs (*Eulemur fulvus collaris*) were relocated to Mandena from a small and threatened block of forest outside the conservation zone. A doctoral student from University of Pisa is following their progress.

I visited Mandena the week before it was officially open and was entranced! It is completely different from the Berenty experience, has been thoughtfully conceived to give tourists as much variety as possible, and the local Antanosy people are involved. At present this is primarily a botanical experience. The six species of lemurs in the Mandena area are still shy, but no doubt will become habituated in time, but you'll see plenty of birds and reptiles. There is a standard circuit which takes three to four hours and includes level paths (the walking is easy) and a rowboat trip. Our pioneering group paddled their own canoes (not very competently!) and I suspect that once the reserve is receiving a regular supply of tourists, local people will do the job. The rowboat takes you down a waterway fringed with pandanus palms (there are six species in Mandena). Then it's a walk back along another forest trail to the visitor centre and tree nursery.

Since my visit, the Mandena conservation zone has secured legal status from the Government of Madagascar. The conservation status of that area is included as part of a *dina* (community agreement) between the two communes in the area, the government ministry and QMM. The *dina* describes the sustainable natural resource management for the whole Mandena zone, of which the conservation zone is an important part. Under the agreement, a brigade of villagers has been established to,

MINING IN THE SOUTH: AN ENVIRONMENTAL AND SOCIOLOGICAL DILEMMA

The dry south of Madagascar has large deposits of ilmenite used to produce titanium dioxide, which is used for paint, paper and plastic. The Canadian company QMM (owned by Rio Tinto), in partnership with the Malagasy government, plans to exploit this mineral resource. The mine would be active for some 60 years, would be the largest such venture in Madagascar and would involve an investment of US$350 million for the mine, a separation plant, a port and roads.

The project could bring 600 direct new jobs plus more indirect jobs to a severely depressed area of the country. Jobs would create prosperity which would reduce the pressure on the environment caused by tavy and the felling of trees for charcoal. The project would involve clearing some of the remaining coastal littoral forest with its endemic flora and fauna.

An RT representative writes: 'Rio Tinto and our Malagasy partner are well aware of the unique natural environment of Madagascar and the worldwide concern that it should be preserved and protected. That is why, since 1987, two sets of social and environmental studies have been carried out: an initial program from 1987 to 1992 and a comprehensive Social and Environmental Impact Assessment (SEIA) which was submitted to the Government of Madagascar in May 2001. Following a thorough review of the SEIA the government issued an environmental permit to the project, along with a series of social and environmental conditions that the company must respect at each phase. One of the key issues is the special botanical interest of the littoral forest that occupies some of the area to be mined. The expert studies concluded that with the appropriate conservation and rehabilitation programs, the mining could proceed with virtually total conservation of fauna values and protection of most floral endemic species including all types of representative forest. As part of its permit conditions, Rio Tinto is committed to a conservation and a rehabilitation program and to plantations of fast growing species that will provide the local population an alternative source of charcoal, fuel and lumber. Further feasibility studies are now underway before an investment decision can be made in mid 2005.'

Jonathan Ekstrom, from Birdlife International, responds: 'The extensive loss of coastal littoral forest which will result from the proposed mine has led to significant criticism of the development, especially given the company's image as a leader in corporate social and environmental responsibility and their published corporate strategic aim of having a net positive impact on global biodiversity. One of the secondary impacts of this mine in a very poor region of a poor country will be significant levels of internal migration, meaning greater pressures on socio-economic infrastructure as well as the environment. For example migration will lead to increased pressures on forest (such as fuelwood collection and charcoal production) and its globally important biodiversity. QMM suggest that an extra 600 jobs will alleviate pressure on Anosy forest, but in fact it is likely that the in-migration will actually lead to an increased pressure on these kinds of natural resources. Solutions are possible, but it will involve QMM / Rio Tinto facing up to such secondary impacts of this unprecedented development in this very poor region of Madagascar.'

amongst other things, patrol the conservation zone to ensure that villages do not cut trees in the zone. Cutting in the conservation zone has now virtually ceased.

Visiting Mandena

The main hotels and tour operators in Taolagnaro will be running day trips, but independent travellers can contact Mrs Lanto at QMM or by calling 2 221 391 or cellphone: 033 1281 532. The reserve is about 10km from Taolagnaro (a beautiful drive) so within cycling distance. Bikes can be hired in town near the Kaleta Hotel. A taxi costs around 75,000Fmg. There is a campsite just outside the boundary of the reserve, and in this area you can walk around without a guide so are free to look for wildlife at your own pace.

The fee to visit the reserve is 40,000Fmg per person, which includes the boat trip. There are currently no additional fees for the guides.

Lac Anony

About 12km south of Amboasary is a brackish lagoon, Lac Anony. There are flamingos here and a large number of other wading birds in a lunar landscape.

Valerie Middleton writes: 'The region around this lake is beautiful and a paradise for both birdwatchers and botanists. We stayed in the "Village des Mineraux Lodge" situated above the small fishing village of Andranobory. This excellent establishment is adapted for research purposes but if no work is being carried out other travellers may also stay. Pre-booking needs to be made through a travel agent in Antananarivo. Access is through the massive sisal plantations and is signposted from the main road.'

Andohahela National Park

This national park (pronounced 'Andoowahela') opened to tourists in 1998, and is a model of its kind. Much thought and sensitivity has gone into the blend of low-key tourist facilities and the involvement of local people, and all who are interested in how Madagascar is starting to solve its environmental problems should try to pay it a visit.

The reserve spans rainforest and spiny forest, and thus is of major importance and interest. A third component is the east/west transition forest which is the last place the triangulated palm (*Neodypsis decaryi*) can be found. These three distinct zones, or 'parcels' (from the French *parcelle*, meaning plot or area of land) make Andohahela unique in its biodiversity.

Andohahela Interpretation Centre (Centre d'Interpretation Andohahela)

Even if you are not able to visit Andohahela itself, do spend some time in this beautifully organised centre. It is a green building on the left-hand side of the road as you leave Taolagnaro. The centre was set up with the help of the Peace Corps and the WWF, for both tourists and – more importantly – the local people. Through clear exhibits, labelled in English, French and Malagasy, it emphasises the importance of the forest and water to future generations of Malagasy, and explains the use of various medicinal plants. Local initiatives include the introduction of fuel-efficient cooking stoves that burn sisal leaves. Wind power is also being investigated. Schools are being built in the area, with educating the next generation on the importance of preserving the environment one of the priorities.

Visiting Andohahela

At the time of writing a visit to most of the national park requires the use of a 4WD vehicle and full camping gear (all provided by tour operators). Fit and properly equipped hikers or cyclists can make it independently, however. Tour operators such as Air Fort Services offer packages to Andohahela. Contact them (page 265) for the latest details and prices.

The national park
Malio (Parcel I – rainforest)

The rainforest area has a trail system and campsites. It has lagged behind the other two 'parcels' because most tourists have visited a rainforest reserve (Périnet or Ranomafana) by the time they reach Taolagnaro. This is part of its appeal… there will be no crowds. The area has all the rainforest requisites: waterfalls, orchids and lemurs (*Lemur fulvus*). It is also popular with birders who come here looking for the rare red-tailed newtonia. To get there (dry season only) you take the paved road out of Taolagnaro for approximately 15km, turn north on a dirt road before the town of Manambaro and go 6km to the nice little village of Malio. Independent travellers can buy a permit at the ANGAP office in Taolagnaro and reach the trailhead by taxi.

Ihazofotsy and Mangatsiaka (Parcel 2 – spiny forest)

Visitors should remember that spiny forest is very hot, so camping/walking here can be quite arduous. That said, for the committed adventurer this is a wonderful area for wildlife, birding and botany. Even if you were to see no animals, the chance to walk through untouched spiny forest – the real Madagascar – gives you a glimpse of how extraordinary this land must have seemed to the first Europeans.

Apart from the fascinating trees and plants unique to this region, you should see sifaka (this is one of the areas where you can observe them leaping on to the spiny trunks of didierea trees without apparent harm), small mammals such as tenrecs (if you're lucky) and plenty of birds endemic to the south, such as running coua and sickle-billed vanga; also many reptiles. Equally you may see nothing! Remember that this is not Berenty; the wildlife tends to be shy, and is inactive during the heat of the day. Be patient.

Of the two spiny forest parcels, Mangatsiaka is the easiest to visit, being only 6km off the main Taolagnaro–Amboasary-Sud road, so ideal for self-sufficient independent travellers. There is a well laid-out trail system and a good campsite. Ihazofotsy is more popular with groups because you need a 4WD to tackle the two-hour access track. Camping is permitted near the village and there is a good trail system through the superb alluaudia trees. An added bonus is the view from a huge domed rock, which is crawling with *Oplurus* lizards.

Tsimelahy (Parcel 3 – transition forest)

I *loved* this place! Apart from reptiles (lizards and snakes), we saw little wildlife but the scenery and plants are utterly wonderful! This region is the only area in which the triangular palm is found; it says something for the rest of the botany that seeing this was not the highlight of our stay. The campsite for Tsimelahy is within a stone's throw of a large deep pool, fed by a waterfall, and fringed with elephant-ear plants. You can slip into the cool water from the smooth rocks and swim to your heart's content.

You can take a 4WD to within a few kilometres of the campsite, then you have a marvellous walk. A choice of two trails run along both shores of the River Taratantsa, affording super views of white flowered *Pachypodium lamerii*, and green forest. My favourite plant was the 'celebrity tree' (*Lazar* in Malagasy or *Cyphostema vitaceae*). It seems to start as a tree, then change its mind and become a true liana (it belongs to this family), draping its droopy top over neighbouring plants. Young Malagasy seeking popularity or success will ask the *mpanandro* (soothsayer) to ask the tree for help.

Another highlight for us was the visit to the little village of Tsimelahy. This is an inspiring example of how a newly established protected area can involve and benefit the local people. There are well-made handicrafts for sale and you will be treated to a rousing song about the forest and its animals from the children in the tiny school room.

Tsimelahy is accessible for independent travellers who are prepared to hike the 12km trail (or 15km road) from Ranopiso. A permit and directions are obtainable from the Interpretation Centre.

Tana to Toamasina

Since the early days of the Merina kingdom, there has been a link from the country's main port and its capital. The route between the two cities will have been established during the expansionist days of King Radama I, when dignitaries were carried by palanquin, and goods were transported on the heads of porters. It gained greater importance after the arrival of teachers from the London Missionary Society, the first Europeans to have a significant influence on Madagascar. They arrived in Tamatave bearing not only the word of God, but technology in the form of printing presses. The track up the escarpment was narrow, difficult and slippery in the rainy season (most of the year) but the royal government refused to build a proper road, fearing this would facilitate an invasion from outside (in fact the French invasion took place by the much easier route from Mahajanga). The first road was built by the French, but maintenance was never a high priority, especially after independence, partly to reduce competition with the state-owned railway. The collapse of the economy in the Second Republic meant that there was no money at all for maintenance and the road became at times almost impassable. However in the 1990s the road was rehabilitated to a high standard with aid from Switzerland and China.

These days many visitors take Route National 2 from the capital. Most are heading for Andasibe but some continue to the coast. The route description here is aimed at those travelling in a private vehicle or by bicycle, but of course taxi-brousse travellers may choose to break their trip at any of the stops along the way. My thanks to Ony Rakotoarivelo for her research on this route. Note: 'PK' are kilometre markers.

Warnings RN2 is notorious for its reckless drivers and high death-toll. Keep alert, especially if on a bicycle. Even if you've never suffered from motion sickness, take precautions on this trip. The macho drivers and winding road are a challenge to any stomach.

RN2: FROM TANA TO MORAMANGA

After the hectic atmosphere of Tana, the journey to Moramanga offers first-time visitors to Madagascar a gentle introduction to rural life here. Rice fields, *hotelys* and roadside stalls selling seasonal fruits line the route, and it is a fine opportunity to observe activities that make up the daily routine of the vast majority of Malagasy people who live outside the major cities.

The 20km of road to **Ambohimangakely** is surrounded by rice fields which, in the early morning, will be filled with local people pursuing the all-important business of supplying their families with rice: digging paddies, sowing rice, transplanting the mature plants, weeding and eventually harvesting (depending on the season of your visit).

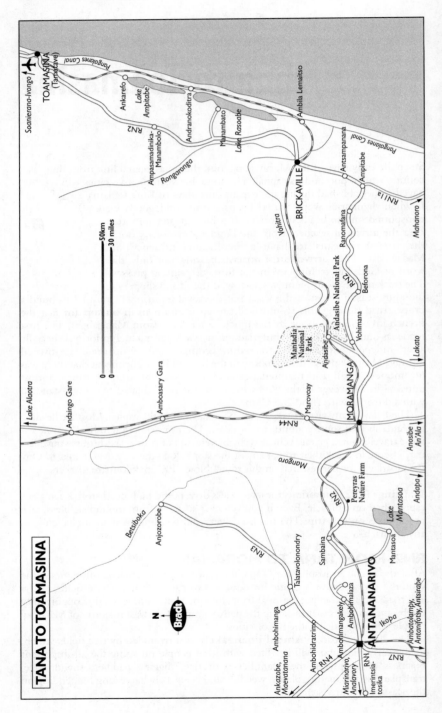

TANA TO TOAMASINA

The following 20km of well maintained road take you through the town of **Ambohimalaza**, steeped in history and tradition (see page 187). By contrast, some 20km later, the road travels past an icon of modern Madagascar. **Sambaina** is home to the first factory of the now famous Tiko empire, owned by President Ravalomanana.

Manjakandriana is the last major town before you descend from the Haut Plateau. Here the flat, straight stretches of road give way to a long series of steep, winding sections and hairpin bends as you head towards the plain below and the small town of **Ambodiamontana**. This descent offers fine views of the forest clinging to the precipitous slopes of the mountains to your left, and a good vantage point from which to survey the next phase of your journey across the flat plains towards Moramanga. If you can take your eyes off the scenery, look out for enterprising locals transporting goods in oil drums balanced on tiny carts down the hair-raisingly steep stretches of road. To your left, water plunges down the flank of a nearby mountain, powering the nearby hydro-electric station across the valley from Ambodiamontana.

As the mountains of the Haut Plateau recede into the distance behind you, the road to Moramanga takes you through numerous small villages, and stretches of thinly populated countryside, the occasional charcoal seller popping up by the side of the road.

Sambaina

This small village 40km from Tana gives an opportunity to stop for a good breakfast. The early-morning weather is likely to be misty and cold.

Pizza Nino (PK 42) Tel: 42 621 01. Run by Yvonne Goldsheider, and serving European/Malagasy food and pizza. Open 06.30–18.30.

Manjakandriana (PK 42)

This largish town 46km from Tana has a good choice of *hotelys* so is an alternative breakfast stop if you have made a pre-dawn start from Tana. The small **Manja Motel** on the left has very simple rooms for 60,000Fmg or 90,000Fmg for double with toilet. A family room costs 120,000Fmg. Continental breakfast is 15,000Fmg. A Malagasy meal with fresh fish is from 19,500Fmg.

The town also has a BOA bank, a hospital, a chemist and petrol station.

Carrying on down the road until you reach PK 62, there's an excuse for another stop.

Mandraka Park On the left side of the road, this is a Malagasy-run collection of wooden bungalows offering accommodation, picnic tables, prepared meals (grilled dishes a speciality) and hikes in the neighbouring forest. Bungalows (shared bathrooms) are 75,000Fmg per night weekdays or 100,000Fmg at weekends. Tel: 22 233 31 or cellphone: 033 1159 409. Meals cost around 25,000Fmg.

Pereyras Nature Farm

Tel/fax: 22 321 01. Formerly known as Mandraka Reptile Farm, this place is well-signposted at Marozevo (PK72) on the right side of the road. It is owned by one of Madagascar's prominent naturalists, André Pereyras. The centre provides the opportunity to see and photograph some of the island's most extraordinary reptiles and invertebrates, but at a price: some of the animals are kept in crowded and stressful conditions. However, recent reports suggest that at least some of the cages are now spacious and perhaps the improvements will continue. My main problem with this place is that although the main purpose of the centre is the breeding (for export) of various butterflies and moths, the demand for reptiles for the pet trade is also satisfied, probably through illegal collecting from the wild.

Visitors pay 25,000Fmg to tour the collection with a guide who costs an additional 10,000Fmg for one to three people, 15,000Fmg for a group of four to six, and 25,000Fmg for more than seven.

About 2km beyond the farm is the village of **Ambodiamontana** where you can have a meal in one of the nice and typically Malagasy *hotelys* along the roadside. Rabbit is a speciality here.

MORAMANGA

Moramanga means, prosaically, 'Cheap Mangoes'. The town experienced a surge of tourist popularity during the 1980s and early '90s when it was used as a dormitory town for Périnet. Now it has slipped back into its status as the last town before Madagascar's most popular reserve. It is worth breaking your journey here – Moramanga is a lively town, and there's quite a bit to see beyond the main road.

Turn left on entering the town and drive for about 800m to have a quick look at the **mausoleum** for the people who died during the uprising in 1947, and then the **Museum of Gendarmerie**. 'Surely the most comprehensive collection in Madagascar, not only police, but cultural, with excellent original exhibits. A must!' (K & L Gillespie) The entrance fee is 10,000Fmg. On weekdays you will need to ask permission to visit at the entrance gate, but at weekends it is open to all 09.00–11.00, and 14.00–17.00.

Telephone code The area code for Moramanga is 56.

Where to stay

Emeraude Tel: 56 821 57; fax: 56 822 35. 32 rooms: double 62,000Fmg, twin 67,000Fmg (shared facilities). En-suite double is 92,000Fmg. Hot water. Breakfast is 15,000Fmg and meals are 35,000Fmg. Probably the best hotel in town.

Hotel Diamant Opposite the church. A new hotel with a total of 18 very comfortable rooms; 5 large rooms have shared facilities for 65,000Fmg, and 5 en-suite rooms for 90,000Fmg. Each room has a small veranda. 8 double rooms are 40,000Fmg with shared facilities.

Grand Hotel Tel: 56 823 81 or cellphone: 033 1162 918. Double or single is 56,000Fmg; continental breakfast is 16,000Fmg and American is 22,500Fmg.

Hotel Restaurant Sarah In the middle of the town, tel: 56 821 08, only two rooms, twin is 60,000Fmg and double is 40,000Fmg shared facilities.

Hotel Restaurant Nadia In the middle of the town; tel: 56 822 43, reportedly good. 12 rooms, 4 singles 48,000Fmg, 5 doubles 60,000Fmg each, twin 85,000Fmg with facilities and hot water. Discotheque at weekends!

Hotel Mirasoa A newish hotel on RN2 about 1km from the centre on the Tana side of town. Tel: 56 821 49. Simple but clean. 10 rooms, double 30,000Fmg and twin bedroom 40,000Fmg, shared facilities.

Hotel Restaurant Fihavanana Tel: 56 820 63. On the right-hand side as you enter town. 10 rooms. Single 30,000Fmg, twin 40,000Fmg, shared facilities; double (large) with en-suite bathroom 60,000Fmg.

Hotel Maitso an'Ala 5 rooms. A very simple hotel, double 25,000Fmg, twin 30,000Fmg.

Where to eat

Au Coq d'Or Tel: 56 820 45. Particularly good for pastries.

Chic restaurant Entering the town, opposite the new petrol station with green and orange

logo, cellphone: 033 1403 394 or 033 1403 392. A very nice small restaurant serving
Malagasy food from 7,000Fmg.
Restaurant La Flore Orientale Tel: 56 820 20; Malagasy, Chinese, European food and
specialising in shrimp dishes. If you order in advance they can prepare any 'exotic' dish of
your choice! Open 10.00–15.00 and 18.00–20.00, 7 days a week.

There are also some Malagasy *hotelys* such as **Hotel Kanto** and Hotel **Voahirana**.

Nightlife
Onno Heuvel, who stayed in Moramanga while exploring the area by mountain
bike, reports: 'There is a cabaret east of the bus station which is lively at the
weekend, and a disco called **Calypso** which is also open at the weekend.'

HEADING NORTH OR SOUTH
Moramanga lies at a crossroads. To the north is the road to Lake Alaotra and to the
south is a rough but interesting road to **Anosibe An' Ala**. Onno Heuvel took this
route on his mountain bike and reports: 'The road is very bad, and climbs up all
the way to the Chutes de Mort, a large waterfall 53km south of Moramanga. This
makes it tough to arrive there in one day, but otherwise this is a great mountain
bike trip. There is also a 4WD taxi-brousse that goes to Anosibe An' Ala.'

Continuing east you reach Andasibe (Périnet) in about half an hour (see page
289).

LAKE ALAOTRA
This is the largest lake in Madagascar and looks wonderful on the map: one imagines
it surrounded by overhanging forest. Sadly, forest has made way for rice, and this is
one of the most abused and degraded areas in Madagascar. Half a million people now
live around the lake, and deforestation has silted it up so that its maximum dry-season
depth is only 60cm. Introduction of exotic fish has done further damage. However,
all is not lost. A grassroots environmental campaign led by Durrell Wildlife
Conservation Trust since 1997 involving festivals and meetings in 72 villages and 28
communes around the lake has led to strong local support to ban marsh burning and
lemur hunting and introduce larger mesh sizes and a closed season for fishing. Local
people recognised the role the marshes play in maintaining local hydrology, providing
a spawning ground for fish and providing weaving materials for Alaotra's renowned
basketry, an important source of income for women.

The entire area of 722,500ha including watershed, rice fields, marshes and lake
was designated as Madagascar's third Ramsar site in 2003, which guarantees
national and regional support for conservation of biodiversity and maintenance of
the ecosystem through sustainable use. It is too late to save Delacour's grebe
(Alaotra little grebe) which is now extinct, and the Madagascar pochard may have
gone the same way; however, work done by the Durrell Wildlife Conservation
Trust has ensured that the Alaotran gentle lemur (Alaotran grey bamboo lemur)
has a future. Not only are these animals breeding happily at Jersey Zoo but annual
monitoring shows that marsh burning has decreased, lemur populations have
stabilised and that fish catches are on the increase. Alaotra provides a great example
of conservation providing benefits for biodiversity and for local livelihoods.

Getting there and away
By *air*
Air Mad flies to Ambatondrzaka (Twin Otter) twice a week. The trip takes 20
minutes and you get great views of the most spectacular erosion gullies.

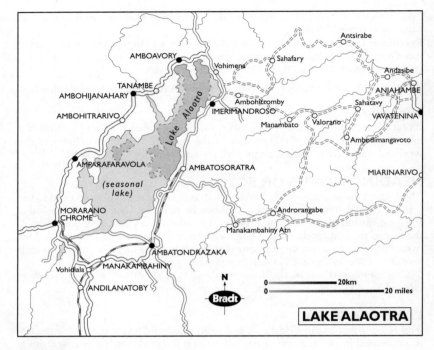

By road

The dirt road (RN44) from Moramanga is one of the new government's road-building priorities because of its importance in transporting rice. At the time of writing, however, it is still a challenging route. A taxi-brousse from Tana to Ambatondrazaka takes 6–10 hours, depending on the state of the road following rains and costs around 75,000Fmg.

Ambatondrazaka

This is the main town of the area, and a good centre for excursions. A tour of the lake by road will take a full day and takes you through village after village where rice, cattle, fishing and geese, with some off-season tomatoes and onions, are the mainstays of rural life. The village **Imerimandroso** gives good views over the lake and nearby **Vohitsoa** is famed for its delicate baskets and mats woven from papyrus from the Alaotra marshes. A visit to Alaotra is not complete without an early morning pirogue ride on the lake, which is calm and mystical after the dirty bustle of the villages. The easiest place to see the Alaotran gentle lemur (bamboo lemur) and waterbirds is at **Andreba Gare** on the east side of the lake, where the villagers have created their own lemur reserve.

Where to stay/eat

Hotel Voahirana BP65, Côte Postale 503. Most rooms have mosquito nets; no en-suite facilities but hot water available. About 45,000Fmg. Good restaurant.

Hotel Max Tel: 54 813 86 Near the train station in Ambatondrazaka, with rooms ranging from 30,000Fmg with shared facilities to 90,000Fmg for rooms with bathroom and TV.

The Smugglers' Path

A steady trickle of adventurers come to Lake Alaotra in order to hike the Smugglers' Path from Lake Alaotra to the east coast. I haven't done this myself and don't intend to – the feedback I've received has been quite negative. The latest report is from Kelyn Akuna, an intrepid teenager who tackled it alone (though he hired a guide) in 2002, carrying an 80lb pack.

'The hike from Imerimandroso to Ambohibe was incredibly hard. It was so hard that the only thing I remember seeing for some time is the narrow red path directly in front of my feet. I am convinced that the people of Madagascar are not familiar with the concept of switchbacks. At times the trail seemed to go straight up and then straight back down. If you had no more than 50 pounds on your back you would be able to enjoy the hike much more. I expected to see a lot of forest, but it was all secondary forest.

'After passing through Antanandava I detoured some so that I would be able to see more of Zahamena. I hiked to Antenina which is a small village just inside the borders of the park. The hike on this day was at first over large rolling hills, and later in primary rainforest (it seemed as though the direction was always up). It took the better part of the day. After Antenina came Tsarasambo, a pleasant little village with loads of coffee trees. After Tsarasambo I went to Salangina, a village rich in cloves. Much like the village I walked to the next day, Sahatavy. From there it is still quite a walk, but you should be able to get to Ambohibe in a day. Once there you can find a taxi-brousse that will take you to Vavatenina.' From here it is easy to get to the east coast road.

J-P COMMERSON

Joseph-Philibert Commerson has provided the best-known quote on Madagascar:

> C'est à Madagascar que je puis annoncer aux naturalistes qu'est la véritable terre promise pour eux. C'est là que la nature semble s'être retirée dans un sanctuaire particulier pour y travailler sur d'autres modèles que ceux auxquels elle s'est asservie ailleurs. Les formes les plus insolites et les plus merveilleuses s'y rencontrent à chaque pas.

> Here in Madagascar I have truly found the naturalist's promised land. Nature seems to have retreated into a private sanctuary, to work on models unlike any she has created elsewhere. At every step one encounters the most strange and marvellous forms.

Commerson was a doctor who travelled with Bougainville on a world expedition in 1766, arriving at Mauritius in 1768. He studied the natural history of that island, then in 1770 journeyed on to Madagascar where he stayed for three or four months in the Fort Dauphin region. His famous description of 'nature's sanctuary' was in a 1771 letter, written from Madagascar, to his old tutor in Paris.

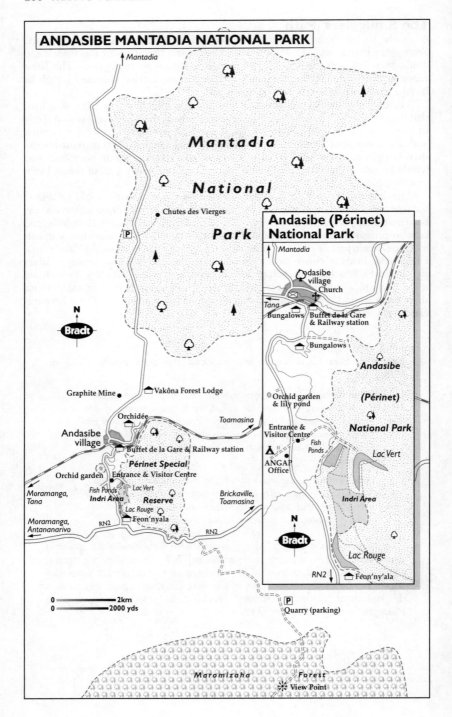

CONTINUING EAST ON RN2

Before reaching Andasibe, it is nice to have a stop at a small village called **Ambolomborona** at PK124 to visit Hotel Juema, a very simple traditional *hotely* on the right-hand side of the road. They can serve you a very simple Chinese soup but if you plan to have lunch there you must give them time to prepare the food. Use the time to watch them making bamboo furniture. If you feel like a rest after all that driving there's a nice thatched-roof chalet.

ANDASIBE MANTADIA NATIONAL PARK

In the late 1990s the long-established reserve generally known by its colonial name of Périnet (but officially, and unpronounceably, Analamazaotra) was combined with Mantadia 20km to the north to form Andasibe Mantadia National Park. Because of its proximity to Tana and its exceptional fauna, this is now Madagascar's most popular reserve, receiving up to 300 visitors a day. These two areas of moist montane forest (altitude: 930–1,049m) provide a variety of lemurs, birds, reptiles and invertebrates which can be seen by any reasonably fit visitor. The experience is enhanced by the quality of the local guides. If you visit only one national park in Madagascar it should be this.

Note that in the winter months of May to August it can feel very cold here, especially when it rains (as it does at that time of year). Hotels without heaters can be quite an ordeal. At any time of year bring warm clothing and adequate waterproofs.

Andasibe village

Few visitors bother to cross the river to look at the village. It's a shame that so little of the tourist revenue has found its way here; you can do your bit by shopping for fruit etc there. 'The village is great to wander around. We found a group of locals sitting on the railway line playing bingo with the caller standing on the platform.' (Sheena Gibson)

Getting there and away
By train

No passenger trains are running on this line at the time of writing.

By road

Taxi-brousses leave from Tana's eastern taxi-brousse station. You will pay less if you take one to Moramanga (a regular stop) and a then a local vehicle to the 25km to the Andasibe turn-off from RN2 or into the village itself.

Where to stay/eat
Category A

Vakôna Forest Lodge BP750, Antananarivo; tel: 22 624 80; fax: 22 230 70; email: izouard@bow.dts.mg; www.hotel-vakona.com. This is Andasibe's luxury hotel, and is only accessible with your own vehicle. Its location near the graphite mine (same ownership) is not idyllic, but the hotel itself works to perfection. The main building has been thoughtfully designed as an octagonal reception area, bar and lounge-dining room with a huge log-fire in the middle (very welcome in the cold season). The upper storey has a shop. The 24 bungalows are quiet and comfortable and there is a swimming pool. Bungalows are 350,000Fmg (high season) and 300,000Fmg (low season). American breakfast is 28,000Fmg. The management is efficient and courteous, and the food delicious: 70,000Fmg for a main meal. Vakôna really is quite something and deserves longer than the normal couple of days so you can relax and enjoy the swimming pool and some horse-riding as well as the usual lemur-viewing. By wandering around on the roads near the hotel you will see quite a bit and have the rare pleasure of doing it on your own. The Vakôna has its own little 'reserve' where former pet lemurs live in relative freedom. These include black-and-white ruffed lemurs and provide excellent photo opportunities. To reach Vakôna from Andasibe, cross the bridge into the village, and take the left fork. The hotel is signposted.

Category B

Hotel Feon' ny ala Tel: 56 832 02. A total of 30 bungalows, 18 with en-suite bathrooms for 138,000Fmg double, 7 cheaper ones with shared facilities; continental breakfast 15,000Fmg, American breakfast 21,000Fmg. Camping area, 10,000Fmg. The name means 'Voice of the Forest' and this is a popular place for visitors who care more about the location of their hotel than its amenities. It is adjacent to the reserve – close enough to hear the indri call (hence its name) – and overlooking the river. There is an orchid garden and resident chameleons. The drawback is that it is reportedly becoming quite shabby. Also the lack of heaters in the cold winter months is a problem, as is the noise: some people complain that the 'voice of the forest' is, at night, the snores of the guests in nearby bungalows. Bring earplugs! The Chinese owners, M and Mme Sum Chuk Lan, are, however, very helpful. The restaurant is good but not excellent (45,000Fmg for a three-course dinner). If you don't want to eat at the hotel you are only a shortish walk from the good snack bar at the entrance to the reserve. The hotel is on the right side of the road that links RN2 to Andasibe.

Hotel Buffet de la Gare Next to the station; tel: 56 832 08. Until 1993 this was the only place to stay in Andasibe, and its list of distinguished guests includes Prince Philip, Gerald Durrell and David Attenborough. Built in 1938 it must once have been appropriate for its role of housing the Great and the Good who wished to visit Périnet, but rooms in the main hotel have deteriorated so much that few people stay here. However, the rooms are still available for 50,000Fmg per night (shared bathroom) and there is talk (and talk...) of renovating it. The more recently built bungalows are fine; there are 8 in a lovely meadow close to the forest about 75m towards the reserve, each has 3 to 4 beds and hot water and – what joy! – fireplaces: 210,000Fmg per night. Less luxurious but perfectly adequate are the seven chalet-type bungalows opposite the Buffet which is 108,000Fmg per night. The dining-room in the main Buffet is truly elegant – fresh flowers on the tables and a marvellous rosewood bar. Good food, too. The menu is 50,000Fmg but you can get a snack from 15,000Fmg. A nice little feature of the dining-room is the *phelsuma* gecko which stuck to the new paintwork near the door; the enthusiastic workman simply applied another coat of paint over the little body and there it remains. It has become a 'what to see' in Andasibe so I'm pleased to hear that it's still here!

Category C

Hotel Orchidee Tel: 56 832 05. This inexpensive hotel is in Andasibe village, away from the made-for-tourists infrastructure. Double is 50,000Fmg, single 35,000Fmg and triple 60,000Fmg. Breakfast is from 8,000Fmg to 17,000Fmg, and a main meal costs between 7,500Fmg and 16,500Fmg. 'I really like it, lots of wood and lovely meals – although it took them a while to arrive! I also enjoyed seeing the orchid collection and the resident tortoise, and glimpsed the cooking facilities which filled me with admiration for those producing the meals.' (FRB).

SAF FJKM Center This NGO is working with local people, training them in sustainable agriculture. They provide inexpensive dormitory accommodation for their volunteers 2km from Andasibe which is open to tourists. There are three bungalows with a double and single bed, shower, toilet and sink for 80,000Fmg per bungalow. There is also dormitory accommodation (communal shower and toilet) for up to 20 people for

17,500Fmg per bed. There is a restaurant which serves meals providing they are ordered in advance (breakfast 6,000Fmg to 10,000Fmg, main meal 10,000Fmg to 25,000Fmg). There may be openings here for volunteer work. Contact : SAF FJKM Moramanga, Lot A 446 Bis, Moramanga 514; tel: 56 822 50; email: saf.mga@simicro.mg or rlbary@netclub.mg.

Camping
You can camp at the entrance to the park or at Hotel Feon' ny ala. Camping is also permitted by the road in Mantadia (but you need your own vehicle).

'Camping behind the ANGAP office (under shelter but on a concrete floor) is free but very basic – just a long drop toilet and no running water. It was also very noisy on Saturday night [when local people were celebrating]. The small restaurant by the park entrance serves fairly expensive food (15,000Fmg for breakfast) but offers good views over the clearing and over breakfast we saw Madagascar harrier hawk, buzzard, cuckoo-roller and black swift fly over! About 40 minutes' walk to Andasibe village (where there are several cheap food options and vegetables for sale) through degraded forest but good birding.

'Probably the best place to camp is Hotel Feon' ny ala (camping on grass lawn with access to flushing toilets and hot shower) but it is a long walk (about an hour) to the village for cheap food.' (Tom Gray)

Permits and guides
You can get your permit from ANGAP in Tana, or at the park entrance (50,000Fmg). Professional film-makers should note that a permit costing 500,000Fmg per person must be purchased in Tana. You will not be allowed in the reserve without the permit.

The Andasibe guides are among the best in Madagascar and an example to the rest of the country for knowledge, enthusiasm and an awareness of what tourists want. The Association des Guides Andasibe (AGA) ensures that standards are maintained. All the guides (there are 21) know where to find indri and other lemurs and many are expert birders. The fee is 60,000Fmg for three hours during the day (group of three); 100,000Fmg for four to six hours; 40,000Fmg for a night walk (group of three). A visit to Mantadia costs 120,000Fmg. On top of the fee guides expect a tip of at least 50,000Fmg per person for two days.

Information and souvenirs
At the entrance to the reserve is a shelter with some information and maps, and nice souvenirs such as T-shirts. There's also a small but interesting museum. The snack bar here is excellent and there's a rather splendid toilet.

Andasibe National Park (Analamazaotra/Périnet)
This 810ha reserve protects the largest of the lemurs, *Indri indri*. Standing about a metre high, with a barely visible tail, black-and-white markings and a surprised teddy-bear face, the indri looks more like a gone-wrong panda than a lemur. The long back legs are immensely powerful, and an indri can propel itself 10m (30ft), executing a turn in mid-air, to hug a new tree and gaze down benevolently at its observers. And you will be an observer: everyone now sees indris in this reserve, and most also hear them. For it is the voice that makes this lemur extra special: whilst other lemurs grunt or swear, the indri sings. It is an eerie, wailing sound somewhere between the song of a whale and a police-siren, and it carries for up to 3km as troops call to each other across the forest. The indris are fairly punctual with their song, but if they oversleep the guides now encourage them with taped

calls (I have mixed feelings about the ethics of this, but it certainly works). They also generally call shortly before dusk, but during the middle of the day they take a long siesta in the canopy so you are unlikely to see them.

Indri are monogamous, living in small family groups of up to five animals, and give birth in June every two years. In Malagasy the indri is called *Babakoto* which means 'Father of Koto'. It is *fady* to kill an indri, the legend being that the boy Koto climbed a tree in the forest to collect wild honey, and was severely stung by the bees. Losing his hold, he fell, but was caught by an indri which carried him on its back to safety.

There are nine species of lemur altogether in Andasibe (including aye-aye), although you will not see them all. You may find the troop of grey bamboo lemurs which are diurnal and sometimes seen near the concrete bridge at Lac Vert, brown lemurs, and perhaps a sleeping avahi (woolly lemur) curled up in the fork of a tree. It is worth going on a nocturnal lemur hunt (the guides are experts at this) to look for mouse lemurs and the greater dwarf lemur that hibernates during the cold season.

Lemurs are only some of the creatures to be found in Andasibe. There are tenrecs, beautiful and varied insects and spiders, as well as reptiles. Sadly the latter are becoming very scarce, as the illegal reptile trade takes its toll. In the old days boys would bring some spectacular Parson's chameleons (bright green and half a metre long) to the trees by the entrance. Now even this artificial display has gone although if you're lucky your guide will leave you while he 'looks' for a chameleon. However, snakes are still quite common, including some handsome boas.

This is also a great place for birdwatching. Specials to look out for include the velvet asity, blue coua and nuthatch vanga.

Leeches can be an unpleasant aspect of the reserve if you've pushed through vegetation and it's been raining recently. Tuck your trousers into your socks and apply insect repellent. If a leech gets through your defences a handy supply of salt will persuade it to let go.

The trails in Andasibe have been carefully constructed, but nevertheless, there is quite a steep ascent (up steps) to the plateau where the indri are found, and to follow these animals you may have to scramble a bit. You may find this difficult if your walking is impaired.

Mantadia National Park

While Andasibe (Périnet/Analamazaotra) is for almost everyone, Mantadia, 20km to the north, is for the enthusiast. The trails are rugged but the rewards are exceptional. Mantadia varies more in altitude (between 800m and 1,260m) than the more popular reserve and consequently harbours different species. What makes it so special is that, in contrast to Andasibe, it comprises virtually untouched primary forest. There are 10,000ha with just a few constructed trails – visitors must be prepared to work for their wildlife – but this is a naturalist's goldmine with many seldom-seen species of mammals, reptiles and birds.

The forest is bisected by the road, with the three trails on the eastern side. Here you may see the beautiful golden-coloured diademed sifaka (*simpona*) and some indri (curiously much darker in colour than in Andasibe). Both these lemur species are getting easier to see as they become habituated to humans. This section of Mantadia has some good, if steep, trails with gorgeous views across the forest and super birdwatching possibilities, including specials such as the scaly ground-rollers, pitta-like ground-roller, and red-breasted coua. 'We (three people) visited with two guides and camped one night beside the road for 100,000Fmg each including transport, which the guides arranged. Stunning wildlife – black-and-white ruffed lemur easily found plus brilliant views of a group of the amazing diadamend sifaka feeding just behind the campsite. Also excellent birds.' (Tom Gray)

There are two main trail areas: the northern Tsokoko circuit at km14 is the toughest and best for wildlife, and a couple of trails to the south. One is an easy two-hour trail which leads up through the forest to a waterfall and lake (*Cascade* and *Lac Sacré*). Bring your swimsuit for a cooling dip in the pool beneath the waterfall. The alternative is the longer Rianasoa circuit.

To do justice to Mantadia you should spend the whole day there, bringing a picnic, and leave the hotel at dawn. You will need your own transport and, of course, a guide. If you stay until dusk you will find a nocturnal walk up to the waterfall very rewarding. Best of all is to camp overnight.

Torotorofotsy and Ampasipotsy
Torotorofotsy Marsh is often added to the itineraries of birding groups, for the rare endemics such as Meller's duck, Madagascar snipe, Madagascar rail, Madagascar crested ibis, Madagascar flufftail, grey emutail and even the very rare slender-billed flufftail. This is also the only known habitat for the golden mantella frog.

An excursion to Torotorofotsy takes all day, involving a three-hour walk down the railway track from Andasibe. A shorter option, where you will see most of the above birds, is Ampasipotsy, which is only 45 minutes' walk from the main road.

FROM ANDASIBE TO TOAMASINA
As you travel towards Brickaville, gradually the lush, green, misty forest of Andasibe starts to give way to a more coastal climate and rapidly changing scenery. After about 40km, the eucalyptus forests are replaced by the first of many travellers' trees, their distinctive (and gigantic) fan-shaped leaves welcoming you to the east. From here on, more and more of these striking plants tower over the surrounding savanna. Of all the areas of Madagascar the east has suffered most heavily from deforestation, but nevertheless, thanks to the efforts of conservation groups (both Malagasy and foreign) this is still a rewarding route.

Vohimana
This is a new forest reserve shortly after the turn-off to Andasibe, near the village of Ambavaniasy between PK 148 and 149. Vohimana is protected through a partnership with local villagers and an NGO, Man and the Environment (www.mate.mg). Together, these groups are working to intensify agriculture and diversify economic development projects in order to reduce the community's dependence on *tavy* farming. 'The reserve has local guides, beautiful hikes with waterfalls and chameleons galore, and well-positioned and appointed (very basic) accommodation in an incredible setting.' (Laurel Brandstetter) Eleven species of lemur are found in the forest, including indri, but these are not yet habituated so are hard to see.

The entrance fee is 25,000Fmg, and accommodation is in three bungalows with lovely views. One bungalow has twin beds and the other two are family rooms with a double bed plus a single bed. Mosquito nets are provided. There is a shared bathroom and toilet. Rates: $US6 per night. There is a kitchen and food can be cooked for you if you bring your own provisions. This is a non-profit organisation so all tourist income is ploughed back into the project. For more information contact MATE at mail@mate.mg.

Beforona
Christina Dodwell recommends a visit to the agro-ecology project here: 'Their guided tour shows how they tackle erosion on the mountain slopes using vetiver

grass, and their terraces of fish ponds and rice fields have an ingenious bamboo-pipe water supply, each pond flowing to another lower down the slope. The centre is run by a local farmer co-operative and a representative is happy to explain to you about their conservation and development work. The tour takes an hour. The tour is free but donations are greatly appreciated. All proceeds go to the co-operative. They have a cheerful little canteen, and dormitories (maximum 25 people per night) for study-groups and overnight visitors. These cost 15,000Fmg per person per night, 30,000Fmg per person for full board. It is possible to make reservation in advance by contacting Mparany at HBP@chemonics.mg with copy to nyrapa@yahoo.fr .'

Ambodiaviavy PK 173
Ony writes: 'While driving down the road I was attracted by the nice garden with flowers and green grass on the left side at where you can see a waterfall called **Andriampotsimbato**. So I stopped and talked to a young man called Lezoma who is ready to fight against poverty, he said, and decided to build a small chalet with a garden for the people passing by. He is charging the visitors a fee of 15,000Fmg per vehicle. It makes a good picnic spot and you can take nice photographs.'

Bedary PK 203
Plan to stop in this small village just to taste the delicious Malagasy food prepared by Mme Evelyne, the owner of the small blue wooden restaurant called **Elegance**. It is clean and peaceful. Meals from 9,000Fmg.

Ranomafana PK 205
Ranomafana means 'Hot water'. This village has a natural **hot spring** which is not exploited since it is considered by the local people to be sacred, and is used instead for asking blessings from the ancestors. The turn-off is just beyond the village before the bridge. Then you take the muddy, slippery path on the right and cross the river on foot during the dry season. 'When I [Ony] went there I had the chance to talk to a couple of local people who had been childless for seven years, but after asking for blessing in this place they have had a baby. I was told that meat or eggs can be cooked in this hot water. If you have time to visit this hot spring, it is better to ask the local people to guide you there.'

There is a post office in this village, and a few *hotelys*. **Restaurant La Girolle** serves Malagasy food for 7,000Fmg. They also have got three very simple rooms and one small bungalow for 50,000Fmg per night.

Manambonitra PK 215,
There are a few *hotelys* along the road and a fruit stall. **Restaurant Ami d'Or** has a nice view from its veranda and is open every day. About 2km before Antsampanana there is a rural (rather scary!) hut in the woods called **Hotel Cabana** which costs 25,000Fmg per night.

Antsampanana
This little town is bursting with stalls offering a huge variety of fruit and vegetables, so perfect for reprovisioning. Nice for photography, too. If you want to dally longer there is the basic **Hotel Espérance** and some restaurants such as Vatosoa, Mirandava, Belle du Jour, Mimosa, Diamant and so on which can serve you Malagasy food. If you are heading west towards Tana you are now about 1½ hours' drive to Andasibe.

Brickaville

After almost 225km of smooth roads and wide open spaces, the potholes, noise and industry of Brickaville can come as a bit of a shock. However fruit, vegetables and friendly *hotelys* can be found there in abundance allowing ample opportunity for re-provisioning and refreshment before heading on towards Toamasina across an enormous, aging (but sturdy) iron bridge over the Rongaronga River.

This is one of those Malagasy towns which has resisted changing its name, despite the efforts of mapmakers. Everyone, Malagasy included, knows it as Brickaville, but its official name is Ampasimanolotra. It lies 134km south of Toamasina.

The town is the centre of sugar cane and citrus production and has a few hotels but few people would stay intentionally. But just in case you're stuck here, below are a few suggestions – and a warning.

Where to stay
Hotel Restaurant Mevasoa 3 bungalows costs 35,000Fmg each per night. Malagasy food 7,000Fmg.
Hotel Bricka cool 7 bungalows: double is 60,000Fmg with bathroom and toilet, and 50,000Fmg with shared bathroom and toilet. Perhaps the best of a poor lot.
Retaurant Florida Near the railway station; Malagasy food.
Hotel des Amis 'You wouldn't put your worst enemies there…' (Rupert Parker) But it's cheap. Double is 25,000Fmg; two small beds is 30,000Fmg; bathroom and toilet outside.

Ambila-Lemaitso

This is a seaside/canalside resort town, where you can happily get stuck for a day or so. But now the trains are not running it is quite hard to reach by public transport.

Where to stay/eat
Hotel Relais Malaky Tel: 56 260 13 or 22 644 68. Probably the best hotel, in a good situation close to the station and overlooking the ocean. Reasonable food. Double rooms (shared bathroom) 75,000Fmg, en-suite doubles for 125,000Fmg. Bungalows are 200,000Fmg. Continental breakfast 15,000Fmg and American breakfast 20,000Fmg.
Ambila Beach About 3km from the station, overlooking the Pangalanes Canal. Nice bungalows, some with cooking facilities. Good value restaurant, friendly staff. About 60,000Fmg upwards.
Hotel les Cocotiers About 90,000Fmg for self-contained bungalows. Good, but about 3km from the station so a bit isolated.

MANAMBATO

This is a picturesque lakeside resort, about 20km northeast of Brickaville, 7km from RN2. The turn-off is at PK 260.5 – the road is muddy and slippery after rain. Lake Rasoabe is part of the Pangalanes Canal system, and Manambato is popular with weekenders from Tana and their children (the bathing is much safer than in the ocean). It is also an access town for boat trips to Ankanin'ny Nofy and Lake Ampitabe (see page 000). A few hotels face the lake and there are wide white-sand beaches. An advantage of Manambato over Ankanin'ny Nofy is that it can be reached by car, although there are also boats from Toamasina. The disadvantage is that there is no public transport there: you need to take a taxi or go on foot.

Where to stay/eat
Chez Luigi Tel: 56 720 20. Very comfortable bungalows, rooms and an excellent restaurant. A room for 4 or 5 people is 225,000Fmg; for 3 people 200,000Fmg (with toilet

and bathroom) and for two is 175,000Fmg; breakfast is 25,000Fmg. Meals cost 70,000Fmg. This is a popular place so you should book in advance for weekends and holidays.

Acacias Tel: 56 720 35 or tel/fax: 22 404 29. Family bungalow: 151,000Fmg, double or twin 131,000Fmg. Meals are 55,000Fmg and breakfast 17,500Fmg.

Hotel Rasoa Beach Tel: 56 720 18, cellphone: 032 0236 187; fax: 56 720 19; email: rasoab@dts.mg. Accommodation varies from 2-person and 4-person bungalows to a 'Tarzan' hut on stilts.10 bungalows. Facing the lake: double 141,000Fmg; for four people 171,000Fmg; family room 191,000Fmg with toilet and bathroom. Facing away from the lake: 120,000Fmg and 150,000Fmg per bungalow. Good food: meals are 55,000Fmg and breakfast is 23,500Fmg. Half-board only.

Au bon coin Zanatany At the entrance to the village, Malagasy-run chalets for budget travellers: 50,000Fmg or 70,000Fmg (shared toilet and bathroom). Very good food for 15,000Fmg.

Hotel Hibiscus Lac Rasoabe 3 simple bungalows for 50,000Fmg, and one for 75,000Fmg (shared facilities). Malagasy food.

Beyond Brickaville, a few glimpses of the ocean and Pangalanes lakes convinces you that you've reached the coast, and then it's a relatively uneventful 93.5km to Toamasina through degraded forest and palm plantations.

Toamasina and the Northeast

Punished by its weather (rain, cyclones), eastern Madagascar is notoriously challenging to travellers. In July 1817 James Hastie wrote in his diary: 'If this is the good season for travelling this country, I assert it is impossible to proceed in the bad.' With this in mind you should avoid the wettest months of February and March, and remember that June to August can be very damp as well. The driest months are September to November, with December and January worth the risk. April and May are fairly safe apart from the possibility of cyclones. The east coast has other problems: sharks and dangerous currents. So although there are beautiful beaches, swimming is safe only in protected areas.

Despite – or perhaps because of – these drawbacks, the northeast is perhaps Madagascar's most rewarding region for independent travellers. It is not yet on the itinerary for many groups, yet has a few beautifully situated upmarket hotels for that once-in-a-lifetime holiday, or wonderful exploratory possibilities for the intrepid backpacker. Much of Madagascar's unique flora and fauna is concentrated in the eastern rainforests and any serious naturalist will want to pay a visit. Other attractions are the rugged mountain scenery with rivers tumbling down to the Indian Ocean, the friendly people, abundant fruit and seafood, and access to the lovely island of Nosy Boraha (Ile Sainte Marie). The chief products of the east are coffee, vanilla, bananas, coconuts, cloves and lychees.

Note: the northeast coast was particularly badly hit by Cyclone Gafilo (see page 4) in March 2004. Although Toamasina escaped unscathed, towns north of Soanierana Ivongo bore the brunt and the infrastructure including roads and bridges may take a while to rebuild.

BACKGROUND INFORMATION
History

This region has an interesting history dominated by European pirates and slave traders. While powerful kingdoms were being forged in other parts of the country,

DISTANCES IN KILOMETRES

Toamasina–Mahambo	90km
Toamasina–Soanierana Ivongo	163km
Toamasina–Mahavelona	60km
Iharana–Sambava	163km
Sambava–Antalaha	89km
Sambava–Andapa	119km

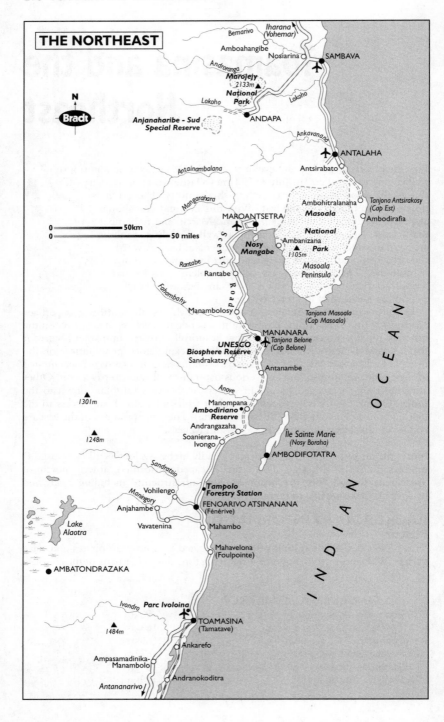

THE NORTHEAST

N
Bradt

Bemarivo
Iharana
(Vohemar)
Amboahangibe
Nosiarina
SAMBAVA
Androranga
Marojejy
2133m
National
Park
Lokoho
Lokoho
Anjanaharibe - Sud
Special Reserve
ANDAPA
Ankavanana
ANTALAHA
Antsirabato
Antainambalana
Mangarahara
Ambohitralanana
Tanjona Antsirakosy
(Cap Est)
MAROANTSETRA
Masoala
Ambodirafia
0   50km
0   50 miles
National
Nosy
Mangabe
Ambanizana
1105m
Park
Rantabe
Masoala
Peninsula
Rantabe
Scenic Road
Fahambahy
Manambolosy
Tanjona Masoala
(Cap Masoala)
MANANARA
Tanjona Belone
(Cap Belone)
UNESCO
Biosphere Reserve
Sandrakatsy
Antanambe
Anove
1301m
Manompana
Ambodiriano
Reserve
Andrangazaha
1248m
Soanierana-
Ivongo
Île Sainte Marie
(Nosy Boraha)
Sandrasio
AMBODIFOTATRA
Vohilengo
Tampolo
Forestry Station
Maningory
FENOARIVO ATSINANANA
Anjahambe
(Fénérive)
Vavatenina
Mahambo
Lake
Alaotra
Mahavelona
(Foulpointe)
AMBATONDRAZAKA
Ivondro
Parc Ivoloina
1484m
TOAMASINA
(Tamatave)
Ankarefo
Ampasamadinika-
Manambolo
Andranokoditra
Antananarivo

INDIAN OCEAN

the east coast remained divided among numerous small clans. It was not until the 18th century that one ruler, Ratsimilaho, unified the region. The half-caste son of Thomas White, an English pirate, and briefly educated in Britain, Ratsimilaho responded to the attempt by Chief Ramanano to take over all the east coast ports. His successful revolt was furthered by his judiciously marrying an important princess; by his death in 1754 he ruled an area stretching from the Masoala Peninsula to Mananjary.

The result of this liaison of various tribes was the Betsimisaraka, now the second largest ethnic group in Madagascar. Some (in the area of Maroantsetra) practise second burial, although with less ritual than the Merina and Betsileo.

Getting around
Although the map shows roads of some sort running almost the full length of the east coast, this is deceptive. Rain and cyclones regularly destroy bridges so it is impossible to know in advance whether a selected route will be usable, even in the 'dry' season. The rain-saturated forests drain into the Indian Ocean in numerous rivers, many of which can be crossed only by ferry. And there is not enough traffic to ensure a regular service. For those with limited time, therefore, the only practical way to get to the less accessible towns is by air. There are regular planes to Nosy Boraha (Ile Sainte Marie), and flights between Toamasina (Tamatave) and Antsiranana (Diego Suarez). Planes go several days a week from Toamasina to Maroantsetra, Antalaha and Mananara, and to Sambava.

For the truly adventurous it is possible to work your way down (or up) the coast providing you have plenty of time and are prepared to walk.

TOAMASINA (TAMATAVE)
History
As in all the east coast ports, Toamasina (pronounced 'Tooamasin') began as a pirate community. In the late 18th century its harbour attracted the French, who already had a foothold in Ile Sainte Marie, and Napoleon I sent his agent Sylvain Roux to establish a trading post there. In 1811, Sir Robert Farquhar, governor of the newly British island of Mauritius, sent a small naval squadron to take the port of Toamasina. This was not simply an extension of the usual British/French antagonism, but an effort to stamp out slavery at its source, Madagascar being the main supplier to the Indian Ocean. The slave trade had been abolished by the British parliament in 1807. The attack was successful, and Sylvain Roux was exiled. During subsequent years, trade between Mauritius and Madagascar built Toamasina into a major port. In 1845, after a royal edict subjecting European traders to the harsh Malagasy laws, French and British warships bombarded Toamasina, but a landing was repelled leaving 20 dead. During the 1883–85 war the French occupied Toamasina but Malagasy troops successfully defended the fort of Farafaty just outside the town.

Theories on the origin of the name Toamasina vary, but one is that King Radama I tasted the seawater here and remarked 'Toa masina' – 'It's salty.'

Toamasina today
Toamasina (still popularly known as Tamatave) has always had an air of shabby elegance with some fine palm-lined boulevards and once-impressive colonial houses. Every few years it's hit by a cyclone, and spends a time in a new state of shabbiness before rebuilding. As you'd expect, it's a spirited, bustling city with a good variety of bars, snack bars and restaurants (updated here by residents Charlie Welch and Andrea Katz with insiders' knowledge). Not many tourists stay here for

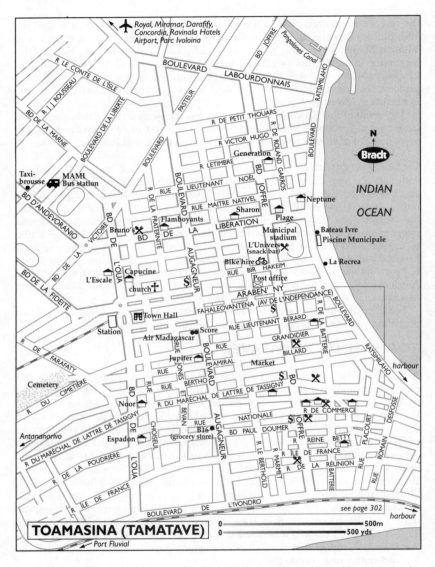

Royal, Miramar, Darafify,
Concordia, Ravinala Hotels
Airport, Parc Ivoloina

INDIAN

OCEAN

TOAMASINA (TAMATAVE)

0 ———————— 500m
0 ———————— 500 yds

any length of time, which is a shame; there is plenty to see and do. For instance the wonderful Parc Ivoloina (see page 308) provides one of the most accessible and delightful natural-history experiences in Madagascar.

Telephone code The area code for Toamasina is 53.

Getting there and away
By road
Route Nationale 2 (RN2) is one of the country's best roads (see *Chapter 11*) and is the fastest and cheapest way of reaching Toamasina from Tana. Vehicles run only

> **THE LEGEND OF DARAFIFY**
>
> Many, many years ago, when Madagascar was still young, the land was surrounded by fresh water. One day a giant named Darafify came striding down the eastern shoreline, carrying a bag of salt over one shoulder. He paused for a rest. A fisherman paddling his pirogue saw what he thought were two enormous trees standing on the edge of the water. These were splendid trees, with fine, straight, brown trunks, just the thing for a new pirogue. So he started to cut the nearest one down with his axe.
>
> Darafify let out a roar of pain and dropped his bag of salt in the water. Since then the sea has been salty.

twice a day, morning or night, and take from six to 12 hours. There is a wide choice of vehicle: bus (auto-car), minibus, and Peugeot station wagon. The large buses are the most comfortable (MAMI is a popular bus company); a night bus may seem like a good option but it is impossible to sleep because of the radio turned up to top volume. It's also more dangerous. Minibuses and Peugeots are faster, and a little more expensive (35,000Fmg).

Book your seat at least a day in advance at the taxi-brousse departure point, Fasan'ny karana, on the road to the airport.

By air

There are daily flights between Tana and Toamasina. The 2004 price is €118 high season, €108 low season. A taxi from the airport into town costs 25,000Fmg.

By rail

The once-famous train from Tana to Toamasina sadly no longer takes passengers. For the time-being, at least, it is for freight only.

By sea and river

Toamasina is one of the starting – or finishing – points for a trip down the Pangalanes Canal. For details of shipping companies see page 346. Most boats leave from Toamasina's Port Fluvial is in the south edge of the town (separate from the harbour).

Getting around

Any taxi ride in the town should cost 5,000Fmg. There is an abundance of *pousse-pousses*.

Tourist information

The **Maison de l'Information** is new and helpful. It is located across the street and then slightly north from the Generation Hotel. The hours are 08.00–11.30 and 14.30–17.00 Monday to Friday, and 08.00–12.00 on Saturdays. Phone 53 343 95, then ask for Noela who runs the office.

Where to stay

Note: Boulevard Ratsimilaho was mostly washed away in the 1994 cyclone Geralda so is not continuous. It now ends just after the crossing of the Pangalanes Canal. To reach the beach hotels in the north of the city you must first go west to catch the road through Tanamakoa then cut back eastward towards the ocean. Best just to take a taxi!

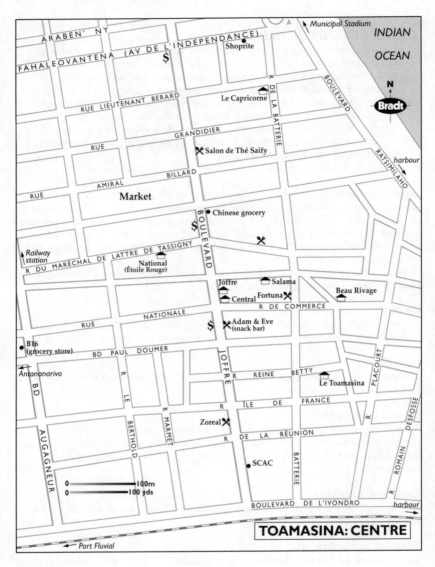

TOAMASINA: CENTRE

Category A

Le Neptune 35 Bd Ratsimilaho (on the seafront); tel: 53 322 26; fax: 53 324 26. The poshest hotel in town, though lacking in character. Swimming pool, good food and nice bar. Credit cards accepted. €65 double.

Hotel Sharon Bd de la Liberation; tel: 53 304 20; fax: 53 331 29; email: sharonhotel@wanadoo.mg or sharonhotel@dts.mg. A high rise concrete building on Bd de la Liberation, 100m west of Hotel Plage, under Italian ownership. All rooms with air-conditioning. The restaurant, Colosseo, serves Italian/European food. Small swimming pool, exercise room etc; mostly a business person's hotel. €61.50.

Hotel Joffre 30 Bd Joffre; tel: 53 323 90. 20 rooms. An atmospheric old hotel with all facilities and very good restaurant. 180,000–200,000Fmg for air-conditioned rooms with en-suite bathroom 'and a seemingly endless supply of hot water'. Some small single rooms for 110,000Fmg, but these are usually reserved for guides and other regulars. Credit cards accepted.

Hotel Le Toamasina Rue Reine Betty; tel: 53 335 49; fax: 53 336 12. 135,000–227,000Fmg, depending on facilities. Comfortable and efficient. Reasonable food. Visa cards accepted.

Category B

Noor Hotel At intersection of Bd Mal Foch and Rue du Mal de Lattre de Tassigny (north side); tel: 53 338 45. 127,000Fmg (air conditioned), 112,000Fmg (with fan). No restaurant, but Jade is round the corner and Vesuvio Pizza is nearby. Credit cards accepted.

Hotel Generation 129 Bd Joffre; tel: 53 321 05; fax: 53 328 34. A nice hotel serving good food.117,000Fmg double with fan, 148,000Fmg with air-conditioning and TV.

Hotel les Flamboyants Bd de la Libération; tel: 53 323 50. About 85,000Fmg for room with fan, 98,000Fmg with air-conditioning. En-suite bathrooms. Good value. Credit cards accepted.

Espadon Hotel Bd de l'OUA; tel: 53 303 86. A concrete high-rise building beyond the Noor Hotel. 85,000Fmg with fan, 135,000Fmg with air-conditioning and TV. Mostly used by business people.

Royal Hotel Route d'Ivoloina; tel: 53 311 15/53 312 81. Another concrete high-rise without much character, but clean and relatively new. 102,000Fmg (shared toilet) to 152,000Fmg (TV and fridge). There are also air-conditioned rooms for 127,000Fmg. Restaurant. Badly located on a busy street away from centre of town.

Concordia Tel: 53 317 42. The closest hotel to airport (within walking distance) on the road towards town. 82,000–100,000Fmg for very nice bungalows with fans and hot water, in a compound which includes a restaurant.

Capricorn 33 Rue de la Batterie; tel: 53 336 51. Large rooms, some with balconies, and en-suite bathrooms; about 59,000Fmg (with fan) to 98,500Fmg with air-conditioning. Closed for renovation at the time of writing.

Central Hotel Bvd Joffre (next to the Joffre Hotel). Tel: 53 340 86; fax: 53 341 19. Nice clean rooms with good mosquito nets, air-conditioning and telephone. Under the same ownership as Restaurant Verandah. Rooms 138,000–203,000Fmg.

Category C

Salama Tel: 53 307 50, on a side street behind Hotel Joffre. 66,000–101,000Fmg, all with fan, hot water, and en-suite toilets and showers. Clean and simple.

Hotel National 13 Rue du Mal de Lattre de Tassigny; tel: 53 322 90. 60,000Fmg to 85,000Fmg (single, with en-suite bathroom) or 110,000Fmg with air-conditioning. A popular backpacker hotel. Most of the cheaper rooms are cell-like, but have fans or barred windows which can be left open. No restaurant.

Hotel Jupiter Bd Auganeur; tel: 53 321 01. 50,000Fmg (shared WC) to 65,500Fmg. Hot water and fan. Concrete building in business district close to the market. Restaurant with Friday cabaret downstairs. Nightclub next door.

Hotel Eden Cellphone: 030 55 850 93; fax: 53 312 90. Appropriately situated near the Adam & Eve Snack Bar on Bd Joffre, opposite the BMOI Bank. Nice but basic rooms: 50,000Fmg for room with shared bathroom to 60,000Fmg for en-suite shower (but shared WC). Fans and hot water in rooms.

Hotel Nado Tel: 53 333 11; fax: 53 333 14; email: sedo@dts.mg. Near to the *bazary kely*. Simple, clean rooms for 62,000 to 116,000Fmg (air conditioned). Simple restaurant in hotel. .

Marotia Hotel Tel: 53 401 99. 'A little off the road that the trucks take to the port: Bd l'Ivondro. Not a very nice part of town and a bit far from restaurants and the centre of town, but nice clean bungalows in the quiet setting of a palm grove which borders the ocean (although it is separated by an unattractive fence). Bungalows from 60,000 to 90,000Fmg. No air-conditioning. Enclosed parking.' (Charlie Welch)

Marotia Annexe Near taxi-brousse station so convenient for late arrival or early departure. Rooms with communal shower 25,000Fmg; en-suite shower 30,000Fmg. Very basic – but very cheap!

Lionel Hotel Convenient location on a side street north of Queen's nightclub (but far enough to avoid the worst of the loud music). A favourite with the Peace Corps crowd. 2-person rooms 50,000 to 70,000Fmg, family rooms 120,000 to 150,000Fmg.

Hotel Plage Bd de la Libération (round the corner from the Neptune); tel: 53 320 90. From 80,000Fmg for double room with cold water to 110,000Fmg for a triple with en-suite bathroom and hot water. Quite clean and comfortable, but the disco is murder and appears to go on 7 nights a week.

Hotel Capucine Cellphone: 032 0451 727. Near the railway station (off Bd Poincaré, opposite the Hotel de Ville). 41,000Fmg for shared shower and WC; 48,000Fmg for en-suite shower (but shared WC). Clean, friendly, but very hot – though you can pay 5,000Fmg for a fan.

Hotel Beau Rivage Rue de Commerce; tel: 53 330 85. 12 rooms, some with fan and balcony. From 35,000Fmg (shared toilet, but shower in room) to 60,000Fmg (fan, shower and toilet in room). Basic and not very clean.

Hotel Numero 1 Opposite the Eaux et Forêts office, a half kilometre from the taxi-brousse station. Shared shower with hot water, friendly management. From 31,000 to 67,000Fmg.

Beach hotels and bungalows

Hotel Miramar Bd Ratsimilaho, Salazamay; tel: 53 332 15; fax: 53 330 13; email: Miramar-hotel444@yahoo.fr. Comfortable chalets and bungalows in a good location (to the north, near the beach). Chalets 170,000Fmg, simple bungalows 210,000Fmg, family bungalows 280,000Fmg. The pool is open to the public, and the hotel is convenient for the airport. Credit cards are not accepted.

Ravinala Tel: 53 308 83; email: fgbaril@dts.mg. On Bd Ratsimilaho on the beach, about 200m north of Hotel Miramar. 9 rooms with fans and hot water, nicely decorated with bamboo. 86,000–116,000Fmg with en-suite WC and shower. Quiet and peaceful; Good restaurant serving European and Malagasy food, and pizza. Friendly people (Vietnamese/Belgian), recommended.

Finaritra Bungalows Tel: 53 339 79, cellphone: 033 1190 707. New, pleasant bungalows with en-suite bathrooms, but quite a way from the centre of town at Mangarano. 50,000Fmg single or double; 80,000Fmg family room. Secure parking. Airport transfers.

Darafify Tel: 53 326 18. In the north of the town, with a good beach location about 2km beyond the Miramar. 80,000–125,000Fmg. Basic bungalows with cold showers and en-suite WC. Good restaurant. For the origin of the name, see box on page 301.

Where to eat

Toamasina is known for its many restaurants. One speciality is *soupe Chinoise,* which can be a meal in itself. Most restaurants open at 19.00.

The following places have been recommended by Toamasina resident, Charlie Welch.

Jade Next door to the Noor Hotel. This is an upmarket Chinese restaurant with good food.

Restaurant Fortuna A very good Chinese restaurant (but slow service). Next to it, under the same management, is **Soupe Chinoise** which opens at 17.00 (as against 19.00) and serves the eponymous soup and noodle specialities.

La Pacifique Rue de la Batterie. A popular and good-value Chinese restaurant just across the road from the Fortuna and serving very good meals at reasonable prices.

La Récrea On the beach, north side. Good food and a nice place to stop for a drink. Live music some weekends.

Bateau Ivre Adjoins the old municipal swimming pool on the east side of the stadium on Bd Ratsimilaho. A bar and restaurant with character. Owners have done a very nice job of fixing up the old municipal pool complex, so you can go there to swim and eat. Moderately priced European food, with seafood a speciality. Live music in the evenings (piano and singer).

Vesuvio Pizzeria Good pizza convenient to the Noor and Espadon Hotel (right across the street). They deliver!

Veranda (formerly Zanatany) One block north of the Hotel Joffre, in an old Creole house with a nicely decorated interior – full of character. European, Malagasy and Chinese food.

Zoreal Bd Joffre, north of the BMOI bank. A local hangout with 2 billiard tables, darts, and bar. French, Creole and Malagasy food, plus excellent pizzas.

Perroquet Bleu On a side road across from the BNI Bank that runs on the side of the Veranda restaurant. An open-air bar and small restaurant which is a local hangout. Pizza and Italian food.

Dragon de Mer Chinese restaurant on side road off Bd Joffre, across from the BMOI Bank. Usually lots of trucks parked around. Very good Chinese food at reasonable prices.

L'Univers. Incorporated into the stadium on its west side. Serves grillades and simple plates. Only restaurant open 24 hours.

Eurasie Located on the road that becomes Route d'Ivoloina, Bd Labourdonnais, but not far from centre of town. Chinese and European food, specializing in Chinese soups which are excellent here and at good prices – a meal unto themselves. Nice décor. They open early in the evenings, at 17.00.

Lilas A very small but clean and pleasant little family-run Chinese restaurant, which adjoins their general store. Short walk from the Concordia Hotel at the end of the Route d'Ivoloina. Good Chinese dishes and soups. Good prices.

Snacks

Adam & Eve Snack Bar 13 Rue Nationale; tel: 53 334 56 (near Hotel Joffre). 'Best cuppa in Madagascar.' Other star features are good prices, strong, hot coffee and delicious samosas (sambos). Particularly good value for breakfast. A long-time favourite with *vazahas*. Always busy, slow service.

Salon de The Saify Good coffee, tea, and pastries.

Glacier Good ice-cream shop on the block behind the Hotel Joffre, near the Pacifique and Fortuna. They also have a good patisserie/bakery. They have opened a second ice-cream shop on the road that goes along the waterfront, Bd Ratsimalaho, not far from the Customs Office.

Brunos Salon de The Another good ice-cream shop and patisserie, which serves good coffee. Just west of the Hotel Flamboyant.

Internet

There are many internet facilities in Toamasina, especially around Bd Joffre and the *bazary be*.

Western Union

There are two offices, one at the BFV Bank on the corner of Av de l'Indépendance and Boulevard Joffre, and the other on Boulevard Augangeur.

Shopping

Shoprite supermarket on the eastern end of Av de l'Indépendance sells everything. The largest supermarket in town, **Score**, has located east of the Air Mad office, on the south side of Av de l'Indépendance. The bookshop **Librairie Fakra** near the market is very good and sells CDs of Malagasy music as well as books and nice postcards.

Car hire

Note: renting a car in Toamasina is more expensive than in Tana.

Aventour Rue Bir Hakeim; tel: 53 322 43.
LCR Bd Joffre; tel: 53 334 69; 53 339 04.
Amazing Grace Rue Victor Hugo; tel: 53 339 58/53 301 52; email: gracetours@simicro.mg

LITTLE MADI – A DIFFICULT DILEMMA
Andrea Katz

Infant bamboo lemurs like 'Madi' just might be the most adorable and appealing primates ever. The temptation to keep one as close to you as you can, for as long as you can, is nearly irresistible (as Hilary can attest!). But Madi's story begins as a sad tale, one that is all too common in Madagascar...

On the east coast, bamboo lemurs (*Hapalemur griseus*) are frequent victims of in-country commerce, a pet-trade that preys upon the sympathy, pity and good intentions of tourists, expats and wealthy Malagasy. Buying and selling of lemurs is illegal but poorly enforced. An infant bamboo lemur is especially vulnerable because the mother 'parks' it in a clump of bamboo, rather than carrying the baby constantly as she moves through the forest. And the birth season coincides with the dry season when Malagasy clear and burn land to plant rice. A villager clearing his fields can just pluck a 'parked' infant off the vegetation and take it home, then try to sell the animal for a little extra income at a nearby market or tourist site.

That's how little Madi came to us at Parc Ivoloina. A well-intentioned tourist bought her from a villager on the beach at Foulpointe. The tourist felt sorry for the little lemur in the basket and thought she would rescue Madi and donate her to the Parc. But in paying any amount of money, no matter how little, the tourist contributed to the pet-trade and encouraged the villager and others to capture more lemurs in the hope of a sale.

Once in our hands, we accepted responsibility to hand-raise Madi since she wasn't yet old enough to be weaned and eat on her own. Hand-raising her was a joy for several weeks. But from experience we knew that if we kept Madi with us for too long, the adorable infant would grow into a troublesome and abnormal lemur when adult. This is true of all lemurs that are hand-raised for several months or more. They won't have a normal behavioural repertoire, making it difficult for them to live compatibly or breed with others of their species.

So we kept Madi at home for only a few weeks, till she was about eight weeks old. Our 12-year-old daughter helped enormously with her care, feeding her every couple of hours with small amounts of formula from a syringe. Madi graduated to lapping formula in a dish and began to chew on tender bamboo shoots, starting to acquire the taste for her natural diet. Then it was time to bring her to Parc Ivoloina where she could be introduced to another young bamboo lemur as her companion and behavioural 'role model'. It nearly broke our daughter's heart to move Madi

SICAM Bd d'Oua; tel: 53 321 04; email: sicam.tamatave@simicro.mg
MR Auto Bd Joffre; tel: 53 308 70, cellphone: 033 1104 991

Bicycle rental
Loulou Location Velos Across from stadium on west side (facing Universe Restaurant); cellphone: 032 0441 483. Rates: 30,000Fmg a day or 7,500Fmg per hour.

Nightlife and entertainment
Pandora Station Near the Hotel Miramar. 'An interesting nightclub. Fun place to go dancing without hassles from night ladies (for men). Safe place for women to dance unhassled as well. Used to serve meals as well but they seem to be moving away from that. Have a "snack" which serves simple things like omelettes, sandwiches, and hamburgers. Décor is imaginative.' (Charlie Welch)

to the Parc, where she wouldn't see her daily and the cuddling would stop. But happily, as a result of her early introduction to other lemurs, Madi has developed into a completely normal bamboo lemur. She doesn't bite and isn't fixated on humans. We have every hope that she will breed one day, perhaps to raise her own infants in a multi-acre forest habitat on the grounds of Parc Ivoloina.

So the dilemma is this... it's hard to turn a blind eye when faced with the chance to 'rescue' an adorable lemur from the villager that carries it in a small, dirty basket, sometimes with a rope around its neck or waist, knowing that the villager has little money to feed the lemur. But as difficult as it is, it's best to leave that one lemur to an uncertain fate in the hands of the person trying to sell it – even if the animal dies. Only this will break the cycle of capture/sale/capture again. Only this will prevent the problems of pet lemurs that bite and the sad cases of lemurs that are tied up or caged at hotels. Those lemurs were hand-raised and treated as pets for too long, perhaps by well-intentioned people who like animals, or perhaps by hotel owners who think that tourists are charmed by lemurs running all over their breakfast table – until those lemurs start biting their guests.

These pet lemurs can never be released into the wild, for several reasons. They are too habituated to humans and will likely approach villagers, making themselves easy prey for re-capture or for the cook pot. They will be unable to identify sufficient food resources in the wild, particularly in times when fruit is scarce. Pet lemurs that have been raised by humans since they were infants won't have developed key survival skills (ie: predator avoidance, arboreal locomotion skills). They won't show normal social behaviour towards other lemurs and will likely be chased or injured by resident populations. And 'domesticated' lemurs are exposed to the diseases and parasites of domestic animals – thus the risk is great that they could introduce these diseases into wild lemur populations.

Madi's story has a happy ending because she's doing great at Parc Ivoloina. But the real issue is that the capture of wild lemurs for the in-country pet trade has a real impact on the survival of local lemur populations. With Madi's removal from her wild group, there is one less female bamboo lemur that will breed in the wild to contribute the future survival of her species. Re-introductions are rarely a solution – they are costly, complicated and require a great deal of planning and risk evaluation. So no matter how great the temptation and the good intentions, don't buy any lemurs or any other wild animal. Help stop the illegal trade in endangered species.

Other night clubs in town are at Neptune, Stone Club (at Hotel Jupiter), and Queens.

Minigolf 18 hole course at the end of Rue de Commerce down from the port entrance. 'Sounds corny but is nicely laid out and kept up with bar and grillade restaurant.' (CW) If you're looking for something completely different to do...

Swimming pool (Piscine Municipal). Already mentioned along with its Bateau Ivre restaurant. A nice place for a dip if you are not staying at the Neptune, Miramar or Sharon. Eat poolside or in the restaurant.

PARC IVOLOINA

This began life in 1898 as a rather grand Botanical Garden but is now a conservation centre and zoo. It is funded by the Madagascar Fauna Group, a consortium of 40 or so zoos from around the world with a special interest in Madagascar. It supports Ivoloina and the reserve of Betampona.

I have been trying to get to Ivoloina for 20 years and finally made it in 2003. I was enchanted! Admittedly I was shown round by the current caretakers, Charlie Welch and Andrea Katz, but even without their guidance a visit here is hugely rewarding, both for what you see and what the MFG is doing in terms of educating the local population about conservation. First the lemurs: in total there are 13 species and subspecies here, including a pair of aye-ayes. Free-ranging lemurs include black-and-white ruffed lemurs, white-fronted lemurs, red-bellied lemurs and grey bamboo lemurs. These offer great photo opportunities, as well as the pleasure of seeing 'zoo animals' living in freedom. There are also reptiles (tortoises, chameleons and boas) and tomato frogs which are unique to the Maroantsetra area.

An interpretive trail leads you through the forest, and there's a 1½km trail running round the perimeter of the lake. In the zoo itself there is a botanical tour, with labelled native trees, and a guide-booklet in French and English. There's a snack bar (which also sells souvenirs) and you can even go on a pirogue trip on the lake!

Do visit the education centre. Grants from the American Embassy and other donors enabled this building to be carefully designed with excellent displays and explanations of the importance of conservation in the area. In addition the centre runs a teacher-training project and a teachers' guide manual for environmental education. Children from the local primary school come here on Saturdays to learn about conservation. This became possible when an American couple visited Ivoloina and asked Charlie and Andrea: 'If you had $10,000 what would you do with it?' The environmental programme is the answer.

The latest scheme is the Model Station, which is on the Station Road just before the zoo entrance. The purpose of the MS is to teach sustainable agriculture techniques to Malagasy cultivators, but it is a worthwhile visit for tourists who are interested in eastern Madagascar's commercial agricultural products and fruits, as well as bee-keeping, and more. It's an easy place to see a wide variety of cultivated plants in a short period of time while strolling along a peaceful winding path. It includes everything from intensive rice-cultivation techniques to vanilla and lychees.

How to visit Ivoloina

Ivoloina is 12km north of Toamasina. The only way to get there is by taxi, which costs around 100,000Fmg (if you want the driver to wait, and then take you back). One of these days they will improve the road and the taxi fare will perhaps come down. The alternative is to hire a bicycle in Toamasina (see page 306).

It is open daily from 09.00 to 17.00; the entrance fee is 25,000Fmg. The best time to visit is late afternoon when the lemurs, including the aye-ayes, are anticipating feeding time. If you are particularly keen to see the aye-aye it is best to contact the MFG office before your visit. It is located on the Route d'Ivoloina just north of the Royal Hotel. The phone number is 53 308 42.

The ideal way to see the park and its animals is by camping overnight (10,000Fmg with your own tent). However, Ivoloina is on the airport side of town so if you are stuck in Toamasina for a few hours between planes there is still time for a short visit.

THE ROUTE NORTH

The road is tarred and in good condition as far as Soanierana-Ivongo. Beyond that it is usually passable as far as Maroantsetra. Then you have to take to the air or journey on foot across the neck of the road-free Masoala Peninsula. An increasing number of good-quality seaside hotels are being built along along the coast.

Even in this first stretch there are alternatives to travelling by car: 'We met a group of four young Frenchmen who were hiking to Fénérive from Tamatave via the beach. First time I had heard of that one. They said it was interesting and seemed to be enjoying themselves. April and May would be a good time, but December to March could really be tortuously hot and uncomfortable.' (C Welch)

Mahavelona (Foulpointe)

The town of Mahavelona is unremarkable, but nearby is an interesting old circular fortress with mighty walls faced with an iron-hard mixture of sand, shells and eggs. There are some old British cannons marked GR. This fortress was built in the early 19th century by the Merina governor of the town, Rafaralahy, shortly after the Merina conquest of the east coast. The entry fee is 15,000Fmg and guided tours are available (in French).

This is becoming a popular beach resort, with the Malagasy as well as *vazaha*. 'There are probably more than 20 hotels and bungalow complexes. Note that the kids, pirogue guys and shell sellers are getting particularly annoying about pestering people on the beach. I hear complaints from tourists.' (C Welch)

Where to stay/eat

Hotel Manda Beach Tel: 57 322 43; also (Tana) 22 317 61. By far the best hotel in the area, located on the Toamasina side of town. Bungalows and safe swimming.
Au Gentil Pêcheur Next door to Manda Beach. Less expensive bungalows and excellent food.
Mangabe Hotel Double bungalows for 180,000Fmg.
Le Foulpointe This restaurant is receiving rave reviews.

Mahambo

A lovely beach resort with safe swimming (but nasty sandfleas, called *moka fohy* in Malagasy). 'Compared to Foulpointe, Mahambo is a much more peaceful scene. Not yet the pestering hordes of salesmen – for now all are calm and wait for clients to come to them. Will probably, sadly, change over time.' (CW)

Where to stay/eat

La Pirogue Tel: 57 301 71. A pleasant new set of bungalows, reasonably priced. Very nicely decorated with all sorts of artisinal products, giant geodes, and even whale bones. Good food. Bungalows 100,000Fmg to 120,000Fmg with cheaper rooms in a block at 80,000Fmg.
Hotel Le Recif Tel: 57 300 50; fax 57 301 32. Bungalows for 80,000Fmg, 20,000Fmg for an extra bed. 'The restaurant is really excellent. The French couple who run it serve wonderful French/European cuisine.' (C Welch)

Hotel Dola Tel: 57 331 01; email: hoteldola_madagascar@voila.fr;
http://hoteledola.site.voila.fr/. 'About a zillion unattractive, tiny, windowless bungalows, but
the place does look well kept. Most of his business comes from meetings and seminars.'
(CW)
Hotel Restaurant Ylang-Ylang Tel. 57 331 00 or 57 300 08; email
mamitina@wanadoo.mg. This is a new very nice bungalow complex, owned and run by a
Chinese family from Fénérive. It's about 70m back. Bungalows 60,000Fmg and familial
100,000Fmg (to 6 people). All with hot water. Restaurant has good cheap food.

Heading west
Between Mahambo and Fenoarivo Atsinanana is a road leading inland to
Vavatenina, where there is basic accommodation in bungalows, and on to
Anjahambe. This town marks the beginning (or end) of the Smugglers' Path to
Lake Alaotra (see page 287).

Fenoarivo Atsinanana (Fénérive)
Beyond Mahambo is the former capital of the Betsimisaraka Empire. There is a
clove factory in town which distils the essence of cloves, cinnamon and green
peppers for the perfume industry. They are not geared up for tourist visits but will
show you round if you ask.
  There are several basic hotels, including Belle Rose Bungalows on the road
leading to the hospital, and an excellent Chinese bakery. Dolphins can sometimes
be seen swimming offshore.

West to Vohilengo
From Fenoarivo a road leads west to Vohilengo. This makes a pleasant diversion
for those with their own transport, especially during the lychee season. 'We arrived
at the start of a six-week lychee bonanza… Along the road to Vohilengo were pre-
arranged pick-up points where the pickers would bring their two 10kg panniers.
Vohilengo is a small village, perfumed with the scent of cloves laid out to dry; the
local *hotely* sells coffee at amazingly cheap prices.' (Clare Hermans)

Tampolo Forestry Station
About 10km north of Fenoarivo is this small forestry station. It is managed by the
agricultural branch of the university, and they have recently opened a nice little
interpretive museum on the grounds. There are paths into the coastal forest that
can be taken with guides. It's a good opportunity to see some of Madagascar's most
endangered flora: the littoral (coastal) forest.

Soanierana-Ivongo
Known more familiarly as 'S-Ivongo', this little town is one of the starting-points
for the boat ride to Sainte Marie. It is also the end of the tarred road

Where to stay/eat
Hotel Espece Basic bungalows for 20,000Fmg. The best budget option. Near the boat
departure point for Ile Ste Marie. Well run by Emile, friendly, with excellent food.
Relais Sainte Marie Nice bungalows for 35,000Fmg.

CONTINUING NORTH (IF YOU DARE!)
From Soanierana-Ivongo the road is unreliable, to say the least. As fast as
bridges are repaired they wash away again. You may have a fairly smooth taxi-
brousse ride with ferries taking you across the rivers, or you may end up walking

for hours and wading rivers or finding a pirogue to take you across. You should get local advice before setting out, especially if you have a lot of luggage to carry or are on a tight schedule. The most recent report (2003 and pre-Cyclone Gafilo) is that a very crowded taxi-brousse took seven hours to make the trip to Manompana.

Andrangazaha

There is just one reason to stop at this little place midway between S-Ivongo and Manompana: Madame Zakia. 'Madame runs the best place north of Tamatave. All vehicles going north stop there to eat. Why? Because Madame feeds the drivers for free, passengers pay. Her food is excellent, bungalows clean with mozzie nets, away from the noise and bustle of town in the bush where you can wait for a lift in quiet comfort.' (Paul & Sarah McBride) Although this report dates from the mid 1990s, a recent traveller confirms that Madame Zakia is still in business.

Manompana

For many years this village, pronounced 'Manompe', was the departure point for Nosy Boraha/Ile Sainte Marie. Because of a spate of recent accidents there are no longer scheduled services to Sainte Marie, but you can find a private boat to take you over. Beware of pirogues, however, which are too small to cross the reef safely.

The village has plenty of charm: 'I loved the place! Even two days sitting outside the epi-bar waiting for transport were a pleasure. The owner and his wife are kind and hospitable, and village life was fascinating.' (FRB)

Around Manompana there is good surfing and swimming, and a small reserve, run by ADEFA, who have an office in the village. As well as guiding you in the reserve, they will take you on a tour of the village, showing a number of interesting things: the bakers oven, coffee being dried on mats, vanilla pods drying in glass coca-cola bottles, sea cucumbers drying on mats before being shipped over to Japan to end up in sushi. You also see how they make their very bitter local drink, *betsa-betsa*, which is made in a week using sugar-cane juice and has about the same alcohol percentage as wine.

Where to stay/eat

Chez Wen-ki's Far end of town; 5 spacious beachfront bungalows with a bucket shower (cold water). Secluded, superb food. Laundry service. Mountain bikes for hire. 'The meals were superb, the bungalows delightful, and M Wen Ki the most enchanting and courteous gentleman imaginable.' (FRB) A bargain at 25,000Fmg.

Chez Lou Lou Central 6 beachfront A-frame bungalows, very clean, good toilets, good seafood.

Mahle Hotel On Mahle Point, 1km from the village. 'Run by an incredibly friendly brother and sister team, the punch coco was the best we tried!' (A Willis) The food is also excellent. This is a very beautiful, ocean-front place with good diving and a lovely nearby forest.

Ambodiriano Reserve

This was set up by two school teachers from Réunion in the mid 1990s, and is now run by the local community, ADEFA (Association de Défense de la Forêt d'Ambodiriano). The small (65ha) reserve incorporates three dramatic waterfalls, above which shelters have been set up for picnics or overnight camping. If you have your own tent it's worth spending the night in order to search for chameleons (always easier by torchlight) and to get the best dawn birdwatching. You may also see lemurs.

A KAYAKING ADVENTURE ON THE EAST COAST
Duncan Murrell

In 2003 I was awarded a Winston Churchill Travelling Fellowship to go on a kayaking trip which would make a significant contribution to my work as an environmental educator, writer and photographer. I chose to begin a circumnavigation of Madagascar which has over 3,000 miles of coastline, and hundreds of unexplored islets, particularly off the northwest coast. I wanted to contribute to a greater awareness of the unique and diverse marine habitats of a country that is much better known for its terrestrial treasures. I have had a long association with humpback whales in SE Alaska, and Madagascar would also give me the opportunity to experience those magnificent animals in a completely different setting.

I started my epic journey at Tamatave at the beginning of September so that I could encounter the migrating whales from Isle Ste Marie up into Antongil Bay. Unfortunately my careful planning came undone on the very first day of the trip because I hadn't reckoned on the power of the surf generated by the thousands of miles of open ocean extending all of the way down to Antarctica. On my first landing on a very exposed and steep beach north of Tamatave my kayak was swamped by the pounding waves and had it not been for the timely arrival of a local young man I would have lost everything. This unexpectedly early calamity had served to bring me into immediate contact with the generosity and hospitality of the Malagasy people. My shivering saviour would accept no reward for his heroics and over the next few days I was visited by many local people who brought me water and plenty of good cheer. I learnt my first Malagasy expression, 'Tsara Be' (very good), and that became the regular mantra as we toasted Madagascar with endless cups of tea and fits of laughter. That really set the tone for future encounters with isolated coastal communities where the inhabitants were always so surprised to see a waterborne *vazaha* landing on their beaches. They would scrutinise my gear with endless curiosity but I never felt for one moment that anything would be stolen, as indeed was the case until I reached larger towns.

The volatile ocean continued to slow my progress towards my first tropical rendezvous with humpbacks and was responsible for inflicting more injuries in addition to the ones that I had sustained on the first day, and which had since become badly infected. I was exploring Nosy Atafana, a group of three beautiful islands protected by a coral reef, and one of four marine parks on the east coast. I was struck by a mighty wave whilst standing on a massive breakwater of a rock that was being pounded by the incoming swells. It was a sledgehammer blow that dashed me against the rocks and gashed my foot wide open. My next destination was a doctor in Mananara and my first course of antibiotics.

MANOMPANA TO MAROANTSETRA

The road north can be an adventure in itself: 'Intending to set out on foot one morning I found myself in the back of a vehicle bound for a nearby village and was subsequently transferred to a lorry ... the experience of watching happy and unconcerned Malagasy cutting down saplings to reinforce bridges, diving into the river to retrieve bits of erstwhile bridge and unloading/reloading the lorry to get it safely across ... then repeating the process just a few kilometres on ... together with negotiation of the near impossible "road" in between ... will stay with me for ever! I suspect too that images of the astounded *vazaha* may stay

The true benefits of having my own water transportation were realised when I was able to paddle along the Masoala Peninsula and up into several of its rivers. Snorkelling in the protected waters of Tompolo gave me a glimpse of the fantastic marine biodiversity that had vanished from a lot of the degraded coastal areas that I had paddled through. It was usual to be up at the crack of dawn and see legions of silhouetted figures armed with sticks poking and prodding the coral in search of octopus or any other marine morsels to fill their baskets. Much of the coral that I had paddled past was dead, perhaps as a result of rising sea temperatures but undoubtedly aggravated by the daily abrasion of feet and sticks.

The coastline between Tompolo and Antalavia is the wildest stretch along the peninsula and is adorned with some of the most curious rocks that I have ever seen. Each smooth boulder appears to be crowned with a set of broken teeth. Farther down the peninsula the River Isava afforded me the deepest penetration into the forest although I was never that far from the small homesteads that are creeping up the rivers. This was the immersion that I was looking for; I was alone and tuned in to every nuance of life around me. Unfortunately I was oblivious to the fact that by wandering up and down the river barefoot I was opening the door to the next, and by far the worst affliction of my trip. What was most likely a parasitic schistosome worm had entered the back of my ankle and started a swelling process that inflated my foot like a balloon. It was excruciatingly painful if I stood upright for more than five to ten minutes. Ironically the gash on my other foot had only just healed.

I had to press onwards towards the outer coast and another tussle with the vagaries of the Indian Ocean; my goal, Antalaha and my next course of antibiotics. On the way someone pointed out that the suspicious looking black spots on my toes were in fact the egg repositories of a parasitic flea. I acknowledged his experience and invited him to scrape the eggs out for me.

The ocean was calming somewhat with the onset of the austral summer but as soon as even moderate swells encounter the submerged reefs they create waves that rise up in an instant and come crashing down with explosive force. It was a marine minefield that called for the greatest vigilance. I had to negotiate narrow passages through the reefs with waves funnelling into them from every quarter. It was gripping stuff but all I could think of was getting over to the relatively placid waters of the west coast. My ocean journey ended in Antalaha for this chapter of my kayaking adventure in Madagascar and my kayak awaits me in Diego Suarez for the next leg, which I hope will be less memorable in some respects.

I am available for school and public lectures. Please contact dunksmurrell@yahoo.com

with those with whom I shared this journey!' It took FRB nine hours to reach Antanambe.

Antanambe

Some 35km north of Manompana, on the edge of the UNESCO biosphere project, is this pretty little town with one of the east coast's nicest hotels.

Chez Grandin The French couple, Alain and Céline Grandin, opened in 1998 and is already deservedly popular. Despite its remote location it verges on the luxury, with gas

BEWARE OF SANDFLIES
Duncan Murrell
The thing about sandflies, as I discovered, is that you don't know the extent of the damage until it's too late. They seem to home in on your back as if they realise that they're evading your detection. I was busy trying to swat a relatively small number on my arms, unaware that my back was being ravaged. Their insidious approach is also abetted by the apparent lack of any noticeable pain from the bites. On two separate occasions my back and the backs of my arms were covered in the horrendously itchy spots. They didn't last for weeks but they certainly itched for days and days and days – and nights especially! Every night I was compelled to emerge from my hammock for a two-handed scratching frenzy. My advice is to put on a long-sleeved shirt when the first one is spotted – even if it appears to be only one – because it's just a decoy. Otherwise they could ruin the whole trip.

cooking, filtered running water, pressure showers and flushing toilets with soft paper, and comfortable beds with mozzie nets. There is a superb restaurant with Creole and French cooking and fresh fish daily. The cost of a bungalow is 50,000Fmg, and 25,000Fmg for a three-course meal. The Grandins arrange tours in the Mananara biosphere reserve, and diving and fishing excursions to a vast reef 1km from the hotel. There is no way to contact Alain and Céline in advance, but it's worth taking pot luck and simply turning up. There is just one problem with this otherwise idyllic place: 'When we were there we were attacked by tiny black sandflies which leave nasty red spots which take weeks to go away – they can cover your body in these in a matter of minutes and it's wise to be careful (we weren't!) Apparently it is a seasonal problem so you might be lucky.' (Rupert Parker) Duncan Murrell had the same problem (see box overleaf).

Hotel Vahibe This is probably the only budget accommodation in the area. The hotel is next to the ferry some 2km north of Antanambe. The owner speaks some English. Around 25,000Fmg.

Visiting the biosphere project

You can either take the easy option of a tour run by Chez Grandin, or do it independently. Permits to visit the reserve can be bought for 50,000Fmg in the ANGAP office adjacent to the hotel and it takes about two hours to walk to the entrance. It's possible to stay overnight in the park in huts but you will need a guide from the town. A nice day excursion is to walk to the edge of the park and skirt round it to a spectacular waterfall which has cold clear pools for swimming.

From Antanambe to Mananara

Ongoing transport becomes increasingly scarce: 'I was short of time so set out on foot the next morning. About 30 exhilarating but exhausting kilometres later I reached a village called **Imorona** where I stayed in accommodation which did not include toilet facilities but I didn't care!' (FRB) From there it is a short hop to Mananara.

Mananara-Nord

Mananara, 185km north of Soanierana-Ivongo at the entrance to the Bay of Antongil, is the only place in Madagascar where one can be pretty much assured of seeing an aye-aye in the wild, on Aye-Aye Island. Some compare this experience to a zoo, but the aye-ayes are not captive (except by the water) and almost everyone loves the experience: 'M Roger, who arranged my visit to Aye-Aye Island, was memorably kind and generous with his time. He and his wife showed me the tortoises they keep in their garden and also their beautiful orchids. You are collected at about 16.00, driven to the appropriate point on the river (near to the Roger home) from which you are rowed across; the aye-ayes appear at about 18.00 and M Roger returns you to your hotel at about 19.00. The trip costs 30,000Fmg. I had a super time, going a little earlier and seeing woolly lemurs (with a gorgeous new baby) and bamboo lemurs too.' (FRB)

Getting there and away
The account by FRB of her journey by road from Soanierana-Ivongo illustrates the joys and perils of this route. You can also travel non-stop. 'The taxi-brousse ride from Mananara back to Tamatave was a delight – even though it was a 26-hour delight of which only three hours were spent asleep!'

For softies the only access to Manara is by Air Mad. The town is on the route from Toamasina to Sambava (the other stop is Maroantsetra). For the overland/oversea journey see below.

Where to stay/eat
Hotel Aye-Aye On the beachfront opposite the airport. Pleasant en-suite bungalows, 61,000Fmg. Good English spoken. The Malagasy owner, Oliver, offers island tours and other excursions, and his wife 'keeps the place ticking over. She was always ready to provide assistance and advice. Best of all is the food: by far the biggest portions I encountered.' (Duncan Murrell)
Chez Roger Basic but adequate. €10 per room, meals €5, breakfast: €2.
Ton-ton Galet A friendly, modest set of bungalows located near the hospital. Good meals and a friendly atmosphere. 'I quite liked the close proximity of pigs & assorted poultry!' (FRB) 30,000Fmg.

What to do in and around town
There is more to do in Mananara than Aye-Aye Island. There's a lively market, a good disco at weekends and the ocean for relaxation. Three kilometres south of the town is a beautiful bay protected by a reef with shallow, safe swimming.

The UNESCO Biosphere Reserve
The easiest way of visiting this reserve seems to be with a tour organised by Chez Grandin in Antanamabe. The area is studied by naturalists and is not easily accessible to tourists. ANGAP have an office in Mananara where English is spoken, if you want to persevere.

Mananara to Maroantsetra
To continue the journey north is an adventure, but that's part of the attraction.

In the early 1990s the intrepid Luc Selleslagh set out in a small boat: 'On the way the sea got rougher and rougher, the waves twice as high as the boat … I thought we were going to end between the sharks. The five other passengers were all sick. I was too afraid to be sick. Finally the captain decided to return!' After that Luc set out on foot. The bridges across the rivers sounded almost as dangerous as the sea but at least he was master of his fate. After two days and one lift he reached Rantabe from where there is at least a vehicle a day heading for Maroantsetra. Luc warns that even in ideal conditions it takes at least eight hours to go the 110km.

In 1998 Rupert Parker did the trip by 4WD vehicle. 'The road is the worst I've ever experienced but also the most spectacular. It hugs the coast climbing up and down through virgin forest right down to the sea, affording stunning glimpses of cliffs and deserted bays if you can divert your attention from holding on for dear life. It took us four hours to do the 40km. There are ferries, broken-down bridges and some sections of the route which are like giant's staircases – huge boulders haphazardly scattered over steep inclines. Definitely Mission Impossible, but because of that the forest is largely uncleared and it's one of the most beautiful areas in Madagascar.'

My latest report is from FRB in 2003. 'I'd very much hoped to continue to follow the coast to Maroantsetra but upon enquiring about transport I discovered that a vehicle had been sent to see how the bridges were...and hadn't returned! This may have changed; when I passed back through Mananara I was told that they were sending a *katkat* to Maroantsetra – but they may just have been teasing me! After my walk from Antanambe I knew that I could not possibly go on foot ... it took me a while to recover from that ... so I had a wonderful journey by boat instead, accompanied for a few magical minutes by leaping humpbacked whales! The coastline was frustratingly visible but the boat journey nonetheless a delight which I wouldn't have wanted to miss, another humbling example of the Malagasy attitude to life and courtesy to *vazahas* ... the sailors even shared their lunch with me, and when we reached Maroantsetra a fellow passenger carried my bag to the hotel.'

Following the cyclones in 2004 the road and bridges are likely to be in a worse condition so boat may still be the only option. If you do go by sea, bear in mind that Madagascar has a poor sea-faring record with several incidences of overcrowded ferries sinking with the loss of all lives.

MAROANTSETRA AND THE MASOALA PENINSULA
Despite difficulty of access and dodgy weather, this is perhaps the leading destination for ecotourists who want to see Madagascar's most important natural habitat in terms of biodiversity – the eastern rainforest, exemplified by Nosy Mangabe and the Masoala Peninsula.

These places require fitness and fortitude but the rewards for nature-lovers are great. Fitness is needed for the hills and mud which are an aspect of all the reserves, and fortitude because this is the wettest place in Madagascar, with the annual rainfall exceeding 5,000mm. The driest months tend to be November and December.

Maroantsetra
Nestled at the far end of the Bay of Antongil, Maroantsetra is Madagascar at its most authentic. Well away from the usual tourist circuits, it is a prosperous, friendly little town, with enough comfortable hotels to make a visit a pleasure for both packaged and independent travellers.

Getting there and away
By air
Most people fly. Consequently flights tend to be booked well in advance. At present flights go on Mondays, Tuesdays, Thursdays, Fridays and Saturdays, but check latest schedules/availability with Air Mad (www.airmadagascar.mg). The 2004 price was €108 high season, €98 low season. The airport is 8km from town.

By land and sea
You can come on foot (and occasional vehicle) from Mananara or hike to/from Antalaha (see page 324). The cargo boat from Ile Sainte Marie no longer serves Maroantsetra but there are occasional vessels from Masoala.

MASOALA COMES TO ZURICH
Janet Mears

A unique ecosystem project has recently come to fruition at Zoo Zurich in Switzerland and is well worth a visit. With input from the Wildlife Conservation Society, Parcs Nationaux Madagascar (ANGAP) and Parc National Masoala, Zoo Zurich is now home to the Masoala biome, some 11,000m^2 of Madagascar rainforest. The brainchild of Dr Alex Rübel, Director of Zoo Zurich, the idea was first conceived in 1992. The Masoala biome gives an impressive snapshot of the Madagascan rainforest and has really captured the natural relationships between the tropical plant and animal worlds under artificial conditions.

There are approximately 100 different plant and tree species in the biome, with 55% of the trees being endemic to Madagascar. About 20% of the 17,000 trees, shrubs and plants in the exhibit were brought in directly from a specially established nursery in Madagascar while others were located in various botanical gardens around the world. With a temperature of 26°C and 80% humidity, there are plants in flower year round.

About 30 species of Malagasy animals, reptiles and birds live in the biome, including a superb group of Aldabran giant tortoises, a species now extinct on Madagascar. As in the real rainforest, you need to use your ears and eyes as you wander between lush green-fringed pathways with the occasional glint of water from the streams running through to lakes. A rustling overhead gives notice that flying foxes are on the move. Then the tiniest of movements on a traveller's palm shows up a large day gecko, slowly making his way along a frond, which takes your eye to a chameleon sitting silently and stationary a few feet away. And, suddenly, a cacophony of noise from deep in the forest disturbs the whispering conversation of the viewing public as four red-ruffed lemurs chase each other out onto the branches above the path. Round bright eyes staring out of dark faces, they look at us, realize we are not a threat, and then run up and down the trees, onto a fallen branch before disappearing back into the forest. Magical.

The Masoala biome has created considerable interest both in Switzerland and further afield. As well as teaching people about Madagascar, the zoo is actively encouraging the public to make donations towards the management of Masoala National Park. They use the maxim 'In Madagascar, an area of rainforest as large as the entire Masoala Hall of Zoo Zurich is destroyed every five minutes. This is not inevitable. With your help, the destruction of the rainforest can be stopped.'

Zoo Zurich is open every day of the year and is a pleasant 15 minute tram ride (no.6) from the Hauptbahnhof. Further details can be found on its website, www.zoo.ch, and at www.masoala.ch, where you can also join the Friends of Masoala.

Where to stay
Relais du Masoala Tel: 22 349 93 (Tana); email: relais@simicro.mg. 15 spacious, palm-thatched bungalows set in 7ha of gardens and coconut groves overlooking the Bay of Antongil. A super place, American owned and very comfortable. There is a swimming pool and the food, including picnic lunches, is excellent. The Relais runs tours to Nosy Mangabe (with optional camping overnight), birdwatching in the Masoala Peninsula, pirogue excursions upriver, whale-watching, and many other trips. The guide Julien

(brother of Maurice and Patrice of Périnet) is a fount of knowledge and takes guests on night walks and other excursions here. Price 300,000Fmg full board.

Motel Coco Beach Tel: 57 720 06. 10 bungalows on the outskirts of town. En suite with cold water 95,000Fmg, shower but no WC 60,000Fmg. Meals in the spacious dining-room are of variable quality. The former owner, Patrice, died in 2000 but his wife, 'Madame Patrice', continues to run the place. One attraction of Coco Beach are the striped tenrecs running about in the garden at night. For excursions contact a man who calls himself 'Rakoto Vazaha'. He has a small company called **Maroa Tour** which offers all sorts of excursions including treks and river trips. Recommended as being helpful and efficient.

Chez Charlotte Opposite Coco Beach, Basic huts ('I never did find the loo') for 25,000–30,000Fmg. Good restaurant.

Hotel Vatsy 8 bungalows for 50,000Fmg and 4 older rooms (noisy and very basic) for 30,000Fmg. Small restaurant.

Hotel du Centre Tel: 57 721 31; email: tsimanova@yahoo.fr. Across from the market offering inexpensive rooms and bungalows. This seemed a very nice place when I checked it out, but a reader was given a room that was dirty with poor plumbing (but possibly not intended for *vazaha*). Best to check your room before deciding to stay here. Rooms 40,000Fmg, meals 15,000Fmg, breakfast 12,500Fmg.

Hotel Maroa Nice quiet bungalows with mosquito nets and en-suite bathroom. 60,000Fmg. Restaurant, but the food was indifferent when I ate there and the service very slow.

Eating and making merry
Restaurant La Pagode Opposite the market. Good food but open only in the evenings.
Rive Droite Open-air restaurant to the right as you come into town from the Coco Beach. 'Good food, but flies can be a nuisance.'

'There's a brilliant disco called the Calypso. Very friendly. Should be 2,500Fmg entrance but vazahas get charged 5,000Fmg. Great atmosphere. The people still do a couple of the traditional dances as well as jive.' (Katie Bloxam)

Excursions
Getting organised
3M Loisirs, on the main street in Maroantsetra, is owned and run by Christian Calvet. This one-stop outfitters will provide everything you need for an expedition: tents, sleeping bags, quad bikes, snorkelling gear – and the excellent English-speaking guide, Emile. Such comprehensive service does not come cheap – one night on Nosy Mangabe for two people cost 450,000Fmg in 2003, but the quality is assured.
 Explorer Madagascar – Bureau des Guides. The centre for organising trips to Masoala and Nosy Mangabe.

Andranofotsy and Navana
It is worth taking a pirogue trip up the Andranofotsy River to the village of the same name. The vegetation and riverlife viewed on the way are fascinating, and the relatively unspoilt village is delightful. This excursion can be arranged through the Relais du Masoala, or independently.

Equally worthwhile is a visit to Navana. Follow the coast east along a beach backed by thickets, through waterways clogged with flowering water-hyacinth and past plenty of forest. You need to cross a lot of water on a pirogue, a regular local service. It takes an hour through little canals and costs very little.

Nosy Mangabe
In fine weather the island of Nosy Mangabe is superb. It has beautiful sandy coves, marvellous trees with huge buttress roots and also strangler figs. And it's bursting with wildlife including, of course, its famous aye-ayes which were released here in the 1960s to prevent what was then thought to be their imminent extinction. If aye-ayes are what you're after, there's little point in coming here just for the day (they are nocturnal) but there is plenty to see on a day visit, including the weird and wonderful leaf-tailed gecko, *Uroplatus fimbriatus*, green-backed mantella frogs, white-fronted brown lemurs and perhaps the black-and-white ruffed lemurs. Leo Barasi spent six days on the island: 'It cost us 175,000Fmg to get to Nosy Mangabe and I don't regret on any of it. OK we

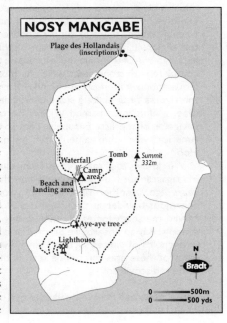

COUNT BENYOWSKI AND OTHER EARLY VISITORS TO MASOALA

Matthew Hatchwell

One of the most fascinating episodes in the history of the European presence in the Masoala region is the extraordinary story of Count Auguste de Benyowski, who established a French colony named Louisbourg on the site of modern-day Maroantsetra in 1774.

A Hungarian aristocrat by birth, Benyowski first arrived in Madagascar in 1772 at the culmination of a series of adventures that had taken him all the way across Russia to the Kamchatka Peninsula, down the Pacific coast of mainland Asia in a commandeered battleship, and finally across the Indian Ocean. Following a brief reconnoitre, Benyowski travelled on to France where he persuaded Louis XV to fund the creation of a new French colony at Maroantsetra which, he argued, could serve later as the basis for claiming Madagascar for France. Like every other early attempt to establish a permanent European settlement in Madagascar, the enterprise was a failure. Benyowski returned to France in 1776, where he met the famous American scientist and diplomat Benjamin Franklin, who inspired him to sail to the New World where he played a minor role in the American War of Independence against the British. Ten years later, he returned to Madagascar with American backing and was killed by French troops after establishing a trading station near Cap Est across the Masoala Peninsula from Maroantsetra.

All traces of Benyowski's original colony have been lost, but at least one 19th century traveller observed finding a stone engraved with the names of some of Benyowski's fellow colonists at a second settlement which they established inland to escape the ravages of malaria. On Nosy Mangabe, many traces remain of European occupation in the 17th and 18th centuries, when first the Dutch and later the French established slave-trading stations there to supply labourers for their colonies elsewhere in the region. It is unknown which of these date from Benyowski's day, although one of the main tourist trails on the island re-traces an earlier path complete with stone steps which he must have used when he established a quarantine station on the island. Many European sailors did not survive the rigours of their long sea journeys and are buried on Nosy Mangabe. One, a Dutchman named Willem Cornelisz Schouten, is famous as the navigator of the first European fleet to round the southern tip of South America, which he named after his native village in the Netherlands, Hoorn.

We know too that Nosy Mangabe was one of the first sites in Madagascar settled by humans when they first arrived some 1500-1700 years ago. Another historical site worth visiting on the island is an enormous boulder at the Plage des Hollandais where Dutch sailors left carved messages for each other during the 1600s. A few decades later, Antongil Bay and nearby Ile Sainte Marie became infamous to sailors as the strongholds of pirates such as Henry Avery and James Plantain. Traces of many of these eras can still be seen in the Masoala region. Others remain to be rediscovered!

Text summarized from Masoala: the Eye of the Forest *(see page 456).*

didn't manage to see any aye-aye, but the rest of the wildlife and the scenery more than made up for it. I loved the leaf-tailed geckos (*uroplatus*), particularly at night when they took on a completely new appearance. Lots of chameleons, including *brookesia*, some very nice boas and several other attractive snakes. The black-and-white ruffed lemurs could be heard from all points of the island and sounded like dying pigs. Best of all, though, were the dolphins and sea turtles that we saw swimming around the bay on our last day – fantastic!'

There is no accommodation on the island – you must camp in the thatched shelters.

Getting there and away
To visit the island you must have a permit. They are available from the Masoala park headquarters next to the Bureau des Guides opposite the market in Maroantsetra, where you can also arrange a boat and a guide (mandatory). The boat trip from Maroantsetra takes 30 minutes.

Exploring the island
Not everyone sees aye-ayes; the best time to view them is between June and September, when they come right down to the Hintsia trees by the shore to feed (but those are also the wettest months). But as described above, there is a wealth of other creatures, and between July and September you have a good chance of seeing humpbacked whales in the bay. The trails are well made and walking, though strenuous, is not difficult.

To complete your experience of Nosy Mangabe climb the hill to the lighthouse. En route you will have the chance to see all sorts of wildlife as well as other sights, sounds and smells. It's a magical island. In rain, though, the paths are slippery and it's pretty unpleasant. And it rains often.

As you leave Nosy Mangabe, ask your boatman to take you to see the old (17th-century) Dutch inscriptions carved on rocks at the Plage des Hollandais. Fascinating! And there is also a recent shipwreck.

The Masoala Peninsula
The peninsula (pronounced 'Mashwahl') is one of the largest and most diverse areas of virgin rainforest in Madagascar, and probably harbours the greatest number of unclassified species. The peninsula's importance was recognised by the French back in 1927 when they created a small reserve there, but independent Madagascar was swift to remove the protection in 1964. However, 230,000ha has now been set aside as a national park.

Visitors should be warned that logging and clearance for agriculture still persists outside the national park and maps of the peninsula tend to be deceptively green. That said, there are still large expanses of virgin forest along with stunning beaches of golden sand dotted with eroded rocks. Some parts of the peninsula, seen on a sunny day, can arguably be described as the most beautiful in Madagascar.

Zoo Zurich has established a link with Masoala (see box on page 317) and are financing some development projects to encourage conservation of the peninsula.

How to visit Masoala National Park
Masoala can be reached only by boat, which takes 3–4 hours from Maroantsetra. For independent travellers, finding a safe but affordable boat is the main difficulty. In 2003 prices ranged from 300,000Fmg to 3,000,000Fmg (per boat) from the Bureau des Guides in Maroantsetra. Alternatively, Rakoto Vazaha at the Coco Beach Hotel may be able to help out.

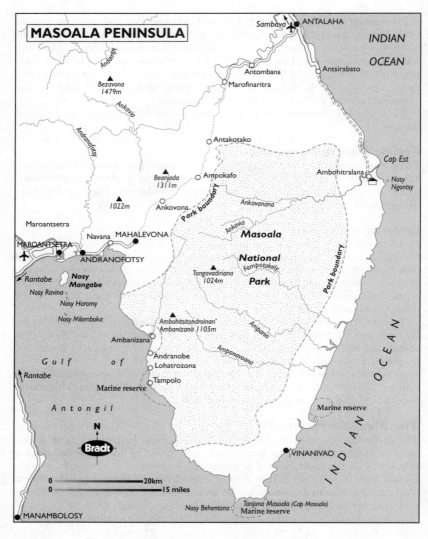

If you can afford an organised tour, take one of the packages offered by the most experienced operator in the region, the hotel Relais du Masoala. It won't be cheap, but you can be assured of the quality of the boat, the camping equipment, and the site chosen for your stay.

Sadly, the best place for visiting the forest changes year by year as pristine forest gives way to cultivation. Although it is depressing to see these changes, it is also encouraging to see the efforts of various conservation agencies to slow the degradation. The preferred place is **Andranobe**, the centre for the research organisation, the Peregrine Fund, and **Lohatrozona**, about 5km to the south. There is a trail from Andranobe or you can reach it in 20 minutes by canoe. The forest a short walk behind the beach is wonderful – very good for red-ruffed lemur, helmet vanga and ground-rollers. Even Bernier's vangas can be seen. Nocturnal

Above Giraffe-necked weevil (*Trachelophorus giraffa*), Ranomafana (NG)
Below right Mating leaf-tailed geckos (*Uroplatus fimbriatus*), Nosy Mangabe (HB)
Below Octopus trees (*Didieracae trolli*) in the dry season, southern Madagascar (HB)

Above Helmet vanga (*Euryceros prevostii*) feeding chicks, Marojejy National Park (NG)

Right Orchids (*Angraecum* sp), Marojejy National Park (NG)

Below Masoala National Park (NG)

walks are also rewarding. **Tampolo** (see below) is a new centre – spectacularly beautiful with simple lodging. New trails have been established around Lohatrozona and Tampolo. Also at Cap Est (Andranoanala).

Masoala lodges
While camping is still popular and gives instant access to the best rainforest, there are a couple of simple lodges half way down the western coast of the peninsula.

Tampolo Lodge Owned by Italian Giuseppe La Marca, this is a collection of rustic huts at Tampolo, one of the most beautiful beaches in Madagascar and adjacent to one of the three Masoala marine parks. 20,000–80,000Fmg; book through Relais du Masoala. The orange-gold sand is backed by the dark green of the rainforest; fresh water runs down from the hillsides into the sea, and comet orchids shine like stars against the dark eroded rocks. The accommodation is very basic (and sanitation almost non-existent) but with surroundings like this, who cares?

Arollodge Completed in July 2003 and run by the energetic Olivier Fournajoux. Palm-thatched bungalows accommodating up to 16 people. Separate toilet and (cold) shower. The huts are set back from the beach so the setting is not quite as nice as Tampolo, but the accommodation is more comfortable. 75,000Fmg (€14) double. Arollodge has an office in Maroantsetra and a website: http://arollodge.free.fr.

Kayak Masoala
This is an eco-tourism company providing a fully inclusive marine and forest experience. From October to January they have set departure dates for the 'Masoala Forest and Sea Expedition' comprising three nights camping on Nosy Behento, an uninhabited island off the tip of the peninsula in the Cap Masoala marine park, and four nights in the rainforest on the Antalavia River near Tampolo marine park. Shorter tours are based at the Antalavia camp only.

What makes these tours really special is that sea-kayaks are used to explore the coastal waters, mangroves, coral reefs and rivers. Additional activities are snorkelling and guided forest walks. Between July and September humpback whales may be seen in the bay.

The price is US$150 per person (sharing) per night. Maroantsetra accommodation is at Coco Beach hotel. Contact via email (kayakmasoala@dts.mg) or through their Swiss agent Zingg Travel (zet@bluewin.ch).

Cap Est
The most easterly point of Madagascar, Cap Est is gradually opening up to adventurous travellers, but has been badly damaged by three cyclones since 2000

and is only slowly recovering. Cap Est can be accessed via boat and on foot from Maroantsetra or, more easily, from Antalaha. Depending on the state of the road, it takes about three hours to reach the town nearest to the cape, **Ambodirafia**, by taxi-brousse. There are two river crossings by ferry. The **Hotel du Voyageur** is a straightforward set up of 16 huts with beds, mosquito nets and buckets for washing. No electricity. (20,000Fmg)

A former upmarket hotel at Cap Est, **La Résidence du Cap**, now run by a Frenchman named Sam, was almost totally destroyed by the cyclones but is still open for business. The littoral forest inland from Cap Est, although severely damaged too by the recent storms, is part of Masoala National Park and an excellent place to see the carnivorous Masoala pitcher plant. Cap Est is also the closest access point on the coast to the impressive Bevontsira Waterfall, 2–3 days' walk inland towards Maroantsetra. Avoid hiking during periods of high rainfall because river crossings may become a problem.

From Maroantsetra to Antalaha the adventurous way
Across the neck of the peninsula
I have heard mixed reports of this five-day hike. The distance is 152km, and in the heat it is very strenuous. Considering that you are mainly passing through secondary forest and cultivated areas, it doesn't attract me as much, say, as hiking the scenically marvellous road from Mananara to Maroantsetra. However, many people want to do it, and will be faced with the choice of going it alone or hiring a guide and porters.

Although it is possible to do it alone, you are advised to find a guide if only to avoid being hassled continuously by locals wanting to guide you. You will need the relevant FTM map, *Antalaha*. If you failed to buy it in Tana there is one in the Motel Coco Beach which you can trace. This is the route:

Day 1 Maroantsetra to Mahalevona, the village beyond Navana, which is described under Excursions. A pleasant 5km walk.

Day 2 Mahalevona to Ankovona. The track climbs into the mountains and there are rivers to cross.

Day 3 Ankovona to Ampokafo. A long trek to Ampokafo which marks the halfway point. Very hilly and very beautiful, with lots of streams and orchids. The village has a small shop.

Day 4 Ampokafo to Analampontsy. Less wild, but still orchids along the way. Most villages en route have shops.

Day 5 Analampontsy to Antalaha. You emerge on to the road at the village of Marofinaritra, about 30km from Antalaha. From here you can get a taxi-brousse to Antalaha.

Via Cap Est
A more scenic (but equally tough) route to Antalaha from Maroantsetra is via Cap Est. You can hire tents and a guide for this trip from 3M Loisirs in Maroantsetra. Alternatively you can do it independently as far as Ampokafo, where you can hire a guide. Loïc Constantin, who told me about this walk, recommends Gervé whom he paid 250,000Fmg. Loïc did the trip in three days, although he recommends a week in order to enjoy the scenery.

From Maroantsetra take a pirogue for 1–2 hours up the River Ankavanana to the village of **Fizoana**. There's a reasonable trail from there to **Ampokafo**, but thereafter the going is tough but the forest increasingly beautiful. A few highlights are the waterfall a half-day's walk from Ampokafo, and Bizono, a further two days' walk, which is an exceptionally lovely village. From the village of **Antanandavahely** it's four hours to the nearest village to Cap Est, **Ambohitralanana**.

Via Masoala

Sebastian Bulmer and Jamie Gibbs did a variation of the Cap Est walk from Antalaha to Maroantsetra in May 2003, following the coast down to the tip of the peninsula. Here is their report:

'Taxi-brousse from Antalaha to **Ambodirafia**, close to Cap Est. Walk from here to the southern tip of Masoala Peninsula. Seven days, including one day off for the Independence Day celebrations. One guide/porter (480,000Fmg) and one porter (420,000Fmg), food and accommodation are extra (rooms are about 10,000–15,000Fmg per night).

'Walking at a gentle pace, staying in villages along the way, empty beaches, mangrove swamps, cleared woodland and a little rainforest towards the end as well as the scars of previous cyclones. Plenty of rivers to ford, either with log "bridges", pirogues or on foot. Independence Day at **Fampotakely** was quite a party, the two *vazahas* creating a serious distraction for the children on their parade! Shortly before arriving at **Sahamalaza** village on day five, we crossed a river with a series of large wooden posts sticking out of the water. After enquiries it was explained that this used to be a bridge capable of carrying vehicles and that up to the 1960s it was possible to drive most of the way down the east coast of the peninsula.

'On entering villages the children tended to run away screaming. It seems their mothers tell them that if they misbehave they will be taken to market and sold to the *vazahas* who will cook and eat them, so two *vazahas* arriving unannounced is a cause for concern! The braver would make a timid reappearance for a game of Grandmother's Footsteps.

'From **Masoala** village there is irregular boat service to **Maroantsetra**, 50,000Fmg per person, slow going and very heavily loaded. Visitors should ensure that they have budgeted for an additional few days whilst awaiting the boat.'

ANTALAHA AND BEYOND
Antalaha

This once prosperous, vanilla-financed town suffered devastating damage from Cyclone Gafilo in March 2004. About 80% of the town is reported to have been destroyed, with 36 dead and 14 missing; 895 people were injured and over 260 thousand made homeless. This should not discourage you from visiting, however. The Malagasy are accustomed to rebuilding following cyclones and need tourism more than ever after a catastrophe of this kind. There are excellent beaches nearby, and this is normally a very pleasant place to spend a day or so.

Getting there and away

The only easy way to get to Antalaha is by plane. The alternatives are the road trip, the trek across the peninsular from Maroantsetra or via Cap Est (see page 324), or perhaps by sea. I have heard that there is a regular boat called the *Masoala* which runs between Toamasina and Antalaha. It costs 250,000Fmg.

Where to stay/eat

Hotel Nanie Pleasant (basic) bungalows, right next to the sea opposite the pier. Next door to a snack-bar serving good pizza. 50,000Fmg.

VANILLA IN MADAGASCAR
Clare and Johan Hermans

Vanilla is the major foreign currency earner for Madagascar, which together with Réunion and the Comoros grows 80% of the world's crop. Its cultivation in Madagascar is centred along the eastern coastal region, the main production centres being Andapa, Antalaha and Sambava.

The climbing plants are normally grown supported on 1.5m high moisture-retaining trunks and under ideal conditions take three years to mature. When the plants bloom, during the drier months, the vines are checked on alternate days for open flowers to hand-pollinate. The pod then takes nine months to develop; each 15–20cm pod will contain tens of thousands of tiny seeds.

The pods are taken to a vanilla processing plant to begin the long process of preparing them for the commercial market. First they are plunged into a cauldron of hot water (70°C) for two minutes, and are then kept hot for two days. During this time the pods change colour from green to chestnut brown. At this stage they are exposed to the sun (mornings only to avoid over-cooking) for three to four weeks.

After maturing, the pods are sorted by size; the workers sit in front of a large rack with 'pigeonholes' for the different lengths. The bundles of sorted pods, approximately 30 to a bunch, are tied with raffia. They are checked for quality by sniffing and bending before being packed into wooden crates with 90% of the product going to the USA for use in the ice-cream industry.

The vanilla used in cultivation in Madagascar is *Vanilla planifolia* which originates from Mexico. It was brought to Madagascar by the French once the secret of hand pollination had been discovered – the flower has no natural pollinator in its foreign home. The culinary and pharmaceutical use of vanilla dates back to pre-Aztec times when it was used as a drink or as an ingredient of a lotion against fatigue for those holding public office. Similarly a native Malagasy vanilla stem can be found for sale in the market in Tana as a male invigorator.

Four different species of vanilla orchid occur naturally in Madagascar, most of them totally leafless. One species can be seen on the roadside between Sambava and Antahala resembling lengths of red-green tubing festooned over the scrub, another is to be found in the spiny forest near Berenty in the south. Most of the native species contain sap that burns the skin and their fruits contain too little vanillin to make cultivation economic.

Uses for vanilla pods

Although conventionally used for cooking, vanilla is also an insect repellent or the wonderful-smelling pods can be put in drawers instead of the traditional pomander to scent clothing or linen.

When cooking with vanilla you can reuse the pods for as long as you remember to retrieve them – wash and dry them after each use. Vanilla does wonders to tea or coffee (just add a pod to the teapot or coffee filter, or grind a dried pod with the coffee beans) and can be boiled with milk to make a yummy hot drink (add a dash of brandy!) or custard. If you take sugar in tea or coffee put some beans in your sugar tin and the flavour will be absorbed. Vanilla adds a subtle flavour to chicken or duck, rice or… whatever you fancy.

Hotel Florida Tel: 88 813 30. On the main street. The best hotel, with air conditioning and hot water. 90,000–125,000Fmg per room, depending on hot or cold water, and with or without air-conditioning.
Hotel du Centre Tel: 88 811 67. In the centre of town, European run, comfortable with good meals.
Hotel Le Cocotier Tel: 88 811 77. Mid price with a good restaurant.
Hotel Ocean Momo The best food in Antalaha. 'For a slap-up feed if you want to push the boat out in luxurious surroundings.'
Vitasoa A budget hotel with a restaurant that serves good, low-cost food.

Continuing north
The road from Antalaha to Sambava and then to Iharana (Vohemar) was in good condition in 2003 with no ferry crossings. It will no doubt have been damaged by the cyclone, however.

SAMBAVA
The centre of the vanilla- and coconut-growing region, and an important area for cloves and coffee production, Sambava merits a stay of a few days. The town is charming, the people are friendly and easy-going, and there is plenty to see and do.

Telephone code The area code for Sambava is 88.

Getting there and away
Sambava has air connections with Tana, Toamasina and Antsiranana (for current schedule see www.airmadagascar.mg) and is accessible by good road from Iharana (Vohemar), taking approximately two hours. The airport is not far from town: you can even walk it if you are a backpacker. Be warned, however, that Sambava is a sprawling town with long distances between most places. The taxi-brousse station is on the northern outskirts, 30 minutes from the centre (shops, post office) and beach hotels are 10–15 minutes beyond that.

Warning Sambava was badly hit by Cyclone Gafilo. Many of the hotels listed below will have been damaged or perhaps destroyed. Contact Sambava Voyages if you need to book one of them in advance.

Where to stay/eat
Category A
Hotel Carrefour BP53; tel: 88 920 60. Situated near the beach, with all mod cons (hot water, air conditioning) although reportedly becoming run-down in 2003. Good food. 130,000Fmg.
Hotel Orchidea Beach Tel: 88 934 38
Le Club Plage Tel: 88 920 64. A posh hotel (two-person bungalows) overlooking the sea, with a swimming pool. From €14 to €18. Also **Hotel Le Club** with conventional rooms. Hotel Le Club offers a choice of several tours, including trekking; they provide transfers to and from the airport, 4WD vehicles with driver, and mountain bikes.
Las Palmas BP28; tel: 88 920 10. Nicely situated by the beach, well run with conscientious and friendly staff. Spacious, air-conditioned bungalows for €28 (double), €25 (single). Hot water but poor water pressure. Good food. Air-conditioned rooms and bungalows. The hotel offers a variety of excursions, such as the Bemarivo River.

Category B
Hotel Esmeralda This is the backpackers' favourite Sambava hotel, pleasantly located with rooms and bungalows overlooking the ocean. Cold water only; en-suite WC.

Hotel Cantonnais A hotel rather than beach bungalows, but in a quiet part of town and most rooms have balconies. There are 5 rooms with toilets; hot water (with good pressure). Good value. The Chinese owner also sells precious stones.

Nouvel Hotel Good value and recommended for its food.

Category C

Chez M Jaoravo 6 rooms on the left side of the cemetery, on the main road. Rooms very hot but clean. Cold water.

Hotel Pacifique Tel: 124. 3 rooms, also bungalows.

Hotel Calypso BP40; tel: 108. An unassuming, reasonably priced hotel in town.

La Romance North of the taxi-brousse station.

All the restaurants at the above hotels serve good meals. Specialist restaurants include **Cantonnais** and **Mandarin** (Chinese) and the **Etoile Rouge** and **Etoile Rouge Annexe**. For do-it-yourself meals head for the *épicerie* to the right of the cemetery. Prices and staff are more user-friendly than in the supermarket.

Things to do
In and around town

Sambava itself is one long main street with parallel dirt roads, so you won't get lost. There is a good market which is known as Bazaar Kely, not because it's small or *kely* (it isn't – and certainly not on Tuesdays, market day) but because there used to be two markets and no-one thought of changing the name when they amalgamated them.

As this is one of the main vanilla-producing areas in Madagascar, a tour of the vanilla factory, Lopat, is interesting and teaches you a lot about the laborious process of preparing one of Madagascar's main exports. Likewise a visit to the coconut plantation (*germoir pépinière*), some 3km south of the airport, is more rewarding than it sounds. You need a permit and a guide so it's easiest to go on an organised tour arranged by one of the hotels.

The highlight for us, however, was a visit to CLUE, the Center for Learning and Understanding English. This lively place was set up by the Peace Corps and welcomes visits from tourists to help the (adult) students practise their spoken English and gain an understanding of a variety of accents. For the visitors it's an excellent chance to learn from the people of the east coast. CLUE is on the main street (you can't miss it) and you should look for Patrice, the Malagasy English teacher. Don't miss this opportunity to do something for cross-cultural understanding. 'A wonderful experience.' (Anne Axel)

North of Sambava is a beautiful beach with safe swimming, and marvellous *Nephila* spiders on their golden webs between the branches of the shady trees.

Excursions further afield

The tour operator Sambava-Voyages (BP28, Sambava 208; tel: +261 20 88 921 10; no email) offers a variety of excursions including Marojejy National Park and the trek from Sambava to Doany. The manageress, Mme Seramila, speaks some English.

River Bemarivo

A pleasant do-it-yourself excursion is up the Bemarivo, though this won't be possible at the end of the dry season – the river is very shallow. Take a taxi-brousse to Nosiarina, on the road north, and look for a pirogue to take you the five-hour journey upriver to Amboahangibe. Anne Axel paid 25,000Fmg for five people plus gear. 'It's a beautiful river trip. The river is wide and there are some small villages that you pass periodically. However, the land by the river has been deforested.'

It is also possible to find a cargo boat to **Amboahangibe**. This is quite a large village with several grocery stores and some houses with rooms. Look for the sign 'Misy Chambres'. These fill up with vanilla-pickers during the harvest. Anne Axel found the last room in town, at the Hotel Fandrosoana. 'It had a captive crocodile in the yard next to the WC.' As an alternative to taking a boat back, it is a pleasant hike along the river, with some interesting above-ground coffins and groves of shady giant bamboos.

CONTINUING NORTH

The road to the next town of importance, Iharana (Vohemar), is excellent and transport is no problem (about two hours). For a description of this pleasant town see *Chapter 14*.

ANDAPA AND AREA

Andapa lies in a fertile and beautiful region, 108km west of Sambava, where much of Madagascar's rice is grown. This is also a major coffee-producing area – to help facilitate export, the EEC provided funding to build an all-weather road in the 1960s. It has been resurfaced subsequently and remains one of the best roads in Madagascar. The journey to Andapa is beautiful, with the jagged peaks of the Marojejy Massif to the right, and bamboo and palm-thatch villages by the roadside. The journey takes about three hours by taxi-brousse.

Where to stay

Hotel Vatasoa (pronounced 'Vats') BP46; Andapa 205; tel: 88 07 078. Comfortable (but sometimes noisy) rooms with hot water for 100,000Fmg, breakfast 17,500Fmg. The food is amazing (but a set meal and not good for vegetarians) and the hotel has all sorts of pluses. There is a large detailed map on the wall of the lounge which shows footpaths and tracks in the area (actually, a reproduction of the FTM 1:100,000 which can be purchased in Tana). For hikers this is invaluable for planning (see *Excursions*). The Chinese owner, Mr Tam Hyok, is 'Mr Andapa'. This dynamic man likes to take a personal interest in his guests and their plans, and will accompany those whom he feels will most benefit from his attentions. He will arrange transfers from Sambava for 500,000Fmg.

Hotel Beanana BP02 No information except that it exists!

Hotel du Centre Basic clean rooms, but a 'less than pleasing WC. Wear sturdy shoes; not for the weak of heart or poor of bowels.' No shower, but acceptable overall.

Where to eat

Mini-Restaurant On the opposite side of the street to the Vatasoa, about a block down the road. Popular with locals and WWF employees.

Restaurant au Bon Plaisir One block away from the taxi-brousse station, on the same street as Hotel du Centre.

Excursions

This is a wonderful area for wandering. At every step you see something interesting from the people or wildlife perspective (in the latter category butterflies, snakes and chameleons) and the scenery is consistently beautiful.

Mr Tam Hyok will have suggestions for more organised sightseeing, including the local cemetery where the dead are interred in coffins above the ground or in the trees.

Hiking

By using the map in the Hotel Vatasoa you can plan a variety of day hikes. Almost any dirt road through villages would bring you the pleasures we experienced on our hike a few years ago. Here are some of the highlights: chameleons in the bushes, coffee laid out to dry on the ground, an entire school of shrieking kids surging up the hill towards us, a village elder matching his stride with ours in order to converse in French, little girls fishing with basket-nets in the irrigation channels, homemade musical instruments, smiles, laughter and stares. It helped that we had our local guide with us who could interpret the village activities. In one place we experienced the power of Malagasy oratory (*kabary*) at full throttle. The theme was communal work. The 20 or so men of the village listened respectfully as the *Président du Fokontany* exhorted them to contribute their labour towards the building of a new fence. Some young men demurred: they would rather pay the let-out fee of 2,500Fmg. The Président discussed the issue with them, explaining the importance of the community working together. By the end of the discussion the young men had started stripping the leaves of a raffia palm to bind up the bamboo poles and begin fence-making.

If you explore off the beaten path, just remember the enormous power you have to change things irreversibly. Your gift or payment will certainly be received with delight and will make you feel warm inside; but will it benefit the village in the long run?

PROTECTED AREAS

In the last decade the area around Andapa has opened two of its most exciting reserves to visitors: Marojejy National Park and Anjanaharibe-Sud Special Reserve. Initially administered by the WWF, these are now under ANGAP control. WWF are very keen to develop ecotourism in this still infrequently visited part of the country, and have made great strides to improve the trails and accommodation in Marojejy. These are some of the most remote and pristine rainforests remaining on the island – and visitors need to be fit and willing to put up with a degree of discomfort.

Anjanaharibe-Sud Reserve

The Anjanaharibe-Sud Special Reserve/Befingotra Forest region, some 20km southwest of Andapa, is an alternative to the magnificent but challenging national park of Marojejy. Anjanaharibe-Sud can be equally rewarding for naturalists with sufficient time to seek out the shy wildlife. This is the most northerly range of the indri which here occurs in a very dark form – almost black. The silky sifaka is also found here, but you are more likely to see the troops of white-fronted brown lemurs. Birders will be on the lookout for four species of ground-roller.

Even without seeing any mammals it is a most rewarding visit, with an easy-to-follow (though rugged) trail through primary forest to some hot springs. The reserve is also a vital element in the prosperity of the area. The Lokoho River, which rises in Anjanaharibe-Sud, is the only source of water for the largest irrigated rice producer in the country.

Befingotra and Andasibe

If you are making your own way to the reserve you will spend some time in these two gateway towns looking for ongoing transport. Befingotra has a couple of *épiceries* with basic supplies (rice, beans etc) and there is a small restaurant. Andasibe is the larger town with several épiceries and hotelys offering a reasonable range of food.

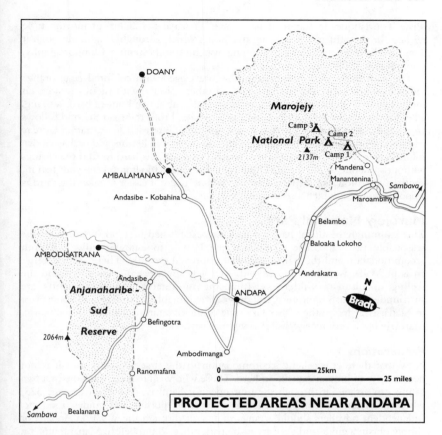

DOANY

Marojejy

National Park

Camp 3
Camp 2
Camp 1
2137m

Mandena
Manantenina
Sambava
AMBALAMANASY
Maroambihy
Andasibe - Kobahina

Belambo

Baloaka Lokoho

AMBODISATRANA
Andrakatra

Andasibe
Anjanaharibe -
ANDAPA

Sud
Befingotra

2064m
Reserve
Ambodimanga

Ranomafana
0 ═══════════ 25km
0 ═══════════════ 25 miles

Sambava   Bealanana

PROTECTED AREAS NEAR ANDAPA

Visiting the reserve

A permit to visit the reserve can be obtained from the Hotel Vatasoa. Mr Tam Hyok can arrange a day visit to Anjanaharibe-Sud, or you can look for another private vehicle for hire in Andapa but it is possible and rewarding to visit it on your own. Camping is permitted and allows you to get the most out of your stay. Anne Axel, who made four lengthy visits to the reserve in 1998, recommends two tough but inexpensive ways of getting there: 'One is to take a taxi-brousse to Andasibe, the last town on the decent road, from where it's a steep two-to-three-hour hike to Befingotra, then another two to three hours to the trailhead; or from Andapa or Andasibe wait for a truck heading for Bealanana and have them drop you off at the reserve.' A guide is not mandatory, but these days the trailhead is very hard to find, so you will probably need to be shown where to enter the forest, and where to find water near the campsite.

If you merely need to be shown the way, and get help carrying gear, look for a guide and/or porters in Andasibe or Befingotra. Be warned, however, that they are unlikely to speak French. Serious naturalists should seek out Gaston Rabemanana, who works for the WWF and is being trained by them as a tourist guide. The Hotel Vatasoa should know where to find him. Gaston will also arrange for transport to the trailhead.

When I was there in 1997 the trailhead was indicated with a nice WWF board:

'Piste Touristique de Ranomafana Source Thermal à 4,260m' giving the time needed for the return trip as being five hours which is roughly right, although it does not allow much time for examining, watching and listening. Or photography. I don't know if the sign is still there.

The path is clearly marked – the trees are tagged with coloured tape: orange indicates the route to the hot springs, and other colours, with metres written on them, show the distance to the campsite – it takes about an hour of brisk walking. The hot springs are an hour beyond the campsite. From the road the trail follows an up-and-down route, slippery at times, but full of interest. On our rather fast day trip we saw no mammals, but campers should see brown lemurs and perhaps indri. John Kupiec reports: 'When you get to the river area it is hard to find the springs without someone to show you. There are three: one is too hot to keep your feet in; another is shallow but it meets a stream which makes it easier to take; the third is a pool to swim in which also merged with stream water.'

Marojejy National Park

This stunningly beautiful national park was established in 1998. You need to be reasonably fit – and able to tolerate the heat – to enjoy it fully, but both accommodation and the trails have been improved recently. There are few other areas in Madagascar to compare with Marojejy for awesome splendour and the feeling of ultimate wilderness. Imposing mountains and craggy cliffs are surrounded by lush rainforests full of wildlife. Notably, Marojejy is the best place in Madagascar to see the silky sifaka, one of the five rarest primates in the world. Marojejy has a very nice website: www.marojejy.com.

Preparations

Now that there is excellent accommodation in the first two campsites it is not necessary to mount an expedition here. Those who wish to go beyond the first two camps can arrange it through the tour operator Sambava-Voyages (see page 328) who will organise a complete package with tents, porters and guides, food etc. Independent travellers should arrange their visit through the WWF in Andapa or simply obtain a guide and permits at the park office, 200m before Manantenina on the left side of the road coming from Sambava. You will need to bring food from Sambava or Andapa. In Manantenina, WWF representatives Will Frank or Clairmont can assist will preparations, while WWF guide Desiré is knowledgeable and entertaining.

There are three campsites at different altitudes, each with its own distinctive flora and fauna. Accommodation at Camp 1 (Camp Mantella) and Camp 2 (Camp Marojejia) now includes comfortable rustic chalets with soft mattresses, pillows and blankets plus covered dining areas with new picnic tables. There is also a flushing loo and 'field shower' at each camp. Camp Marojejia has a stunning covered shelter and dining area overlooking the forest and peaks.

In the national park

The path from Manantenina to the park entrance is mainly level with occasional modest climbs and near the start there is a river to wade through twice (shallow in the dry season). The path takes you through rice paddies and cultivated areas where there is little shade from the sun (or rain). After 2.7km you arrive at the village of Mandena, then it's a further 2.9km to the park entrance where there is a good map showing the trails and distances. Once in the park proper the trail takes you 4.3km through rainforest to the first camp, Camp Mantella. This first stretch from road to camp will take about four to five hours.

Camp Mantella, at 425m, is situated in the heart of superb lowland rainforest. There are six mosquito-proof chalets here, each with three beds. In this area you stand a good chance of seeing helmet vanga (*Euryceros prevostii*) and various ground-rollers. You may also see white-fronted brown lemurs. Camp Marojejia (750m) is a further hour's walk along a well-engineered trail, and lies at the transition between lowland and mid-altitude rainforest. It sits opposite an amazing outcrop of rock cloaked in rainforest. This is one of the most spectacular views you could ever imagine waking up to. The areas above Camp Marojejia are best for observing the silky sifaka (*Propithecus diadema candidus*) which have now been habituated, although it can still take time and luck to track them down.

Above Camp Marojejia the trail becomes very steep and continues right through all the altitudinal zones to the peak of the Marojejy Massif at 2137m. Camp 3 (1380m) is nothing more than a handful of cleared tent pitches on a ridge top. The forest here is more stunted because of the altitude, but is still good for silky sifaka, and birds such as rufous-headed ground roller and yellow-bellied sunbird asity. The frogs in the nearby stream are diverse and abundant. A viewing platform has been built on the ridge shortly before Camp 3 – the vista is breathtaking.

The camp is used to facilitate treks to Marojejy peak – a four- to five-hour climb. 'It's one of the most spectacular walks I've ever done – fantastic views over rainforest-clad ridges, amazing mountains and above the tree line bizarre moorland-type habitat. There are dwarf palms (30cm high) with little chameleons in them. The view from the top is awesome and the feeling of space and wilderness is the greatest I've experienced. But it's very tough and only for those who are extremely fit.' (NG)

Each year there continues to be considerable improvements in the quality of trails and accommodation. Though Marojejy remains a somewhat challenging park, it is far more hospitable than in the recent past. Soon it may even be possible to drive to the park entrance and forgo the initial two-hour walk to the park boundary.

Thanks to Nick Garbutt for the original report and updates, and the additional information from Erik Patel of Cornell University, who spent two years here studying silky sifakas.

The breast-leaper... It is a small animal which attaches itself to the bark of trees and being of a greenish hue is not easily perceived; there it remains with its throat open to receive the flies, spiders and other insects that approach it, which it devours. This animal is described as having attached to the back, tail, legs, neck and the extremity of the chin, little paws or hooks like those at the end of a bat's wing with which it adheres to whatever it attaches itself in such a manner as if it were really glued. If a native happens to approach the tree where it hangs, it instantly leaps upon his naked breast, and sticks so firmly that in order to remove it, they are obliged, with a razor, to cut away the skin also.
Samuel Copland, *History of the Island of Madagascar,* 1822

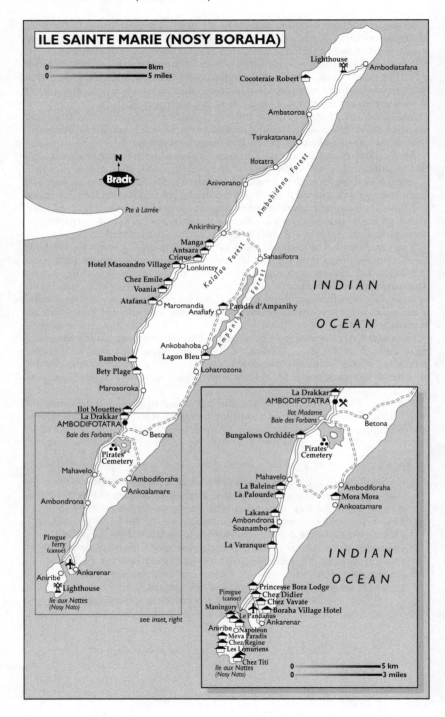

ILE SAINTE MARIE (NOSY BORAHA)

0 ——— 8km
0 ——— 5 miles

Lighthouse
Ambodiatafana
Cocoteraie Robert

Ambatoroa

Tsirakatanana

Ifotatra

Ambohidena Forest

Anivorano

Pte à Larrée

Ankirihiry

Manga
Antsara
Crique
Hotel Masoandro Village
Lonkintsy
Sahasifotra

Kalalao Forest

Chez Emile
Voania

Atafana
Maromandia
Anafiafy
Paradis d'Ampanihy

Ampanihy Forest

Ankobahoba
Lagon Bleu
Lohatrozona

Bambou
Bety Plage

Marosoroka

INDIAN

OCEAN

Ilot Mouettes
La Drakkar
AMBODIFOTATRA
Baie des Forbans
Betona

Pirates
Cemetery

Mahavelo
Ambodiforaha
Ankoalamare

Ambondrona

Pirogue
ferry
(canoe)

Aniribe
Ankarenar

Lighthouse
Ile aux Nattes
(Nosy Nato)

see inset, right

La Drakkar
AMBODIFOTATRA
Ilot Madame
Baie des Forbans
Betona

Bungalows Orchidée
Pirates
Cemetery

Mahavelo
La Baleine
La Palourde
Ambodiforaha
Mora Mora
Ankoatamare

Lakana
Ambondrona
Soanambo

La Varanque

INDIAN

OCEAN

Princesse Bora Lodge
Chez Didier
Chez Vavate
Boraha Village Hotel
Pirogue
(canoe)
Maningory
Le Pandanus
Ankarenar
Aniribe
Napoleon
Meva Paradis
Chez Regine
Les Lemuriens
Chez Titi
Ile aux Nattes
(Nosy Nato)

0 ——— 5 km
0 ——— 3 miles

Ile Sainte Marie
(Nosy Boraha)

Ile Sainte Marie is 50km long and 7km at its widest point. The only real town is Ambodifotatra (pronounced 'Amboodifoot<u>a</u>rtr'). Other small villages comprise bamboo and palm huts. The island is almost universally known as Sainte Marie – few people use its Malagasy name, Nosy Boraha. Here is a cliché of a tropical island with endless deserted beaches overhung by coconut palms, bays protected from sharks by coral reefs, hills covered with luxuriant vegetation, and a relative absence of unsightly tourist development. Most travellers love it: 'As soon as we saw the island from the air, we were ready to ditch our travel plans and spend the rest of our trip nestled in paradise. Everything about the island is intoxicating: the smell of cloves drying in the sun, the taste of coco rum and the warmth of the sea.'

Sainte Marie unfortunately – or perhaps fortunately, given the dangers of overdevelopment – has a far less settled weather pattern than its island rival, Nosy Be. Cyclones strike regularly and you can expect several days of rain and wind all year round, but interspersed with calm sunny weather. The best months for a visit seem to be June and mid-August to December, although a reader tells me she twice had perfect weather in January, and another reports that in July most days were sunny and hot, but with frequent light rain overnight or in the morning, and fairly strong winds from the south.

For an all-inclusive package to Sainte Marie, with various options for excursions and transport by boat from Soanierana-Ivongo, contact Sainte-Marie Loisirs, BP3650, Isoraka, Antananarivo; tel/fax: 22 611 40; email: corossol@malagasy.com. Bookings can also be made through soanambo.tana@simicro.mg.

Telephone code The area code for Ile Sainte Marie is 57.

BACKGROUND INFORMATION
History
The origin of the Malagasy name is obscure. It means either 'Island of Abraham' or 'Island of Ibrahim', with probable reference to an early Semitic culture. It was named Ile Sainte Marie by European sailors when the island became the major hide-out of pirates in the Indian Ocean. From the 1680s to around 1720 these pirates dominated the seas around Africa. There was a Welshman (David Williams), Englishmen (Thomas White, John Every and William Kidd) and an American (Thomas Tew) among a Madagascar pirate population which in its heyday numbered nearly one thousand.

Later a Frenchman, Jean-Onésime Filet ('La Bigorne'), was shipwrecked on Sainte Marie while escaping the wrath of a jealous husband in Réunion. La Bigorne turned his amorous attentions with remarkable success to Princess Bety, the daughter of King Ratsimilaho. On their marriage the happy couple received Nosy Boraha as a gift from the king, and the island was in turn presented to the mother country by La Bigorne (or rather, put under the protection of France by Princess Bety). Thus France gained its first piece of Madagascar in 1750.

Getting there and away
By air
Air Madagascar flies every day from Tana and Toamasina to Sainte Marie. From Tana it's €137 (high season) and €125 (low season) and from Toamasina €71 and €65. All flights are heavily booked, especially in July and August, so you should try to make your reservations well in advance. Make sure your hotel reconfirms your return flight (or do it yourself at the Air Mad office in the north part of Ambodifotatra).

By boat
A motor launch runs between Soanierana-Ivongo, at the end of the surfaced road north of Toamasina, and Ambodifotatra. The service is daily (not Sundays), except when the weather is bad when you may have to wait up to a week. The boat leaves Ambodifotatra (Ilot Madame) at 08.00 and S-Ivongo at about 10.30. The trip takes 2½ hours.

Getting around the island
There is a taxi-brousse service, at least up the west coast. Prices are higher than on the mainland (about 10,000Fmg from the airport to Ambodifotatra) but they will sometimes pick you up at a pre-arranged time. Look out for the cheaper *taxi asaka*, yellow taxi-brousse. Once or twice a week it goes as far as Cocoterie Robert (about 120,000Fmg). It's worth flagging down any vehicle. Most will stop and charge the standard rate.

Most hotels have bikes for rent (the French for mountain bike is VTT). You'll pay around 50,000Fmg per day. Bikes are cheaper at Ambodifotatra. You can see quite a lot of the island by bike, but don't reckon on covering much ground – the roads are very rough and most bikes in poor condition (check the brakes!).

You can hire motorbikes opposite the Hotel Soanambo and mopeds are also available in Ambodifotatra.

WHERE TO STAY
Almost all Ile Sainte Marie's hotels are ranged along the west coast of the island (so they suffered the full force of Cyclone Gafilo), with only a few in the east or on Île aux Nattes in the south. Prices here are for high season – usually November to mid January, and July to October but dates vary from hotel to hotel. Almost all offer reduced rates during the low season.

Most hotels have their own vehicles and meet the incoming planes. If you have not pre-booked check with the driver that there is room at their hotel before climbing aboard.

If you are on a tight budget beware of staying at one of the distant hotels. You will be obliged to buy their (often pricey) meals and transport will be expensive.

Note: Ile Ste Marie was badly hit by cyclone in early 2004. At the time of writing some were closed for repairs – I hope just temporarily.

West coast hotels
These hotels are listed in geographical order, from south to north. Their price/quality category is given in brackets.

Chez Vavate (*Category C*) BP21; tel: 57 401 15. 6 rooms/bungalows. On first appearance an unprepossessing collection of local huts built on a ridge to the north of the airstrip. Don't be taken in by first impressions, the food here is wonderful (the *punch coco* also ensures that you spend your evenings in a convivial haze) and the relaxed family atmosphere makes this a very popular place with young travellers. This is one of the longest-established hotels in Ile Ste Marie (I stayed here on my first visit in 1984 when it had already been going for six years). There are six large bungalows comprising 12 rooms. Each has a mosquito net and shower, but the toilet is shared. The cost per room is 65,000Fmg. One 6-person bungalow has an en-suite bathroom and costs 165,000Fmg. Meals are 40,000Fmg and breakfast 20,000Fmg. A courtesy vehicle meets the flights (5,000Fmg) but otherwise you need to walk and it is a quite a strenuous 1½km from the airport. Take the wide grassy track which runs parallel to the airstrip then veers to the left up a steep hill. Chez Vavate employs a guide, Amadé, who is knowledgable and friendly.
Chez Didier (*Category C*) The first place you come to (on the right) as you walk up the road from the airport. Noisy, basic, but very cheap at 30,000Fmg.
Princesse Bora Lodge (*Category A*) BP13, Ile Sainte Marie; tel: 57 040 03, cellphone: 032 0709 047; fax: 57 401 47; email: bora@wandadoo.mg; www.princesse-bora.com. Within walking distance of the airport, but transfers are usually through zebu-cart. Owned by François-Xavier Mayer, whose family has been on Ste Marie for over two centuries, and his partner and architect of the hotel, Sophie de Michelis, this beautifully designed hotel is the best on the island. Everything about it is excellent: the management, the food, the location, and the whale-watching trips. Many other hotels offer whale-watching, but as far as I know only François brings in a scientific element so that visitors are collecting data about the whales as well as watching them. There are 6 luxury and 9 double bungalows; only the luxury ones have twin beds; the others have doubles only. Rates (half board) per person vary according to the number of people occupying a room, from €55 (4 people, luxury) to €75 (double) and €85 (single). There are discounted rates for 5 nights. Credit cards accepted. The hotel runs a private plane service from Tana in the high season (700,000Fmg one way). Mountain bikes for hire.
Bungalows de Vohilava (*Category B*) Tel/fax: 57 401 40 & 57 402 50; email: vohilava@malagasy.com. 10 bungalows about 3km from the airport. 120,000Fmg (single), 225,000Fmg (double). There is a restaurant but these are mainly self-catering with fully-equipped kitchens; suppliers come daily to sell fresh food. Whale-watching 200,000Fmg.
La Varanque (*Category B*) Primarily a restaurant but with a few clean, simple bungalows.
Soanambo (*Category A*) BP22; tel: 57 401 37 & 22 536 06 (Tana), cellphone: 033 1141 425; email: hsm@dts.mg. 3km from airport, 10km from Ambodifotatra. 40 rather characterless bungalows of varying sizes and prices, from €42 double to €67 double in a condominium and €335 for the 3-roomed Royal Suite. Breakfast is €4 and dinner €12. There's a lovely garden with *Angraecum* orchids and a terrace bar/restaurant from which you can watch the whales. One of the best – and longest – private beaches in Ste Marie. Swimming pool. Bicycles and motorbikes available for hire. Credit cards accepted.
Lakana (*Category B*) BP2; tel: 57 401 32; fax: 57 401 33; email: lakana@fyd.mg. 5km from the airport. 6 simple but very comfortable wooden bungalows, including 4 perched along the jetty; from €29 to €31 per person. Mountain bikes for hire. Visa cards accepted.
La Palourde (*Category C*) Tel: 57 403 07. 4 clean bungalows on the beach with en-suite cold shower; hot water on request. 60,000Fmg. The Malagasy/Mauritian owner is a great cook, especially if meals are ordered in advance.
Hotel La Baleine (*Category C*) Tel: 57 401 34. About 7km from the airport, 8 rustic bungalows owned by Albert Lanton. Communal bathroom with cold water. Very good food. With the proceeds of the hotel, Albert sponsors a youth football club and other local projects. The only negative point is that the beach is not particularly nice here… but who cares?

Bungalows Orchidée (*Category A*) Tel: 57 400 54. Located 3km south of Ambodifotatra, 12km from the airport. 10 bungalows, 4 double rooms. €38 double; breakfast €4; dinner €9. Hot water, air conditioning, watersports, excursions. Bookings may be made in Tana, tel: 22 237 62/270 15; fax: 22 269 86. Also in Tamatave: tel: 53 333 51/53 337 66. Credit cards accepted. Closed May 2004 due to cyclone damage.

Manaus Gargotte (*Category C*) 3 basic bungalows (homemade) with outside toilets; located between Vanilla Café and Orchidée. 20,000Fmg. Clean, friendly, with terrific food for 27,000Fmg.

Hotel Zinnia (*Category C*) Tel: 57 400 09; fax: 57 400 32. Right by the harbour wall at Ambodifotatra. 6 bungalows at about 25,000Fmg for a double, with hot water, fans and outside flushing toilet. Good, neat and pleasant restaurant with excellent food and 'the best coffee on Sainte Marie'. Mountain bikes for hire at 25,000Fmg a day.

Hotel La Bigorne (*Category C*) Tel: 57 401 23. About 200m south of the Air Madagascar office in Ambodifotatra. A good bar/restaurant which also has 1 room and 2 bungalows in the back garden.

Le Drakkar (*Category C*) Tel: 57 400 22. 1km north of Ambodifotatra. Simple bamboo bungalows with cold shower. Rooms from about 25,000Fmg. The main building is an old colonial house with lovely décor and a sitting-/dining-room on the water's edge. Convenient for an early-morning boat departure.

Ilot Mouettes (*Category B*) Tel: 57 401 00, cellphone: 032 0236 937. 4km north of Ambodifotatra. 4 bungalows set in 24ha including its own beach. 5-person bungalow 125,000Fmg, 2-person bungalows 50,000Fmg. Prices do not include meals. Family-run by Françoise and Renée, a local couple; very friendly (but no English spoken!), terrific food.

Hotel Bety Plage (*Category A*) 6km north of Ambodifotatra. Beautifully landscaped, but the position right by the road is not perfect. Noisy generator. From €15; breakfast €3, dinner €8. Closed May 2004 due to cyclone damage.

Hotel Bambou (*Category C*) Between Ambodifotatra and Loukintsy. Inexpensive beach huts, with a superb view of the sunset over a pristine sandy bay – and friendly.

Atafana (*Category C*) BP14; tel: 401 54. Two sets of bungalows, about 15 minutes from each other, about 4km south of La Crique, well run by the Noel family. Described by some as having the best location, on a private bay, with good food and very friendly. Rooms with baths (hot water) are 100,000Fmg; cold-water shower and wash-basin are 80,000Fmg. Camping is permitted for 10,000Fmg. Communal flushing toilets. Power comes from a generator until about 21.00. Excellent swimming at the northern beach. Residents can rent two mountain bikes and a rowing pirogue.

Hotel Voania (*Category C*) Roughly 200m from the Atafana. On a clean beach, raked every morning to get rid of rocks and flotsam. 18,000Fmg for a basic double bungalow; more for those with a cold shower. Next to the local village, but the newest part is private and secluded. No electricity, but equipped with powerful pressure lanterns. The restaurant is slightly cheaper than Atafana's.

Chez Emilie (*Category C*) About 1km north of the Atafana. 'The beach and bungalows are almost as good as Atafana (but no hot water). But it is Emilie and her food that makes it such a fantastic place to stay. Emilie is a super-charming, always cheerful lady, and she served the best meals that we ate during our three week stay in Madagascar.' (Øyvind Sæthre)

Hotel Masoandro Village (*Category A*) Tel/fax: 57 401 03; email: masoandro@simicro.mg. Under the same ownership as Soanambo, this is a group of 12 bungalows, local style, each with a sea view. A lovely location opposite Pointe Larée (just south of La Crique). €56 per double bungalow (high season) or €40 (low season); single €44 (€32). Meals €12. Diving and snorkelling. Excursions to the Forêt d'Ampanihy or camping on Pointe Larée. Mountain bikes for hire. Good English spoken.

La Crique (*Category B*) BP1. Tel/fax: 57 401 60 (mornings only); email: lacrique@dts.mg. €22–30. Deservedly popular, these are bungalows with shared facilities in one of the prettiest locations, 1km north of Lonkintsy, with a wonderful ambience and delicious (but expensive) food. In September you can watch humpbacked whales cavorting offshore. Often full, so try to book ahead. Electricity from 18.00 to 20.00 only. Transport to/from the airport costs about 40,000Fmg, and there is a regular minibus to town. Mountain bikes available. Guided tours across the island. Very tiring (it will take 2–3 hours each way) but worth it for the beautiful beach and swimming on the other side.

Hotel Antsara (*Category B*) 300m north of La Crique. 5 beach bungalows, plus 8 more on a slope further from the sea. Rooms from about 35,000Fmg, with or without WC or bathroom. Excellent Réunionnaise-French hosts. Snorkelling gear available. Has a noisy disco, but only at weekends.

Hotel Manga (*Category C*) Manga Gargota, Sainte Therese (BP515). This recommended budget hotel is about 900m north of La Crique, at the end of the paved road.

La Cocoteraie (*Category A*) BP29. In the extreme north of the island, described by one who knows as 'the most beautiful beach in the world', and has recently added 40 more bungalows. Under the same ownership as Soanambo so room prices the same: €56 per double bungalow (high season) or €40 (low season); single €44 (€32). Meals €12. Transport from the airport is expensive, however.

East Sainte Marie

Restaurant Bungalows Paradis d'Ampanihy (*Category B*) On the river close to Anafiafy, opposite the Forêt d'Ampanihy. Run by Helène, a Malagasy woman, and her family. A basic bungalow with mosquito net is about 30,000Fmg, more for those with shower. Four-course meals in a beautiful dining-room with outside tables and several tame lemurs. A pirogue trip across the river to the Forêt d'Ampanihy and back is only about 4,000Fmg per person. 10 minutes' walk to the sea.

Hotel Lagon Bleu (*Category C*) On the east coast, near Marofilao, 7km from Anafiafy. A smallish cosy site, but clean and peaceful.

Hotel C'est La Vie (*Category B*) Nord Ilampy (east coast, more or less opposite Ambodifotatra). A new, South-African run set of bungalows with 'the best views on the island'.

Mora Mora Hotel (*Category A*) Ambodiforaha; tel: 57 401 14; fax: 57 400 48. 13 bungalows, 9 with en-suite bathrooms. Half-board 200,000Fmg per person; lunch 50,000Fmg. This Italian-owned place specialises in boat trips to watch whales (US$30) or for watersports including diving. Some visitors have been disappointed that it does not have a beach and is a bit isolated. Airport/town transfers 25,000Fmg. Closed May 2004 due to cyclone damage.

Boraha Village (*Category A*) Tel: 57 400 71; email: boraha@dts.mg or boraha-village@wanadoo.fr; www.boraha.com. A French-owned hotel with 10 bungalows (doubles) all facing the sea. No beach, but a lovely verandah projecting into the sea. Specialises in deep-sea fishing. Weekly package for a double bungalow (half-board) which includes airport transfers is €276 per person. Closed May 2004 due to cyclone damage.

Ile Aux Nattes

This is becoming the preferred place to stay for those wanting more peace and isolation. See page 342 for a description of the island and its accommodation.

WHERE TO EAT
Ambodifotatra

Restaurant La Jardine serves good, inexpensive food and is recommended for breakfast. Homemade hot croissants with hot chocolate, and friendly people. The

Hotel Antsara is recommended for its inexpensive set dinner. **Bar-Restaurant Le Barachois** is across the road from the harbour, next to the ferry booking office, and has 'the most comprehensive menu encountered anywhere'. Quite inexpensive, and the tables on the porch are fine for people-watching.

Anafiafy
Restaurant Bar Bleu gets rave reviews!

Maromandia
Chez Charles 'Very cheap, plentiful food beautifully served by candlelight.' (S Blachford). Order in advance.

Ile Aux Nattes
A tradition is a day trip to this little island for lunch. A variety of hotels now serve good food. See page 342.

AMBODIFOTATRA
The town is growing and has several boutiques and a patisserie which runs out of bread in the late morning. The **market** is on Tuesdays and Thursdays. There's a **bank**, open 07.30–10.30, and 13.30–15.00, which will change travellers' cheques. There are **fax and email** facilities at Safan Baleine.

HUMPBACK WHALES OF MADAGASCAR
Duncan Murrell

Every year humpback whales migrating from their summer feeding grounds in Antarctica arrive in the waters off Madagascar between July and September to mate, give birth and nurture their young. Humpback whales, like several other species of whales, migrate between their colder, high latitude feeding grounds to the warmer shallow waters around tropical islands or on continental shelves. There is more food available in the nutrient-rich waters of polar regions than in tropical waters but the calves have insufficient insulating blubber to protect them from colder water. It takes one and a half months for the whales to travel the 3,000-mile journey from Antarctica during which they lose up to a third of their bodyweight. As with all of the baleen whales, the gestation period of 10–12 months is closely linked to the timing of their annual migration.

The majority of the whales end up in the relatively protected and shallow waters of Antongil Bay but many can be observed either in transit or lingering between Isle Sainte Marie and the mainland, often in very close viewing distance of the shore; this is especially true between Atafana and Antsara where the channel narrows considerably. They can also be seen passing Fort Dauphin early and late in the season, and a few travel up the west coast and can be viewed near Anakao and Morondava.

Humpback whales are undoubtedly one of the most entertaining of whales because of their exuberant displays of breaching (jumping), lobtailing (tail slapping) or pec slapping (flipper slapping). Males competing for females often indulge in forceful displays of head lunging and slapping to create surges and explosions of water to intimidate their rivals. In their feeding grounds they often deploy a unique feeding strategy where they herd their prey with bubbles.

But probably the behaviour that the humpback whale is most renowned for is its singing. The male produces one of the most complex songs in the animal

Sightseeing

There are some interesting sights around Ambodifotatra and the Baie des Forbans which are an easy cycle ride from most of the hotels. In the town itself there is a **Catholic church** built in 1837, which serves as a reminder that Ile Sainte Marie had been owned by France since 1750. As a further reminder of French domination there is a **war monument** to a French-British skirmish in 1845.

The **Pirates' Cemetery** is just before the bay bridge to the town (when coming from the south). A signposted track, not usable at high tide, leads to the cemetery. It takes 20 minutes and you don't need a guide (though it may be hard to shake off the pestering kids). This is quite an impressive place, with gravestones dating from the 1830s, one with a classic skull and crossbones carved on it, but not many graves. There is a 1,000Fmg charge to visit the cemetery.

The **town cemetery** is worth a visit, though it lacks the story-book drama of the pirates' final resting place. The graveyard is about 6km north of Ambodifotatra, at Bety Plage on the right side of the road.

EXPLORING THE ISLAND

The best way to explore Ile Sainte Marie is by bike (hard work), motorbike or on foot. In the low season, if you are fit and energetic, you could walk or cycle around most of the island and take your chance on places to stay. During peak seasons most of the hotels would be full.

kingdom using a great variety of sounds spanning the highest and lowest frequencies audible to the human ear. These songs are in a constant state of evolution and as the season progresses, new themes may be added or old ones changed. Each whale changes its song to keep in tune with other singers. As a result the song heard at the end of the season is quite different from the song heard at the beginning. When the whales return the following year, they resume singing the version in vogue at the end of the previous breeding season. Many whalewatching boats are now equipped with hydrophones (underwater microphones) to enable visitors to listen to their singing. Their haunting songs really elicit both the mystery and the majesty of these incredible animals.

Up until recently the humpbacks of Madagascar were one of the least studied and understood populations in the world. In the last few years researchers have been using DNA testing, satellite tagging, photographic identification and other methods to increase our knowledge of this significant population. In 2000 Madagascar's Ministry of the Environment wholeheartedly endorsed new laws governing whalewatching to protect the whales along their migration route. Training has been provided to instruct local students and faculties from Malagasy universities in research techniques and for local ecotourism representatives to encourage safe, enjoyable, and conservation-oriented whalewatching procedures. The humpback whales are a fantastic offshore bonus for the visitor, and as with the rest of Madagascar's dwindling natural treasures there is no room for complacency.

Humpback whales have been protected since 1966 and their numbers are recovering very slowly. Before they were hunted intensively in the 19th century, humpbacks probably numbered about 150,000 worldwide; today's estimates range from 25,000 to 35,000. Increased demands on their habitat, including unregulated whalewatching, will continue to threaten the likelihood that they will ever recover fully.

One option is the boat tour round the island offered by Il Balenottero Dive Centre (see page 343). You don't have to be a diver to enjoy this – swimmers and snorkellers will find it equally rewarding. Each of the three nights is spent in a different small hotel.

Crossing from west to east

Although possible to do on your own, it's easy to get lost so many young men have made a lucrative business of guiding visitors to the Indian Ocean side of the island. Many overcharge and have no information except for the route. The walk across the island takes about 2½ hours. Another starting point for the walk across the island is Antsara. If you take a guide for the island crossing, be sure to agree on the price first.

It is well worth taking a pirogue trip to explore the coast around the northeastern peninsula with its Forêt d'Ampanihy: 'The beach was the most beautiful I have ever seen. The colour of the water was a mixture of deep blue and emerald green. There weren't any other tourists – in fact I saw only three other people, fishermen, the whole time I was there. I ate a leisurely lunch then walked along the beach for miles. I would hate to see this place spoiled by tourism – it's so pristine!' (AA). 'A quite dramatic pirogue trip along the river, as the trees met overhead to form a tunnel. The pirogue will take you to an inlet where the peninsula is at its narrowest, and it's a five-minute walk to the sea on the other side. The coral reef is several hundred metres offshore, so you need another pirogue to dive there – diving from the shore is too dangerous because of the tidal flow. Absolutely deserted, with huge trees on the shore and here and there a lone fisherman.' (Jeremy and Lindie Buirski). Note: these reports date from a few years ago; I have had no recent news.

The far north

About one hour's walk from La Cocoteraie Robert is a beautiful and impressive *piscine naturelle*, with a waterfall, a big pool and enormous basalt rocks.

ILE AUX NATTES (NOSY NATO)

To many people this little island off the south coast of Ile Sainte Marie is even better than the main island. Being car-free it is much more peaceful. 'If I were to do the trip again, I'd split my time equally between both islands. Nosy Nato is about as fantasy-islandesque as it gets. Pristine beaches, quiet villages, hidden bungalows, excellent restaurants.' (Debbie Fellner) The circumference of the island is 8km, and it takes at least three hours to walk round it. Don't try this at high tide – there are some tricky bits to negotiate past often rough seas.

There is much to see during a short walking tour, including the island's unique – and amazing – orchid *Eulophiella roempleriana*, known popularly as *l'orchidée rose*. It is 2m high with deep pink flowers.

The best beach is at the north of the island: 'crystal clear, shallow water, calm tide, soft sand – absolute paradise!'

A pirogue transfer here from near the airport on Sainte Marie costs about 12,000Fmg round trip. They will take you direct to your chosen hotel.

Where to stay/eat

Maningory (*Category A*) BP22; tel: 57 402 60; cellphone: 032 0709 005/06; email: maningory@dts.mg; www.madagascar-contacts.com/maningory. Well-equipped bungalows built in the local style on a nice beach, some facing the sea. Twin room 240,000Fmg, double 235,000Fmg; meals in the large, pleasant bar-restaurant 60,000Fmg. Diving school. This

hotel, on the east coast of the island, suffered no damage in the cyclone.
Napoléon (*Category A*) Tel: 57 401 26/7; fax: 57 401 36. Or (Tana) tel: 22 207 20; fax: 22
677 70. Napoléon, who died in 1986, was a charismatic character who 'ruled' – in various
guises – this little island and enjoyed entertaining *vazaha*. His place is now owned by the
Soanambo group but the simplicity befitting Ile aux Nattes has been maintained. Bungalows
are €10–20 depending on facilities. There's a restaurant, where Napoléon's famous *poulet au
coco* is still served to appreciative diners. Closed in May 2004 due to cyclone damage.
Le Pandanus (*Category B*) Tel: 57 401 28; a double bungalow is 70,000Fmg with shared
bathrooms.
Meva Paradis (*Category B*) Tel: 57 402 71, cellphone: 032 0220 780. This collection of palm-
thatched bungalows fronting the white-sand beach is well named: it seemed close to perfection
when I looked round in 2003. Rooms in the main house (double bed, en-suite bathroom) are
€37.50, and a bungalow is €44 (or 175,000Fmg). Half-board for 2 people is €65.
Les Lemuriens (*Category B*) 10 comfortable A-frame huts, many with bay views and
balconies, at the southern end of the island. 50,000Fmg without shower, 75,000Fmg en
suite. Very good restaurant with a pleasant atmosphere.
Chez Regine (*Category C*) 6 quiet bungalows with shared toilets for 60,000Fmg. Very
peaceful and friendly; excellent food. No way of pre-booking, as far as I know, so just turn up!
Chez Titi and **La Petite Traversée** are two small hotels on the west of the island.

WATERSPORTS AND ACTIVITIES
Snorkelling and diving
The shallows around Sainte Marie are ideal for snorkelling and diving, although
the island's inshore waters are overfished by local Malagasy. Lobsters (crayfish) are
very much in evidence in and around the reefs, of which there are many, six to ten
metres down in clear water and close to Atafana and La Crique. There are also
several huge coral 'tables', some nearly two metres wide, but unfortunately a
number have been broken off by fish traps.

Divers should read the box on safety on page 121; and everyone should watch
out for the vicious spines of sea urchins (see pages 252–3).

Il Balenottero Dive Centre Tel/fax: 57 400 36 (Ambodifotatra) or tel: 22 450 17 (Tana);
email: ilbalenottero@simicro.mg; www.ilbalenottero.com. Italian owned. A well run and
professional dive centre located in Ambodifotatra. Very good equipment, organised dive
trips to wrecks as well as the coral reefs. Whale-watching, and swimming with the whales!
Prices: whale watching €33, diving €33 (10 dives €267). They also organise a four-day
boat excursion round the island for €133 (€260 if do two dives per day).
Le Lemurien Palme Dive Center Cellphone: 032 0460 734; email:
lemurienpalme@aol.com; www.lemurien-palme.com. Christina Dodwell, an expert diver,
reports this to be 'a newly established outfit run by two ex-paramedic women who are very
helpful and professional.' Their office is in Ambodifotatra.

The following hotels offer diving:

Club Nautique Princesse Bora Tel: 57 401 47; email: bora@dts.mg
Maningory (Île aux Nattes) Tel: 57 402 20
Mora Mora Tel: 57 401 14

Whale-watching
July through September is the best time to see humpback whales; you can watch
them from the beach from any of the hotels or take a boat excursion (offered by
many of the hotels and diving clubs). See box on pages 340–1.

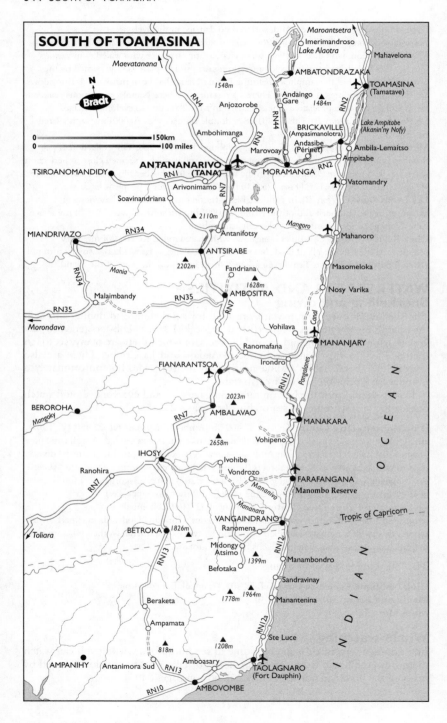

SOUTH OF TOAMASINA

Bradt

Maevatanana

N

0 ————— 150km
0 ————— 100 miles

Maroantsetra
Imerimandroso
Lake Alaotra
Mahavelona

1548m

AMBATONDRAZAKA

Andaingo Gare
1484m
TOAMASINA
(Tamatave)

Anjozorobe

RN4

RN3

RN44

BRICKAVILLE
(Ampasimanolotra)
*Lake Ampitobe
(Akanin'ny Nofy)*

Ambohimanga

Marovoay
Andasibe
(Périnet)
Ambila-Lemaitso
Ampitabe

TSIROANOMANDIDY

ANTANANARIVO
(TANA)

RN1

MORAMANGA
RN2
Vatomandry

Arivonimamo
RN7

Soavinandriana

▲ 2110m
Ambatolampy

Mangoro

Antanifotsy
Mahanoro

MIANDRIVAZO
RN34

ANTSIRABE

Mania
2202m
Masomeloka

Fandriana
1628m
Nosy Varika

RN34
Malaimbandy
RN35
AMBOSITRA

RN35
RN7
Vohilava
Canal

Morondava
Ranomafana
MANANJARY
Irondro

FIANARANTSOA
Pangalanes

RN12

2023m

BEROROHA
RN7
AMBALAVAO
MANAKARA

Mangoky
2658m
Vohipeno

IHOSY
Ivohibe

Ranohira
Vondrozo
FARAFANGANA
Manombo Reserve

RN7
Mananivo

Mananara
VANGAINDRANO
Tropic of Capricorn

BETROKA
1826m
Ranomena
RN12

Midongy
Atsimo
1399m
Manambondro

Befotaka

Beraketa
Sandravinay

Ampamata
1778m 1964m
Manantenina

818m
RN12a

AMPANIHY
Antanimora Sud
RN13
1208m
Ste Luce

Amboasary
TAOLAGNARO
(Fort Dauphin)

RN10
AMBOVOMBE

I N D I A N   O C E A N

South of Toamasina

This chapter covers the increasingly visited Pangalanes Lake resorts to the south of Toamasina. It touches on the little-visited (but surely that's part of the attraction) towns that may be accessed via the Pangalanes Canal, before rejoining the good road which joins the two seaside towns of Manakara and Mananjary, and continues to the pleasant town of Farafangana. After Vangaindrano the road/track becomes unpredictable, although a trickle of adventurous travellers manage to reach Taolagnaro (Fort Dauphin).

The Pangalanes region is a stronghold of the Betsimisaraka, the second largest ethnic group in Madagascar. Perhaps because of the isolation imposed by lack of transport, there have been fewer mixed marriages here so the culture has remained remarkably pure.

PANGALANES

This series of lakes was linked by artificial canals in French colonial times for commercial use, a quiet inland water being preferable to an often stormy sea. Over the years the canals became choked with vegetation and no longer passable, but they are gradually being cleared so that in future there may once again be an unbroken waterway stretching 665km from Toamasina to Vangaindrano (see box on page 348). Currently 430km are, in theory, navigable, and some tour operators offer one- to four-day trips down the canal. Surprisingly, I have never heard of anyone taking their own kayak or canoe down the canals; it must certainly be an option.

The quiet waters of the canal and lakes are much used by local fishermen for transporting their goods in pirogues and for fishing. The canal and ocean are separated by about a kilometre of dense bush, so it is not easy to go from one to the other.

In recent years Pangalanes has been developed for tourism, with lakeside bungalows and private nature reserves competing with the traditional ocean resorts for custom. The tourist centre is **Lake Ampitabe** which has broad beaches of dazzlingly white sand, clean water for swimming, and a private nature reserve with several introduced species of lemur.

DISTANCES IN KILOMETRES

Toamasina–Vatomandry	190km
Vatomandry–Mahanoro	125km
Mahanoro–Nosy Varika	86km
Manakara–Farafangana	109km

Getting there and away
The normal way
Each hotel provides its own transport for booked-in guests. Reaching the lodges at Akanin'ny Nofy on Lake Ampitabe from RN2 involves a drive to Manambato, at the edge of Lake Rasoabe (see page 295), followed by a 45-minute boat journey along Pangalanes. You can also take a motor launch from the Port Fluvial in Toamasina. The ride takes 1½ hours and is most enjoyable, giving a good flavour of the lakes and connecting canal, and the activities of the local people. It's nice to see the speed boats slow down to a crawl when they pass the laden pirogues, to avoid capsizing them in the wash.

Shipping companies
There are a few shipping companies, all situated on Boulevard Joffre in Toamasina. These are:
Softline 25 Bd Joffre; tel: 53 329 75 or (Tana) 22 341 75
Hibiscus (Hotel Pangalane); tel: 53 334 03
Calypso Tours (at Eden Hotel); tel: 53 312 90 or 030 55 850 93; email: calypsotours@netcourrier.com

The adventurous route
Independent travellers can take a taxi-brousse to Manambato and then hope to find a pirogue to take them further. Alternatively, take a taxi-brousse to Brickaville and walk along the railway track 12km to Ambila-Lemaitso (you will need to ask a local person to show you the way). From here you may be fortunate enough to find a cargo boat or pirogue going down the canal or, as Taco Melissen did in 2000, you can walk along the beach. This is a wild and beautiful option, but you must be well prepared and carry enough water. There is a small village after about 17km which sells water and other provisions, but after that it's just empty beach until you reach Lake Ambitabe.

LAKE AMPITABE
This isolated lake is accessible (for tourists) only by boat so is delightfully quiet and peaceful.

There are three sets of beach bungalows at Ankanin'ny Nofy, which means 'House of Dreams'. Quoted prices usually include a double bungalow, plus transfers and meals. Phone the agencies in Tana or Toamasina (details below) for latest prices and availability.

Village Atafana Tel: 53 223 64. Or reservations in Tana through the agency MTB, 20 Rue Ratsimilaho (Isoraka, near the Colbert); tel: 22 223 64; postal address: BP121. 2- to 3-person bungalows on a lovely stretch of beach; excellent meals and excursions.
Hotel Les Pangalanes Tel: 53 334 03

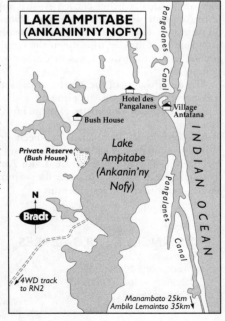

LAKE AMPITABE
(ANKANIN'NY NOFY)

Pangalanes Canal

Hotel des Pangalanes
Village Antafana

Bush House

Lake Ampitabe (Ankanin'ny Nofy)

Private Reserve (Bush House)

Pangalanes Canal

INDIAN OCEAN

N

4WD track to RN2

Manambato 25km
Ambila Lemaintso 35km

or 53 321 77. 12 bungalows, 4 double, 2 twin, and 4 with 4 beds. 180,000Fmg double; meals 55,000Fmg.

Bush House Book through Boogie Pilgrim, 40 Av de l'Indépendance, Tana; tel: 22 258 78; fax: 22 625 56; email: contact@boogie-pilgrim.net. 3 rooms and 9 bungalows. German-run, comfortable, in a beautiful situation. Rates (full board): single room €40, double room €30 per person; bungalows €48 single and €36pp double. Transfer from Manambato: €104 per boat (max 6 people). Bush House has been highly praised by readers: 'Definitely the best night of the trip. The food, the accommodation and the people were all exceptional.'

Le Palmarium

The flora of this small (35ha) private reserve is focused on a large variety of palms, hence its name. It is an hour's walk along the beach and well worth the 35,000Fmg entrance fee. Although it's more a zoo than a real reserve in that most of the lemurs have been introduced and are fed regularly, they are free-ranging but tame enough to make photographing normally rare species easy and rewarding. The owners claim to have 12 species including aye-aye and indri.

Lac aux Nepenthes

A few kilometres from Bush House. Here there are literally thousands of pitcher plants – a terrific sight!

Vohibola

This is a new project run by MATE (Man and the Environment) which is in the early stages of being developed for tourism. It is 45 minutes south of Ankanin'ny Nofy by boat. Project coordinator, Barbara Mathevon, writes: 'Vohibola is one of the two largest remaining fragments of littoral forest in Madagascar.The site is in an interesting area in the middle of lakes, the Canal des Pangalanes and the Indian Ocean. The forest is delimitated at the north by Tampina and in the south by Andranokoditra, both fishermen's villages located on a narrow sandbank. We have a path in the forest for hiking with a lot of plant and bird observations, and we're setting up an organisation with tour operators to get tourists into the forest. Local operators (Boogie Pilgrim) can organise tours to Vohibola.

'Access is by boat from Manambato or from Tamatave to Andranokoditra which is worth visiting. We have local representatives there for the payment of entrance fees (25,000Fmg) and who can prepare a picnic by the ocean for 15,000Fmg.' An ecotourism programme is being planned, but at present the infrastructure is basic. However, there is simple accommodation in two bungalows near the village for 30,000Fmg. For more information check the website www.mate.mg.

THE SOUTHEAST COAST

For most people this begins with Mananjary, which is linked to the highlands by both air and road. Adventurous souls, however, can slowly make their way south, leaving RN2 after Brickaville.

The route south from Toamasina to Mananjary

Few travellers make this challenging journey which offers an excellent opportunity to get well off the tourist track and experience the way of life of the Betsimisaraka people.

There is a road (and taxi-brousses) south to Mahanoro, via Vatomandry. Then it's a question of luck, taking whatever transport you can find, to Mananjary and the beginning of the tarred road. I wish someone would do this and tell me about it!

CANAL DES PANGALANES – THE WATER HIGHWAY OF THE EAST COAST

Colin Palmer

I was fortunate enough to go to Madagascar to study the potential for increasing the use of the waterways. Water transport is generally far better from an environmental point of view, yet experience from many countries (Thailand is a prime example) has shown that waterways are all too often overlooked in the rush for 'development' through road building.

A prime place for our study was the Canal des Pangalanes, which offers an exceptional opportunity to provide communications and access for many of the coastal communities of the east coast. That was how I came to be exploring the extraordinary and unexpectedly beautiful waterways of eastern Madagascar. To the south of Toamasina a wild expanse of natural lagoons and waterways fill the low plains behind the surf-pounded beach.

The Canal des Pangalanes was created in colonial times to provide a safe means of transport along the east coast. The shore is surf beaten and the few harbours are shallow and dangerous. The inland water passage provided a safe alternative and around the turn of the century regular ferry services were in operation. The canal interconnected the natural rivers and lagoons, where necessary cutting through the low-lying coastal plain. At intervals it crosses rivers which flow to the sea, providing access for fishermen and ensuring that the level is stable.

The waterways fell into disuse, but in the 1980s a grand project to rehabilitate them was carried out. Silted canals were dredged, new warehouses built and a fleet of modern tug barge units purchased to operate a cargo service. That may once have worked, but now the warehouses and quaysides are empty and the tug barge units lie in a jumbled array in the harbour at Toamasina.

Meanwhile, local people make good use of the waterways. Mechanised ferries run from Toamasina and every house along the way seems to have its wooden pirogue. The communities face the water and for many people it is the only reliable means of transport, especially in the wet season. It is also a vital source of livelihood and the stakes of fish traps almost fill the channels, while fields of cassava line the banks. Piles of dried fish, wood and charcoal stand in heaps awaiting collection by the returning ferries. Coming from the town, they

Vatomandry

The name means 'Sleeping Rocks' from two flat, black rocks close to the shore. This was an important town in its time, growing from a small settlement on the east bank of the River Sandramanongy to the administrative centre of the Hova government in the pre-colonial 19th century. At this time, Vatomandry was a prosperous port and merchandise was carried by porters to the capital along the paths of the eastern forest. Present-day Vatomandry marks the end of the navigable part of the Pangalanes Canal so is likely to become an increasingly popular resort. The town was severely damaged by a cyclone in 2003 which killed 68 people, so current facilities are unknown. The town boasts one good hotel, the **Hotel Pangalanes** (tel: 53 340 335). Doubles from 40,000Fmg.

Mahanoro

The name means 'Who makes happy' but whether Mahanoro will have this effect on a visitor is unknown since I've been unable to get any first-hand are overflowing with people competing for space with beer crates, bicycles, sacks of food and all the other paraphernalia of life.

Nowadays, navigation on the canal starts at the Port Fluvial in Toamasina, but it once ran further north. There is a loop that runs around behind the town and connects to the sea, and from there another channel runs north at least as far as the first river, and to Mahavelona according to the map.

From Toamasina, navigation is said to be possible as far as the stretch between Masomeloka and Nosy Varika, where it is blocked by siltation. This may just mean 'blocked' for commercial vessels and perhaps pirogues would have no problems. Beyond Nosy–Varika it opens up again as far as Mananjary. The Cartographia map shows it continuing almost as far as Farafangana, but there are references that say it goes further, to Vangaindrano. Either way, that's a total distance of more than 600km from Mahavelona. What an adventure to explore the full length!

To travel on the Pangalanes is a joy – well, most of it is. Start at Toamasina and you get the worst bit over and done with quickly. Boats leave from the bleak Port Fluvial, with its empty warehouses and jumble of discarded tug barge units.

The first, man made, cut of the canal runs south from the town, past the oil refinery. The air is thick with the smell of hydrocarbons and greasy black outfalls show all too clearly the source of the grey slime that coats the water hyacinth, the only thing that seems to be able to grow. But persevere and soon you start to pass family canoes tied to the bank and the slender, deeply loaded ferry boats pushed by struggling outboard motors. As the water starts to clear, the vegetation recolonises the riverbank and the pervasive odour of industrialisation slips away.

The artificial straightness of the first sections gives way to twisting channels and the wider expanses of lagoons and lakes – a world where communities of thatched wooden houses cluster around small landing places, grey rectangles in a canvas of green and blue, delineated here and there by the stark white of sandy beaches.

Those planning an exploration of the Pangalanes in their own canoe should buy maps no 6 and 8 of the 1:500,000 series published by FTM (see page 181). French sea charts also show the canal.

information on it! The town is to the north of the Mangoro River, so most of the places of interest are watery (although there is said to be a Merina fortress here). 18km to the north are the impressive Chutes de Sahatsio, also the Nosy Volo gorge.

Nosy Varika

The name means 'Lemur Island' but I think you'd be lucky to see any *varika* (brown lemurs) here now.

The most interesting excursion in the area is to the Chutes de la Sakaleona, a waterfall which plunges 200m, but this requires an expedition of several days.

MANANJARY AND MANAKARA

These two pleasant seaside towns have good communications with the rest of Madagascar and are gaining popularity among discerning travellers, especially now the railway from highlands to coast has been rehabilitated.

Getting there and away

Mananjary is usually reached by road from Ranomafana, and Manakara is the end (or beginning) of the railway journey from Fianarantsoa (see page 211). The road between the two towns is surfaced, but badly potholed. Even so, the journey by taxi-brousse takes only four hours. Mananjary and Manakara are linked by air with Tana and Taolagnaro several times a week. The Air Mad office in Manakara is in the Hotel Sidi.

Mananjary

This formerly nice little town is losing popularity. 'Life seems to have left. People told me everything had moved south to Manakara and that the town was abandoned.' (Johan Bjørkås). Mananjary was also badly hit by Cyclone Gafilo so, at the time of writing, is in rather a sorry state. However, it comes to life every seven years when it holds a mass circumcision ceremony. The next one will be in 2007.

The town is accessible by good road and taxi-brousse from Ranomafana.

Telephone code The area code for Mananjary is 72

Where to stay/eat

Auberge Ambohitsara Tel: 22 267 21; fax: 22 630 49; email: irma@dts.mg. Probably the best hotel in town. Bungalows for 125,000Fmg; full-board is 100,000Fmg per person. Transfer by boat from Mananjary to Ambohitsara for 960,000Fmg.

Jardin de la Mer Tel: 72 940 80; fax: 72 942 24. A pleasant set of beach bungalows; 120,000Fmg per bungalow (two beds); single 103,000Fmg. Hot showers and WC en suite. Disappointing restaurant.

Sorafahotel (formerly Solimotel) Bd Maritime; tel: 72 942 85 or 72 092 01. Bungalow 92,000Fmg; rooms: 87,000Fmg; single is 77,000Fmg. Breakfast 14,000Fmg and continental breakfast 20,500Fmg. The second best hotel with the best food.

Chez Stenny Tel: 72 942 66. About 1km north of town. Friendly and clean small guesthouse with 2 rooms (40,000Fmg) and 3 bungalows (50,000Fmg).

Route des Epices Tel: 72 940 90. Good restaurant on R25 just before the cathedral. English spoken. Tours organised.

Manakara

This town at the end of the line is experiencing a surge of popularity. The two leading hotels come highly praised by several readers so for this reason alone it is worth staying a few days. The town itself has its fans: 'The Allée des Filaos running between ex-colonial buildings and the ocean makes the waterfront a very attractive part of town. The new town and station are across the river bridge and of no interest. *Pousse-pousses* provide the best local transport.' (Andrea Jarman) The taxi-brousse station is some way from the centre of town; take a *pousse-pousse* if your bags are heavy.

You should not swim in Manakara because of dangerous currents and sharks. But the sea is infinitely rewarding anyway: 'We absolutely fell in love with the beach (except for trash piles and human excrement). The combination of the offshore reef, the breakers, the wide sand strip, the grass and other foliage, then the first line of pine trees… gave the place a park-like atmosphere. The breakers alone proved fascinating, partly because of the endless interplay between the incoming and outgoing surf.' (John Robertson)

Stuart Riddle warns against taking a pirogue trip to see the Pangalanes; a disappointing experience in many ways.

Telephone code The area code for Manakara is 72.

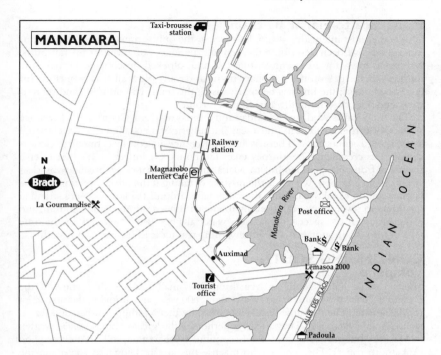

Where to stay/eat

Le Vanille 'Large rooms with bathroom, a double bed, a fridge and a balcony, costs 105,000Fmg. Mosquito nets provided. It's in a quiet part of town, on the road to Farafangana, just opposite the stadium. The owners are Malagasy and they serve the best food I've tasted in Madagascar, and also among the most reasonable. Dinner 25,000Fmg, and desert 4.000Fmg. The meat is really well cooked, and the pepper-sauce is just delicious.' (Johan Bjørkås)

Padoula Chambres d'Hôtes Lot 1B 132 Manakare-Be 316, Manakara; tel: 72 216 23. Locally run by Perline, simple but very clean. Prices vary from 45,000Fmg to 56,000Fmg, and there is also a campsite which is 10,000Fmg per person. Campers can use the hotel shower. This beach-side hotel has maintained its high standards and is universally praised by readers and the volunteers from Akany Avoko who have stayed here. 'I can't say enough about how friendly the owners were and how great the scenery is (right on the ocean). The food was great as well, though you have to order in advance. We thought we should branch out and try some other restaurants, but ended up wishing we had eaten at Padoula every night! Very reasonable prices and the *Bananas Crème Josephine* dessert is incredible!' (Heather Bomsta) 'Very welcoming, beautiful view of the sea, hostess speaks very good English and is an excellent Malagasy cook. Very reasonable prices.' 'Possibly the nicest hotel I have experienced in Madagascar! The owner incredibly helpful.'

Parthenay Club Tel: 72 216 63. A club for the locals with some tourist bungalows. Double with shared bathroom is 65,000Fmg; and en-suite double is 90,000Fmg.

Eden Sidi Hotel Unlike its seedy relative, this is an upmarket set of bungalows 12km south of Manakara.

Sidi Hotel Tel: 72 212 85. 'What a dump!' (SR). But If you're stuck, it does have beds.

Lemasoa 2000 A restaurant at the Allée des Filaos end of the bridge. 'There you can enjoy stunning views of the Manakara River (if you get tired of stunning views of the ocean) and the food isn't bad either. And cheap.' (S Riddle)

Manakara to Fianar by train

This is the most interesting – and, let's face it, the only – train ride in Madagascar. Since 1995 I've been describing the heroic experiences of adventurous rail-buffs, waiting in town for an eternity while the train plucked up courage to make the journey, then stuck on the stationary train for days... Now all that is finished (or is it? See below): the line has been privatised, the trains run on time, and there is even a booklet describing the attractions en route.

The train leaves Wednesday, Friday and Sunday at 07.00. Get to the ticket office at 06.00 or earlier so you can find a seat. Ticket prices are 60,000Fmg first class and 40,000Fmg second class. There is little difference in comfort, but first class is slightly less crowded. The journey takes ten hours. Or longer... 'It's best to take the train from Fianar downhill to Manakara – less chance of breakdowns (less stress on old engines). We made the mistake of taking it the other direction and the engine couldn't make it up into the mountains around Fianar. We were stranded for hours in several not-very-friendly towns with hordes of begging children, and missed most of the spectacular scenery/waterfalls because it was dark by the time we got into the mountains. The unrewarding trip took 15 hours.' (Tom Voth)

CONTINUING SOUTH
Vohipeno

Situated some 45km south of Manakara, this small town is the centre of the Antaimoro tribe who came from Arabia about 600 years ago, bringing the first script to Madagascar. Their Islamic history is shown by their clothing (turban and fez, as well as Arab-style robes). They are the inheritors of the 'great writings', *sorabe*, written in Malagasy but in Arabic script. *Sorabe* continue to be written, still in Arabic, still on 'Antaimoro paper'. The scribes who practise this art are known as *katibo* and the writing and their knowledge of it give them a special power. The writing itself ranges from accounts of historical events to astrology, and the books are considered sacred.

Farafangana

On the map this appears to be a seaside resort, but its position near the mouth of a river means that the beach and ocean are not easily accessible. The town is a prosperous commercial centre, with well-stocked shops and a busy market and is the last place that you can change travellers' cheques or foreign currency if travelling south.

According to Frankie Kerridge, the locals do not swim – they say the sea is full of monsters – so they watch football instead. The Farafangana team frequently comes top in the Madagascar league.

Telephone code The area code for Farafangana is 73 – but phones rarely work here!

Getting there and away

Air Madagascar flies from Tana to Farafangana and on to Taolagnaro about twice a week.

A taxi-brousse from Tana to Farafangana takes about 24 hours, but most people will arrive here via Manakara. Farafangana is only two or three hours away on a good road.

Where to stay/eat

Coco Beach Beach-side bungalows on the southern outskirts of the town, just beyond the lighthouse.

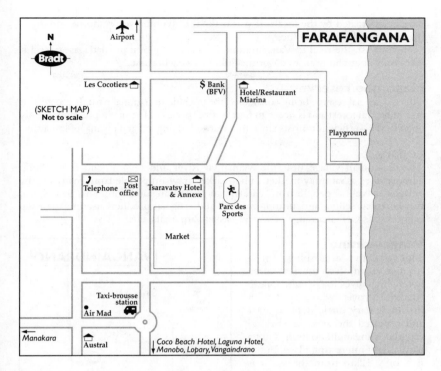

Laguna More bungalows about 4km south of Farafangana.

Hotel Les Cocotiers BP135, Fenoarivo, Faranfangana; tel: 73 911 87 or 73 911 88. Near the post office, this is an upmarket hotel with en-suite bathrooms and hot water. 110,000Fmg. Good restaurant.

Chez Abba Tel: 73 911 85. About 40,000Fmg for a seafront bungalow with a simple bucket shower.

Miarina (formerly Les Tulipes Rouges) The rooms are all called after different shades of red! Now primarily a restaurant but it still has some rooms. Good food and safe parking.

Tsaravatsy Hotel Tel: 73 910 36. Popular with Malagasy; good restaurant (Malagasy and Chinese specialities). Cold water, shared facilities. 30,000Fmg.

Le Croustillant bakery Good selection of breads and croissants across the road from Les Cocotiers.

Les Mimosas Salon de Thé Opposite Les Cocotiers. Lots of imported goodies available (at a price).

Austral Hotel Tel: 73 912 77; fax: 73 912 57; email: austral@netclub.mg

West to Ihosy (maybe)

If you are seriously adventurous and want to try to reach Ihosy (which looks entirely practical on the map) you will need to go on foot, with a guide. You can do the first section, to **Vohitranambo**, by taxi-brousse. The next goal is **Vondrozo**, about 50km away, which is passable by vehicle but has no public transport. You will have to hope to hitch a ride. You can continue by car as far as the **Vevembe** region at which point the passable road ends and jungle has taken over. You will probably need a guide to proceed on foot (or with a mountain bike) to the next stretch of passable road at **Ivohibe** because of the numerous trails that have been created by the locals. If you make it to Ivohibe you're home and dry – there are taxi-brousses to Ihosy.

In contrast, the road to Vangaindrano is 'one of the best in Madagascar' and it takes only about an hour to cover the 70km by taxi-brousse.

Manombo reserve

This is a special reserve being considered for upgrade to national park. It protects an area of littoral forest and is home to four or five species of lemur. At present it is only open to self-sufficient tourists since the nearest lodging is Farafangana, 30km away.

Lopary

This is a small village near the Mananivo River and recommended by Philip Thomas for its Saturday market. 'The market draws in people from many nearby villages as well as people from Farafangano and Vangaindrano. This is a typical rural market, selling agricultural produce and artisinal products used in the rural economy, as well as a range of woven basketware, mats, etc.'

Vangaindrano

This has the atmosphere of a frontier town; few tourists come here which gives it a certain appeal. Marko Petrovic, who stayed with his missionary uncle here in 2001 and explored the area (see below) reports: 'Vangaindrano itself is not a particularly interesting place, but as it is only 12km from the sea it is worth making this trip along a road which has been beautifully repaired because Madagascar's minister in charge of roads comes from that area. The road runs parallel with the enormous River Mananara, which flows past Vangaindrano. It is interesting to watch the fishermen who live by the sea going out into the 10ft waves in their narrow wooden pirogues. I swam there many times enjoying the amazing power of the waves, but was always careful not to go too far out because currents can very quickly take you

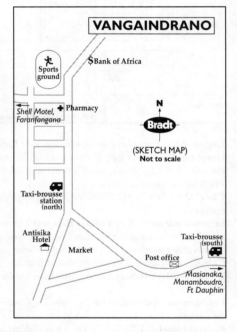

in the direction of Australia! Sharks, too, are a possible danger although I never saw any. The beach is beautifully sandy but beware of rocks under the water.'

Marko says his adventure-loving uncle (Mompera – Father – Klemen) would probably be happy to meet and advise (in French) travellers wishing to explore the area. He is based at the Catholic church in Vangaindrano.

Where to stay/eat

There are several small hotels including the **Antsika** and perhaps the **Zorah** (if it is still open) which is about a half kilometre from the town centre, on the left-hand side as you enter town from the north. The best-quality hotel is probably the new

Shell Motel (named for its petrol station rather than bivalves) which is to the north of the town.

From Vangaindrano to Taolagnaro (Fort Dauphin)

Vangaindrano is the end of the road for most people, but you can continue further. Since the last edition of this book the road (RN12) has been improved somewhat and a small number of backpackers and mountain-bikers successfully make their way to Serious Civilisation at Taolagnaro, 230km to the south.

Philip Thomas, an anthropologist who knows the area well, says: 'There is an almost daily taxi-brousse service as far as the village of **Manambondro**, 58km to the south of Vangaindrano. Midway to Manambondro is the ferry-crossing point at Masianaka, where there is now a lively settlement on the north bank where people can get both food and shelter. Manambondro village boasts a hotel with its own eatery, the Eden, although both can be classed as rudimentary. There are occasionally vehicles going further south than this although they are not always able to take passengers. People say the road will be improved further still, but they've been saying this for a very long time...'

Marko Petrovic's report of his journey by motorbike which appeared in the last edition is still valid. At least the conditions are probably not worse! 'At the end of my stay my uncle and I decided to tackle the RN12 from Vangaindrano to Fort Dauphin with small (50cc) motorbikes because bigger ones would have been awkward crossing rivers by dugout canoes. We set off one Sunday afternoon, laden with food, spare clothes, tools and carrying extra fuel because there would be no petrol station until Fort Dauphin. The first hurdle was crossing Lake Masianaka, which would have been straightforward if the ferry hadn't been *simba* (broken down). We persuaded the ferry operators to tie two canoes together so we could lay the motorbikes across them. The rowers, my uncle and I, squatted in what space was left, doing our best to keep as still as possible. After that the road became a mud bath fit for a hippo. As light waned we just ploughed straight through the mud – an incredible thrill! We spent that night in Manambondro. The next day we had to cross another river, again using canoes. Several dozen zebu swam with us, only their horns, nose and humps protruding above the water. The next obstacle was a bridge that looked so rickety we carried the bikes across gingerly, one by one. The road became a roller-coaster ride, winding its way up and down and round the hills that separate the sea from the mountains that run parallel to the coast. We reached **Sandravinanay** by early afternoon and decided to call it a day. We spent the night sheltering in the wooden church, listening to the rain pattering on the roof.

'Next morning we were advised by the locals to take the bikes by canoe down the River Sandra as far as the sea, where we followed tracks left by lobster-merchants' trucks on the beach and later rejoined RN12, which is really no more than a rough dirt track. Before we reached **Manantenina**, the largest town between Vangaindrano and Fort Dauphin, we crossed two rivers which actually had functioning ferries, although we had to bribe the ferrymen to take us across. The final stretch, from Manantenina to Fort Dauphin (110km), took us a whole day but the road was marginally better and all five ferries were operating. Some ferries are operated by pulling on a rope which is stretched across the river. A constant hazard was the numerous streams crossing the road which in places are deep enough to drown a motorbike. We reached Fort Dauphin after four days on the "road" exhausted but happy.'

This is a route for the true adventurer with a small motorbike or mountain bike. Or a sturdy pair of legs and a backpack. Go for it!

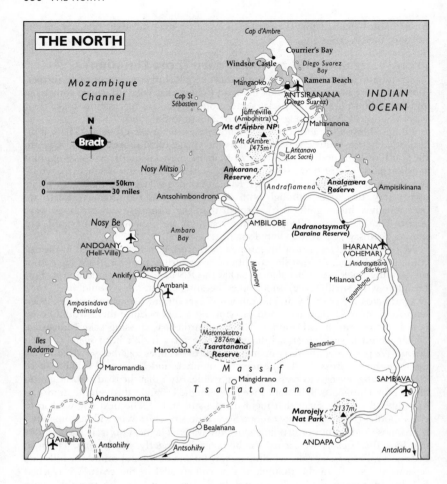

The North

The north of Madagascar is characterised by its variety. With the Tsaratanana massif (which includes Madagascar's highest peak, Maromokotro, 2,876m) bringing more rain to the Nosy Be area than is normal on the west coast, and the pocket of dry climate around Antsiranana (Diego Suarez) which has seven months of dry weather with 90% of the 900mm of rain falling between December and April, the weather can alter dramatically within short distances. With changes of weather go changes of vegetation and its accompanying fauna, making this region particularly interesting for botanists and other naturalists.

This is the domain of the Antankarana people. Cut off by rugged mountains, the Antankarana were left to their own devices until the mid-1700s when they were conquered by the Sakalava; they in turn submitted to the Merina King Radama I, aided by his military adviser James Hastie, in 1823.

Roads in the area are being improved and Antsiranana is losing its isolation. Distances are long, however, so most people prefer to fly between the major towns.

ANTSIRANANA (DIEGO SUAREZ)
History
Forgivingly named after a Portuguese captain, Diego Suarez, who arrived in 1543 and proceeded to murder and rape the inhabitants or sell them into slavery, this large town has had an eventful history with truth blending into fiction. An often-told story, probably started by Daniel Defoe, is that pirates in the 17th century founded the Republic of Libertalia here. Not true, say modern historians.

Most people still call the town Diego. The Malagasy name simply means 'Port' and its strategic importance as a deep-water harbour has long been recognised. The French installed a military base here in 1885, and the town played an important role in World War II when Madagascar was under the control of the Vichy French (see box on page 362). To prevent Japanese warships and submarines making use

DISTANCES IN KILOMETRES

Ambondromamy–Antsiranana	737km
Antsohihy–Ambanja	218km
Antsiranana–Ambilobe	131km
Antsiranana–Ankarana	120km
Antsiranana–Ambanja	240km
Antsiranana–Anivorano	75km
Antsiranana–Daraina	247km
Antsiranana–Vohemar	294km

of the magnificent harbour and thus threatening vital sea routes, Britain and the allies captured and occupied Diego Suarez in 1942. There is a British cemetery in the town honouring those killed at this time.

Antsiranana today

This is Madagascar's fifth largest town (population about 80,000) and of increasing interest to visitors for its diverse attractions. The harbour is encircled by hills with a conical 'sugar loaf' plonked in one of the bays to the east of the town. From the air or the top of Montagne des Français, Antsiranana's superb position can be appreciated but the city itself is in the usual state of decay, though with a particular charm. The port's isolation behind its mountain barrier and its long association with non-Malagasy races have given it an unusually cosmopolitan population and lots of colour: there are Arabs, Creoles (descendants of Europeans), Indians, Chinese and Comorans. In 2004 Antsiranana was badly hit by Cyclone Gafilo which inflicted severe damage to the town with 85 dead and around 118,000 made homeless. Some of the infrastructure may not have been rebuilt by the time you visit, so make allowances.

Almost everyone enjoys Diego. It is colourful, compact, has some great eateries, a good beach and of course the excellent nearby reserves. This is a pleasant town for wandering; take a look at the market – one of the largest and most colourful in Madagascar – poke around the harbour, and investigate a few souvenir shops. If you want to relax on a beach for a few days, stay at Ramena.

The name 'Joffre' seems to be everywhere in and around the town. General Joseph Joffre was the military commander of the town in 1897 and later became Maréchal de France. In 1911 he took over the supreme command of the French armies, and was the victor of the Battle of the Marne in 1914.

Telephone code The area code for Antsiranana is 82.

Getting there and away
By air

There are flights from Tana (returning the same day) via Mahajanga on most days, also regular flights from/to Nosy Be. Twin Otters link Antsiranana with the east coast towns of Iharana (Vohemar), Sambava and Toamasina.

There are taxis waiting at the airport but they set their own price: an extortionate 50,000Fmg for the 6km to the town centre. A cheaper alternative is to walk to the main road and wait for a taxi-brousse.

By road

The overland route between Ambaja (nearest town to Nosy Be) and Antsiranana is popular. Much tougher, but possible is the road to Iharana (Vohemar). Both routes are described later in this chapter. The company Anila Transport will also provide comfortable road transport to Ambilobe for about 20,000Fmg.

Where to stay
Category A

Panorama A new hotel on the road to Ramena. Tel: 82 225 99; fax: 82 235 60. 12 bungalows with private shower and terrace set in spacious gardens with a swimming pool. €70 double; breakfast €4.

King's Lodge 8km east of Antsiranana. Tel: 82 225 99; fax: 82 235 60; email: infoking@compro.mg; www.kingdelapiste.de. Well designed, set on a gentle slope backed by a hill, with a shaded terrace and sea view. Under the same ownership as King de la

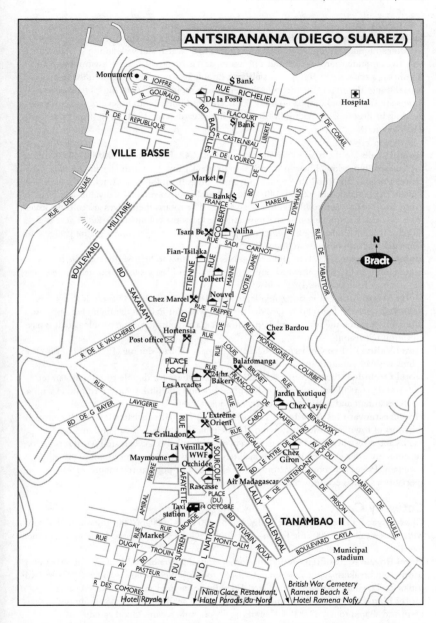

ANTSIRANANA (DIEGO SUAREZ)

Monument

R JOFFRE

R GOURAUD

RUE RICHELIEU

$ Bank

De la Poste

R DE L REPUBLIQUE

R DE L'REPUBLIQUE

BD BASCILLES

R FLACOURT

$ Bank

R DE CORAIL

Hospital

R CASTELNEAU

RUE DE L'OUREO

DE LA LIBERTE

VILLE BASSE

RUE DES QUAIS

BOULEVARD MILITAIRE

Market

AV DE

Bank $

Bank $

FRANCE

V MAREUIL

RUE D'IMHAUS

RUE DE COLBERTE

Tsara Be

Valiha

RUE SADI CARNOT

RUE DE L'ABATTOIR

N

Bradt

Fian-Tsilaka

BD SAKARAMY

BD ETIENNE

RUE MARNE

RUE NOTRE DAME

Colbert

Nouvel

Chez Marcel

RUE DE LA

RUE FREPPEL

R DE LE VAUCHERET

Hortensia

Post office

RUE DE

RUE LOUIS

Chez Bardou

RUE MONSEIGNEUR COURBET

PLACE FOCH

RUE FRANÇOIS

RUE BRUNET

Balafomanga

24 hr Bakery

Les Arcades

LAVIGERIE

BD DE G BAYER

RUE

RUE

RUE DE CABOT

Jardin Exotique

Chez Layac

RUE MAHEY

BENIOWSKY

L'Extrême Orient

La Grilladon

RUE RIGAULT

AV DU POIVRE

La Venilla

WWF

Orchidée

Chez Giron

Maymoune

RUE SOURCOUF

BD LE MYRE DE VILERS

AV DE L'INTENDANT

GL CHARLES DE GAULLE

Rascasse

RUE LAFAYETTE

AV PIERRE

PLACE (DU) 14 OCTOBRE

Air Madagascar

AV DE LALLY

R DE L'INTENDANT

RUE DE PRISON

Taxi station

AV AMIRAL

RUE LABORDE

RUE

Market

DUGAY

TROUIN

BD SYLVIAN ROUX

TOILENDAL

TANAMBAO II

BOULEVARD CAYLA

Municipal stadium

RUE

BD PASTEUR

AV

R DES COMORES

AV D L SUFFREN

R DU NATION

MONTCALM

AV D L NATION

British War Cemetery
Ramena Beach &
Hotel Ramena Nofy

Nina Glace Restaurant,
Hotel Paradis du Nord

Hotel Royale

Piste (see page 365). Good restaurant. Rooms €39; meals €8. Bill Love reports that 'a pair of giant day geckos has taken up residence in the dining-room since the hotel cats disappeared.'

Hotel Colbert 51 Rue Colbert; tel: 82 232 89; fax: 82 232 90; email: hicdiego@dts.mg. 27 air-conditioned rooms with en-suite bathrooms. Safe deposit boxes in each room. 230,000Fmg. Good restaurant but expensive.

Category B

Le Jardin Exotique 24 Rue Françoise de Mahy; tel: 82 219 33; email: lejardinexotique@dts.mg; www.lejardinexotique.net. 'Warm and welcoming service with only five en-suite rooms set around a pleasant patio garden with a small swimming pool. Room 1 is a self-catering bungalow with one double bedroom and a kitchen/living-room, 150,000Fmg. Room 3 is the nicest of the remaining rooms at 95,000Fmg.' The 2 other rooms are smaller and cost 85,000Fmg. Fans, mosquito nets (with holes); only a curtain dividing bathroom from bedroom. Breakfast in the garden for 15,000Fmg (expensive for what you get).

Hotel Escale On the road to the airport; tel: 82 213 42. From about 100,000–115,000Fmg for a double bungalow. I have no reports on its quality but it's worth checking out.
Hotel Paradis du Nord Rue Villaret Joyeuse, across from the market; tel: 82 214 05. 82,000Fmg (single), and 92,000–140,000Fmg double. All en suite. Good value since everything works – air-conditioning, hot water… The rooms themselves are cell-like except for No 1 which is marvellously spacious and overlooks the colourful market. There is a pleasant balcony dining-room (with good food), a laundry service, and a secure garage (you can rent cars from here, including 4WD).
Hotel de la Poste BP121; tel: 82 220 44. Near Clémenceau Sq, overlooking the bay. A superb location but few other redeeming features when I last visited (admittedly a few years ago – it may have improved).
Hotel Maymoune 7 Rue Bougainville; tel: 82 218 27. About 140,000Fmg. It may have improved since the last report: 'Decidedly seedy, with music from the nightclub opposite thumping through the walls until 3am.' However, a big plus for some people is that it has CNN on television!
Hotel Valiha 41 Rue Colbert; tel: 82 221 97; email: valiha@ddt.mg. 127,000Fmg for clean rooms with air conditioning and hot water.
Hotel Orchidée Rue Surcouf; tel: 82 210 65. 75,000Fmg for double room with fan (en suite), and 100,000Fmg with air-conditioning. Friendly, helpful, Chinese-run hotel with a small restaurant and a few rooms for around 50,000Fmg.
Hotel/restaurant les Arcades Place Foch. Tel: 82 231 04; email:arcades@blueline.mg. In the heart of town, opposite the town hall. The typical French colonial building has 8 rooms and a restaurant and bar. There's a courtyard and also a cybercafé.) Most rooms are en suite, but 2 have shared bathroom facilities. 3 rooms have air-conditioning, the others have fans. Prices per room vary from €5 to €13.50. The popular restaurant serves specialities such as coconut crab curry and paella.

Category C

Chez Layac 35 Rue François de Mahy; tel: 82 210 21. 41,000–56,000Fmg for double room with shared toilet, 75,000Fmg for en-suite double. Good value. A good place to meet other travellers.
Hotel Royale Rue Suffren, around the corner from the Paradis du Nord. About 50,000Fmg per person; breakfast about 7,000Fmg. Cell-like rooms but clean, and with fans. Lockers with padlocks. The interior rooms are quieter. Friendly, some English spoken. Good value.
Hotel Fian-tsilaka 13 Bd Etienne; tel: 82 223 48. 52,000Fmg for a basic room with wash-basin and shared toilet. 82,000–102,000Fmg for en-suite rooms. Good restaurant.
Hotel la Rascasse Rue Surcouf, opposite Air Mad; tel: 82 223 64. Good value rooms from 85,000Fmg (shared toilet) to 100,000Fmg for en-suite facilities, but the place is pretty seedy: 'The restaurant and the terrace are mostly occupied by lonely men and easy-going girls.' (CH)
Chez Yvette Giron Villa Elise, 0512D0110, Polygone III Route de la SIM, Diego Suarez 201; tel: 220 89. Not a hotel, but rooms in a private house for 50,000Fmg per night; breakfast 18,000Fmg. Recommended by Debbie Fellner: 'Yvette Giron's home is

beautiful, safe and clean, within walking distance of downtown, and she provides an excellent breakfast.'

Where to eat
Balafomanga Tel: 82 228 94. A French-run, expensive restaurant, with excellent food. Try the marinated zebu or coco shrimp.
La Venilla Up the road from the Hotel La Rascasse and opposite the WWF office. Arguably the best restaurant in town, yet still keeps its prices reasonable. Especially recommended for breakfast, when little else is open.
La Grilladon Av Sourcouf (not far from the WWF office). An upmarket restaurant with a pool table and outdoor bar; excellent food. Try the fish with mushroom and aubergine.
Halmah Resto Rue Roi Tsimiaro. Where the locals eat, and always busy. Good value.
Restaurant Libertalia Offers a few good, low-priced meals on the first floor. There's also a lovely garden restaurant. 'This has to be the best for a Friday night! We had a full moon, good food, great music, prostitutes dancing for their expats.'
L'Extrême Orient A popular restaurant near Air Mad; inexpensive, good food.
La Rosticceria Rue Colbert; an excellent Italian restaurant with veranda. 'The owner makes her own lemon/cream liqueur and will ply you with it despite protestations!'
Chez Marcel Bd Etienne, across the street from the Nouvel Hotel. Closed for renovation in 2003.
Tsara Be Opposite the Valiha on Rue Colbert. 'Managed by an expat from Toulouse and staffed by locals, the restaurant serves very good fresh food at reasonable prices. Le Patron is exceptionally jovial and welcoming and makes it his business to mingle with visitors and get to know them. Good ambiance, highly recommended.'

Snacks and fast food are easy to find. The **Hortensia**, near the post office, does fast food all day. If your hotel does not serve breakfast, go to the **Boulangerie Amicale**, between La Rascasse and the cinema. Excellent hot rolls and *pain au chocolat*. **Glace Gourmande**, on Rue Colbert, probably serves the best ice-cream in town, and is recommended for breakfast. The **bakery** on Rue François de Mahey, around the corner from the Libertalia, sells baguettes day and night. And ice-cream.

Nightlife
Vahinée Bar Rue Colbert, opposite BNI-CL bank. 'The food is adequate, the atmosphere and the staff sublime.' (JG)

Cybercafés
There are several, including one opposite the new (but not open) Grand Hotel on Rue Colbert which costs 1,000Fmg per minute.

Ramena
This beach resort is growing fast and provides a pleasant alternative to staying in Diego. Ramena is about 18km from the town centre, 45 minutes from the airport. Get there by taxi-brousse or by private taxi (about 75,000Fmg round trip). It's a beautiful drive around the curve of the bay, with some fine baobabs en route. The road down to the beach is just after the Fihary Hotel.
As well as a selection of hotels and restaurants, there is a disco along the beach.

Where to stay/eat
Meva Plage Hotel At Meva beach, near Ramena; cellphone: 032 0471 522 or 032 0478 242; email: mevaplagehotel@blueline.mg or atyla@wanadoo.mg. 7 rooms. Probably the best of the beach hotels. €40 per person per night; meals €12.

THE BATTLE OF DIEGO SUAREZ
John Grehan

In the days before mass air-transportation, Madagascar's geographical location gave the island immense strategical importance. In World War II, British convoys to the Middle East and India sailed round the north of Madagascar, passing the great French naval base of Antsirane (now Antsiranana) at Diego Suarez. Antsirane, its harbour facilities completed in 1935, was France's most modern colonial port with a dry dock that could accommodate 28,000 ton battleships and an arsenal capable of repairing the largest of guns.

It was evident to both the Allied and Axis Powers that whoever held Diego Suarez controlled the western Indian Ocean. As the French authorities in Madagascar were firm supporters of the German-influenced Vichy Government, Britain believed that it had to occupy the island before it was handed over to her enemies. So, in the spring of 1942, Britain mounted *Operation Ironclad*, its first ever large-scale combined land, sea and air operation, to capture Diego Suarez as the initial step in occupying the whole island.

A force of some 13,000 troops with tanks and artillery, supported by 46 warships and transport vessels and 101 aircraft of the Fleet Air Arm, assembled to the north of Cap d'Ambre before dawn on 5 May 1942. The narrow entrance to Diego Suarez Bay was known to be powerfully defended by large-calibre artillery so the British decided to land in Courrier Bay and march across country to take Antsirane from the landward side.

The first troops to land were Commandos, who captured the small battery that overlooked Courrier Bay. The French and Senegalese defenders were still asleep and the position was taken with little loss of life. However, a small French force ensconced in an observation post on the summit of Windsor Castle could not be dislodged. For two days the French clung to their eyrie, despite repeated bombardments from the Royal Navy and attacks by the Fleet Air Arm and the Commandos.

With the beaches secured, the main British force landed and began its march upon Antsirane. Meanwhile, the Fleet Air Arm depth-charged and torpedoed the French warships and submarines at anchor in Diego Suarez Bay and bombed Arrachart airfield. But the defenders were now at their posts and an intense battle for possession of Diego Suarez began.

Some three miles to the south of Antsirane the French had built a strong defensive line across the isthmus of the Antsirane Peninsula. Devised by General Joffre in 1909, it comprised a trench network and an anti-tank ditch strengthened

La Case en Falafy (Chez Bruno); cellphone: 032 0267 433; www.godzilla.ch/case_en_falafy. Thatched bungalows, en-suite showers (but water supply dodgy), a swimming pool of sorts and an open-air kitchen/bar/restaurant.

Residence du Nosy Lonjo Tel: 82 294 00. On the way to Ramena, overlooking the island of Nosy Lonjo.

Fihary Hotel Tel: 82 228 62/294 15; fax: 294 13. 15 chalets with modern bathrooms, hot water, mosquito nets, a large restaurant (super food, only they often run out!) with a terrace. About 125,000Fmg.

Badamera Near the beach, friendly, wonderful food. Huts or rooms for about 50–80,000Fmg with communal bathrooms.

Ramena Nofy Bungalows about 180,000Fmg. Very clean and quiet, with working fans. 2 minutes from the beach. Delicious food, especially fish.

by forts and pillboxes housing artillery and machine-guns. For two days the British forces assaulted the French line without success and with mounting losses.

The breakthrough came on the evening of 6 May when a British destroyer charged through the entrance of Diego Suarez Bay under the guns of the French batteries. The destroyer successfully landed a body of 50 Marines onto the quay. This tiny force stormed through the town, capturing the main barracks and the artillery headquarters. This disruption in their rear finally broke the defenders' resolve and when the main frontal attack was renewed the French line was overrun.

The fighting resulted in more than 1,000 casualties. The British commander submitted recommendations for more than 250 decorations, including three posthumous Victoria Crosses.

Britain's vital route to the east had been secured – but only in the nick of time. Barely three weeks after the capture of Antsirane, a Japanese submarine flotilla arrived off the coast of Madagascar. In a daring night raid the Japanese attacked the ships in Diego Suarez Bay, sinking one supply ship and severely damaging the flag ship of the British expedition, the battleship *Ramillies*.

With the island's main naval base in British hands, it was expected that the French Governor General, Armand Annet, would bow to the inevitable and relinquish control of the whole island. However, despite months of negotiations, Annet refused to surrender and Britain was forced to mount further military operations.

In September 1942, British and Commonwealth troops landed at Majunga and Tamatave. Brushing aside all attempts to stop and delay them, the Allies captured Tananarive only to find that Annet had retreated to the south of the island. But when a South African force landed at Tuléar, Annet realised that he was trapped.

The French strung out surrender negotiations until one minute after midnight on 6 November – exactly six months and one day after the start of the British attack upon Diego Suarez. The significance of this was that French troops involved in a campaign lasting longer than six months were entitled to a medal and an increased state pension!

After a brief period of British Military Administration, the island was handed over to General de Gaulle's Free French movement. The key naval base of Antsirane, however, remained under British control until 1944.

John Grehan is the author of The Forgotten Invasion, *see Further Reading in the Appendix.*

Restaurant Emeraude 'Walk down the road to the beach from Hotel Fihary. Turn left on to the beach at the pier. This is the first restaurant you'll come to. Excellent.'
Hotel Oasis Poor location in the middle of the village; rooms 60,000Fmg. Good restaurant.

An excursion from Ramena

Angela Slater and David Pollard recommend the following walk to the **Baie des Dunes** (part of the Orangea Peninsula which forms the southeastern arm of the entrance to the bay). Since part of the route passes through a military zone you will need to buy a permit from one of the sentries which costs 15,000Fmg. An ID (passport) is usually needed. 'The walk is best done early in the morning or late afternoon because of the heat; also carry plenty of water. It starts from the village of

Ramena. You will need a permit to pass through the Orangea military zone. This costs 15,000Fmg each and you'll need to show your passport for indentification. Walk along the metalled road towards the headland – straight on from the bungalows rather than down to the beach – which will take you to the military installation where you will have to show your pass to the gatehouse. Once in the camp follow the signs to the lighthouse or dunes past the barracks then along an open stretch to the hillside and follow the obvious track along the contour. Bird life is very good: two species of vanga (sickle-billed and Chabert's), bee-eaters and kestrels.

'The track continues past some ruined buildings and there is a signpost to the lighthouse. Carry on along the track, which can be hard going at times in the soft sand, and then the view opens up seaward. A word of caution at this point: if you leave the track to look at the view (which I can recommend as there are white-tailed tropic-birds) be careful of the cliffs. All along the walk there are numerous animal tracks, mainly land crabs but some reptiles also. Then you arrive at the Baie des Dunes; the bay itself is overlooked by an old gun emplacement. On the beach to the right of this there is a stretch of white sand gently sloping to the sea; to the left there is a remnant reef with pools, then a steep drop off into the water, excellent for snorkelling. In front of the emplacement there is a small island which is accessible from the beach.

'The whole area is excellent for wildlife, especially the pools, and there is the potential to spend the whole day here exploring if you bring a packed lunch. Further over in the same woodland we found crowned and Sanford's brown lemur.'

Boat trips

You can arrange to be taken by boat to 'a wonderful small island. Two hours in a choppy sea, but worth it. Fish caught by boatmen cooked on the beach. About 100,000Fmg per person.'

Sightseeing and half-day excursions
British cemetery

On the outskirts of town on the road that leads to the airport, the British cemetery is on a side road opposite the main Malagasy cemetery. It is well signposted. Here is a sad insight into Anglo-Malagasy history: rows of graves of the British troops killed in the battle for Diego in 1942, and the larger numbers, mainly East African and Indian soldiers serving in the British army, who died from disease during the occupation of the port. Impeccably maintained by the Commonwealth War Graves Commission, this is a peaceful and moving place.

Montagne des Français (French Mountain)

The mountain gets its name from the memorial to the French and Malagasy killed during the allied invasion in 1942. Another sad reminder of a war about which the locals can have had little understanding. There are several crosses but the main one was laboriously carried up in 1956 to emulate Jesus's journey to Calvary.

It is a hot but rewarding climb up to this high point with splendid views and some nearby caves. Go early in the morning for the best birdwatching (and to avoid the heat of the day). Take a taxi 8km along the coast road towards Ramena beach, to the start of the old road up the mountain. This is 50m before the King's Lodge. The footpath is marked with red paint about 300m along the track on the left. 'In the area of *tsingy* just before the high cliffs we spotted Sandford's brown lemurs. Many more small footpaths extend from left to right and make enjoyable walking including some which lead to the obvious large cave high above King's Lodge. Since early 2000 these cliffs and the interior of the cave have become a mecca for rock climbers where French groups have put up many bolted routes. Full details of these can be found at the Kings Lodge.' (V & J Middleton)

Apparently the flora and fauna are much more rewarding on the Indian Ocean side of the mountain.

EXCURSIONS FROM ANTSIRANANA

Antsirana is the starting point for several outstanding excursions, some nearby and possible in a day, some requiring several days. The most popular is Montagne D'Ambre, with Ankarana the goal for walkers and naturalists. With a 4WD you can also spend a few days visiting the far north at Cap d'Ambre and Windsor Castle.

Getting organised

Many hotels in Diego will be able to put you in touch with someone who will organise a tour you. Perhaps more risky than the established companies below but more personal and often more enjoyable for this reason. The following individual is recommended by Alex Sandell and Ben Kelly who had a wonderful trip to Ankarana with him (though he speaks only French – no English).

Jasmin Ravalohery Cellphone: 032 0405 662. 'Genuine, friendly, interesting and very enthusiastic.'

Tour operators

Nature et Océan 5 Rue Cabot, BP436, Antsiranana. They run 4WD vehicles to places of interest such as Montagne d'Ambre, Ankarana, Antanavo, Windsor Castle, Courrier's Bay and Ambilobe. They also run sea trips and fishing expeditions. Madagascar Airtours also has an office here.

Le King de la Piste Bd Bazeilles, Antsiranana; tel/fax: 82 225 99. This agency, run by Jorge Pareik (German), is the best in town for trips by 4WD (minimum two people) to hard-to-reach places such as Windsor Castle, Cap d'Ambre and Analamera. Jorge and his Malagasy wife also organise excursions by motorbike or mountain bike. Prices are very high (and you must pay in cash – credit cards are not accepted) but most people consider it worth it for the efficient service.

Ecotours Adjacent to the Hotel Rascasse, Rue Sourcouf. 'Not only is this one of the cheapest operators, the patron also has English-speaking guides… Having spent a week with me, both of them now know a great deal about Britain's involvement in Madagascar in World War Two!' (John Grehan)

Zanatany Tours BP475, Antsiranana; tel: 82 237 88; fax: 82 224 44. This outfit is run by one of Madagascar's best guides to the north, Hyacinthe (Luc Hyacinthe Kotra), and his team which includes Angelin and Angelic who are known by many visitors for their outstanding knowledge of Ankarana. They specialise in natural history tours to reserves such as Ankarana, Analamera and Daraina, providing all necessary camping equipment and 4WD vehicles. A highly recommended, slightly cheaper alternative to King de la Piste.

Car and bike hire

ADA Location (Batiment SICAM), Bd Duplex; tel: 82 224 98; email: sicam.diego@simicro.mg. A Peugeot 106 costs 241,000Fmg per day including a driver.
Hotel Paradis du Nord Sometimes has cars plus drivers.
The Blue Marine 67 Colbert (near the Nouvel Hotel). Bike hire.

Windsor Castle and Courrier's Bay

A half-day drive (4WD) or full-day bike excursion takes you to the fantastic rock known as Windsor Castle. This monolith (visible from Antsiranana and – better –

if you arrive by ship) is steep-sided and flat-topped, so made a perfect lookout point during times of war. The views from there are superb. It was fortified by the French, occupied by the Vichy forces, and liberated by the British. A ruined staircase still runs to the top (if you can find it). There is some *tsingy* here, and many endemic water-retaining plants including a local species of pachypodium, *P. baronii windsori*.

To get there take the road that runs west towards Ampasindava, where you turn right (north) along a rocky road, then left towards Windsor Castle. The road continuing north is the very rough one to Cap d'Ambre. The stone staircase to the top of Windsor Castle is not easy to find, and alternative routes sometimes bring you to dense forest or an impassable rock face. Sven Oudgenoeg, who also initially failed to find the staircase, enlisted the help of a local fisherman who acted as a guide and showed him the path. He gives these precise instructions: 'Drive exactly 28.2km from Diego Suarez towards Cap d'Ambre; here you come to a fork in the road. The 'main' road (once metalled, now potholed) continues towards Cap d'Ambre, the left branch goes to Windsor Castle. After 4.2km the road passes through a clump of mango trees where it divides into two paths. Take the one to the left which leads along a steep ridge to the foot of the ruined staircase. The way up the staircase is not always clear, so you have to apply a little logic, but it can be done, and takes about an hour to the top.' John and Valerie Middleton give an alternative (2001): 'A much easier and more interesting ascent route is to follow the less steep ridge to the one mentioned until it is possible to traverse leftwards beneath the large rock face. This leads directly to the steps to the top. The northwest side of Windsor Castle is reported to be superior for its flora and fauna but requires a camp en route from the Courrier's Bay road. Incidently, this road is cut off for around five hours at high tide for about 60m.'

This is a hot, dry climb. Take plenty of water and allow yourself enough time. Courrier's Bay, half an hour beyond Windsor Castle, is an exceptionally fine beach.

Cap d'Ambre

In the last edition of this guide I wrote: 'I have yet to hear of a traveller who has reached the Cape. This is a very difficult and potentially dangerous trip and should not be undertaken lightly'. John and Valerie Middleton (who else?) rose to the challenge in 2003 and sent this report: 'Our main objective was one of plants and karst. The road is surprisingly easy; in fact the slowest bit is the first 10km from Antsiranana. It is approximately 75km to the Cap and this should take no more than seven hours with photo stops – and the views are often superb with both the Indian Ocean and Mozambique Channel at once. The obvious route via a straight road north is poor due to the tide covering the track and making it extremely muddy most of the time. The best way is via the villages of Bedarabe and Ambatonjanohavy in the east. The final tip beneath the lighthouse is an amazing wilderness of fantastic wave eroded limestone. The lighthouse itself has a 10cm wide crack all down one side and is currently not working. Beneath this on the landward side, several old lighthouse buildings house the friendly keeper and another family. He keeps a record of visitors and we were surprised to see so many – about 15 in September and October alone!' Which goes to show that you shouldn't believe everything you read in a guidebook – even this one!

The Middletons add: 'On our return we camped beneath La Butte at the northern end of the escarpment at the opposite end of which is Windsor Castle. Our interest was to explore the not inconsiderable areas of *tsingy* and associated plants but also found the whole plateau gave excellent walking opportunities. The several large outcrops were almost all as impressive as Windsor Castle.'

Lac Antanavo (Lac Sacré)

The sacred lake is about 75km south of Antsiranana, near the small town of Anivorano. It attracts visitors more for its legends than for the reality of a not particularly scenic lake and the possibility of seeing a crocodile. The story is that once upon a time Anivorano was situated amid semi-desert and a thirsty traveller arrived at the village and asked for a drink. When his request was refused he warned the villagers that they would soon have more water than they could cope with. No sooner had he left than the earth opened, water gushed out, and the mean-minded villagers and their houses were inundated. The crocodiles which now inhabit the lake are considered to be ancestors (and to wear jewellery belonging to their previous selves. So they say).

The crocodiles are sometimes fed by the villagers, so you may do best to book a

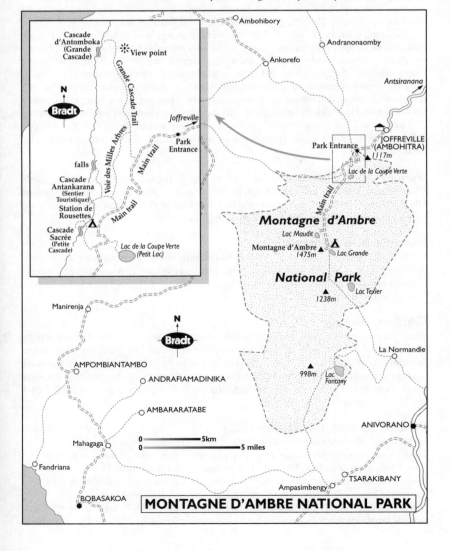

tour in Diego; the tour operator should know when croc feeding day is. There are two smaller lakes nearby which the locals fish cautiously – often from the branches of a tree to avoid a surprise crocodile attack.

MONTAGNE D'AMBRE (AMBER MOUNTAIN) NATIONAL PARK

This 18,500ha national park was created in 1958, the French colonial government recognising the unique nature of the volcanic massif and its forest. The park is part of the Montagne d'Ambre Reserves Complex which also includes the Special Reserves of Ankarana, Analamera and Forêt d'Ambre. The project, initiated in 1989, is funded by USAID, the Malagasy government and the WWF; it was the first to involve local people in all stages of planning and management. The aims of conservation, rural development and education have largely been achieved. Ecotourism has been encouraged successfully with good information and facilities now available.

Montagne d'Ambre National Park is a splendid example of upland moist forest, or montane rainforest. The massif ranges in altitude from 850m to 1,475m and has its own micro-climate with rainfall equal to the eastern region. It is one of the most visitor-friendly of all the protected areas of Madagascar, with broad trails, fascinating flora and fauna, a comfortable climate and readily available information. In the dry season vehicles can drive right up to the main picnic area, giving a unique opportunity (in Madagascar) for elderly or disabled visitors to see the rainforest and its inhabitants.

The name comes not from deposits of precious amber, but from the amber-coloured resin which oozes from some of its trees and is used medicinally by the local people.

Warning Antsiranana is now firmly on the itinerary of cruise ships, with Montagne d'Ambre the focus of the day's excursion. This means that upward of 100 passengers will pour into the park. Independent travellers may wish to visit the port to check if a ship is due before planning their visit.

Permits and information

Permits (50,000Fmg) and a very good information booklet are available at the park entrance. The ANGAP office is on the outskirts of town towards the airport. Permits are also available here.

It is compulsory to take a guide.

Getting there

The entrance to the park is 27km south of Antsiranana, 4km from the town of Ambohitra, or Joffreville as almost everyone still calls it. Taxi-brousses leave Antsiranana at 07.00 for Joffreville, and return at 14.00. The journey takes about an hour (the road is tarred). A private taxi is cheaper than organising the trip through a tour operator. This has always seemed the perfect place for a good-quality hotel and now –hooray! – there are two.

Where to stay/eat (Joffreville)

Le Domaine de Fontenay Cellphone: 033 1134 581; email: cts@dts.mg; www.lefontenay-madagascar.com. One of Madagascar's best hotels. Double rooms €120, suite €163. 'Owned and run by Marie-Jose de Spéville and Karl-Heinz Horner. Great food, amazingly clean, comfortable, and professionally run establishment with en-suite rooms in a beautiful garden. English-speaking, friendly people.' (Keri Harvey)
Nature Lodge Tel: 320 71712306; www.naturelodge-ambre.com. 7 very comfortable bungalows, with a tastefully designed bar and restaurant. Friendly, excellent food. Double

rooms €40, meals €9. This lodge can also be booked through the restaurant Grill du Rova in Tana; tel: 22 356 07.

La Benedictine This is a convent in Joffreville that serves meals. 'A community-style dinner served to everyone present at one large table by nuns. They have a gift shop there too.' (Bill Love)

Accommodation in the park

There are shelters and bunk beds in the park for visitors equipped with their own sleeping bags (bring your own food). From the wildlife point of view, staying in or near the park is far preferable to making a day trip from Antsiranana.

There is a campsite (often crowded) at the car-park/picnic area (known as Station de Rousettes) where a visitor centre is being built.

Weather

The rainy season (and cyclone season) is from December to April. The dry season is May through August, but there is a strong wind, *varatraza*, almost every day, and it can feel very cold. The temperature in the park is, on average, 10°F cooler than in Antsiranana, it is often wet and muddy, and there may be leeches. So be wary of wearing shorts and sandals however hot and dry you are at sea-level. Bring rain gear, insect repellent and even a light sweater.

The most rewarding time to visit is during the warm season: September through November. There will be some rain, but most animals are active and visible, and the lemurs will have babies.

Flora and fauna

Montagne d'Ambre is as exciting for its plants as for its animals. A very informative booklet gives details and illustrations of the species most commonly seen. All visitors are impressed by the tree-ferns and the huge, epiphytic bird's-nest ferns which grow on trees. The distinctive *Pandanus* is also common, and you can see Madagascar's endemic cycad. Huge strangler figs add to the spectacle.

Most visitors want to see lemurs and two diurnal species have become habituated; Sanford's brown lemur (a subspecies of brown lemur) and the crowned lemur. Male Sanford's lemurs have white/beige ear-tufts and side-whiskers surrounding black faces, whilst the females are of a more uniform colour with no whiskers and a grey face. Crowned lemurs get their names from the triangle of black between the ears of the male; the rest of the animal is reddish brown. Females are mainly grey, with a little red tiara across the forehead. Both sexes have a lighter-coloured belly; in the female this is almost white. Young are born from September to November.

Other mammals occasionally seen are the ring-tailed mongoose and – if you are really lucky – the fosa. And there are five species of nocturnal lemur.

'At eye-level you may spot some large chameleons – although the drive up from Antsiranana is a better hunting ground for these reptiles which are often seen crossing the road. Also look carefully on the forest floor and low vegetation as this is the place to find several different leaf-mimic *brookesia* chameleons (some little more than 2cm long). There are other lizards like the spectacular *Paroedura* gecko, plus pill millipedes rolling into a perfect ball, many frogs, butterflies and mysterious fungi.' (Nick Garbutt)

Even non-birders will be fascinated by the numerous species here: the Madagascar crested ibis is striking enough to impress anybody, as is the paradise flycatcher with its long, trailing tail feathers. The locally endemic Amber Mountain rock thrush is tame and ubiquitous, and the black-and-white magpie robin is often seen. The jackpot, however, is one of Madagascar's most beautiful birds: the pitta-like ground-roller.

Trails, waterfalls and lakes

The park has, in theory, 30km of paths, but many of these are overgrown although they are gradually being cleared and renamed. The best, and most heavily used, trails lead to the Petit Lac, the Jardin Botanique, and two waterfalls, Cascade d'Antomboka (Grande Cascade) and Cascade Sacrée (Petite Cascade). There is also a Sentier Touristique with another lovely waterfall at the end.

The three waterfalls provide the focal points for day visitors. If time is short and you want to watch wildlife rather than walk far, go to the **Cascade Sacrée**. This is only about 100m along the track beyond the picnic area (Station de Rousettes) and on the way you should see lemurs, orchids and birds galore. Take a small path on your left to the river for a possible glimpse of the white-throated rail and the malachite kingfisher. The Cascade Sacrée is an idyllic fern-fringed grotto with waterfalls splashing into a pool. In the hot season there is a colony of little bats (I don't know the species) twittering in the overhang to the right of the pool.

The **Sentier Touristique** is also easy and starts near the Station de Rousettes (walk back towards the entrance, cross the bridge and turn left). The path terminates at a viewpoint above **Cascade Antankarana**: a highly photogenic spot and a good place to find the forest rock thrush and other birds.

The walk to the **Cascade d'Antomboka** is tougher, with some up and down stretches, and a steep descent to the waterfall. There is some excellent birdwatching here, some lovely tree-ferns and a good chance of seeing lemurs – especially if you bring a picnic which includes bananas… On your way back you'll pass a path on the right (left as you go towards the waterfall) marked **Voie des Mille Arbres** (formerly Jardin Botanique); don't be misled into thinking this will lead you to the rose-garden. It's a tough roller-coaster of a walk, but very rewarding, and eventually joins the main track.

Another easy walk from Station de Rousettes is the viewpoint above the crater lake, **Lac de la Coupe Verte**.

A full day's walk beyond Station de Rousettes takes you to a crater lake known as **Lac Maudit**, or Matsabory Fantany, then on for another hour to **Lac Grand**. Beyond that is the highest point in the park, **Montagne d'Ambre** (1,475m) itself. Unless you are a fit, fast walker it would be best to take two days on this trek and camp by Lac Grand. That way you can wait for weather conditions to allow the spectacular view.

Night walks

Now that there is accommodation in Joffreville, night walks are easily arranged. Nick Garbutt reports: 'The drive up to the park after dark can be amazing for chameleons – I've regularly found five to seven species, plus tree boas and some frogs.' In the forest two types of leaf-tailed gecko are often seen, *Uroplatus sikorae* and *U. ebenaui*.

ANALAMERA SPECIAL RESERVE

This 34,700ha reserve is in remote and virtually unexplored deciduous forest some 20km southeast of Montagne d'Ambre, and is the last refuge of the very rare Perrier's black sifaka (*Propithecus diadema perrieri*) which few people have been fortunate enough to see. The reserve is now open to visitors and, for the enthusiast, easily merits between two and four nights' camping. There are no facilities of any kind, so visitors must be totally self-sufficient.

To reach the reserve from Antsiranana you drive 50km south on the main road, and are then faced with a further 11km on a dreadful stretch which is impassable in the rainy season. Guides and porters can be organised in the nearby village of Menagisy, but it is more sensible to arrange the visit through an operator in Antsiranana, such as Le King de la Piste or Zanatany Tours. In addition to the black sifaka, you may also see crowned lemurs, Sanford's brown lemurs and endangered birds such as the white-breasted mesite and Van Dam's vanga.

ANKARANA SPECIAL RESERVE

About 108km south of Antsiranana is a small limestone massif, Ankarana. An 'island' of *tsingy* (limestone karst pinnacles) and forest, the massif is penetrated by numerous caves and canyons. Some of the largest caves have collapsed, forming isolated pockets of river-fed forest with their own perfectly protected flora and fauna. Dry deciduous forest grows around the periphery and into the wider canyons. The caves and their rivers are also home to crocodiles, some reportedly six metres long. The reserve is known for its many lemur species, including crowned and Sanford's brown lemur, and also the inquisitive ring-tailed mongoose, *Galidia elegans*, but it is marvellous for birds, reptiles and insects as well. Indeed, the 'Wow!' factor is as high here as anywhere I have visited.

Ankarana is a Special Reserve (18,220ha) and is rightly among the most popular western reserves, although at present it is a hiking and camping trip only.

Where to stay (outside the park)

Two readers have recommended 'basic huts for visitors' near the east entrance of the reserve. These cost about 25,000Fmg. Rebecca Pierce gives the owner's name as Toly Aurelian. Whether these are the same huts as enjoyed by Alex Sandall (see below) I'm not sure, but they certainly provide a good alternative to an all-inclusive camping tour.

A set of bungalows is also being built on the south side of the reserve, south of Campement d'Andrafiabe (Camp des Américains).

Permits and guides

A permit for Ankarana should be purchased from ANGAP) in Antsiranana or Tana. A guide is compulsory. Most live in Matsaborimanga, but are available at the ANGAP office at Mahamasina.

Getting there and away

With a 4WD vehicle you can drive all the way to the main campsite, Campement Anilotra (Camp des Anglais), in the dry season. Most drivers approach from the north, turning off at Anivorano and heading for the village of Matsaborimanga. Allow five hours for this drive from Antsiranana.

By far the most interesting way to get there, however, is to hike in from RN6, a good tarred road which runs between Ambanja and Antsiranana The journey to the village of Mahamasina takes about three hours from Ambanja or 2½ hours from Antsiranana and is easily made by taxi-brousse or ordinary taxi. There is an ANGAP office near the trailhead at the 108km sign on the road. It's a super walk of about 11km in to the reserve; allow 2½ to 3 hours. The first part is down a wide track, then, after about 20 minutes, you turn right down a gully and cross a river. Shortly after that the trail levels out, enters some beautiful forest (you are now in one of the wide canyons). A huge *ficus* marks the halfway point and a steep gully indicates that you are arriving at Campement Anilotra.

On the way back, if you use the same route, your guide will take you along an alternative trail to visit the bat caves – a tough scramble, but well worth it.

Organised tours

It is not easy to do Ankarana independently. You need transport and a guide anyway, so it makes sense to take an organised tour (see page 365 for a list of recommended tour operators). Levels of organisation and comfort vary considerably, so your choice will probably depend on your budget. At the top end of the market is Le King de la Piste or Zanatany, which will cost you around 2,300,000Fmg for two people, three days/two nights. This will include good-quality tents, meals and transport. 'They were the only tour operator who would take us to the west side of Ankarana (this was mid June). It was top notch. Our guide, Zac, was incredibly knowledgeable, charming, spoke very good English and was a deft hand at flicking scorpions off clothes. So early in the season, we had the place pretty much to ourselves, which must make all the difference when exploring the caves.'

At the other end of the comfort scale, but ideal for toughies, is to stay outside the reserve and hike in. This was the choice of Alex Sandell and Ben Kelly who paid Jasmin Ravalohery an all-inclusive price of 500,000Fmg per person (for five people). 'The journey from Diego was entertaining and educational in itself, with various stops to buy a couple of chickens for dinner, rescue chameleons from the road and visit a market. We stayed in a collection of small Malagasy huts right at the east entrance to the park where there was a basic but functional long-drop toilet and bucket shower. Jasmin and his wife cooked up delicious Malagasy delicacies for dinner on both nights. There was a *lot* of walking during our 1½ days in the park. On Day 1 we saw the Petit Tsingy and Bat Cave (fabulous!) which took six hours. On Day 2 we walked 9½ hours to visit Lac Vert and the Grand Tsingy. Not for the faint-hearted but it was hugely enjoyable and even conquered without complaint by the 11-year-old in our group! The walk itself was what gave us all the most enjoyment: to find yourself at once in a dry and open savanna-type environment, then in the cool shade of a green forest spotting snakes, birds, sleeping nocturnal lemurs and mischievous diurnal lemurs, and then cross a dry riverbed to find yourselves in a dry, barren, grey forest with the sun beating down on you is really quite striking. The extremes of the ecosystems here are unlike anything I've seen before.'

Campsites

The main campsite, formerly known as Camp des Anglais (following the Crocodile Caves Expedition), has been renamed **Campement Anilotra**. It is equipped with long-drop toilets and picnic tables. There are three separate areas, so although it tends to get crowded you can usually escape from other travellers. Note that the camp offers considerably more shade than Campement d'Andrafiabe, as well as a chance to bathe in the river running through the cave. However, as the reserve becomes more popular, so does the likelihood of finding this campsite fully occupied. The water supply is a good ten minutes' walk away down a slippery slope.

The usual alternative campsite is **Campement d'Andrafiabe** (Camp des Américains), which is handy for the Andrafiabe Cave. It has a water supply and toilets, but can get very crowded. At the time of writing 'it has deteriorated into a hell-hole'. Very possibly by the time you read this, is will have been renovated.

An increasingly popular camp is **Camp des Africains** (it seems to have kept its old name) which has long-drop toilets and picnic tables. Water is a problem – it's hard to

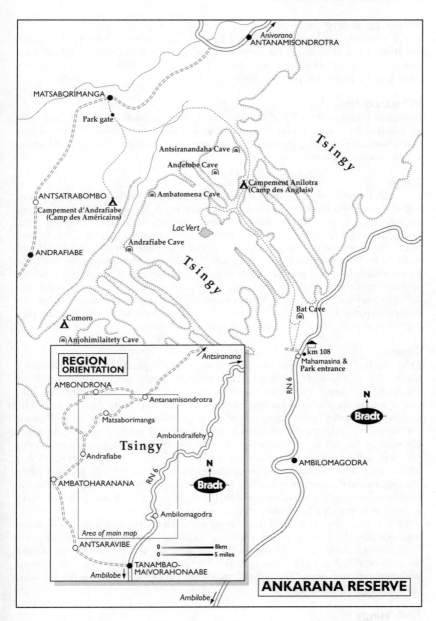

ANKARANA RESERVE

get to in the dry season so you need to bring water with you. There is a bat cave nearby and some small *tsingy* about half an hour's walk away, but to reach the main *tsingy* you must walk 32km round trip. This camp is good for wildlife with crowned lemurs, lepilemurs and the beautiful russet-coloured *Galidia elegans* mongoose.

Camp de Fleur is about two hours from Campement Anilotra and is a good base for visiting Lac Vert and some of the best *tsingy*.

What to bring

You'll need strong shoes or boots, a daypack, a two-litre water bottle, insect repellent, torch (flashlight) for the caves plus spare batteries. And earplugs. Not just because of the snoring from other campers – the lepilemurs and cicadas of Ankarana are highly vocal!

What to see

Ankarana reminds me of J-P Commerson's famous quote: 'At every step one encounters the most strange and marvellous forms.' Everything is strange and marvellous: the animals, the birds, the plants, the landscape. The main things to see are *tsingy* and caves.

Tsingy

Although found in other countries, *tsingy* is very much a Madagascar phenomenon and you won't want to leave Ankarana without seeing it. If staying at Anilotra Camp, the best *tsingy* is about two hours away, over very rugged terrain, just beyond the beautiful crater lake, Lac Vert. This is a very hot, all-day trip (start early, in the cool of the day, bring a picnic and plenty of water) and is absolutely magnificent. Board walks have been constructed to allow safe passage over the *tsingy*, protecting the fragile rock while you admire the strange succulents such as *Pachypodium* which seem to grow right out of the limestone. Lac Vert is as green as its name, and if you are crazy enough you can hike down a steep, slippery slope to the water's edge. An easier alternative is *Le Petit Tsingy* which is found just 15 minutes from the campsite. Although smaller, there are similar plants and also lemurs.

Caves

From Andrafiabe Camp you can explore the gigantic passageways of Andrafiabe Cave. 'We don't believe that even the most claustrophobic person could get claustrophobia here! This is well worth a visit with an exit halfway through into one of the spectacular canyons from where an interesting return can be made. The Crocodile Caves in the southern end of the reserve seem to be little visited but are well worth the effort – the situation is spectacular and the passageways are huge. We went in for almost a kilometre to the first lake but did not find any crocodiles (the rest of the cave is more or less dry at this time of year [September]).' (V & J Middleton) 'The crocodile cave …was easily walkable in about 30 minutes from the entrance to the eastern end where it took a steep, rocky climb to go out into the sunken forest. I saw croc tail drag marks, but no live ones. Fish and large eels were trapped in interior puddles and sections of river.' (Bill Love).

Don't miss the wonderful bat caves, especially Crystal Cave. 'This is an underground fairytale land of sparkling stalagmites and stalactites. Bring a headlamp or flashlight – hiking over such delicate terrain can be tricky and dangerous. You'll feel like a mouse in the Bat Cave with its towering walls pocked with bat and swift nests. The ground crawls with cockroaches and is littered with bat carcasses.' (D Fellner)

Red 'tsingy'

Sheena Gibson reports: 'About an hour from Diego, on the east side of the road to Ankarana, is an area of red *tsingy*. This is absolutely fantastic and much more photogenic that the normal grey *tsingy*. It is off the beaten track and you need a 4WD to reach it.' This is actually not true *tsingy* but eroded sandstone (as opposed to limestone). Tour operators specialising in Ankarana should know about the 'red tsingy' and be able to take you there.

OVERLAND FROM ANTSIRANANA TO SAMBAVA

A taxi-brousse from Antsiranana (Diego) to Ambilobe (on RN6) takes about three hours. After that, the trouble begins because the road is truly awful. 'It took us at least 21½ hours to cover some 150km. We left Ambilobe in the early afternoon (after having been told to be ready for 6.30 that morning) travelling in what is known as a *camion Kosovo* through the night and arrived in Vohemar around eleven the next day, battered, bruised and exhausted.' (Sebastian Bulmer)

If you survive this first section, however, it is plain sailing from Iharana (Vohemar) to Sambava down one of the best roads in Madagascar.

Ambilobe
Where to stay/eat
Hotel Nord 90,000Fmg for a large, clean room with hot water.

Daraina
Daraina is a small town around 70km northwest of Iharana; the road is bad to very bad (impossible in the wet season) and the journey takes about three hours in a taxi. There is only one reason to stop here: you can see one of the rarest species of sifaka. Nick Garbutt sent the following report:

'There's not a lot in Daraina except a couple of *hotelys* serving regular *hotely* fare and it's often murderously hot, but the nearby forests are home to the beautiful golden-crowned sifaka (*Propithecus tattersalli*) – one of the rarest of all lemurs and listed as one of the 25 most threatened primates in the world.

'A Malagasy NGO called FANAMBY has set up an office and project to work with the local communities and try to preserve the forests and the sifaka. One of their aims is to establish a network of protected areas in the region (currently none of the forests where the sifakas live is protected). The region has deposits of gold and is rich in semi-precious stones. This is one of the factors causing conflict with the establishment of a park.

'Visitors are required to pay a fee of 40,000Fmg to the Mayor of Daraina to go and see the sifakas – 25,000Fmg of this goes to Daraina, and 15,000Fmg to the village near where the sifakas can be seen.

'The village is called Andranotsimaty and is accessible by 4WD (45 minutes from Daraina) or by walking (1½ hours). The people here scrape a living by mining for gold and the forests near the village are scarred with deep pits that have been excavated. However, the sifakas in the forests adjacent to the village are common and very easy to see. It is possible to camp in the forest near Andranotsimaty.'

For more information contact Serge Rajaobelina at FANAMBY, BP8434, Antananarivo 101; tel/fax: 261 20 22 288 78; email: fanamby@fanamby.org.mg; www.fanamby.org.mg.

Iharana (Vohemar)
More than one reader has said that this pleasant beach resort town is *the* place to recover from some rough travelling. It has all the right ingredients: a comfortable (but not expensive) hotel and some wonderful food. And a beach. There are enjoyable walks to be taken in the area too. It is also still something of a Cinderella in tourist terms: often gets ignored in favour of better-known resorts. Cyclone Gafilo did a fair amount of damage here, however.

Getting there and away
The easiest way to get here is to fly to Sambava then take a taxi-brousse for the two-hour road journey. The very rough trip from Antsiranana is described earlier.

The alternative is to fly (by Twin Otter) from Antsiranana or Nosy Be (note that even Air Mad uses the old name, Vohemar). The Air Mad office is hard to find; it's tucked away in the Star Breweries yard!

Where to stay
Sol y Mar Excellent bungalows in a beautiful setting by the shore with shower and WC. Prices from 80,000Fmg for a basic bungalow to 160,000Fmg for one facing the ocean, with hot water. 'Just a few paces from my room into the sea for a splendid swim. Also had good food.' (Philip Jones). 'The *punch coco* is out of this world, and the lychee punch isn't bad either. The meals, when the French co-owner is cooking, are really superb!' Recent reports (2003) confirm this place is still the tops (but they may have been damaged by the cyclone).
Poisson d'Or Basic, with a good restaurant.
Railouvy Across from the Poisson.

Where to eat
Hotely Kanto A terrific place for meals, run by Madame Elizabeth, who as well as being very friendly is a tremendous cook. Her speciality is *ravitoto* with coconut.
La Florida You can order almost anything in this restaurant: calamari, shrimp coco, *soupe Chinoise* etc, all for a very reasonable price.

OVERLAND FROM ANTSIRANANA TO AMBANJA AND NOSY BE
RN6 has recently been improved, and this route is popular with travellers heading for Nosy Be – but there is plenty to see in the area so it is a shame to rush. The journey from Antsiranana to Ambanja at present takes about five hours for the 240km journey.

The first place to break your journey is Ambilobe (see page 375). Then on to Ambanja (two hours), which merits a stay of a day or two.

Ambanja
This is a pleasant little town set amid lush scenery.

Telephone code The area code for Ambanja is 86.

Getting there and away
Most people stopping at Ambanja are on their way to or from Nosy Be. Josephine Andrews offers these hints for the trip to Antsiranana. 'There are some fixed-time taxi-brousses which leave at 11.00 and 13.00 (those big nine-place Peugeots) for Diego. There is a little office near to the main market in the north of the town. Otherwise there are always vehicles of every description heading north from the same market, or south from the little market at the far south of town.'

Where to stay/eat
Hotel Palma Nova Probably the best hotel in Ambanja, and close to the town centre. About 70,000Fmg for a clean, en-suite, air-conditioned room. Excellent breakfasts.
Hotel Patricia A perennial *vazaha* favourite. Run by M Yvon and his wife (Chinese/Malagasy) who go out of their way to be helpful. Rooms vary in quality and price, so there is something to suit everyone. Usually shut in the afternoon (for siesta) so be prepared to wait. There is an excellent Malagasy cookbook for sale here, written by M Yvon's sister.
Hotel Bougainvilleas Rooms have a shower and WC.
Sambirano Tel: 86 920 60. Low-priced rooms.

Ankify

This beautiful area of coast is being developed as a resort. It is the departure point for ferries and water taxis (*kinga*) to Nosy Be and has two lovely (*Category A*) hotels.

Where to stay

Le Dauphin Bleu BP33, Ambanja; tel: 320 235 083; email: info@ledauphinbleu.com; www.ledauphinbleu.com (German language). 250,000Fmg including breakfast. 7 stone bungalows with hot water and breakfast served on its beach terrace. A lovely hotel a few kilometres beyond the Baobab, with a view of Nosy Komba. German-owned, with a large garden and a private beach.

Le Baobab BP85, Ambanja; tel: 86 614 37 or (Antsiranana) 82 293 64 or (Tana) 22 222 95. Located about 2km northwest of the dock area, nestled between rocky cliffs and a beach that overlooks Nosy Komba. Very pleasant bungalows with separate bathrooms, hot water, table fans, mosquito nets. About €23. Bill Love, who stays here regularly, writes: 'The grounds are beautifully planted in bougainvillea, palms, ylang-ylang etc, with paved paths between cottages. The restaurant/bar is located on top of another hill, is open-air under a huge thatched roof, and is very comfy and with a great view of the bay… Crowned lemurs pass over the trees over the road nearby, and lower life-forms abound on evening flashlight walks down the road outside the hotel.' Bill adds: 'The panther chameleons residing locally are among the most beautiful of all – greenish bodies with brilliant blue bands.' In his 2003 report Bill adds: 'Nadina Yuon now manages Le Baobab. Very friendly, speaks English very well.'

Hotel la Mer Cellphone: 032 0482 261; email: info@hotel-la-mer.com; www.hotel-de-la-mer.com. The hotel is only a few minutes from a beach where swimming is possible, and 4.5km from the ferry at Ankify. Or you can organise transfers to Nosy Be by boat from the hotel. Transfers from Ambanja to the hotel costs €12. Two bungalows and three rooms, with 'huge bathrooms, WC and bidet, European standard.' 130,000Fmg per bungalow, 200,000Fmg for a room. 'Highly recommended. It is run by a very efficient German woman, Regina Kunzke, and we were extremely impressed. The food is excellent and views over the bay stunning.' (R Pierce)

Tsaratanana

Adventurous travellers look at a map of Madagascar and long to climb its highest mountain. However, Tsaratanana is not normally open to tourists and those who have tried to penetrate it for scientific research have had a rough time. In a nutshell, this mountain is largely deforested, waterless, trail-less and hot. That said, there is a tour operator in Tana who will take you to the top: Madamax (see page 105).

Continuing south from Ambanja to Mahajanga

For a description of this journey see *Chapter 16*.

BAYS AND INLETS ACCESSIBLE TO YACHTS

The bays below could be reached by adventurous hikers or cyclists (many are near villages) but are visited mainly by yachties (lucky devils!).

Russian Bay (Helondranon Ambavatoby)

This is a beautiful and remote place opposite the Nosy Be archipelago. It provides excellent anchorages, all-round shelter and is a traditional 'hurricane hole'. The marine life in the bay itself is terrific, offering wonderful snorkelling and diving, especially in the reefs outside the entrance. There is excellent fishing too. In the right season (October to December), whales are commonly sighted in the bay. This is one of the best spots in which to seek the very rare whale shark. The beaches are known turtle-nesting sites. The sambirano and moist tropical deciduous woods there harbour abundant birdlife, reptiles and lemurs, and there is a choice of trails for day hikes.

The bay's name dates back to an incident in 1905, during the Russo-Japanese war, when a Russian warship, the *Vlötny*, anchored there. The order was to attack any passing Japanese ship, but the crew took one look at life in Madagascar and realised that they did not wish to wage war nor to return to Russia. They had barely organised a mutiny before their officers gave in, having taken one look at the lovely Malagasy women. The ship was hidden in the reaches of Russian Bay and twice emerged to trade with pirate vessels in the Mozambique Channel before they ran out of fuel for the boilers. The Russians were decimated by malaria, but the survivors quickly adapted to their new home, living by fishing. The last one died in 1936. The Russians sold anything they could remove from the ship, but the remains can still be seen at low tide.

Baramahamay Bay (Maroaka)

The Baramahamay River is navigable for about 3km inland and provides a beautiful, well-sheltered anchorage with verdant hills behind sunny, white beaches. The wide bay is conspicuous as a large gap in the coastline. Yachties should approach on the north side of the bay and anchor near the villages in 8m over sand and mud. These villages are known also for their blacksmiths, who make large knives and *pangas*. One of the small villages here is known for its wild honey, and there is a pool with good drinking water.

Your chances of seeing the (very rare) resident Madagascar fish eagles here are good.

Berangomaina Point

The bay inside this headland is an attractive, well-sheltered anchorage. Good visibility is needed to access the bay, however, as there are many scattered reef patches. The channel is at its deepest on the north side, where the depth exceeds 15m right up to the reef. Anchor off the beach before the village, in 10m over a mud bottom. This place is for self-sufficient travellers only, no provisions are available.

Nosy Be

16

The name means 'Big Island' and is pronounced 'Nossy Bay' by the local Sakalava people, although 'Noos Bay' is nearer the highlands pronunciation. It is blessed, in the driest months, with an almost perfect climate (sunshine with brief showers). Fertile and prosperous, with the heady scent of ylang-ylang blossoms giving it the tourist-brochure name of 'Perfumed Isle', this is the place to come for a rest – providing you can afford it. Compared with the rest of Madagascar, Nosy Be is expensive.

Nosy Be developed tourism long before mainland Madagascar, so inevitably the island seems touristy or 'commercialised' to adventurous travellers. However, Nosy Be provides a taste of everything that is special to Madagascar, from wonderful seafood to beaches, from chameleons to lemurs, so for this reason is ideal for those with very limited time who are looking for a hassle-free holiday. It also has several options for real luxury – not always easy to find in Madagascar.

All of the easily accessible beaches on Nosy Be have now been taken over by hotels. None is perfect for swimming – they shelve too gradually so the water is shallow at high tide and a long walk out at low tide. There are sometimes the vicious sand-flies known locally as *moka fohy* (see box, page 314).

Those determined to find an undeveloped area should study the FTM map of Nosy Be (scale 1:80,000), which is readily available in Tana and Hell-Ville. It is very detailed and marks beaches. Note, however, that the reserve of Lokobe is out of bounds to tourists, and many of the 'roads' are impassable to vehicles.

Telephone code The area code for Nosy Be is 86.

HISTORY

Nosy Be's charms were recognised as long ago as 1649 when the English colonel, Robert Hunt, wrote: 'I do believe, by God's blessing, that not any part of the world is more advantageous for a plantation, being every way as well for pleasure as well as profit, in my estimation.' Hunt was attempting to set up an English colony on the island, at that time known as Assada, but failed because of hostile natives and disease.

Future immigrants, both accidental and intentional, contributed to Nosy Be's racial variety. Shipwrecked Indians built a magnificent settlement several centuries ago in the southeast of the island, where the ruins can still be seen. The crew of a Russian ship that arrived during the Russo-Japanese war of 1904–5 are buried in the Hell-Ville cemetery. Other arrivals were Arabs, Comorans and – more recently – Europeans flocking to Madagascar's foremost holiday resort.

When King Radama I was completing his wars of conquest, the Boina kings took refuge in Nosy Be. First they sought protection from the Sultan of

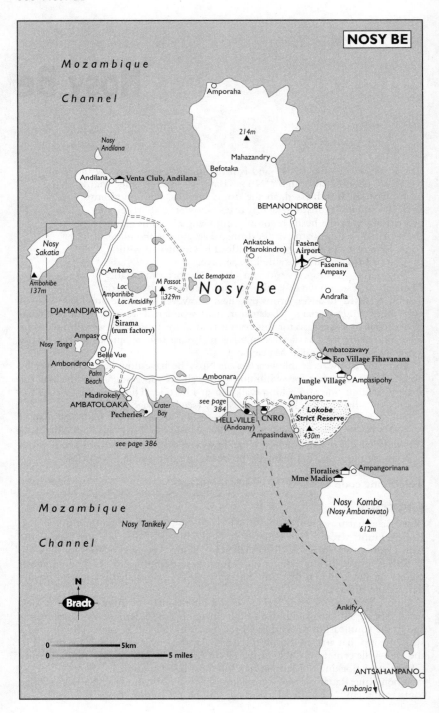

NOSY BE

Mozambique

Channel

Nosy
Andilana

Andilana Venta Club, Andilana

Amporaha

214m

Mahazandry
Befotaka

BEMANONDROBE

Nosy
Sakatia

Ambohibe
137m

Ambaro

Lac
Amparihibe
Lac Antsidihy

M Passot
329m

Lac Bemapaza

Nosy Be

Ankatoka
(Marokindro)

Fasène
Airport

Fasenina
Ampasy

Andrafia

DJAMANDJARY

Sirama
(rum factory)

Ampasy

Nosy Tanga

Belle Vue

Ambondrona
Palm
Beach

Madirokely
AMBATOLOAKA
Pecheries

Crater
Bay

Ambonara

Ambatozavavy
Eco Village Fihavanana

Jungle Village Ampasipohy

Ambanoro

see page
384

see page 386

HELL-VILLE
(Andoany)

CNRO

Ampasindava

Lokobe
Strict Reserve

430m

Floralies
Mme Madio

Ampangorinana

Nosy Komba
(Nosy Ambariovato)

612m

Mozambique

Channel

Nosy Tanikely

N

Bradt

0 ————— 5km
0 ————————— 5 miles

Ankify

ANTSAHAMPANO

Ambanja

Zanzibar, who sent a warship in 1838 then, two years later, they requested help from Commander Passot who had docked his ship at Nosy Be. The Frenchman was only too happy to oblige and asked Admiral de Hell, the governor of Bourbon Island (now Réunion), to place Nosy Be under the protection of France.

The island was formally annexed in 1841.

Note Nosy Be is probably the fastest-changing destination in Madagascar. New businesses open and others close on a monthly basis, and inflation is affecting prices. Telephones often don't work so organising your visit in advance by phone (or email) is not easy. Irene Boswell, who helped update this chapter, stresses 'All information is relative – expect surprises.'

GETTING THERE AND AWAY
By air
There are regular flights from Tana, Mahajanga and Antsiranana, and international flights from Réunion. And – if all goes according to plan – there will be direct flights from Milan by the time you read this.

Taxis from the airport operate on a fixed rate (too changeable to quote here).

By boat from Mahajanga
The *Jean-Pierre Calloc'h* leaves Mahajanga on Fridays arriving in Nosy Be the following day. It returns on Mondays. The times vary according to the tides. This is more a cruise than a ferry, with a first and second class lounge, a bar, a disco, televisions and comfortable airline seats. It costs 350,000Fmg first class, 300,000Fmg second class, and 200,000Fmg third class. Cars cost 1,350,000Fmg plus tax. Contact details, cellphone: 032 0221 686; fax (Mahajanga): 62 226 86. This ferry is also the main supplier of fresh fruit and vegetables to Nosy Be.

From Ankify or Antasahampano
Nosy Be's nearest mainland town of any size is Ambanja; taxis leave from outside the Hotel de Ville for Ankify or Antsahampano, the departure points for the twice-daily car ferry. The sailing time (and port) depend on the tides. The trip takes 2? to 3 hours and costs 7,500Fmg. This ferry can take two vehicles (240,000Fmg). The alternatives are steamboat (*vedette*) which, being smaller, are less tied to the tides and often call first at Nosy Komba, and speedboats. These leave 'hourly' (Malagasy time); the cost is 25,500Fmg. *Vazahas* sometimes get asked for a lot more – up to 200,000Fmg – so try to find out what the locals pay. The journey takes about half an hour.

If you are taking the ferry back from Nosy Be to Ankify, check the board outside the ferry office in Hell-Ville (*A M Hassanaly et fils*). If you have a vehicle, book it on the ferry here.

GETTING AROUND THE ISLAND
There is one well-maintained road, from the airport to Andilana via Hell-Ville. All the others are tracks, sometimes rendered impassable by cyclones. Transport (on the good road) is by taxi-be or private taxi (of which there are plenty).

Taxi
Shared taxis are relatively inexpensive, costing a flat rate. Private taxis also operate on a fixed rate, but these are usually negotiable. Prices are rising too fast to quote accurately here.

Car, bike, motorcycle and plane hire
Many of the hotels rent out mountain bikes and mopeds/motorbikes. If you hire a motorbike, check your insurance policy: many companies will not insure you against motorbike accidents! Prices vary according to power: about 100,000Fmg for a 125cc (half day) to 200,000Fmg for a 350cc.

Nosy Red Cars Ambataloaka. Rent out self-drive Minimokes for two people. 99,000Fmg. Enquire at your hotel.

Nos Autos Car Hire (Hell-Ville) BP48; tel: 86 611 24/ 86 611 51. 5 minibuses, 12 cars, 2 4WD vehicles.

Boat trips
Numerous individuals and companies offer boat excursions. Many of the operators look out for *vazaha* at the port. Others visit the hotels. The two below are just a sample.

Soconet (Daniel) Camp Vert, Hell-Ville; tel: 86 610 79; fax: 86 615 92. The leader in cheap and cheerful day-trips to Nosy Komba and Nosy Tanikely.

Patrick Usually meets *vazahas* as they arrive in Hell-ville; offers boat trips to a variety of destinations.

ACTIVITIES
Watersports
Yachting
Alefa BP89, Madirokely; tel/fax: 86 615 89, cellphone: 032 0712 707; email: alefa@simicro.mg. Round-island luxury pirogue trip. Trips last from two to 22 days, camping with cooks, tents etc provided.

Indian Ocean Charters For specialised sailing/diving holidays. South African run, visit www.indianoceancharters.com or email seaducer@tiscali.co.za or call Greg on cellphone: 033 1432 717 (Nosy Be).

Madanautique Owner Christian Joly; cellphone: 032 0707 213; email: chrisjoly@dts.mg; www.madanautique.com. Excellent catamarans for hire, usually for a week.

Madavoile (also known as **Blue Planet**) BP110, Ambatoloaka; tel: 86 616 37; cellphone: 032 0422 355; email: madplanet@simicro.mg; www.madavoile.com. Well-run sailing trips; efficient and helpful.

Diving
The once-lovely coral around Nosy Be itself has sadly been destroyed, but the pristine little islands of the region offer the best diving in Madagascar (though all coral was damaged by Cyclone Gafilo). May to October are the recommended months.

Blue Dive BP250, Hell-Ville (Ambataloaka); tel: 86 616 31, cellphone: 032 0720 720; email: info@bluedive-madagascar; www.bluedive-madagascar.com

Forever Dive (Mandirokely); cellphone: 032 0712 565; email: forever.dive@simicro.mg; forever-dive.fr.st

Madagascar Dive Club Tel: 86 614 18. Behind the Marlin Club Hotel. Member of PADI International Resort Association.

Madaplouf Bemoko (between Djamanjary and Andilana); tel: 86 612 69; email: madaplouf@wanadoo.mg. Run by a doctor and marine biologist.

Manta Dive Club BP326, Hell-Ville (Madirokely); cellphone: 032 0720 710; email: manta@wanadoo; www.mantadiveclub.com

Oceane's Dream BP173, Ambataloaka, Nosy Be 207; cellphone: 032 0712 782; email: oceaned@wanadoo.mg; www.oceanesdream.com. Organises diving trips to many of the outlying islands and even to the Comoros. Run by Laurent Duriez.

Sakatia Dive Inn BP186, Hell-Ville; tel: 86 614 62, cellphone: 032 0712 675; email: sakatia@wanadoo.mg. See Nosy Sakatia (page 395).

Tropical Diving (Centre International de Plongée) Annexe Coco Plage, Ambataloaka, BP212; tel: 614; cellphone: 03 207 127 90; fax: 84 610 91; email: tropicaldiving@simicro.mg. Specialise in night-diving and underwater photography. Swiss owned.

Deep-sea fishing

Manou Tel: 86 616 12, cellphone: 032 0444 527; email: manoufishing@simicro.mg

Fishing World Cellphone: 032 0712 513; email: fishingworld@simicro.mg; www.fishing-world.fr.st

Nosy Be Fishing Club Cellphone: 032 0479 854

Centre Nautique Rapala Cellphone: 032 0252 307

Barracuda Ambataloaka Tel: 86 620 66, cellphone: 032 0262 992; email: barracuda@simicro.mg

Souvenir shopping

The large number of tourists visiting Nosy Be has made this one of Madagascar's main centres for souvenir production, and provides a unique chance to buy direct from the makers and benefit the local people. Mind you, much of the stuff for sale in boutiques and stalls comes from Tana. Unique to Nosy Be/Nosy Komba are the carved pirogues, clay animals and 'Richelieu' curtains and tablecloths.

Handicraft sellers frequent the road to the port and there are some high-quality goods in Hell-Ville's many boutiques. The best shops in town are **Chez Abud**, which has the widest variety of goods, and **Arts Madagascar** which also has a good selection at reasonable prices. **Parfum de Mangues** is recommended as having a good turnover of stock and friendly, helpful sales staff. It is near the Oasis snack bar.

HELL-VILLE (ANDOANY)

The name comes from Admiral de Hell rather than an evocation of the state of the town. Hell-Ville is actually quite a smart little place (at least by Malagasy standards), its main street lined with boutiques and tourist shops. There is a market selling fresh fruit and vegetables (which may also be purchased from roadside stalls) and an interesting cemetery, especially if you are around on All Souls Day (November 1).

Where to stay in Hell-Ville

There is a good choice of inexpensive hotels in Hell-Ville. For budget travellers a night or two here while you investigate the cheaper beach hotels is almost essential. Things change so fast in Nosy Be that you are certain to find places to stay that are not listed in this chapter.

Category B

Hotel Abud Tel: 86 610 55. A 5-storey building centrally located above Chez Abud souvenir shop. 30 comfortable small rooms, with or without en-suite toilet, 80,000–130,000Fmg. Some rooms have balconies overlooking the street. Restaurant.

Hotel Diamant 10 La Batterie (near Hotel de la Mer); tel: 86 614 48; email: madexof@metclub.mg. 10 comfortable air-conditioned rooms. 131,000Fmg.

La Plantation Cellphone: 032 0267 797; email: computerservice@wanadoo.mg. Better known as a restaurant but rooms available for 150,000Fmg.

Le Saloon Rue Gallieni, opposite the town hall; tel: 86 617 09. 50 air-conditioned rooms.

Le Clerac Tel: 86 632 62, cellphone: 032 0211 162. 65,000–100,000Fmg. Rooms with balconies.

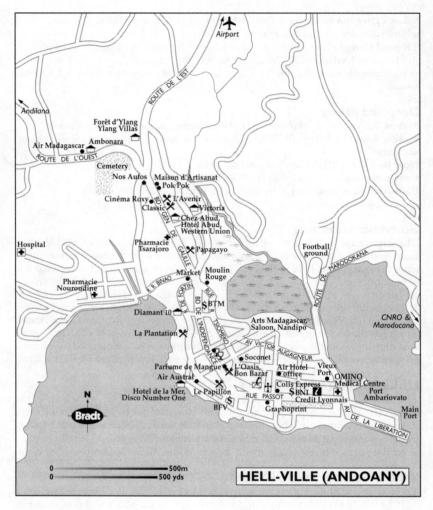

HELL-VILLE (ANDOANY)

Category C

Hotel de la Mer Bd du Docteur Manceau; tel: 86 613 53. The once infamous 'Hotel de Merde' had a brief renaissance but has once again fallen on hard times. Check it out before staying here. 40,000–80,000Fmg. There's a great view from the restaurant.

Hotel Diana Off the main street near Hotel Abud; cellphone: 032 0211 631. Prices range from 55,000Fmg to 120,000Fmg. Some en-suite rooms, others with shared WC/shower.

Hotel George V La Poudrière. Tel: 86 615 61. Eight rooms with fans. 65,000Fmg.

Where to eat in Hell-Ville

Le Papillon Tel: 86 615 82. On the right (as you walk towards the harbour) just before the Catholic church, where Bd de l'Indépendance becomes Rue Passot. Good food, especially pizzas.

La Plantation Cellphone: 032 0267 797. In the Battery area behind the market. Recommended (2004) as being 'a very nice place with sometimes delicious food, run by a

European couple with long experience in catering. The meals are served outside on a typical veranda, overlooking a lively Malagasy quarter.'
Le Manava Above the Moulin Rouge Disco. Tasty food, huge quantities, and very reasonable prices. Currently (2004) the best bargain in Hell-Ville.

Cybercafé
Oasis Bon-Bazar Tel: 86 611 78. Opposite the Papillon. An excellent and low-priced snack bar and cybercafé on the main road, opposite BVF bank. Fresh croissants and *pain au chocolat* daily. Good cakes and ice-cream and a terrace where you can eat them and watch the world go by.

Nightlife
Vieux Port A popular place at the old port. 'Wild nights, usually gets going around 22.00, with live music. Great *salegy* and reggae music. 5,000Fmg to get in but drinks expensive.' (JA)
Moulin Rouge Discotheque Not far from the market; tel: 86 610 36. Serves pizzas during the day and disco every night from 21.30 until dawn.
Disco Number One In a basement beneath the Hotel de Mer. Thursdays and Saturdays.
Bar Nandipo Tel: 86 613 52. French-run bar in the centre of Hell-Ville (near the town hall), popular with expats. Pool table and darts. The best place for a Happy Hour cocktail.

Music festival
The Donia music festival is held each Pentecost (May). A four-day celebration takes place in the Hell-Ville football ground southeast of town. Groups come here from Mauritius, Réunion and Seychelles as well as all parts of Madagascar. 'I would highly recommend a visit. A great party, friendly crowd and good music. But be prepared for the basic (ie: non-existent) loo facilities.' (Sebastian Bulmer) And all for 5,000Fmg. Hotels get very booked up at this time. For more information contact Philip Hardcastle at the Ylang Ylang Hotel (Ambataloaka).

BEACH HOTELS
Most visitors prefer to stay in beach hotels located along the sandy western coast. Hoteliers separate these into seven zones, including Hell-Ville and Nosy Komba. For simplification I have used (mostly) the same divisions, although there are now hotel developments all down the west coast so this is fairly arbitrary. There is also beach accommodation in other areas such as Lokobe and some of the outlying islands. These are listed under the appropriate headings.

Note that if you choose a hotel north of Dzamandzar you will not easily find transport to Ambataloaka or Hell-Ville if you fancy a meal elsewhere or some nightlife. So these hotels are perfect for those who mainly want to relax.

The prices are for high season (mid-July to mid-September, and over the Christmas holiday). Low-season rates are cheaper. Below is just a sample of what is available: with the speed of change in Nosy Be it is impossible to keep up!

This listing is from north to south.

Andilana
Northern Nosy Be is the most beautiful part of the island, though it has succumbed to development. It is 45 minutes' drive from Hell-Ville.

VentaClub Andilana Tel: 86 634 60; fax: 86 634 61; email: andilana.ricevimento@ventaglio.com; www.ventaclub-andilana.com. This is the only all-inclusive hotel in Madagascar, using the tried and tested Club Med format. 'They give you a green bracelet when you arrive, and this entitles you to three sumptuous meals a day (lunch and dinner is five-course with heaps of fresh shellfish and fish), all drinks, snacks, tea, coffee, watersports, etc; Italian-owned now and super-professional people, service, et al. The perfect tropical island holiday spot.' (Keri Harvey). Rates per person range from €106–127 (single) to €85–102 (double) but remember that absolutely everything is included. Facilities for disabled travellers too. Note: this resort must be prebooked **Belvédère** Tel: 86 611 22. A few simple bungalows with some more comfortable rooms. Lovely view. Below is the restaurant **Chez Loulou** which does excellent meals and a fantastic Sunday buffet.

Ambaro

Corail Noir Tel: 86 634 47; fax: 86 635 17; email: corailnoir@netclub.mg. Alex Sandell and Ben Kelly loved this hotel (2003). 'Built and managed by a friendly and enthusiastic Italian/Malagasy couple, it is an incredibly attractive, comfortable and relaxing place to unwind. There are about 16 rooms (ground-floor rooms with little front garden, first floor with balcony) plus ten bungalows with decks out front. Spaced amongst beautiful and well-maintained grounds, with a fabulous open-air bar/restaurant and swimming pool, the whole complex sits next to the beach looking out across the sea and to Nosy Sakatia.

Buildings are mostly made from stone, bamboo and palm leaves and decorated very simply in natural colours and accessories'. A double bungalow is €55 per person. Meals (half-board) €20.

Le Grand Bleu Auberge Tel: 86 634 08; email: legrandbleu@dts.mg; www.legrandbleunosybe.com. A new, French-owned hotel on east side of the road. 10 simple but comfortable bungalows set high on a hill with a splendid view across the island. Lovely swimming pool. €39 per bungalow; meals €7.50. Airport transfer €11 (round trip).

Auberge Orangea Tel: 86 610 67, cellphone: 032 0221 9212; email: orangea@wanadoo.mg; www.orangea-nosybe.com. A new, French-owned hotel on the beach, with a beautiful garden.10 nice bungalows. Double with fan: €50; main meal: €40. Swimming pool.

Belle Vue (Djamandjary area)

Djamandjary is an ugly small town with some strange igloo-shaped cement structures which, long ago, were provided by a relief organisation as cyclone-proof housing. They are, indeed, indestructible, and have mostly been abandoned by the villagers

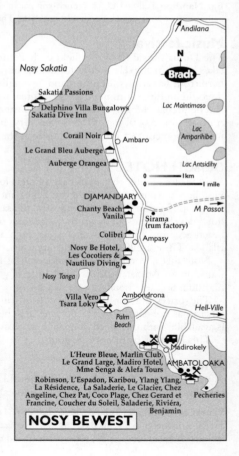

NOSY BE WEST

who have tired of waiting for them to fall down in the time-honoured Malagasy way. Opposite the town is a sugar cane and rum-processing factory, SIRAMA. This is due to be privatised and local opinion is that land by the sea will be sold off for hotel development. Although the beach here is uninspiring (it shelves too gradually for good swimming) it is shaded by coconut palms, and a chain of hotels stretches down the coast as far as Ambataloaka. Each hotel rakes away the dead seaweed that the high tide deposits daily on the beach.

Chanty Beach BP172; tel: 86 614 73; fax: 86 614 74; email: cherz@wanadoo.mg; http://travel.to/Chanty-Beach. 2 luxury 2-person self-catering apartments with spacious veranda, equipped with air conditioning/fans and telephones, near a good beach north of Hotel Vanila. €75–90 double; meals €13–15.

Hotel Vanila BP325; tel: 86 615 23; fax: 615 26; email: vanilahotel@simicro.mg; www.vanila-hotel.com (good, clear website). 3km north of Dzamandzar. 30 airy rooms for €67–92 standard double (depending on season), €79–105 with air-conditioning. Probably the best hotel in Nosy Be; very well managed, with a lovely swimming pool and usually excellent food.

Colibri (Chez Rick & Daniéle) BP83; tel: 86 615 69; fax: 86 612 57. A friendly, family-owned place with just 3 bungalows, set in a lovely garden. Meals taken communally with the owners.

Nosy Be Hotel Tel: 86 614 30; fax: 86 614 06; nosy.be.hotel@simicro.mg; www.nosybehotel.com. Italian/French owned. The most popular mid-range hotel in the area; 7 bungalows, 36 rooms, some with air-conditioning, others with fans. Swimming pool. Prices range from €72 to €180 depending on the room and season. Expensive food.

Ambondrona and Madirokely

South of Djamandjary; some prefer this area to the busier, noisier Ambataloaka. If you don't want to eat at your hotel it's close enough to walk to Ambataloaka and get a taxi back.

Marlin Club BP205; tel: 86 610 70, cellphone: 032 0712 762; fax: 86 614 45; email: marlin.club@simcro.mg. 16 rooms plus a few bungalows. €110–150. Very comfortable, price includes breakfast. A good beach-restaurant. Watersports and deep-sea fishing.

L'Heure Bleue Tel: 86 614 21. Three 2-storey family bungalows for 350,000Fmg and 8 simple bungalows for €55 with breakfast. Swimming pool. Hot meals in the evening only (cold buffet at lunchtime). A popular, and beautifully situated hotel with stunning views over Ambataloaka Bay.

Madiro Hotel BP218, Madirokely; tel/fax: 86 614 18 or 86 617 42; email: madiro@simicro.mg. Italian-owned. 15 comfortable bungalows set round the swimming pool in a beautiful garden. All have fans and fridges. €55–65. Tours offered include camping trips to other islands, water-skiing, parasailing. Also a scuba-diving centre.

Le Grand Large BP89 Madirokely; tel/fax: 86 615 84. 14 rooms with air conditioning and hot water. Excellent location, but reportedly becoming a little seedy. First floor (best view) €48, ground floor €42.50. Meals €8. Water scooters; three boats for excursions.

Tsara Loky BP160; tel: 86 610 22. Malagasy run. 6 simple bungalows with fans, showers and WC; 6 rooms with shared bathroom. €18.50 for a room, €29 for a bungalow.

Chez Madame Senga Madirokely. 4 simple bungalows with WC, shower and fan; very good value at about 70,000–100,000Fmg. Good restaurant.

Hotel Robinson Tel: 86 614 36, cellphone: 032 0261 503; email: robinsonchezjoel@wanadoo.mg. On the junction for Ambataloaka and Madirokely. 6 bungalows with shower, WC and fan. 75,000–175,000Fmg, depending on the location.

Ambatoloaka (and Daresalama)

Once up a time this was a charming fishing village. Now it is the main tourist centre on Nosy Be. It offers the best options for inexpensive places to stay as well as luxury accommodation, and is also the liveliest place on the island so if you're looking for nightlife, this is where it's at.

Category A

Hotel l'Espadon Tel: 86 614 28; cellphone: 032 0261 473; email: hotel_espadon@malagasy.com. Swiss-owned. 11 bungalows, 9 rooms. Very comfortable with air conditioning, TV etc. Between €54 and €90, depending on location of room. Sunday barbeque. Meals 35,000–60,000Fmg. Breakfast 25,000Fmg. Specialise in deep-sea fishing.

Les Boucaniers BP411; tel: 86 620 38, cellphone: 032 0267 520; email: boucaniers@wanadoo.mg; www.hotel-lesboucaniers.com. On the hillside opposite Chez Gérard et Francine (so not on the beach). 18 tastefully furnished bungalows. Satellite TV in the bar. €36–45 (low season), €40–50 (high season).

Category B

Hotel L'Ylang Ylang BP110; tel: 86 614 01; fax: 86 614 02; email: hotel@lylang@wandoo.mg; www.hotel-lylangylang.com. 12 rooms, 8 with fans, 4 with air-conditioning. All rooms en-suite with wall safe and mini bar. The best hotel in this category; British owned and very good value at €42 double including breakfast. 'Fantastic surroundings, excellent cuisine, friendly service, and the nicest waiter on the entire island.' Airport transfer €12. Visa cards accepted.

Chez Gérard et Francine BP193; tel: 86 614 09, cellphone: 032 0712 793; email: ligeretfran@simicro.mg . Comfortable family house, at a good, quiet location at the southern end of Ambatoloaka; 9 rooms, some with en-suite shower. Deservedly popular so usually full. €40 (double).

Hotel Coco Plage BP159; cellphone: 03 207 769 64. 11 rooms for about €35. About 1km south of the village.

Chez Pat Cellphone: 032 4 024 786 or 032 0479 315; email: patricia.chaponnay@wanadoo.fr. 6 renovated rooms on the beach. Bar and restaurant on a beautiful terrace overlooking the beach. Serve French dishes and pizza. 200,000–250,000Fmg depending on the season.

La Résidence Ambatoloaka BP130; tel: 86 610 91; fax: 86 616 43.This once-popular place is under new management but is struggling to regain its former position; the restaurant is said to be very good, however. 12 air-conditioned en-suite rooms and a good terrace/lounge. Double rooms €30.

Hotel Benjamin (Villa Razambe) Tel: 86 060 93, cellphone: 032 0240 813; email: hotelbenjamin@simicro.mg; www.hotelbenjamin-nosybe.com. 6 very comfortable bungalows, each with a terrace, set in a nice garden with a swimming pool. Very good value at €26 (double); breakfast €3.

Category B/C

La Riviéra Route d'Ambataloaka; tel: 86 614 05 or 86 612 26. 5 bungalows with en-suite bathrooms; hot water; fans. 130,000Fmg without breakfast.

La Saladarie Tel: 86 614 52. Being rebuilt after cyclone damage.

Coucher du Soleil Hotel & Restaurant BP134; tel/fax: 616 20. 7 very clean and comfortable bungalows with en-suite bathroom (basic showers, new toilets). Not on the beach, but sea view; 100,000–125,000Fmg; breakfast 12,000Fmg.

Where to eat

Most of the main hotels have good restaurants, with **L'Ylang Ylang** particularly recommended, but Ambataloaka has always been renowned for its little restaurants serving delicious food. Local resident Irene Boswell writes: 'The best eating places may now be the *gargottes* in Ambataloaka. We have had some dreadful meals in some of the expensive hotels and there is often a set menu with no choice.'

Chez Angeline Tel: 86 616 21. Before the arrival of big-time tourism in Nosy Be, this was its most popular little restaurant, famous for its seafood and *poulet au coco*. It has just been renovated so worth checking out.

Baobab Kafé Opposite the Résidence Ambatoloaka. Serves snacks as well as main meals.

Karibou Tel: 86 616 47. Good Italian food, including pizzas.

La Saladerie Tel: 86 614 52. Salads and sandwiches.

Le Glacier Drinks, snacks and ice-cream.

Soleil A lively bar/restaurant.

La Saladarie Tel: 86 614 52. This salad specialist was badly damaged in the cyclone but was formerly deservedly popular.

Graines de Soleil (Formerly Au Fin Gourmet). Under new ownership. Quality not yet known.

Nightlife

Le Djembe 'The best-equipped nightclub in the whole of Mada: air conditioning, high-tech lighting and special effects, mirrored walls ... even a waterfall behind the bar.' (S Edghill) Price fluctuates. 5,000Fmg at the time of writing, but may revert to its former 10,000Fmg.

Le Jackpot A gambling place next to the Djembe nightclub. More downmarket than Le Casino.

Le Casino Set on a hillside like an old plantation house, diagonally opposite on the right as you leave Ambataloaka. Fruit machines, roulette, blackjack etc. Live music on Saturday nights.

La Sirène Opposite Le Djembe (if one is closed the other will be open).

Le Lion d'Or Not far from Le Djembe. A bar frequented mainly by local people; dancing on Saturday nights.

PRACTICALITIES
Medical care

Espace Médicale This well-respected organisation has opened on the road to Hell-Ville. There is always a doctor on call.

Pharmacies

There are two well-stocked pharmacies in Hell-Ville. One of them is always open as a *Pharmacie de Garde* for emergencies (this changes each week but the taxi drivers usually know as there are announcements on the radio). **Pharmacie Tsarajoro** is on the main street north of the market, almost opposite Chez Abud; tel: 86 613 82. **Pharmacie Nouroudine** is in Andavakatoko not far from the small market to the west of town down the road from the main market; tel: 86 610 38. There is also a good pharmacy, TOKO, in Mandirokely, near Ambataloaka.

Money

Very few hotels take credit cards. Banks and their hours are listed below, but note that they usually work only a half day before a holiday.

Banks

BNI (Credit Lyonnais) On the road down to the port, it often has the best exchange rates. Open Mon–Fri, 08.00–15.30. Travellers' cheques, Gives cash advances on Visa.

BOA Closest bank to the market, on Rue Gallieni. Open Mon–Fri, 07.30–11.30 and 14.30–16.30. Gives cash advances on MasterCard (but takes all day). Representative for Western Union.
BFV Close to Oasis, almost opposite the post office. Open Mon–Fri, 07.30–11.30, and 14.00–16.00. Gives cash advances on Visa. Representative for Western Union.

Photo shop
Graphoprint in Hell-Ville (opposite the Catholic church) do next-day service for developing prints, and sell film and camera batteries. Also photocopying service.
DMT In Hell-Ville (main street). Same services as Graphoprint.

Supermarkets, yacht supplies and repairs
The best supermarket is said to be **Big Bazar** in Daresalama, near Ambataloaka. In Hell-Ville the supermarket **Leader Price** has a wide range of goods including yacht supplies. There are two branches, one next to Graphoprint, and the other near the petrol station. There is also an Italian-owned supermarket at Djamanjary. **Mécabe**, in Hell-Ville, sells spare parts for yachts and will facilitate repairs.

Airline offices
Air Madagascar Located in the northern part of Hell-Ville; tel: 86 613 57. Open Mon–Fri, 08.00–11.00 and 14.00–17.00; Sat: 08.00–09.30.
Agence Ario Rue Passot, Hell-Ville; tel: 86 612 40; email: arionos@dts.mg. Represents Air Mauritius and Air Austral. Open Mon–Fri, 08.00–12.00, and 14.00–17.00; Sat: 08.00–10.00.

EXCURSIONS
Mont Passot
A popular excursion used to be the trip to the island's highest point, Mont Passot. However, the road was washed away in the cyclone, so perhaps the tourist hordes will now make way for those with the energy to hike up. I hope so! En route there are good views of a series of deep-blue crater lakes, which are said to contain crocodiles, as well as being the home of the spirits of the Sakalava and Antakarana princes. Supposedly it is *fady* to fish there, or to smoke, wear trousers or any garment put on over the feet, or a hat, while on the lakes' shores. That said, it may be the tourists have frightened the spirits away, since my local informant has never heard of this prohibition. It is, in any case, difficult to get down to the water since the crater sides are very steep.

The 'road' to the peak runs from Djamandjary; hikers or bikers should make a day excursion of it and take a picnic. If the authorities repair the road and Mont Passot regains its former popularity with cruise groups, those looking for solitude with a view should keep away.

Lokobe
Nosy Be's only protected area, Lokobe, is a Strict Reserve and as such is not currently open to visitors (plans for it to become a national park seem to have been shelved). However, it is possible to visit the buffer zone on the northeast side of the peninsula where permits are not required. The two little villages here, **Ambatozavavy** and **Ampasypohy**, have embraced tourism with enthusiasm and the whole area now bears little comparison with the unspoilt place I so delighted in over a decade ago. However, a visit here still offers a glimpse of village life in Nosy Be and is an informative and enjoyable excursion.

Guided day excursions to Lokobe are now commonplace: it takes around one hour by pirogue from Ambatozavavy to Ampasipohy. This trip is still a good option for those who cannot spend the night (see *Where to stay*). During the course of the day you are served a traditional lunch and taken on a tour of the forest (now sadly very degraded) where your guide will explain the traditional uses of various plants and points out a variety of animals. You are bound to see a lepilemur (this is *L. dorsalis*), that often spends its day dozing in the fork of a favourite tree or tangle of vines rather than in a hole. You should also see black lemurs (they are fed bananas in the forest) and probably a ground boa and chameleons (that have been placed there just in advance of your arrival). The chameleons here are the panther species (*Furcifer pardalis*) and in the breeding season (November to May) the male is bright green and the female a pinkish colour. The villagers grow vanilla and peppers, and a wide range of handicrafts can be bought direct from the maker.

Where to stay
Eco-village Fihavanana BP203, Ambatozavavy; tel: 86 612 36; email: delto207@dts.mg. Designed for ecotourists rather than beach fanatics; Swiss-managed. 9 very comfortable, spacious palm-thatched bungalows with hot showers and solar-powered. 200,000Fmg (high season), meals 35,000Fmg. Transfer from Hell-Ville costs about 25,000Fmg for two people. The manager can organise trips with local fisherman, but they also have their own Zodiac. An excellent feature is the Lokobe Nature Trail which can be walked at night so is of particular interest to those devoted to reptiles and nocturnal fauna of all kinds.
Jungle village BP208, Hell-Ville; cellphone: 032 0430 803; email: contact@junglevillage.net; web: www.junglevillage.net. 6 lovely basic bungalows in Ampasypohy, run by Marc Dehlinger. Beautifully located; €30 per bungalow. Dinner 35,000Fmg.

Ambanoro and the CNRO Museum
Ambanoro was formerly the site of the Black Lemur Forest Project which is sadly no longer functioning. The closure of this centre reduces the interest in a visit to this area but it is still a pleasant walk with enough to see to make it worth a half day excursion. The area was once an important Indian community, and there are the ruins of an ancient mosque, half-hidden by enormous sacred fig trees, and an elaborate Indian cemetery. Ambanoro was once the capital of Nosy Be (its other name, Marodokana, means 'Many Shops') and was a thriving port and trading centre up until the rise of Hell-Ville in the early 1800s.

The CNRO (Oceanographic Research Institute) museum is about 2km from town on the road to Ambanoro. It is becoming increasingly run-down, but if you can find someone to let you in you can see examples of preserved fish (including a baby hammerhead shark) and a very good local seashell collection (weekday mornings only).

NOSY KOMBA AND NOSY TANIKELY
No visit to Nosy Be is complete without an excursion to these two islands. Nosy Komba's main attraction is the black lemurs, and the marine national park of Nosy Tanikely lures snorkellers and bird enthusiasts.

Getting there and away
All the Nosy Be hotels do excursions to Nosy Komba which is usually combined with Nosy Tanikely. Most will let you do the sensible thing of taking an overnight break in Nosy Komba, and then rejoin the boat the following day for Nosy Tanikely. For Nosy Komba alone it is much cheaper to go by pirogue. Go to the small pirogue port (Port Ambariovato, to the east of the main port in Hell-Ville). The pirogues

leave at around 11.00 each day after the morning's shopping in Hell-Ville. The trip should cost from 5,000 to 15,000Fmg. If you are a group of six or more, you can find a fast boat from the main port for around 25,000Fmg per person to Nosy Komba.

The best time to visit these two popular islands is out of the main tourist season. If you decide to fix your own trip at the harbour (rather than through your hotel) question the boat-owner carefully about what 'all inclusive' actually means. Is snorkelling gear included? It will cover lunch but how about drinks? (Some operators charge high prices for *all* drinks, not just alcohol.) Is the Nosy Komba reserve fee included? And bananas to feed to the lemurs? It's better to know all this before you set out.

Yachties approaching from Nosy Be should wait until Nosy Vorona ('Bird Island' – the island with the old lighthouse) then bear 020 degrees. Good anchorage in 3–7m over sand and mud.

Nosy Komba (Nosy Ambariovato)

Once upon a time Nosy Komba was an isolated island with an occasional boat service, a tiny, self-sufficient village (Ampangorinana), and a troop of semi-tame black lemurs that were held to be sacred so never hunted. Now all that has changed. Tourists arrive in boat-loads from Nosy Be and from passing cruise ships which can land over 100 people.

Komba means 'lemur' (interestingly, it is the same as the Swahili word for bushbaby which of course is the African relative of the lemur) and it is the lemurs

LEMUR BEHAVIOUR
Alison Jolly

Female lemurs tend to be dominant over males. This is drastically different from our nearer relatives, the monkeys and apes, where males dominate females in the vast majority of species. In some lemur species, like the ringtails and the white sifaka of Berenty, males virtually never challenge females. In others, like brown lemurs, it is nearer fifty-fifty, depending on the individual's character. The black lemurs of Nosy Komba are intermediate. Their females are likely to dominate males but are not certain to. If you are feeding them, the blond females are apt to be in the forefront of the scrimmage with only a few of the black males. Watch to see who grabs food from whom and – even more telling – who does not dare grab.

Female dominance also applies to sex. An unwilling female chases off a male, or even bites him. Or she may just sit down with her tail over her genitals – a perfect chastity belt. A lemur's hands can't hold another's tail, so if she puts it down, or just sits down, he is flummoxed. And in most lemur species, he would never dream of challenging her desires.

Also note the way the males rub their wet, smelly testicles and anal region on the females, Some females do not appreciate this and tell them off with a snarl. Males may also rub their bottoms on branches to scent-mark them. Then they may rub their heads on the branch in order to transfer the scent to their forehead.

You can tell a lot about a lemur's mood by where it is looking – a long hard stare is a threat, quick glances while head-flagging away is submissive. The tail, though, won't tell you much except how the animal is balanced on a branch or your shoulder. They use tails to keep track of each other, but not to signal mood.

BITING THE HAND THAT FEEDS IT
Alison Jolly

Be careful when feeding lemurs. They may scratch you with their fingernails in their eagerness, or give you an accidental nip while trying to get the food. Much more important: never try to catch a lemur with your hands, just let it jump on you as it wants. If you constrain it, it will react as though a hawk has grabbed it and give you a slash with its razor-sharp canines. Especially do not let children feed lemurs unless they are warned never to hold on. These are wild animals, not pets.

that bring in the visitors. During the 1980s the villagers made nothing out of these visits apart from the sale of clay animals which they glazed with the acid of spent batteries. Then they instigated a modest fee for seeing the animals and increased the variety of handicrafts. Now that Nosy Komba is on some cruise-ship itineraries they have taken on the works: 'tribal dancing', face decoration, escorted walks… anything that will earn a dollar or two.

With all the demands on your purse, it sometimes takes a bit of mental effort to see the underlying charm of Ampangorinana, but it is nevertheless a typical Malagasy community living largely on fishing and *tavy* farming (witness the horrendous deforestation of their little island; when I first visited in 1976, it was almost completely covered with luxuriant trees) but it is the black lemurs that provide the financial support (and probably prevent further degradation of their environment). The ancestor who initiated the hunting *fady* must be pleased with himself. If you want the lemurs-on-your-shoulders experience and the chance to see these engaging animals at close quarters you should definitely come here. Only the male *Eulemur macaco* is black; the females, which give birth in September, are chestnut brown with white ear-tufts.

Nosy Komba also provides an excellent opportunity for observing lemur behaviour (see box opposite) and for taking a close look at one of our relatives. Look at a lemur's hands. You will see the four flat primate fingernails (such wonderfully human hands!) and the single claw (on the hind feet, not on the hands) which is used for scratching, and as an ear-pick.

A small fee is charged to see the lemurs, and en route to Lemur Park everyone in the village will try to sell you something. Since you are buying direct from the grower/maker, this is the best place to get vanilla and handicrafts (carved *pirogues*, clay animals and unusual and attractive Richelieu 'lace' tablecloths, curtains and bedspreads). The handicrafts here are unlike any found on the mainland, so it is worth bringing plenty of cash (small change). If you intend to buy a bedspread (and this is the best place to do so) you will need at least 300,000Fmg for a double-bed size.

One of the former glories of Nosy Komba, its coral, has sadly almost completely disappeared so snorkelling is no longer rewarding. The sea and beach near the village are polluted with human waste, but there is a good swimming beach round to the left (as you face the sea).

The best way to visit Nosy Komba is by yourself, or in a small group, and avoid the 'rush hour' (09.30–10.30). When there are few other tourists, Nosy Komba is a tranquil place, so consider an overnight stay or a stay of a few days. The available accommodation is comfortable enough and cheaper than beach options on Nosy Be. Given time to explore, it is possible to find and watch lemur groups away from 'Lemur Park' or to take a hike up the hill for spectacular views of the whole of Nosy Be (the top of Nosy Komba, at 630m, is higher than any point on Nosy Be), but start early before it gets too hot and bear in mind that there is little left of the primary forest; just secondary growth with lots of bamboo.

Where to stay

Auberge La Pirogue Cellphone: 032 0744 040; www.la-pirogue.com. A touch of luxury on Nosy Komba ! Beautiful bungalows located in the peaceful south of the island. Full board €146, half-board €126.

Chez Bernie Bernie and Remo have 4 good-quality bungalows. €69 full board (which includes unlimited boat hire).

Les Floralies BP107, Nosy Be; cellphone: 032 0220 038; email: floralieskomba@wanadoo.mg. French-run bungalows and one beach house beautifully situated at the end of the quietest beach, with en-suite shower and toilet. €55 including breakfast. Bar and restaurant. An additional series of backpacker bungalows, Les Bungalows de la Gare, have been added. These cost only about 25,000Fmg.

Hotel Lémuriens BP185, Nosy Be. Under new ownership. 6 bungalows with shower and WC, or shared facilities. €20 per night.

Hotel Madame Madio BP207. 8 simple bungalows (shared facilities); 3 bungalows with en-suite bathrooms. Order other meals in advance.

Jardin Vanille Cellphone: 032 0712 707; email: jardinvanille@wanadoo.mg. Simple but comfortable bungalows.

Nosy Tanikely

Although now much visited, this is still a lovely little island. The island is a marine reserve and it is for the snorkelling that most people visit it. And the snorkelling is still good, despite the hundreds of tourist boats dropping their anchors, and tourist feet stepping on the coral. In clear water you can see an amazing variety of marine life – coral, starfish, anemones, every colour and shape of fish, turtles, lobsters…

With this new world beneath your gaze there is a real danger of forgetting the passing of time and becoming seriously sunburnt. Even the most carefully applied sunblock tends to miss some areas, so wear a T-shirt and shorts.

Don't think you have finished with Nosy Tanikely when you come out of the water; at low tide it is possible to walk right round the island. During your circumambulation you will see (if you go anticlockwise): a broad beach of white sand covered in shells and bleached pieces of coral, a couple of trees full of flying foxes and – in the spring – graceful white tropic-birds flying in and out of their nests in the high cliffs. At your feet will be rock pools and some scrambling, but nothing too challenging.

Then there is the climb up to the lighthouse at the top of the island for the view.

OTHER ISLANDS IN THE NOSY BE ARCHIPELAGO
Nosy Sakatia
This rather bare island lies off the west side of Nosy Be. There are some well-run hotels here catering for divers.

Where to stay
Sakatia Passions Tel: 86 614 62; www.sakatia-passions.com. Lovely bungalows set amid coconut palms. €146–160. Deep-sea fishing and diving a speciality.
Sakatia Dive Inn Cellphone: 032 0712 675; email: sakatia@wanadoo.mg. 6 rustic bungalows with mosquito nets, basins and WC, 350,000Fmg per day; also 5 A-frame tents

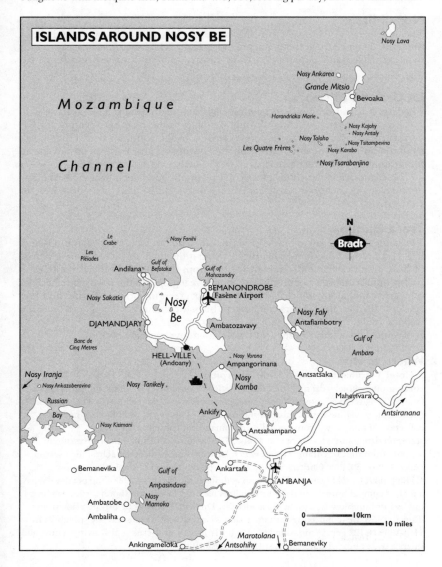

ISLANDS AROUND NOSY BE

at a cheaper rate. Communal facilities. Family-style dining. As the name implies, this place offers diving courses and excursions.

Delphino Villa Bungalows Tel: 86 61 668. [I have not had confirmation that this place is still open.]. 4 charming, rustic traditional Malagasy bungalows. 45,000Fmg per night (without breakfast) with refreshingly inexpensive drinks.

These places welcome visitors from boats. The channel between Nosy Be and Nosy Sakatia provides safe anchoring some 150m off the beach at 5m over a sandy bottom, if you don't wish to anchor off Hell-Ville – but beware strong tidal currents.

Nosy Mitsio

The archipelago of Nosy Mitsio lies some 60–70km from Nosy Be and about the same distance from the mainland. This is the Maldives of Madagascar, with two exclusive (and expensive) fly-in resorts on stunningly beautiful small islands.

La Grande Mitsio

The largest island is populated by local Malagasy – Antakarana and Sakalava, who survive on their denuded island through farming, cattle and goats. Overgrazing has devastated the island but some forest remains in the southern part. Huge basalt columns are a prominent feature on the northwest tip, used as an adventure playground by enterprising goats.

The island attracts yachties to its coral reefs and good anchorages. Maribe Bay provides good anchorage, protected between two hills. This is a good area for seeing manta rays.

Tsara Banjina

The name means 'good to look at' and this is a small but incredibly beautiful island. The red, grey and black volcanic rocks, rising quite high at its centre, have a mass of lush, green vegetation clinging to them, from baobabs and other large trees to pachypodium and tiny rockery plants. But its real glory are the pure white beaches of coarse sand, along which lap a crystal-clear green/indigo sea. Turtles and rays rest near the beaches. Divers can be kept busy for a couple of days, and there are walking trails.

Yachties can anchor off the southwest, at 6m over a sandy bottom.

Where to stay

L'Hotel Tsarabajina Contact details: main office (Tana) tel: 22 285 14; fax: 22 285 15; email: groupe.lhotel@dts.mg. Paris office: 23 Rue Truffaut, 75017 Paris; tel: 01 44 69 15 00; fax: 01 44 69 15 55; email: lhotelparis@prat.com; www.groupelhotel-madagascar.com (a good, clear website for Tsarabajina and Anjajavy). This is a beautifully designed collection of bungalows, constructed predominantly of natural materials and accommodating just a few people at a time. The building containing the bar/restaurant is separate from the 20 A-frame chalets which have en-suite bathrooms. Rates: high season (April 1–Nov 30, plus Christmas holiday) €137pp double, €177 single; low season: €112pp double, €137 single. There is an additional tourist tax of 3,000Fmg per day. 'What a perfect ending! Superb snorkelling, dolphins feeding close to the shore, turtles hatching out by our bungalow ... a piece of paradise!' (J Dudley) Transfers by private plane from Tana to Nosy Be (connecting with international arrivals) €263 one way; by speedboat from Hell-Ville (€122 per person round trip). This is also a world-class scuba-diving centre, and offers a wide range of watersports such as windsurfing.

The owners of Tsarabanjina also have Anjajavy (see page 410) so encourage visitors to stay at both places.

Nosy Ankarea

Another beautiful place to spend a few luxurious days. There are some gorgeous, sun-drenched beaches and the low hills make for pleasant walking excursions. 'The island is superb. Fabulous pachypodiums, flamboyants etc. Surrounded by coral reefs in an azure sea. The forest on the island is relatively undisturbed, due to numerous *fadys* and the fact that no one lives there except Marlin Club tourists. It is possible to climb up the highest hill (219m – quite steep but well worth it) to reach a plateau covered with pachypodiums and lots of weird and wonderful other succulents. From here you can see all of Nosy Mitsio and the surrounding reefs.' (Josephine Andrews)

Here is the **Marlin Club Ecohotel Annex** with 6 luxury tents, with beach parasols, showers and toilets. First-class meals in a thatched restaurant built around a huge baobab tree. Contact Marlin Club Hotel (page 387) for details.

Les Quatre Frères (The Four Brothers)

These are four imposing lumps of silver basalt, two of which are home to hundreds of nesting seabirds, including brown boobies, frigate birds and white-tailed tropic-birds. A pair of Madagascar fish eagles nest on one of the rocks. The sides drop vertically to about 20–30m, and divers come here because three of the boulders can be circumnavigated during one vigorous dive. Yachties can anchor to the southeast of Nosy Beangovo, roughly 100m from the mouth of a cave, at a depth of about 10m. Currents reach up to one knot. The best marine life is in the lee. There are huge caves, spectacular overhangs and rockfalls in the area.

Nosy Iranja

About 1¼ hours by boat from Nosy Be, or transfer by helicopter can be arranged. When I visited the island in the mid-1990s it was a beautiful and peaceful island inhabited by fisherfolk, and an important breeding reserve for hawksbill turtles. Then the luxury hotel was built. Initial dismay has turned to admiration at how well it has been designed and for the excellent management.

The good news is that the turtles are being protected and there is a good interpretation centre so visitors understand the importance – and rarity – of these marine animals. 'An absolute paradise. They ask you to leave your name at reception if you want to be woken in the night to see sea turtles if they come out of the sea to lay their eggs. We were fortunate to have experienced this and impressed at the true conservation work carried out. Highly recommended.' (R Pierce)

Island Dreams Hotel

The 28 or so bungalows circle the whole island so each has a sea view, there is a restaurant, a fitness centre, watersports and all the extras that you would expect in a luxury resort. Their website is www.iranja.com. Accommodation is from €60pp (in a four-person bungalow) to €170 (single). Meals are €28 half-board or €43 full-board. Transfers from the airport at Nosy Be are €92, or €80 from the harbour. Book through their operations centre on Rue Raimbault (BP56, Nosy Be 207; tel: 86 616 90).

Nosy Kivinjy

Otherwise known as Sugarloaf Rock, this is a great basalt boulder with 'organ pipes' formations on one side. Not recommended for diving (poor) or anchorage (very insecure). There are strong northeast-flowing currents around the islet.

Nosy Mamoko
This little island is at the southwest end of Ampasindava Bay. Known among the yachting fraternity for its exceptional shelter in all weather, it is a lovely, tranquil spot for a few days' relaxation. Nosy Mamoko is on the itineraries of two or three operators, based in Nosy Be, who organise lengthy trips into the region. There is good fishing here and whale-watching from October to December. Good anchorage is found in the channel between the island and the mainland, in 15m over a sandy bottom.

Nosy Radama
The Radama islands, which lie to the far south of Nosy Be and thus are only really accessible to yachties, compete with the Mitsios for the best diving sites in the northeast of Madagascar. They are set in a breathtaking coastline of bays backed by high mountains. Most of these high sandstone islands are steep-sided above and below water and covered with scrub, grass and trees. Sharp eroded rock formations, however, render the remaining forest rather difficult to explore.

Nosy Kalakajoro
The northernmost island, featuring dense, impenetrable forest on the south side. There are good beaches on the southern side and snorkelling is worthwhile off the southeast. Yachts should anchor 100m off the southeast side in 10–12m over good holding sand and mud, to get protection from the north-to-west winds.

Nosy Berafia (also known as Nosy Ovy – Potato Island)
This is the largest of the group, but the environmental degradation is terrible. Nearly all the trees have been cut and goats have completed the destruction of its flora. Red soil weeps from gaping scars into the surrounding water. If you still want to visit, boats can anchor off the east side, near a protected rocky outcrop.

Nosy Valiha
A small island which is privately owned so you should not visit without permission.

> 'There are some birds the size of a large turkeycock which have the head made like a cat and the rest of the body like a griffin; these birds hide themselves in the thick woods, and when anyone passes under the tree where they are they let themselves fall so heavily on the head of the passengers that they stun them, and in the moment they pierce their heads with their talons, then they eat them.'
> Sieur de Bois, 1669

The West

The west of Madagascar offers a mostly dry climate, deciduous forest (with some excellent reserves to protect it), and endless sandy beaches with little danger from sharks. The region is the fastest growing in Madagascar in terms of tourist development, the poor roads doing little to deter the building of new beach hotels, some of which depend on fly-in tourism. Because of the lack of roads and agreeable climate this is the ideal area for mountain bikers or walkers. Adventurous travellers will have no trouble finding a warm welcome in untouristed villages, their own deserted beach and some spectacular landscapes.

This is the region to see one of Madagascar's extraordinary natural wonders: the *tsingy*. Pronounced 'zing', this is exactly the sound made when one of the limestone pinnacles is struck by a small stone (they can be played like a xylophone!). Limestone karst is not unique to Madagascar, but it is rare to see such dramatic forms, such an impenetrable forest of spikes and spires. The endemic succulents that struggle for a foothold in this waterless environment add to the unworldly feeling of a *tsingy* landscape.

Opposite major rivers the sea water along the west coast is a brick-red colour: 'like swimming in soup', as one traveller put it. This is the laterite washed into the rivers from the eroded hillsides of the highlands and discharged into the sea: Madagascar's bleeding wounds.

HISTORY

The west is the home of the Sakalava people. For a while in Malagasy history this was the largest and most powerful tribe, ruled by their own kings and queens. The Sakalava kingdom was founded by the Volamena branch of the Maroserana dynasty which emerged in the southwest during the 16th century. Early in the 17th century a Volamena prince, Andriamisara, reached the Sakalava River and gave its name to his new kingdom. His son, Andriandahifotsy (which means 'White Man'), succeeded him around 1650 and, with the aid of firearms acquired from European traders, conquered the southwestern area between the two rivers, Onilahy and Manambolo. This region became known as the Menabe. Later kings conquered first the Boina, the area from the Manambolo to north of present-day Mahajanga, and then the northwest coast as far as Antsiranana.

By the 18th century the Sakalava Empire occupied a huge area in the west, but was divided into the Menabe in the south and the Boina in the north. The two rulers fell out, unity was abandoned, and in the 19th century the area came under the control of the Merina. The Sakalava did not take kindly to domination and sporadic guerrilla warfare continued in the Menabe area until French colonial times.

The Sakalava kingdom bore the brunt of the first serious efforts by the French to colonise the island. For some years France had laid claims (based on

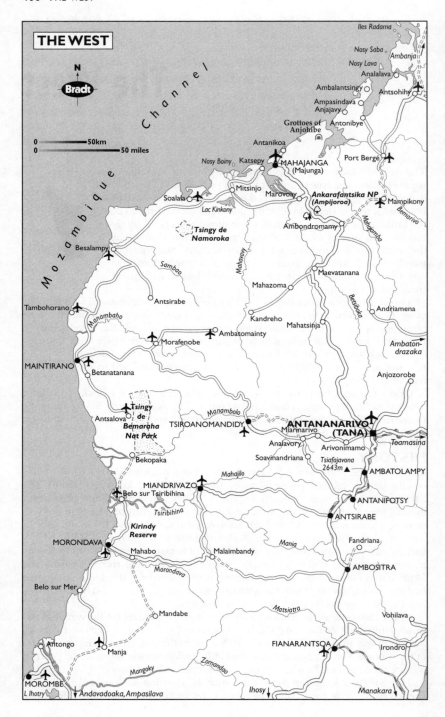

THE WEST

N

Bradt

0 ——— 50km
0 ——— 50 miles

Iles Radama

Nosy Saba
Nosy Lava

Ambanja

Analalava

Mozambique Channel

Ambalantsingy
Antsohihy

Ampasindava
Anjajavy

Antonibye

Grottoes of
Anjohibe

Antanikoa

Nosy Boiny Katsepy

MAHAJANGA
(Majunga)

Port Bergé

Mitsinjo

Soalala

Marovoay

*Ankarafantsika NP
(Ampijoroa)*

Mampikony

Lac Kinkony

Bemarivo

Mahajamba

Ambondromamy

*Tsingy de
Namoroka*

Mahavavy

Maevatanana

Samboa

Besalampy

Mahazoma

Betsiboka

Andriamena

Antsirabe

Kandreho

Mahatsinja

*Ambaton-
drazaka*

Tambohorano

Manambaho

Morafenobe

Ambatomainty

Anjozorobe

MAINTIRANO

Betanatanana

Manambolo

TSIROANOMANDIDY

**ANTANANARIVO
(TANA)**

*Tsingy
de
Bemaraha
Nat Park*

Antsalova

Miarinarivo

Analavory

Arivonimamo

Toamasina

Bekopaka

Soavinandriana

*Tsiafajavona
2643m* ▲

AMBATOLAMPY

Mahajilo

MIANDRIVAZO

Belo sur Tsiribihina

ANTANIFOTSY

Tsiribihina

ANTSIRABE

*Kirindy
Reserve*

Fandriana

Mania

MORONDAVA

Mahabo

Malaimbandy

Morondava

AMBOSITRA

Belo sur Mer

Mandabe

Matsiatra

Vohilava

Antongo

Manja

FIANARANTSOA

Irondro

MOROMBE

Mangoky

Zomandao

L Ihotry

↓Andavadoaka, Ampasilava

Ihosy ↓

Manakara ↓

KING RADAMA II

The son of the 'Wicked Queen' Ranavalona, King Radama II was a gentle ruler who abhorred bloodshed. He was pro-European, interested in Christianity (although never formally a Christian) and a friend of William Ellis, missionary and chronicler of 19th-century Madagascar. After Radama's death, Ellis wrote: 'I have never said that Radama was an able ruler, or a man of large views, for these he was not; but a more humane ruler never wore a crown.' With missionaries of all denominations invited back into Madagascar, intense rivalry sprang up between the Protestants sent by Britain, and the Jesuits who arrived from France. Resentment at the influence of these foreigners over the young king and disgust at the often rash changes he instigated boiled over in 1863, and only eight months after his coronation he was assassinated, strangled with a silken sash so that the *fady* against shedding royal blood was not infringed.

The French–British rivalry was fuelled by the violent death of the king, even to the extent that Ellis was accused of being party to the assassination. But was Radama really dead? Both Ellis and Jean Laborde believed that he had survived the strangling and had been allowed to escape by the courtiers bearing him to the countryside for burial. Uprisings, supposedly organised by the 'dead' king, supported this rumour. In a biography of King Radama II, the French historian Raymond Delval makes a strong case that the ex-monarch eventually retreated to the area of Lake Kinkony and lived out the rest of his life in this Sakalava region.

treaties made with local princes) on parts of the north and northwest, and in 1883 two fortresses in this region were bombarded. An attack on Mahajanga followed. This was the beginning of the end of Madagascar as an independent kingdom.

The Sakalava people today

The modern Sakalava have relatively dark skins. The west of Madagascar received a number of African immigrants from across the Mozambique Channel and their influence shows not only in the racial characteristics of the people, but also in their language and customs. There are a number of Bantu words in their dialect, and their belief in *tromba* (possession by spirits) and *dady* (royal relics cult) is of African origin.

The Sakalava do not practise second burial. The quality of their funerary art (in one small area) rivals that of the Mahafaly: birds and naked figures are a feature of Sakalava tombs, the latter frequently in erotic positions. Concepts of sexuality and rebirth are implied here. The female figures are often disproportionately large, perhaps recognising the importance of women in the Sakalava culture.

Sakalava royalty does not require an elaborate tomb since kings are considered to continue their spiritual existence through a medium with healing powers, and in royal relics.

GETTING AROUND

Roads are being improved but driving from town to town in the west can still be challenging and in much of the area the roads simply aren't there. There are regular flights to the large towns and a Twin Otter serves many of the smaller ones.

MAHAJANGA (MAJUNGA)
History
Ideally located for trade with East Africa, Arabia and western Asia, Mahajanga has been a major commercial port since 1745, when the Boina capital was moved here from Marovoay. One ruler of the Boina was Queen Ravahiny, a very able monarch who maintained the unity of the Boina which was threatened by rebellions in both the north and the south. It was Mahajanga which provided her with her imported riches and caught the admiration of visiting foreigners. Madagascar was at that time a major supplier of slaves to Arab traders and in return received jewels and rich fabrics. Indian merchants were active then, as today, with a variety of exotic goods. Some of these traders from the east stayed on, the Indians remaining a separate community and running small businesses. More Indians arrived during colonial times.

In the 1883–85 war Mahajanga was occupied by the French. In 1895 it served as the base for the military expedition to Antananarivo which established a French Protectorate. Shortly thereafter the French set about enlarging Mahajanga and reclaiming swampland from the Bombetoka River delta. Much of today's extensive town is on reclaimed land.

Mahajanga today
Mahajanga today is a hot but breezy town with a large Indian population and enough local colour and interesting excursions to make a visit of a few days well worthwhile.

The town has two 'centres', the Town Hall (Hotel de Ville) and statue of Tsiranana (the commercial centre), and the streets near the famous baobab tree. Some offices, including Air Madagascar, are here. It is quite a long walk between the two – take a *pousse-pousse*, of which there are many. There are also some smart new buses, and taxis which operate on a fixed tariff.

A wide boulevard follows the sea along the west part of town, terminating by a lighthouse. At its elbow is the Mahajanga baobab, said to be at least 700 years old with a circumference of 14m.

Telephone code The area code for Mahajanga is 62.

Getting there and away
By air
There is an international flight into Mahajanga from Moroni, Comoros Islands, on Mondays and Wednesdays with Air Madagascar, and daily flights from Tana – sometimes twice daily. There are also regular Air Mad flights from Nosy Be and a once-weekly one from Antsiranana (Diego Suarez).

The airport is near the village of Amborovy; 6km northeast of the town. If you don't want to take a taxi, taxi-brousses pass close to the airport.

By road
Mahajanga is 560km from Tana by the well-maintained RN4. Taxi-brousses and a comfortable minibus usually travel overnight, taking 15–18 hours. For details of the minibus phone 22 601 66 or email fifiabe@hotmail.com. It's a lovely trip (at least until it gets dark) taking you through a typical Hauts Plateaux landscape of craggy, grassy hills, rice paddies and characteristic Merina houses with steep eaves supported by thin brick or wood pillars. 'Try to be awake for crossing the Betsiboka: a huge red river with big rocks tossed about. Concentrate on the scenery, not the strength of the bridge supports.' (F Kerridge)

DISTANCES IN KILOMETRES

Antananarivo–Ampijoroa	466km
Ampijoroa–Mahajanga	110km
Antananarivo–Mahajanga	572km
Antananarivo–Morondava	665km
Miandrivazo–Morondava	274km
Morondava–Belo sur Tsiribihina	106km

This is a popular drive for those with their own vehicle, with the option of a stop at the forest of Ambohitantely at the Tana end, and Ampijoroa/Ankarafantsika near Mahajanga. You should allow about 14 hours for the trip

The taxi-brousse station in Mahajanga is on Avenue Philbert Tsiranana.

By sea

Sadly, in 2004 the ferry *Samson* which used to ply between Moroni and Mahajanga sank in the tempestuous seas caused by Cyclone Gafilo.

However, you can still access Mahajanga from Nosy Be with the comfortable ferry *Jean-Pierre Calloc'h*, which sails weekly and takes 20 hours. Cellphone: 032 0221 686, or tel/fax: 62 226 86. It is operated by Malagasy Sambo Ligne, Quai Barriquand, and leaves Mahjanga on Fridays, arriving Saturdays, and returns on Mondays. Departure times vary according to the tides. For full details and prices see page 381.

For the truly adventurous, why not try to hitch a ride on a cargo boat? Colin Palmer writes: 'We spent a lot of time in the harbour and saw a number of sailing cargo boats that serve the northwest and west... What better way to access Maintirano, Belo and Morondava?'

Where to stay

Note: Mahajanga rivals Nosy Be in the quality of its best hotels. They really *are* Category A with swimming pools and all mod cons.

Category A

Hotel Coco Lodge 49 Rue de France; tel: 62 230 23/62 238 18; fax: 62 226 92; email: contact@coco-lodge.com. 17 smart, spacious air-conditioned rooms, with en-suite bathrooms; minibar, all spotlessly clean. The rooms are built around a central courtyard with a lovely swimming pool. 175,000Fmg per room. They do breakfasts but not lunches or dinners. 'Very friendly management – the most efficient I have ever encountered in Madagascar!' (D Schuurman)

Anjary Hotel 9 Rue George V; tel: 62 237 98 or 62 238 07; fax: 62 229 49; email: anjaryhotel@dts.mg. 44 rooms. A new, smart, centrally located hotel, used mostly by business people. Double en-suite rooms with TV and phone for €20, twin rooms €22, suite €25.

La Piscine Hotel La Corniche, Bd Marcoz; tel: 62 241 72/73/74; fax: 62 239 65; email: piscinehotel@madatours.com. A new, upmarket French-owned hotel with a huge swimming pool and an open-air restaurant overlooking the ocean. 31 double rooms for 450,000Fmg, 2 suites (650,000Fmg) and 4 twin rooms. Phone, air conditioning, TV (cable), minibar. Nightclub.

Le Tropicana Oasis Gatinière, Rue Administrateur Lacaze, Mangarivotra; tel: 62 220 69; email: hotel-tropicana@tiscali.fr; www.hotel-majunga.com. This fine hotel-restaurant is up the hill from the Don Bosco school behind the cathedral, in a 1930s' French colonial house. It's small enough to feel intimate (6 rooms), with air conditioning, satellite TV etc.

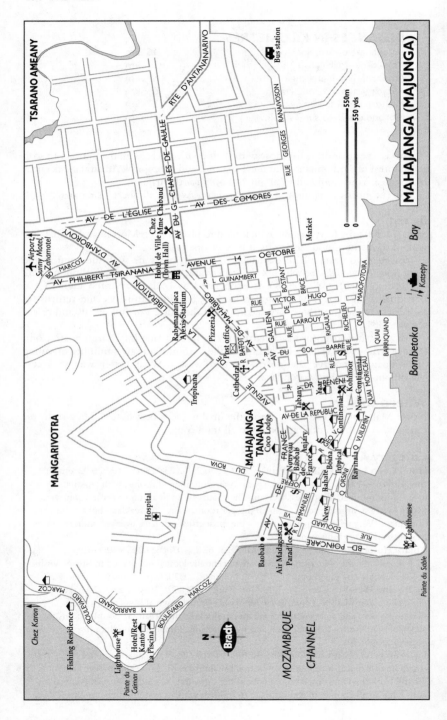

MAHAJANGA (MAJUNGA)

€30 per room. Swimming pool, excursions to the Anjohibe caves etc. French and Malagasy cuisine. 'The dining is superb. Even on an oppressively hot day you can escape from the dust of urban Mahajanga and sit on the terrace with friends over lunch… telling stories of exotic places and pretending you are Joseph Conrad.' (Mark Ward)

Sunny Hotel Route d'Amborovy; tel: 62 235 87 or (Tana) 22 263 04; fax: 22 290 78; email: rasseta@dts.mg or rasseta@blueline.mg. 30 well-equipped rooms, with air-conditioning; safe, minibar; cable TV etc, only 5 minutes' drive from the airport so ideal for an early departure. Large swimming pool; tennis courts and even a fitness centre. Excellent food. Excursions; car hire. The only negative is the caged lemurs (but see box on page 239).

Zaha Motel Tel: 62 225 55/237 20; fax: 62 237 11; email: zahamotel.mjn@malagasy.com. At Amborovy beach (not far from the airport, and 8km from Mahajanga). Rooms about 233,000Fmg, bungalow 423,000Fmg, including breakfast. This is a slightly vulgar, large hotel complete with activities such as tennis, volleyball and so on. It offers a cool alternative to staying in Mahajanga, but you need your own transport and there are now nicer places to stay. It has a good beach, however, with blue, not red, sea.

Chalet aux Bougainvilliers Grand Pavois beach (12km north of Mahajanga); tel/fax: 62 224 20; louloua@wanadoo.mg. Since there is just one chalet, this is an option for a couple who want to get away from it all. The chalet is in a beautiful location, in a garden with lots of flowers and a small waterfall. It has a small kitchenette and outside bathroom. A simple restaurant on the beach below serves fresh food. €25 per night.

Category B

Hotel de France 10 Rue de Maréchal Joffre; tel: 62 237 81; fax: 62 223 26; email: h.france@dts.mg. One of the oldest hotels in Mahajanga, conveniently located in the centre of town. 20 air-conditioned rooms with en-suite bathrooms. 250,000Fmg (single), 275,000Fmg (double). Tours organised.

New Hotel 13 Rue Henri Palu; tel: 62 221 10; fax: 62 293 91. 20 rooms: about 120,000Fmg. Bathrooms en suite, hot water, TV and phone, and a good restaurant.

New Continental Av de la République; tel: 62 225 70; fax: 62 241 19. Double room with fan, 140,000Fmg, air-conditioning 150,000Fmg. TV, phone, en-suite bathrooms. Town centre hotel, Indian-owned, well run.

Le Nouveau Baobab Rue du Maréchal Joffre, just off Av de France. About 150,000Fmg for air-conditioned en-suite rooms.

Hotel Voanio Tel: 62 238 78. About 75,000Fmg (with fan) to 126,000Fmg (double, air-conditioned). All rooms en suite. In a quiet part of town; clean and friendly.

Hotel Ravinala Quai Orsini; tel: 62 229 68. From about 92,000Fmg (fan, en-suite facilities) to 117,000Fmg (TV, phone, air-conditioning).

Hotel Fishing Residence: 58 Bd Marcos, La Corniche; cellphone: 032 0468 220. 10 rooms, 5 bungalows. €20–30. As the name implies, they specialise in deep-sea fishing.

Category C

Chez Chabaud Tel: 62 233 27, cellphone: 032 0706 734; fax 62 233 27; email nico@dts.mg. Mme Chabaud's daughter, Brigitte, runs a newly refurbished hotel near the Hotel de Ville (Town Hall). 18 rooms, 12 with en-suite facilities, for 75,000Fmg, and 6 with shared facilities for 50,000Fmg. The restaurant opposite is run by Brigitte's sister, Christiane, who also runs the legendary restaurant in Katsepy. All the family speaks English.

Chez Karon Tel 62 226 94; fax 62 293 44. A nice hotel in a pleasant seaside location (at the so-called Village Touristique). 24 rooms. Good food. Tours organised.

Hotel Tropic 22 Rue Flacourt (near the port); tel: 62 236 10. 8 rooms; the most basic have en-suite cold shower and shared WC. Clean and comfortable, but avoid the lower-storey rooms which have no windows. About 95,000Fmg.

Hotel Kanto Bd La Corniche; tel: 62 229 78. Overlooking the sea about 2km north of the town. 47,000Fmg (double, shared toilet) to 82,000Fmg (en-suite double, air-conditioning). Good restaurant. There's an annexe near the central market: corner of Av de la République and Rue Henri Palu.
Le Boina 14 Rue Flacourt; tel: 62 224 69. About 60,000Fmg with shower.
Yaar Hotel Rue Paul Henri; tel: 62 230 12. Near the New Hotel. 8 rooms. Single room with en-suite toilet, about 50,000Fmg.

Where to eat
Snack le Grilladin 32 Av Galleni Ampasika. An above-average Indian restaurant with an extensive menu. Tandoori and vegetarian specialities. 10,000–15,000Fmg for the main dish.
Kohinoor Restaurant Indian restaurant with good food and kitsch décor. One of the few places to do a vegetarian dish of the day.
Pakiza Av de la République, near the New Continental. A great variety of ice-creams and milkshakes, also good for breakfast. Terrific tamarind juice.
Bar Tabany A popular meeting place in the west part of town, near the market.
Salon de Thé Saify Near the post office and cathedral. A perennial favourite for breakfast and snacks.
Parad'Ice Next to the Air Madagascar office off Bd Poincaré. 'The best ice-cream in Madagascar – the passion-fruit ice-cream is out of this world!' They also serve wonderful breakfasts.

Cybercafé
Near the Hotel de France.

Maps
The Librairie de Madagascar (on Avenues de Mahabido and Gallieni) reportedly has a good selection of maps including the FTM one of the Mahajanga region.

Sightseeing
Regional tourist office Direction inter-regional du Tourism: Mr Desiré Saramba; Bd Marcos, Ampisikina, Mahajanga. Tel 62 228 72
Maderi Tour Rue Fules Ferry, Mahajanga Be (BP1087, Mahajanga); tel: 62 023 34. This company owns the new Antsanitia Beach Hotel (see page 408) and also the catamaran *Komagari*. This is described by Derek Schuurman as 'the best catamaran I have been on anywhere around Madagascar'. It sleeps four (two cabins). Maderi Tour arranges catamaran trips north to Nosy Be, and also 4WD excursions on land.

Mozea Akiba Museum
Situated about 4km from the centre of town, near the Plage Touristique (take a taxi, and allow half an hour to get there). The rewarding result of co-operation between the universities of Mahajanga and Gotland, Sweden, the museum has a display showing the history of the region, as well as an exhibition of paleontology and ethnology, and photos and descriptions of some of Mahajanga's tourist sights such as the Cirque Rouge and Grottes d'Anjohibe. Signs are in French and some English. Photography is forbidden. Hours: 09.00–11.00, 15.00–16.00, Tuesday to Friday only.

Fort Rova
This impressive fort at Ambohitrombikely, 20km southeast of Mahajanga, was built on the highest point in the region in 1824 by King Radama I. The entrance has been restored, and it is worth a visit for the views and sense of history.

Day excursions
Cirque Rouge
About 12km from Mahajanga and 2km from the airport (as the crow flies). This is a canyon ending in an amphitheatre of red, beige and lilac-coloured rock eroded into strange shapes: peaks, spires and castles. The canyon has a broad, sandy bottom decorated with chunks of lilac-coloured clay. It is a beautiful and dramatic spot and, with its stream of fresh water running to the nearby beach, makes an idyllic camping place.

As a day trip a taxi will take you from Mahajanga and back, but make sure the driver knows the way: there are no signposts. A cheaper alternative is to take a taxi-brousse from the street west of Chez Chabaud (opposite the BOA bank). This will take you to the intersection of the Zaha Motel and airport, from where you can walk the final 6km. Give yourself at least one hour to look around. Late afternoon is best, when the sun sets the reds and mauves alight.

Katsepy
Katsepy (pronounced 'Katsep') is a tiny fishing village across the bay from Mahajanga which is reached in 45 minutes by ferry. This runs twice a day: 07.30 (08.30 Sundays and holidays) and 15.30, returning an hour later (so the last ferry back is 16.30). The trip takes just under an hour and costs 5,000Fmg one way.

For at least three decades there has been only one reason to go to Katsepy: to dine at **Chez Chabaud** (cellphone: 032 0706 734 and email: nico@dts.mg). I still go weak at the knees remembering my meal there in 1984, while researching the first edition of this book. The place has had its ups and downs in the 20 years since then (including an arson attack by a disgruntled employee) but Derek Schuurman and Lalaina Ramaroson have sent me this encouraging report: 'Madame Chabaud herself now commutes between Madagascar and France, and has passed her legendary culinary skills on to her daughter Christiane, who has done a sterling job of running Chez Chabaud in Katsepy, as well as the branch in Mahajanga with her sister's help. We took a catamaran cruise to Katsepy in April 2004 and discovered that there is good reason for the international publicity this incredibly remote little restaurant has been given. We agreed that it (and the Mahajanga branch of Chez Chabaud) boasts the best food in all of Madagascar and that, as you know, is saying a *lot*!' In 2004 Derek and Lalaina's meal cost 80,000Fmg – that's £5/$9!

There is accommodation here too: seven separate bungalows with en-suite facilities (showers and modern flush loos) and very comfortable beds. 75,000Fmg double and 85,000Fmg for a family room.

What to do in Katsepy
Mostly lie around recovering from the meal, but there is a wildlife possibility – though one with a sad history which I've just traced back through seven editions of this guidebook. In the late 1980s one of the highlights of the visit was a small troop of rare crowned sifakas which lived in Madame Chabaud's garden. They only lasted one edition, so to speak: by the early 1990s they'd been killed and eaten by the villagers. But there were reports of equally rare Decken's sifakas near the village. These met the same fate. But now Derek Schuurman and Lalaina Ramaroson write: 'There remains a healthy population of crowned sifaka in the protected parcel of dry forest around the Katsepy lighthouse. Access to this forest is allowed only to accredited scientists at present, but Christiane says that it is possible to arrange a car to take guests to the edge of the forest, where the Sifakas can often be seen.' Christiane can also arrange trips to a nearby sugar cane factory (always a useful source of rum!) or to Lake Kinkony.

FURTHER AFIELD
Nosy Boiny (Nosy Antsoheribory)
This is a small island, about a kilometre long, in Boina Bay, with some fascinating ruins of an Arab settlement established around 1580 after a Portuguese raid on the mainland. The settlement thrived until 1750, when the Sakalava conquered the area. In its heyday the town, known as Masselage, probably supported a population of about 7,000. The ruins include several cemeteries, houses and mosques. 'The surface of the island is scattered with pottery. There are also many baobabs.' (Dan Carlsson)

To reach the island start from Katsepy and continue by road to the village of Boeny-Ampasy on the west side of the bay. There are some bungalows here. A 1¹/₂-hour boat journey brings you to Nosy Boiny. Patrice Kerloc (tel: 62 236 62) can arrange trips here and to the Grottes de Anjohibe.

Anjohibe caves
The Grottes de Anjohibe are 82km northeast of Mahajanga and accessible only by 4WD vehicle, and then only in the dry season. There are two places to visit, the caves themselves and a natural swimming pool above a waterfall. The caves are full of stalactites and stalagmites (and bats), and have 2km of passages. Bill Love wrote in 2003: 'The drive took over three hours one way via very dusty, moderately bumpy roads. Sifakas seen en route. The ancient, rusty staircases seemed a bit creaky; they certainly can't last much longer. Flashlights a must to enjoy properly! The cave was spectacular inside.'

To reach the caves turn left at the village of Antanamarina, from where it is another 5km. Then, to cool off, return to the village and take the road straight ahead to the waterfall and pools. There are natural pools both above and below the waterfall. To add to the excitement there may be crocodiles in the lower pool.

Dan Carlsson of Project Madagascar (Sweden) excavated these caves in 1996. 'It seems as though the caves have been used for normal living but also as a place of sacrifice. We found...pottery with ash, charcoal and animal bones... also several hippopotamus bones believed to be some million years old.'

Birding trips in the Betsiboka Delta
Keen birders will want to go out into the Betsiboka Delta to visit islets which are the haunt of the very rare Bernier's teal and Madagascar sacred (white) ibis. Many of the hotels can arrange a boat for this trip, including Christiane Chabaud.

Antsanitia Beach Resort
Derek Schuurman writes: 'Maderi Tour is opening an upscale beach hotel at the exquisite Antsanitia Beach, which is about one hour's drive by 4WD north of Mahajanga. The spacious, tastefully designed en-suite chalets are about 250,000Fmg per night, full board.

FLY-IN RESORTS NORTH OF MAHAJANGA
If you look on a map of Madagascar, you'll see a glorious expanse of nothingness along the indented coastline between Mahajanga and Nosy Be. This is where two entrepeneurs have established fly-in resorts which come (in my opinion) as close to perfection as you could hope for.

Lodge des Terres Blanches
About 100km from Mahajanga, and 25km south of Anjajavy, is a lodge that really does qualify for the cliché 'best kept secret' (at least from English-

speaking tourists) since I've had great difficulty in getting details but finally Dr Ilya Eigenbrot has come up trumps with the following mouth-watering description.

'Jacky Cauvin is a former bush pilot with a great eye for those all-important criteria – location, location and location! He was the original owner of the plot on which the luxury complex of Anjajavy now stands, and has moved his bungalows to a new location which he "…spotted from the air, liked, and bought…"

'He provides basic, but very comfortable accommodation in six wooden bungalows (each sleeps two in a double bed) by a gorgeous white beach fringed with forest in which parrots, lovebirds and sifaka, as well as many reptiles and other wildlife, abound.

'The bungalows are spotlessly clean and have running water and showers – the temperature depends on the time of day – and toilets.

'Food and drink are included in the price (€170–230 per night) and the meals are eaten together in the larger wooden 'lodge' building, where there is also a bar with a fridge at the guests' disposal. If you want to go on a longer hike, or to be dropped off in a cove somewhere for the day, picnics can be arranged.

'There are two boats with which Jacky takes guests out for trips – sometimes as passengers to watch other guests fish for sailfish and marlin on the grand banks 30km out to sea (you have to pay to charter the boat if you wish to actually fish yourself – €300 per day – but everyone gets to eat the fish afterwards), but mostly just to some beautiful coves along the coast, or islands studded with majestic baobabs, or eroded limestone formations that look like something from a science fiction novel, or even recently discovered graves of an unknown tribe in caverns on the coast.

'On the other hand, if you haven't got your sea legs, or are just looking for absolute relaxation, why not lie back in a hammock with a book and a cold beer while sifakas snort in the trees, or go for a wander through the forests, where you might encounter the odd zebu and lots of wilder creatures… Then perhaps a bit of snorkelling off the beach in a calm, warm sea…

'And then, it must be dinnertime again…

'The electricity is on for a couple of hours in the evening (for reading lights only, there are no sockets in the bungalows) and a fluorescent light running off a battery is available all the time.

'The meals (not recommended for vegetarians) are a great way to practise your French: Jacky's English is impeccable, but most of his guests are francophone, and Jacky is a fantastic host and raconteur over a glass of his 'rhum arrangé' (sugar cane rum infused with spices) after sunset, as well as being extremely knowledgeable about local Sakalava culture and Malagasy flora and fauna.

'To get there, you need to get to Mahajanga airport, where Jacky will pick you up in his little four-seater plane and whisk you off. Needless to say, he is an excellent pilot, and the 40-minute, low-altitude flight, touching down on a runway that Jacky himself describes as "like something in a Disneyworld ride" is exhilarating. Alternatively, he can pick you up by boat from the port at Mahajanga, both plane and boat transfers cost €140 return (from/to Mahajanga) per person. There is no vehicle access.

'A real gem!!!'

How to book

Terres Blanches can only be booked through the tour operator Anthurium Hotels, on Réunion (tel: 00262 (0)262 93 13 93; fax: 00262 (0)262 93 17 97; email: resa@anthurium.com; www.anthurium.com).

Jacky has only an Iridium satellite phone, so communicating with him directly is costly and subject to long delays. If you need further information, Dr Ilya Eigenbrot has kindly offered to help: email: ilya@eigenbrot.com or mobile: 07770 392801.

Anjajavy

I don't often experience real luxury, but Anjajavy is about as good as you can get in Madagascar. But the point of Anjajavy is not that it's just another luxury seaside hotel, it's that it includes a large area of Madagascar's dwindling dry deciduous forest. This is what makes it special – it's the only protected area between Mahajanga and Nosy Be, and the hotel management has every incentive to ensure that the fauna and flora not only survive but flourish, for this is what brings tourists to Madagascar.

Wildlife viewing here is effortless. When I was there in late June, a troop of Coquerel's sifaka visited a fruiting tree near one of the villas promptly at 3.30 each day. Sometimes they were joined by common brown lemurs and at night our torch beam picked out the eyes of perhaps a dozen mouse lemurs. Then there were the birds – flocks of bright green grey-headed love-birds. sickle-billed vangas, crested couas and vasa parrots, to name just a few. Reptiles are common. You may see ground boas and hog-nose snakes and plenty of chameleons – most common is Oustalet's chameleon, Madagascar's largest species. We were particularly impressed with the local guide, Matoary, a gentle, mature man who has a wealth of experience to share. It was he who told us about the *kononono* (see box on page 423). This sort of knowledge cannot be taught – English and scientific names can.

There's a cave, too, spectacular enough with its stalactites and stalagmites to be worth a visit, but with the addition of countless Commerson's leaf-nosed bats. Another cave has the skulls of extinct lemur species embedded in the rocks.

Then there are the coral reefs, *tsingy*-like limestone outcrops, pristine beaches and extensive mangrove forests … not to mention total comfort, brilliant service and superb food! Anjajavy is under the same ownership as Tsarabanjina (Nosy Be) so visitors are encouraged to stay at both hotels (though this is not insisted on). Three nights is the minimum stay, five allows you to appreciate all that this amazing place has to offer.

Anjajavy l'hôtel Tana office: Lot VW 105, Ambohimitsimbina (BP876), Antananarivo; tel: 261 20 22 285 14; fax: 22 285 15; email: groupe.lhotel@dts.mg; www.groupelhotel-madagascar.com. Paris office: 23 Rue Truffaut, 75017 Paris; tel: 01 44 69 15 00; fax: 01 44 69 15 55; email: lhotelparis@prat.com. 25 villas sleeping up to 60 guests. One villa is adapted for disabled travellers. Prices (three nights): €884 per person (double) high season (April 1–November 30) or €796 low season. This *includes* transfer by private plane from Tana, and all meals, excursions that do not involve motor transport, and a full range of sports activities.

ANKARAFANTSIKA NATIONAL PARK (FORMERLY AMPIJOROA FORESTRY STATION)

This is one of the relatively few areas of protected western vegetation, so it is good news that it has now been upgraded to a national park (with an unpronounceable name so I suspect that many people will continue to call it Ampijoroa). This is a super reserve. It is easy to get to, thrilling to visit with an abundance of wildlife of all kinds, and with clear, level or stepped paths which make hiking a pleasure. The arrival of accommodation next to the park is the last ingredient in making this a 'must' for anyone with an interest in the wildlife of this region.

Ampijoroa /Ankarafantsika straddles RN4 from Mahajanga. The main part of the reserve is on the southern side of the road (on your right coming from Mahajanga), with Lac Ravelobe to the north.

I am grateful to Derek Schuurman for updating this section.

Getting there and away
From Mahajanga
The reserve is 120km from Mahajanga. It takes about two hours to make the journey by car, and if you are in a private vehicle it is worth stopping at Lac Amboromalandy, a reservoir which is an excellent place to see waterfowl. Taxi-brousses leave town early in the morning heading for Tana, so this is a much cheaper option (about 10,000Fmg).

Note the excellent examples of Sakalava tombs at the 16km marker outside Mahajanga, to your left as you're driving to Ankarafantsika.

From Tana
RN4 from Tana is in good condition and the journey by taxi-brousse should take no more than 10 hours, costing around 75,000Fmg. It leaves the Gare du l'Ouest at 8.00 and 16.00. Coming from Tana it is easy to miss Ampijoroa, so look out for Andranofasika. This little town lies on a T-junction where a road turns off to Ambatoboeni; you will recognise it by the triangle of grass with blue-painted concrete benches and a map of Madagascar. Ankarafantsika is 4km further on.

Where to stay
Gite d'Ampijoroa This new, and very welcome building is a 5-room, locally managed guesthouse with 2 twin rooms and 3 double rooms for 85,000Fmg per room. The rooms are fairly small, very neat, with very comfortable beds with mosquito nets. Guests are provided with towels, etc so there is no need to bring your own. Candles and a bottle of mineral water are also provided. Facilities are communal: 2 new flush toilets and 2 (cold) showers, plus a basin with mirror at the bathroom entrance. There is electricity and the lighting in the rooms is very good (the candles are for powercuts). Note that there are no wall sockets in the rooms. Each room has a different name and features colourful paintings of local wildlife on the walls. For information and bookings contact Direction Inter-Regional de l'ANGAP, 14, Rue Philibert Tsiranana, Mahajanga; tel 62 226 56. Some upmarket new chalets are being constructed at the side of Lake Ravelobe. These will have en-suite bathrooms and should be open by the time you read this.

Camping
The campsite has been upgraded: there are tent platforms with shelters and a kitchen which campers may use. There are also communal ablution facilities for campers. 70,000Fmg, equipment included.

There is also another campsite run by the women's association of Ambodimanga, a village a few kilometres from the national park entrance along the main road in the direction of Andranofasika and Tana.

Where to eat
Meals for guests of the gite are provided at the small, simple **Restaurant La Pigargue**, (four tables), close to the roadside. Breakfast is 7,500Fmg, and a main meal costs 10,000Fmg.

Dila Restaurant Andranofasika (the nearby town). This is a nice option for those with their own transport: the food is excellent and very reasonably priced, the place spotless, yet it's a genuine local place rather than a tourist establishment.

Permits and guides

Permits cost the usual 50,000Fmg and are available at Ankarafantsika.

There are nine guides, six of whom speak English. They cost 25,000Fmg to 40,000Fmg per day, depending on the circuit. Maximum five people per guide. Night walks are 40,000Fmg.

Information, souvenirs and local culture

There is now also a visitors' information centre and souvenir shop with excellent T-shirts. One of the interesting things visitors can learn is about the *doany,* a place where *tromba,* or trance ceremony (see page 16) take place. The *doany* is a small house decorated in white and red and surrounded by a fence. A mural depicts the possessed individual communicating with spirits (including that of the dead king) to ask for protection and blessings. A zebu is then sacrificed and its entrails left in the lake for the crocodiles. A similar ceremony takes place annually on New Year's day at Lake Ravelobe.

There are several *fady* in the area, mostly pertaining to the lake (women must not wash in the lake during menstruation and nothing can be washed – or sacrificed – at the lake on a Saturday). There is also a *fady* against eating pork.

Flora and fauna of Ankarafantsika

This is typical dry, deciduous forest with sparse understorey and lots of lianas. In the dry winter season many of the trees have shed their leaves, but in the wet months the forest is a sea of bright greens. Conspicuous is the tree with menacing spines, the *Hazom-boay,* or *Hurac crepitances.*

Wildlife viewing in Ampijoroa starts as soon as you arrive. Right beside the parking area is a tree that Coquerel's sifaka use as a dormitory. They are extremely handsome animals with the usual silky white fur but with chestnut-brown arms and thighs. On your walks you may also see mongoose lemur, western woolly lemur and the sportive lemur if the guide shows you its tree. This is the only place in the world where you might see the recently discovered (1998) golden-brown mouse lemur, *Microcebus ravelobensis,* named after Ampijoroa's Lake Ravelobe. There are always lots of reptiles (two new species of *brookesia* chameleons were discovered there recently), and this is a birder's paradise. 'Within minutes we found sicklebill, Chabert's and hook-billed vangas all nesting round the campsite… and then the highlight: white-breasted mesites which walk just like clockwork toys.' (Derek Schuurman). John and Valerie Middleton recommend a walk to the 'Canyon': 'Perhaps the finest walk we did here. It's a 4km walk through the forest and across the savannah to an amazing multi-coloured erosion feature. On this route we pretty well saw all the bird, animal and plant life that this park has to offer in daytime.'

Circuits

Much has been done to maintain and upgrade the trail system in the park. There is a view point, Belle Vue, on a hilltop from where there is a fantastic view over the Ankarafantsika forest. A bench has thoughtfully been put there so visitors can relax and enjoy the lemurs and birds in the trees around them.

Trails developed for visitors include:

Circuit Coquereli: Two hours. Recommended for first time visitors as an introductory walk. Good for sifaka and brown lemurs. Grading: easy.

Circuit Retendrika Three hours. More focused on botany. The guides take visitors on a trail where the trees are labelled. Guides will give an account of the medicinal, magical or edible properties of the various trees and plants. It's also good for birds. Grading: moderate.

Pachypodium visit Not so much a circuit as a visit to one of the park's particular attractions. Grading: medium.

Baobab Trail 2 hours. To save time, you may wish to drive in the direction of Andranofasika, then take a walk near the south side of Lake Ravelobe. You traverse some raffia-dominated forest and rice paddies, cross a new hanging bridge (built in November 2003) and end up at some spectacular, very tall baobabs *Adansonia madagascariensis*. Grading: easy.

Circuit Source de Vie 3–4 hours. Best for visitors who wish to gain an insight into local culture and everyday life of the rural community in and around the park. Grading: moderate.

Circuit Ankarokaroka 3–4 hours. A hike through forest and some savannah, and also to the canyon (recommended by the Middletons – see above). Grading: moderate.

Nocturnal walks 1½ hour. A night walk usually starts at 19.00 and is an essential part of a visit to this national park. It is the only time you will see mouse lemurs, including the recently discovered golden-brown mouse lemur (*Microcebus ravelobensis*), and it's also much easier to spot chameleons at night. The most commonly seen local species is the rhinoceros chameleon. Grading: easy.

Boat trip There is a boat for excursions on Lake Ravelobe. The lake is no longer considered safe for walking – or swimming – because of several crocodile attacks in recent years. One of Ampijoroa's best guides was lost to a crocodile a few years ago.

Projet Angonoka
Ampijoroa is also home to the Angonoka Tortoise Programme, or Projet Angonoka, operated by the Durrell Wildlife Conservation Trust. This is one of Madagascar's most successful captive breeding projects. After many years of research and much trial and error, the ploughshare tortoise – the world's rarest tortoise – is now breeding readily and is now being reintroduced to the Baly Bay area – its original habitat. Equally rare, the attractive little flat-tailed tortoise (*kapidolo*) is also being bred here.

The site has been upgraded and fortified since the theft of a large number of ploughshare tortoises in the 1990s. An exciting addition to the DWCT site is the *rere* or Madagascar big-headed/side-necked turtle, an endangered endemic freshwater turtle confined to the western lakes. Breeding success of the *rere* has been excellent, and some 150 of the captive-bred turtles have already been released into one of the lakes in the park.

Because of the extra security required to safeguard these rare animals, it is possible for tourists to glimpse them only through a chain-link fence.

KATSEPY TO MITSINJO, LAKE KINKONY AND SOUTH
Mitsinjo and Lake Kinkony
Taxi-brousses sometimes meet the ferry at Katsepy for the onward journey to **Mitsinjo** (and vehicles taking the ferry are almost certainly bound for that town). The journey takes about three hours.

'Mitsinjo is a lovely town with a wide main street, trees with semi-tame Decken's sifakas, a general store that has a few rooms available, and Hotely Salama which serves wonderful food and cold beer!' (Petra Jenkins). Not far from Mitsinjo is **Lac Kinkony** (a protected area). Petra reports: 'About once a week in the dry season the fishermen of Lac Kinkony do a supply run to Mitsinjo and you may be able to get a lift. The lake is wonderful. It boasts fish eagles, flamingoes, sacred ibis ... need I say more? It is free from bilharzia but the northeastern end is a bit silty for swimming. Cadge a lift by pirogue and you've got paradise! Crocodiles are friendly and don't bother swimmers (!).'

John Kupiec enjoyed a pirogue and walking trip with Patrick, the English-speaking son of the owner of Hotely Salama. They stayed away for five days and saw plenty of wildlife as well as the lovely lakeside scenery. On the southern part of the lake is the little village of **Antseza** which has a Thursday market where you may be able to reprovision if you are camping. In the lake is a small island, Mandrave. The legend is that this island rose up in the lake after the boats of the invading Merina had been sunk by the Sakalava. It is a sacred island with many *fady*: you may not wear gold jewellery on the lake and if you have gold teeth you must not speak while on the lake! No-one can live on the island, nor urinate there, nor approach too close to the sacred tamarind tree that grows there (although prayers may be offered to it). A Sakalava king is buried beneath the tree.

An alternative hard way to reach Mitsinjo is to attempt it by *boutre* or cargo boat (see box on page 416) or you can take the soft(er) option of rafting the River Mahavavy with the specialist river-runners, Remote River Expeditions. See page 442.

Soalala and beyond

From Mitsinjo you may be able to make your way to Soalala although there is no longer any road transport there. Perhaps you can catch a motor *vedette* from Mahajanga. These go (irregularly) to Soalala to collect prawns, crabs and fish. John and Valerie Middleton write: 'This is a fascinating port and well worth visiting. It contains several very large African baobabs and impressive Pachypodiums. It was previously a French fort and at least two ancient cannons can be seen on the seafront. There are many good eating places but nowhere to stay unless camping. We managed to stay in the compound of the Forestry and Water Department where there was a good water supply, albeit shared by a constant stream of ever-friendly locals. Across the bay is a new, massive French shrimp farm and if it is intended to take a vehicle across written permission needs to be obtained to cross the farm's land. The old village vehicle ferry no longer crosses to the old road although passenger ferries do make the crossing. From here are occasional taxi-brousses.'

There is an air service (Twin Otter, once a week) out of Soalala, or you can go on to **Besalampy**, which is also served by Twin Otter. Then you can continue to make your way down the coast, taking cars, *pirogues* or whatever transport presents itself. This route is practical only in the dry season and for rugged and self-sufficient travellers. You can fly out of Tambohorano and Maintirano (and other towns – check the Air Mad timetable). Good luck!

Tsingy de Namoroka

This is a Strict Nature Reserve, and as such is not generally open to tourists so make your arrangements through a tour operator; the Middletons organised their trip through Madagascar Air Tours. This is their report: 'The route south to **Vilanandro** takes about three hours by vehicle and passes through some magnificently varied landscapes. One 10km section in the middle contains evergreen forest and swampland with a multitude of different ferns and dense stands of raffia palms. In other sections small lakes provide excellent birdwatching. Vilanandro is a delightful village; we found one bar which sold only beer, about four small shops, nowhere to stay, and very, very friendly people. One family allowed us to camp in their compound from where we made daily forays into the reserve. To do this we carried an ANGAP guide from Soalala, the ANGAP representative in Vilanandro, a local guide, and three villagers with tools to build/rebuild the road as we went along! We spent three days exploring Namoroka and would definitely say that the *tsingy*, the birdlife, the plants and the scenery are amongst the best we had seen in Madagascar. Places visited include the almost 5km-long cave of Anjohiambovonomby and its amazing associated canyons, the stunningly beautiful sacred spring of Mandevy with its scented water-flora of white Aponogetons, and the many large dolines, washed pure white by the winter rains and surrounded by superb *tsingy* and flora.'

CONTINUING BY ROAD FROM MAHAJANGA
Marovoay
About 50km from Mahajanga a road branches off the RN4 and leads to Marovoay (12km). Formerly the residence of the Boina kings, the town's name means 'Many Crocodiles'. When the French attacked the Malagasy forces assembled in Marovoay in 1895 in their successful drive to conquer Madagascar, it is reported that hundreds of crocodiles emerged from the river to devour the dead and dying. Malagasy hunters have since got their revenge, and you would be lucky to see a croc these days. Colin Palmer, a self-confessed 'boat anorak', reports: 'Marovoay is just a nice place to hang out. It has warm, friendly people and a port to wander in. This was evidently quite important in French times, but is now silted up and disused by large vessels. However, local people still make use of it as a market for their produce from the delta. An exuberant lady called Seraphine has just opened **Hotel Standard** in the main street. Her food was good and she showed us round the rooms – which looked clean, if simple. She speaks expressive, voluble French and a little English.'

Rejoining RN4 you pass through **Ankarafantsika National Park** (Ampijoroa) – see page 410 – to meet RN6, the road to Antsiranana, at Ambondromamy. Here you have the choice of the easy road south or the deceptively short route north to Ambanja and Nosy Be.

THE ROUTE NORTH
The 'road' to Antsohihy
This road is about to be improved using EU funding, so this may be your last chance for a typically Madagascar experience, as described by some intrepid travellers a few years ago!

The following are from Colin Palmer and Stuart Edgill who had their own 4WD vehicles. 'At Ambondromamy the road forks and you turn left on to the RN6, marked as a red road on the map. This was presumably a good metalled road in colonial times, but this is certainly not the case now. It immediately became a heavily rutted track with the occasional glimpse of a crumbling fragment of tarmac giving a hint of its former glory. There were many deviations off the main route into the scrub to avoid the most badly rutted sections obviously caused by lorries during the rainy season. Our average speed on this 84km section to Mampikony was 15km/h!

'As we approached **Mampikony** I saw what at first I took to be paddy fields, but I found to my surprise these were fields of onions. Mampikony is the centre of onion production in Madagascar, even exporting them to Réunion.'

THE SAILING CARGO BOATS OF THE NORTHWEST
Colin Palmer

The hot, dry plains northwest of Madagascar are cut by the mighty Betisboka and Sofia rivers, which deposit their red silt into sprawling deltas lined with mangrove forests. The Indian Ocean surf of the east coast is replaced by the gentler waters of the Mozambique Channel. Water transport can make safe use of the sea – the deltas provide protection for fleets of fast outrigger fishing boats while larger sailing cargo boats ply their trade along the coast.

A huge area of the country between Mahajanga and Maintirano is devoid of roads and things are not much better as far south as Morondava. For many places in this remote region, the only way to move goods and people is by boat.

Almost uniquely in the modern world, the ports along this coast are served by non-mechanised sailing cargo boats, owned and operated by the Vezo people – primarily fisherfolk from the southwest who have diversified into the ownership and operation of cargo boats.

Two quite different designs operate side by side. The 'Arab' lateen-rigged (one large triangular sail) boutres and the 'European' gaff-rigged bateaux. The boutres are built in a time-honoured tradition that relies on the eye of the builder to get the shape right, while the bateaux are built to plans and templates most probably introduced by the French. Perhaps this was an attempt to 'improve' the local boutres, but if so the improvement seems to be lost on the locals. New boats being built in Mahajanga (and probably elsewhere) are almost exclusively in the boutre tradition.

This clash of boatbuilding techniques is an example of East meeting West, or at least East meeting modern West. The Eastern approach to building boats is to think of the planking as the hull of the boat and build it first. The ribs are added later, simply as something to stiffen the hull. In the West we once did things the same way, as the Viking ships show. But there is another approach that may have been introduced by the Romans, where the ribs are set up first to get the shape, and the planks bent round them to keep the water out.

In Madagascar, the result of either method is a stout, flat bottomed boat that can find its way into the silting creeks of the northwest deltas as well as hold its own in the open seas of the Mozambique Channel. Business seems to be thriving and the boats are well cared for and expertly sailed. Facilities on board are basic, but it ought to be possible for intrepid travellers to hitch a ride along the coast. Those who do will be fortunate indeed to experience some of the last seagoing cargo boats to earn their livings under sail.

Accommodation is limited **to Hotel La Mampikony** – 'Rooms at 25,000Fmg; best deal of the trip, but basic!' (CP) or **Les Cocotiers** – '40,000Fmg with cold shower, loo down the corridor, palissander wood floors, and a terrace by the road where we ate and watched the world go by. Everywhere there were onions, on the stalls, on lorries, loose being sorted or in sacks waiting to be transported…. you have got to know your onions in Mampikony!' (SE)

The next town of importance is **Port Bergé** (Boriziny), 82km away on a road just as poor. Onions give way to tobacco and cotton. This is a pleasant town with at least two hotels, the **Zinnia** ('filthy, smells, rats') and **Le Monde** ('immaculate, friendly'. Family rooms for 60,000Fmg; good value). The road improves from Port Bergé to Antsohihy, so the 133km stretch can be done in about five hours.

Antsohihy

Pronounced 'Antsooee', this town is a good centre for exploration, and accessible by Twin Otter as well as taxi-brousse. Like many towns in Madagascar it is built on two levels. 'I am afraid we all found the place a bit depressing, it having passed from the stage of splendid decay to being truly run-down. We visited the "port", basically a creek, eventually leading out to sea, capable of taking very small cargo ships.' (SE)

Where to stay/eat

Hotel Blaina Thatched bungalows with en-suite bathrooms, about 70,000Fmg. By far the best accommodation in town.

Hotel de France In the upper town, by the main square.

Hotel La Plaisance On the opposite side of the square to Hotel de France. 'It had fewer squashed and flying mosquitoes in the rooms than the Hotel de France. 40,000Fmg, cold shower, loos on the second-floor landing (some rooms are on the opposite side of the road). All ground-floor rooms in effect open on to the street. It also had a bar and small dance-floor downstairs where there is a Friday disco.' (SE)

Getting there and away

If you are using a taxi-brousse, approach from the north rather than the terrible road to the south. It takes about 10 hours from Ambanja. There are Twin Otter flights between Mahajanga, Analalava, Antsohihy and Ambanja.

Excursions from Antsohihy

Antsohihy is situated on a fjord-like arm of the sea which becomes the River Loza. There is a regular boat service to **Ananalava**, an isolated village accessible in the dry season by taxi-brousse but otherwise only by boat or plane (Twin Otter). This area is worth investigating. 'A friend recently was up near Analalava and was raving about the coastline. This is where there is the marine tsingy,' writes a researcher friend. The Paradise Hotel is inexpensive, and the owner of the *épicerie* across the road from the Paradise has a few rooms to let. 'I loved the maze of paths on both sides of the village. There is a *fady* in effect on one stretch of the river. At one time this area was ruled by a queen and many trees may not be cut down and there are other taboos. In the boat everyone removed their hats when we passed. There is still a powerful queen in the area who occasionally grants an audience. In her presence you must ask your question to the guard who repeats it to the queen. Her answer is made the same way.' (J Kupiec)

Nosy Saba

From Ananalava you may be lucky enough to find a sturdy boat to take you to this almost perfect island for a few days. I have been here twice and doubt if any island comes closer to paradise. There is fresh water, a few fishermen's huts (abandoned in the rainy season), coconut palms, curving bays of yellow sand, a densely forested section with clouds of fruit-bats, coral, chameleons…

If arriving by yacht, the anchorage south of the eastern tip gives good shelter from the north to northwest winds. Anchor 100m off the beach over a sand shelf 1.5–4m deep. The edge of the shelf drops off steeply. Close to the shore are shallow coral patches. But further out, watch the strong tidal currents: the northwest-flowing ebb makes a rolling swell. The water is very clear and a remarkable number of large game fish can be seen even when snorkelling along the island's edge southwest of the anchorage. The coral is excellent, and rewarding scuba-diving can be had along the drop-off.

Nosy Lava

The large island of Nosy Lava ('Long Island') lies temptingly off Ananalava. *Don't go there!* Why not? It's Madagascar's Devil's Island, a maximum security prison housing the country's most vicious murderers. By all accounts the prisoners lead pretty enjoyable lives: women from nearby Ananalava are said to cross over by pirogue to fraternise with the prisoners. They've also been provided with electricity and other mod cons not available to ordinary folk. One Malagasy informant commented that 'Nosy Lava is more like a holiday camp than a prison'. Nosy Lava had a brief moment in the international spotlight in 1993 when two notorious convicts boarded the yacht *Magic Carpet* and murdered its South African/German occupants.

From Antsohihy into the interior

Two roads run from Antsohihy in an easterly direction into the lush and mountainous interior: a lovely area for the adventurous to explore.

A tarred road runs southeast to Mandritsara, a small town set in beautiful mountainous scenery. Taxi-brousses leave every morning, passing through **Befandriana Nord** where there is a hotel, the **Rose de Chine**.

Mandritsara

The name means 'Peaceful' (literally 'Lies Down Well'), and was reportedly bestowed on it by King Radama I during his campaigns. There are several hotels here including **Hotel Pattes**, a nice little place with excellent food.

Mandritsara also, surprisingly, has one of the best hospitals in Madagascar, the **Baptist Missionary Hospital.** Tom Savage writes: 'The hospital is called Hopitaly Vaovao Mahafaly (HVM for short) which means Good News Hospital. They are great, and people travel far and wide to get there. They also have a regular turnover of medical students on their electives from all over the world. The doctor in charge there is British: Dr David Mann.'

Mandritsara is linked with the outside world by Twin Otter.

Bealanana

An alternative (paved) road from Antsohihy runs northeast to Bealanana, 'a muddy, scruffy highland town with friendly people'. The town is quite high, and the temperate climate with ample rainfall allows the cultivation of potatoes and a great variety of fruit.

Hotel Ramagasy is family-run and friendly; basic rooms around 20,000Fmg. **Hotel La Crête** has double rooms with basin and shower (but probably cold water). The hotels will arrange for a taxi-brousse to pick you up for the return trip (four hours) to Antsohihy or Abatoriha. The road is good; the vehicles are not.

West from Antsohihy

Just to show that nothing is beyond my more adventurous readers, here is an account from Valerie and John Middleton, whose interest is limestone karst and the plants that grow there. 'From Ansohihy we drove quickly to Marovantaza where we hired a local guide to show us the way westwards to **Antonibe**. This is a true wilderness route with few people, many challenges, some good deciduous forest, many birds and many Coquerel's sifaka. Antonibe is a large, hot, friendly town close to Narinda Bay. There is nowhere to stay and the few *hotely*s, bars and shops are difficult to find. After obtaining permission from the mayor to proceed further we collected yet another guide and headed for **Amboaboaka**, an even friendlier village situated amongst some superb cone karst scenery. Much to the villagers' interest we camped within the village. The following day we were taken by the headman and several village elders to view the karst where we found many interesting succulent plants and visited four previously unexplored and very beautiful caves including one, Ampahito Valakely, some 800m in length. This karst is reasonably close to Anjajavy and as such is a possible excursion from there.

'From Amboaboaka we returned to Antonibe and then headed up Narinda Bay to **Ampasindava**. This route is very spectacular and for its final 3–4km involves driving along the beach. This is passable only for two hours either side of low tide and even then we had waves coming in through the window! And we have photos to prove it! We again camped in the centre of the village which has superb views across the bay. Our route then took us across the peninsula and through more cone karst to **Ambalantsingy**, a beautiful sleepy fishing village on the edge of some massive mangrove swamps. Our purpose here was to visit, with the aid of a local pirogue (25,000Fmg), the karstic islands in the very beautiful Morambe Bay. These islands, which were probably originally land-formed cones, had become even more eroded with some undercutting at low tide of up to 6m. The *tsingy* is good, the plants almost primeval, and the setting breathtaking.'

Antsohihy to Ambanja

Stuart Edgill continues his saga: 'The next day, after croissants and coffee at the taxi-brousse station, we set off on the road to Ambanja, 217km away, marked white on the map. Be careful not to continue on the RN31: you need, in effect, to turn left at a rain barrier (a barrier which is closed when the road is impassable during the rainy season) about 15km from Antsohihy. This road turned out to be no worse, and in some places better, than the road before. Although unmetalled, the road was flat and firm; also here the terrain was more open, making it easier to drive around the heavily rutted parts. Children ran away from us here. Our friend says it was because they have been told that *vazaha* drink their blood to gain strength or kidnap them. Another thing was that all the way along this route the children called out for empty mineral water bottles, presumably to collect water in.

'As we began to near Ambanja after **Maromandia** we began to climb and suddenly the scrub land gave way to tropical vegetation and cashew trees. We left Ansohihy at 6am and arrived at Ambanja at about 5pm.'

MAINTIRANO AND REGION

Maintirano, a small port due west of Tana, has been somewhat out on a limb, with very few foreign visitors. Bishop Brock, an indefatigable cyclist, provided most of the following information in 1996. I have had no reports since then. Come on, someone!

The road from Tsiroanomandidy to Maintirano

'I cycled from Tana to Maintirano, thence to Morondava, a distance of about 1,100km, of which only about 250km was tarred. The ride from Tsiroanomandidy to Maintirano is a difficult trek through a rugged, arid wilderness, that requires a large degree of self-sufficiency. Although there is ample water, it's not always conveniently located and at times I carried up to eight litres. There is no formal accommodation, and only one shop and *hotely* in Ambaravaranala, Beravina and

MOONLIGHT IN BELOBAKA

Jolijn Geels

From Tsiroanomandidy we went to Belobaka by taxi-brousse, and that is where the road ends – in a small town with no electricity, no toilets and no hotels. After presenting ourselves to the *maire* and the *gendarmerie*, we were offered a room in the newly built 'city hall' which was not yet in use. The room was on the first floor, and it was completely empty. Water was provided in a bucket, and the 'toilet' was 'past the *gendarmerie* to the left behind the bushes'. From Belobaka we would have to walk to Ankavandra, the starting point of our Manambolo River trip.

Most of the time Belobaka is very dark at night, with only candles and oil lamps to provide a little light. However, on a clear night when the moon is full, a bluish light, casting sharp shadows, shines over Belobaka and the streets that otherwise are so quiet come alive. In this remote town, the children sing and dance to a full moon!

It was our first night in Belobaka. After our evening meal and a bucket shower in a hidden corner, we retreated to the balcony on the first floor where we sat and talked for a while. Then we heard singing, clapping, drumming and a lot of laughter! On the square just next to our 'hotel' many children of all ages and some adults were dancing, clearly visible in the light of the full moon. Running up and down the street, challenging a second group of kids to improve on their performance, they seemed to make up their game as they went along. All of a sudden they were chanting '*Vazaha! Vazaha!*' and the whole spectacle moved towards our balcony where they put up a real show for us. Of course we sang along as best as we could when they started singing some well known French songs. Did we understand Malagasy? they asked. Well, not really, but we told them what words we knew, and every attempt we made to say something

Morafenobe. I camped in the bush, stayed in villages and with a family in Morafenobe. Crossing the Bangolava between Ambaravaranala and Beravina was difficult, and crossing the northern tip of the Plateau du Bemaraha east of Maintirano was brutal riding. The scenery was magnificent and varied, however, at times being so wide open that the sense of isolation was almost overwhelming. It took me eight days to cover this 438km.'

This road is also travelled by trucks and 4WD taxi-brousses. Bishop recommends that you look for a vehicle in Tsiroanomandidy, rather than Tana. The journey should take two to three days.

Maintirano

This small western port is attractive for people who want to get off the beaten track. Nothing much happens here. Bishop points out that although it appears to be a seaside town on the map, 'it's as though the town has turned its back on the sea: virtually nothing in Maintirano overlooks the ocean.' However, he found it one of the friendliest towns in Madagascar (no doubt its isolation has something to do with this). 'I was constantly entertained by local families (and the Catholic missionaries) and one man insisted that I take all my meals with his family during my stay there.'

The best hotel is the **Laizama**.

Maintirano is one of the places served by Air Mad (Twin Otter) on its Tana–Mahajanga run, so there is an alternative to the overland journey. You can also float down the Manambolo River (see page 440).

in their language triggered outbursts of laughter. It was just wonderful! At times we felt a bit silly, like a king and queen being cheered by a crowd, but what a happy crowd it was!

Then, without warning, the party was over and the children dispersed. Within minutes the streets of Belobaka were completely empty and silent.

The following day we had plenty of things to do: we made enquiries about the walk to Ankavandra, we started to look for a guide, we had agreed to meet a few people, and we wanted to buy some supplies for the walk. We had many visitors enjoying tea and cold drinks on our balcony. While we were sitting there, the singing and dancing started again. One of our visitors explained that these spontaneous celebrations occur every four weeks if the sky is clear and the streets of Belobaka are moonlit.

The show went on. The children invited us to join them in the streets to sing and dance and clap with them. It seemed as if the whole world revolved around the children of Belobaka, as if time stood still while we shared songs and laughter. How much time had passed I really couldn't tell, but like the night before all of a sudden the party seemed to come to an end. However, this time the children didn't leave in silence. We shook many hands and wished them '*tafandria mandry!*', which is Malagasy for 'good night' or 'sleep well'. They wished us '*tafandria mandry*' too, and as they walked away in small groups, they happily chanted '*tafandria mandry!*' again and again until they had reached their homes. Then there was silence.

When we woke up next morning we heard, below our window, '*tafandria mandry, vazaha!*', and then laughter. Of course we replied, and there was more laughter. That day we were leaving for Ankavandra. As we walked the streets to do our last bit of shopping, it still echoed '*tafandria mandry!*' in a shy but conspiratorial way. It made us smile from ear to ear.

Telephone code The area code for Maintirano is 69.

From Tsiroanomandidy to Ankavandra, via Belobaka

Jolijn Geels and Herman Snippe made their way by road and trail to the head of the Manambolo River and thence to Belo Sur Tsiribihina. For a synopsis of this wonderfully adventurous trip, see page 440.

FROM MAINTIRANO TO MORONDAVA

Continuing by bicycle, Bishop Brock writes: 'This is somewhat easier than the Tsiroanomandidy to Maintirano stretch, and there are major towns/villages every day or two. Some self-sufficiency is still required, though, and water was a problem south of Bekopaka (all the rivers were dry; I had to get water from village wells). Although this route gives free access to the Tsingy de Bemaraha, in my opinion it is not a very interesting bike ride.'

Again, there is an alternative to cycling this route: 'The road is currently being served by a 6WD taxi-brousse that passes each way about once a week.'

Tsingy de Bemaraha National Park

Until *National Geographic* magazine published photos of the *tsingy* in 1987, very few people – even the Malagasy – knew of this impenetrable wonderland. Until 1998 it was closed to tourists; only scientists could visit the Réserve Naturelle Intégrale du Tsingy de Bemaraha. Now it is a national park, and well worth the effort of getting there. The scenery rivals anything in Madagascar and it's a treasure-house for botanists. At 152,000ha it is one of Madagascar's largest protected areas. It lies to the south of Maintirano, with the River Manambolo forming the southern border of the park, cutting a spectacular gorge through the limestone.

The main point of access is at **Bekopaka** on the north bank of the Manambolo River. Here is the main park entrance and from it leads a network of well-constructed paths and walkways through the best areas at the reserve's southern extremity. Some of the paths take you through and up on to the *tsingy* (eroded limestone pinnacles), where boardwalks have been constructed for safer access. However, some of the terrain is still tough going and is really only suitable for those who are reasonably fit (and thin – there are some tight squeezes through gaps in rocks).

Adjacent to the park entrance is a lake which has a pair of highly endangered Madagascar fish eagles. Other water birds include Madagascar jacana, white-faced whistling duck, Humblot's heron and purple heron.

Some 25km further to the north are the famous areas of *grande tsingy* – imposing limestone pinnacles up to 50m in height, with equally impressive canyons and gorges. There are now paths leading to this area and constructed walkways allow limited access into the area. Reaching the area, however, remains a real challenge – from Bekopaka it's a full day trek and all supplies must be taken with you. Bring plenty of water and a packed lunch.

Naturalist and photographer Nick Garbutt writes: 'Bemaraha is undoubtedly a very special place and well worth visiting, but it's not without its frustrations. After my first visit in 1998 I reported on the inflexibility of the ANGAP administration – something I hoped would relax once the new park found its feet. Sadly this has not proved to be the case. Although some improvements are evident, the ANGAP attitudes remain intransigent – this is a park run by a rule-book which can be problematic for those with wildlife as their major interest.

'There are set circuits to walk, lasting between 1½ and 8 hours and different rates are charged according to the length of the circuit. Most of these circuits run through a combination of forest areas and *tsingy*. However, if, for instance, your principle interest is the wildlife, the system doesn't allow you to concentrate in the forest areas and miss out the other bits, or combine the forest portions of different set circuits. The park official at the gate is adamant that each circuit has to be completed before the next can begin. There are no nocturnal walks allowed either. This is disappointing as the forests of Bemaraha undoubtedly harbour some spectacular nocturnal lemurs and other wildlife.' Nick is not alone in his criticisms, but all visitors report the helpfulness of the guides and staff, so once the bureaucracy allows them to run the park for the benefit of its visitors, it should be a superb experience for all.

Pirogue rides on the Manambolo River up through the adjacent gorge are also available – but only in the morning. These are highly recommended. There are spectacular cliffs and wonderful forest on either side, and it's possible to see groups of Decken's sifaka and red-fronted brown lemurs basking in the early morning sun.

For up-to-date information on the national park check their website: www.tsingy-madagascar.com.

Flight of fantasy

Charter flights from Morondava (either returning to Morondava or landing in Belo sur Tsirabihina) over the *grande tsingy* are spectacular. The flight up from Morondava takes about 35 minutes; the pilot will then fly back and forth over

ANT-LIONS (KONONONO)

In the reserves of the south and west – or anywhere that trails are sandy rather than muddy – one of the most enjoyable pursuits for sadists is feeding the ant-lions. Look for a small, conical pit in the sand, find an ant or other small insect, and drop it in. There'll be a flurry of activity at the bottom of the pit – grains of sand will be thrown up to smother the ant – and it will either be pulled dramatically down into the depths of the pit or manage to escape with its life. For full details of this extraordinary animal see page 52.

Children in the northwest of Madagascar have recognised the decorative potential of these creatures and call them *Kononono* which means 'nipple-badge'. Once you persuade one to grasp a soft piece of skin (ie: a nipple) it will hang on for hours! The name teaches you another Malagasy word: *nonono* which means nipple. Think of the sound of a baby sucking, and you'll recognise the onomatopoeia!

the best areas of *tsingy*. 'The views and spectacle are utterly amazing – massive needles of rock interspersed with pristine forest. When the pilot drops down low, it's even possible to see brilliant white Decken's sifaka sitting in the trees. I was so engrossed in taking photos I was violently sick at the end of the flight!' (Nick Garbutt)

Getting there

Bekopaka is reached in about 10 hours from Morondava, if you have your own 4WD vehicle. Access is not easy by public transport, even in the dry season. From the north, the park can be reached from Antsalova, which has an air service. Most people, however, approach from the south, where the nearest town accessible by taxi-brousse from Belo Tsiribihina is Ankilizato (not to be confused with the town of the same name east of Morondava) which is 57km north of Belo. From there you must either walk (porters can be hired) or take a zebu-cart the 24km to Bekopaka.

The most practical option is to organise a car and driver in Morondava, but hire the required guide from the ANGAP office in Bekopaka. When settling the car-hire price, check whether the cost of crossing the Tsiribihina and Manambolo rivers is included. The cost per vehicle for the ferry is 100,000Fmg and 25,000Fmg respectively.

Organised tours

The hotels Bouganvilliers, Baobab Café, La Masoandro (Chez Maggie) and Morondava Beach in Morondava all organise tours by 4WD to the Bemaraha.

Where to stay in Bekopaka

Auberge de Tsingy (Chez Ibrahim) Lots of atmosphere and friendly, helpful staff. Simple 2-person bungalows, shared facilities, for 45,000Fmg. Breakfast 15,000Fmg and main meals (with good vegetarian options) for 45,000Fmg. Tours of the park are organised by the hotel.

Hotel Relais de Tsingy A beautifully situated set of 6 bungalows (total capacity 20) with en-suite bathrooms and hot water, overlooking the lake with wonderful views. Double rooms 250,000Fmg; breakfast 15,000Fmg, meals 55,000Fmg.

Camping

A camp ground has been set aside on the north shore of the Manambolo, right next to the park entrance. It's very picturesque with groves of mango trees that provide good shade and a basic toilet. 15,000Fmg per tent per night. You must provide your tent and all camping equipment. There is also an adjacent snack bar with basic meals for around 15,000Fmg and cold drinks.

Belo sur Tsiribihina

Apart from being the town at the end of the River Tsiribihina (see *River trips*, page 439), this place has little to offer. The famous Avenue of Baobabs is nearer Morondava and an easy excursion from there. Likewise Kirindy, though travellers coming from the north can visit both attractions on their way to Morondava. Tsiribihina means 'Where One Must Not Dive', supposedly because of the crocodiles. Be warned!

Arriving from the north you have to cross the river by ferry to get to the taxi-brousse station for Morondava. There is no timetable and the journey takes half an hour.

Where to stay/eat

Hotel du Menabe The quality of the rooms is unknown, but this hotel is not recommended for meals: 'Devoid of atmosphere, has the slowest service I've ever experienced, and the food was unimpressive' (SR)

Grande Lumière Opposite the Menabe. 8 bright, clean rooms with cold shower.

Restaurant Pacifique Near the market. Good food, especially the crevettes.

Mad Zebu Restaurant Despite its rather surprising name, recommended as the best restaurant in Belo.

MORONDAVA

The Morondava area was the centre of the Sakalava kingdom and their tombs – sadly now desecrated by souvenir hunters – bear witness of their power and creativity.

This was evidently a popular stopping place for sailors in the past and they seem to have treated the natives generously. In 1833, Captain W F W Owen wrote of Morondava: 'Five boats came alongside and stunned us by vociferating for presents and beseeching us to anchor.'

Today Morondava is the centre of a prosperous rice-growing area (and has successfully introduced ostrich farming to Madagascar!). For tourists it is best known as a seaside resort with a laid-back atmosphere. This friendly coastal town is the southern gateway to many of the attractions of the western region and is the centre for visiting the western deciduous forest, the famous baobabs, Belo su Mer

DIVING CENTRES IN THE SOUTHWEST

There are coral reefs down much of the west coast, and whilst the Toliara region remains the most popular for diving, other specialised centres are being developed in the Morondava–Morombe stretch of coast.

Menabe Plongée (Belo Sur Mer) BP384, Morondava; tel: 95 524 51; email: Mena.belo@ad.com

Laguna Blu/Manta Diving Centre (Ampasilava-Andavadoaka, near Morombe); www.lagunabluresort.com

and the Tsingy de Bemaraha National Park.

In March 2004, Cyclone Galifo battered Morondava as it returned to the island from the Mozambique Channel after inflicting heavy damage in the north. Although damage was widespread, the town is picking up the pieces and moving ahead.

The Morondava Tourism group (GOTOM) is working with hoteliers and tour operators in the cyclone recovery process and will be opening an office in town to co-ordinate the promotion and expansion of tourism in the region. Francois Vahiako, head of the newly formed Morondava Guides Association (GROP), is reachable at Les Bougainvilliers.

Telephone code The area code for Morondava is 95.

Getting there and away
By road
Morondava is 700km from Tana and served by a once-good road. Driving time from Tana to Morondava ranges between 12 and 15 hours depending on current road and weather conditions. A MAMI minibus leaves the Anosibe depot in Tana in the afternoon, arriving the following morning. The road is not bad until the 120km stretch between Miandrivazo and Malaimbandy, which can take six hours. The trip by taxi-brousse from Antsirabe took Stuart Riddle 16 hours and cost 100,000Fmg. The taxi-brousse station in Morondava is about 40 minutes' walk from the beach hotels at Nosy Kely – a hot, tiring hike when carrying a backpack.

See also *Travelling between Morondava and Toliara*, page 433.

If you are driving, note that there is no diesel between Antsirabe and Morondava.

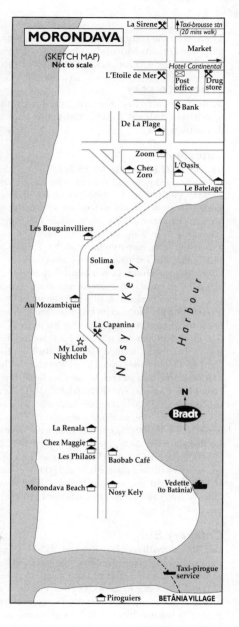

By air
There is a daily service from Tana or Toliara, and the Twin Otter calls here after visiting smaller west-coast towns including Belo Tsiribihina, Manja, and Morombe.

By sea

There is a new ferry, or *Taxi be de la Mer*, which runs, perhaps daily (or every other day), south from Morondava to Morombe via Belo sur Mer. Enquire at the Hatea café. See page 435 for onward transport from Morombe.

Where to stay

Most hotels are clustered along the beach on the peninsula known as Nosy Kely, which has suffered from some major damage from erosion, with others in the downtown area.

Category A

Baobab Café Nosy Kely; tel: 95 520 12; fax: 95 521 86; email: baobab@blueline.mg. 16 air-conditioned rooms all with en-suite facilities, minibar, TV, and hot water. 190,000–450,000Fmg depending on quality and facilities. Extra bed 50,000Fmg. Superb food: 'The fresh fish and seafood are sensational; there's none finer in Madagascar.' (Nick Garbutt) Breakfast 25,000Fmg, menu 75,000 Fmg.The hotel backs on to the river on the east side of Nosy Kely. Billiards available and the large pool which is open, for a small fee, to non-residents. Airport transfer 15,000 Fmg pp. Organising tours to the baobabs, Kirindy and Tsingy. See Excursions from Morondava.

Chez Maggie Hotel 'Le Masoandro' Nosy Kely; tel: 95 523 47; fax: 95 527 90; cell phone: 320 203 486; email: info@chezmaggie.com; www.chezmaggie.com. 2 two-storey chalets and 6 spacious bungalows, all with en-suite facilities, air-conditioning, fans and hot water. 250,000Fmg per room; extra bed 50,000Fmg. A lovely garden setting directly on the beach. Excellent restaurant with full service bar open to non-residents. Breakfast 22,000–30,000Fmg; menu 75,000 Fmg. Swimming pool, airport transfers and laundry service. Excursions include Ave of the Baobabs, Kirindy Forest and Tsingy de Bemaraha. See *Tour Operator and Guides*. The hotel changed hands in 2003 with a new Malagasy/American partnership and has been recently renovated.

Hotel Les Philaos Nosy Kely; tel: 95 521 02. 18 rooms, apartment style, 9 with air-conditioning: 130,000–225,000Fmg; 9 with fans: 90,000Fmg. All rooms have a small kitchen. A very nice, secluded hotel beyond Chez Maggie. No restaurant but they can serve breakfast for 20,000–25,000Fmg. Under the same ownership as the Hotel Central.

Le Renala 'Sable d'Or', Nosy Kely; tel: 95 522 29. 8 bungalows with air conditioning, 285,000Fmg; 5 with fans: 255,000Fmg; all with one double and one single bed. Also, 2 apartments with one double bed: 225,000 Fmg and 4 rooms with air conditioning: 165.000Fmg. All with en-suite facilities. Solid wooden bungalows in Nosy Kely (next to Chez Maggie) surrounded by landscaped gardens and grass. Breakfast 22,000–30,000Fmg; meals: 45,000Fmg.

Category B

Les Bougainvilliers Nosy Kely; tel: 95 521 63; fax: 95 520 23. 9 double bungalows plus 4 rooms, all with en-suite facilities, hot water and fans; 98,000Fmg, extra bed 20,000Fmg. 4 simple rooms with double bed and shared facilities: 50,000 Fmg. Good food. Breakfast 15,000–32,000Fmg; meals 43,000Fmg. Visa cards accepted. Friendly staff. They organise a variety of excursions including the Tsingy de Bemaraha. Manager Francios Vahiako is the head of the Morondava Guide Association and available to assist with arranging guides/tours throughout the area.

Hotel Morondava Beach Tel/fax 95 523 18; cellphone: 020 3204 692 28; email: mbeach@blueline.mg; www.hgi-mbeach.com. 15 bungalows, with air conditioning 149,000Fmg; with fan 89,000–120,000Fmg; extra bed 30,000Fmg. Breakfast: 17,000–25,000Fmg; meals (good): 45,000 Fmg. 4WD hire.Offers a full range of excursions Including the Tsingy de Bamaraha.

Hotel les Piroguiers Betania. Tel: 95 526 19; email: piroguiers@yahoo.fr. 4 bungalows on stilts: about 85,000Fmg. Menu about 54,000Fmg. This one of Jim Bond's 'best discoveries in recent years' and Jim knows the area well. Betania is 'a delightful Makoa fishing village across the river, famous for its fabulously large, sunbathing pigs'. Take a *taxi-pirogue* (500Fmg) or a *vedette* (2,500Fmg). The hotel is owned by Pascal and Bodo Boisard, who are involved members of the Betania community. 'The food is excellent – particularly recommended is Bodo's wonderful fish in saffron and coconut sauce. They also have 12 horses on which you can do trips further south along the coast. In the rainy season, swimming across the mouths of the rivers with your horse, holding on to its mane… well, there's nothing quite like it!'

Hotel Continental Downtown. 6 rooms all with air conditioning and TV for 150,000Fmg, 13 rooms with fan 45,000Fmg. Breakfast 15,000–20,000Fmg. 4WD vehicles for rent.

Category C

Hotel L'Oasis Route de Batellage; tel: 95 522 22; email: vazahabe@dts.mad.
4 en-suite rooms with double beds, some with air conditioning. 60,000Fmg. A near-beach hotel, family-run and very friendly. Good restaurant and bar. Breakfast: 10,000–20,000Fmg; sea food à la carte: 10,000–20,000Fmg. Often with live music, drums and reggae performed by the owner and local musicians. 'My tip for an evening meal. The owner was so genuinely friendly, and as a lone diner he made me feel extremely comfortable and welcomed. And the food was fantastic!' (Stuart Riddle). Mountain bikes available here. See *Tour operator and guides*, Jean la Rasta.

Hotel Central Tel: 95 523 78. On the main street, newish and recently renovated. Hot shower and WC. No restaurant but breakfast served.

Hotel Menabe Near the market. 20 spacious rooms with en-suite bathroom (cold water) but reportedly buggy and noisy: a church bell next door tolls all night. 40,000–55,000Fmg. Breakfast available: 22,000–25,000Fmg.

Hotel Le Batelage A 4-storey hotel near the Oasis. 8 en-suite rooms with double bed and fans; 50,000–75,000Fmg. Breakfast: 12,500Fmg; meals à la carte 7-20,000Fmg.

Zoom Hotel Up the road from the Oasis. 8 rooms with double beds and fans: 60,000Fmg. No restaurant, but can provide breakfast upon request..

Where to eat

Just before *la crise politique*, Jonathan Ekstom (see *Pretty Polly*, page 430), wrote a detailed and mouthwatering booklet on the restaurants of Morondava. This has been updated and will be available at Chez Maggie.

Renala On the seafront and specialising in seafood. Recommended are the prawns, grilled or in coconut sauce and *steak du thon*.

Le Masoandro or **Sunshine** (Chez Maggie Hotel). Offers a varied menu with excellent seafood and ambience. Speciality of the house: crab sautéed with garlic.

Baobab Café Full menu with open BBQ, several specials including sole with lemon and fish or poultry breast with vanilla. 'I particularly recommend going there for breakfast for the wonderful warm croissants. The café has a great view and friendly staff. You can then use their lovely pool and shop on site for excellent T-shirts. ' (S Riddle)

La Sirene Located in town with quality seafood at a reasonable price.

Drug Store Mini Resto Across from the market. Best value snack bar in town.

Mada Bar 'Small, relaxed, and has excellent food' (SB) In front of My Lord disco in Nosy Kely.

Campanina Across the road from My Lord disco. Serves good Italian food and pizza.

Hatea Just south of Bougainvillier on Nosy Kely: a small restaurant, and snack bar with cybercafe.

Cybercafés
There are three in Morondava, at the Hatea, the Oasis Hotel and downtown.

Nightclub
My Lord Nosy Kely
Banacafe Opposite My Lord (said to be the better of the two)

Tour operator and guides
Baobab Tours Located at the Baobab Café (same contact details), they offer a large selection of vehicle and boat trips, including excursions to Kirindy, deep-sea fishing, the Tsingy de Bemaraha National Park and flights over the *tsingy*. Their prices are high, however.
Gerard Ravoajanahary World-renowned birder and multi-lingual naturalist in residence at the MaggieLa Masoandro (Chez Maggie) Hotel. Along with personally guiding excursions in the Morondava area, Gerard leads river tours throughout Madagascar. Contact via the Chez Maggie.
Michael Golfier Recommended as an English-speaking guide/fixer. Tel: 95 52 140
Jean le Rasta (Rasta Jean) Recommended by several travellers as being 'efficient, reliable and charismatic'. Speaks some English. Contact through the Hotel Oasis.

Excursions from Morondava
Baobabs
This is the region of the splendid Grandidier's baobab, *Adansonia grandidieri*, best seen at the Avenue of the Baobabs. Also popular are Les Baobabs Amoureux (two entwined baobabs), and there's a Sacred Baobab as well. Mountain bikes are available at some of the hotels and are an excellent way to see the baobabs. Beware of the heat, flies and thorns on the road. By car or taxi, the **Avenue of the Baobabs** is 45 minutes from Morondava. Try to get there shortly before sunset (or – better – sunrise) for the best photos. **Les Baobabs Amoureux** are another half hour or so away. Nearby is a lake which is very good for birdwatching.

There used to be two *baobabs sacrés* ('sacred baobabs'), one near Kirindy and one near the turn-off from the main road to Belo. Sadly the latter one fell down in the cyclone. The remaining baobab, a chunky *Adansonia rubrostipa* (not the stately *A. grandidieri*) has signs of offerings nearby and *lambas* tied to the branches.

Several of the famous baobabs are reportedly in bad condition due in part to cyclone damage, and in part through pollution of the water from the sugar cane factory.

Namahora
If you arrive by air you will pass through this small town on the way to Morondava from the airport. There is a very lively Friday market, and the place is of historic interest, being the site of the Sakalava defeat of the Merina back in the 19th century. The name means 'Place Where They Were Tied' (ie: the captive Merina). If you want to stay, there is a small hotel on the edge of town, nearest the airport.

Zebu market
If you are in Morondava on Friday it's worth visiting the Marché des Zebus, held at **Analeiva**, the first village outside Morondava on the road to Tana.

Sakalava tombs: a warning
Although the Menabe region is famous for its tombs, some things of obvious interest to tourists should be left alone. This applies particularly to the famous erotic carvings on tombs in the area around Morondava.

PRETTY POLLY
Jonathan Ekstrom

Anyone who has spent time in Madagascar will realise that the Malagasy are not the most monogamous of peoples. The same is true for the island's parrots. The greater vasa parrots of Madagascar are those big black squawking things you can see flying around the forest canopy. They are not the prettiest of parrots, having drab brownish-black plumage, long necks and even bald heads for some of each year. Perhaps there is a moral emerging in this story already, for vasa parrots also have one of the most exhilarating sex lives of any animal on Earth. It's the females that are dominant over the males (they're 25% bigger!) and they pursue the little chaps ardently all through September and October. It's the girls that do the chasing. And they seem to know what they're doing as most females end up with four to eight different mates.

You can imagine what a headache this is for the males, having to compete to fertilise the eggs of the female with all your best buddies. The male parrots have risen to the challenge, however, with some utterly unbelievable evolutionary adaptations. For a start they have a penis. Birds in general don't have a penis, both sexes just have cloacal openings which are pressed together to transfer the sperm. Not so for vasa parrots. The males have evolved a penis somewhat bigger than a golfball which they erect out of their cloaca as and when they need it. Courtship before sex takes an appropriately long time, several weeks in fact, and on the big day the female might consort with a half dozen males before settling down with one at midday in some shaded corner of the forest canopy. And of course this is not ordinary love-making, at least not for the bird world.

Sex in most species of birds like robins and sparrows doesn't look that fun, to be honest – it's all over pretty quick with a kiss of the cloacas lasting a couple of seconds, and both partners then wander off in different directions apparently pretending they don't know each other. Not so in vasa parrots: sex lasts a full two hours with the male and female locked together in passionate coitus, rather like the dog family. Tied together for two hours you can see them crooning over each other, preening their partner's plumage, squawking when things get

These carvings are fertility symbols, and often depict figures engaged in sexual activities which the Sakalava consider *fady* to practise. One example is oral sex. Erotic carvings of this kind can nowadays be seen in cultural museums in larger towns such as Tana or Toliara, and small replicas are often carved and sold as souvenirs – erotica always has a ready market. In the early 1970s unscrupulous art dealers pillaged the tombs around Morondava, removing nearly all the erotic carvings. As a result, the Sakalava now keep secret the location of those tombs which still have carvings. As one guide reported: 'Some of the graveyards are for the tourists, but most are secret – for the people.'

RESERVES NORTH OF MORONDAVA

The dry deciduous forests between the rivers Morondava and Tsiribihina are of great biological importance. Indeed, this is one of the most threatened forest types in the world. Many endemic species of flora and fauna are found here; the area is particularly rich in reptiles such as tortoises, snakes and a variety of lizards. The fosa is common in these forests and eight species of lemur are found, including a bit rough…it's a real event. So much so that it frequently attracts onlookers: a whole crowd of parrots can turn up to watch. Sometimes things get a bit out of hand and some of her other boyfriends get a bit frisky and try jumping on top of the copulating pair, sometimes managing to disturb them and have a go themselves. However, it's all down to the female's choice as she has the beak and claws to control her diminutive boyfriends.

Well, after such persistent promiscuity, when it comes to feed the chicks you can imagine the confusion. The males have normally found several girlfriends for themselves as well, and these avian harems often mean it's not clear which chicks belong to which dad. It's the males that do all the work bringing in the food and you can see the lads (carrying fruits and seeds freshly gathered from the forest), vexing over which of their girlfriends to feed next. Once again the females don't just sit back and see what happens, they sing long and complex songs to attract their boyfriends in to feed them. Each female has her own unique song, so November in the forests of Madagascar is rather like a huge singing contest where females with chicks compete to be the best singer. And it works – females singing longer or more complex songs attract more males and get more food. The males benefit from feeding the best singing girlfriends because these are also the strongest birds with the most chicks in the nest.

Greater vasa parrots have the most complex sex life of any parrot so far studied. Scientists think most other species of parrot are probably monogamous and have the same partner their whole life – making parrots real bastions of chastity in the avian world. So vasas have broken all the rules and are pillars of promiscuity instead. That's evolution in isolation for you. Like so much of Madagascar's wildlife, if you leave some normal, decent-living animals by themselves in the middle of the Indian Ocean for a few dozen million years they are bound to come up with something bizarre.

Dr Jonathan Ekstrom is an ecologist with BirdLife International, Cambridge, UK. He did his Ph.D research on the greater vasa parrot in western Madagascar. In addition to his work with BirdLife he is a freelance writer and co-director of an Earth Education programme for children (www.noboundary.org).

white sifaka and the rare pale fork-marked lemur and Madame Berthe's mouse lemur, the world's smallest primate weighing in at only 30g. The giant jumping rat, Madagascar's most charming rodent, is unique to this small area.

There are three protected areas between the two rivers: Andranomena, Analabe and Kirindy. Heading north from Morondava, the first one you come to is **Andranomena**, a Special Reserve under the control of ANGAP which has an office in the village of Andranomena, where permits may be purchased and a guide hired (compulsory) to take you on the trails.

Analabe is a private nature reserve owned by M Jean de Heaulme, of Berenty fame. There are, as yet, no facilities for tourists. Analabe lies 60km north of Morondava, to the west of Kirindy by the village of Beroboka. In addition to forest it contains some mangrove areas as well as marshes and lakes typical of coastal plain.

Kirindy

This is one of the most rewarding natural areas in Madagascar. At time of writing it is not a reserve but three conservation groups are involved in plans to include it in a new protected area. Until a few years ago its sole purpose was the sustainable 'harvesting' of trees, but despite the selective logging, the wildlife here is abundant. This is the only place where you may see the giant jumping rat and the narrow-striped mongoose.

Kirindy is also *the* place to see fosa (*Cryptoprocta ferox*). Madagascar's largest carnivore has become much easier to see in recent years. Jonathan Ekstrom reports: 'They mate voraciously over four days between November 5 and 20. It's pot luck but you would be guaranteed good views. There are camera teams there every year to film it!' Richard Lewis of the Durrell Wildlife Conservation Trust (one of the three NGOs working here) adds: 'Kirindy is still the best place to see fosa (I had my trainers stolen by them last year).'

Accommodation is, at present, pretty basic but even if you normally dislike roughing it, you should try to stay the night here. Day visitors see far less than those able to observe wildlife at the optimum time of dawn and dusk, and a night-time stroll is usually an exceptional wildlife experience with nocturnal lemurs and chameleons every few paces and – if you are really lucky – the giant jumping rat.

Getting there and away
Kirindy is about 65km northeast of Morondava – about two hours by poor road (in a private vehicle) or three tedious hours by taxi-brousse.

It is much easier to take a package tour through one of the hotels in Morondava such as the Bougainvilliers, Boabab Café, Continental and Chez Maggie.

When to go
The giant jumping rat is one of the most endangered mammals in Madagascar, so it's worth choosing the optimum months for seeing it. These animals are seldom seen during the cold months and tend to keep out of sight when there is a full moon. However, in the warm wet season you are very likely to see one on the road. If you have a have a strong torch or spotlight it will 'freeze', giving you an excellent view. Jon Ekstrom writes: 'Note that the weather is extremely predictable. The rains start at the end of November or beginning of December. Before then the forest is dry, no leaves on the trees, and birds are easy to see. September and October are the best months. November is getting hot but still OK (and remember you might get lucky with those mating fosa!). December to March is very hot and humid, and the road is often impassable. January and February terrible, terrible horseflies!'

Where to stay
There are eight bungalows with twin or double beds with mosquito nets, and sheets and blankets but bring your own sleeping bag just in case. Facilities are fairly basic: limited electricity, outdoor (cold) shower and a few long-drop toilets. Cost: 50,000Fmg, or you can camp for 25,000Fmg. There is also a small restaurant (cold beer!); simple meals cost about 10,000–25,000Fmg.

Information, permits and guides
The entrance fee is 50,000Fmg. A guide (compulsory) costs 30,000Fmg per hour for two people (day walk) or 40,000Fmg for a night walk.

Kirindy Marathon
July 2004 saw the first running of the Giant Jumping Rat Marathon in the forest. This was a special event to raise awareness of the endangered local species and to provide training and markets for local people to sell handicrafts. For information on future marathons enquire at Chez Maggie (Gary Lemmer).

TRAVELLING BETWEEN MORONDAVA AND TOLIARA

There are two slow routes, road and road-and-sea. Or you can fly between the two main cities via Morombe.

By road

If you insist on doing it this way, you are in for a long and adventurous trip. 'We endured a three-day, three-night journey on a truck called *OK Zaza* for 100,000Fmg. Went from Morondava via Miandrivazo, Antsirabe, Fianar, Ihosy and Tuléar. A trip that could only be described as legendary... by the third day the three of us [*vazaha*] had lost the plot and so all got rottenly drunk on rum and warm coke. Suddenly the music was fab, the truck was great, and we ended up having a very funny night...' (S Blachford).

By road and sea

One couple spent 60 hours just getting from Morondava to Morombe! In theory there is a weekly boat, or you can hire a pirogue. Once in Morombe you can get a taxi-brousse for the onward journey. Failing this you can find road transport between Morondava and Belo Sur Mer, and there's a daily taxi-brousse (dry-season only) between Morombe and the Ifaty road-head north of Toliara. The sea stretch in the middle can be done (adventurously!) by pirogue.

By air

My advice is to fly! There is a flight one northbound and one southbound flight a week.

Belo Sur Mer

Not to be confused with Belo Sur Tsiribihina, this Vezo village 70km south of Morondava is a place you either love or hate. To enjoy it you need to be there in the coolest time of year. 'In the hot season Belo is a hell-hole of inescapable heat and insufficient drinking water.' A well has just been built now in the village and so drinking water is less of a problem.

The village itself is a collection of small houses and huts, on the border of a small lagoon, shrouded in palm trees; each family keeps a pig which is allowed to forage at night – Belo's mobile garbage disposals. There are huge cargo vessels (*boutres*) among the coconut palms at the Belo lagoon, and these are still built using exactly the same designs as the pirates used centuries back (see box on page 416). Belo is also the base for visiting a cluster of nine interesting offshore islands. The largest island is **Nosy Andravano**, but there are numerous islets. Those to the north are mere sandbanks, but the islands to the south have vegetative cover. Nomadic Vezo fishermen live on the northerly islands for six months of the year. There are shark carcasses and turtle shells left to dry on the sand, and fish and shark fins are salted in troughs. Each of the islands is fringed by coral reefs, although to view the healthy coral you may have to snorkel out up to 2km off the coast. You can hire a *pirogue* from Belo Sur Mer, from 25,000Fmg per day, to take you around the islands. Remember to bring your own drinking water and enough food for yourself and the piroguers if you intend to camp on the islands. Rob Conway, Eucare researcher who updated this section, warns 'Those islands south of Nosy Andravano are infested by rats that have a remarkable ability to chew through anything'.

The area is being developed fast. There are already two discos in Belo and small restaurants are being opened. The crab here is highly recommended and available all year round.

Getting there and away

Adventurers can go by pirogue, but 'Watch out for some flash English-speaking guides who will try to charge 600,000Fmg for this trip'. It should cost around 125,000Fmg, but most *vazaha* settle for 400,000Fmg. It takes about eight hours to sail to Belo from Morondava. Another option is to hitch from Morondava to the intersection for Belo Sur Mer and then hitch again to the village itself. A taxi-brousse also runs, temperamentally, from Morondava.

A new (2004) option sounds the most enticing. Gary Lemmer reports: 'There is now a *taxi be de la mer*, a well-equipped ship which does a daily (maybe) run Morondava/Belo/Morombe. It costs 100,000Fmg to Belo, and 250,000Fmg to Morombe.' For information and bookings enquire at the Hatea Café in Morondava.

Four-wheel-drive vehicle hire is available at several hotels in Morondava and motorboat transport may be arranged with the Baobab Café to Belo and Andravaho Island. The cost ranges from 2,000,000 to 3,350,000Fmg for 6-8 people.

Where to stay

Hotel le Dauphin 6 bungalows for 75,000Fmg. Transfers from Morondava by speedboat, 250,000Fmg per person, or motorised pirogue, 150,000Fmg. For further details contact Chez Maggie in Morondava.

Marina de Belo Sur Mer Once highly recommended, this hotel has changed ownership and now receives less enthusiastic reports, mainly because 'the prices are now much higher, without the organisation that one would expect'. However, if you want to see Belo in comfort, with transport laid on, this is the only option. You can book the hotel (and find out the latest prices) through Espace Océan, next to Hotel de La Plage in Morondava. This hotel runs some excellent tours, taking you to see baobabs and a lake of flamingoes (if they're there), then snorkelling. This tour costs about 780,000Fmg.

Menabe Another upmarket, well-run hotel which also has a diving school which offers courses and (expensive) tours from Belo Sur Mer to the fringing reefs of the islands.

There are now numerous other hotels open in Belo Sur Mer, which start from about 50,000Fmg. Also there's a report that bungalows are being developed on Nosy Andravano by the owner of Hotel Zoom in Morondava. Problems, however, have been encountered as no drinking water is available on the island.

If you have your own tent, you can arrange for a pirogue to take you to one of the islands and pick you up a couple of days later. If you do this, make sure you bring enough drinking water!

For more information on the Eucare marine conservation project check their website: www.eucarenet.com.

Morombe

This small, rather isolated town, has reinvented itself for the 21st century. In the 1996 edition of this book Chris Balance wrote: 'Morombe clearly died when the French left, but 9,000 souls remain and they spend their time walking up and down the only street, very slowly, shaking hands with each other and discussing the possibility that someone might build a proper road to them someday.' After the total eclipse of 2001 I wrote: 'The citizens now walk briskly up and down the street, shaking hands, and lamenting that the tourists have gone and there is still no decent road to their town.' In 2004 Alexander Elphinstone of Blue Ventures writes: 'Contrary to Chris Balance, I feel that Morombe is a town that rocks every night of the week. It's the only Malagasy town I visited where the locals are partying Monday through Sunday. Friendly people, for whom tourism is still a novelty. Be aware of over friendly local girls in bars; unfortunately I think Morombe is a place visited by old French men looking for such girls.'

There is still no decent road to Morombe. It deserves a (short) visit, however. In 2001 I very much liked this unpretentious seaside town, with its pleasant beach, active fishing village and mangroves.

Getting there and away
By road
Morombe is usually accessible by taxi-brousse from Ifaty, north of Toliara. There are two roads north. One, that hugs the coast, is sandy and in poor condition, and the 200km journey takes about ten hours. In a private 4WD vehicle, however, it is a worthwhile prospect because of the breathtaking scenery en route. 'On your left is the blue sea and white sand, and on your right is the incredible spiny forest, where the Mikea people live. This is a paradise for birders, and for baobab lovers. Normally it takes 8–10 hours to drive from Ifaty to Andavadoaka or Ampasilava. It is practicable only between the end of June and early November. The car can get stuck in the sand forever without the help of villagers to pull you out.' (Nivo Ravelojaona)

The taxi brousse route (inland) is through the spiny forest, but is not nearly as beautiful. This 240km journey can take from 12 hours to 24 hours. 'Do not attempt it during the rainy season, it once took a Blue Ventures team three days! This bus leaves daily, at 6.00am from Toliara going north, and usually at 3.00am from Morombe going south (buy a ticket the evening before and ask the driver to pass by your hotel at 3.00am) – although occasionally it leaves at 8.00pm or midnight.' (Alexander Elphinstone)

By sea
As reported for Belo, there is now a *taxi be de la mer*, a well-equipped ship, which does a weekly run Morondava/Belo/Morombe. It costs 100,000Fmg to Belo, and 250,000Fmg to Morombe.

By air
Morombe Airport can take only Twin Otters but it is a short hop from Morondava. The Air Mad service runs twice a week from Toliara and Tana (via Morondava). There are no taxis at the airport and it's about a 20-minute walk into town.

Where to stay/eat
Hotel Baobab 16 concrete bungalows on the beach on the south side of the town. With fan 150,000Fmg, with air-conditioning 175,000Fmg. Good restaurant. The most expensive hotel but a recent visitor reports that 'the bungalows are drab, and the restaurant has no atmosphere'. Bookings (Tana) tel: 22 427 01.

Lakana Volamena BP30 Morombe; tel: 618. New, but basic rooms grouped round a central courtyard, some with bathrooms. 80,000–150,000Fmg without shower, 200,000–250,000Fmg with shower (prices may come down now the eclipse tourists have gone). Finished just in time for the eclipse, this is a very pleasant hotel, right on the beach just north of the Baobab, French managed, serving good food. It is of a similar standard to Baobab but with much more atmosphere.

Other hotels include the **La Croix du Sud** and the **Hotel Crabe** (in the northern part of town). These are 'simple what-you-see-is-what-you-get type

MADAGASCAR'S CORAL REEFS

Alasdair Harris – Blue Ventures

Madagascar's 3000km of submerged coral banks and fringing, barrier and patch reefs represent some of the most extensive and well-developed reef ecosystems in the Indian Ocean. The world famous *Grand Récif* barrier reef of Toliara and neighbouring reefs in the southwest of the country constitute one of the West Indian Ocean's largest coral reef systems, extending some 400km in length, and representing a significant biodiversity 'hotspot' for the region. Much of this biodiversity remains, to date, unknown to science.

These rich but fragile natural resources sustain coastal economies, providing revenue from fisheries, aquaculture and tourism, as well as sustenance for a largely poverty-stricken population of 15 million people, which is increasing at a rate of 3.2% per annum. It has been estimated that at least half of all tourists arriving in Madagascar each year visit a coral reef area.

Climate change, El Niño, and the associated increases in sea surface temperatures have resulted in severe coral bleaching events in Madagascar in recent years and represent the greatest natural threat to these systems. A study on the massive 1998 bleaching event estimated a loss of US$7,000–8,200 million in net present value terms for the Indian Ocean. Bleaching events are increasing in their frequency and severity when summer heat causes sea surface waters to reach their annual maximum temperatures, and current estimates suggest bleaching could become an annual event in the next 25–50 years.

Though very little data was taken in the years preceding large-scale bleaching in Madagascar, dive operators in the tourist centres of Anakao and Ifaty have claimed almost 100% mortality of hard corals in shallow sites.

In addition to large-scale natural threats, local populations have significant effects on the health of Madagascar's coral reefs. Poor land-use practices are one of the primary anthropogenic threats to coastal biodiversity, and large areas of coastal and upland forest have been destroyed by rapid expansion of slash-and-burn agricultural systems. Wide-scale burning has exacerbated soil erosion, which now affects more than 80% of Madagascar's total land area. Elevated levels of siltation on coral reefs, in particular in west Madagascar, have already been widely reported, most notably on near-shore reefs close to the mouths of rivers, such as the Onilahy and Fiherenana rivers near Toliara.

Other anthropogenic impacts on Madagascar's coastal environment include coral, sand and rock mining, mangrove destruction, destructive and unregulated fishing, most of which are linked to poverty, inadequate planning and legislation combined with a lack of political capacity for instituting methods to address these problems.

places: a bed with mosquito net and something resembling a shower, for 25,000Fmg per night.' (AE)

Sightseeing

Morombe rewards those with time to stroll. It's quite a prosperous-looking little town, with some spacious houses in the north and a bustling fishing village of wooden huts to the south. Like so many Malagasy seaside towns, it is very spread out with no obvious sign of a centre.

The collection of species such as octopus and sea cucumbers for commercial export generally rely on methods that destroy the physical structure of the reef. Furthermore, net fishing in near-shore habitats such as mangroves, intertidal pools and seagrass beds may cause serious declines in reef fish species that use the coast as a nursery area.

Despite the biodiversity, economic importance and vulnerability of Madagascar's coastal areas and coral reefs, they have all but been ignored from a conservation perspective, primarily because they do not harbour the same endemicity that is seen in terrestrial ecosystems.

There is now a critical need for better knowledge and understanding of Madagascar's marine and coastal ecosystem processes, and for better access to information and technical capacity to devise management solutions. For example, it is essential to monitor the impacts of bleaching and the recovery rates of coral reefs, in order to incorporate resilience and resistance factors into the future selection and management of protected marine areas.

Blue Ventures, a UK-based not-for-profit operator is an example of one of the few organisations dedicated to facilitating projects to enhance coral reef conservation and research in Madagascar. Their work seeks to integrate coral reef research, education and conservation in the remote village of Andavadoaka, at the northern end of the reef system that extends from the Grand Recif of Toliara. The economy of Andavadoaka's coastal community of approximately 2000 Vezo is entirely marine based. Blue Ventures has established a permanent marine research program in Andavadoaka, which has resulted in the identification of a number of sites that were either able to resist or recover from the bleaching events of 1998. One of the goals of the project is to create a system of small marine protected areas off the coast of Andavadoaka. These no-take zones will be designed to fulfil a number of purposes including:

- conservation of coral reef, seagrass and intertidal habitats,
- protection of breeding grounds for fisheries production, and
- the development of sustainable alternatives to reef based fishing such as eco-tourism initiatives and establishment of pelagic fish aggregation devices (FADs).

As a result of these developments, and in the context of the recent Durban Initiative and renewed interest in Madagascar's coastal ecosystem, Andavadoaka presents a unique opportunity for the creation of a coastal zone management pilot program aiming to incorporate sustainable tourism, fisheries development and locally managed marine conservation.

For more information on other marine conservation efforts in Madagascar see page 456, or visit http://www.blueventures.org (email research@blueventures.org).

If you continue south along the beach beyond the Hotel Baobab you will come to a rewarding group of mangroves where you can watch mud-skippers. Behind this area are some local tombs; we did not investigate these, respecting the local *fady* against such visits.

Andavadoaka and Ampasilava

These two villages are adjacent to each other by 'one of the best beaches in Madagascar', some 45km to the south of Morombe. Coming south from

Morombe, you first reach Andavadoaka then, 5km further on, Ampasilava. The drive there is varied and very beautiful. Ask in Morombe about taxi-brousses (usually three per week), or any possible lifts (if a lift is available most people, especially some of the Indian shop owners, will know). The journey by road takes around two hours. The alternative is to take a pirogue from Morombe, which takes about five hours, and hitch a lift back, or to organise your trip in Toliara via one of the regular supply boats.

Andavadoaka has been described as the only coastal village in Madagascar whose setting rivals that of Fort Dauphin. The area can boast the richest marine ecosystem on the southwest coast, and has therefore become the home for many migrating fishermen, as well as a developing tourist resort. The diving is far superior to any that can be found at Anakao, Toliara or Ifaty, with some sites having guaranteed sightings of potato groupers and Napoleon wrasses. Manta rays, whales, sharks and turtles are seen quite regularly and phenomenal 'megapods' of up to 500 dolphins have also been sighted in recent years. Humpback whales may be seen between June and October (as well as some migrant stragglers outside these months), as they migrate to and from their breeding grounds to the north. The area also hosts the marine organisation Blue Ventures (www.blueventures.org) who are working closely with the local fishing communities as well as the University of Toliara's Institut Halieutique et des Sciences Marines (IHSM).

Tom Savage of Blue Ventures reports: 'Aside from its unique marine and coastal environment, Andavadoaka is often visited by baobab botanists since it is home to a rare diversity of these unique species. You can take a half-hour zebu ride or a one-hour stroll from the village to see these trees. The beaches in the area, including those of the nearby island Nosy Hao (pronounced 'Nosy Oa') are spectactular. The shallow tidal lagoon provides a relatively safe spot for swimming and snorkelling. When swimming it is worth keeping an eye out for local pirogues, which can move at several knots and have collided with swimmers in the past. Tourists are encouraged to spend a few days in Andavadoaka because of the difficulty in getting there. It is well worth it.

'The sheer remoteness and isolation of the region has prevented tourism from having a significant impact here, which is probably the main reason why Andavadoaka is still so unspoilt. So if you do plan to visit this ecologically sensitive region, please bring biodegradable washing products. (This should apply to the whole of Madagascar.) It is also worth remembering when ordering certain seafood dishes (eg: lobster) that the more you order, the less you are likely to find when snorkelling! If you snorkel in the lagoon, you will notice the dramatic impact that fishing has had, even without the impact of tourism.'

Where to stay/eat

Hotel Coco Beach Email: delpo1@copefrito.com. Owner Olivier del Pierre. A charming and extremely friendly French-owned hotel, with rustic but comfortable beach bungalows in one of the most beautiful settings in southern Madagascar, offering extraordinary panoramic views. The friendly staff run the low-key hotel in a family manner, whereby you can request food, which is generally excellent, at most times. The management is able to organise diving and snorkelling. Bookings can be made through Chez La La, Toliara (see page 240). Price: around 75,000Fmg. Coco Beach is becoming Increasingly popular and can be booked out during Christmas and New Year.

Laguna Blu Resort Ampasilava; tel: 00 816 21 01 20 75; email: lagunabluresort@lagunabluresort.com; www.lagunabluresort.com. Classy, Italian-owned bungalows for €46 single, €92 double. Excellent facilities with Western mattresses, good food, extremely comfortable bungalows and hot and cold running water, which for this part of the country is no mean feat. Very little English spoken. The Manta scuba-diving/snorkelling centre is based here. The manager, Sandro, is an Italian doctor who also runs a clinic for local people.

The village is bound to expand its tourist accommodation. At the time of writing, Madame Ramasay (a local *épicerie* owner) is building small huts for tourists on Nosy Hao. She also has a few small guest rooms in Andavadoaka and other shop owners are following her lead.

Miandrivazo

Said to be the hottest place in Madagascar. The town lies on the banks of the Mahajilo, a tributary of the Tsiribihina, and is the starting point for the descent of that river. Supposedly the name comes from when King Radama was waiting for his messenger to return with Rasalimo, the Sakalava princess of Malaimbandy with whom he had fallen in love. He fell into a pensive mood and when asked if he was well replied '*Miandry vazo aho*' – 'I am waiting for a wife.'

It's a ten-hour journey from Morondava by car or taxi-brousse, with one infamously bad stretch of road between Miandrivazo and Malaimbandy.

Where to stay/eat

Le Relais de Miandrivazo BP22. On the main square. Comfortable rooms with mosquito nets. Reasonable food, good atmosphere. Intermittent water.
Hotel Laizama 'A simple but homely hotel – we often found ducks in the shower – with very helpful management. We ate at the Buvette Espoir in town. Meals must be booked in advance; great value.' (R Harris and G Jackson)
Hotel Chez la Reine Rasalimo Tel: 95 438. Concrete bungalows on a hill overlooking the river. Very friendly staff with a good restaurant. Double rooms with mosquito nets and fans: 90,000Fmg; triple 100,000Fmg.

Descending the Tsiribihina River

This is a popular trip (see below) and can easily be set up from Miandrivazo. The guides have organised themselves into the Association Guide Piroguier Miandrivazo (AGPM) which seems very professional. Wherever you are staying, someone from AGPM will find you.

José Rakotomamonjy and his wife Soul are warmly recommended by Thomas Feichtinger of Austria, not only for the canoe trip down the Tsiribihina but for other excursions. José is knowledgable about wildlife and speaks good French and some English. Soul comes along as the cook. José can be found at the Bar Amical in Miandrivazo.

Rebecca Pierce recommends **Baba Voyages** (cellphone: 032 0413 919; www.babavoyages.com) for organising the trip. 'They were very efficient, had a sign outside their office saying "Contre la Corruption" and we had an excellent English-speaking guide called Daniel. We took a bone-rattling zebu cart at the end of our journey to get to the road to Morondova – what an experience!'

RIVER TRIPS

Trips down the lazy western rivers of Madagascar are becoming increasingly popular, and can be done as an organised tour or independently. Most tour operators use fast (but noisy) motorboats, some use inflatable rafts while local people use pirogues.

The four main western rivers that are navigable are the Tsiribihina, the Mangoky, the Manambolo and the Mahavavy. The former is quite easy to do independently, but the others are more challenging and you are advised to go with the specialist tour operators such as Mad'Cameleon and Remote Rivers Expeditions.

Tsiribihina River

This is a three- to five-day trip, with the starting point in Miandrivazo. The birdlife viewed from the river is excellent, and there is a good chance of seeing lemurs, chameleons and snakes. Nights are spent camping on the riverbank. Some river-goers report it too hot to sleep in a tent, in which case a mosquito net is absolutely essential. At the end of the wet season the trip changes dramatically: camping on the beach is impossible due to the high river so you walk to the nearest village, and the trips are much shorter due to the faster-flowing river.

The trip should not be undertaken lightly: 'Long, long days paddling in the searing heat ... I got sunburnt in spite of Factor 15 sunblock, and chewed to death by mosquitoes, despite extra-strong repellent. But I'm glad I did it ...' (Sarah Blachford)

This is an easy trip to arrange independently. Opinions vary on whether it should be organised locally or before you arrive in Miandrivazo. 'It is significantly cheaper to book through AGPM than through agents in Tana. The problem is that communication with Tana is very difficult, so you have to wait until you get to Miandrivazo to book.' (Colin Palmer) Another reader comments: 'I suggest that organisation of a river trip in Tana or Antsirabe is preferable to organisation in Miandrivazo, and that travellers discuss all aspects of their trip in detail.'

'When staying in local villages during our descent, our guide didn't ever make the attempt to bridge the communication gap between us and the villagers when we would have loved, indeed would have paid, to be shown how they weave raffia fibre so effectively. An enthusiastic guide would have organised that and broken the ice between mute hosts and guests. As a traveller approached by a guide, be assertive enough to say no to an inadequate or unenthusiastic guide even if the trip sounds good. There will be plenty of enthusiastic, friendly guides around if you are patient.' (Tim Ireland)

Other readers who have organised their own trips on the Tsiribihina add the following points:

- Find out the language of your paddler. Do they speak any English or indeed French?
- Look at the pirogue before agreeing to anything, and go for a test run.
- Don't assume the paddlers are guides and know about the wildlife.
- Do your own food shopping or tell your paddlers exactly what you want. You should also pay for the food for your paddlers.
- A mosquito net is essential; a tent advisable.

Manambolo River

The descent of the Manambolo can be arranged through the tour operator Mad'Cameleon (see page 442) or through Remote River Expeditions (see advert on page 427). On an organised tour the trip takes three days (though five allows for some rest and sightseeing), beginning at Ankavandra. This is a spectacular trip through the untouched homeland of the Sakalava. On the third day you pass through the dramatic Manambolo gorge between towering limestone cliffs, and through the Tsingy de Bemaraha Reserve. The chances of seeing the area's special wildlife, such as Decken's sifaka and the Madagascar fish eagle, are high.

It's rare for anyone to do the Manambolo independently, but Herman Snippe and Jolyjn Geels achieved it in 1999. They took a variety of taxi-brousses from Tana to Tsiromanomandidy and on to Belobaka. From here they hired a guide to take them on foot to Ankavandra along the Route de Riz used by rice porters. This walk took three days and was 'wonderful' although they warn of a shortage of drinking water in the dry season. There have been recent reports of bandits in this area, so it is best to check prior to making the journey. Ankavandra is pretty much owned and run by a Mr Nouradine, who owns the only hotel and river-worthy pirogues. The trip downriver cost Herman and Jolijn about US$125 (a high price for Madagascar). The price included two piroguiers and their food. In April, after rain, the two-and-a-half-day descent of the river was thrilling and spectacularly beautiful.

Getting from Bekopaka to 'civilisation' at Belo sur Tsiribihina was an adventure in itself! Herman and Jolijn walked for a day before finding a tracteur-brousse – a tractor towing a trailer crowded with passengers – to take them the final stretch.

Mangoky River

The journey from Beroroha to Bevoay (approx 160km) runs through an extremely isolated region in the southwest of the island, with no roads north or south of the river for more than 100km. This calm water stretch offers expansive beaches for camping and many yet-to-be-explored side canyons. The Mangoky passes through sections of dry deciduous forests which are dominated by perhaps the largest baobab forest on Earth. There are at least three species, the predominant being the huge *Andonsonia grandidieri*.

The seclusion of the river and undisturbed aspect make it extremely rich with bird and other wildlife. Lemurs found include the Verreaux's sifaka, red-fronted and ring-tailed, and a number of nocturnal species. The list of birdlife is long and includes Thamornis warbler, Sakalava weaver, Archbold's newtonia, peregrines, Madagascar buzzards, cuckoo-rollers and many herons and egrets. There are at least four species of coua (*gigas*, *coquereli*, *cursor* and *ruficeps*) and two vanga (*Xenopirostris xenopirostris* and *Falculea palliata*). Gatherings of knob-billed and white-faced whistling ducks have been seen in flocks of up to one thousand.

'Given the vast unexploited area along the river, its rich wildlife and the sheer beauty of the river itself, perhaps the Mangoky deserves to be designated Madagascar's first national river reserve.' (Gary Lemmer).

Mahavavy River

Another 'special' from Remote River Expeditions, this river was first explored in 1998. The rafting team put in at Kandreho and ended in Mitsinjo. The area was extremely rich in both lemurs and birds, with large expanses of beautiful forest. Lemur-viewing was far superior to the other western rivers. 'For sheer numbers, proximity, and ease of viewing, the Mahavavy was superb, mainly for the two subspecies of Verreaux's sifaka (*deckeni* and *coronatus*) and *Eulemur fulvus rufus*.

'The outstanding areas for these species were around the Kasijy forest and the riverine tamarind gallery forest between Bekipay and Ambinany. To give some ideas of densities in both the Kasijy area and also the forest between Bekipay and Ambinany, I can say that a short foray into the forest, moving maybe 200–300m, staying one hour, would produce five to six families of sifaka, which were remarkably unconcerned by our presence. Red-fronted brown lemurs were very numerous, especially in Kasijy. The Mahavavy is very rich in birds; the most exciting sightings of the trip were of Madagascar fish eagles (a total of six).' (Conrad Hirsh).

Tour operators running river trips

Most of the main ground operators listed in *Chapter 4* organise river trips on comfortable vessels with good food and camping equipment, and experienced guides.

Specialist operators include:

Mad'Cameleon Tel: 22 630 86; fax: 22 344 20; email: madcam@dts.mg. Canoe trips on the Manambolo River.
Remote River Expeditions www.remoterivers.com. Take small groups on all the main rivers of Madagascar and regularly pioneer new trips.
Madamax Tours Tel (Tana): 22 351 01; www.madamax.com. River trips near Antananarivo and throughout the island.

Appendix 1

HISTORICAL CHRONOLOGY

AD 000	Approximate date for the first significant settlement of the island.
800–900	Dates of the first identifiable village sites in the north of the island. Penetration of the interior begins in the south.
1200	Establishment of Arab settlements. First mosques built.
1500	'Discovery' of Madagascar by the Portuguese Diego Dias. Unsuccessful attempts to establish permanent European bases on the island followed.
1650s	Emergence of Sakalava kingdoms.
Early 1700s	Eastern Madagascar is increasingly used as a base by pirates.
1716	Fénérive captured by Ratsimilaho. The beginnings of the Betsimisaraka confederacy.
1750	Death of Ratsimilaho.
1787	The future Andrianampoinimerina declared King of Ambohimanga.
1795/6	Andrianampoinimerina established his capital at Antananarivo.
1810–28	Reign of Radama I, Merina king.
1818	First mission school opened in Tamatave.
1820	First mission school opened in Antananarivo.
1828–61	Reign of Ranavalona I, Merina queen.
1835	Publication of the Bible in Malagasy, but profession of the Christian faith declared illegal.
1836	Most Europeans and missionaries leave the island.
1861–63	Reign of Radama II, Merina king.
1861	Missionaries re-admitted. Freedom of religion proclaimed.
1863–68	Queen Rasoherina succeeds after Radama II assassinated.
1868–83	Reign of Queen Ranavalona II.
1883	Coronation of Queen Ranavalona III.
1883–85	Franco-Malagasy War.
1895	Establishment of full French protectorate; Madagascar became a full colony the following year.
1897	Ranavalona III exiled first to Réunion and later to Algiers. Merina monarchy abolished.
1917	Death of Ranavalona III in exile.
1942	British troops occupy Madagascar.
1946	Madagascar becomes an Overseas Territory of France.
1947	Nationalist rebellion suppressed with thousands killed.
1958	Autonomy achieved within the French community.
1960	June 26. Madagascar achieves full independence with Philibert Tsiranana as president.
1972	Tsiranana dissolves parliament and hands power to General Ramanantsoa who forges links with Soviet Union.

1975	Lieutenant-Commander Didier Ratsiraka is named head of state after a coup. The country is renamed the Democratic Republic of Madagascar and Ratsiraka is elected president for a seven-year term.
1976	Ratsiraka nationalises large parts of the economy and forms the AREMA party
1986	Ratsiraka changes position and promotes a market economy.
1991	Demonstrations and strikes. Ratsiraka orders security forces to open fire on the crowds outside the presidential palace demanding his resignation. About 130 people are killed.
1992	Under pressure of demonstrations, Ratsiraka introduces democratic reforms replacing the socialist system, but is forced to resign.
1993	Albert Zafy elected president in the country's first multi-party elections. The birth of the Third Republic.
1996	Albert Zafy impeached.
1997	Didier Ratsiraka re-elected president.
2000	December. AREMA wins in most of the cities, apart from Antananarivo, in provincial elections. 70% of voters boycott the elections.
2001	May. Senate reopens after 29 years, completing the government framework provided for in the 1992 constitution.
2001	December. First round of presidential elections. Marc Ravalomanana claims the election was rigged and refuses to take part in a run-off. This leads to six months of turmoil.
2002	July. *La Crise Politique* ends and Marc Ravalomanana becomes president.

Appendix 2

THE MALAGASY LANGUAGE
Some basic rules
Pronunciation

The Malagasy alphabet is made up of 21 letters. C, Q, U, W and X are omitted. Individual letters are pronounced as follows:

a	as in 'father'
e	as in the a in 'late'
g	as in 'get'
h	almost silent
i	as ee in 'seen'
j	pronounced dz
o	oo as in 'too'
s	usually midway between sh and s but varies according to region
z	as in 'zoo'

Combinations of letters needing different pronunciations are:

ai	like y in 'my'
ao	like ow in 'cow'
eo	pronounced ay-oo

When k or g is preceded by i or y this vowel is also sounded after the consonant. For example *alika* (dog) is pronounced Aleekya, and *ary koa* (and also) is pronounced Ahreekewa.

Stressed syllables

Some syllables are stressed, others almost eliminated. This causes great problems for visitors trying to pronounce place names, and unfortunately – like in English – the basic rules are frequently broken. Generally, the stress is on the penultimate syllable except in words ending in na, ka and tra when it is generally on the last syllable but two. Words ending in e stress that vowel. Occasionally a word with the same spelling changes its meaning according to the stressed syllable, but in this case it is written with an accent. For example, *tanana* means 'hand', and *tanána* means 'town'.

When a word ends in a vowel, this final syllable is pronounced so lightly it is often just a stressed last consonant. For instance the sifaka lemur is pronounced 'She-fak'. Words derived from English, like *hotely* and *banky*, are pronounced much the same as in English.

Getting started

The easiest way to begin to get a grip on Malagasy is to build on your knowledge of place names (you have to learn how to pronounce these in order to get around) and to this end I have given the phonetic pronunciation in the text. As noted in the text, most place names mean something so you have only to learn these meanings and – hey presto! – you have the elements of the language! Here are some bits of place names:

An-, Am-, I-	at, the place where	Manga	blue or good
Arivo	thousand	Maro	many
Be	big, plenty of	Nosy	island
Fotsy, -potsy	white	Rano, -drano	water
Kely	small	Tany, tani-	land
Kily	tamarind	Tsara	good
Mafana	hot	Tsy, Tsi	(negative)
Maha	which causes	Vato, -bato	stone
Mainti	black	Vohitra, vohi-,	hill
Maintso	green	bohi-	

In Malagasy the plural form of a noun is the same as the singular form.

Vocabulary
Social phrases

Stressed letters or phrases are underlined.

English	Malagasy	Phonetic pronunciation
Hello	Manao ahoana	Mano _own_
Hello	Salama	Sal_aa_m
(north & east coast)	Mbola tsara	M'boola tsara
What news?	Inona no vaovao?	_Inan vowvow?_
No news	Tsy misy	Tsim_ees_

These three easy-to-learn phrases of ritualised greetings establish contact with people you pass on the road or meet in their village. For extra courtesy (important in Madagascar) add *tompoko* (pronounced 'toomp'k') at the end of each phrase.

Simple phrases for 'conversation'

English	Malagasy	Phonetic pronunciation
What's your name?	Iza no anaranao?	Eeza nan_ara_now?
My name is	Ny anarako	Ny an_ara_koo
Goodbye	Veloma	Vel_oo_m
See you again	Mandra pihaona	Mandra pi_oo_n
I don't understand	Tsy azoko	Tsi az_ook_
I don't know	Tsy haiko	Tsi haikou
Very good	Tsara tokoa	Tsara t'k_oo_
Bad	Ratsy	Rats
Please/Excuse me	Aza fady	Aza_fad_
Thank you	Misaotra	Mis_ow_tr
Thank you very much	Misaotra betsaka	Mis_ow_tr bets_ak_
Pardon me		
(ie: may I pass)	Ombay lalana	M'_buy_ lalan
Let's go	Andao andeha	And_ow_ and_ay_
Crazy	Adaladala	Adalad_al_
Long life! (Cheers!)	Ho ela velona!	Wellav_ell_!

If you are pestered by beggars try:

I have nothing	Tsy misy	Tsim_ee_ss
(there is none)		
Thank you, I don't need it	Misaotra fa tsy mila	Mis_ow_tr, fa tsi meel
Go away!	Mandehana!	Man day _han_

Note: The words for yes (*eny*) and no (*tsia*) are hardly ever used in conversation. The Malagasy tend to say '*yoh*' for yes and '*ah*' for no, along with appropriate gestures.

Market phrases

How much?	*Ohatrinona?*	*Ohtreen?*
Too expensive!	*Lafo be!*	*Laff be!*
No way!	*Tsy lasa!*	*Tsee lass!*

Basic needs

Where is…?	*Aiza…?*	*Ize…?*
Is it far?	*Lavitra ve izany?*	*Lavtra vayzan?*
Is there any…?	*Misy ve…?*	*Mees vay…?*
I want…	*Mila … aho*	*Meel … a*
I'm looking for…	*Mitady … aho*	*M'tadi … a*
Is there a place to sleep?	*Misy toerana hatoriana ve?*	*Mees too ayran atureen vay?*
Is it ready?	*Vita ve?*	*Veeta vay?*
I would like to buy some food	*Te hividy sakafo aho*	*Tayveed sakaff wah*
I'm hungry	*Noana aho*	*Noonah*
I'm thirsty	*Mangetaheta aho*	*Mangataytah*
I'm tired	*Vizaka aho*	*Veesacar*
Please help me!	*Mba ampio aho!*	*Bampeewha!*

Useful words

village	*vohitra*	*voo-itra*
house	*trano*	*tran*
food/meal	*hanina/sakafo*	*an/sakaff*
water	*rano*	*rahn*
rice	*vary*	*var*
eggs	*atody*	*atood*
chicken	*akoho*	*akoo*
bread	*mofo*	*moof*
milk	*ronono*	*roonoon*
road	*lalana*	*lalan*
town	*tanana*	*tanan*
river (large)	*ony*	*oon*
river (small)	*riaka*	*reek*
ox/cow	*omby/omby vavy*	*oomby/omb varve*
child/baby	*ankizy/zaza kely*	*ankeeze/zaza kail*
man/woman	*lehilahy/vehivavy*	*layla/vayvarve*

Appendix

MADAGASCAR'S MAMMALS AND WHERE TO SEE THEM

Nick Garbutt

Although there are relatively few species (compared with mainland Africa), Madagascar is an exceptional place to watch mammals. Of course, everyone wants to see lemurs but for those with time, patience and a little luck, there is far more to see. Listed below are the best places to try and see Madagascar's mammals. Species marked with an asterisk (*) are nocturnal.

Lemurs

Common name	Scientific name	Distribution/Where to see
Grey mouse lemur	*Microcebus murinus**	The dry forests of the west and spiny forests of the south. Best sites Ampijoroa Forestry Station, Kirindy Forest and Berenty Reserve.
Brown mouse lemur	*Microcebus rufus**	Throughout the eastern rainforest belt. Andasibe-Mantadia National Park Ranomafana NP.
Pygmy mouse lemur	*Microcebus myoxinus**	Currently known only from the Kirindy Forests area.
Golden-brown mouse lemur	*Microcebus ravelobensis**	Currently known only from the forests of Ampijoroa. Ampijoroa Forestry Station.
Hairy-eared dwarf lemur	*Allocebus trichotis**	Central and northeastern lowland rainforests. Analamazaotra Reserve.
Greater dwarf lemur	*Cheirogaleus major**	Eastern rainforests. Ranomafana National Park and occasionally seen in Andasibe-Mantadia NP
Fat-tailed dwarf lemur	*Cheirogaleus medius**	Dry forests of the south and west. Ampijoroa Forestry Station and Kirindy Forest.
Coquerel's dwarf lemur	*Mirza coquereli**	Dry forests of the west and moist forests of the Sambirano region. Kirindy Forest and secondary forests near Ambanja in the northwest.
Eastern fork-marked lemur	*Phaner furcifer furcifer**	Rainforest centred around the Masoala Peninsula. Ambanizana and Andranobe on the Masoala Peninsula.

448

Pariente's fork-marked lemur	*Phaner furcifer parienti★*	Sambirano region in the northwest. Ampasindava Peninsula and the forests around the village of Beraty.
Pale fork-marked lemur	*Phaner furcifer pallescens★*	Dry forests of the west. Kirindy Forest.
Amber Mountain fork-marked lemur	*Phaner furcifer electromontis★*	Montagne d'Ambre, Ankarana and Analamera region of northern Madagascar. Montagne d'Ambre National Park and Ankarana Reserve.
Weasel sportive lemur	*Lepilemur mustelinus★*	Northern half of the eastern rainforest belt. Marojejy National Park, Anjanaharibe-Sud Reserve and Masoala National Park.
Small-toothed sportive lemur	*Lepilemur microdon★*	The southern half of the eastern rainforest belt. Andasibe-Mantadia National Park and Ranomafana National Park.
Northern sportive lemur	*Lepilemur septentrionalis★*	Forests of the extreme north. Ankarana Reserve and Montagne d'Ambre National Park.
Grey-backed sportive lemur	*Lepilemur dorsalis★*	Sambirano region and offshore islands in the northwest. Lokobe Reserve on Nosy Be.
Milne-Edwards sportive lemur	*Lepilemur edwardsi★*	Dry forests of the west, north of the Manambolo River. Ampijoroa Forestry Station.
Red-tailed sportive lemur	*Lepilemur ruficaudatus★*	Dry forests of the west, south of the Manambolo River. Kirindy Forest.
White-footed sportive lemur	*Lepilemur leucopus★*	Spiny and gallery forests of the south and southwest. Berenty Reserve, Hazafotsy and Beza-Mahafaly Reserve.
Eastern grey bamboo lemur	*Hapalemur griseus griseus*	Eastern rainforest belt. Andasibe-Mantadia National Park and Ranomafana National Park.
Western grey bamboo lemur	*Hapalemur griseus occidentalis*	Sambirano region in the northwest, Namoroka, Soalala and Tsingy de Bemaraha regions in the west. Sambirano River Valley near the village of Benavony.
Lake Alaotra reed lemur	*Hapalemur griseus alaotrensis*	Reed and papyrus beds and surrounding marshes of Lake Alaotra. Southwest shore of Lake Alaotra.
Golden bamboo lemur	*Hapalemur aureus*	Rainforests of Ranomafana and Andringitra in the southeast. Ranomafana National Park.
Greater bamboo lemur	*Hapalemur simus*	Rainforests of the southeast. Ranomafana National Park.

Ring-tailed lemur	*Lemur catta*	Spiny forests and gallery forests of the south and southwest and the Andringitra Massif. Berenty Reserve, Beza-Mahafaly Reserve and Isalo National Park.
Mongoose lemur	*Eulemur mongoz*	Dry forests of the northwest. Tsiombikibo forest near Mitsinjo and Ampijoroa Forest Station.
Crowned lemur	*Eulemur coronatus*	Forest of the extreme north. Ankarana Reserve, Montagne d'Ambre National Park and Analamera Reserve.
Red-bellied lemur	*Eulemur rubriventer*	The eastern rainforest belt (mid to high elevations). Ranomafana and Marojejy National Parks.
Common brown lemur	*Eulemur fulvus fulvus*	Dry forests of the northwest and central eastern rainforests. Ampijoroa Forest Station and Andasibe-Mantadia National Park.
Sanford's brown lemur	*Eulemur fulvus sandfordi*	Forests of the far north. Montagne d'Ambre National Park and Ankarana Reserve.
White-fronted brown lemur	*Eulemur fulvus albifrons*	Rainforests of the northeast. Nosy Mangabe and Anjanaharibe-Sud Reserves, Marojejy and Masoala National Parks.
Red-fronted brown lemur	*Eulemur fulvus rufus*	Dry forests of the west and rainforests of the southeast. Kirindy Forest and Ranomafana National Park.
White-collared brown lemur	*Eulemur fulvus albocollaris*	Rainforest between the Manampatra and Mananara rivers in the southeast. Manombo Reserve and the forests to the west of Vondrozo.
Collared brown lemur	*Eulemur fulvus collaris*	Rainforests of the extreme southeast. Andohahela National Park and St Luce Private Reserve.
Black lemur	*Eulemur macaco macaco*	Sambirano region and offshore islands in the northeast. Lokobe Reserve on Nosy Be and the neighbouring island of Nosy Komba.
Blue-eyed black lemur	*Eulemur macaco flavifrons*	Forests just south of the Sambirano region in the northwest. Forests to the southwest of Maromandia and the vicinity of Marovato-Sud.
Black-and-white ruffed lemur	*Varecia variegata variegata*	Eastern rainforests. Nosy Mangabe Reserve, Ranomafana and Mantadia National Parks.
Red ruffed lemur	*Varecia variegata rubra*	Rainforests of the Masoala Peninsula. Andranobe and Lohatrozona in Masoala National Park.

Eastern avahi	*Avahi laniger*	Throughout the eastern rainforest belt. Andasibe-Mantadia National Park and Ranomafana National Park.
Western avahi	*Avahi occidentalis*	Western and northwestern Madagascar. Ampijoroa Forest Station.
Diademed sifaka	*Propithecus diadema diadema*	Central and northeastern rainforests. Mantadia National Park.
Milne-Edward's sifaka	*Propithecus diadema edwardsi*	Southeastern rainforests. Ranomafana National Park.
Silky sifaka	*Propithecus diadema candidus*	Northeastern rainforests (at higher elevations). Marojejy National Park.
Perrier's sifaka	*Propithecus diadema perrieri*	Dry forests in the extreme north between the Lokia and Irodo rivers. Analamera Reserve.
Verreaux's sifaka	*Propithecus verreauxi verreauxi*	Dry forests of the west, south of the Tsiribihina River and spiny forests of the south and southwest. Berenty Reserve, Beza-Mahafaly Reserve, Hazafotsy and Kirindy Forest.
Coquerel's sifaka	*Propithecus verreauxi coquereli*	Dry forests of the northwest. Ampijoroa Forestry Station.
Decken's sifaka	*Propithecus verreauxi deckeni*	Western Madagascar, between the Manambolo and Mahavavy rivers. Tsiombikibo forest near Mitsinjo and Tsingy de Bemaraha National Park near Bekopaka.
Crowned sifaka	*Propithecus verreauxi coronatus*	Dry forests between the Mahavavy and Betsiboka rivers. The Bongolava Massif and areas south of the Manambolo River. Near the lighthouse north of Katsepy and the forest around Anjamena on the banks of the Mahavavy River.
Golden-crowned sifaka	*Propithecus tattersalli*	Forest fragments between the Manambato and Loky rivers in northeast Madagascar, 6km northeast of Daraina.
Indri	*Indri indri*	Central eastern and northeastern rainforests. Andasibe-Mantadia National Park and Anjanaharibe-Sud Reserve.
Aye-aye	*Daubentonia madagascariensis*★	Eastern rainforests and western dry forests. Nosy Mangabe Reserve and Île mon Désir (Aye-aye Island) near Mananara.

Other mammals
Carnivores

| Fanaloka or striped civet | *Fossa fossana*★ | Rainforest of the east and north, the Sambirano in the northwest and the dry forests of the extreme north. Ranomafana National Park and Ankarana Reserve. |
| Falanouc | *Eupleres goudotii*★ | Eastern rainforests and dry forests of the northwest and extreme north. Montagne d'Ambre and Ranomafana National Parks. |

Fosa	*Cryptoprocta ferox*	All native forests. Kirindy Forest and Ankarana Reserve.
Ring-tailed mongoose	*Galidia elegans*	Native forests of the east, north and west. Ankarana Reserve and Ranomafana National Park.
Narrow-striped mongoose	*Mungotictis decemlineata*	Dry forests of the west, south of the Tsiribihina River. Kirindy Forest.

Tenrecs

Common tenrec	*Tenrec ecaudatus*★	All native forest areas. Andasibe-Mantadia National Park, Ranomafana National Park, Kirindy Forest and Ampijoroa Forestry Station.
Greater hedgehog tenrec	*Setifer setosus*★	All native forest types. Andasibe-Mantadia National Park and Nosy Mangabe Reserves and Ranomafana National Park.
Lesser hedgehog tenrec	*Echinops telfairi*★	Dry forest of the west and spiny forest and gallery forests of the south. Ihazafotsy, Berenty, Ifaty and Beza Mahafaly Reserve.
Lowland streaked tenrec	*Hemicentetes semispinosus*	Eastern rainforests. Andasibe-Mantadia National Park and Ranomafana National Park.
Highland streaked tenrec	*Hemicentetes nigriceps*	Higher altitudes on the eastern escarpment and central highlands. Andringitra National Park.
Large-eared tenrec	*Geogale aurita*★	Dry forests of the west and the spiny forest and gallery forest areas of the south and southwest. Kirindy Forest and Beza Mahafaly Reserve.

Rodents

Giant jumping rat	*Hypogeomys antimena*★	Western dry forest between the Andranomena and Tsiribihina rivers. Kirindy Forest.
Red forest rat	*Nesomys rufus*	Eastern rainforests. Ranomafana National Park.
Lowland red forest rat	*Nesomys audeberti*	Lowland eastern rainforests. Ranomafana National Park.

Bats

Madagascar flying fox	*Pteropus rufus*★	Eastern rainforests, western dry forests and southern gallery forests. Berenty Reserve, Nosy Tanikely off Nosy Be.
Commerson's leaf-nosed bat	*Hipposideros commersoni*★	Anjavy caves. Ankarana.

Appendix 4

FURTHER INFORMATION
Books

Madagascar's historical links with Britain and the current interest in its natural history and culture have produced a century of excellent books written in English. This bibliography is a selection of my favourites in each category. Note that many are out of print but may be found second-hand.

General – history, the country, the people

Bradt, H *Madagascar* (World Bibliographical Series), Clio (UK); ABC (US) 1992. An annotated selection of nearly 400 titles on Madagascar, from the classic early works to those published in the 1990s.

Brown, M *A History of Madagascar* D Tunnacliffe, UK 1996. The most accurate, comprehensive and readable of the histories, brought completely up to date by Britain's foremost expert on the subject.

Covell, M *Madagascar: Politics, Economics and Society* Frances Pinter, UK (Marxist Regimes series) 1987. An interesting look at Madagascar's Marxist past.

Crook, S *Distant Shores: by Traditional Canoe from Asia to Madagascar* Impact Books, UK 1990. The story of the 4,000-mile Sarimanok Expedition by outrigger canoe across the Indian Ocean from Bali to Madagascar. An interesting account of an eventful and historically important journey.

Dodwell, C *Madagascar Travels* Hodder & Stoughton, UK 1995. An account of a journey through Madagascar's most remote regions by one of Britain's leading travel writers.

Drysdale, H *Dancing with the Dead: a Journey through Zanzibar and Madagascar* Hamish Hamilton, UK 1991. An account of Helena's journeys in search of her trading ancestor. Informative, entertaining and well-written.

Ellis, W *Madagascar Revisited* John Murray, UK 1867. The Rev William Ellis of the LMS was one of the most observant and sympathetic of the missionary writers. His books are well worth the search for secondhand copies.

Eveleigh, M *Maverick in Madagascar*, Lonely Planet Journeys, 2001. A well written account of an exceptionally adventurous trip in the north of Madagascar.

Fox, L *Hainteny: the Traditional Poetry of Madagascar* Associated University Presses, UK and Canada 1990. Over 400 beautifully translated *hainteny* with an excellent introduction to the history and spiritual life of the Merina.

Gehan, John *The Forgotten Invasion: The Story of Britain's First Large-Scale Combined Operation, the Invasion of Madagascar 1942* Historic Military Press 2005. The first detailed account of a little-known aspect of Anglo-Malagasy history by a leading military historian.

Lanting, F *Madagascar, a World out of Time* Robert Hale, UK 1991. A book of stunning, and somewhat surreal, photos of the landscape, people and wildlife.

Murphy, D *Muddling through in Madagascar* John Murray, UK 1985. An entertaining account of a journey (by foot and truck) through the highlands and south.

Parker Pearson, Mike & Godden, Karen *In Search of the Red Slave* Sutton Publishing, UK 2002. An archaeological team goes in search of Robert Drury. An absorbing account which reads like a whodunnit, but is equally interesting as a portrait of the Tandroy people.

Sibree, J *Madagascar Before the Conquest: the Island, the Country, and the People* T Fisher Spong, C *Madagascar: Rail and Mail* Indian Ocean Study Circle, 2003. Available from Keith Fitton, 50 Firlands, Weybridge, Surrey KT13 OHR. £12 plus postage. A monograph detailing the country's philately and railways.

Unwin, UK 1896. With William Ellis, Sibree was the main documenter of Madagascar during the days of the London Missionary Society. He wrote many books on the island, all of which are perceptive, informative, and a pleasure to read.

Ethnology

Bloch, M *From Blessing to Violence* Cambridge University Press, UK 1986. History and ideology of the circumcision ritual of the Merina people.

Mack, J *Madagascar: Island of the Ancestors* British Museum, London 1986. A scholarly and informative account of the ethnography of Madagascar.

Mack, J *Malagasy Textiles* Shire Publications, UK 1989.

Powe, E L *Lore of Madagascar* Dan Aiki Publications (530 W Johnson St, Apt 210, Madison, WI 53703) USA 1994. An immense work – over 700 pages and 260 colour photos – with a price to match: $300. This is the only book to describe in detail, and in a readable form, all 39 ethnic groups in Madagascar.

Rund, J *Taboo: a Study of Malagasy Customs and Beliefs* Oslo University Press/George Allen & Unwin, UK 1960. Written by a Norwegian Lutheran missionary who worked for 20 years in Madagascar. A detailed study of *fady*, *vintana* and other Malagasy beliefs.

Sharp, L A *The Possessed and the Dispossessed: Spirits, Identity and Power in a Madagascar Migrant Town* University of California Press, USA 1993. Describes the daily life and the phenomenon of possession (*tromba*) in the town of Ambanja.

Wilson, P J *Freedom by a Hair's Breadth* University of Michigan, USA 1993. An anthropological study of the Tsimihety people, written in a clear style and accessible to the general reader.

Natural history
Literature

Attenborough, D *Zoo Quest to Madagascar* Lutterworth, UK 1961. Still one of the best travel books ever written about Madagascar, with, of course, plenty of original wildlife observations. Out of print, but copies can be found.

Durrell, G *The Aye-aye and I* Harper Collins, UK 1992. The focal point is the collecting of aye-aye for Jersey Zoo, written in the inimitable Durrell style with plenty of humour and travellers' tales.

Jolly, A *A World Like Our Own: Man and Nature in Madagascar* Yale University Press, 1980. The first and still the best look at the relationship between the natural history and people of the island. Highly readable.

Jolly, A *Lords and Lemurs* Houghton Mifflin, Boston 2004. The long-awaited sequel to *A World Like Our Own*. Alison Jolly knows Berenty better than anyone and writes about it better than anyone. This is a marvellous blend of scientific – and anthropological – fact in a book that reads like a novel. It's funny, engrossing, and often surprising.

Preston-Mafham, K *Madagascar: A Natural History* Facts on File, UK and US 1991. The most enjoyable and useful book on the subject. Illustrated with superb colour photos (coffee-table format), it is as good at identifying strange invertebrates and unusual plants as in describing animal behaviour.

Quammen, D *The Song of the Dodo* Hutchinson, UK 1996. An interesting account of island biogeography and its implications for nature reserves.

Thompson, P *Madagascar: The Great Red Island* UK 2004. A self-published account of travels in Madagascar by a botanist so of particular interest to plant-lovers. There's a useful appendix on plant names. Available from the author, tel: 01588 672106, email: peterthompson@burwaynet.com.

Tyson, P *The Eighth Continent: Life, Death and Discovery in the Lost World of Madagascar.* Perennial (HarperCollins), 2001. An American journalist's description of accompanying four scientific expeditions in Madagascar, with American, British and Malagasy scientists. This is interspersed with extensive information on Madagascar's history, archaeology and natural history.

Wilson, J *Lemurs of the Lost World: Exploring the Forests and Crocodile Caves of Madagascar* Revised 1995 and available from the author (see page 457). An interesting and informative account of the Ankarana expedition and subsequent travels in Madagascar.

Specialist literature and guides

Bradt, H; Schuurman, D; Garbutt, N *Madagascar Wildlife: a visitor's guide* Bradt Travel Guides (UK); Globe Pequot Press (USA) 2001 (2nd edition). A photographic guide to the island's most interesting and appealing wildlife, and where best to see it.

Dransfield, J & Beentje, H *The Palms of Madagascar* Royal Botanic Gardens, Kew, UK 1996. A beautiful and much-needed book describing the many palm species of Madagascar.

Dorr, Laurence J; *Plant Collectors in Madagascar and the Comoro Islands* Royal Botanic Gardens, Kew, UK 1997. Biographical and bibliographical information on over 1,000 individuals and groups.

Du Puy, D; Cribb P; Bosser J; Hermans J & C *The Orchids of Madagascar* Royal Botanic Gardens, Kew, UK 1999. A checklist of all known Malagasy orchid species, along with a complete bibliography, superbly illustrated with colour photos. Pricey (£49.50) but orchid enthusiasts will not care.

Garbutt, N *Mammals of Madagascar* Pica Press (UK) 1999. Comprehensive, with wonderful photos and black-and-white illustrations, as well as authoritative text. My only complaint is it's too heavy to be used as a field guide. [But may come out in paperback]

Glaw, F; Vences, M *A Field Guide to the Amphibians and Reptiles of Madagascar* 1994. A thorough guide to the herpetofauna of Madagascar. In Britain this is available through the NHBS.

Goodman, Steven & Benstead, Jonathan *The Natural History of Madagascar* Chicago University Press 2004. The most thorough and comprehensive account yet published. The island's geology, climate, human ecology and impact, marine ecosystems, plants, invertebrates, fish, amphibians, reptiles, birds, mammals and conservation written by authorities in their field. A hefty 1709 pages with a price to match (£59.50).

Hillerman, F E; Holst, A W *An Introduction to the Cultivated Angraecoid Orchids of Madagascar* Timber Press, USA. Includes a good section on climate and other plant life.

Inventaire Ecologique Forestier National Published in 1996 by the Direction des Eaux et Forêts. A brave and welcome attempt to make the island's botany more accessible.

Martin, J *Chameleons* Facts on File, USA; Blandford, UK 1992. Beautifully illustrated with photos by Art Wolfe; everything a chameleon aficionado could hope for.

Mittermeier, M et al *Lemurs of Madagascar* Conservation International 1994. A detailed field guide to all Madagascar's lemurs.

Morris, P; Hawkins, F *Birds of Madagascar: a Photographic Guide* Pica Press, UK 1999. I find this well-respected guide difficult to use in the field (too heavy, no distribution maps) but the authoritative text and photos provide serious birders with the details they need for reliable identification.

Rauh, W *Succulent and Xerophytic Plants of Madagascar* Strawberry Press, Mill Valley, CA, USA 1995 & 1998. Two of the five intended volumes on the subject. Detailed and comprehensive; lavishly illustrated with photos.

Rübel, Alex, Hatchwell, Matthew & MacKinnon, James *Masoala: the Eye of the Forest* Theodor Gut Verlag, Switzerland 2003. A photographic book on the Masoala National Park. Available from the NHBS.

Sinclair, I; Langrand, O *Birds of the Indian Ocean Islands* Struik, South Africa 1999. The most user-friendly of the field guides to Madagascar's birds but currently out of print. Clear layout with good illustrations and distribution maps allow for quick reference on the trail.

Where to buy books on Madagascar

Discover Madagascar (Seraphine Tierney) 7 Hazledene Rd, Chiswick, London W4 3JB; tel: 020 8995 3529; www.discovermadagascar.co.uk. Seraphine puts out a catalogue of books on Madagascar which are in print but may be hard to find in conventional outlets. She also sells Malagasy music cassettes and CDs.

Mad Books (Rupert Parker) 151 Wilberforce Rd, London N4 2SX; tel: 020 7226 4490; email: Rupert@madbooks.co.uk; www.madbooks.co.uk. Rupert specialises in old and rare (out-of-print) books on Madagascar, and will send out his catalogue on request. He will also search for books.

Eastern Books of London 81 Replingham Rd, London SW18 5LU; tel/fax: 020 8871 0880; email: info@easternbooks.com; www.easternbooks.com. An antiquarian bookseller (shop, catalogue and website) specialising in rare and out-of-print books on Madagascar and the Indian Ocean.

Editions Karthala (France) 22–24 Bd Arago, 75013 Paris. This French publisher specialises in Madagascar, both for new titles and reprints.

Natural History Book Service (NHBS) 2 Wills Rd, Totnes, Devon TQ9 5XN; tel: 01803 865913; fax: 01803 865280; www.nhbs.com

Useful addresses
Conservation bodies

Association Nationale de Gestion des Aires Protégées (ANGAP)
BP 1424, Antananarivo; tel: 22 415 54/22 415 38; email: angap@dts.mg.
Contact: Mme Chantal Andrianarivo.

Marine conservation
Central

Office National de l'Environnement (Marine and Coastal Unit)
BP 822, Antananarivo; tel: 22 556 24/22 552 76; email: one@pnae.mg
Contact: Mme Haja Razafindrainibe.

Centre National de Recherche Environnementale (CNRE) (Coastal Management Unit)
BP 1739, Antananarivo; tel: 22 630 27; email: cnre@dts.mg
Contacts: Dr Jean Maharavo; Prof Germain Refeno.

WWF Madagascar (Marine Programme)
BP 738, Antananarivo; tel: 22 348 85; email: wwfrep@dts.mg
Contact: Dr Rémi Ratsimbazafy.

Wildlife Conservation Society (Marine Programme)
BP 8500, Antananarivo; tel: 22 528 79; email: wcsmad@dts.mg
Contact: Mr Herilala Randriamahazo.

Regional

Institut Halieutique et des Sciences Marines (IH.SM)
BP 141, Toliara; tel: 94 435 52; email: ihsm@syfed.refer.mg
Contact: Dr Man Wai Rabevenana.

Centre National de Recherche Océanographique (CNRO)
Hell-Ville, Nosy Be. Contact: The Director.

Useful websites
General
www.madagascar-contacts.com – information on hotels, tour operators, etc.
www.air-mad.com – information from Air Madagascar.
www.madonline.com – chat and general information.
www.fco.gov.uk – British Foreign Office advice on safety.
www.unusualdestination.com – tour specialists based in South Africa.

Natural history
www.wwf.panda.org (international) – World Wide Fund for Nature.
www.wwf.org (USA).
www.wemc.org.uk – World Conservation Monitoring Centre.
www.duke.edu/web/primate – Duke University Primate Center.
www.conservation.org – Conservation International.

Bradt Travel Guides

Africa by Road	£13.95	Kabul Mini Guide	£9.95
Albania	£13.95	Kenya	£14.95
Amazon	£14.95	Kiev City Guide	£7.95
Antarctica: A Guide to the Wildlife	£14.95	Latvia	£12.95
The Arctic: A Guide to Coastal		Lille City Guide	£5.95
Wildlife	£14.95	Lithuania	£12.95
Armenia with Nagorno Karabagh	£13.95	Ljubljana City Guide	£6.95
Azores	£12.95	London: In the Footsteps of	
Baghdad City Guide	£9.95	the Famous	£10.95
Baltic Capitals: Tallinn, Riga,		Macedonia	£13.95
Vilnius, Kaliningrad	£11.95	Madagascar	£14.95
Bosnia & Herzegovina	£13.95	Madagascar Wildlife	£14.95
Botswana: Okavango Delta,		Malawi	£12.95
Chobe, Northern Kalahari	£14.95	Maldives	£12.95
British Isles: Wildlife of Coastal		Mali	£13.95
Waters	£14.95	Mauritius	£12.95
Budapest City Guide	£7.95	Mongolia	£14.95
Cambodia	£11.95	Montenegro	£12.95
Cameroon	£13.95	Mozambique	£12.95
Canada: North – Yukon, Northwest		Namibia	£14.95
Territories	£13.95	Nigeria	£14.95
Canary Islands	£13.95	North Cyprus	£12.95
Cape Verde Islands	£12.95	North Korea	£13.95
Cayman Islands	£12.95	Palestine with Jerusalem	£12.95
Chile	£16.95	Panama	£13.95
Chile & Argentina: Trekking		Paris, Lille & Brussels: Eurostar Cities	£11.95
Guide	£12.95	Peru & Bolivia: Backpacking &	
China: Yunnan Province	£13.95	Trekking	£12.95
Cork City Guide	£6.95	Riga City Guide	£6.95
Croatia	£12.95	River Thames: In the	
Dubrovnik City Guide	£6.95	Footsteps of the Famous	£10.95
East & Southern Africa:		Rwanda	£13.95
Backpacker's Manual	£14.95	St Helena, Ascension,	
Eccentric America	£13.95	Tristan da Cunha	£14.95
Eccentric Britain	£11.95	Serbia	£13.95
Eccentric Edinburgh	£5.95	Seychelles	£12.95
Eccentric France	£12.95	Singapore	£11.95
Eccentric London	£12.95	South Africa: Budget Travel Guide	£11.95
Eccentric Oxford	£5.95	Southern African Wildlife	£18.95
Ecuador, Peru & Bolivia:		Sri Lanka	£12.95
Backpacker's Manual	£13.95	Sudan	£13.95
Ecuador: Climbing & Hiking	£13.95	Svalbard	£13.95
Eritrea	£12.95	Switzerland: Rail, Road, Lake	£12.95
Estonia	£12.95	Tallinn City Guide	£6.95
Ethiopia	£13.95	Tanzania	£14.95
Falkland Islands	£13.95	Tasmania	£12.95
Faroe Islands	£13.95	Tibet	£12.95
Gabon, São Tomé & Príncipe	£13.95	Uganda	£13.95
Galápagos Wildlife	£14.95	Ukraine	£14.95
Gambia, The	£12.95	USA by Rail	£12.95
Georgia with Armenia	£13.95	Venezuela	£14.95
Ghana	£13.95	Your Child's Health Abroad	£9.95
Iran	£12.95	Zambia	£15.95
Iraq	£14.95	Zanzibar	£12.95

WIN £100 CASH!
READER QUESTIONNAIRE

**Send in your completed questionnaire for the chance to win
£100 cash in our regular draw**

All respondents may order a Bradt guide at half the UK retail price – please
complete the order form overleaf.

(Entries may be posted or faxed to us, or scanned and emailed.)

We are interested in getting feedback from our readers to help us plan future Bradt
guides. Please complete this quick questionnaire and return it to us to enter into
our draw.

Have you used any other Bradt guides? If so, which titles? . . . .
. . . .

What other publishers' travel guides do you use regularly? . . . .
. . . .

Where did you buy this guidebook? . . . .

What was the main purpose of your trip to Madagascar (or for what other reason
did you read our guide)? eg: holiday/business/charity etc. . . . .
. . . .

What other destinations would you like to see covered by a Bradt guide?
. . . .

Would you like to receive our catalogue/newsletters?

YES / NO (If yes, please complete details on reverse)

If yes – by post or email? . . . .

Age (circle relevant category) 16–25   26–45   46–60   60+

Male/Female (delete as appropriate)

Home country . . . .

Please send us any comments about our guide to Madagascar or other Bradt Travel
Guides. . . . .
. . . .
. . . .
. . . .

Bradt Travel Guides
19 High Street, Chalfont St Peter, Bucks SL9 9QE, UK
Telephone: +44 (0)1753 893444 Fax: +44 (0)1753 892333
Email: info@bradtguides.com
www.bradtguides.com

CLAIM YOUR HALF-PRICE BRADT GUIDE!

Order Form

To order your half-price copy of a Bradt guide, and to enter our prize draw to win £100 (see overleaf), please fill in the order form below, complete the questionnaire overleaf, and send it to Bradt Travel Guides by post, fax or email. Post and packing is free to UK addresses.

Please send me one copy of the following guide at half the UK retail price

Title	Retail price	Half price
. . . .	. . . .	. . . .

Please send the following additional guides at full UK retail price

No	Title	Retail price	Total
. . .	. . . .	. . . .	. . . .
. . .	. . . .	. . . .	. . . .
. . .	. . . .	. . . .	. . . .

Sub total . . . .
Post & packing outside UK . . . .
(£2 per book Europe; £3 per book rest of world)
Total . . . .

Name . . . .

Address . . . .

Tel . . . .   Email . . . .

☐ I enclose a cheque for £ . . . . made payable to Bradt Travel Guides Ltd

☐ I would like to pay by VISA or MasterCard

  Number . . . .   Expiry date . . . .

☐ Please add my name to your catalogue mailing list.

Send your order on this form, with the completed questionnaire, to:

Bradt Travel Guides/MAD
19 High Street, Chalfont St Peter, Bucks SL9 9QE
Tel: +44 (0)1753 893444 Fax: +44 (0)1753 892333
Email: info@bradtguides.com
www.bradtguides.com

NOTES

Index